Encyclopedia of Islamic Herbal Medicine

Encyclopedia of Islamic Herbal Medicine

JOHN ANDREW MORROW

McFarland & Company, Inc., Publishers
Jefferson, North Carolina, and London

Library of Congress Cataloguing-in-Publication Data

Morrow, John A. (John Andrew), 1971–
Encyclopedia of Islamic herbal medicine / John Andrew Morrow.
p. cm.
Includes bibliographical references and index.

ISBN 978-0-7864-4707-7
softcover : 50# alkaline paper ♾

1. Herbs — Therapeutic use — Encyclopedias. 2. Materia medica, Vegetable — Encyclopedias. 3. Medicine, Arab — Encyclopedias. 4. Islam — Encyclopedias. I. Title.
RM666.H33M665 2011 615.3'2103 — dc23 2011034281

British Library cataloguing data are available

Manufactured in the United States of America

McFarland & Company, Inc., Publishers
Box 611, Jefferson, North Carolina 28640
www.mcfarlandpub.com

To Rachida with love

Table of Contents

THE ENCYCLOPEDIA

Acknowledgments

I would like to thank my wife Rachida Bejja and my sons Yā-Sīn and Ṭā-Hā for lovingly supporting my scholarship. I would also like to thank my parents, Lisette and Andy Morrow, for providing me with the best education possible and for always encouraging my academic endeavors.

I am most grateful to Rachida Bejja for painstakingly proofreading the Arabic transliteration. I am equally grateful to my colleagues Abū Dharr Héctor Manzolillo, a professional translator by trade, Dr. Ginny Lewis, an associate professor of German at Northern State University, in Aberdeen, South Dakota, and Dr. Qudsia Nizami, an assistant professor of *'Ilm al-Advia* at the prestigious Hamdard University in India, and co-author of *Classification of Unānī Drugs: With English and Scientific Names*, for ensuring the accuracy of the Spanish, German, and Unānī botanical names. Besides reviewing the names of the herbs covered in this encyclopedia, Professor Nizami updated my information regarding Unānī institutes of higher learning throughout the world. Special thanks must also be given to the outstanding reference librarians at Northern State University who helped me obtain even the most obscure books that I required to complete my research.

I am indebted to Professor Barbara Castleton from al-Akhawayn University in Morocco for proofreading the work and providing important corrections and suggestions. I am most moved by her kindness, generosity, support and encouragement, and count myself honored to have her as a colleague.

I am also honored to have counted on the criticism of the following: Dr. Andrew J. Newman, Reader in Islamic Studies and Persian, and Graduate School Director at the University of Edinburgh, who researches the legal bases of Islamic medical theory and practice; Dr. Fabrizio Speziale, a specialist in the history of Islamic medicine from the Université Sorbonne Nouvelle–Paris 3; Suleman Said, M.Sc., Researcher III for the Division of Basic Biomedical Sciences at the University of South Dakota's Sanford School of Medicine, and the author and coauthor of a vast number of scientific studies; Dr. Diego Estomba, a medical doctor, coroner, and specialist in rheumatology, who has written about Mapuche Indian ethnobotany in Patagonia; and especially Deni Bown, the esteemed British herbalist and author of *The Encyclopedia of Herbs and Their Uses*, a work that has been a great source of information and inspiration for me. These distinguished herbalists, scholars, scientists, medical doctors and specialists reviewed this publication, providing valuable insight and advice.

Any errors that remain in this work are mine alone, of course.

Note on Arabic Transliteration

Arabic Letter	*Transliteration*
ء	’
ب	b
ت	t
ث	th
ج	j
ح	ḥ
خ	kh
د	d
ذ	dh
ر	r
ز	z
س	s
ش	sh
ص	ṣ
ض	ḍ
ط	ṭ
ظ	ẓ
ع	‘
غ	gh
ف	f

Arabic Letter	*Transliteration*
ق	q
ك	k
ل	l
م	m
ن	n
ه	h
و	w
ي	y
ة	t/h
ه	h

SHORT VOWELS

Arabic Letter	*Transliteration*
َ	a
ُ	u
ِ	i

LONG VOWELS

Arabic Letter	*Transliteration*
ا & ى	ā
وُ	ū
ي	ī

DIPHTHONGS

Arabic Letter	*Transliteration*
وَ ْ	aw
يَ ْ	ay
يِّ	iyy
وُّ	uww

ّ = *SHADDAH*
(DOUBLED LETTERS)

Arabic Letter	*Transliteration*
بّ	bb
Etc.	Etc.

DIALECTAL VOWELS

Arabic Letter	*Transliteration*
َ	e
ُ	o

DIALECTAL DIPHTHONGS

Arabic Letter	*Transliteration*
يَ ْ	ei

The method of transliteration is based mainly on the one employed by Ghulam Sarwar, with some minor modifications regarding the representation of diphthongs and the *shaddah*. We have also chosen to ignore the initial *hamzah*. We have only applied diacritical marks to Arabic works and authors. We have generally not placed diacritics on names of Urdu, Persian, or other provenance. While it is customary to say *subḥānahu wa ta‘ālā* after the name Allāh, *‘alayhi al-salām* after the name of the Prophet, and *raḍiyya Allāhu ‘anhu* after the names of the companions, we have chosen to drop them, to maintain the flow of the English. While these phrases are not included, they are intended, and readers are free to use them.

Introduction

While most educated readers are familiar with Muḥammad as a prophet and statesman, few are aware that he also practiced herbalism and should thus be considered the founding father of what is known as Prophetic medicine. Known in Arabic as *ṭibb nabawī* or *ṭibb al-nabī*, Prophetic medicine became one of the foundational elements of *ṭibb unānī*, which literally means Ionian or Greek medicine, a broader form of phytotherapy which synthesizes aspects of ancient Arab, Greek, Persian, Ayurvedic, and Chinese medicine.[1] Known in the West as Arabic, Islamic or Eastern medicine, Unānī medicine is widely practiced throughout the Muslim world, from Morocco to India. Despite its popularity, Unānī medicine is a branch of herbalism which is little known in the West. Unfortunately, like the Islamic religion, Islamic medicine suffers from an image problem outside of the Muslim world.

Since Islamic medicine originated in the Middle East, its repertoire of herbs is quite different from that of Western herbalism, though the two traditions do have a number of herbs in common. Among the herbs commonly used in Islamic herbalism are acacia, aloeswood, gum arabic, black seed, camphor, cucumber, date, fenugreek, fig, frankincense, gourd, grape, henna, jujube, jasmine, lemon, myrobalan, myrrh, plantain, pomegranate, quince, saffron, sandalwood, senna, sumac, Syrian rue, tamarisk, and wormwood. With some exceptions, most Westerners are unfamiliar with the varied medicinal uses of the majority of these herbs and plants.

While the Unānī pharmacopeia includes thousands of medicinal herbs, this encyclopedia focuses exclusively on the herbs revealed in the Qur'ān and found in the Sunnah (the teachings of the Prophet), the primary texts of all Islām, and central to the Sunnī tradition, as well as those herbs noted by the Twelve Imāms considered by most Shī'ite Muslims to be the divinely appointed spiritual successors to the Prophet. These herbs form the foundation of Islamic herbalism. As such, we will focus on the nearly one hundred herbs from the Prophetic pharmacopeia, as opposed to the thousands of herbs from the Unānī pharmacopeia.

Consequently, a note about the scope of this work is in order: This encyclopedia is first and foremost about Prophetic herbalism. Prophetic herbalism, it should be specified, relies exclusively on the herbal prescriptions of the Prophet and, for Shī'ites, the Twelve Imāms. Although Unānī herbalism does embrace Prophetic herbalism, it draws principally from Ionian or Greek medicine, with additions from Persian, Ayurvedic, and Chinese medicine. While Unānī medicine has a strong theoretical foundation based on balancing humors, the herbalism of the Prophet had no underlying medical theory: it was a pure form of phytotherapy. It was only later, due to the influence of Unānī medicine, that the Greek concept of the humors was introduced into Prophetic medicine. As Kowalchik and Hylton explain, "Although the Arabs were initially quite empirical in their approach, drawing from Hippocratic principles, in the end, the Galenic concept of medicine, based on mechanical laws of anatomy, logic, and physiology, prevailed."[2] Galen, of course, believed that medical doctors needed to be guided by theory rather than observation. Guided by Avicenna, Arab physicians embraced the humoral theory, leading to a theoretical rather than evidence-based approach to medicine. The symbolic split between Galenic medicine and modern Western medicine can be traced back to Paracelsus (1493–1541 C.E.) who tossed Avicenna's *Canon of Medicine* into the fire in 1527, signifying his break from Galenic medicine. Casting aside theory, Paracelsus insisted on the importance of experimental knowledge.

Besides the significant difference in size of their *materia medica*, Prophetic herbalism and Unānī herbalism appealed to different sectors of society. As Claudia Liebeskind explains,

> Prophetic medicine was aimed at a different audience from the technical Galenic texts. Whereas Unānī medical writings were only appreciated by a small educated elite, *ḥadīth*-based prophetic medicine appealed to the common man. Moreover, whilst Unānī *ṭibb* was predominantly urban-based, the overwhelming majority of the population lived in the countryside.[3]

While much of Unānī medicine is more secular in character, "Prophetic medicine ... was always religious in character."[4] In fact, many religious Muslims rejected the secular nature of Greek medicine as heathen, and insisted on following Prophetic medicine, which is considered of divine origin, and the product of revelation. True knowledge, they believed, came from God, and not from Galen or Avicenna.[5] The antagonism was accentuated by the fact that many practitioners of Greco-Arabic medicine were non–Muslims while most practitioners of Prophetic medicine were religious scholars. The mosque became the center of Prophetic medicine, while hospitals and universities became the center of Unānī medicine. Although there were conflicts between both traditions, they were never totally independent, but overlapped with one another.[6] Attempts to reconcile both traditions were made by Dhahabī (d. 1348), and al-Azraq, among others, who combined the herbal teachings of the Prophet along with those of Hippocrates and Avicenna.[7]

The distinction between Prophetic medicine and Unānī medicine is particularly clear-cut in India and Pakistan, where "Indo-Muslim physicians today would rarely, and never within (*unānī*) health care and research institutions, define their medicine as Islamic, but as Greek."[8] The adjective *yūnānī* is quite uncommon in the Indian Arabic and Persian precolonial medical literature where the discipline was simply called *ṭibb* or "medicine."

The earliest known Indo-Persian medical work which uses the term *yūnānī* in its title dates to the 18th century. It was only during the colonial period that Indo-Muslim physicians sought to differentiate their system of medicine from other forms of traditional Indian medicine by using the Arabic adjective *yūnānī*, which means "Ionic" or "Greek."

The adjective *yūnānī* also served the purpose of differentiating Unānī medicine from Prophetic and Islamic medicine, which had absorbed magic and folk-healing practices. Responding to colonial criticism that Indo-Muslim medicine was unscientific, traditional practitioners sought to distance themselves from the sphere of the sacred, removing any religious aspects from their medical system. As Speziale points out, "Important external influences acted on this process of de–Islamization."[9] These included the writings of Orientalists like Edward G. Browne, who asserted in his *Arabian Medicine* (1921) that Arabic or Islamic medicine was mostly the product of the Greek mind.

Although most Indo-Muslim practitioners embraced the new *yūnānī* denomination, not all leading physicians agreed with this linguistic innovation and its implications: the de–Islamization of Islamic medicine. Hakim 'Abd al-Lateef (d. 1970), who came from a leading family of physicians from Lucknow, strongly opposed the ongoing process of synthesis with colonial science. In *The Indian Relation of our Medicine*, he argued that *ṭibb* was not simply of Greek origin, but a synthesis of Greek, Arabic, Iranian, and Indian medicine. Since the Indian aspect tended to prevail in India, he argued that the system should be called *Hindustani ṭibb*. As Speziale explains, "Rahman Faruqi, author of the first known history of Indo-Islamic medicine in Urdu, did not define the tradition as *Yūnānī* but *Islāmī ṭibb*."[10] After independence, the new *Unānī* term became the official denomination for all institutions of Islamic medicine established by the Indian Ministry of Health.

Despite its popularity in the Muslim world, Islamic herbalism is a field which has attracted little attention in the Western world and the broader world health arena. In the past several decades, very few books have been published on Islamic herbalism in European languages. The most important material available includes translations of Ibn Sīnā, Ibn Buṭlān, al-Kindī, al-Samarqandī, al-Suyūṭī, al-Ḥusayn and 'Abd Allāh ibn Bisṭām al-Nīsābūrī, and Ibn al-Jawziyyah, aimed primarily at scholarly audiences. While some books on Prophetic herbalism are available in the English language, they tend to be completed by religious writers and are generally poorly written and researched, a difference more notable when contrasted with those completed by Western Orientalists and Arabic-speaking academics from the Islamic world.

If one were to peruse the shelves on healthcare and herbal medicine in libraries, book and health food stores, one would find titles dealing with the herbal traditions from Europe, the Americas, India, and China. One would be hard pressed to find references to Islamic, Prophetic, Unānī or Muslim medicine in any of these books, much less titles devoted entirely to this rich herbal tradition. In contrast to the popularity of Ayurveda and yoga, Islamic herbalism and Ṣūfī healing have a negligible presence in the alternative health care market in the Western world. This is an odd state of affairs considering that phytotherapy plays such a fundamental role in the Islamic world, where 80 percent of people rely on traditional medicines for primary health care, most of which involve the use of plant extracts.[11]

In India, a country with a large Muslim minority, there are roughly 30,000 registered Unānī practitioners, with many more practicing along hereditary lines. There are over 100 fully staffed Unānī hospitals, close to one thousand Unānī dispensaries, 40 colleges (including 7 offering postgraduate training), including one National Institute of Unani Medicine at Bangalore which offers only postgraduate courses, as well as numerous regional and clinical research institutes.[12] Almost 95 percent of prescriptions in India are plant-based in the traditional systems of Unānī, Ayurveda, homoeopathy and Siddha.[13] In Pakistan 70 to 80 percent of the population, particularly in rural areas, uses complementary and alternative medicine.[14] Unānī medicine is also very popular in Afghanistan, Iran, Malaysia, the Middle East, the Maghreb and Islamic Africa. The popularity of Islamic medicine in the Muslim world can be seen by the continued publication of classical works on Prophetic medicine, as well as modern commentaries of these primary sources, in Arabic, Persian, Urdu and Western languages.[15] The popularity of Unānī medicine can also be seen in the global spread of institutions which provide training in this form of traditional *ṭibb*.[16]

Muslim medicine remains relevant, partially because it forms an integral part of Islām. The word "Islām" is derived from the Arabic root *slm*, which has a basic meaning of peace and safety. Muslims are enjoined to submit to God, and live in peace and harmony with nature. According to the Qur'ān, Adam was made the Vicegerent (*khalīfah*) of God on earth (2:30). In Islām, human beings are guardians of nature as they have been entrusted by God with the care of creation. As the Prophet explained, "The world is beautiful and green, and verily Allāh has made you its guardians, and He sees how you acquit yourselves [of your responsibility.]"[17] The Qur'ānic attitude towards nature is one of reverence. According to Islām, God created the world in balance (*mīzān*) and it is the duty of human beings to preserve that balance. While resources are to be used, they must always be honored, and must never be exploited as Allāh warns against spreading corruption on earth (2:11; 2:27; 2:205; 3:63; 5:33; 5:64; 7:56; 7:74).

In the Qur'ān, Almighty Allāh says, "There is not an animal on earth, nor a bird that flies on its wings, but they are communities like you" (6:38). The Prophet Muḥammad said, "The creatures are the family of Allāh: and He loves most those who are kind to his family."[18] He also said, "Whoever is kind to the creatures of Allāh is kind to himself."[19] The Prophet prohibited cruelty to animals, and specifically forbade making animals fight for sport, cursing animals, striking their faces or branding their faces; instead, he demanded they be treated kindly.

This is relevant to herbalism in that, considering the Islamic attitude towards the environment, Muslim herbalists should be at the forefront of the campaign against the medicinal use of animal parts from endangered or threatened species. As scientific studies have proven, many effective and ethical alternatives exist which can help bring to an end cruel practices such as bile extraction from caged black bears, and reduce, if not eliminate, the demand for animal products derived from international poaching.[20] The sections on animal parts found in Unānī, Ayurvedic, and Chinese medical manuals should stress the existence of effective substitute materials, and urge practitioners to avoid the use of animal-harvested *materia medica*.[21] After all, we are herbalists, not animalists.

The Qur'ān points people to nature as the source of health and well-being. Almighty Allāh instructs people to "Eat of the good things Allāh has provided, lawful and good" (5:88; 2:168). For Muslims, food and medicine form part of the same continuum. They follow the adage of Hippocrates, who said, "Let your food be your medicine, and your medicine be your food." As far as Muslims are concerned, the key to good health can be found in the Qur'ān and the Sunnah.

According to the Qur'ān and the Sunnah, the traditions of the Prophet Muḥammad and his Household, the cure for every illness is to be found in nature. This is precisely what the Prophet meant when he stated, "He who has put disease on Earth has also placed its remedy there"[22]; and "Verily, Allāh sent the disease and sent the cure, creating for every disease a cure from plants and honey, since both are curative."[23] Echoing the words of his forefather, the Prophet Muḥammad, Imām Ja'far al-Ṣādiq said, "Allāh has sent down the illness and the cure. He has not created an illness without making a cure for it."[24]

Islamic medicine is synonymous with natural medicine. The very word for drug in Arabic is *'aqqār* (plural *'aqāqīr*) which means stump, shrub, or seed, and is also applied to roots, branches, and twigs. Although the word came to embrace drugs of all origins, its original meaning referred to drugs of natural origin. As Allāh says in a *ḥadīth qudsī* or sacred saying, "I will not heal you until you have received medical treatment."[25] Hence, when the Prophet says "O servants of Allāh, take medicine"[26] and "Accept treatment and use medicine,"[27] he was referring fundamentally to phytotherapy. In fact, the Prophet and the Imāms only prescribed herbs for the treatment of illness, and warned their followers against some of the potential dangers of mainstream allopathic medicine.

Although they cautioned against excessive reliance on drugs, the Prophet and the Imāms received medical treatment when required. Like all herbalists, they knew when plants were needed and when drugs and surgery were needed. Although they can benefit from herbal supplementation, major, and life-threatening, conditions always require immediate modern medical attention. If modern medicine is often more effective when it comes time to treating major illnesses, traditional medicine can be effective in preventing minor problems from developing into major, life-threatening illnesses. Both have an essential, but different, role to play in preventing illness and treating disease. This complementary approach, between the religiously based Prophetic medicine and the more "secular" Greek medicine, has a long tradition in the Islamic world.

In its broader sense, Islamic medicine, it must be recalled, became the guardian of Galenic medicine. It was largely through medical universities and bimaristans in Baghdad, Cairo, Córdoba, and Salerno that Arabic-Islamic medicine spread throughout Europe. The Crusades also played an important role in the dissemination of Arabic-Islamic pharmaceutical expertise in the Western world. As Campbell comments, "the European medical system is Arabian not only in origin but also in its structure. The Arabs are the intellectual forebears of the Europeans."[28]

Many Muslims, both past and present, have excelled in various areas of medical science, following the Prophet's promise that "He who heals a Muslim obtains the mercy of Allāh."[29] If anything, Islām opposes the myopic vision of modern medicine, which fails to appreciate the multiple dimensions of health, and pays strict attention to synthetic drugs as opposed to natural medicines. Islamic medicine represents the naturopathic dimension missing from modern allopathic medicine. The integration of both traditional and modern health care is espoused by the World Health Organization:

> In developing countries, where more than one-third of the population lacks access to essential medicines, the provision of safe and effective traditional and alternative remedies could become a important way of increasing access to health care. One way to ensure this is to integrate traditional medicine into the formal health system, thus ensuring better safety and adequate follow-up for patients.[30]

Although the present encyclopedia focuses exclusively on Prophetic herbalism, it must always be remembered that the Islamic approach to health care is holistic in nature, devoting as much attention to spiritual medicine, known as *al-ṭibb al-jismānī*, and spiritual and psychological medicine, known as *al-ṭibb al-rūḥānī* or *al-ṭibb al-qalb*. As Abū Zayd al-Balkhī (d. 934) explained in his *Maṣāliḥ al-abdān wa al-anfus* (*Sustenance for Body and Soul*), human beings are composed of both body and soul; hence, human existence cannot be healthy without this *ishtibāk* or interweaving.[31] As Seyyed Ḥossein Naṣr has noted, "traditional Islamic medicine functioned in a world in which unity reigned, and spirit, soul, and body had not become totally separated with the former being cast aside as irrelevant, as is the case of much of modern medicine."[32]

The Islamic view of health is completely consistent with the definition of the term provided by the World Health Organization: a state of complete physical, mental, and social well-being. For a Muslim, spirituality, physical hygiene, a sound diet, regular exercise, discipline, strong family ties, wholesome entertainment, a healthy sex life, intellectual development, a strong work ethic, and harmonious social relations are all part of the Islamic way of life.[33]

As an indication of the importance placed on spiritual well-being, a book like the *Ṭibb al-a'immah* or *The Medicine of the Imāms*, devotes half of its content to herbs and half to prayers, invocations, Qur'ānic cures, charms, amulets, and talismans. The Arabic bibliography on spiritual medicine is vast, including classical works by Ibn al-'Arabī, Abū Bakr Muḥammad ibn Zakariyyah al-Rāzī, Abū al-Faraj 'Abd al-Raḥmān ibn 'Alī ibn al-Jawzī,

Muḥammad Mahdī Abū Dharr al-Narāqī, and many more.[34] For modern English-language works which combine health and spirituality, readers can consult the works of Narāqī, Khumaynī, Muṭahharī, Tabāṭabā'ī, and Mūsawī Larī.[35]

The Prophet himself divided knowledge into two fields, *'ilm al-abdān*, the knowledge of medicine, and *'ilm al-adyān*, the knowledge of religion, equating the importance of medicine with that of the religious sciences. Manifesting the importance of medicine, Imām 'Alī stated that "The sciences are three: jurisprudence for religion, medicine for the body, and grammar for language."[36]

The most distinguished herbalists from the Prophet's Household included the Sixth and the Eighth Imāms: Ja'far al-Ṣādiq — who pioneered the principles, rules, and science of medicine, teaching over 4,000 students — and 'Alī al-Riḍā, the attributed author of the *al-Risālah al-dhahabiyyah fī al-ṭibb* (*The Golden Treatise on Medicine*), which is the oldest known work which synthesizes Galenic and pre–Islamic medicine into the Islamic medical tradition.[37]

Persian Shī'ahs were among the most prominent early Islamic physicians. The Safavid period in particular was a golden age for Shī'ite medicine. Despite the minority status of Shī'ite Muslims in much of the Muslim world, "Shī'ite medical literature spread to a certain degree throughout numerous parts of the Islamic world well into colonial and current times."[38]

Shī'ite herbalists appear to have operated in a more supportive sphere than many Sunnī herbalists, who were hampered by the authorities' attempts to impose control and "orthodoxy" on the vocation. Since it had been taught by the Prophet and the Imāms, herbal medicine was fully endorsed by the Shī'ite scholars of Islām. As Shaykh al-Mufīd expressed regarding traditional Islamic herbalism, "Medicine is correct (*ṣaḥīḥ*), and knowledge of it is established (*thābit*), and is through revelation. The religious scholars have only taken it from the prophets."[39] In fact, until the 21st century, it was quite common for Shī'ite Muslim religious scholars (*'ulamā'*) to earn their living as *ḥakīms* or practitioners of herbal medicine.

Despite Prophetic medicine's deep Islamic roots, Ibn Khaldūn (d. 1406) characterized it as "definitely not part of divine revelation but ... something customarily practiced among the Arabs [before the rise of Islām]."[40] Inspired by the words of Ibn Khaldūn, scholars like Irmeli Perho claim that Prophetic medicine was fabricated by traditionalist Muslim scholars.[41] Edward Granville Browne asserted that "Arabian medicine" was "for the most part Greek in origin" while J. Christoph Bürgel went as far as describing Prophetic medicine as "quackery piously disguised."[42] However, as Hakim Said Mohammad has shown, Islamic medicine originates from the Prophet Muḥammad and was further developed by Muslim herbalists throughout the ages.[43] As Seyyed Ḥossein Naṣr explains, "The 'medicine of the Prophet' is in a sense part and parcel of the Prophetic Sunnah with all that this participation implies."[44] Since the Prophet's Sunnah was pervasive, it could not neglect such an important area of life as that of health and medicine.[45] As Naṣr explains, the prophetic traditions concerning medicine were compiled during the early Islamic period.[46] Prophetic medicine remained distinct while interacting with Greek, Persian, and Indian medicine, producing a synthesis known as Islamic medicine.[47] As Muḥammad Ḥamīdullāh explains:

> Medical works were translated from Syrian, Greek, Pehlevi, and Sanskrit, among other languages. Muslim physicians benefited from them. They tested the herbal treatments they contained and soon produced their own original works which were superior to those of the ancients since they were able to synthesize the wisdom from around the entire world: from the Greeks, the Indians, and even the Chinese.[48]

Pre-Islamic medicine employed a relatively narrow range of plants while Prophetic herbalism uses approximately one hundred. Many of the herbs mentioned by the Prophet and the Imāms were not readily available in Arabia and did not form a part of pre–Islamic Arab medicine. Herbs are mentioned over one hundred times in the Holy Qur'ān and in the traditions of the Prophet, all of which pre-date the translation of Greek works on medicinal herbs.[49] Hence, it makes no chronological sense to claim that the prophetic traditions regarding herbal medicine are of Greek origin.

Far from being a stagnant replica of Greek medicine, "Arabian medical practice flourished, stirring changes and spurring advances."[50] Arabic culture not only preserved the gains of the classical Greek and Roman period, it elaborated upon them.[51]

From both a culinary and medical perspective, the Muslims were not mere imitators: they were active appropriators. Rather than simply regurgitating foreign medical material, Muslims built upon it, introducing new herbs and new applications which are not found in Greek, Ayurvedic, and Chinese medicine. Bürgel's claim that Prophetic medicine relies on the fabrications of charlatans can be dismissed on the basis of *'ilm al-rijāl*, the science of men, which corroborates the authenticity of the medicinal traditions in question, and on the basis of botany and scientific studies which confirm the medicinal properties of the plants in question. Muslim traditionalists have been diligent in determining the authenticity of medical traditions and dismissing those that are false.[52] This does not mean, however, that there are no quacks or charlatans parading around as Islamic herbalists and Sufi healers with fraudulent credentials. As Ḥassan Kamal explains,

> The decline of Islamic medicine began at the end of the 12th century as a result of changes in Caliphate, or internal troubles and of military defeats. Magic and superstition filtered in, and books of pseudo-scientific character began to appear.[53]

Works like the *Libro de dichos maravillosos* are saturated with sorcery, witchcraft, ritual sacrifices, and Satanic invocations.[54] In reality, such works represent remnants of pre–Islamic pagan practices.

While modern medicine has manifested its marvels, it has steadily strayed from its herbal origin, to the point that many physicians view phytotherapy with skepticism. They point out that the same herb may be viewed as a stimulant in one herbal tradition while it is viewed as a sedative in another. However, as Imām Ja'far al-Ṣādiq and Imām Mūsā al-Kāẓim explained,

> [E]ach body is accustomed to its conditioning, which means that something which may be beneficial for an illness which affects certain people in one region may kill others in the same region who use it for that same illness. What is suitable with one habit is not suitable for those whose habits differ."[55]

Preparation, the parts of an herb employed, and other variables can greatly impact the ways in which a substance affects the human body, which may also enhance the perceptions of "disparities" in different herbal traditions. Opponents of herbal medicine often fail to mention that the properties of plants vary depending on their strain and the region in which they are grown. For example, the senna from the Old World is much stronger than its cousin from the New World.

The opposition to herbal medicine seems shortsighted considering the fact that 25 percent of modern medicines are made from plants first used traditionally[56] and as much as 67 percent to 70 percent of modern medicines are derived from natural products.[57] Common drugs like aspirin, atropine, colchicine, digoxin, ephedrine, morphine, paclitaxel, quinine, and vinblastine, to cite a few examples, all have a botanical origin. Despite thousands of years of use, and tens of thousands of scientific studies confirming the safety and effectiveness of herbal components, the United States Food and Drug Administration (FDA) continues to claim that only modern pharmaceuticals are tried, tested, and true, and only double-blind studies are authoritative.

However, as any search of PubMed will confirm, more than 20,000 studies have been conducted on medicinal herbs.[58] The vast majority of these are lab studies which focus on standardized extracts of active components. Many herbalists reject this selective approach, and insist that the entire herb should be subject to study. However, it is not necessarily the entire herb that produces the therapeutic benefit. In many cases, the benefit is derived from the active element. Hence, it is perfectly logical and scientifically sound to focus on the active component. Studies, however, should not limit themselves to isolating plant constituents. They should also focus on studying the synergistic effects of the combined constituents. As Chevallier explains,

> dividing up a medicinal herb into its constituent parts cannot explain exactly how it works in its natural form. The whole herb is worth more than the sum of its parts, and scientific research is increasingly showing that the active constituents of many herbs ... interact in complex ways to produce the therapeutic effect of the remedy as a whole.[59]

A systematic review conducted by Guo, Canter, and Ernst demonstrated that 1,345 randomized clinical trials have been conducted on individual herbs.[60] While these double-blind human trials on whole herbs are somewhat scarce when compared to the tens of thousands of studies devoted to isolated active components, they demonstrate that randomized controlled trials of individualized herbal medicine are entirely feasible. Unfortunately, herbs are rarely considered candidates for large-scale clinical trials as medical researchers expect proof of efficacy or at least evidence of safety.[61] So the medical industry refuses to endorse herbal remedies due to "lack of clinical trials," while at the same time it generally blocks herbal research at the clinical trial level.

Herbal "purists," however, believe that the scientific approach is far removed from the methods of herbal medicine. They argue that such studies are conducted by agents of pharmaceutical companies who endeavor to extract bioactive fractional substances from plants for the purpose of creating a chemical drug or attracting funding for drug research. These critics insist that such studies cannot be used in any sense to "prove" the validity of an herbal application in healing. While the study of a single active component cannot categorically prove the efficacy of an entire herb, it most certainly helps support claims of its therapeutic benefits. If herbalists claim that a plant is an antibiotic, and a scientist identifies, extracts, and establishes the antibiotic activity of its active ingredient, that scientist has most certainly confirmed the medicinal property attributed to the plant. It may not provide a full picture of the plant's potential, but it presents a part. Rather than rejecting such studies, herbalists should encourage them as they may lead to complete studies of the plants in question.

Among the various herbal traditions today, we notice a struggle between those who wish to preserve their tradition intact, and those who wish to enrich it with elements from other traditions as well as modern elements. In India, Unānī medicine is divided into two camps, the followers of Hakim Ajmal Khan, who founded the Unānī Ṭibbiya College in 1921, and which is affiliated with Delhi University, and the followers of Hakim 'Abd al-'Aziz (1855–1911), the leader of the Lucknow tradition, associated with the Takmil al-Ṭibb College. The first group believes in advancing Unānī medicine through further integration with other systems of medicine, including Ayurveda, and modern Western medicine. The second group opposes the assimilation of outside medical concepts, and believes that Islamic medicine should advance within its own conceptual framework without resorting to outside assistance.[62]

Like the Wahhābīs, who believe in following the Qur'ān and *ḥadīth* literally, there are Unānī herbalists who treat Avicenna's *Qānūn* as if it were the Qur'ān. Neither Avicenna nor the great Unānī herbalists of the past were uncritical of their sources. As Claudia Liebeskind explains, "Although al-Rāzī (865–925 C.E.) relied heavily on his Greek predecessors, especially Galen — many of his texts have the same titles as Galen's — he was not afraid to criticize or correct the Greek texts whenever he found them wanting."[63] As his work *Doubt on Galen* implies, Rāzī, as well as physicians like Ibn Zuhr, maintained a critical mentality. They did not accept Greek ideas unquestionably. Rather, they viewed them as a challengeable basis for further enquiry. Ibn al-Nafīs, the author of a *Sharḥ al-Qānūn* (*Commentary on the Canon*), made it clear in his introduction that he read, respected, and followed Galen, but not blindly, and did not hesitate to criticize him when he believed he departed from the truth and accurate observation.[64]

As a result of their emphasis on experimentation and empiricism, writers like Rāzī, Majūsī, Zahrawī, Ibn Sīnā, Ibn Zuhr, and Ibn al-Nafīs came to new conclusions on the basis of new results and observations. The experiments conducted by al-Rāzī and Ibn Zuhr, for example, contradicted the Galenic theory of humors and the Galenic theory of the heart. Open-minded and brilliant as Avicenna was, he would never agree with a fundamentalist approach to medicine.

This essentialist attitude which is exemplified by certain scholars is quite common in the Muslim world and explains the scholarly stagnation it has suffered from for the past five hundred years. Herbal medicine will not advance if its practitioners remain opposed to progress, an attitude which can only be characterized as one of "herbal fundamentalism."

The conflict between tradition and progress is also found among Ayurvedic practitioners. As Robert Svododa explains,

> Many Ayurvedists, practitioners and educators alike, are convinced that Ayurvedic doctrines are so fundamentally archaic that Ayurveda can only be saved as a medical system by extensively integrating the tenets of modern medicine into its structure to form an "integrated" medical system. Those authorities who support a *suddha* (pure) Ayurveda are equally convinced that the fundamentals of Ayurveda are superior to those of modern medicine, and that only certain useful technological advances need be considered for adoption into the Ayurvedic armamentarium. Integrated practitioners try to position themselves as innovators who battle against blind orthodoxy, while the "pure" faction sees itself as fighting a rearguard action to prevent the destruction of the Indian cultural environment while remaining open to worthwhile innovation.[65]

On the one hand, the purists fear that an integrated syllabus will destroy the theoretical foundation of Ayurveda, reducing it to a hybridized form of allopathic medicine. On the other hand, the integrationists are inordinately hostile towards the theoretical foundation of Ayurveda. As a result of this antagonism, the medical practice of Ayurveda "oscillates between the two extremes of pure Ayurveda and an untrained use of modern medicines."[66] The solution, however, is not to be found in these two extremes. Ayurveda does not have to become part of modern medicine, nor does Ayurveda have to remain frozen in time. Ayurveda can complement Western medicine, and Western medicine can complement Ayurveda, drawing from the strong points from each respective tradition.

The antagonism between classical and post-classical schools of medicine is encountered in many medical traditions, and whether a third medical science, combining tradition with modernity, can be created is questionable, as herbal medicine and modern medicine have fundamental foundational differences. While traditional herbal systems are holistic, Western medicine is atomistic. While traditional herbal systems believe in the synergistic properties of whole herbs, Western medicine focuses on active chemical entities and studies in vitro and in vivo effects according to entirely different biochemical parameters. As Shankar and

Manohar observe, "If we believe the absence of chemistry to be a serious lacuna in indigenous science, we would have to concede that the absence of a holistic [approach] in modern science is as serious a lacuna."[67] Bridging the differences between traditional medicine and modern medicine will definitely be difficult. Chinese physicians, for example, have not created a third medical tradition: they simply practice two different traditions simultaneously.

Although there are Unānī and Ayurvedic purists who reject the validity of the scientific approach, many representatives of these rich herbal traditions see science as a complement, and not a threat. As the *Ayurvedic Pharmacopoeia of India* explains,

> Ayurveda has never been static. Its practitioners had been innovative and dynamic in the therapeutic practice and carried on clinical trials out of the local flora and discovered newer medicine with the same therapeutic values as the classical drugs which might have been then either locally unavailable or perhaps demanding heavy prices.[68]

The same can be said with Unānī phythotherapists in India and Pakistan, particularly those at Hamdard University, who are actively engaged in the scientific study of medicinal herbs for the purpose of confirming or refuting their traditional uses.

Although scientific studies are of great value in establishing the effectiveness of drugs, there are some serious concerns about the objectivity of this approach as it is practiced in real-world situations today. According to an ABC report cited in "Death by Medicine," 90 percent of clinical trials funded by pharmaceutical companies conclude that a drug is effective while only 50 percent are approved in independent clinical trials.[69] In 2004, a study published in the *Canadian Medical Journal Association* found that industry funded trials are more likely to be associated with statistically significant pro-industry findings, both in medical trials and surgical interventions.[70] Clearly, the objectivity of such trials has to be called into question. If it is not outright scientific prostitution, it is certainly a serious conflict of interest.

Unlike contemporary synthetic drugs, herbal medicines have been used for thousands of years. Herbalists learned the properties of plants through observation, trials, tests, and, in some traditions, spiritual insight. Ancient researchers tested plants on animals, on themselves, and on others, carefully documenting their findings and transmitting them through oral and written tradition to their disciples. Avicenna, in particular, introduced clinical trials, randomized controlled trials, and efficacy tests in his *Canon* in the 9th century.[71] It was an herbalist from al-Andalus, Abū al-'Abbās al-Nabātī, the teacher of Ibn al-Bayṭār, who introduced the experimental scientific method in the 13th century. He employed empirical techniques to test, describe, and identify medicinal herbs and used his findings to distinguish between unverified reports, and those that were supported by tests and observation. As a result of his efforts, herbal medicine eventually evolved into the science of pharmacology.[72]

The Prophet Muḥammad was well aware of dangerous herbs and forbade their use. According to Mujāhid, the Messenger of Allāh prohibited people from taking harmful and potentially deadly medicine. Prohibited plants include toxic drugs such as *saqmuniyyah* (*Convolvulus scammonia* L.), *al-tākūk* (*Euphorbia* resin), *shubrum* (*Euphorbia officinarum* L.), *ḥanẓal* (*Citrullus colocynthis* Schrad.), and *'alqam* (*Ecballium elaterium* A. Richard).[73] When the Andalusian herbalist Ibn Ḥabīb was asked his opinion regarding these herbs, he said that their use was prohibited and that they could only be used in cases of such extreme need that their use was made imperative. He also insisted that such substances should only be administered by a person of authority who was well-versed in medical treatment.[74]

When the Caliph al-Mā'mūn queried Imām

'Alī al-Riḍā regarding medical matters, he responded, "I have of it knowledge of what I have personally tested and came to know about its accuracy by experience and by the passage of time in addition to what I was told by my ancestors." In many traditions, the Imāms assured believers that the herbal combinations they prescribe have been "proved by experience."

Al-Rāzī, who died in 925 C.E., argued that all drugs, even those known for their efficacy since ancient times, should be accepted or discarded only after experimental trials (*al-tajribah*). The Muslims, like the Europeans, Indians, and Chinese before them, only accepted medicinal herbs into their *materia medica* on the basis of empirical evidence. Bīrūnī, for example, was the first Muslim to chronicle the discovery of tea and its therapeutic effects. Bīrūnī explains that it was only after it had been tried and tested that tea leaves were entered into Chinese therapeutics.[75] As Muḥammad Ḥamīdullāh explains, Muslim herbalists "tested herbal treatments" from Syriac, Greek, Pahlavi, Sanskrit, and other sources, before accepting them into Islamic medicine's *materia medica*.[76]

According to herbal traditions throughout the world, the knowledge of plants is divine in origin.[77] Among the Hindus, it is believed that Ayurveda was a gift from the gods. In the Bible, God states, "Behold, I have given you every plant yielding seed which is upon the face of all the earth, and every tree with seed in its fruit; you shall have them for food" (Genesis 1:30). In total, the Bible mentions approximately 150 medicinal plants. In the Qur'ān, God says, "And the Earth We have spread out (like a carpet); set thereon mountains firm and immovable; and produced therein all kinds of things in due balance" (15:19). Besides those revealed in the Qur'ān, the *ḥadīth* literature mentions over one hundred medicinal herbs.

From the dawn of creation of the present time, herbal wisdom has been passed down from initiate to initiate, and from generation to generation. There were Chaldean herbalists over 5,000 years ago, and Assyrian clay tablets from 3000 B.C.E. describe some 250 medicinal herbs. The records of Hammurabi (c. 1800 B.C.E.), King of Babylon, include instructions for the use of herbal medicine. One of the most ancient herbal texts in existence is the Ebers Papyrus, believed to have been written about 1500 B.C.E., which contains a collection of prescriptions and formulae covering a wide range of uses. This invaluable document provides the properties and uses of more than 800 medicinal drugs, including myrrh, mastic, frankincense, wormwood, aloes, opium, onion, garlic, acacia, and date blossoms.[78] In the library of Sardana-palus or Ashurbanipal, which dates from 650 B.C.E., Assyrian and Babylonian clay tablets have been found which reveal the uses of two hundred and fifty herbs, including anise, jasmine, oleander, cardamom, cumin, turmeric, mandrake, poppy, and many other medicinals.[79]

The ancient Egyptians also had a sophisticated knowledge of herbs by 3000 B.C.E. Medical schools flourished at Heliopolis, Sais, and other sites. Three of the most prominent physicians of Pharaonic medicine included Neterhotep (c. 3200 B.C.E.), Imhotep (c. 2800 B.C.E.), and Amenhotep son of Hapu (c. 1550 B.C.E.). Their prescriptions included castor oil, frankincense, myrrh, styrax, colocynth, juniper, acacia, beer, milk, and other medicinals.

Chinese medicine is the oldest uninterrupted herbal tradition, tracing back to several thousand years B.C.E. The most ancient herbal tome in existence is *Yellow Emperor's Classic of Internal Medicine*. Dated to c. 1000 B.C.E., it is attributed to Huang Di, the founding father of Chinese medicine, who lived from c. 2697–2595 B.C.E.

The Hindus have another one of the oldest and richest herbal traditions in the world. Although the Vedas, a large body of sacred Hindu texts dating from at least 2000 B.C.E., mention hundreds of medicinal herbs, the earliest surviving Ayurvedic texts originate from the fourth century B.C.E. They include the *Sushruta Samhita*, which lists approximately 700 medicinal plants, and the *Charaka Samhita*, which lists approximately 500 herbal drugs. Like many Persian physicians who relocated to Baghdad during the Golden Age of Islamic scholarship and science, "several Indian doctors migrated there and helped propagate and assimilate the teaching and practice of the Indian system of medicine in the new Muslim society."[80]

Unlike other herbal traditions that waned over time, and were largely supplanted by Western medicine, Ayurvedic medicine remains particularly strong in India. Currently, "[t]here are over 100 undergraduate institutions teaching Ayurveda, and 24 postgraduate teaching and doctorate granting institutions."[81] Approximately twenty-one colleges and hospitals provide training in the preparation and dispensation of Ayurvedic medicine. There are about thirteen central pharmacies which distribute Ayurvedic medicines to over 4,769 licensed pharmacies. There are also 1,349 government hospitals, 8,300 government dispensaries, and 16,313 hospital beds assigned for Ayurvedic use, not to mention the many nursing homes and clinics which operate in this tradition.[82] Although these statistics may seem impressive, India only allocates 4 percent of its national health budget to Ayurveda, investing 96 percent of its resources in modern medicine.[83]

The ancient Greeks also had an advanced knowledge of herbal medicine. Some of the most ancient herbals in the Western world include *Historia Plantarum*, *Enquiry into Plants* and *Growth of Plants* by Theophrastus (371–c. 287 B.C.E.), which lists 500 plants, *Natural History* by Pliny the Elder (23–79), which covers approximately 900 plants, *De materia medica* by Dioscorides (c. 40–90), which surveys over 600 plants, and *De simplicibus* by Galen (129–200/217), which is so complete that no Greek or Roman botanists ever attempted to supersede it.

With the decline and eventual downfall of the Roman Empire, Greco-Roman classics came dangerously close to disappearing. Thanks to the Arabic-Islamic patronage, however, ancient Greek medical works were translated into Arabic, and disseminated throughout the Muslim world by scholars, scientists, and translators like Ḥunayn ibn Isḥāq (809–873) in such cultural centers such as the *Bayt al-Ḥikmah* in Baghdad, the *Dār al-Ḥikmah* in Cairo, and the School of Translators in Toledo. As Shankar and Manohar explain,

> Before the end of the third/ninth century almost all the important Greek medical writings from Hippocrates to Galen and his commentators up to the first/seventh century were rendered into Arabic, either directly or from the Syriac versions. Further information was added to Arabic medical knowledge from Sanskrit, Coptic, and other sources.[84]

As a result of Islamic efforts, Greco-Arabic-Islamic medicine spread into Europe, laying the foundations of modern medicine. In its traditional form, Greco-Arabic-Islamic-Eastern medicine continues to flourish under the title of *Ṭibb-e Unānī* or *Ṭibb-e Islāmī* in much of the Muslim world.[85]

The Persians were particularly famous for their medicinal knowledge. The city of Jundīshāpūr, founded in 271 C.E. by Shāpūr I, the Sassanid king, was home to the world's oldest known teaching hospital, which also included a library and a university. The doctor of the Prophet Muḥammad, Hārith ibn Kaladah (d. 634), was a graduate of the medical university of Jundīshāpūr. The city continued to produce physicians for centuries, from pre–Islamic times into the Umayyad dynasty. Caliphs such as al-Hādī (d. 786), and Ḥārūn al-Rashīd (d. 809) were all supplied with medical experts from Jundīshāpūr.

Western Europeans were also highly advanced in the field of herbal medicine, as were the Anglo-Saxons and the indigenous peoples of the Americas, with the latter surpassing even the Chinese and Hindu peoples in the number of medicinal plants employed.

While Western medicine draws from one to two centuries of experience, herbal medicine draws from thousands of years of observation. Herbalists contend that historical medical records and herbals are underutilized resources As far as phytotherapists are concerned, herbs are the single most studied medicinals on the market, their properties known, and their effectiveness proven on the basis of historical use and similar use of closely related herbs for the same purpose by indigenous peoples from geographically dispersed areas.

As the World Health Organization confirms, three-quarters of plants that provide active ingredients for prescription drugs were investigated by researchers because of their traditional herbal uses. Eighty percent of the 120 active compounds currently isolated from higher plants show a positive correlation between their modern therapeutic use and the traditional use of the plants from which they are derived.[86] At least 7,000 medicinal compounds from the modern pharmacopeia are derived from medicinal herbs.[87]

It comes as no surprise, then, that many herbs are similar to modern drugs in their effects. According to scientific studies, the antioxidative activity of *Costus discolor* is comparable to that of alpha-tocopherol; the antioxidative activity of *Anethum graveolens* is comparable to dl-alpha-tocopherol and quercetin; *Crithmum maritimum* L. and *Foeniculum vulgare* Miller have antioxidant capacities comparable to that of alpha-tocopherol and butylated hydroxytoluene (BHT); the methanolic extract of henna leaves possesses antioxidative activity comparable to that of ascorbic acid; *Musa acuminata* and *Musa balbisiana* possess antioxidative activity comparable to melatonin and vitamin E; the hypoglycemic activity of a dialyzed fenugreek seed extract is comparable to that of insulin; fenugreek polyphenolic extract has cytoprotective effects comparable to silymarin, a known hepaprotective agent; *Zingiber officinale* possesses antihyperglycemic activity comparable to that of gliclazide; *Salvadora persica* extract is comparable to other oral disinfectants and antiplaque agents like tricolsan and chlorhexidine gluconate if used at a very high concentration; *Lawsonia inermis* possesses an anti-inflammatory effect which is not significantly different from that of phenylbutazone; *Hibiscus rosa-sinensis* leaf extract possesses hypoglycemic activity similar to tolbutamide; *Apium graveolens* possesses significant hepaprotective activity comparable with the drug silymarin; and *Narcissus* species from Spain almost all possess HIV-1 inhibitory activity, some of which are comparable to dextran sulfate but without the cytotoxicity. In some cases, clinical trials have demonstrated that medicinal herbs are actually superior to modern medicine.

Skeptics of herbal medicine may claim that only modern pharmaceuticals are safe. Statistics, however, would challenge that contention with research indicating that FDA-approved drugs kill more Americans each year than were killed during the Vietnam War. Although many prescription drugs lead to death due to misapplication, many of them can be lethal when used as prescribed. Some of these deadly drugs, often hastily approved by the FDA, include Thalidomide, FenPhen, Acutane, Vioxx, Celebrex, Rezulin, Ketek, and Avandia.

An average of 783,936 people in the United States die every year from mistakes in the delivery, dosage or application of conventional medicine, including 100,000 to 200,000 from prescription drugs.[88] Accidental death from prescription drugs is now the fourth leading cause of death in the United States. In addition, according to the American Association of Poison Control Centers, there were 230 reported deaths from supplements from 1983 to 2004, with yearly numbers rising from 4 in

1994 to 27 in 2005, an average of 11 deaths per year.[89] In 2004, the FDA reported its own results; it had received 260 reports of death caused by supplements since 1989, an average of 10 per year.

It should be noted that most of the deaths blamed on supplements were the result of overdoses of minerals, vitamins, and non-herbal products like melatonin and glucosamine. Ephedra abuse, by individuals who use it as an appetite suppressant and a stimulant, has resulted in 155 deaths over eleven years; however, over-the-counter anti-inflammatory drugs are responsible for around 40,000 deaths per year. According to U.S. poison control centers, herbs and specialty products accounted for the second lowest incidence of reports: 13 deaths over the course of eleven years.

Increasingly, scientific studies are coming forth confirming the medicinal value of plants. As we will see in the following pages, in vivo, in vitro, animal studies, and double-blind, placebo-controlled human trials have confirmed what herbalists like Muḥammad, the Messenger of Allāh, knew over a millennium before. While many herbs have been shown to be effective in the treatment of a wide array of ailments, readers will wonder why they are rarely made into medicines. The answer is unapologetically and unethically economic. As far as pharmaceutical companies are concerned, there is no point in investing 250 to 900 million dollars getting a natural product approved by the FDA as a new drug, when natural products cannot be patented. Since a natural herb is a gift of the Earth, it cannot expand their bottom line nor extend their economic power and influence.

In order to get around these legal and economic obstacles, some pharmaceutical companies are seeking to patent specific elements found in herbs or producing genetically engineered plants. By doing so, they would "own" and control the organism, thus securing their dollars and cents. They have even introduced terminator technology which ensures that any seeds produced by crops become sterile, and have created strains of seeds which will not sprout unless they are sprayed by a proprietary product.

As we explained earlier, this encyclopedia focuses exclusively on the foundational phytotherapy of the Prophet Muḥammad and the Twelve Imāms of his Pure Progeny. Our primary Shīʿite sources include the *Ṭibb al-a'immah*, the main text of the Twelver Shīʿite medical tradition.[90] We have consulted the large annotated Arabic version edited by Muḥsin ʿAqīl as well as the short English translation completed by Batool Ispahany.[91] The Arabic edition is valuable in that its notes include many prophetic traditions regarding herbs not found in the text. As for the English edition, Ispahany has taken care to correctly identify the herbs in question. The only shortcoming in this volume is it does not offer the scientific names of the herbs along with their common British English names. The botanical names, of course, are essential in order to avoid misidentification of the herbs.

Our primary Shīʿite sources also include Maḥmūd ibn Muḥammad al-Chaghhaynī's (d. 7th c.) *Ṭibb al-nabī*, Kulaynī's *al-Kāfī*, ʿAmilī's *Wasā'il al-shīʿah*, Ṭabarsī's *Mustadrak al-Wasā'il*, Majlisī's *Biḥār al-anwār*, and Imām ʿAlī al-Riḍā's *al-Risālah al-dhahabiyyah fī al-ṭibb*, all consulted in their original Arabic.[92] Rather than search through hundreds of volumes of *aḥādīth*, readers can find most of the Shīʿite traditions on the subject in the excellent anthologies prepared by Muḥsin ʿAqīl such as *Ṭibb al-Nabī*, *Ṭibb al-Imām ʿAlī*, and *Ṭibb al-Imām al-Ṣādiq*.[93]

Our primary Sunnī sources on Islamic herbalism are the *sittah al-ṣiḥāḥ*, the six books of sound traditions, along with other compilations of *aḥādīth*. We have also consulted the *Ṭibb nabawī* books by ʿAbd al-Malik Ibn Ḥabīb (d. 852–53), Abū al-Qāsim ibn Ḥabīb al-Nisābūrī (d. 860), Aḥmad ibn Muḥammad ibn al-Sunnī (d. 975), Jalāl al-Dīn 'Abd al-Raḥmān ibn Abū Bakr al-Sūyūṭī (d. 1505), Ibn Qayyim al-Jawziyyah (d. 1350), Shams al-Dīn Muḥammad ibn Aḥmad ibn 'Alī ibn Ṭūlūn (d. 1546) Aḥmad ibn 'Abd Allāh ibn Aḥmad ibn Isḥāq Abū Nu'aym al-Iṣbahānī (d. 1038), and Shams al-Dīn Abū 'Abd Allāh Muḥammad ibn Aḥmad al-Dhahabī (d. 1348).[94] With the exception of the last named, we have consulted all of these books in their original Arabic.

Where translations exist, we have compared them to their original source. When the translations were sound, we replicated them as such. Unfortunately, many translations of prophetic traditions are faulty in both style and content. For example, Aḥmad Thomson's translation of Sūyūṭī's *Medicine of the Prophet* misidentifies many herbs. The English edition was the basis for other translations, thus perpetuating the errors. For a first-rate translation of Ibn al-Jawziyyah, readers are referred to Penelope Johnstone's professionally completed translation.[95]

Rather than deal with the thousands of herbs used in Unānī medicine, we have focused on approximately one hundred herbs mentioned by the Prophet and the Imāms. For the sake of simplicity, we have selected only traditions referring specifically to one, two or three herbs, leaving more complex pharmacological preparations for subsequent study.

Due to the fact that we have used many different editions of the same book, CD-ROM sources, as well as online editions such as *al-muḥaddith*, during the course of our research, we have followed the Islamic tradition of simply citing the source of prophetic traditions, without always including page numbers. We have followed the same rule for botanical dictionaries and other books which are organized alphabetically or are well-indexed. Other sources, however, are fully documented, and follow the format of the American Medical Association, with minor modifications.

Also for the sake of simplicity, we have used the short titles of the Arabic works, and have abbreviated the names of the publishers. We have included diacritical marks on Arabic words and names to ensure proper pronunciation. We have not, however, applied diacriticals to words and names in Urdu, Persian, or other languages. Although this work is written in American English, we have maintained the Canadian and British spelling of words as they appear in some of the bibliographical references.

Each entry commences with the common English name of the herb in question along with the Classical Arabic name employed in the Qur'ān or Sunnah. This is followed by the scientific name of the herb, the family of plants to which it belongs, along with its English, French, Spanish, German, Urdu, and Modern Standard Arabic translations. Since this encyclopedia is directed to Western audiences, we have not included the names of the plants in other Eastern languages. Unless relevant to the proper identification of polemical plants, we have not listed the common Arabic names of the plants due to reasons of dialectal divergence. To avoid confusion, we have generally listed the names of the herbs in Classical Arabic, as well as their botanical name in Modern Standard Arabic.

It is important to note that, with the exception of herbs which have remained relatively stable over the course of the centuries and millennia, fruits and vegetables have evolved enormously. If, in most cases, the herbs mentioned by the Prophet and the Imāms are still in existence today, the fruits and vegetable varieties they refer to have long been lost. In fact, as Biggs, McVicar, and Flowerdew point out, "Fruit has evolved greatly, the varieties from the pre–World War II period have now completely disappeared."[96] So, even when we correctly identify the species of fruits and vegetables mentioned by the Prophet and the Imāms, their specific variety is often impossible to ascertain.

Even the oldest heirloom varieties of vegetables only date back five hundred to one thousand years. In fact, the majority of heirloom varieties date back one to two hundred years.[97]

After the botanical information and common names, we include a safety rating which ranges from generally safe to deadly. In our opinion, Duke's division of herbs into "as safe as coffee" or "safer than coffee" is inadequate and, as the author admits, an "oversimplification."[98] For the sake of safety, we prefer to err on the side of caution when dealing with potentially dangerous herbs. Much of the information regarding the toxicity of the herbs in question has been drawn from the *Plants for a Future* database which is available online.[99] The *PDR for Herbal Medicines* also includes a good "Side Effects Index," "Drug/Herb Interactions Guide," and "Safety Guide."[100] For shorter works which provide precautionary information, readers can consult *Mosby's Handbook of Herbs and Natural Supplements* or the *Herbal Medicine Handbook.*[101]

The safety rating is followed by the "Prophetic Prescription" in which we provide the herb's direct and indirect authorization from the Qur'ān, the Prophet, or the Twelve Imāms. The term "Prophetic Prescription" encompasses both the Qur'ān, which was delivered by the Prophet, and the teachings of Muḥammad (the Sunnah)—these being accepted as authentic in Sunnī Islām—and the sayings of the Twelve Imāms, who, according to the largest sect of Shī'ite Islām, were the spiritual, political, and intellectual heirs of the Messenger of Allāh. These traditions interest us more for the herbs they prescribe than for the medieval descriptions of diseases which they provide. Attempting to decipher the actual diseases being described in ancient prophetic traditions would require another voluminous study. Readers who are not familiar with the whole "culture of authority" should also be prepared for the repetitious references and quotes from the Prophet and the Imāms.

Our inclusion of Shī'ite traditions is an important contribution to scholarship in the field. In the twenty-first century, no scholar of Islām can make claims to objectivity without considering both Sunnī and Shī'ite traditions in the study of any Islamic subject.

The prophetic traditions we have relied upon, both Sunnī and Shī'ī, are primarily authentic [*ṣaḥīḥ*] or reliable [*ḥasan*] according to the standards of Muslim scholarship. Others may be weak, and some may even be spurious. It should be understood, however, that in the science of men, known as *'ilm al-rijāl* in Arabic, the standards used for authenticating a tradition vary greatly. The very same *ḥadīth* may be deemed authentic by one traditionist or *muḥaddith* and be denounced as weak or spurious by another. Although many of the traditions we have cited are sound or good, some are weak and others are uncorroborated and apocryphal. Since all traditions, from faithful to fallacious, contributed to the creation of Islamic herbalism, it is important to cite all material relating to the subject. Whenever *aḥādīth* are cited, they are cited on the authority of their narrators who bear the ultimate responsibility for the accuracy of the words being rendered. Whenever one reads, "The Messenger of Allāh said" or "The Imām said" it must always be implicitly preceded by "It is related on the authority of so and so."

The "Prophetic Prescription" is followed by a section addressing issues in identification. This section is of paramount importance since the exact identification of the herb is imperative. In order to ensure the most accurate identification of the herbs in question, we have relied on both classical and modern Arabic dictionaries, including *Lisān al-'arab*, the *Hans Wehr Dictionary of Modern Written Arabic*, and Larousse's *al-Mu'jam al-'arabī al-asāsī.*[102] We have relied on both classical Arabic botanical dictionaries, including Bīrūnī's *Book on Pharmacy and Materia Medica*, Abū Sa'īd 'Abd al-Malik ibn Qurayb al-Aṣma'ī's *Kitāb al-nabāt*, and Abū Ḥanīfah al-Dīnawarī's *Kitāb al-nabāt*, as well as modern Arabic botanical dictionaries including Ismā'īl Zahedī's *Botanical Dictionary: Scientific Names of Plants in English, French, German, Arabic, and Persian Languages*, Moustapha Nehmé's *Dictionnaire étymologique de la Flore du Liban*, and Moḥamed Walīd Assouad's *Dictionnaire des termes botaniques*, among many others.[103] The surveys of Saudi Arabian flora conducted by James P. Mandaville, Shahina A. Ghazanfar, and Shaukat 'Alī Chaudhary were also invaluable in attempting to identify otherwise contentious herbs.[104] *The Handbook of Medicinal Plants of the Bible* by James A. Duke was also useful since the Bible and the Qur'ān refer to a very similar botanical environment.[105]

While the Arabic originals of Ibn al-Qayyim al-Jawziyyah and Sūyūṭī are useful for locating prophetic traditions on Islamic herbalism, they are rarely useful in helping identify the herbs in question. This also applies to classical dictionaries like *Lisān al-'arab*. The descriptions they provide of the herbs in question are rarely specific enough to ensure their accurate botanical identification; hence the value of Dīnawarī's *Kitāb al-nabāt* and Bīrūnī's *Kitāb al-ṣaydanah*. As Bernard Lewin explains, Dīnawarī's work was the main source of knowledge about the botanical nomenclature of Classical Arabic for philologists, lexicographers, and writers on botanical and pharmacological matters.[106] Bīrūnī's book is of great value since it lists the names of each herb in Arabic, Syriac, Persian, Greek and Latin, as well as other languages and dialects. Thanks to the polyglotic nature of his dictionary, most of the herbs he describes can be identified with scientific accuracy.

Unfortunately, some of the herbs mentioned by the Prophet have been misidentified and mistranslated into English by translators of Islamic traditions, and books on Prophetic medicine. The reasons the herbs mentioned by Muḥammad have been erroneously identified and wrongly rendered into English are multiple. The fact that many of the authors and translators of works on Islamic herbalism are not herbalists themselves plays a role; the main shortcoming of translators, however, comes from their lack of linguistic competence in classical Arabic. This is evidenced by their inaccurate transliterations of Arabic words and a complete confusion of short vowels. Unable to read Arabic according to its own vocalic system, they read it as if it were Urdu or Persian, and the result is a misleading transliteration. The Persian and Urdu influence, however, is not limited to the transliteration; it actually taints the translation itself. The Persian and Urdu languages include many words of Arabic origin. Many Persian and Urdu speakers assume that the meaning of the borrowed word is the same as it was in the Arabic original. While this is occasionally true, it cannot be taken for granted, since many of these words have adopted new shades of meaning. Although many of the Unānī names for plants are of Arabic and Persian origin, they do not always refer to the same plants in Arabic and Persian as they do in *Unānī ṭibb*. Morphology is often more important than etymology. In many cases, the description of the plant, along with its properties, can provide a more precise identification than a common name. To avoid any confusion, it is imperative to refer to the Latin botanical names of plants, which are universal in usage. (It should be noted, however, that discrepancies exist due to the use of different naming systems in past eras, and that complete standardization under one system is still a work in progress.)

Even translators who are proficient in Arabic seem to confuse the colloquial and classical languages, neglecting the semantic shifts which have occurred in the regional dialects over the course of the intervening centuries. As Arabic speakers moved out of Arabia and established themselves throughout the Middle East and North Africa, they came across new types of plant life. Rather than coining new terms for the flora they encountered, they used their old semantic repertoire to describe new realities. At times, the plant name used in Arabia was applied to a plant from the same family in North Africa. Such was the case with words like *rayḥān*, which was applied to entirely different types of aromatic plants. The same Arabic word applies to different plants in different regions of the Arab world. The word *zaʿtar*, for example, is a generic Arabic name applied to a group of herbs from the genera *Origanum*, *Calamintha*, *Thymus*, and *Satureja*. Herbalists have long been aware of the confusion inherent in the common names of plants. Therefore, in order to properly identify a plant, it is always essential to employ its Latin botanical name.

One of the limitations of previous books on Prophetic medicine is the failure of translators to justify their identification of the herbs in question. According to Farooqi, the methods he used in identifying herbs was "beyond the scope" of his study. Since the identification of plants is notoriously difficult, it is all the more important for scholars to explain the basis of their identification. Although certain well-known plants can be identified using gas chromatography, the only method of definitively identifying most plants is by comparison with the type specimen in an herbarium, which requires the services of a botanist well-trained in taxonomy and the regional flora. With Prophetic traditions we are limited to literary evidence as opposed to physical evidence.

It should be stressed that Unānī physicians and herbal experts are well aware of the issues of identification, and many leading scholars, particularly associated with Hamdard University in India and Pakistan, and such schools as Aligarh University, include experts in Arabic linguistics, and have been studying issues of plant identification for more than two hundred years. Our criticism, of course, does not extend to these brilliant Ḥakīms, physicians, and scholars, whose authoritative works can be referred to with confidence. Our criticism is directly mainly towards some religious writers and translators.

When one peruses the works of some religious writers and translators, one inevitably observes mistakes and contradictions that are the result of a less-than-firm grasp of the Arabic language, and of botany. As can easily be appreciated, misidentifying a plant poses a great peril. Religious writers and translators who produce poorly researched works may give all sorts of different botanical names for a single Arabic plant, completely misidentify herbs, or fail to warn readers about significant side effects and dangers related to their use.

As any botanist can attest, and contrary to the claims of too many widely read works on Prophetic herbalism, the Prophet never saw a pumpkin or squash in his life; there were only gourds in Arabia at that time. As botanical history confirms, pumpkins and squash come from the Americas and only reached Europe, Africa, and the Middle East after 1492. Similarily, many authors assert that corn — beyond doubt a New World plant — is mentioned in the Qur'ān. Clearly this is impossible, if one uses "corn" in its modern sense to mean maize, as too many "authorities" do. "Corn" has long been used to refer to any important cereal or grain crop, but to claim that pre–Columbian mentions of corn in Old World materials refer specifically to maize is wholly without basis.

It is also incorrect to claim that the Qur'ān mentions wild cherries, lemons, black seed, and fenugreek, as some authors do, as none of these plants are mentioned in the Muslim scripture. Classical botanists like al-Bīrūnī complained that much of the Arab material on herbs had been mistranslated from the original Greek sources and was virtually incomprehensible:

> One cannot decipher what was meant and this kind of negligence unfortunately has become all

> too common a characteristic among us. Were this not so, the books left by the Greek master, Dioscorides, Galen, and Pawlus Arbāsiyūs [Paulus Aegineta], which have been already rendered into Arabic, would have been sufficient for us. But unfortunately, we cannot depend on them; and since several rectifications and emendations have been introduced in the texts of their works, we cannot derive full benefit from them.[107]

According to al-Bīrūnī, rather than contributing to science and scholarship, "The translators of these words have done one great disservice to us."[108]

Hakim Mohammad Said, arguably the greatest Unānī scholar of the twentieth century, recognized also that changes in meaning have taken place over the past millennium.[109] The *Hamdard Pharmacopoeia* (1997) also admits, "The question of giving correct botanical ... name of the drugs mentioned in original Unānī literature was a controversial task."[110] The authors of the work admit that the identity of some herbs is so obscure that their origin can only be inferred on the basis of their pharmacological properties, and in some cases there is so little information that even this was not possible.

One of the essential contributions of this encyclopedia is the careful identification of the herbs in question, thereby clearing up mistakes and mistranslations. While we cannot claim perfection, we can claim due diligence. If we have misidentified any herb in question, it will not be the result of negligence. Since we have provided the grounds for our identification, the work of subsequent scholars will be facilitated and advances can be made more easily.

After making every effort to properly identify the herb in question, we provide readers a section called "Properties and Uses." These therapeutic properties are drawn from a combination of herbal traditions. It should be stressed, however, that we have not included every single property and use attributed to the herbs in question.

The Western herbals we have relied upon include Deni Bown's authoritative *Encyclopedia of Herbs and Their Uses*, Kathi Keville's *Herbs: An Illustrated Encyclopedia*, Fetrow and Avila's *Complete Guide to Herbal Medicines*, Balch's *Prescription for Herbal Healing*, Fern's *Plants for a Future*, and Maude Grieve's *A Modern Herbal*, among many others.[111]

Our Arabic/Islamic/Unānī medical sources include *Indusyunic Medicine: Traditional Medicine of Herbal, Animal, and Mineral Origin in Pakistan* by Khan Usmanghani, Aftab Saeed, and Muhammad Tanweer Alam, *The Handbook on Unānī Medicines with Formulae, Processes, Uses and Analysis* by the National Institute of Industrial Research, the *Hamdard Pharmacopoeia of Eastern Medicine* by Hakim Mohammed Said, the *Classification of Unānī Drugs* by Ahmad, Nizami, and Aslam, and the *Index of the Arab Herbalist's Materials* by Wataru Miki, which is based on a dozen authoritative works on herbalism.[112] Our Ayurvedic sources include *The Ayurvedic Pharmacopoeia of India* by the Ministry of Health and Family Welfare, *Indian Medicinal Plants: An Illustrated Dictionary* by C.P. Khare, and *Plants that Heal* by H.K. Bakhru.[113]

We have opted for a global approach to document the usage of herbal substances in healing, drawing from various herbal traditions. We have attempted to strike a balance between Western and Eastern herbals. We have even included *King's American Dispensatory*, commonly known as King's Dispensary, which is a homeopathic reference. While it may be argued that such a work cannot be slipped into herbal recommendations, many homeopathic remedies are derived from herbs. As far as we are concerned, herbology, homeopathy, and aromatherapy are all interrelated as opposed to isolated fields of study.

While some may object to the use of Grieve's *A Modern Herbal*, the work remains of value when used critically and selectively. We do agree that the work is dated, and that it is based, in part, on folklore. However, as

Hakim Said observed, "Folklore and medicine are, after all, inseparable and Lord Tood, the Nobel Laureate in chemistry, has rightly pointed out that some of the future major medical discoveries may, after all, reside in folklore, if correctly interpreted and investigated."[114] From a more modern perspective, the work does contain many mistakes. Still, for her time, Grieve was a repository of traditional Western European herbalism for which, we believe, she deserves a degree of respect. Even those authors who at times fault Grieve have, at other times, recommended or relied upon her work.

Some may question our combining herbal properties and uses from various traditions, complaining that some of the uses are not proven and are not referenced in their particular pharmacopeia. However, as al-Bīrūnī made explicitly clear, "there is no limit on the experience and analogical reasoning on the use of drugs. Were this not so, Desqūrīdas [Dioscorides] would have fixed it and Jālīnūs [Galen] would have fixed the number of drugs."[115] All herbal traditions can learn from each other, discover new herbs and new uses, thereby expanding their *materia medica* through an eclectic approach. Such was the attitude of great Islamic herbalists of the past who "collected outer knowledge from many lands — from Egypt, Greece, Rome, India, and China — and unified it to obtain the best prescriptions."[116]

Since the medicinal properties of herbs are intrinsic, and not dependant on the dictates of any given herbal tradition, we have listed the various properties without distinguishing between the properties found within various herbal traditions, or those of modern medicine. Simply because a particular property is unknown to one tradition, and simply because a particular use is unknown to another tradition, does not mean that they do not exist.

Although we have mentioned the major traditional properties of the herbs in question, sourcing these traditions to numerous encyclopedias and botanical dictionaries, we cannot claim to have included all of their possible properties according to every herbal tradition. For an overwhelming list of activities, readers can consult the reference works by James A. Duke and the pharmacopeias from the various herbal traditions.

After listing the traditional properties of the herb in question, we offer a section called "Scientific Studies," which synthesizes the most recent research on phytotherapy. We searched in excess of 100,000 medical articles, read approximately 10,000 of them, and selected roughly 1,000 for our notes. This section provides the medicinal properties of the herbs in question according to modern medical science. By including a section on traditional properties followed by a section on scientific studies, we hope to combine the established traditional uses from classical sources, along with recent scientific investigation of their validity.

In the United States traditional herbalism has yet to be integrated into the allopathic medical system. While many medical doctors in England and Western Europe are open to alternative medicine, and Chinese doctors regularly combine traditional Chinese medicine (TCM) and modern medicine, having been trained in both, there remains a great deal of skepticism among North American physicians.[117] This makes it that much more important to include scientific evidence from medical journals to support an herb's use, rather than simply presenting the traditional properties of the herbs in question. Physicians will not accept the use of an herb because "Galen said it is good for you." As scientists, scholars, and consumer rights advocates insist, case histories, testimonials, and subjective evidence are often used by quacks to justify their exaggerated claims. Unless provided with empirical evidence from medical journals, physicians will remain unconvinced when it comes to claims about the medicinal qualities of various herbs.

Since many proponents of allopathic medicine are skeptical when it comes to the medicinal properties of plants, we have provided a multitude of studies confirming the fact that they contain active medicinal substances. Such studies may not definitively prove the validity of an herbal application. However, they certainly help prove that herbs are not inert substances. The studies we quote often confirm the properties attributed to them by the various herbal traditions of the world.

Rather than reproducing medical studies in their entirety, we have summarized them, focusing on their findings, which we reproduce integrally or by means of paraphrase. The information in the "Scientific Studies" section is drawn directly from medical journals. We have made every effort to maintain a balance between providing a degree of technical medical information sufficient to satisfy the medical and scientific community, and sheer readability. In the event that a reader is not familiar with scientific terms, we have provided a "Glossary of Medical Terminology" at the end of the work.

When surveying the section on scientific studies, readers should understand the difference between different types of trials. In-vitro refers to a trial conducted in an artificial environment like a test tube. An in-vitro trial is sufficient to determine the active elements in an herb. For example, the antioxidative activity of an herb can be determined through an in-vitro trial of some of its isolated elements. In-vivo refers to a trial conducted within a living organism. This can involve an animal trial, conducted mainly on mice, rats, rabbits, and dogs, or a trial conducted on people.

Readers need to understand that not all trials are equal. Trials can be rated as poor, moderate, good, or excellent, depending on how they are conducted. All scientific studies are subject to peer-review. Results need to be replicable through repeated trials. Merely because one scientist or group of scientists report a particular finding, it is not deemed valid without due scientific process. A single study is simply insufficient, since there are many variables that can affect results. Just like Muslim jurists say "Allāh knows best," when recognizing the possibility of human error, so do scientists, who announce their results by saying they only "suggest" or "may" affirm a finding. Hence, one cannot base one's conclusions on a single study. One needs to look at an entire body of research on a subject. The best studies are always those which are in-vivo. Human studies are superior to animal studies because drugs affect animals differently than people. The validity of a study increases if it is double-blind, placebo-controlled, and randomized. The longer the study and the larger the number of participants, the more authoritative the results will be. Naturally, any study needs to be independently confirmed.

Unlike other books which include sections on the administration of herbs, we have decided not to include a section on dosage. The treatments cited in the scientific studies are not prescriptions and should never be adopted as a therapeutic dosage. The herbs in this encyclopedia have a wide range of applications, modes of preparation, and administrations for a multitude of ailments. Further, with the exception of minor illnesses, self-diagnosis and self-medication is always discouraged due to potential dangers. With more serious illnesses like diabetes, even minor changes in diet can provoke serious complications, potentially leading to death. As such, readers should seek the advice of both professional herbalists and qualified medical practitioners prior to commencing any course of treatment. The present work is meant for informational purposes only, and is not intended as a substitute for consulting with a health care provider. As such, the author and publisher are not responsible for any adverse effects or consequences resulting from the use of any of the herbs discussed in this book.

This encyclopedia is the result of decades of study, and ten years of scholarship and sacrifice. Our role in this academic endeavor was more of a compiler than a creator, and more of an investigator than an innovator. If anything, we are merely a receptacle, an heir of the ancients, a rock on the road, and a link in a chain, bringing the past to the present, and forging a path for phytotherapy into the future. If any good comes from this work, then all praise is due to God, and all thanks belongs to the Prophet, the Imāms, and all the scholars, botanists, herbalists, and scientists on whose work we have relied. In closing, we hope and pray that this publication will foster a greater appreciation and understanding of Islamic herbalism, leading to further research in the field and potential health benefits for all of humanity. *Allāh yu'ṭīkum al-ṣiḥḥah* (May Allāh grant you the best of health).

Notes

1. The proper Arabic transliteration for Ionian or Greek is *Yūnānī*. However, since the *Unānī* spelling is so prevalent, we have opted to follow the most readily identifiable form.

2. Kowalchik C, Hylton W. *Rodale's Illustrated Encyclopedia of Herbs*. Emmaus, PA: Rodale Press, 1987: 323.

3. Liebeskind C. Unānī medicine of the subcontinent. *Oriental Medicine: An Illustrated Guide to the Asian Arts of Healing*. Van Alphen J, Aris A, Ed. London: Serindia Publications; 1995: 45.

4. Ibid.

5. Prioreschi P. *A History of Medicine: Byzantine and Islamic Medicine*. Omaha: Horatius P, 2001: 346.

6. Sengers G. *Women and Demons: Cult Healing in Islamic Egypt*. Leiden: Brill, 2003: 56.

7. Prioreschi P. *A History of Medicine: Byzantine and Islamic Medicine*. Omaha: Horatius P, 2001: 346–347.

8. Speziale F. Linguistic strategies of de–Islamization and colonial science: Indo-Muslim physicians and the Yūnānī denomination. *IIA Newsletter* June 2005; 37: 18.

9. Speziale F. Linguistic strategies of de–Islamization and colonial science: Indo-Muslim physicians and the Yūnānī denomination. *IIA Newsletter* June 2005; 37: 18.

10. Speziale F. Linguistic strategies of de–Islamization and colonial science: Indo-Muslim physicians and the Yūnānī denomination. *IIA Newsletter* June 2005; 37: 18.

11. Sandhya B, Thomas S, Isabel W, Shenbagarathai R. Ethnomedicinal plants used by the Valaiyan community of Piranmalai Hills (Reserved Forest), Tamil Nadu, India: A pilot study. *African J Trad Complementary and Alternative Medicines* 2006; 3(1): 101–114; Fetrow CW, Avila JA. *The Complete Guide to Herbal Medicines*. Springhouse: Springhouse Corporation, 2000: 1.

12. In India, there are seven postgraduate institutes which offer training in Unānī medicine. They are: AIMIJ Unānī Medical College in Mumbai, which is affiliated with Bombay University; Ajmal Khan Ṭibbia College, which is affiliated with Aligarh Muslim University; Ayurvedic and Unānī Ṭibbia College in New Delhi, which is affiliated with the University of New Delhi; the Faculty of Unānī Medicine in New Delhi, which is affiliated with Hamdard University in New Delhi; the Government Nizamia Ṭibbia College, which is affiliated with the NTR University of Health Sciences in Hyderabad; the Government Unānī Medical College, which is affiliated with the University of Madras in Chennai; and the National Institute of Unānī Medicine, which is affiliated with the RG University of Health Science in Bangalore.

13. Satyavati GV, Gupta AK, Tandon N. *Medicinal Plants of India*. New Dehli: Indian Council of Medical Research; 1987.

14. Hussain SA, Saeed A, Ahmed M, Qazi A. Contemporary role and future prospects of medicinal plants in the health care system and pharmaceutical industries of Pakistan. http://www.telmedpak.com/doctorsarticles

15. In Arabic, this includes recent editions of Dhahabī, Ibn Qayyim al-Jawziyyah, Jalāl al-Dīn al-Sūyūṭī, 'Abd al-Malik ibn Ḥabīb, 'Alī al-Riẓā, Shams al-Dīn Muḥammad ibn 'Alī ibn Ṭūlūn, modern compilations by Muḥammad ibn Abī al-Fatḥ Ba'lī, Muḥammad ibn Mufliḥ al-Maqdisī, Ḥasan Shamsī Bāshā, Maḥmūd Nāẓim Nasīmī, Najīb Kilānī, and Muḥammad 'Alī Barr, among many others. See: Ba'lī M. *Saḥīḥ al-ṭibb al-nabawī*. Bayrūt: Dār Ibn Ḥazm, 2004; Ibn Ṭūlūn S. *al-Manhal al-rawī fī al-ṭibb al-nabawī*. al-Riyyāḍ: Dār 'Ālam al-kutub; 1995; *Ibnal-Ṭibb al-nabawī*. Ed. MA Barr. Dimashq: Dār al-Qalam; 1993; Riẓā, A al-.*al-Risālah al-dhahabiyyah*. Qum: Maṭba'at al-Khayyām; 1982; *Ibn Khamsūn faṣlan fī al-tadāwī wa-al-'ilāj*. al-Riyyāḍ: Dār 'Ālam al-Kutub, 2000; *B Qabasāt min al-ṭibb al-nabawī*. Jiddah: Maktabat al-Sawādī; 1991; *Nas al-Ṭibb al-nabawī wa-al-'ilm al-ḥadīth*. Dimashq: al-Sharikah al-Muttaḥidah; 1984; *K Fī Bayrūt:* Mu'assasat al-Risālah; 1980; *Bārr al-Sanā wa al-sanawāt*. Jiddah: Maktabat al-Sharq al-Islāmī; 1992;—. *Hal hunāk ṭibb nabawī*. Jiddah: al-Dār al-Sa'ūdiyyah; 1409 [1988]. There are also several Persian books on the medicine of Imām 'Alī al-Riẓā, including *Ṭibb al-Riẓā: Ṭibb va bihdasht*, *Ṭibb al-Riẓā: Ṭibb va Darman Dar Islām*, and *Ṭibb al-Ṣādiq*, by Murtada 'Askarī, among many more.

16. Training in Unānī medicine can be acquired in India, Pakistan, Bangladesh, Sri Lanka, Iran, Saudi Arabia, Kuwait, United Arab Emirates, China, the United Kingdom, and South Africa. In Bangladesh, individuals can complete their studies at the Government Ṭibbia College in Jalalabad. There are ten institutions in the country involved in teaching Unānī medicine and another five devoted to Ayurvedic medicine. These institutions offer a four-year diploma course, along with a six-month internship, and attract approximately 400 students per year. In 1989–90, the Government Unānī and Ayurvedic Degree College was opened. Affiliated with the University of Dhaka, the college offers a five-year degree course and a one-year internship in its 100-bed traditional medical hospital. In Pakistan, there are 30 colleges teaching Unānī medicine in the private sector as well as one college in the private sector. Students can complete a four year degree course in Eastern medicine, as well as a Ph.D. in Eastern Medicine at Hamdard University. In Sri Lanka, the Insti-

tute of Indigenous Medicine, which is affiliated with the University of Colombo, offers a five-year degree course in Unānī medicine. In Iran, training is available at the Traditional Medicine and Materia Medica Research Center (TMRC) which forms part of Shaheed Beheshti Medical University. Graduates are permitted to practice traditional Iranian medicine. In the United Arab Emirates, students who complete graduate and postgraduate studies in Unānī medicine are authorized to practice traditional *ṭibb* after passing a qualifying examination. A degree course in Uighur Medicine (Greco-Arabic Medicine) is also offered at Xinjiang Uighur Medical College in China. In South Africa, Cape Town University offers a two-year diploma course in Unānī Medicine for healthcare providers; as well as a five-year Bachelor of Unānī Tibb Medicine. In the United Kingdom, a two year diploma in Eastern medicine can be completed at the Mohsin Institute of Ṭibb in Leicester. Training in Unānī medicine is also available from the Center of Islamic Medicine in Kuwait as well as the Center for Traditional Medicine in Saudi Arabia.

17. Muslim. *Jāmi' al-ṣaḥīḥ*. al-Riyyāḍ: Bayt al-Afkār; 1998.

18. Bukhārī M. *Ṣaḥīḥ al-Bukhārī*. al-Riyyāḍ: Bayt al-Afkār; 1998; Murata S. *The Tao of Islām*. Albany: SUNY P; 1992: 178.

19. Amin M. *Wisdom of the Prophet Muḥammad*. Lahore: Lion Press; 1945.

20. Zhang J. Alternatives to the use of endangered species in Chinese medicine. *Proceedings of the Second Australian Symposium on Traditional Medicine and Wildlife Conservation*. March 1999. http://www.environment.gov.au/biodiversity/trade-use/publications/symposium/alternatives.html

21. The *Hamdard Pharmacopeia* includes a list of 48 animal drugs used exclusively in Unānī medicine (5), along with a list of 92 animal drugs used in both Ayurvedic and Unānī medicine (5). The *Handbook on Unānī Medicines* also features numerous animal drugs (529–613), as does the *Indian Materia Medica* (135–234).

22. Tirmidhī M. *al-Jāmi'*. al-Qāhirah: Muṣṭafā al-Bābī al-Ḥalabī; [1937–].

23. Ibn Ḥabīb A. *Mukhtaṣar fī al-ṭibb/Compendio de medicina*. Ed. C Álvarez de Morales and F Girón Irueste. Madrid: Consejo Superior de Investigaciones Científicas; 1992: 44.

24. Nisābūrī A. *Islamic Medical Wisdom: The Ṭibb al-a'immah*. Trans. B Ispahany. Ed. AJ Newman. London: Muḥammadī Trust; 1991: 75.

25. Majlisī MB. *Usages et bons comportements en Islām*. Trans. AA al-Bostani. Paris: Séminaire Islamique; 1990: 60.

26. This tradition is found in Abū Dāwūd, Tirmidhī, al-Ḥākim, Nisā'ī, Ibn Mājah, Ibn Sunnī, and Abū Nu'aym. A variant is found in Ibn Ḥamīd and Abū Nu'aym.

27. Sūyūṭī J. *As-Sūyūṭī's Medicine of the Prophet*. Ed. A Thomson. London: Ṭā-Hā Publishers; 1994.

28. Campbell D: *Arabian Medicine and its Influence on the Middle Ages*. Vol. 1. Kegan Paul. London: Trench, Trübner, 2001; 69–77.

29. Ibn Ḥabīb A. *Mukhtaṣar fī al-ṭibb/Compendio de medicina*. Ed. C Álvarez de Morales and F Girón Irueste. Madrid: Consejo Superior de Investigaciones Científicas; 1992: 45.

30. How safe is traditional medicine? World Health Organization. July 11, 2005. http://www.who.int/features/qa/20/en/index.html

31. Deuraseh N. Physical medicine and spiritual medicine in Islām: an interweaving. *The Yale Journal for Humanities in Medicine*. Jan. 19 2007. http://yjhm.yale.edu/essays/ndeuraseh3.htm

32. Naṣr SḤ. Preface. *The Medicine of the Prophet*. Ibn Qayyim al-Jawziyyah. Trans. P Johnstone. Cambridge: The Islamic Texts Society; 1998: xviii.

33. In his study of Bukhārī's "Chapter on Medicine," Deuraseh found that most of the prophetic traditions relate to preventive medicine rather than therapeutic medicine. See: Deuraseh N. Health and medicine in the Islamic tradition based on "The book of medicine" (*Kitāb al-ṭibb*) of *Ṣaḥīḥ al-Bukhārī*. *JISHIM* 2006; 5: 2–14.

34. Ibn al-'Arabī. *Mujarrabāt ibn 'Arabī fī al-ṭibb al-rūḥānī*. Ed. M 'Aqīl. Bayrūt: Dār al-Maḥajjah, 2006; Rāzī, M. *La médecine spirituelle/Ṭibb al-rūḥānī*. Trans. R Brague. Paris: Flammarion, 2003;—. *The Spiritual Physick of Rhazes*. Trans. A Arberry; Narāqī MM. *Jāmi' al-sa'ādāt*. Najaf: Jāmi'at al-Najaf al-Dīniyyah; 1963.

35. Narāqī MM. *L'éthique musulmane*. Trans. AA al-Bostani. Paris: Séminaire Islamique; 1991; Mūsawī Lārī M. *Problèmes moraux et psychologiques*. Trans. Nahid Chahbazī. Qum: Mūsawī Lārī; 1987; Khumaynī R, Mutahharī M, Ṭabāṭabā'ī MH. *Luz interior*. Trans. AD Manzolillo. Buenos Aires: Editorial Jorge Luis Vallejo; 1997; Khumaynī R. *Forty Ḥadīth: An Exposition of Ethical and Mystical Traditions*. Trans. M Qarā'ī. Islamic Propagation Organization; 1989.

36. Speziale F. La *Risālah al-dhahabiyyah*, traité médical attribué a l'Imām 'Alī al-Rizā. *Luqmān* 2004; 20: 2: 12, 15.

37. As Speziale has made clear, claims that Imām 'Alī al-Riḍā authored the *Risālah* are weak. As this specialist points out, it appears to have been compiled, if not written, by Muḥammad ibn Jumhūr, who attributed it to the Imām for the sake of authority. In any event, the *Risālah* and its many commentaries consolidated the reputation of al-Rizā as a healer. Not surprisingly, the shrine of the Imām in Mashhad once contained a hospital in which 'Imad al-Dīn Shīrāzī, the famous physician, used to work. See: La *Risālah al-dhahabiyyah*, traité médical attribué a l'Imām 'Alī al-Rizā. *Luqmān* 2004; 20: 2: 18–19, 30.

38. Speziale F. La *Risālah al-dhahabiyyah*, traité médical attribué a l'Imām 'Alī al-Rizā. *Luqmān* 2004; 20: 2: 9.

39. Nisābūrī A. *Islamic Medical Wisdom: The Ṭibb al-a'immah*. Trans. B Ispahany. Ed. AJ Newman. London: Muḥammadī Trust; 1991: xxix.

40. Nisābūrī A. *Islamic Medical Wisdom: The Ṭibb al-a'immah*. Trans. B Ispahany. Ed. AJ Newman. London: Muḥammadī Trust; 1991:x.

41. Perho I. *The Prophet's Medicine: A Creation of the Muslim Traditionalist Scholars*. Helsinki: Kokemäki; 1995.

42. Browne EG. *Arabian Medicine*. Cambridge: Cambridge University Press; 1962: 2, 5–6; Burgel JC. *Secular and Religious Features of Medieval Arabic Medicine. Asian Medical Systems: a Comparative Study*. Ed. C Leslie. Berkeley and Los Angeles: University of California Press; 1972: 44–62.

43. Said, H. *al-Ṭibb al-islāmī: A Brief Survey of the Development of Ṭibb (Medicine) during the Days of the Holy Prophet Mohammad and in the Islamic Age, and Presented on the Occasion of the World of Islām Festival, London, April–June 1976*. Karachi: Hamdard National Foundation; 1976.

44. Naṣr SḤ. Preface. *The Medicine of the Prophet*. Ibn Qayyim al-Jawziyya. Trans. P Johnstone. Cambridge: The Islamic Texts Society; 1998: xvii.

45. Naṣr SḤ. Preface. *The Medicine of the Prophet*. Ibn Qayyim al-Jawziyya. Trans. P Johnstone. Cambridge: The Islamic Texts Society; 1998: xxi

46. Naṣr SḤ. Preface. *The Medicine of the Prophet*. Ibn Qayyim al-Jawziyya. Trans. P Johnstone. Cambridge: The Islamic Texts Society; 1998: xvii–xviii

47. Naṣr SḤ. Preface. *The Medicine of the Prophet*. Ibn Qayyim al-Jawziyya. Trans. P Johnstone. Cambridge: The Islamic Texts Society; 1998: xviii.

48. Ḥamīdullāh M. Introduction. *Kitāb al-nabāt: Le dictionnaire botanique d'Abū Ḥanīfah al-Dīnawarī*. Cairo: Institute Français d'Archéologie Orientale du Caire; 1973: 10–11.

49. The Qur'ān refers to herbs, foods, and crops over 150 times, mentioning more than 28 specifically, including manna (2: 57; 7: 160; 20: 80–81), date palm (2: 266; 6: 99; 6: 141; 13: 4; 16: 11; 16: 67; 17: 91; 18: 32; 19: 23; 19: 25; 20: 71; 23: 19; 26: 148; 36: 34; 50: 10; 54: 20; 55: 11; 55: 68; 69: 7; 80: 29), olive (6–99; 6–141; 16–11; 23–20; 24–35; 95: 1–4; 23: 20), grape (2–266; 6–99; 13–4; 16–11; 16–67; 17–91; 18–32; 23–19; 36–34; 78–31,32; 80–28), pomegranate (6–99; 6–141; 55: 55–68), fig (95: 1–4); cedar (34: 15–16; 56: 27–33; 53: 7–18), tamarisk (34: 15–16); *miswāk* (34: 16), camphor (LXXVI: 5); ginger (LXXVI: 17), lentil (2: 61), onion (2: 61), garlic (2: 61), cucumber (2: 61); acacia (61: 27–33), gourd (37: 139–146), mustard (21: 47; 31: 16), sweet basil (60: 12), *zaqqūm* (17: 60; 37: 62–68; 44: 43–48; 56: 52–56; 61: 89), dry thorns (88: 6–7); trees (2: 35; 7: 10–22; 14: 24–26; 16: 10–68; 17: 60; 20: 120; 22: 18; 23: 20; 24: 35; 27: 60; 28: 30; 31: 27; 36: 80; 37: 62, 64; 146; 44: 43; 48: 18; 55: 6; 56: 52, 72); fruits (2: 22, 25; 126; 155, 266; 6: 99; 141; 7: 57; 130; 13: 3; 14: 32, 37; 16: 11, 67, 69; 18: 34, 42; 23: 19; 35: 27; 36: 35, 57; 37: 42; 38: 51; 41: 47; 43: 73; 44: 55; 47: 15; 52: 22; 55: 11, 52, 68; 41: 20, 32; 77: 42; 80: 31), leaves (6: 59; 7: 22; 20: 121), grain (2: 261; 6: 59, 95, 99; 21: 47; 31: 16; 36: 33; 50: 9; 60: 12; 78: 15; 80: 27), agricultural crop (6: 141; 16: 11; 18: 32; 26: 148; 32: 27; 39: 21; 44: 26; 48: 29; 49: 29), fodder (80: 31–32), vegetables (2: 61; 80: 26–28), and plants (2: 61, 261; 3: 37; 6: 99; 7: 58; 10: 24; 15: 19; 16: 11, 65; 18: 45; 20: 53; 22: 5; 23: 20; 26: 7; 27: 60; 31: 10; 36: 36; 37: 146; 50: 7,9; 57: 20; 71: 17; 78: 15; 80: 27).

50. Kowalchik C, Hylton W. *Rodale's Illustrated Encyclopedia of Herbs*. Emmaus, PA: Rodale Press; 1987: 322.

51. Chevallier A. *The Encyclopedia of Medicinal Plants*. New York: DK, 1996: 19.

52. Ibn Qayyim al-Jawziyyah, for example, felt that the traditions regarding lentils, rice, watermelon, purslane, eggplant, pomegranate, grapes, endive, leek, carrot, and harissa were falsified.

53. Kamal Ḥ. *Encyclopedia of Islamic Medicine*. Cairo: General Egyptian Book Organization; 1975: 21.

54. Labarta A. *Libro de dichos maravillosos: misceláneo morisco de magia y adivinación*. Madrid: Consejo Superior de Investigaciones Científicas Instituto de Cooperación con el Mundo Árabe; 1993.

55. Nisābūrī A. *Islamic Medical Wisdom: The Ṭibb al-a'immah*. Trans. B Ispahany. Ed. AJ Newman. London: Muḥammadī Trust; 1991: xxix–xxx.

56. World Health Organization. Traditional medicine. May 2003. http://www.who.int/mediacentre/factsheets/fs134/en/

57. Ministry of Environment & Forests, Government of India. *State of the Environment Report*. New Delhi: Ministry of Environment & Forests, Government of India, 2001: 77–79. Examples of conventional drugs derived from plants include: colchine, derived from *Colchicum autumnale*, digoxin/lanoxin, derived from *Digitalis* spp., tubocurarine, derived from *Chondrodendron tomentosum*, ephedrine, derived from *Ephedra sinica*, etoposide, derived from *Podophyllum peltataum*, physostigmine, derived from *Physostigma venenosum*, reserpine, derived from *Rauvolfia serpentina*, scopolamine, derived from *Datura stramonium* and *Duboisia* spp., taxol, derived from *Taxum brevifolia*, and vincristine, derived from *Catharanthus roseus*. See: Blumenthal M. *The ABC Clinical Guide to Herbs*. Austin: American Botanical Council; 2003: xvii. Other commonly used plant-based drugs include aspirin, atropine, codeine, morphine, paclitaxel, quinine, as well as vinblastine and vincristine.

58. As of September 29, 2009, PubMed listed 20,237 research papers which included the word "phytotherapy."

59. Chevallier A. *The Encyclopedia of Medicinal Plants*. New York: DK; 1996: 11.

60. Guo R, Canter PH, Ernst E. A systematic review of randomized clinical trials of individualized herbal medicine in any indication. *Postgraduate Medical Journal* 2007; 83: 633–637. The *ABC Clinical Guide to Herbs* provides overviews of 571 clinical trials conducted on individual whole herbs. See: Blumenthal M. *The ABC Clinical Guide to Herbs*. Austin: American Botanical Council; 2003.

61. Eldin S, Dunford A. *Herbal Medicine in Primary Care*. Amsterdam: Elsevier Health Sciences, 1999: 92–93.

62. Liebeskind C. Unānī medicine of the subcontinent. *Oriental Medicine: An Illustrated Guide to the Asian Arts of Healing*. Van Alphen J, Aris A, Ed. London: Serindia Publications; 1995: 56–57.

63. Liebeskind C. Unānī Medicine of the Subcontinent. *Oriental Medicine: An Illustrated Guide to the Asian Arts of Healing*. Van Alphen J, Aris A, Ed. London: Serindia Publications; 1995: 48.

64. Hamarneh S, Anees MA. *Health Sciences in Early Islām*. San Antonio: Noor Health Foundation and Zahra Publications; 1983: 163.

65. Svododa R. Theory and practice of Ayurvedic medicine. *Oriental Medicine: An Illustrated Guide to the Asian Arts of Healing*. Van Alphen J, Aris A, Ed. London: Serindia Publications; 1995: 67.

66. Shankar D, Manohar R. "Ayurveda today: Ayurveda at the crossroads." *Oriental Medicine: An Illustrated Guide to the Asian Arts of Healing*. Van Alphen J, Aris A, Ed. London: Serindia Publications; 1995: 102.

67. Shankar D, Manohar R. Ayurveda today: Ayurveda at the crossroads. *Oriental Medicine: An Illustrated Guide to the Asian Arts of Healing*. Van Alphen J, Aris A, Ed. London: Serindia Publications; 1995: 103.

68. *The Ayurvedic Pharmacopoeia of India*. Part 1. Vol. IV. New Delhi: Ministry of Health and Family Welfare, 2004: xv.

69. Null G, Dean C, Feldman M, Rasio D, Smith D. Death by medicine. *Life Extension Magazine*. August 2006. http://www.lef.org/magazine/mag2004/mar2004_awsi_death_01.htm; Fraser J. Statistics prove prescription drugs are 16,400 percent deadlier than terrorists. *Newstarget*. July 5, 2005. http://www.newstarget.com/009278.html

70. *Bhandari, Busse, Jackowski, Montori, Schunemann, Sprague, Mears, Schemitsch, Heels-Ansdell, Devereaux*. Association between industry funding and statistically significant pro-industry findings in medical and surgical randomized trials. *CMAJ* 2004; 170(4): 477–480. See, also: Bubela T, Boon H, Caulfield T. Herbal remedy clinical trials in the media: a comparison with the coverage of conventional pharmaceuticals. *BMC Medicine* 2008; 6: 35. http://www.biomedcentral.com/1741-7015/6/35

71. Tschanz DW. Arab roots of European medicine. *Heart Views* 2003;4(2); Eldredge JD. The randomised controlled

trial design: unrecognized opportunities for health sciences librarianship. *Health Information and Libraries J.* 2003; 20, 34–44; Bloom BS, Retbi A, Dahan S, Jonsson E. Evaluation of randomized controlled trials on complementary and alternative medicine. *IJ of Technology Assessment in Health Care.* 2000; 16(1), 13–21; Brater DC, Daly WJ. Clinical pharmacology in the Middle Ages: principles that presage the 21st century. *Clinical Pharmacology & Therapeutics.* 2000; 67(5), 447–450; Daly WJ, Brater DC. Medieval contributions to the search for truth in clinical medicine. *Perspectives in Biology and Medicine*. 2000; 43 (4), 530–540.

72. Toby H. *The Rise of Early Modern Science: Islām, China, and the West.* Cambridge: Cambridge University Press, 2003: 218.

73. Ibn Ḥabīb A. *Mujtaṣar fī al-ṭibb/Compendio de medicina.* Ed. C Álvarez de Morales and F Girón Irueste. Madrid: Consejo Superior de Investigaciones Científicas; 1992: 67/35.

74. Ibn Ḥabīb A. *Mujtaṣar fī al-ṭibb/Compendio de medicina.* Ed. C Álvarez de Morales and F Girón Irueste. Madrid: Consejo Superior de Investigaciones Científicas; 1992: 67/35.

75. Bīrūnī, AR al-. *al-Bīrūnī's Book on Pharmacy and Materia Medica.* Ed. and trans. HM Said. Karachi: Hamdard National Foundation; 1973: 84–85.

76. Ḥamīdullāh M. "Introduction." *Kitāb al-nabāt: Le dictionnaire botanique d'Abū Ḥanīfah al-Dīnawarī.* Cairo: Institute Français d'Archéologie Orientale du Caire; 1973: 11.

77. For more on the subject, see: Budge EA. *The Divine Origin of the Craft of the Herbalist.* London: Society of Herbalists; 1928.

78. Said HM. *Hamdard Pharmacopoeia of Eastern Medicine.* Delhi: Sri Satguru Publications; 1997: vii.

79. Said HM. *Hamdard Pharmacopoeia of Eastern Medicine.* Delhi: Sri Satguru Publications; 1997: viii.

80. Hamarneh S, Anees MA. *Health Sciences in Early Islām.* San Antonio: Noor Health Foundation and Zahra Publications; 1983: 218–219.

81. Shankar D, Manohar R. Ayurveda today: Ayurveda at the crossroads. *Oriental Medicine: An Illustrated Guide to the Asian Arts of Healing.* Van Alphen J, Aris A, Ed. London: Serindia Publications; 1995: 101.

82. Shankar D, Manohar R. Ayurveda today: Ayurveda at the crossroads. *Oriental Medicine: An Illustrated Guide to the Asian Arts of Healing.* Van Alphen J, Aris A, Ed. London: Serindia Publications; 1995: 101.

83. Shankar D, Manohar R. Ayurveda today: Ayurveda at the crossroads. *Oriental Medicine: An Illustrated Guide to the Asian Arts of Healing.* Van Alphen J, Aris A, Ed. London: Serindia Publications; 1995: 101.

84. Shankar D, Manohar R. Ayurveda today: Ayurveda at the crossroads. *Oriental Medicine: An Illustrated Guide to the Asian Arts of Healing.* Van Alphen J, Aris A, Ed. London: Serindia Publications; 1995: 155.

85. Hamarneh S, Anees MA. *Health Sciences in Early Islām.* San Antonio: Noor Health Foundation and Zahra Publications; 1983: 209.

86. Fabricant SD, Farnsworth NR. The value of plants used in traditional medicine for drug discovery. *Environmental Health Perspectives* 2001; 109: 69–74.

87. Holmes C. *Summary Report for the European Union: 2000–2005.* York: Agricultural and Rural Strategy Group, 2005.

88. Null G, Dean C, Feldman M, Rasio D, Smith D. Death by medicine. *Life Extension Magazine* August 2006. http://www.lef.org/magazine/mag2004/mar2004_awsi_death_01.htm; Fraser, J. Statistics prove prescription drugs are 16,400 percent more deadly than terrorists. *Newstarget* July 5, 2005. http://www.newstarget.com/009278.html.

89. Hurley D. Diet supplements and safety: some disquieting data. *New York Times.* Jan. 16 2007. http://www.nytimes.com/2007/01/16/health/16diet.html?pagewanted=print

90. Nīsābūrī A. *Ṭibb al-a'immah.* Bayrūt: Dār al Maḥajjah al-Bayḍā'; 1994.

91. Nisābūrī A. *Islamic Medical Wisdom: The Ṭibb al-a'immah.* Trans. B Ispahany. Ed. AJ Newman. London: Muḥammadī Trust; 1991.

92. M Chaghhaynī. *Ṭibb al-nabī or Medicine of the Prophet.* Elgood C. Trans. *Osiris* 1962; 14: 33–192; Kulaynī M. *al-Kāfī.* Ṭihrān: Maktabat al-Sadūq; 1961; 'Amilī H. *Wasā'il al-shī'ah.* Bayrūt: al-Mu'assasah; 1993; Ṭabarsī H. *Mustadrak al-Wasā'il*. Bayrūt: Mu'assasat Āl al-Bayt; 1987–1988; Majlisī M. *Biḥār al-anwār.* Ṭihrān: Javad al-Alavi; 1956; Bār MA. *Al-Imām al-Riẓā wa risālatuhu fī al-ṭibb al-nabawī.* Bayrūt: Dār al-manāhil; 1991.

93. 'Aqīl M. *Ṭibb al-Nabī.* Bayrūt: Dār al-Maḥajjah al-Bayḍā,' 2000; *Ṭibb al-Imām 'Alī.* Bayrūt: Dār al-Maḥajjah al-Bayḍā'; 1996; *Ṭibb al-Imām al-Ṣādiq.* Bayrūt: Mu'assasat al-A'lamī; 1998. For more Shī'ite sources on the subject of Prophetic medicine, see: Speziale F. La *Risālah al-dhahabiyyah,* traité médical attribué a l'Imām 'Alī al-Rizā. *Luqmān* 2004; 20: 2: 1–11.

94. Ibn al-Sunnī A. *Ṭibb al-Nabī.* Ed. Ö Recep. Marburg/Lahn [E. Symon Foto-Druck]; 1969; Sūyūṭī J, M Chaghhaynī. *Ṭibb al-nabī or Medicine of the Prophet.* Elgood C. Trans. *Osiris* 1962; 14: 33–192; Sūyūṭī J. *al-Raḥmah fī al-ṭibb wa al-ḥikmah.* al-Qāhirah: al-Maktabah al-Muḥammadiyyah, [196–]; Ibn Qayyim al-Jawziyyah, M. *al-Ṭibb al-nabawī.* Bayrūt: Dār al-Kitāb; 1985; Ibn Ṭulūn S. al-Manhal al-rawī fī al-ṭibb al-nabawī. Ed. 'Azīz Bayk. Riyyāḍ: Dār 'ālam al-kutub; 1995; Iṣbahānī AN al. *Mawsū'at al-ṭibb al-nabawī.* Ed. MKD al-Turkī. Bayrūt: Dār Ibn Ḥazm, 2006; Dhahabī S. *al-Ṭibb al-nabawī.* Bayrūt: Dār al-Nafā'is, 2004; Ibn Ḥabīb A. *Mujtaṣar fī al-ṭibb/Compendio de medicina.* Ed. C Álvarez de Morales and F Girón Irueste. Madrid: Consejo Superior de Investigaciones Científicas; 1992; Nīsābūrī. *Ṭibb al-a'immah.* Bayrūt: Dār al-Maḥajjah al-Bayḍā'; 1994.

95. Johnstone P, trans. *Medicine of the Prophet.* Ibn Qayyim al-Jawziyyah. Cambridge: The Islamic Texts Society; 1998.

96. Biggs M, McVicar J, Flowerdew B. *Vegetables, Herbs, and Fruit: An Illustrated Encyclopedia.* Buffalo/Richmond Hill: Firefly Books, 2006: 138.

97. For photos of heirloom varieties, readers can consult the catalogues prepared by Seed Savers Exchange (http://www.seedsavers.org) and Baker Creek Heirloom Seeds (http://rareseeds.com). For images of plants from the time of the Prophet, readers can consult the 5th century edition of *De Materia Medica* by Dioscorides. Since Muḥammad lived from 570 to 632 C.E., the work gives a good idea of the variety of plants which existed during the period.

98. Duke JA. Introduction. *Handbook of Medicinal Herbs.* Boca Raton: CRC Press; 2002.

99. See: *Plants for a Future: Edible, Medicinal, and Useful Plants for a Healthier World.* http://www.pfaf.org/index.php

100. *PDR for Herbal Medicines.* Montvale, NJ: Medical Economics Company, 2000.

101. Skidmore-Roth L. *Mosby's Handbook of Herbs and Natural Supplements.* St. Louis: Mosby; 2001; Herbal Medicine Handbook. Springhouse, PA: Springhouse; 2001.

102. Cowan JM. Ed. *Arabic-English Dictionary: The Hans Wehr Dictionary of Modern Written Arabic.* New York: Spoken Language Service; 1976; *Mu'jam al-'arabiyyah al-asāsiyyah.* Bayrūt, 1989.

103. Assouad MW. *Dictionnaire des termes botaniques.* Librairie du Liban: Bayrūt, 2002; Bīrūnī AR al-. *al-Bīrūnī's Book on Pharmacy and Materia Medica.* Ed. and trans. By HM Said. Karachi: Hamdārd National Foundation; 1973; al-Aṣma'ī AM. *Kitāb al-nabāt.* Cairo: Maktabat al-mutanabbi; 1972; Dīnawarī AH. *Kitāb al-nabāt: Le dictionaire botanique d'Abū Ḥanīfah al-Dīnawarī.* al-Qāhirah: Institut Français d'Archéologie Orientale du Caire; 1973; Dīnawarī AH. *Kitāb al-nabāt/The Book of Plants.* Ed. Bernhard Lewin. Bayrūt: Dār al-Qalam; 1974; Nehmé M. *Dictionnaire étymologique de la flore du Liban.* Bayrūt: Librairie du Liban, 2000; Zahedi E. *Botanical Dictionary: Scientific Names of Plants in English, French, German, Arabic, and Persian Languages.* Tehran: University of Tehran Press; 1959.

104. Chaudhary SA. *Flora of the Kingdom of Saudi Arabia.* al-Riyyāḍ: Ministry of Agriculture and Water; 1999; Ghazanfar SA. *Handbook of Arabian Medicinal Plants.* Boca Raton: CRC Press; 1994; Mandaville JP. *Flora of Eastern Saudi Arabia.* London: Kegan Paul; 1990.

105. Duke, James A. *Handbook of Medicinal Plants of the Bible.* Boca Raton: CRC Press; 2007.

106. Dīnawarī AH. *Kitāb al-nabāt/The Book of Plants.* Ed. Bernhard Lewin. Bayrūt: Dār al-Qalam; 1974: v.

107. Bīrūnī, AR al-. *al-Bīrūnī's Book on Pharmacy and Materia Medica.* Ed. and trans. HM Said. Karachi: Hamdard National Foundation; 1973: 9.

108. Bīrūnī, AR al-. *al-Bīrūnī's Book on Pharmacy and Materia Medica.* Ed. and trans. HM Said. Karachi: Hamdard National Foundation; 1973: 9.

109. Said HM. *Hamdard Pharmacopoeia of Eastern Medicine.* Delhi: Sri Satguru Publications; 1997: vi.

110. Said HM. *Hamdard Pharmacopoeia of Eastern Medicine.* Delhi: Sri Satguru Publications; 1997: xiii.

111. Balch PA. *Prescription for Herbal Healing.* New York: Avery, 2002; Bown D. *Encyclopedia of Herbs and their Uses.* Montreal: RD Press; 1995; Felter HW, Lloyd JU. *King's American Dispensatory.* 1898. http://www.henriettesherbal.com/eclectic/kings/index.html; Fern K. *Plants for a Future: Edible, Medicinal, and Useful Plants for a Healthier World.* Clanfield: Permanent Publications; 1997. http://www.pfaf.org/; Fetrow CW, Avila JR. *The Complete Guide to Herbal Medicines.* Springhouse: Springhouse Corporation, 2000; Grieve M. *A Modern Herbal: The Medicinal, Culinary, Cosmetic and Economic Properties, Cultivation and Folklore of Herbs, Grasses, Fungi, Shrubs, and Trees, with all their Modern Scientific Uses.* 1931. New York: Dover Publications; 1982. http://www.botanical.com/botanical/mgmh/mgmh.html; Keville K. *Herbs: An Illustrated Encyclopedia.* New York: Friedman/Fairfax; 1994.

112. Ahmad, F, Nizami Q, Aslam M. *Classification of Unānī Drugs with English and Scientific Names.* Delhi: Maktaba Eshaatul Qur'ān; 2005; National Institute of Industrial Research. *The Handbook on Unānī Medicines with Formulae, Processes, Uses and Analysis.* Delhi: Asia Pacific Business P; 2004; Said HM. *Hamdard Pharmacopoeia of Eastern Medicine.* Karachi: Times Press; 1969; Usmanghani K. *Indusyunic Medicine.* Karachi: University of Karachi; 1997; Miki W. *Index of the Arab Herbalist's Materials.* Tokyo: Institute for the Study of Languages and Cultures of Asia and Africa; 1976.

113. Khare CP. *Indian Medicinal Plants.* New York: Springer, 2007; Ministry of Health and Family Welfare, *The Ayurvedic Pharmacopoeia of India.* New Delhi: Ministry of Health & Family Welfare; 1978–2000; Bakhru HK. *Foods that Heal: The Natural Way to Good Health.* Delhi: Orient Paperbacks, 997. http://www.indiangyan.com/books/healthbooks/food_that_heal/date.shtml.

114. Bīrūnī, AR al-. *al-Bīrūnī's Book on Pharmacy and Materia Medica.* Ed. and trans. HM Said. Karachi: Hamdard National Foundation; 1973: v.

115. Bīrūnī, AR al-. *al-Bīrūnī's Book on Pharmacy and Materia Medica.* Ed. and trans. HM Said. Karachi: Hamdard National Foundation; 1973: 6.

116. Shaykh Fadhlalla Haeri. "Foreword." *Health Sciences in Early Islām.* Hamarneh S, Anees MA. San Antonio: Noor Health Foundation and Zahra Publications; 1983: 17.

117. According to one study, 70 percent of medical students in England considered nonconventional therapy to be useful (46). Another study found that 86 percent of training general physicians had a positive attitude towards nonconventional therapy (46). Kayne, S.B. *Complementary therapies for pharmacists.* London: Pharmaceutical Press, 2002. In the U.S., however, only fifty seven percent of physicians have a positive attitude towards incorporating complementary and alternative medicine. Wahner-Roedler DL, Vincent A, Elkin PL, Loehrer LL, Cha SS, Bauer BA. Physicians' attitudes toward complementary and alternative medicine and their knowledge of specific therapies: a survey at an academic medical center. *Evidence-Based Complementary and Alternative Medicine* 2006; 3(4): 495–501. As a result of scientific studies which support the safe and effective use of some of the more well-researched herbs, the level of credibility in herbs continues to increase among members of the conventional medical community in the U.S. See, Blumenthal M. *The ABC Clinical Guide to Herbs.* Austin: American Botanical Council; 2003; xxii.

The Encyclopedia

Acacia / *Samrah*

Family: Fabaceae

Botanical Name: *Acacia* spp.

Common Names: *English* Acacia, wattle; *French* Acacia; *Spanish* Acacia; *German* Akazie; *Urdu/Unānī* Babul, Keekar, Mughilan, Ummughilan; *Modern Standard Arabic* Samrah, Sunt, Shawkah miṣriyyah

Safety Rating: Generally Safe *Acacia* is generally considered safe for most people when used as directed. It may, however, interfere with the rate of absorption of oral drugs.

Prophetic Prescription: It is related that while at war, the Prophet and his companions had nothing to eat but the leaves of *ḥublah* (acacia) and *samar* (acacia).[1]

Issues in Identification: According to Ghazanfar, *Acacia tortilis*, which grows in the foothills and gravel plains of northern Oman, is known as *samar* and *samrah*.[2] Chaudhary also identifies *samar* as *Acacia tortilis* and says that it is widely distributed in Saudi Arabia, although it is absent in the south and in the west, south of Yanbu.[3] Farooqi also identifies *samrah* with acacia, but holds that it refers to *Acacia spirocarpa*. According to Duke, *Acacia raddiana* Savi is known as *somer* in Arabia and Yemen. While the precise species consumed by the Prophet and his companions may be subject to debate, ample evidence supports it as having been a type of acacia.

According to Farooqi, acacia leaves are not edible.[4] However, referencing the *U.S. Army Survival Manual*, published by the U.S. Department of Defense, we find that the young leaves, flowers, and pods of acacia are indeed edible raw or cooked.[5] The *Oxford Companion to Food* also confirms that "most varieties are edible in parts (for example, seeds, roots, gummy exudations)."[6] Finally, the *World Encyclopedia of Food* points out that many types of acacia, like *Acacia seyal*, yield pods and seeds that can be dried into flour for breadmaking.[7]

Properties and Uses: Acacia is astringent, demulcent, aphrodisiac, nutritive, and expectorant.

Scientific Studies: *Antidiarrheic Activity* A decoction of *Acacia arabica* bark was in the British Pharmacopoeia for the treatment of diarrhea.

Antibacterial Activity A decoction of *Acacia arabica* bark was included in the British Pharmacopoeia as an astringent gargle, lotion, or injection. According to Maude Grieve, a liquid extract of *Acacia arabica* was administered in India for its astringent properties.

In a study conducted by the University of Fort Hare in South Africa, the methanol extracts of *Acacia nilotica*, another form of acacia, showed significant inhibition against Gram-positive and Gram-negative bacteria, while acetone extracts of these plants inhibited most of the species.[8]

Chemopreventive Activity In a controlled animal trial at the University of Rajasthan in India, the leaf extract of *Acacia nilotica* was found to have significant chemopreventive and antimutagenic activity, followed by the flower extract, and then the gum.[9]

Anti–Hepatitis C Activity In a Toyama Medical and Pharmaceutical University study in Japan, methanol and water extracts of *Acacia nilotica* showed significant inhibitory activity against the hepatitis C virus using in vitro assay methods.[10]

Anti-HIV Activity In a study conducted by Toyama Medical and Pharmaceutical University, in Japan, methanol and aqueous extracts of *Acacia nilotica* bark and pods showed considerable inhibitory effects against HIV-1.[11]

Acacia Notes

1. Bukhārī M. *Ṣaḥīḥ al-Bukhārī*. al-Riyyāḍ: Bayt al-Afkār, 1998; Muslim. *Jāmi' al-ṣaḥīḥ*. al-Riyyāḍ: Bayt al-Afkār, 1998.
2. Ghazanfar SA. *Handbook of Arabian Medicinal Plants*. Boca Raton: CRC Press, 1994.
3. Chaudhary SA. *Flora of the Kingdom of Saudi Arabia*. al-Riyyāḍ: Ministry of Agriculture and Water, 1999.
4. Farooqi MIH. *Medicinal Plants in the Traditions of Prophet Muḥammad*. Lucknow: Sidrah Publishers, 1998: 96.
5. Dept. of the Army. *U.S. Army Survival Manual*. Washington: Dept. of the Army, 1957. http://www.survivaliq.com/survival/edible-and-medicinal-plants-acacia.htm
6. Davidson A. *The Oxford Companion to Food*. Oxford: Oxford University Press, 1999: 2.
7. Coyle LP. *The World Encyclopedia of Food*. New York: Facts on File, 1982: 3.
8. Kambizi, Afolayan. An ethnobotanical study of plants used for the treatment of sexually transmitted diseases (njovhera) in Guruve District, Zimbabwe. *Ethnopharmacol* 2001; 77(1): 5–9.

9. Meena, Kaushik, Shukla, Soni, Kumar. Anticancer and antimutagenic properties of *Acacia nilotica* (Linn.) on 7,12-dimethylbenz(a)anthracene-induced skin papillomagenesis in Swiss albino mice. *Asian Pac J Cancer Prev.* 2006; 7(4): 627–632.
10. Hussein, Miyashiro H, Nakamura, Hattori M, Kakiuchi, Shimotohno. Inhibitory effects of Sudanese medicinal plant extracts on hepatitis C virus (HCV) protease. *Phytother* 2000; 14(7): 510–516.
11. Hussein, Miyashiro, Nakamura, Hattori, Kawahata, Otake, Kakiuchi, Shimotohno. Inhibitory effects of Sudanese plant extracts on HIV-1 replication and HIV-1 protease. *Phytother* 1999; 13(1): 31–36.

Almonds *see* Nuts

Aloe/*Ṣabir, Ṣabr*

Family: Asphodelaceae

Botanical Name: *Aloe vera*

Common Names: *English* Aloe vera; *French* Aloès; *Spanish* Áloe vera; *German* Aloë, Echte Aloe; *Urdu/Unānī* Ailwa, Musabbar, Faiqra, Usarah-e-Ghikawar; *Modern Standard Arabic* Alwah, Alwah ḥaqīqiyyah, Ṣabr, al-Ṣabir, Ṣabbār, Sawlah

Safety Rating: Generally Safe to Potentially Dangerous Although allergic reactions may occur in sensitive individuals, aloe vera gel is generally regarded as safe when applied to the skin. Effective for minor skin abrasions and small cuts, it has not proven useful in the treatment of deep surgical wounds. Whole leaf preparations, in which the latex has not been removed, should only be ingested under expert supervision due to their potentially irritating properties. Since they can cause harm to the kidneys and the gastrointestinal tract, laxative products made from aloe should only be ingested under expert supervision. The use of aloe as a laxative must be avoided by patients suffering from colitis, Crohn's disease, irritable bowel syndrome, inflamed hemorrhoids, intestinal obstruction, abdominal pain, or kidney problems. Due to the potential potassium loss induced by aloe preparations, aloe preparations containing its latex should not be used concurrently with cardiac medications such as antiarrhythmics, cardiac glycosides, thiazide diuretics, corticosteroids, and licorice. Due to its laxative effect, aloe can interfere with the absorption of oral drugs. Aloe products should be avoided during menstruation, pregnancy and lactation, and should not be consumed by small children. Aloe vera gel, which contains its latex, is an abortifacient. Internal use of aloe vera should not exceed one week.

Prophetic Prescription: The Prophet Muḥammad stated that "[a]loe (*ṣabir*) and watercress (*thafā'*) are both cures for an illness."[1] The Messenger of Allāh was once approached by a man who complained about his eyes. The Prophet told him to "Cover them with aloe."[2] The Prophet said that aloe brightens the face, and is best applied at night.[3] He said, "These two bitter medicines are so good: aloe (*ṣabir*) and garden cress (*thafā'*)."[4] As for Imām Ja'far al-Ṣādiq, he prescribed aloe vera as one of three ingredients employed for the inflammation of the eyes, the other two being myrrh (*al-murr*), and camphor (*al-kāfūr*).[5]

Issues in Identification: There is no question that the *ṣabir* referred to by the Prophet is *Aloe*. For Turkī, it refers specifically to *Aloe vera*.[6] Dīnawarī said that the plant looks like *al-sawsan al-akhḍar*, although it leaves are denser, and that when pressed, it produces a juice which coagulates like gelatin. He also explains that it is widespread in Oman, but that the best *ṣabir* comes from Socotra.[7] Presently part of the 'Adan Governorate of the Republic of Yemen, Socotra is a small archipelago of four islands and islets in the Indian Ocean, some 350 kilometers south of the Arabian peninsula off the coast of Somalia. According to Bīrūnī, *ṣabir* is also known as *maqar*, which Said identifies as *Aloe*, *Aloe vera*, and *Aloe perryi*.[8]

As Ghazanfar explains, there are roughly 25 species of *Aloe* which occur in Arabia, mainly in Saudi Arabia. *Aloe vera*, known as *ṣabar* and *ṣaqal*, is found throughout Arabia in the foothills and wadis. *Aloe dhofarensis*, known as *ṣubr* in Omani Dhofari Arabic and as *ṭuf* in the Omani Jibbali dialect, is endemic to Dhofar where it occurs in the drier regions. *Aloe tomentosa*, known as *ḥir* in the Yemeni dialect and as *ṣabbār* in the Saudi dialect, is commonly found in Saudi Arabia at about 2,000 meters, in rocky mountainous areas. Other species occurring in Saudi Arabia include *Aloe inermis* and *Aloe perryi*. All of these species of *Aloe* are currently used in Arabian herbalism for the treatment of swollen, itchy, or inflamed eyes.[9] Since the medicinal properties of the various *Aloe* species are similar, the Prophet may have been referring to aloe in general, and not one species in particular. If the aloe of the Prophet was the same as the aloe from the New Testament, then it was probably *Aloe vera* as Duke and Michael Zohary believe.

Properties and Uses: *Aloe barbadensis* (syn. *A. vera*) is an intensely bitter, pungent, and potent stimulating purgative which is antibacterial, antifungal, antiviral, antiallergenic, emmenagogue, anthelmintic, detersive for ulcers, and anti-inflammatory. In small doses, it is stomachic and tonic while in large doses it is purgative.

Internally, aloe vera is used for chronic constipation, poor appetite, stomach inflammation, digestive problems, and in colonic irrigation. It is never given to pregnant women or to patients with hemorrhoids or irritable bowel syndrome. Since the leaves are strongly purgative, they require great care with dosage. In order to prevent griping in laxative formulations, it is usually combined with *Foeniculum vulgare* or *Tamarindus indica.* Aloe vera is also used internally for the treatment of acne, aids, arthritis, asthma, bleeding, blindness, bursitis, cancer, the common cold, colitis, constipation, depression, diabetes, glaucoma, hemorrhoids, lack of menstruation, seizures, stomach ulcers, and varicose veins.

Externally, aloe vera is used for burns, scalds, sunburn, wounds, eczema, and to prevent nail biting. It is used topically as a pain reliever for sore nipples and to relieve itching of chickenpox. As Ghazanfar explains, the juice of *Aloe dhofarensis* leaves is used for treating headaches, to relieve pain in limbs and joints, skin rash, wounds, swollen or itchy eyes, diabetes and constipation. *Aloe tomentosa* leaves and sap are used for skin problems, for treating wounds, and inflammation of the eyes. *Aloe perryi,* which is native to Yemen, is swallowed with water for treating constipation, to regulate menstruation, and for inducing abortion.[10]

SCIENTIFIC STUDIES: *Wound-Healing Activity* Clinical evidence has shown *Aloe vera* to be a wound-healing agent, useful in treating burns, cuts, wounds, scars, and ulcers.[11] According to laboratory studies, the fresh leaf enhances healing of wounded cells and promotes the growth of normal cells.[12] Aloe is an excellent emollient with an outstanding ability to regenerate damaged tissue, from skin ulceration and burns to frostbite, burns, and full face dermabrasion.[13] The topical effects of aloe vera appear to be the result of its wound-healing, anti-inflammatory, moisturizing, emollient, and antimicrobial actions.[14] According to one study, topical aloe gel may improve wound healing.[15] *Aloe vera,* however, seems to impair healing of deep wounds.[16]

Dermatological Activity Aloe is also valuable in skin care, treating acne, aging skin, allergies, itching, and eczema.[17] It is used in hair care for hair loss, dandruff, and psoriasis.[18] According to a double blind study of 60 people with mild to moderate symptoms of psoriasis, aloe vera cream was shown to be helpful.[19] In another study, aloe gel appeared to make hydrocortisone cream work better.[20] There is evidence that it effectively regenerates injured nerves and is successful in healing leg ulcerations and severe acne and that it promotes hair growth.[21] In one study, frostbite patients who were treated with a product containing 70 percent aloe suffered only from a 7 percent infection rate while those who received no aloe had a 33 percent rate of amputation.[22]

Antiperiodontitis Activity One study injected aloe extracts into the diseased areas of 128 patients suffering from varying degrees of periodontosis. Within one week, symptoms ceased and pain decreased in all patients.[23]

Immunostimulating Activity Acemannan, a water-soluble polysaccharide found in aloe vera, is a potent immune system stimulant.[24] Acemannan has shown promise in treating viral infections like HIV, particularly in its early stages.[25] It may also hold promise for treating diabetes and reducing triglycerides and blood sugar.[26] Aloe has been shown to lower blood sugar levels in diabetic mice.[27] While the clinical work on the effects of aloe vera on heart disease is limited, it was found to help prevent heart attacks in those who suffer from heart problems or who have a family history of heart disease.[28] Studies have shown that daily consumption of aloe vera juice lowers blood pressure and cholesterol levels by 12 to 14 points in a matter of weeks.[29]

Laxative Activity Aloe is taken internally for chronic constipation (particularly when induced by iron supplements), poor appetite, digestive disorders, immune system enhancement, asthma, and colonic irrigation. Aloe vera is rarely prescribed without a carminative, like *Foeniculum vulgare* or *Tamarindus indica,* to moderate the tendency to intestinal griping caused by the crystalline part of aloe called aloin. In commercial juice and gel, the aloin is removed from the leaf, making it soothing to intestinal irritations, peptic ulcers and colitis. Hence, any warnings apply to aloe latex used as a laxative, not the aloe gel or juice commonly consumed by health enthusiasts.[30]

Antiasthma Activity According to one study, the oral administration of *Aloe vera* for six months produced positive results in the treatment of asthma.[31]

Antiulcer Activity Studies have demonstrated the effectiveness of aloe in treating stomach lesions of peptic ulcer patients. In a study of twelve patients with X-ray confirmed duodenal ulcers, all demonstrated complete recovery after one year of consuming a tablespoon of an emulsion of *Aloe vera* gel in mineral oil once daily.[32]

Antiarthritic Activity Aloe is widely used, both as a liniment and as a drink, to reduce swelling, the pain of arthritis and rheumatism. In animal trials, aloe vera has shown positive results in the treatment of arthritis.[33]

Antidiabetic Activity In the Arabian Peninsula, diabetics consume aloe to help control their blood glucose levels. The effectiveness of aloe in reducing blood sugar levels in non-insulin-dependent individuals was confirmed in a clinical trial. Patients who took one teaspoon of aloe daily for 4 to 14 weeks saw their fasting blood sugar levels reduced by half, without loss of body weight.[34]

Aloe Notes

1. Abū Dāwūd S. *Sunan Abū Dāwūd.* Bayrūt: Dār Ibn Ḥazm, 1998.

2. Sūyūṭī J. *As-Sūyūṭī's Medicine of the Prophet.* Ed. A Thomson. London: Ṭā-Hā Publishers, 1994: 73.

3. Abū Dāwūd S. *Ṣaḥīḥ Sunan Abū Dāwūd.* Riyyāḍ: Maktab al-Tarbiyyah, 1989.

4. Abū Dāwūd S. *Ṣaḥīḥ Sunan Abū Dāwūd,* Riyyāḍ: Maktab al-Tarbiyyah, 1989.

5. Nisābūrī A. *Islamic Medical Wisdom: The Ṭibb al-a'immah.* Trans. B. Ispahany. Ed. AJ Newman. London: Muḥammadī Trust, 1991: 04.

6. Iṣbahānī AN al-. *Mawsū'at al-ṭibb al-nabawī.* Ed. MKD al-Turkī. Bayrūt: Dār Ibn Ḥazm, 2006.

7. Dīnawarī AH. *Kitāb al-nabāt: Le dictionaire botanique d'Abū Ḥanīfa al-Dīnawarī.* al-Qāhirah: Institut Français d'Archéologie Orientale du Caire, 1973: 95–96.

8. Bīrūnī, AR al-. *al-Bīrūnī's Book on Pharmacy and Materia Medica.* Ed. and trans. HM Said. Karachi: Hamdard National Foundation, 1973.

9. Ghazanfar SA. *Handbook of Arabian Medicinal Plants.* Boca Raton: CRC Press, 1994.

10. Ghazanfar SA. *Handbook of Arabian Medicinal Plants.* Boca Raton: CRC Press, 1994.

11. Lawless J, Allan J. *Aloe Vera: Natural Wonder Cure.* Thorsons: London, 2000: 50–57.

12. Compton MS. *Herbal Gold.* St. Paul: Llewellyn, 2000: 132.

13. Tyler VE., Foster S. *Tyler's Honest Herbal.* 4th ed. New York: Haworth Press, 1999: 30; Lucas RM. *Miracle Medicine Herbs.* West Nyack: Parker, 1991: 100–101.

14. Robson MC, Heggers JP, and Hagstron WJ. Myth, magic, witchcraft, or fact? *Aloe vera* revisited. *J Burn Care Rehab* 1982; 3: 157–162; Davis RH, Kabbani JM, and Maro NP: *Aloe vera* and wound healing. *J Am Pod Med Assoc* 1987; 77: 165–169; Davis RH, Leitner MG, and Russo JM. *Aloe vera,* a natural approach for treating wounds, edema, and pain in diabetes. *J Am Pod Med Assoc* 1988; 78: 60–68; Rowe TD, Loevell BK, and Parks LM: Further observations on the use of Aloe vera leaf in the treatment of third-degree X-ray reactions. *J Am Pharm Assoc* 1941; 30: 266–269; Rowe TD: Effect of fresh *Aloe vera* gel in the treatment of third-degree Roentgen reactions on white rates. *J Am. Pharmacol Assoc* 1940; 29: 348–350; Lushbaugh, CC and Hale DB. Experimental acute radiodermatitis following beta radiation. V. Histopathological study of the mode of action of therapy with *Aloe vera. Cancer* 1953; 6: 690–698.

15. Chithra, P, et al. Influence of *Aloe vera* on collagen characteristics in healing dermal wounds in rats. *Mol Cell Biochem* 1998; 181(1&2): 71–76.

16. Schmidt JM, et al. *Aloe vera* dermal wound gel is associated with a delay in wound healing. *Obstet Gynecol* 1991; 78: 115–117.

17. Lawless J, Allan J. *Aloe Vera: Natural Wonder Cure.* Thorsons: London, 2000: 58–63.

18. Lawless J, Allan J. *Aloe Vera: Natural Wonder Cure.* Thorsons: London, 2000: 64–66.

19. Syed TA, Ahmad A, Holt AH, et al. Management of psoriasis with *Aloe vera* extract in a hydrophilic cream: a placebo-controlled, double-blind study. *Trop Med Internat Health* 1996; 1: 505–509.

20. Davis RH, et al. *Aloe vera* as a biologically active vehicle for hydrocortisone acetate. *J Am Pod Med Assoc* 1991; 81(1): 1–9.

21. El Zawahry, M., et al. *Intern. Journ. Dermat.* 1973; 12(1): 68–74.

22. Heggers, J.P., et al. *Journ. Amer. Med. Tech.* 1979; 41: 293.

23. Benenson V. *Extract of Aloe: Supplement to Clinical Data.* Moscow: Medexport: Moscow Stomatologic Inst.

24. Sheets MA, et al. Studies of the effect of acemannan on retrovirus infections: Clinical stabilization of feline leukemia virus-infected cats. *Mol Biother* 1991; 3: 41–45; Hart LA, et al. Effects of low molecular weight constituents from *Aloe vera* gel on oxidative metabolism and cytotoxic and bactericidal activities of human neutrophils. *Int J Immunol Pharmacol* 1990; 12: 427–434; Kemp, MC, et al. In vitro-evaluation of the antiviral effects of acemannan on the replication and pathogenesis of HIV-1 and other enveloped viruses: Modification of the processing of glycoprotein precursors. *Antiviral Res* 1990; 13(Suppl. 1): 83; Womble D and Helderman JH: Enhancement of all responsiveness of human lymphocytes by acemannan. *Int J Immunopharmacol* 1988; 10: 967–974; Peng SY, et al. Decreased mortality of Norman murine sarcoma in mice treated with the immunomodulator, acemannan. *Mol Biother* 1991; 3: 79–87.

25. Compton MS. *Herbal Gold.* St. Paul: Llewellyn, 2000: 132; Anonymous: *Aloe vera* may boost AZT. *Med Tribune* 1991: 4; McDaniel, HR, et al. An increase in circulating monocyte/macrophages (MM) is induced by oral acemannan in HIV-1 patients. *Am J Clin Pathol* 1990; 94: 516–517; Pulse TL and Uhlig E: A significant improvement in a clinical pilot study utilizing nutritional supplements, essential fatty acids and stabilized Aloe vera juice in 29 seropositive, ARC and AIDS patients. *J Adv Med* 1990; 3: 209–230; Singer J: A randomized placebo-controlled trial of oral acemannan as an adjunctive to anti-retroviral therapy in advanced HIV disease. *Int. Conf AIDS* 1993; 9(1): 494.

26. Tyler VE, Foster S. *Tyler's Honest Herbal.* New York: Haworth Press, 1999: 30.

27. Ajabnoor MA: Effect of aloes on blood glucose levels in normal and alloxan diabetic mice. *J Ethnopharmacol* 1990; 28: 215–220.

28. Lawless J, Allan J. *Aloe Vera: Natural Wonder Cure.* Thorsons: London, 2000: 70.

29. Lawless J, Allan J. *Aloe Vera: Natural Wonder Cure.* Thorsons: London, 2000: 70–71.

30. Goldberg B. *Alternative Medicine: The Definitive Guide.* Fife, Washington: Future Medicine, 1995: 262.

31. Shida T, et al. Effect of *Aloe* extract on peripheral phagocytosis in adult bronchial asthma. *Planta Medica* 1989; 51: 263–266.

32. Blitz, JJ. Smith JW, Gerard JR. *Aloe vera* gel in peptic ulcer therapy: preliminary report. *J Am Osteopathol Soc* 1963; 62: 731–735.

33. Lawless J, Allan J. *Aloe Vera: Natural Wonder Cure.* Thorsons: London, 2000: 71–72.

34. Harm. *Research* 24(4): 288–294; 1986.

Aloeswood / *'Ūd al-Ḥindī*

Family: Thymelaeaceae
Botanical Name: *Aquilaria* spp.

Common Names: *English* Aloeswood, agarwood; *French* Bois d'oud; *Spanish* Áloe indio, Palo de Áloe; *German* Erlenholz, Agarholz, Adlerbaum, über die Aloe; *Urdu/Unānī* Agar, Ood, Ood-e-Gharqi, Ood-e-Hindi; *Modern Standard Arabic* 'Ūd al-hindī, 'Ūd al-bukhūr, 'Ūd al-raṭb

Safety Rating: Generally Safe *Aquilaria* is generally considered safe when used as directed under expert supervision. Considering that the wood and oil of *Aquilaria* are the most expensive in the world, and considering that the tree is a threatened species, its medicinal use should be discouraged.

Prophetic Prescription: The Messenger of Allāh said, "Aloeswood (*'ūd al-ḥindī*) is a cure for seven diseases. When it is inhaled, it treats sore throats, when it is placed in the mouth, it treats pleurisy."[1] He also said, "Use aloeswood (*'ūd al-ḥindī*) for it cures seven diseases, and pleurisy is one of them."[2] In another instance, a mother brought her son to the Prophet seeking treatment for his tonsils. The Prophet said, "Why do you pain your children by pressing their throats! Use aloeswood (*'ūd al-ḥindī*) for it cures seven diseases, one of which is pleurisy. It is used as a snuff for treating throat and tonsil disease and it is inserted into one side of the mouth of one suffering from pleurisy."[3] According to Ibn Ḥabīb, the Prophet used to use aloeswood (*'ūd al-ḥindī*) as a snuff to treat headaches. The Andalusian herbalist also explained that the costus (*kust*) of aloeswood should be rubbed with sesame and *zanbaq* (*Iris germanica* L.) prior to use.[4]

Issues in Identification: Although the Arabic *'ūd* has the general sense of wood, stick, pole, branch, twig, stalk, cane, and reed, it also refers in a specific sense to aloeswood. Elgood and Turkī identify *'ūd* as aloeswood, without specifying a scientific name.[5] Said says that *'ūd* refers to aloeswood, including *Aquilaria agallocha* (a synonym for *A. malaccensis*).[6] Johnstone identifies it as *Aquilaria malaccensis*[7] while Álvarez Morales and Girón Irueste identify it as *Aloexylon agallochum* Lour.[8] According to Duke, the aloeswood of the Old Testament refers to *Aquilaria malaccensis*, which is known in Arabic as *ūd*, *ūd al-ḥindī*, and *ūd al-jūj*, among other dialectal words. *Aquilaria agallocha* is known in Moroccan Arabic as *'ūd kameira*.[9]

According to Bīrūnī, *'ūd al-hindī* is also known as *al-maqr*.[10] According to most translators, *'ūd al-ḥindī*, which literally means "Hindu wood" or "Indian wood," refers to aloeswood. According to Sūyūṭī, "The best *'ūd* is called *qamarī*, and the best of this is tinged with blue. *'Ud* is also known as *'alūt*. Indian *'ūd* is another name for *'ūd*."[11] Bīrūnī describes the *qamarī* variety as light, somewhat whitish, and non-greasy.[12] As Abū Dāwūd and Sūyūṭī note, aloeswood (*'ūd*) is sometimes referred to as *kust al-ḥindī* or *qust al-ḥindī*. Although aloeswood is also known as Indian or Hindu costus, it must not be confused with costus or *Saussurea lappa*. Indian costus is not the same product as costus. Modern incense traders are categorical in asserting that *'ūd*, known as Lignum Aloes, aloeswood, agarwood, agarci wood, and eagle wood, is the sweet perfumed wood from the Aquila tree.

According to Farooqi, the assumption that *'ūd al-ḥindī* refers to *Aquilaria agallocha* is "scientifically and historically absolutely wrong."[13] He claims that during the time of the Prophet, only the root of costus (*Saussurea lappa*) obtained in Kashmir was traded from India and that the Arabs were not aware of agar or aloeswood, which was found only in Annam. However, as Said has established, the *'ūd* identified by Bīrūnī is indeed *Aquilaria malaccensis*.[14] Ghazanfar also confirms that *Aquilaria* is known in Arabia as *'ūd* and its perfume continues to be highly prized to this day.[15] Shaykh Hakim Moinuddin Chishti also identifies *'ūd* as aloeswood.[16]

As Eric Hansen explains in "The Hidden History of Scented Wood," historians are uncertain when aloeswood first reached the Middle East.[17] They are certain, though, that aloeswood has been present in the region since ancient times. References to aloeswood are found in the Old Testament. Historians of China like Friedrich Hirth and W.W. Rockhill put the date as far back as the 10th century B.C., when King Solomon began trade with the south Arabian Sabaean kingdom, which was already trading with merchants on the Malabar coast of India. Aloeswood is also mentioned in written accounts by Arab and Chinese travelers and merchants dating from the first century of the modern era, a time of accelerating trade among the Arabian Peninsula, the Malabar Coast, and China. At this time, frankincense and myrrh from Oman and the Hadramout region of southern Arabia were being traded in the Far East. It is thus reasonable to assume that a reciprocal trade in aloeswood would have traveled on the same maritime routes.

Farooqi's claim that aloeswood was only found in Annam is also incorrect. The Chinese role in the aloeswood trade is considered to have been significant since the Han Dynasty (206 B.C.–A.D. 220), when Imperial perfume blenders used it along with cloves, musk, costus-root oil and camphor. In fact, it was in response to increasing domestic and international demand for aloeswood that Chinese traders ventured into Annam, now part of Vietnam, where they encountered an abundance of top-quality trees. This new source of supply converted the Chinese traders into wholesalers and middlemen, securing their dominion on the aloeswood market, a position they retain to this day.

Farooqi's claim that aloeswood was not traded among the Arabs during the time of the Prophet is equally erroneous. The aloeswood trade with the Arab world was well-established in pre–Islamic times. As Eric Hansen explains, Arab and Persian traders had established settlements on the outskirts of Canton as early as 300 C.E., and a Chinese traveler named Fa-Hien noted the wealth of the Arab *'ūd* traders from the Hadramout and Oman who lived comfortably in Ceylon. The aloeswood trade continued into Islamic times. Writing in the sixth century, the Greek geographer, Cosmas Indicopleustes, noted that the China-Ceylon–Middle East trade included large shipments of aloeswood.

In his book *Silsilat al-tawārīkh* (*Chain of Chronicles*), Zayd ibn Ḥasan of Siraf (now in Iran) relates the experiences of two ninth century traders: Ibn Wahhāb of Basra, and another named Sulaymān. Although they traveled at slightly different times, both reported on the price and availability of aloeswood in both Basra and Baghdad. Their trading routes traversed the Arabic Gulf to the Maldives, Ceylon, the Nicobar Islands, and then on to Canton by way of the Straits of Malacca and the South China Sea. According to Zayn ibn Ḥasan, Sulaymān saw Arab and Persian traders playing a game similar to backgammon. He mentions that the pieces were occasionally made of rhinoceros horn or ivory, but that they were most commonly made of fragrant aloeswood. Thus, a reliable chain of reference confirms that aloeswood has a 3,000 year history in the China, Japan, and the Middle East, and that it was well-known in both pre–Islamic and Islamic Arabia.

PROPERTIES AND USES: Aloeswood, sometimes referred to as agarwood, is the resinous wood from the genus *Aquilaria*, an evergreen tree native to northern India, Laos, Cambodia, Malaysia, Indonesia, and Vietnam. Rare and precious, aloeswood is the most expensive wood in the world. Aloeswood is an aromatic, astringent, stimulant, stomachic, laxative, tonic herb used to treat nausea, nervous disorders, regurgitation, and weakness in the elderly. It is considered an aphrodisiac, diuretic, antimicrobial, carminative, cholagogue, deobstruent, and tonic. It is used to relieve epilepsy, to treat smallpox and rheumatism, and to relieve spasms in the digestive and respiratory systems, including shortness of breath. It is used to treat illness during and after childbirth, chills, general pains, to lower fever, to combat cirrhosis of the liver as well as cancer. It has also been used as a treatment for lung and stomach tumors. It is purgative in large amounts. Chinese, Tibetan, Ayurvedic and Unānī physicians have all used agarwood in their practice to treat various diseases, including mental illness. It is used internally in Unānī medicine for anemia, amenorrhea, atonic dyspepsia, obstructive jaundice, painful piles, and as an anthelmintic. Externally, the powder is dusted over wounds to expedite healing. Farooqi's claim that "Agar bark has never been considered a useful medicine either in Unānī medicine or Ayurveda" is incorrect.[18] As Deni Bown states, "It has a long history of use in traditional Chinese, Ayurvedic, and Unānī medicine."[19]

SCIENTIFIC STUDIES: *Antitumor Activity* According to an animal study conducted by Wonkwang University in South Korea, the aqueous extract of *Aquilaria agallocha* stems possess inhibitory effects on passive cutaneous anaphylaxis.[20] The stem bark of *Aquilaria malaccensis* has also been shown to possess anticancer compounds.[21] Further studies have shown other anticancer properties of aloeswood.[22]

Nervous System Depressant Activity In an animal study conducted by the Institute for Oriental Medicine in Japan, the benzene extractable compounds of agarwood were shown to possess potent central nervous system depressant activities, supporting its use in Oriental medicine as a sedative.[23]

Aloeswood Notes

1. Sūyūṭī J. *As-Sūyūṭī's Medicine of the Prophet.* Ed. A Thomson. London: Ṭā-Hā Publishers, 1994: 83; Bukhārī M. *Ṣaḥīḥ al-Bukhārī.* al-Riyyāḍ: Bayt al-Afkār, 1998.
2. Ibn Ḥanbal A. *Musnad al-Imām Aḥmad ibn Ḥanbal.* Bayrūt: Mu'assasat al-Risālah, 1993.
3. Bukhārī M. *Ṣaḥīḥ al-Bukhārī.* al-Riyyāḍ: Bayt al-Afkār, 1998; Muslim. *Jāmi' al-ṣaḥīḥ.* al-Riyyāḍ: Bayt al-Afkār, 1998.
4. Ibn Ḥabīb A. *Mujtaṣar fī al-ṭibb/Compendio de medicina.* Ed. C Álvarez de Morales and F Girón Irueste. Madrid: Consejo Superior de Investigaciones Científicas, 1992: 56/22.
5. Elgood C. Trans. *Ṭibb al-nabī* or *Medicine of the Prophet.* Sūyūṭī J, M Chaghhaynī. Osiris 1962; 14: 38; Iṣbahānī AN al-. *Mawsū'at al-ṭibb al-nabawī.* Ed. MKD al-Turkī. Bayrūt: Dār Ibn Ḥazm, 2006.
6. Bīrūnī, AR al-. *al-Bīrūnī's Book on Pharmacy and Materia Medica.* Ed. and trans. ḤM Said. Karachi: Hamdard National Foundation, 1973.
7. Johnstone P, trans. *Medicine of the Prophet.* Ibn Qayyim al-Jawziyyah. Cambridge: The Islamic Texts Society, 1998.
8. Ibn Ḥabīb A. *Mujtaṣar fī al-ṭibb/Compendio de medicina.* Ed. C Álvarez de Morales and F Girón Irueste. Madrid: Consejo Superior de Investigaciones Científicas, 1992.
9. Davidson A. *The Oxford Companion to Food.* Oxford: Oxford University Press, 1999: 7.
10. Bīrūnī, AR al-. *al-Bīrūnī's Book on Pharmacy and Materia Medica.* Ed. and trans. HM Said. Karachi: Hamdard National Foundation, 1973.
11. Sūyūṭī J. *As-Sūyūṭī's Medicine of the Prophet.* Ed. A Thomson. London: Ṭā-Hā Publishers, 1994: 82.
12. Bīrūnī, AR al-. *al-Bīrūnī's Book on Pharmacy and Ma-*

teria Medica. Ed. and trans. HM Said. Karachi: Hamdard National Foundation, 1973.
13. Farooqi MIH. *Medicinal Plants in the Traditions of Prophet Muḥammad*. Lucknow: Sidrah Publishers, 1998: 55.
14. Bīrūnī AR al-. *al-Bīrūnī's Book on Pharmacy and Materia Medica*. Ed. and trans. HM Said. Karachi: Hamdard National Foundation, 1973.
15. Ghazanfar SA. *Handbook of Arabian Medicinal Plants*. Boca Raton: CRC Press, 1994.
16. Chishti SHM. *The Book of Sufi Healing*. Rochester, Vermont: Inner Traditions International, 1991: 118; *The Traditional Healer's Handbook*. Rochester, Vermont: Healing Arts Press, 1991: 323.
17. Hansen E. The hidden history of scented wood. *Saudi Aramco World* 2006; 51: 6. http://www.saudiaramcoworld.com/issue/200006/the.hidden.history.of.scented.wood.htm
18. Farooqi MIH. *Medicinal Plants in the Traditions of Prophet Muḥammad*. Lucknow: Sidrah Publishers, 1998: 55.
19. Bown D. *Encyclopedia of Herbs and Their Uses*. Westmount: RD Press, 1995: 240.
20. Kim, Lee, Lee, Kim, Song, Lee, Kim. Effect of the aqueous extract of Aquilaria agallocha stems on the immediate hypersensitivity reactions. *J* 1997; 58(1): 31–38.
21. Gunasekera, Kinghorn, Cordell, Farnsworth. Plant anticancer agents. XIX Constituents of Aquilaria malaccensis. *J* 1981; 44(5): 569–572.
22. Gunasekera, Kinghorn, Cordell, Farnsworth. Plant anticancer agents. XIX Constituents of Aquilaria malaccensis. *J* 1981; 44(5): 569–572.
23. Okugawa, Ueda, Matsumoto, Kawanishi, Kato. Effects of agarwood extracts on the central nervous system in mice. *Planta* 1993; 59(1): 32–36.

Anabasis/*Ashnān*

FAMILY: Chenopodiaceae

BOTANICAL NAME: *Anabasis aphylla*; *Anabasis articulata*

COMMON NAMES: *English* Anabasis, Jointed Anabasis; *French* Anabasis; *Spanish* Anabasis; *German* Anabasis; *Urdu/Unānī* Ashnan, Gazran, Ghasol, Chogan, Kakal; *Modern Standard Arabic* Ashnān

SAFETY RATING: DANGEROUS The annual branches of anabasis contain the alkaloid anabasine, which is a botanical insecticide.[1] Besides being toxic to invertebrates, anabasis can cause poisoning in mammals.[2] In high doses, anabasine produces a depolarizing block of nerve transmission, leading ultimately to death by asystole.[3] Symptoms of anabasine poisoning resemble those of nicotine poisoning. Anabasine is believed to be teratogenic in swine when consumed in large amounts.[4]

PROPHETIC PRESCRIPTION: According to Imām Ja'far al-Ṣādiq, "Eating anabasis (*ashnān*) weakens the knees, and destroys semen."[5]

ISSUES IN IDENTIFICATION: While it is known as *agram*, *'ajram*, *balbal*, *shenan*, *tatir*, *ujirim*, and *ushnān* in colloquial Arabic, *ashnān* is the Classical Arabic term for anabasis. *Ashnān* is a synonym for *shībah*. In Yemen, it is known as *shajar abyaḍ*; in Syria it is known as *dukn al-shaykh*; and in Egypt it is known as *shawk al-aḥmar*. The particular species of *ashnān* mentioned by the Imām is more difficult to determine. It may refer to *Anabasis aphylla*, which extends from Europe to Russia, including Siberia and northern China, and which is very common in Central Iran. It is much more likely, however, that it refers to *Anabasis articulata* or jointed anabasis, which is found in the Levant and the Arabian Peninsula. This is also the view of Duke, who identifies the Biblical *shuni* as *Anabasis articulata*.

PROPERTIES AND USES: Although *Anabasis aphylla* is used medicinally in some parts of the world, little is known about its properties and uses. The pharmacological properties of the plant have recently been the subject of several Russian and Chinese studies which are unavailable in other languages.

The medicinal properties of *Anabasis articulata* are more widely known. The plant is considered to have antismoking, insecticidal, myorelaxant, respirastimulant, and sialogogue activities. It also happens to be a fairly potent rodenticide. The mashed plant is combined with mud and blood and applied to goat lesions by Lebanese goat-herders. The Lebanese also apply the fresh leaf tea or dry plant ashes to running sores. High in potassium and saponins, *Anabasis articulata* is used as a detergent for washing purposes due to its foaming and cleaning properties.

SCIENTIFIC STUDIES: *Antimicrobial Activity* According to a study conducted by the China Agricultural University in Beijing, *Anabasis aphylla* contains some antimicrobial compounds. The researchers concluded that the antimicrobial agents could be used to control plant and animal diseases.[6]

Anabasis Notes

1. Komarov VL et al. *Flora SSSR 1934–1964*; Wu Zhengyi & P. H. Raven et al., eds. *Flora of China 1994*.
2. Shatrov AP. Poisoning of sheep with Anabasis aphylla and A. solsa. 1962 *Veterinariia Moscow* 1962; 39(8): 49–54.
3. Mizrachi N, Levy S, Goren Z. Fatal poisoning from nicotiana glauca leaves: identification of anabasine by gas-chromatography/mass spectrometry. *Journal of Forensic Sciences* 2000; 45(3): 736–741.
4. Notes on poisoning: Nicotiana tabacum. Canadian Biodiversity Information Facility. Government of Canada 2008-03-18. http://www.cbif.gc.ca/pls/pp/ppack.info?p_psn=186&p_type= all&p_sci=sci&p_x=px.
5. Majlisī M. *Biḥār al-anwār*. Ṭihrān: Javad al-Alavi, 1956.
6. Du, Wang, Hao, Li, Peng, Wang, Liu, Zhou. Antimicrobial phenolic compounds from Anabasis aphylla L. *Nat* 2009 Mar; 4(3): 385–8

Apples / *Tuffāḥ*

Family: Rosaceae

Botanical Name: *Malus domestica*

Common Names: *English* Apple tree; Apple (fruit); *French* Pommier; Pomme (fruit); *Spanish* Manzano; Manzana (fruit); *German* Echter Apfelbaum; Apfel (fruit); *Urdu/Unānī* Saib, Tuffah; *Modern Standard Arabic* Tuffāḥ

Safety Rating: Generally Safe to Potentially Deadly Apples are generally safe. The seeds, however, contain cyanide, and should not be consumed, as ingesting large quantities of them can cause death.

Prophetic Prescription: While most English-speakers are familiar with the sayings, "An apple a day keeps the doctor away," and "eating an apple before bed will make a doctor beg his bread," few are aware of the concrete medicinal benefits of apples. The Imāms of the Household of the Prophet, however, were quite cognizant of the medicinal value of the apple and its particular applications. Imām Muḥammad al-Bāqir said, "When you wish to eat apples, sniff them and then eat them, for if you do that every illness and danger will be expelled from your body and everything caused by winds will subside."[1]

Imām Ja'far al-Ṣādiq, for example, gave a general endorsement of apples for a broad range of illnesses. "If people knew what was in apples," he said "they would treat their illnesses only with them."[2] In a longer variant of the tradition, the Imām added "because they are the most beneficial for the heart, and the fastest acting, especially when they are ripe."[3] Imām al-Ṣādiq also mentioned that "Apples help ripen the stomach."[4] On another occasion, he said, "We cure ourselves with apples."[5]

In another narration, Imām Ja'far al-Ṣādiq is more specific, and recommends apples for febrile conditions: "Give apples to those among you who have fever for nothing is more beneficial."[6] When fever was mentioned to the Imām, he said: "We, Ahl al-Bayt, only treat ourselves by pouring cold water on ourselves and by consuming apples."[7] In another tradition, Imām al-Ṣādiq said, "Apples extinguish the heat, cool down the inside, and it remove fever."[8] He also said, "Apples remove fever, and lowers [body] temperature."[9] In a longer version of the same tradition, the Imām said, "I sent for some apples in order to eat them so that they can lower my temperature, cool down my inside, and to remove fever."[10]

A man from a zone affected by an epidemic sent a letter to the Imām. The Imām replied in writing that he should "Use apples and eat them."[11] The man did so and he was cured. On one occasion, the Imām advised a person with a nose-bleed to consume apples. He did so, and the bleeding subsided.[12] On another occasion, he instructed a man suffering from a nose-bleed to drink apple sauce saying "Give him apple sauce (*sawīq al-tuffāḥ*) to drink." He did so, and was healed.[13] Finally, the Imām also affirmed that "I do not know of anything better against poisons than apple sauce (*sawīq*)."[14]

Issues in Identification: It is the consensus that *tuffāḥ* is Arabic for apple. Writing in the 4th century, Palladius mentioned thirty-seven varieties of apples.[15] Ibn Ḥabīb (790–853), the Andalusian herbalist, said, "The apple has a great many varieties, some sweet, some sour, and some in between."[16] One of the companions of Imām Ja'far al-Ṣādiq was surprised to see the Imām eating apples. Regarding apples, the companion commented that "people hate them," suggesting that the apples consumed by the Imām were of the tart variety.[17] During Dīnawarī's (828–896) time, apples were grown abundantly in Arabia (*bilād al-'arab*).[18] Unfortunately, Dīnawarī does not identify the specific regions of "the land of the Arabs" where apples were cultivated in large quantities.

For all intents and purposes, bilād al-'arab or the Islamic Empire stretched from al-Andalus in Western Europe to India. Since eastern Turkey is the center of diversity of the genus *Malus*, it is possible that he included the region as part of Greater Arabia. Considering that apples are produced in colder regions, it seems unlikely that apples were grown in Arabia proper, although they can be grown in northern Iraq, most of Iran, North Africa, Spain, and Portugal. We know for certain that they were being cultivated in al-Andalus in the 9th century. In 1080, Ibn Bassāl wrote *The Book of Agriculture* which contains information on many crops grown in Islamic Spain, including apples.[19] It is the consensus of scholars that Muslims were responsible for bringing sweet apples from Turkey or Persia into North Africa and al-Andalus.[20] As regards the apples consumed by the Prophet and the Imāms, they were likely brought by caravan to Arabia from Persia or Syria.[21] It should also be noted that during the Middle Ages, apples were eaten as "vegetables," and not as fruit. They were even included in soups.[22]

Properties and Uses: Apples are a nutritious fruit rich in vitamin C, a generous amount of calcium, 50 percent more vitamin A than oranges, and they are rich in potassium and phosphorus. Apples possess alkalizing, sedative, diuretic, laxative, hydrating, and cholesterol-lowering properties. They are used to prevent constipation and treat diarrhea, stomach disorders, anemia, headaches, eye infections, dry cough, gout, skin problems, rheumatism, kidney stones, high blood pressure, and heart disease. In addition, the bark of the apple tree is tonic and febrifuge.

SCIENTIFIC STUDIES: *Anticancer Activity* According to research, apples may reduce the risk of colon cancer, prostate cancer, and lung cancer.[23] Apples contain vitamin C, as well as a host of other antioxidant compounds, which may reduce the risk of cancer by preventing DNA damage. While they contain less fiber than other fruits, the fiber content in apples helps regulate bowel movements, thus reducing the risk of colon cancer.

Cholesterol-Lowering Activity Since they are fat-free, a source of fiber, and bulky for their caloric intake, apples may help with heart disease, weight loss, and controlling cholesterol. Research indicates that a diet high in potassium helps reduce the risk of heart attacks. Interestingly enough, Ibn Buṭlān (d. c. 1068) observed that sweet apples comforted the heart.[24]

Diuretic Activity Apples have a considerable diuretic effect that aids in bringing down blood pressure to normal levels. Apples reduce the supply of sodium chloride to a minimum, thus relieving the kidneys. In addition, the high level of potassium in apples helps lower the sodium level in tissues. The malic acid contained in apples is believed to neutralize uric acid and afford relief to the sufferers; hence, Ibn Buṭlān's assertion that sour apples were good for an inflamed liver.[25]

Neurodegenerative Disorders Apples show potential in protecting the brain from neurodegenerative diseases like Alzheimer's and Parkinsonism. A study conducted by Cornell University found that the naturally occurring antioxidants found in fresh apples protect nerve cells from neurotoxicity induced by oxidative stress.[26] Although all apples are high in phytonutrients, the amount of phenolic compounds in apple flesh varies from year to year, season to season, and growing region.

Apples Notes

1. Nisābūrī A. *Islamic Medical Wisdom: The Ṭibb al-a'immah*. Trans. B. Ispahany. Ed. AJ Newman. London: Muḥammadī Trust, 1991: 179.
2. Nisābūrī A. *Islamic Medical Wisdom: The Ṭibb al-a'immah*. Trans. B. Ispahany. Ed. AJ Newman. London: Muḥammadī Trust, 1991: 61.
3. Ṭabarsī H. *Mustadrak al-Wasā'il*. Bayrūt: Mu'assasat Āl al-Bayt, 1987–1988.
4. Majlisī M. *Biḥār al-anwār*. Ṭihrān: Javad al-Alavi, 1956.
5. Nisābūrī A. *Islamic Medical Wisdom: The Ṭibb al-a'immah*. Trans. B. Ispahany. Ed. AJ Newman. London: Muḥammadī Trust, 1991: 69.
6. Nisābūrī A. *Islamic Medical Wisdom: The Ṭibb al-a'immah*. Trans. B. Ispahany. Ed. AJ Newman. London: Muḥammadī Trust, 1991: 76; Ṭabarsī H. *Mustadrak al-Wasā'il*. Bayrūt: Mu'assasat Āl al-Bayt, 1987–1988.
7. Majlisī M. *Biḥār al-anwār*. Ṭihrān: Javad al-Alavi, 1956.
8. Ṭabarsī H. *Mustadrak al-Wasā'il*. Bayrūt: Mu'assasat Āl al-Bayt, 1987–1988.
9. Majlisī M. *Biḥār al-anwār*. Ṭihrān: Javad al-Alavi, 1956.
10. Majlisī M. *Biḥār al-anwār*. Ṭihrān: Javad al-Alavi, 1956.
11. Ṭabarsī H. *Mustadrak al-Wasā'il*. Bayrūt: Mu'assasat Āl al-Bayt, 1987–1988.
12. Majlisī M. *Biḥār al-anwār*. Ṭihrān: Javad al-Alavi, 1956.
13. 'Amilī H. *Wasā'il al-shī'ah*. Bayrūt: al-Mu'assasah, 1993.
14. 'Amilī H. *Wasā'il al-shī'ah*. Bayrūt: al-Mu'assasah, 1993; Majlisī M. *Biḥār al-anwār*. Ṭihrān: Javad al-Alavi, 1956.
15. Bianchini F, Corbetta F. *The Complete Book of Fruits and Vegetables*. New York: Crown, 1976: 126.
16. Ibn Ḥabīb A. *Mujtaṣar fī al-ṭibb/Compendio de medicina*. Ed. C Álvarez de Morales and F Girón Irueste. Madrid: Consejo Superior de Investigaciones Científicas, 1992: 93.
17. Majlisī M. *Biḥār al-anwār*. Ṭihrān: Javad al-Alavi, 1956.
18. Dīnawarī AH. *Kitāb al-nabāt/The Book of Plants*. Ed. Bernhard Lewin. Bayrūt: Dār al-Qalam, 1974: 218; Dīnawarī AH. *Kitāb al-nabāt/The Book of Plants*. Ed. Bernhard Lewin. Uppsala/Wiesbaden: A.-B. Lundequistska Bokhandeln and Otto Harrassowitz, 1953: 140.
19. Juniper BE, Mabberley DJ. *The Story of the Apple*. Portland: Timber Press, 2006: 132.
20. Juniper BE, Mabberley DJ. *The Story of the Apple*. Portland: Timber Press, 2006: 132.
21. Tannahill R. *Food in History*. New York: Stein and Day, 1973; 126; 174.
22. Toussaint-Samat M. *A History of Food*. Trans. Anthea Bell. West Sussex: Wiley-Blackwell, 2009: 570.
23. Stanford Comprehensive Cancer Center. Information about cancer. http://cancer.stanford.edu/information/nutritionAndCancer/reduceRisk/
24. Ibn Buṭlān, *The Medieval Health Handbook: Tacuinum sanitatis*. Ed. L Cogliati Arano. Trans. O Ratti and A Westbrook. New York: George Braziller, 1976: 10.
25. Ibn Buṭlān, *The Medieval Health Handbook: Tacuinum sanitatis*. Ed. L Cogliati Arano. Trans. O Ratti and A Westbrook. New York: George Braziller, 1976: 186.
26. Lee KW, Kim YJ, Kim DO, Lee HJ, Lee CY. J. Major phenolics in apple and their contribution to the total antioxidant capacity. *Agric Food Chem*. 2003; 51: 22: 6516–6120.

Banana/*Ṭalḥ*

FAMILY: Musaceae

BOTANICAL NAME: *Musa* x *paradisiaca*

COMMON NAMES: *English* Banana; *French* Bananier; Banane (fruit); *Spanish* Plátano, Banano; *German* Echte Banane; *Urdu/Unānī* Keylaa, Mawz; *Modern Standard Arabic* Mawz, Ṭalḥ

SAFETY RATING: GENERALLY SAFE Bananas are generally considered safe for most people.

Prophetic Prescription: The Holy Qur'ān describes *ṭalḥ* as a tree of Paradise (56:29).

Issues in Identification: According to both classical and modern Arabic dictionaries, the meaning of the word *ṭalḥ* includes both acacia and bananas. The Hans Wehr dictionary says that *ṭalḥ* is a variety of acacia (*Acacia gummifera*) as well as banana tree. Farooqi claims that the *ṭalḥ* of the Qur'ān is acacia and not bananas. Indeed, in support of this, Muḥammad Aṣad used the term "acacia" in his translation of the Qur'ān. Duke has also asserted that the Arabic *ṭalḥ* refers to *Acacia seyal* Delile.

According to Bīrūnī, however, the *ṭalḥ* mentioned in the Qur'ān is believed by most commentators to be the banana. He describes it as *manḍūd*, which means that its fruits are aligned like the teeth of a comb. He also describes *ṭalḥ* as being *makhḍūd*, which means thornless, thus distinguishing it from jujube, which has menacing thorns."[1] *Ṭalḥ* is defined as banana in several classical and modern interpretations of the Qur'ān. Although 'Abdullāh Yusuf 'Ali decided not to translate *ṭalḥ* into English, Picktall translated the term as "plantains."

As Mohammad Al-Zein and Lytton John Musselman explain, "Although banana is not native to Arabia, it is very likely that Arabs were familiar with bananas, as they were first cultivated in the Mediterranean region ... at the time of the rise of Islām."[2] It is believed that the banana was present in isolated regions of the Middle East during the time of the Prophet and there is no doubt that the spread of the banana followed the spread of Islām. Besides being mentioned in the Qur'ān and the *ḥadīth*, bananas were brought to Palestine by Muslim conquerors in the year 650. They are also mentioned in texts in Palestine and Egypt dating from the tenth century, and later appear in North Africa and al-Andalus. During medieval times, the bananas grown in Granada were said to be the best in the entire Arab world.[3] According to botanists, the banana was undoubtedly introduced into east Africa by the Arabs.[4]

The word banana is derived from the Arabic *banān*, which means the extremities of the fingers. Considering that bananas are sweet, their mention would make more sense in the Qur'ānic context of heaven. The adjective used to describe them in the Qur'ān, *talḥ*, means neatly stacked or piled one above another. A critical reading of verses 27–33 of Surah 56 suggests *talḥ* is mentioned as a source of shade, something that an acacia bush could not provide. While both meanings are possible, the strongest argument is in favor of the banana. According to Dīnawarī, some people say that *ṭalḥ* refers to *mawz barrī*, or the wild banana, which produces small green fruits that never ripen.[5] Dīnawarī says that wild miniature bananas grow in Oman, where they are called *al-bardā*.[6]

Properties and Uses: According to Maude Grieve, the banana is of more interest for its nutrient content than for its medicinal purposes. Banana root has some employment as an anthelmintic and has been reported useful in reducing bronchocele. Plantain juice has also been used as an antidote for a snakebite. According to Bakhru, bananas are beneficial for intestinal disorders, constipation, diarrhea, dysentery, arthritis, gout, anemia, allergies, kidney disorders, tuberculosis, and urinary disorders. They are also useful in weight loss, menstrual disorders, and in treating wounds and burns.

Scientific Studies: *Antioxidative Activity* According to an in-vitro study conducted by the Universidad de los Andes in Venezuela, banana extracts from *Musa acuminata* and *Musa balbisiana* were shown to possess antioxidative activity comparable to melatonin and vitamin E.[7]

Antifungal Activity In a study conducted by the Chinese University of Hong Kong, a thaumatin-like protein, isolated from the emperor banana, was found to possess antifungal activity and to slightly inhibit HIV-1.[8] According to a study conducted by Pondicherry University in India, strain FP10, a bacterial isolate from banana, possesses innate potential of fungal antibiosis and can be used as a biofertilizer as well as a biocontrol agent.

Antidiabetic Activity According to an animal study conducted by Vidyasagar University in India, the herbal formulated drug MTEC, which consists of aqueous-methanol extract of *Musa* x *paradisiaca*, *Tamarindus indica*, *Eugenia jambolana*, and *Coccinia indica* provided significant protection in fasting blood glucose and serum insulin levels in rats with induced diabetes.[9]

Anti-inflammatory Activity According to an animal study conducted by Mukogawa Women's University in Japan, corosolic acid, a constituent of banana leaves, ameliorates hypertension, abnormal lipid metabolism, and oxidative stress, as well as an inflammatory state. These results imply that corosolic acid may be beneficial in preventing atherosclerosis-related diseases.[10]

Antiulcer Activity According to an animal trial conducted by Banaras Hindu University in India, the methanolic extract of *Musa sapientum* var. *paradisiaca* showed greater ulcer-protective effect in non–insulin-dependent diabetes mellitus than glibenclamide, an anti–diabetic drug, and sucralfate, an ulcer protective drug.[11] In another animal study, various preparations of dried, unripe plantain banana were found to be antiulcerogenic against aspirin-induced ulceration and were effective as a prophylactic treatment in healing ulcers already induced by aspirin.[12]

Antimalarial Activity According to the archives of *Flora Medicinal*, an ancient pharmaceutical laboratory that supported ethnomedical research in Brazil for more than 30 years, *Musa* x *paradisiaca* is one of eighty species indicated to treat malaria by Dr. J. Monteiro da Silva and his co-workers.[13]

Antivenom Activity In a study conducted by the University Federal de Minas Gerais in Brazil, researchers verified the activity of *Musa* x *paradisiaca* against the toxicity of snake venom. When mixed with snake venom, *Musa* x *paradisiaca* extract significantly inhibited phospholipasa A2, myotoxic, and hemorrhagic activities and lethality in mice. However, when mice received *Musa* x *paradisiaca* extract and venoms without previous mixture or by separated routes, they were not protected against venom toxicity. According to these results, *Musa* x *paradisiaca* extract does not protect against the toxic effects of snake venoms in vivo, but was very effective when the experiments were done in vitro.[14]

Antilithiactic Activity According to an animal study conducted by Kasturba Medical College in Manipal, *Musa* x *paradisiaca* stem juice was found to be effective in reducing the formation and also in dissolving preformed kidney stones.[15]

Banana Notes

1. Bīrūnī, AR al-. *al-Bīrūnī's Book on Pharmacy and Materia Medica*. Ed. and trans. HM Said. Karachi: Hamdard National Foundation, 1973: 44.

2. Al-Zein M, Musselman LJ. The Quranic *Ṭalḥ*: banana or acacia? *2004 Botany Conference*. http://www.2004.botanyconference.org/

3. Watson A. *Agricultural Innovation in the Early Islamic World*. New York: Cambridge University Press, 1983: 54.

4. Bianchini F, Corbetta F. *The Complete Book of Fruits and Vegetables*. New York: Crown, 1976: 176; Watson A. *Agricultural Innovation in the Early Islamic World*. New York: Cambridge University Press, 1983: 54.

5. al-Dīnawarī AH. *Kitāb al-nabāt: Le dictionaire botanique d'Abū Ḥanīfa al-Dīnawarī*. al-Qāhirah: Institut Français d'Archéologie Orientale du Caire, 1973.

6. Dīnawarī AH. *Kitāb al-nabāt: Le dictionaire botanique d'Abū Ḥanīfa al-Dīnawarī*. al-Qāhirah: Institut Français d'Archéologie Orientale du Caire, 1973.

7. Perez-Perez EM, Rodriguez-Malaver AJ, Padilla N, Medina-Ramirez G, Davila J. Antioxidant capacity of crude extracts from clones of banana and plane species. *J Med Food*. 2006; 9(4): 517–523.

8. Ho VS, Wong JH, Ng TB. A thaumatin-like antifungal protein from the emperor banana. *Peptides*. 2007; 28(4): 760–766.

9. Mallick C, Mandal S, Barik B, Bhattacharya A, Ghosh D. Protection of testicular dysfunctions by MTEC, a formulated herbal drug, in streptozotocin induced diabetic rat. *Bio Pharm Bull*. 2007; 30(1): 84–90.

10. Yamaguchi Y, Yamada K, Yoshikawa N, Nakamura K, Haginaka J, Kunitomo M. Corosolic acid prevents oxidative stress, inflammation and hypertension in SHR/NDmcr-cp rats, a model of metabolic syndrome. *Life Sci*. 2006; 79(26): 2474–2479.

11. Mohan Kumar M, Joshi MC, Prabha T, Dorababu M, Goel RK. Effect of plantain banana on gastric ulceration in NIDDM rats: role of gastric mucosal glycoproteins, cell proliferation, antioxidants and free radicals. *Indian J Exp Biol*. 2006; 44(4): 292–299.

12. Best R, Lewis DA, Nasser N. The antiulcerogenic activity of the unripe plantain banana (*Musa* species). *Br. J Pharmacol*. 1984; 82(1): 107–116.

13. Botsaris AS. Plants used traditionally to treat malaria in Brazil: the archives of *Flora Medicinal*. *J Ethnobiol Ethnomedicine*. 2007; 3(1): 18.

14. Borges MH, Alves DL, Raslan DS, Pilo-Veloso D, Rodrigues VM, Homsi-Brandeburgo MI, de Lima ME. Neutralizing properties of *Musa* x *paradisiaca* L. (*Musaceae*) juice on phlospholipase A2, myotoxic, hemorrhagic and lethal activities of crotalidae venoms. *J Ethnopharmacol*. 2005; 98 (1–2): 21–29.

15. Prasad KV, Bharathi K, Srinivasan KK. Evaluation of *Musa* (*Paradisiaca* Linn. *cultivar*)—'Puttubale' stem juice for antilithiatic activity in albino rats. *Indian J Physiol Pharmacol*. 1993; 37(4): 337–341. (Author's note: The scientific name used in this study is technically incorrect.)

Barley / *Sha'īr*

FAMILY: Gramineae

BOTANICAL NAME: *Hordeum vulgare*

COMMON NAMES: *English* Common Barley; *French* Orge commune; *Spanish* Cebada; *German* Saatgerste, Gerste; *Urdu/Unānī* Jao, Shaeer; *Modern Standard Arabic* Sha'īr

SAFETY RATING: GENERALLY SAFE Barley is generally considered safe for most people. However, it should not be fed to nursing mothers as it suppresses lactation.

PROPHETIC PRESCRIPTION: According to many authorities, the Messenger of Allāh would often eat barley bread.[1] When anyone was indisposed, he used to call for a barley porridge (*talbīnah*) to be made. He would say, "Indeed it mends the heart of the sorrowful, and relieves the heart of the sick; just as one of you removes dirt from her face with water."[2] It is reported that when Imām 'Alī ibn Abī Ṭālib was recovering from an illness, the Prophet told him to eat barley and beet root (*silq*) as a tonic.[3]

On several occasions, the Most Noble Messenger recommended the consumption of *talbīnah*, a barley porridge prepared after boiling barley with milk and sweetening it with honey. He used to say, "[Barley] porridge (*talbīnah*) gives comforts to the heart and lessens its grief."[4] Whenever a person of the family of the Prophet fell ill, he ordered the preparation of barley gruel, explaining that "It removes grief from the heart of the patient. It removes weakness as you remove dirt from your face by washing it."[5]

'Ā'ishah, one of the wives of the Prophet, said that the Messenger of Allāh always recommended barley soup to those suffering from fever.[6] She used to order the preparation of (barley) porridge (*talbīnah*) for sick people and used to say "though the patient may dislike it, it is highly beneficial for him."[7] In another tradition, the Messenger of Allāh said, "By Allāh who holds my life in His hands, this removes the dirt from your stomach as you remove dirt from your face by washing it." The consumption of barley is recommended in numerous *aḥādīth* in Nisā'ī, Abū Dawūd, Bukhārī, Ibn Mājah, Tirmidhī, and Aḥmad.

The Imāms from Ahl al-Bayt (the Prophetic Household) also extolled the medicinal value of barley. Imām Muḥammad al-Bāqir said, "How great is the blessing of [barley] porridge (*sawīq*) If a person drinks it when he is full, it is wholesome for him and digests the food. If he drinks it when he is hungry, it fills him. The most excellent provision on a journey and at home is [barley] porridge (*sawīq*)."[8] As Imām Muḥammad al-Bāqir expressed, "How great is the blessing of [barley] porridge (*sawīq*). If a person drinks it when he is full, it is wholesome for him and digests the food. If he drinks it when he is hungry, it fills him. The most excellent provision on a journey and at home is [barley] porridge (*sawīq*)."[9]

Regarding barley porridge, Imām Ja'far al-Ṣādiq said, "[Barley] porridge (*sawīq*) produces flesh and strengthens the bone."[10] In another tradition, he said that "Drinking [barley] porridge (*sawīq*) with oil produces flesh, strengthens the bone, thins the skin, and increases libido (*bāh*)."[11]

Imām Ja'far al-Ṣādiq stated, "[Barley] porridge (*sawīq*) extracts bitterness and phlegm from the stomach, and prevents seventy kinds of disease."[12] He also explained that "He who drinks [barley] porridge (*sawīq*) for forty mornings [in a row] his shoulders will become filled with strength."[13] He stated, "Three handfuls of dried sawīq on an empty stomach dries the bitterness and the phlegm until none of it remains."[14] He also taught that "Dried [barley] porridge (*sawīq*) removes whiteness (*al-bayāḍ*)."

On one occasion, a man approached Imām Ja'far al-Ṣādiq and said, "O son of the Messenger of Allāh, a child has been born with moisture (*al-billa*) and weakness." The Imām said, "What prevents you from [giving him] [barley] porridge (*sawīq*)? Make him drink it, and tell your wife to take it, for it produces flesh and strengthens the bones and you will beget only strong children."[15] The Imām also said, "Give your children sawīq to drink when they are small for it produces flesh and strengthens the bone."[16] He also recommended [barley] porridge (*sawīq*) to treat fever, saying, "Give the feverish person *sawīq* that has been washed three times to drink."[17] Imām Ja'far al-Ṣādiq also said, "[w]hen dry *sawīq* (meal of parched barley) is taken on an empty stomach, it allays the heat and calms the bile; when it is crushed and then drunk, it does not do that."[18]

When 'Abd al-Raḥmān ibn Kathīr fell ill from stomach pain and diarrhea, the Imām ordered him to take *sawīq al-jāwras* along with cumin water. He did as instructed, and was healed. Known in Arabic as *dukhn* and *kanab*, among other colloquial terms, the Persian loan-word *jāwras* applies to small seeds like those of wheat or barley, the porridge prescribed by the Imām may have been made of farina or barley. When another one of his companions became ill, he said, "Give him barley porridge (*sawīq al-sha'īr*) to drink. He will be cured, Allāh-willing, for it is nutritious for the inside of the sick person."[19]

According to Imām 'Alī al-Riḍā barley bread is much better than wheat bread, just as the importance of the Ahl al-Bayt is greater than that of the common people. He explained that every prophet sent by Allāh had blessed the person who eats barley bread or barley porridge. The Imām said that any person who eats these two things will never suffer from any type of stomach ache. He said that barley bread and barley porridge has been the strength-giving food of the prophets and pious people. According to Imām Ja'far al-Ṣādiq, the best food for loose bowels is barley bread. He also said that barley bread alleviates all bodily pains.

The Imāms of Ahl al-Bayt also included barley in their "comprehensive medication" which was indicated in cases of scorpion or snake bites.[20] They also recommended the application of barley and saffron water around the eyes to remove puffiness as well as for coldness of the abdomen and fluttering of the heart.[21]

Issues in Identification: It is the consensus that *sha'īr* is Arabic for barley or *Hordeum vulgare*. According to Mandaville, beyond human uses, cultivated barley is often used by Saudi Bedouins for livestock fodder in summer or when grazing is otherwise unavailable, indicating its sustaining elements.[22]

Properties and Uses: Barley is a sweet, warming herb that stimulates appetite, improves digestion, and suppresses lactation.[23] Barley shoots are diuretic, while the seed sprouts are demulcent, expectorant, galactofuge, lenitive and stomachic. In some cases, the seed sprouts can act as an abortifacient. They are also used to treat dyspepsia caused by cereals, infantile lacto-dyspepsia, regurgitation of milk, and breast distension. Barley seeds are digestive, emollient, nutritive, febrifuge, and stomachic. They are taken internally as a nutrient particularly for babies and febrile conditions. Barley is also used in a poultice for burns and wounds as it soothes irritated tissues. Al-Kindī's used barley flour as a dental medicine to sweeten the breath and to strengthen the gums.[24] Barley seeds have also been traditionally used to treat tumors. Germinated barley seeds have a hypoglycemic effect preceded by a hyperglycemic action.

Due to its high nutritional value, rich in vitamins B and E, it is given to those who are convalescent in the form of barley water or an extract of malt. It is used internally for digestive disorders like gastritis and is particularly indicated in the treatment of indigestion in babies. Barley water is soothing to the bowel when there is inflammation or diarrhea. All of this was well-known in medieval times when Ibn Buṭlān noted that barley improves the faculty of expulsion and is easily digested.[25]

Barley is used in catarrhal affections of the respiratory organs and is beneficial for pharyngitis and cough. It is highly beneficial in the treatment of urinary disorders like nephritis and cystitis and is an effective diuretic. It is also indicated for excessive lactation, hepatitis, and Candida albicans infection. The germinated seed is used for abdominal bloating while the malt extract is used for weak digestion.

Barley water is used for poor appetite, digestion during convalescence, and is a good remedy for kidney problems. Hordenine, an alkaloid with properties similar to ephedrine, is produced in the root of the germinating grain, and is therefore of value in the treatment of asthma and bronchitis. Barley flour, combined with salt, honey, and vinegar, can be applied to ease itchy skin. One caution: Because of its ability to suppress lactation, barley is not given to nursing women.

The cholesterol-lowering properties of barley have long been known in the Middle East where it is known as the "heart medicine." It possesses antiviral and anticancer activity as well as potent antioxidants, including tocotrienols. It has also shown great promise in the treatment of diabetes.

SCIENTIFIC STUDIES: *Antidiabetic Activity* In a 12-week animal study conducted by Konkuk University in South Korea, malted barley extract was found to alleviate many of the symptoms of diabetes, offering promise as a therapeutic supplement for the normalization of blood glucose levels in humans with hyperglycemia, as well as patients with non–insulin-dependent diabetes mellitus.[26]

According to a 16-week animal study conducted by the University of Yamanashi in Japan, a barley diet was shown to significantly decrease systolic blood pressure, and it lowers cholesterol.[27] The study concluded that high fiber intake has beneficial effects on systolic blood pressure and blood lipids levels, suggesting that fiber intake should be increased in individuals who have diabetes mellitus in order to help prevent complications.

In an animal study completed by King's College in the UK, researchers found that a diet containing barley had a modulating effect on the symptoms of diabetes.[28] Researchers postulated that the beneficial effect of barley resided in its very high level of chromium. According to NutriGuard Research, preliminary studies suggest that compounds in barley malt have similar activity as Metformin, a common diabetic drug, but without its side effects.[29]

Antihepatitic, Cholesterol-Lowering, and Anticancer Activity Other documentation indicates that barley may be of aid in the treatment of hepatitis, the lowering of cholesterol levels, and the prevention of bowel cancer.[30]

Barley Notes

1. Tirmidhī M. *al-Jāmi' al-ṣaḥīḥ*. al-Qāhirah: Muṣṭafā al-Bābī al-Ḥalabī, [1937–]; Bayhaqī A. *Sunan al-kubrā*. Bayrūt: Dār Ṣadīr, 1968.

2. Ibn Qayyim al-Jawziyyah M. al-Ṭibb al-nabawī. Bayrūt: Dār al-Kitāb, 1985; Tirmidhī M. *al-Jāmi' al-ṣaḥīḥ*. al-Qāhirah: Muṣṭafā al-Bābī al-Ḥalabī, [1937–]; Bayhaqī A. *Sunan al-kubrā*. Bayrūt: Dār Ṣadīr, 1968.

3. Ibn Mājah M. *Sunan*. N.p.: n.p, n.d.; Ibn Ḥanbal A. *Musnad al-Imām Aḥmad ibn Ḥanbal*. Bayrūt: al-Maktabah al-Islāmiyyah, 1969; Tirmidhī M. *al-Jāmi' al-ṣaḥīḥ*. al-Qā hirah: Muṣṭafā al-Bābī al-Ḥalabī, [1937–].

4. Muslim. *Jāmi' al-ṣaḥīḥ*. al-Riyyāḍ: Bayt al-Afkār, 1998.

5. Ibn Mājah M. *Sunan*. Trans. MT Anṣārī. Lahore: Kazi Publications, 1994.

6. Sūyūṭī J. *As-Sūyūṭī's Medicine of the Prophet*. Ed. A Thomson. London: Ṭā-Hā Publishers, 1994: 73.

7. Bukhārī M. *Ṣaḥīḥ al-Bukhārī*. al-Riyyāḍ: Bayt al-Afkār, 1998.

8. Nisābūrī A. *Islamic Medical Wisdom: The Ṭibb al-a'immah*. Trans. B. Ispahany. Ed. AJ Newman. London: Muḥammadī Trust, 1991: 80–81.

9. Nisābūrī A. *Islamic Medical Wisdom: The Ṭibb al-a'immah*. Trans. B. Ispahany. Ed. AJ Newman. London: Muḥammadī Trust, 1991: 80–81.

10. 'Amilī H. *Wasā'il al-shī'ah*. Bayrūt: al-Mu'assasah, 1993.

11. 'Amilī H. *Wasā'il al-shī'ah*. Bayrūt: al-Mu'assasah, 1993.

12. 'Amilī H. *Wasā'il al-shī'ah*. Bayrūt: al-Mu'assasah, 1993.

13. 'Amilī H. *Wasā'il al-shī'ah*. Bayrūt: al-Mu'assasah, 1993.

14. 'Amilī H. *Wasā'il al-shī'ah*. Bayrūt: al-Mu'assasah, 1993.

15. Nisābūrī A. *Islamic Medical Wisdom: The Ṭibb al-a'immah*. Trans. B. Ispahany. Ed. AJ Newman. London: Muḥammadī Trust, 1991: 111.

16. Amilī H. *Wasā'il al-shī'ah*. Bayrūt: al-Mu'assasah, 1993.
17. 'Amilī H. *Wasā'il al-shī'ah*. Bayrūt: al-Mu'assasah, 1993.
18. Nisābūrī A. *Islamic Medical Wisdom: The Ṭibb al-a'immah*. Trans. B. Ispahany. Ed. AJ Newman. London: Muḥammadī Trust, 1991: 80.
19. 'Amilī H. *Wasā'il al-shī'ah*. Bayrūt: al-Mu'assasah, 1993.
20. Nisābūrī A. *Ṭibb al-a'immah*. Bayrūt: Dār al-Maḥajjah al-Baydā,' 1994.
21. Nisābūrī A. *Ṭibb al-a'immah*. Bayrūt: Dār al-Maḥajjah al-Baydā,' 1994.
22. Mandaville JP. *Flora of Eastern Saudi Arabia*. London: Kegan Paul, 1990.
23. Bown D. *Encyclopedia of Herbs and Their Uses*. Westmount: RD Press, 1995: 294.
24. Levey M, al-Khaledy N, eds. *The Medical Formulary of al-Samarqandī*. Philadelphia: University of Pennsylvania Press, 1967: 196, note 185.
25. Ibn Buṭlān, *The Medieval Health Handbook: Tacuinum sanitatis*. Ed. L Cogliati Arano. Trans. O Ratti and A Westbrook. New York: George Braziller, 1976: 205.
26. Hong H, Jai Maegn W. Effects of malted barley extract and banana extract on blood glucose levels in genetically diabetic mice. *J* 2004; 7(4): 487–490.
27. Li, Wang, Kaneko, Qin, Sato. Effects of fiber intake on the blood pressure, lipids, and heart rate in Goto Kakizaki rats. *Nutrition*. 2004; 20 (11–12): 1003–1007.
28. Mahdi GS, Naismith DJ. Role of Chromium in barley in modulating the symptoms of diabetes. *Ann* 1991; 35(2): 65–70.
29. McCarty MF. Nutraceutical resources for diabetes prevention: an update. *Med* 2005; 64(1): 151–158.
30. Chevallier A. *The Encyclopedia of Medicinal Plants*. London: Dorling Kindersley, 1996.

Basil/*Rayḥān, Ḥūk*

Family: Labiataea

Botanical Name: *Ocimum* spp.

Common Names: *English* Basil, sweet basil; *French* Basilic, Herbe royale; *Spanish* Albahaca; *German* Echtes Basilienkraut, Basilikum; *Urdu/Unānī* Rayhan, Shahsafaram, Aspargham, Asfargham, Asfaram, Tulsi; *Modern Standard Arabic* Rayḥān, Ṣa'tar hindī, Ḥūk, Ḥabaq, Bādharūj

Safety Rating: Generally Safe to Dangerous Although sweet basil is considered safe as a culinary herb, it contains estragole, which is carcinogenic and genotoxic. For this reason, it should not be taken in medicinal doses for more than a couple of weeks, and should never be consumed medicinally by women who are pregnant or lactating, or by infants and toddlers. In medicinal amounts, sweet basil may cause stomach upset or diarrhea. The herb should only be consumed medicinally under expert supervision.

Prophetic Prescription: When speaking of Paradise, the Qur'ān refers to *rayḥānah*, which is translated into English as "Gardens of Delight" by both Yusuf 'Ali and Picktall, and "Garden of Bliss" by Aṣad (56:88–89). According to the Prophet Muḥammad, "Whoever is offered a gift of sweet basil (*rayḥān*) should not refuse it, for it is light to carry and has a sweet scent."[1] In speaking of his grandsons, Ḥasan and Ḥusayn, the Messenger of Allāh said, "They are like sweet basil (*rayḥān*) to me."[2]

According to Imām Ja'far al-Ṣādiq, "Sweet basil (*al-ḥūk*) is the herb of the prophets, peace be upon them, for it has eight benefits: it helps digest food, it opens what was closed, it gives flavor, it makes food appetizing, it improves the circulation of the blood, and it protects against leprosy (*judhām*); in fact, if it remains in one's body, it kills the entire disease."[3]

Issues in Identification: It is the consensus that *rayḥān* is Arabic for both basil and sweet basil. According to Hans Wehr, *rayḥān* is Arabic for *Ocimum basilicum*. There is debate, however, as to which type of basil referred to by the Prophet. For Said, *rayḥān* refers to wild basil, which is also known as *athbah* and *athabah*.[4] Ibn al-Jawziyyah says that *rayḥān* is the name of the myrtle plant in North Africa.[5] He says that the people of Arabia known the myrtle plant as *rayḥān*, while the inhabitants of Iraq and Syria give the name *rayḥān* to the holy basil plant, also known as monk's basil (*Ocimum filamentosum*). He says that wild basil or Persian *rayḥān* is known in Arabic as *ḥabaq*. Johnstone has followed Ibn al-Jawziyyah in identifying *rayḥān* as any sweet smelling plant.[6] In his index, Turkī translates *rayḥān* as both "myrtle" and "aromatic plant."[7] Elgood, however, identifies *rayḥān* as sweet basil.[8]

Although the term *rayḥān* can apply generally to any sweet smelling plant, its specific meaning refers to sweet basil. As Ibn Ṭūlūn explains, *rayḥān* is a term of Persian origin used by the Arabs to refer to myrtle (*al-ās*).[9] We can also be fairly certain that the Prophet did not refer to bush basil or small leaved basil which is known as *shāhasfaram* or *rayḥān ṣa'tarī*. *Shāhasfaram* is identified by Dīnawarī as *ḍaymurān*, *ḥūk*, '*unjuj*, and *rayḥān al-barr*, which means wild basil.[10] According to Mandaville, a few plants of *Ocimum basilicum* are cultivated around gardens in eastern Saudi Arabia and some are occasionally found as an apparent escape in oases.[11] Sweet basil is known as *mashmūm* and *rayḥān* in the Saudi dialect. According to Ghazanfar, *Ocimum basilicum* is found throughout Arabia, both cultivated and as an escapee.[12]

Properties and Uses: Basil is a restorative,

warming, aromatic herb that relaxes spasms, lowers fever, improves digestion, and is effective against bacterial infections and internal parasites. It is considered exhilarant, expectorant, antiperiodic, diuretic, emmenagogue, antiseptic, cordial, cephalic, diuretic, and nervine. Internally, it is used internally for flatulence, feverish illnesses, poor digestion, pain relief, stomach ulcers, nausea, insomnia, influenza, rheumatism, high blood sugar, low spirits, and exhaustion. Externally, it is used as an antiseptic to treat acne, insect stings, inflammation, and skin infections. According to Ghazanfar, *Ocimum basilicum* is used in Arabia for the treatment of cataracts, colds, abdominal pains, and diarrhea.[13]

SCIENTIFIC STUDIES: *Antioxidant and Antibacterial Activity* Basil is a potent antioxidant and a free radical scavenger.[14] It is also antibacterial, insecticidal, and antimicrobial, manifestations that also point to potential applications for food packaging.[15] In a study conducted by the Bulgarian Drug Agency, the essential oil of basil obtained from the aerial parts of *Ocimum basilicum* has a strong inhibitory effect against multi-drug resistant clinical isolates from the genera *Staphylococcus, Enterococcus* and *Pseudomonas*.[16] Since these bacteria are widespread and pose serious therapeutic difficulties, the results of this study are encouraging.

Antidiabetic Activity Studies suggest that basil contains hypolipidemic substances that may be of benefit as a therapeutic tool in hyperlipidemic subjects. In a controlled animal trial conducted by University Mohammed I in Morocco, *Ocimum* extract was shown to lower total cholesterol, triglycerides, and LDL-cholesterol by 56 percent, 63 percent and 68 percent.[17] The hypolipidemic effect exerted by basil was found to be markedly higher than the effect induced by fenofibrate treatments. Another study, conducted by the University of Jos in Nigeria, found that intraperitoneal injection of 400mg/kg of the methanolic extract of *O. gratissimum* significantly reduced plasma levels in normal and diabetic rats by 56 and 68 percent respectively.[18]

In a randomized placebo-controlled, single blind trial, conducted by Azad University of Agriculture and Technology in India, *O. sanctum* and *O. album* were found to have a hypoglycemic effect, manifesting reductions of 17.6 percent and 7.3 percent in the levels of fasting and postprandial blood glucose, with mean total cholesterol levels showing a mild reduction. As a result of these findings, basil leaves may be prescribed as an adjunct to dietary therapy and drug treatment in mild to moderate diabetes.[19] In an animal study conducted by Satsang Herbal Research and Analytical Laboratories in India, the oral administration of 95 percent ethanolic extract of *O. sanctum* was confirmed to possess blood glucose lowering effects.[20]

Antithrombotic Activity In a controlled study conducted by Xinjiang Medical University in China, *O. basilicum* was found to possess an inhibitory effect on induced platelet aggregation. The effect was dose-dependent and resulted in an antithrombotic effect which developed progressively over 7 days and disappeared over 3 to 7 days.[21]

Gastro-Intestinal Healing Activity In a study conducted by Centro Médico de México, the aqueous and methanolic extract of *Chiranthodendron pentadactylon, Hippocratea excelsa* and *Ocimum basilicum* were found to be the most potent in treating gastrointestinal disorders, with inhibition values ranging from 68.0 to 87.6 percent.[22] In another study, conducted by Lagos State University in Nigeria, the inhibitory effects of *Ocimum gratissimum* was confirmed against *Shigella dysenteriae*.[23] These results increase the support for the use of medicinal plants like basil for the treatment of gastrointestinal disorders such as diarrhea.

Chemopreventive Activity In a study conducted by Chiang Mai University in Thailand, sweet basil was found to have the highest antiproliferative activity on human mouth epidermal carcinoma and murine leukemia.[24] In an animal study conducted by Jawaharlal Nehru University in India, basil leaf was found to possess chemopreventive properties, to detoxify xenobiotics, to induce antioxidants, and to effectively inhibit carcinogen-induced tumor incidence at the peri-initiational level.[25] These results demonstrate the potential of the essential oil of basil for cancer treatment.

Therapeutic Activity in Myocardial Infraction In an animal study conducted by the All India Institute of Medical Sciences, *Ocimum sanctum* was found to have therapeutic and prophylactic value in the treatment of myocardial infarction.[26]

Antiulcer Activity In a study conducted by the University of Delhi, the fixed oil of *O. basilicum* was found to possess significant antiulcer activity against aspirin, indomethacin, alcohol, histamine, reserpine, serotonin and stress-induced ulceration in experimental animal models.[27] The researchers involved conclude that *O. basilicum* fixed oil may be considered to be a drug of natural origin which possesses both anti-inflammatory and antiulcer activity.

Anti-HIV Activity The greatest potential of basil, however, seems to be in the area of AIDS research. In an in-vitro study conducted by the Osaka Prefectural Institute of Public Health, *Ocimum basilicum* "Cinnamon" showed potent inhibitory effects against HIV-1 induced cytopathogenicity in MT-4 cells.[28]

Basil Notes

1. Bukhārī M. *Ṣaḥīḥ al-Bukhārī*. al-Riyyāḍ: Bayt al-Afkār, 1998; Tirmidhī M. *al-Jāmi' al-ṣaḥīḥ*. al-Qāhirah: Muṣṭafā al-Bābī al-Ḥalabī, [1937–].
2. Bukhārī M. *Ṣaḥīḥ al-Bukhārī*. al-Riyyāḍ: Bayt al-Afkār, 1998.
3. Majlisī M. *Biḥār al-anwār*. Ṭihrān: Javad al-Alavi, 1956.
4. Bīrūnī, AR al-. *al-Bīrūnī's Book on Pharmacy and Materia Medica*. Ed. and trans. HM Said. Karachi: Hamdard National Foundation, 1973.
5. Ibn Qayyim al-Jawziyyah M. *al-Ṭibb al-nabawī*. Bayrūt: Dār al-Kitāb, 1985.
6. Johnstone P, trans. *Medicine of the Prophet*. Ibn Qayyim al-Jawziyyah. Cambridge: The Islamic Texts Society, 1998.
7. Iṣbahānī AN al-. *Mawsū'at al-ṭibb al-nabawī*. Ed. MKD al-Turkī. Bayrūt: Dār Ibn Ḥazm, 2006.
8. Elgood C. Trans. *Ṭibb al-nabī or Medicine of the Prophet*. Sūyūṭī J, M Chaghhaynī. Osiris 1962; 14: 38.
9. Ibn Ṭulūn S. *al-Manhal al-rawī fī al-ṭibb al-nabawī*. Ed. 'Azīz Bayk. Riyyāḍ: Dār 'ālam al-kutub, 1995.
10. Dīnawarī AH. *Kitāb al-nabāt/The Book of Plants*. Ed. Bernhard Lewin. Bayrūt: Dār al-Qalam, 1974: 203.
11. Mandaville JP. *Flora of Eastern Saudi Arabia*. London: Kegan Paul, 1990.
12. Ghazanfar SA. *Handbook of Arabian Medicinal Plants*. Boca Raton: CRC Press, 1994.
13. Ghazanfar SA. *Handbook of Arabian Medicinal Plants*. Boca Raton: CRC Press, 1994.
14. Gülçin, *Elmastas, Aboul-Enein*. Determination of antioxidant and radical scavenging activity of Basil (*Ocimum basilicum* L. Family *Lamiaceae*) assayed by different methodologies. *Phytother* 2007 Apr; 21(4): 354–361.
15. Wannissorn, Jarikasem, Siriwangchai, Thubthimthed. Antibacterial properties of essential oils from Thai medicinal plants *Fitoterapia*. 2005; 76(2): 233–236; *Pavela*. Insecticidal activity of certain medicinal plants. *Fitoterapia*. 2004; 75(7–8): 745–749; *Suppakul, Miltz, Sonneveld, Bigger*. Antimicrobial properties of basil and its possible application in food packaging. *J* 2003; 51(11): 3197–3207.
16. Opalchenova, Obreshkova. Comparative studies on the activity of basil — an essential oil from *Ocimum basilicum* L. — against multidrug resistant clinical isolates of the genera *Staphylococcus, Enterococcus* and *Pseudomonas* by using different test methods. *J* 2003; 54(1): 105–10.
17. Amrani, Harnafi, Bouanani, Aziz, Caid, Manfredini, Besco, Napolitano, Bravo. Hypolipidaemic activity of aqueous *Ocimum basilicum* extract in acute hyperlipidaemia induced by triton WR-1339 in rats and its antioxidant property. *Phytother* 2006; 20(12): 1040–1045.
18. Aguiyi, Obi, Gang, Igweh. Hypoglycaemic activity of *Ocimum gratissimum* in rats *Fitoterapia*. 2000; 71(4): 444–446.
19. Agrawal, Rai, Singh. Randomized placebo-controlled, single blind trial of holy basil leaves in patients with non–insulin-dependent diabetes mellitus. *Int* 1996; 34(9): 406–409.
20. Kar, Choudhary, Bandyopadhyay. Comparative evaluation of hypoglycaemic activity of some Indian medicinal plants in alloxan diabetic rats. *J* 2003; 84(1): 105–108.
21. Tohti, Tursun, Umar, Turdi, Imin, Moore. Aqueous extracts of *Ocimum basilicum* L. (sweet basil) decrease platelet aggregation induced by ADP and thrombin in vitro and rats arterio — venous shunt thrombosis in vivo. *Thromb Res*. 2006; 118(6): 733–739.
22. Velazquez, Calzada, Torres J, Gonzalez F, Ceballos G. Antisecretory activity of plants used to treat gastrointestinal disorders in Mexico. *J* 2006; 103(1): 66–70.
23. Ilori, Sheteolu, Omonigbehin, Adeneye AA. Antidiarrhoeal activities of *Ocimum gratissimum* (Lamiaceae). *J* 1996; 14(4): 283–285.
24. Manosroi, Dhumtanom, Manosroi. Anti-proliferative activity of essential oil extracted from Thai medicinal plants on KB and P388 cell lines. *Cancer* 2006; 235(1): 114–120.
25. Dasgupta, Rao, Yadava. Chemomodulatory efficacy of basil leaf (*Ocimum basilicum*) on drug metabolizing and antioxidant enzymes, and on carcinogen-induced skin and forestomach papillomagenesis. *Phytomedicine*. 2004; 11(2–3): 139–151.
26. Sharma, Kishore, Gupta, Joshi, Arya. Cardioprotective potential of ocimum sanctum in isoproterenol induced myocardial infarction in rats. *Mol* 2001; 225(1): 75–83.
27. Singh. Evaluation of gastric antiulcer activity of fixed oil of *Ocimum basilicum* Linn. and its possible mechanism of action. *Indian* 1999; 37(3): 253–257.
28. Yamasaki, Nakano, Kawahata, Mori, Otake, Ueba, Oishi, Inami, Yamane, Nakamura, Murata, Nakanishi. Anti-HIV-1 activity of herbs in Labiatae. *Biol* 1998; 21(8): 829–833.

Beans/*Bāqalā*

FAMILY: Fabaceae

BOTANICAL NAME: *Vicia faba*

COMMON NAMES: *English* Broad Bean, Fava Bean, Brown Fava Bean, Faba Bean, Field Bean, Bell Bean, Tic Bean; *French* Haricot; *Spanish* Alubia, Judía; *German* Bohne; Weiße bohne, Wörterbuch; *Urdu/Unānī* Baqla, Faul; *Modern Standard Arabic* Fūl, Bāqalā

SAFETY RATING: GENERALLY SAFE Since broad beans are rich in tyramine, they should be avoided by patients taking monoamine oxidase inhibitors (MAO). Raw broad beans contain vicine, isouramil, and convicine, toxic glycosides which can cause "favism," a potentially fatal form of hemolytic anemia which occurs in individuals who suffer from the hereditary condition known as glucose-6-phosphate-dehydrogenase deficiency (G6PD). The disease can be caused by consuming broad beans as well as by inhaling its pollen. Approximately 1 percent of white people and 15 percent of black people are susceptible to the disease.

PROPHETIC PRESCRIPTION: According to Imām Ja'far al-Ṣādiq, "Eating fava beans (*bāqalā*) increases bone marrow in the legs, increases the brain, and produces fresh blood."[1] The Imām also said, "Eat fava beans (*bāqalā*) with its skin for it burnishes the stomach."[2]

ISSUES IN IDENTIFICATION: The *fūl* or beans mentioned by the Imām refers to broad beans or *Vicia faba*, a species of bean native to North Africa and to southwest Asia, and which has been cultivated at least since ancient Egyptian times.

PROPERTIES AND USES: Broad beans are highly nutritive. Their seedpods are diuretic.

SCIENTIFIC STUDIES: *Parkinson-Controlling Ac-*

tivity According to a study conducted by Istanbul University, broad beans (*Vicia faba*) are a natural source of L-dopa, a substance used medically in the treatment of Parkinson's disease. The consumption of broad beans is said to be a natural means of prolonging "on" periods in patients who have "on-off" fluctuations.[3]

According to a small human trial conducted by the Tel Aviv Elias Sourasky Medical Center in Israel, the ingestion of broad beans (*V. faba*) produces a substantial increase in L-dopa plasma levels, which correlates with a substantial improvement in motor performance. The researchers concluded that their findings may have implications for the treatment of Parkinson's Disease, particularly in patients who have mild symptoms.[4]

According to a small human trial conducted at the same medical center, the consumption of broad beans after 12 hours without treatment for Parkinsonian symptoms resulted in substantial improvement during the next four hours.[5]

Potential Value in Treating Hypertension, Heart Failure, Renal Failure, and Liver Cirrhosis According to a study conducted by Tel Aviv Sourasky Medical Center, the consumption of broad beans, which are ubiquitously rich in easily absorbable L-dopa, greatly increase urinary sodium and dopamine. As such, the researchers suggest that broad beans might be of value in treating hypertension, heart failure, renal failure, and liver cirrhosis in which natriuresis and diuresis are medically beneficial.[6]

Beans Notes

1. ʻAmilī H. *Wasā'il al-shīʻah*. Bayrūt: al-Mu'assasah, 1993.
2. ʻAmilī H. *Wasā'il al-shīʻah*. Bayrūt: al-Mu'assasah, 1993.
3. Apaydin, Ertan, Ozekmekçi S. Broad bean (*Vicia faba*) — a natural source of L-dopa — prolongs "on" periods in patients with Parkinson's disease who have "on-off" fluctuations. *Mov* 2000 Jan; 15(1): 164–6.
4. Rabey, Vered, Shabtai, Graff, Harsat, Korczyn. Broad bean (*Vicia faba*) consumption and Parkinson's disease. *Adv* 1993; 60: 681–4.
5. Rabey, Vered, Shabtai, Graff, Korczyn. Improvement of parkinsonian features correlate with high plasma levodopa values after broad bean (*Vicia faba*) consumption. *J* 1992 Aug; 55(8): 725–7.
6. Vered, Grosskopf, Palevitch, Harsat, Charach, Weintraub, Graff. The influence of Vicia faba (broad bean) seedlings on urinary sodium excretion. *Planta* 1997 Jun; 63(3): 237–40

Beet/*Silq*

FAMILY: Chenopodiaceae
BOTANICAL NAME: *Beta* spp.

COMMON NAMES: *English* Beet, Beetroot, sugar beet; *French* Betterave; *Spanish* Remolacha, Betabel, Acelga; *German* Echter Mangold, Rübe; *Urdu/Unānī* Chuqandar, Silq; *Modern Standard Arabic* Silq, Banjar, Shamandar, Libdān

SAFETY RATING: GENERALLY SAFE

PROPHETIC PRESCRIPTION: The Prophet once advised Imām ʻAlī ibn Abī Ṭālib to eat beet root and barley when he was convalescing.[1] According to Imām Jaʻfar al-Ṣādiq, "Allāh, may He be honored and glorified, protected the Jews from leprosy (*judhām*) by the eating of beets, and the extraction of their roots."[2] The Imām also said that "Eating beets protects against leprosy (*judhām*)."[3] Al-Ṣādiq related that "A group of Jews was affected by whiteness (*al-bayāḍ*). God revealed to Mūsā: 'Order them to eat beef with beets.'"[4] In another tradition, al-Ṣādiq said, "Beef and beet broth removes whiteness (*al-bayāḍ*)."[5]

ISSUES IN IDENTIFICATION: It is the consensus that *silq* is Arabic for beet, although a debate continues as to which particular type of beet it identifies. According to Said and Johnstone, *silq* refers to *Beta vulgaris*.[6] According to Akīlī, it encompasses *Beta vulgaris*, *Beta cicla*, and *Beta vulgaris* var. *foliosa*.[7] For Álvarez Morales and Girón Irueste, *silq* refers to *Beta vulgaris* var. *cicla*.[8] Since the Prophet merely said *silq*, we can assume that he referred to beet in the generic sense since *Beta vulgaris* is known as *silq mabdhūl*, *libdān*, *ḍirs al-kalb*, *fujl bū al-layl*, while *Beta silvestris* is known as *banjar barrī* and *jāru al-nahr*. As Muḥammad ʻAlī Barr explains, *banjar* and *shamandar* are other Arabic synonyms for *silq*.[9]

According to Mandaville, *Beta vulgaris* is known only as a weed of farm fields or ruderal sites in eastern Saudi Arabia where it is rare or occasional.[10] According to Chaudhary, *Beta vulgaris* ssp. *maritima* is known in Saudi Arabic as *salq barrī*. It is native to Western Europe, the Middle East, and Western Asia. In Saudi Arabia, it is found as an occasional weed around cultivated areas.[11]

The Prophet, however, could not have been referring to yellow beets, which have been known since at least 1583, and which may very well date from the Middle Ages.[12] He was certainly not referring to sugar beets, which were developed in Upper Silesia (now Poland) during the 1740s.[13] The beets which existed during the Prophet's time were red and white varieties which were known to the ancient Greeks and Romans.[14] The classical Greeks and Romans, however, only used the leaves of beets in salads. It was only much later that beets were cultivated for their roots. The Prophet could only have prescribed beet leaves, as opposed to beet roots, to Imām ʻAlī. As Davidson explains,

> [Beets] are descended from the sea beet, *B. maritima*, a wild seashore plant growing around the Mediterranean and Atlantic coasts of Europe and N. Africa. This has only a small root, but its leaves and stems are sometimes eaten. Early Greek writers such as Theophrastus referred to the cultivation of this plant. By about 300 B.C. there were varieties with edible roots.[15]

As Bianchini and Corbetta relate,

> The beets described by Horace and Cicero must have been vastly different from the ones used today. Those grown in Roman times were probably more appreciated for their leaves than for the rest of the plant. Our red beet, with the roundish root, cannot therefore boast a long history. Red beets in the wild state grow along the coasts of western Europe and North Africa.... The cultivated red beet originated in Germany and was then introduced into Italy around the fifteenth century.[16]

The varieties of beets that most people are familiar with are all modern varieties. Even the oldest heirloom varieties such as "Golden Beet," "Early Wonder," "Chioggia," "Crosby's Egyptian," "Mammoth Red Mangel," and "Detroit Dark Red," only date back to the 1800s. According to some experts, the oldest variety of beet still existing is the crapaudine, which possibly dates back one thousand years. This is still five hundred years short of any species which may have existed during the lifetime of the Prophet.

Properties and Uses: *Beta vulgaris* is a fleshy root used as a source of sugar or in salads and cookery. It is a rich source of carbohydrates, a good source of protein, and has high levels of important vitamins, minerals, and micronutrients. It is also a good source of dietary fiber, and has virtually no fat. Beets also contain higher levels of folic acid than most other vegetables. The leaves of the plant are rich in minerals and vitamins, particularly vitamins A and C, beta-carotene and other carotenes, potassium, iron, and folic acid. In fact, the leaves of *Beta vulgaris* have a similar vitamin and mineral content to spinach (*Spinacea oleracea*).

Beta vulgaris has been used medicinally since ancient times. Beets are considered beneficial for the blood, due to their high iron content. They are used to treat digestive problems, skin problems, headaches, toothaches, fever, and lethargy. Beets are regarded as a laxative, and a decongestant. They are used to treat bad breath, coughs, and hemorrhoids. They are also considered an aphrodisiac, perhaps due to their boron content, a mineral which plays a role in the production of human sex hormones. Since it is a particularly rich source of betaine, a mood modifier, *B. vulgaris* is used in the treatment of clinical depression. Betaine is also used to treat a genetic condition called homocystinuria, and is also an effective treatment for alcohol-induced liver failure, as it promotes the regeneration of livers cells and facilitates the conversion of fats. Beets also contain anticancer properties, including the alkaloid allantoin, which was shown to have antitumor effects in the 1960s. In the 1990s, cell culture and animal studies confirmed the significant tumor-inhibiting and antimutagenic properties of beetroot juice, likely resulting from the combined effects of betanin, allantoin, vitamin C, and other compounds such as farnesol and rutin. Recent research strongly suggests that beetroot can help prevent cancer. Beetroot is also considered to prevent illness by stimulating the immune system.

Scientific Studies: *Antidiabetic Activity* According to an animal study conducted by Istanbul University in Turkey, the extract of *Beta vulgaris* L. var. *cicla* was found to have a protective effect on the liver in diabetes mellitus.[17]

Antiherpetic Activity In an in-vitro study conducted by the Universidad de Antioquia in Columbia, the extracts of nine species of plants were tested for their potential antitumor and antiherpetic activity.[18] The aqueous extract from *Beta vulgaris* showed some antiherpetic activity with acceptable therapeutic indexes. The species was considered a good candidate for further activity-monitored fractionation to identify active principles.

Anti-influenza Activity In one study, an aqueous *Beta vulgaris* extract was repeatedly administered to mice by intranasal instillation, prior to intranasal inoculation of influenza virus. The extract conferred a partial protection against the experimental influenza infection. In short, there was a significant decrease in the hemagglutination titers recorded in mouse lung homogenates, a decrease in mortality rate, and an increase in the mean survival time as compared with the untreated, virus-inoculated controls.[19]

Anti-inflammatory Activity In a study conducted by the Jordan University of Science and Technology, the ethanolic extract of *Beta vulgaris* was shown to possess an anti-inflammatory effect, confirming its traditional use in painful and inflammatory conditions.[20]

Beet Notes

1. Tirmidhī M. *al-Jāmi' al-ṣaḥīḥ*. al-Qāhirah: Muṣṭafā al-Bābī al-Ḥalabī, [1937–]; Abū Dāwūd S. *Ṣaḥīḥ Sunan Abū Dāwūd*, Riyyāḍ: Maktab al-Tarbiyyah, 1989.
2. 'Amilī H. *Wasā'il al-shī'ah*. Bayrūt: al-Mu'assasah, 1993.
3. Ṭabarsī H. Mustadrak al-Wasā'il. Bayrūt: Mu'assasat Āl al-Bayt, 1987–1988.
4. 'Amilī H. *Wasā'il al-shī'ah*. Bayrūt: al-Mu'assasah, 1993.
5. 'Amilī H. *Wasā'il al-shī'ah*. Bayrūt: al-Mu'assasah, 1993.
6. Bīrūnī, AR al-. *al-Bīrūnī's Book on Pharmacy and Ma-*

teria Medica. Ed. and trans. HM Said. Karachi: Hamdard National Foundation, 1973; Johnstone P, trans. *Medicine of the Prophet*. Ibn Qayyim al-Jawziyyah. Cambridge: The Islamic Texts Society, 1998.
7. Ibn al-Qayyim al-Jawziyyah. *Natural Healing with the Medicine of the Prophet*. Pearl Publishing. Trans. M al-Akīlī. Philadelphia, 1993.
8. Ibn Ḥabīb A. *Mujtaṣar fī al-ṭibb*/*Compendio de medicina*. Ed. C Álvarez de Morales and F Girón Irueste. Madrid: Consejo Superior de Investigaciones Científicas, 1992.
9. Ibn Ḥabīb A. *al-Ṭibb al-nabawī*. Ed. MA Barr. Dimashq: Dār al-Qalam, 1993.
10. Mandaville JP. *Flora of Eastern Saudi Arabia*. London: Kegan Paul, 1990.
11. Chaudhary SA. *Flora of the Kingdom of Saudi Arabia*. al-Riyyāḍ: Ministry of Agriculture and Water, 1999.
12. Weaver, WW. *Heirloom Vegetable Gardening*. Owl Book, New York: Henry Holt, 1997: 82.
13. Weaver, WW. *Heirloom Vegetable Gardening*. Owl Book, New York: Henry Holt, 1997: 83.
14. Weaver, WW. *Heirloom Vegetable Gardening*. Owl Book, New York: Henry Holt, 1997: 83.
15. Davidson A. *The Oxford Companion to Food*. Oxford: Oxford University Press, 1999: 70.
16. Bianchini F, Corbetta F. *The Complete Book of Fruits and Vegetables*. New York: Crown, 1976: 80.
17. Ozsoy-Sacan, KarAbülut-Bulan, Bolkent, Yanardag, Ozgey. Effects of chard (Beta vulgaris L. var. cicla) on the liver of the diabetic rats: a morphological and biochemical study. *Biosci* 2004; 68(8): 1640–1648.
18. Betancur-Galvis, Saez, Granados, Salazar, Ossa. Antitumor and antiviral activity of Colombian medicinal plant extracts. *Mem* 1999; 94(4): 531–535.
19. Prahoveanu, Esanu, Anton, Frunzulica. Prophylactic effect of a Beta vulgaris extract on experimental influenza infection in mice. *Virologie* 1986; 37(2): 121–123.
20. Atta, Alkofahi. Anti-nociceptive and anti-inflammatory effects of some Jordanian medicinal plant extracts. *J Ethnopharmacol*. 1998; 60(2): 117–124.

Ben/*Bān*

FAMILY: Moringaceae

BOTANICAL NAME: *Moringa oleifera*

COMMON NAMES: *English* Ben, Horseradish tree; *French* Huile de Ben ou Behen; *Spanish* Rá bano picante; *German* Meerrettichbaum, Behenbaum, Behennussbaum, Klärmittelbaum, Trommelstockbaum; *Urdu*/*Unānī* Sahajana, Sohanjana; *Modern Standard Arabic* Bān

SAFETY RATING: DANGEROUS TO DEADLY *Moringa oleifera* contains the alkaloid spirochin, a potentially fatal nerve paralyzing agent. In clinical tests conducted in India in the 1980s, leaf extracts of *Moringa oleifera* were found to be 100 percent abortive at doses equivalent to 175 mg/kg of starting dry material. The roots of the plant are typically shredded and used as a condiment in the same fashion as horseradish. Due to the dangers posed by the plant, its consumption as both a condiment and a medicine should be strongly discouraged if not prohibited.

PROPHETIC PRESCRIPTION: The Prophet Muḥammad said, "Whoever anoints himself with the oil of ben before Satan he will not be harmed, Allāh, the Exalted, willing."[1] Ibn al-Jawziyyah quotes a supposedly spurious *ḥadīth* which states, "Oil yourselves with *bān*, for it will put you in good favor with your womenfolk."[2] While not well-founded, the content of the tradition may be valid. When the oil of ben was mentioned to Imām Muḥammad al-Bāqir, he described it as "[a] male oil (*duhn dhakar*) and an excellent oil, the oil of ben." Imām 'Alī ibn Abī Ṭālib explained that "[t]he best oil is the oil of ben. It is a protection and it is masculine, a security from every affliction. So anoint yourselves with it, for the Prophets, blessings of Allāh be on them, used to use it."[3]

ISSUES IN IDENTIFICATION: It is the consensus of Arabic and Unānī botanists that *bān* is Arabic for ben. The only scholar to claim otherwise was Elgood, who translated the word as "coffee bean."[4] The translator seems to have confused the Arabic words *bunn* and *ban*/*bān*. The Arabic *bunn* derives from the Amharic *bunc* and *bunna*, which means coffee, while the word *ban*/*bān* refers to *Moringa oleifera* or the horseradish tree from Arabia and India.

As botanists are well aware, coffee hails from in or around Kaffa, in southwest Ethiopia, where African tribes uses to prepare it as food. Coffee, as a drink, developed later, not as a hot drink, but as an alcoholic beverage derived from the fermented juice of the ripe cherries. As Stobart relates, "The usual story is that the plant was brought from Ethiopia to the Yemen. Dates vary from A.D. 575 to A.D. 850 ... its use must have been very local, for it took almost a thousand years to reach Cairo, at least in noticeable amounts, and the first coffee shop was not opened there until 1550."[5]

According to Meyers, the very first coffee shop, Kiva Han, was opened in Constantinople in 1457. In Europe, the first coffee shop was opened in Italy in 1645. Coffee shops were opened in England in 1652, in southern France in 1664, in Paris in 1672, and in Berlin in 1721.[6] As Kowalchik and Hylton explain, "It wasn't until A.D. 1000 that Arabs learned to boil coffee and serve it hot."[7] And it was not until several hundreds of years that the Arabs learned to roast and ground the beans before boiling them.[8] Chronologically speaking, the Prophet and the Twelve Imāms could never have referred to coffee beans.

Aṣmaʿī says that *bān* is a synonym for *shūʿ*.[9] Dīnawarī describes *bān* as a tree that grows tall like *athal*, with soft wood which is somewhat hollow inside, and fruits like beans (*lūbiyā*) horns, but greener, which contains seeds which are used to make oil.[10] According to Akīlī, the Arabic *bān* refers to *Moringa pterygosperma*.[11] This is highly unlikely because *M. pterygosperma* is found in India, Pakistan, parts of East Asia, and tropical Africa. For Johnstone, *bān* refers to *Moringa aptera*.[12] While we opt for *Moringa oleifera*, other oil producing plants from the Moringaceae family are equally plausible.

According to Chaudhary, *Moringa oleifera* is originally a native of Pakistan and India. It is a cultivated tree in Saudi Arabia. According to Chaudhary, *Moringa peregrina* is widely distributed in the western heights of Saudi Arabia. It is found in northeast tropical Africa and the Middle East, one variety wild, and the other cultivated.[13] As Ghazanfar explains, *M. peregrina* is found throughout Arabia on rocky, hilly areas. The seeds of *M. peregrina* are used to produce ben oil, which is used in perfumery and lubrication. *Moringa peregrina* is still known as *shū'* in Omani Arabic.[14]

Properties and Uses: *Moringa oleifera*, known as horseradish tree, ben oil tree or drumstick tree, is a nutritious, diuretic, laxative herb that is an expectorant, galactalogue, antibacterial, and it is a rubefacient when applied topically. It contains a potent antibiotic. The oil, which is pressed from the seeds, is a galactagogue, rubefacient, antiscorbutic, and diuretic, as well as a stimulant and a purgative. In Unānī medicine, ben oil is used as a laxative and antispasmodic, and in the Ayurveda, as an emmenagogue and aphrodisiac. Ben oil contains various acids, including two alkaloids which have the same action as epinephrine. The oil from the nut is commonly found in Muslim medical texts. The oil, which has no taste, smell, or color, is exceptionally resistant to oxidization. Due to the fact that it does not go rancid, it is a useful ingredient in foods and pharmaceutical products. Internally, the young leaves of the ben tree are used for insufficient lactation. They are often added to shellfish dishes to counteract any toxins. The bark and gum are used for tuberculosis and septicemia. The juice of the root is used for asthma, gout, rheumatism, enlarged spleen and liver, bladder and kidney stones, and inflammatory conditions. Externally, the bark, root, and gum are used for boils, ulcers, glandular swellings, infected wounds, skin diseases, dental infections, snakebites, and gout. As Ghazanfar explains, *Moringa peregrina* oil is used to treat headache, fever, abdominal pain, and constipation. It is also used for burns, back pain, muscle aches, and during labor at childbirth.[15]

Scientific Studies: *Cardiostimulating, Circulatory Stimulating, Antitumor, Antipyretic, Antiepileptic, Anti-inflammatory, Antiulcer, Antispasmodic, Diuretic, Antihypertensive, Cholesterol-Lowering, Antioxidant, Antidiabetic, Hepaprotective, Antibacterial, and Antifungal Activity* According to the University of Agriculture in Faisalabad, *Moringa oleifera* has an impressive range of medicinal uses with high nutritional value. Research has confirmed that various parts of the plant act as cardiac and circulatory stimulants, possess antitumor, antipyretic, antiepileptic, anti-inflammatory, antiulcer, antispasmodic, diuretic, antihypertensive, cholesterol lowering, antioxidant, antidiabetic, hepaprotective, antibacterial and antifungal activities.[16]

Wound-Healing Activity In an animal study conducted by Bharati Vidyapeeth Deemed University in India, the aqueous extract of leaves of *Moringa oleifera* was shown to possess significant wound-healing properties.[17] In a study conducted by the Defense Research and Development Establishment in India, the administration of *M. oleifera* seed powder with arsenic was found to significantly protect animals from oxidative stress and in reducing tissue arsenic concentration. Administration of *M. oleifera* seed powder could also be beneficial during chelation therapy.[18]

Waste-Water Cleaning Activity A large number of studies have demonstrated that *Moringa oleifera* seed coagulant has great potential for use in the treatment of wastewater. *Moringa oleifara* seeds contain a high quality edible oil and water soluble proteins that act as effective coagulants for water and wastewater treatment.[19] *Moringa oleifera* pods have been successfully employed as an inexpensive and effective sorbent for the removal of organics such as benzene, toluene, ethyl benzene, and cumene from aqueous solutions.[20] *Moringa oleifera* has been shown to absorb lead from contaminated water.[21] It has also been shown to effectively remove arsenic from water.[22] *Moringa oleifera* seeds contain natural polyelectrolytes which can be used as coagulants to clarify turbid waters. In laboratory tests, direct filtration of turbid surface water with seeds of *S. potatorum* or *M. oleifera* as coagulant produced a substantial improvement in its aesthetic and microbiological quality. The method appears suitable for home water treatment in rural areas of developing countries. These natural coagulants produce "low risk" water; however, additional disinfection or boiling should be practiced during localized outbreaks or epidemics of enteric infections.[23] The polypeptide of *Moringa oleifera* possesses a bactericidal activity capable of disinfecting heavily contaminated water. The polypeptide has been shown to efficiently kill several pathogenic bacteria, including antibiotic-resistant isolates of *Staphylococcus*, *Streptococcus*, and *Legionella* species. This polypeptide displays the unprecedented feature of combining water purification and disinfectant properties.[24] Research has shown that shelled *Moringa oleifera* seeds are a cost-effective, environmentally friendly, and safe way to remove toxic metals from domestic water supplies.[25]

Antitumor Activity A study conducted by ER-GenTech and Ferrara University in Italy found that *Moringa oleifera* inhibits the interactions between nuclear factors and target DNA elements mimicking sequences recognized by the nuclear factor kappaB. Extracts inhibiting both NF-kappaB binding activity and tumor cell growth might be a source for antitumor compounds, while extracts inhibiting NF-kappaB/DNA interactions with lower effects on cell growth could be of interest in the search of compounds active in inflammatory diseases, for which inhibition of NF-kappaB binding activity without toxic effects should be obtained.[26]

Antifungal Activity In an in-vitro study conducted by the Academia Sinica in Taiwan, the ethanol extracts of *M. oleifera* demonstrated antifungal activities against dermatophytes such as *Trichophyton rubrum*, *Trichophyton mentagrophytes*, *Epidermophyton floccosum*, and *Microsporum canis*. Isolated extracts could be of use for the future development of anti-skin disease agents.[27]

Antiurolithiatic Activity According to an animal study conducted by K.L.E.S's College of Pharmacy in India, the root-wood of *M. oleifera* possesses significant antiurolithiatic activity.[28]

Antioxidative Activity According to a study conducted by the National Botanical Research Institute in India, the seeds of *Syzygium cumini* have high total phenolic contents and high antioxidative activity. *Moringa oleifera* was also found to be rich source of kaempferol.[29]

Anticancer Activity In a study conducted by the Federal University of Ceara in Brazil, the anticancer potential of 11 plants used in Bangladeshi folk medicine was examined. Among all tested extracts, only three extracts, including *M. oleifera*, could be considered as potential sources of anticancer compounds.[30]

Anti-inflammatory Activity According to an animal study conducted by the Laboratoire de Pharmacologie et de Physiologie in Senegal, the aqueous root extract of *M. oleifera* reduces carrageenin-induced edema to the same extent as the potent anti-inflammatory drug indomethacin. These results provide further evidence that the roots of *M. oleifera* contain anti-inflammatory principle that may be useful in the treatment of the acute inflammatory conditions.[31]

Antiherpetic Activity In a study conducted by Chulalongkorn University in Thailand, twenty Thai medicinal plant extracts were evaluated for anti-herpes simplex virus type 1 activity. Eleven of them inhibited plaque formation of HSV-1. *Moringa oleifera* was among three herbs which were also effective against thymidine kinase-deficient HSV-1 and phosphonoacetate-resistant HSV-1 strains. The daily administration of *Moringa oleifera* extract significantly delayed the development of skin lesions, prolonged the mean survival times and reduced the mortality of HSV-1 infected mice. There were no significant difference between acyclovir and *Moringa oleifera* in the delay of the development of skin lesions, and no significant difference between acyclovir and *Moringa oleifera* in mean survival times. Toxicity of the plant extract was not observed in treated mice. It was concluded that *Moringa oleifera* may be a possible candidate for an anti–HSV-1 agent.[32]

Antioxidative Activity In a study conducted by Annamalai University in India, administration of *Moringa oleifera* extract significantly decreased hepatic marker enzymes and lipid peroxidation with a simultaneous increase in the level of antioxidants.[33]

Antifungal Activity In a study conducted by the University of Maiduguri in Nigeria, the aqueous extract of *Moringa* seed was shown to be a potent biofungicide.[34]

Chemomodulatory Activity In a controlled animal study conducted by Gauhati University in India, the chemopreventive potential of *Moringa oleifera* drumstick extract was demonstrated against chemical carcinogenesis.[35]

Ruminal Antifermentation Activity According to a study conducted by the University of Hohenheim in Germany, *Moringa oleifera* was found to reduce rumen fermentation, providing a possible alternative to critical synthetic feed additives such as antibiotics for high yielding dairy cows.[36]

Cholesterol-Lowering Activity In a 120-day animal trial conducted by The M.S. University of Baroda in India, oral administration of *Moringa oleifera* lowered serum cholesterol, phospholipid, triglyceride, VLDL, LDL, cholesterol to phospholipid ratio and atherogenic index, but increased HDL ratio (HDL/HDL-total cholesterol). The study demonstrated that *Moringa oleifera* possesses a hypolipidemic effect.[37]

Anti-Hypoglycemic Activity In an animal study conducted by Satsang Herbal Research and Analytical Laboratories in India, the oral administration of 95 percent ethanolic extract of *Moringa oleifera* was confirmed to possess blood glucose lowering effects.[38]

Radioprotective Activity In a study conducted by the Kasturba Medical College in India, the pretreatment of methanolic leaf extract of *Moringa oleifera* was found to confer significant radiation protection to the bone marrow chromosomes in mice, leading to a higher survival rate after lethal whole-body irradiation.[39]

Antihyperthyroidism Activity According study conducted by Devi Ahilya University in India, extracts from *Moringa oleifera* aqueous leaf extract may help regulate hyperthyroidism.[40]

Antihypocholesterolemic Activity According to an animal study conducted by the University of Nigeria, administration of the crude leaf extract of *Moringa oleifera*, along with high-fat diet, decreased serum, liver, and kidney cholesterol levels by 14.35 percent, 6.40 percent, and 11.09 percent. The effect on the serum cholesterol was statistically significant. The study concluded that the leaves of *Moringa oleifera* have definite hypocholesterolemic activity, validating their pharmacological use in India.[41]

Antitumor Activity In a study conducted by the University of the Philippines four *Moringa oleifera* ethanol extracts demonstrated inhibitory activity against Epstein-Barr virus-early-antigen, three of which showed very significant activities. Based on the in vitro results, niazimicin was further subjected to in vivo test and found to have potent antitumor promoting activity in the two-stage carcinogenesis in mouse skin. On the basis of these results, niazimicin has been proposed as a potent chemopreventive agent in chemical carcinogenesis.[42]

Anti-inflammatory, Antispasmodic, and Diuretic Activity According to an animal study conducted by the Center for Mesoamerican Studies on Appropriate Technology in Guatemala City, hot water infusions of flowers, leaves, roots, seeds and stalks or bark of *Moringa oleifera* demonstrated antispasmodic activity.[43]

Antifertility Activity Several animal studies have confirmed that *Moringa oleifera* Lam. possesses antifertility activity. *Moringa olefeira* was shown to render the uterus non-receptive, thus preventing fertilized eggs from being welcomed by the unprepared uterus.[44] *Moringa Olefeira* shows potential as a type of herbal birth control.

Abortifacient Activity According to an animal study conducted by the Central Drug Research Institute in Lucknow, the aqueous of 90 percent ethanol extracts of *Moringa oleifera* leaves were found to be 100 percent abortive at doses equivalent of 175 mg/kg of starting dry material.[45] *Moringa oleifera* extracts might be used to develop a safe herbal abortifacient.

Ben Notes

1. Nisābūrī A. *Ṭibb al-a'immah.* Bayrūt: Dār al-Maḥajjah al-Bayḍā', 1994: 119.
2. Ibn Qayyim al-Jawziyyah M. *Al-Ṭibb al-nabawī.* Bayrūt: Dār al-Kitāb, 1985.
3. Nisābūrī A. *Ṭibb al-a'immah.* Bayrūt: Dār al-Maḥajjah al-Bayḍā', 1994: 119.
4. Elgood C. Trans. *Medicine of the Prophet.* J Sūyūṭī, M Chaghhaynī. *Osiris* 1962; 14: 71.
5. Stobart T. *Herbs, Spices, and Flavoring.* Woodstock, NY: Overlook Press, 1982: 87.
6. Meyers H. "Suave molecules of mocha:" coffee, chemistry, and civilization. *New Partisan: Politics, Culture, Arts* 2005. http://newpartisan.squarespace.com/home/suave-molecules-of-mocha-coffee-chemistry-and-civilization.html; Toussaint-Samat M. *A History of Food.* Trans. Anthea Bell. West Sussex: Wiley-Blackwell, 2009: 689.
7. Kowalchik C, Hylton W. *Rodale's Illustrated Encyclopedia of Herbs.* Emmaus, PA: Rodale Press, 1987: 94.
8. History of roasting coffee. http://www.caffepronto.com/education/roast.php
9. al-Aṣma'ī AM. *Kitāb al-nabāt.* Cairo: Maktabat al-mutanabbi, 1972.
10. Dīnawarī AH. *Kitāb al-nabāt/The Books of Plants.* Ed. Bernhard Lewin. Uppsala/Wiesbaden: A.-B. Lundequistska Bokhandeln and Otto Harrassowitz, 1953: 75.
11. Ibn al-Qayyim al-Jawziyyah. *Natural Healing with the Medicine of the Prophet.* Pearl Publishing. Trans. M al-Akīlī. Philadelphia, 1993.
12. Johnstone P, trans. *Medicine of the Prophet.* Ibn Qayyim al-Jawziyyah. Cambridge: The Islamic Texts Society, 1998.
13. Chaudhary SA. *Flora of the Kingdom of Saudi Arabia.* al-Riyyāḍ: Ministry of Agriculture and Water, 1999.
14. Ghazanfar SA. *Handbook of Arabian Medicinal Plants.* Boca Raton: CRC Press, 1994.
15. Ghazanfar SA. *Handbook of Arabian Medicinal Plants.* Boca Raton: CRC Press, 1994.
16. Anwar, Latif, Ashraf, Gilani. *Moringa oleifera*: a food plant with multiple medicinal uses. *Phytother* 2007; 21(1): 17–25.
17. Rathi, Bodhankar, Baheti. Evaluation of aqueous leaves extract of *Moringa oleifera* Linn for wound healing in albino rats. *Indian* 2006; 44(11): 898–901.
18. Gupta, Dubey, Kannan, Flora. Concomitant administration of *Moringa oleifera* seed powder in the remediation of arsenic-induced oxidative stress in mouse. *Cell* 2007; 31(1): 44–56.
19. Bhuptawat, Folkard, Chaudhari. Innovative physicochemical treatment of wastewater incorporating *Moringa oleifera* seed coagulant. *J* 2007; 142(1–2): 477–482.
20. Akhtar, Moosa, Bhanger, Iqbal. Sorption potential of *Moringa oleifera* pods for the removal of organic pollutants from aqueous solutions. *J* 2007; 141(3): 546–556.
21. Nadeem, Mahmood, Shahid, Shah, Khalid, McKay. Sorption of lead from aqueous solution by chemically modified carbon adsorbents. *J* 2006; 138(3): 604–613.
22. Kumari, Sharma, Srivastava, Srivastava. Arsenic removal from the aqueous system using plant biomass: a bioremedial approach. *J* 2005; 32(11–12): 521–526.

23. Babu, Chaudhuri. Home water treatment by direct filtration with natural coagulant. *J* 2005; 3(1): 27–30.
24. Suarez, Entenza, Doerries, Meyer, Bourquin, Sutherland, Marison, Moreillon, Mermod. Expression of a plant-derived peptide harboring water-cleaning and antimicrobial activities. *Biotechnol* 2003; 5; 81(1): 13–20.
25. Sharma, Kumari, Srivastava, Srivastava. Home water treatment by direct filtration with natural coagulant. *Bioresour* 2006; 97(2): 299–305.
26. Lampronti, Khan, Bianchi, Ather, Borgatti, Vizziello, Fabbri, Gambari. Bangladeshi medicinal plant extracts inhibiting molecular interactions between nuclear factors and target DNA sequences mimicking NF-kappaB binding sites. *Med* 2005; 1(4): 327–333.
27. Lampronti, Khan, Bianchi, Ather, Borgatti, Vizziello, Fabbri, Gambari. Bangladeshi medicinal plant extracts inhibiting molecular interactions between nuclear factors and target DNA sequences mimicking NF-kappaB binding sites. *Med* 2005; 1(4): 327–333.
28. Karadi, Gadge, Alagawadi, Savadi. Effect of *Moringa oleifera* Lam. root-wood on ethylene glycol induced urolithiasis in rats. *J* 2006; 105(1–2): 306–311.
29. Bajpai, Pande, Tewari, Prakash. Phenolic contents and antioxidative activity of some food and medicinal plants. *Int* 2005; 56(4): 287–291.
30. Costa-Lotufo, Khan, Ather, Wilke, Jimenez, Pessoa, de, de. Studies of the anticancer potential of plants used in Bangladeshi folk medicine. *J* 2005; 99(1): 21–30.
31. Ndiaye, Dieye, Mariko, Tall, Sall, Faye. [Contribution to the study of the anti-inflammatory activity of *Moringa oleifera* (*moringaceae*)]. *Dakar* 2002; 47(2): 210–212.
32. Lipipun, Kurokawa, Suttisri, Taweechotipatr, Pramyothin, Hattori, Shiraki. Efficacy of Thai medicinal plant extracts against herpes simplex virus type 1 infection in vitro and in vivo. *Antiviral* 2003; 60(3): 175–180.
33. Ashok, Pari. Antioxidant action of *Moringa oleifera* Lam. (drumstick) against antitubercular drugs induced lipid peroxidation in rats. *J* 2003; 6(3): 255–259.
34. Donli, Dauda. Evaluation of aqueous *Moringa* seed extract as a seed treatment biofungicide for groundnuts. *Pest* 2003; 59(9): 1060–1062.
35. Bharali, Tabassum, Azad. Chemomodulatory effect of *Moringa oleifera*, Lam, on hepatic carcinogen metabolising enzymes, antioxidant parameters and skin papillomagenesis in mice. *Asian* 2003; 4(2): 131–139.
36. Hoffmann, Muetzel, Becker. Effects of *Moringa oleifera* seed extract on rumen fermentation in vitro. *Arch* 2003; 57(1): 65–81.
37. Mehta, Balaraman, Amin, Bafna, Gulati. Effect of fruits of *Moringa oleifera* on the lipid profile of normal and hypercholesterolaemic rabbits. *J* 2003; 86(2–3): 191–195.
38. Kar, Choudhary, Bandyopadhyay. Comparative evaluation of hypoglycaemic activity of some Indian medicinal plants in alloxan diabetic rats. *J* 2003; 84(1): 105–108.
39. Rao, Devi, Kamath. In vivo radioprotective effect of *Moringa oleifera* leaves. *Indian* 2001; 39(9): 858–863.
40. Tahiliani, Kar. Role of *Moringa oleifera* leaf extract in the regulation of thyroid hormone status in adult male and female rats. *Pharmacol* 2000; 41(3): 319–323.
41. Ghasi, Nwobodo, Ofili. Hypocholesterolemic effects of crude extract of leaf of *Moringa oleifera* Lam in high-fat diet fed wistar rats. *J* 2000; 69(1): 21–5.
42. Guevara, Vargas, Sakurai, Fujiwara, Hashimoto, Maoka, Kozuka, Ito, Tokuda, Nishino. An antitumor promoter from *Moringa oleifera* Lam. *Mutat* 1999; 440(2): 181–188.
43. Caceres, Saravia, Rizzo, Zabala, De, Nave. Pharmacologic properties of *Moringa oleifera*. 2: Screening for antispasmodic, anti-inflammatory and diuretic activity. *J* 1992; 36(3): 233–237.
44. Prakash, Pathak, Shukla, Mathur. Uterine histoarchitecture during pre and post-implantation periods of rats treated with aqueous extract of *Moringa oleifera* Lam. *Acta* 1987; 18(2): 129–135; Shukla, Mathur, Prakash. Histoarchitecture of the genital tract of ovariectomized rats treated with an aqueous extract of *Moringa oleifera* roots *J* 1989; 25(3): 249–261; Shukla, Mathur, Prakash. Biochemical and physiological alterations in female reproductive organs of cyclic rats treated with aqueous extract of *Moringa oleifera* Lam. *Acta* 1988; 19(4): 225–232; Shukla, Mathur, Prakash. Antifertility profile of the aqueous extract of *Moringa oleifera* roots. *J Ethnopharmacol.* 1988; 22(1): 51–62.
45. Nath, Sethi, Singh, Jain. Commonly used Indian abortifacient plants with special reference to their teratologic effects in rats. *J* 1992; 36(2): 147–154.

Black Seed/*al-Ḥabbah al-Sawdā', Shūnīz*

FAMILY: Ranunculaceae

BOTANICAL NAME: *Nigella sativa*

COMMON NAMES: *English* Black seed, black cumin, common fennel flower, Roman coriander, nutmeg flower, fitches; *French* Nigelle, Nielle, Cumin noir; *Spanish* Ajenuz, Comino negro, Falso comino; *German* Echter Schwarzkümmel; *Urdu/Unānī* Kalonji, Shoneez; *Modern Standard Arabic* Ḥabbah al-sawdā', Shūnīz

SAFETY RATING: GENERALLY SAFE *Nigella sativa* seems to be generally safe for most people when consumed as directed in therapeutic doses.

PROPHETIC PRESCRIPTION: Black seed is one of the most famous herbs used in Islamic phytotherapy. In a famous *ḥadīth*, the Messenger of Allāh said, "black seed is a cure for every disease except death."[1] In another tradition related by Bukhārī, we learn that the companions of the Prophet used to take five to seven black seeds, crush them, combine them with oil, and apply it to their nostrils. Ibn Ḥabīb also confirms that the Prophet used to prescribe black seed as snuff.[2] In a more detailed tradition, the Prophet Muḥammad said, "In black seed is a healing from every illness except *al-sām*." It was said, "O Messenger of Allāh, what is *al-sām*?" He replied, "Death." Then he said, "These two [honey and black seed] are not predisposed to the heat or the cold or to natural constituents, but they are both a healing wherever they are."[3] In another *ḥadīth*, the Messenger of Allāh said, "Let these black seeds fall upon you for they contain a cure for every disease except death."[4] He also said, "The best medicine is cupping, costus (*qusṭ*), and black seed (*shūnīz*)."[5] According to Ibn Ḥabīb, the Prophet used to take black seed soaked in honey every morning and evening to preserve his memory and to fight phlegm.[6]

According to Imām Ja'far al-Ṣādiq, "Black seed (*ḥabbah al-sawdā'*) is a cure for every illness, and it was the beloved [herb] of the Messenger of Allāh, may the peace and mercy of Allāh be upon him." He was told, "People claim that it is Syrian rue (*ḥarmal*)." He said, "No, it is *shūnīz*. Were I to ask the companions [of the Prophet] to show me the beloved [herb] of the Messenger of Allāh, may the peace and blessings of Allāh be upon him, they would show me *shūnīz*."[7] According to the Imām, "In *shūnīz* there is a cure for every disease. I take it for fever, headache, inflammation of the eyes (*ramad*), and stomach pain. For every pain that I suffer from, Allāh, may He be honored and glorified, heals me with it."[8]

Imām Ja'far al-Ṣādiq recommended black seed to a companion who suffered from abdominal pain. He also prescribed a mixture of black seed and honey for cases of colic.[9] On one occasion, a man came to Imām Ja'far al-Ṣādiq complaining of painful rumbling in the belly. The Imām said, "What prevents you from taking black seed, and honey for it? It contains a cure for every illness but death."[10] On yet another occasion, a man complained to the Sixth Imām that he suffered from excessive urination. The Imām advised him to "Take *shūnīz* at the end of the night."[11]

Imām 'Alī al-Riḍā recommended the use of black seed to protect against the common cold. As he stated, "Do not hesitate to smell narcissus for it protects against the cold in winter, and so does black seed."[12]

ISSUES IN IDENTIFICATION: According to Bīrūnī, *ḥabbah al-sawdā'* is known as *ḥabbat al-barakah*, *al-sawdā'*, *kammūn aswad*, as well as the Persian name of *shūnīz*.[13] Ibn al-Jawziyyah, Dīnawarī and Ibn Ḥabīb also state that *ḥabbah al-sawdā'* is *shūnīz*.[14] Johnstone claims that *shūnīz* refers to *Papaver somniferum* (poppy).[15] This is incorrect as the Arabic term for *Papaver somniferum* is *nu'mān al-kabīr*. Turkī, however, attempts to make a distinction between *ḥabbah al-sawdā'*, as *Nigella sativa* seed, and *shūnīz*, as black coriander, when they refer to the same source.[16]

Although it sounds like a general name, applicable to any dark seed, the term "black seed" is indeed a botanical term in classical Arabic. Scientifically speaking, "black seed" refers specifically to *Nigella sativa*, a small Asiatic annual, native to Syria, not in any way related to the fennel, but belonging to the buttercup family, Ranunculaceae. It is grown to a limited extent in southern Europe and occasionally in other parts of the world. It is found only as a cultivated plant in Arabia.

It is important not to confuse black seed with other dark seeds. As the Hans Wehr Dictionary explains, *ḥabbah al-sawdā'* refers to any black seed in colloquial Arabic, such as fennel seed, cumin, black pepper, black mustard, black caraway, terebinth fruit, and coriander seed. Even classical writers have been confused regarding the origin of "black seed." According to sources cited by Ibn al-Jawziyyah, *ḥabbah al-sawdā'* is *khardal* (mustard) or the green grain, the fruit of the terebinth (*buṭm*), views which he discards.[17]

Akīlī has translated *ḥabbah al-sawdā'* as black cumin and Aḥmad Thomson and Hakim Chishti have rendered it as coriander seed.[18] As Turkī confirms, *ḥabbah al-sawdā'* refers to *Nigella sativa* seed.[19] When this mistake was pointed out to Hakim Chishti, he responded, "in *The Traditional Healers Handbook*, I purposefully made substitutions."[20] He cited the introduction from his *Traditional Healers Handbook* which says,

> Another matter relating to selection of herbs is that some herbs used in *Ṭibb* in India or Afghanistan are not available in the United States (they may be in Europe). As an example, embelic myrobalan is used in several formulas in the original formulary of *Mizān-ul-Ṭibb*. This herb has great tonic and restorative powers, but it is, for all practical purposes, unavailable in the West. Therefore, in consultation with other Ḥakīms, I arrived at *equivalent substitutions* [emphasis added]; using readily available ingredients, according to the imbalance being treated.[21]

Despite this defense, Hakim Chishti has clearly stated in his book that black seed or *ḥabbah al-sawdā'* is coriander seed, when this is not the case. The name "coriander seed" appears nowhere in Duke's extensive list of common names for *Nigella sativa*. It is well-known that black seed is *Nigella sativa* and calling it coriander can cause confusion. The author has not said that coriander seed is a substitution for *ḥabbah al-sawdā'*. He has claimed that *ḥabbah al-sawdā'* is coriander seed.

The confusion regarding the identity of black seed traces as far back as the Prophet's time. After he said, "Black seed contains a cure for every disease," his companions brought him some black pepper. The Prophet told them "This is not it." They then brought him *shūnīz* and he said, "This is it!"[22]

Laiq 'Ali Khan claims that the Arabs did not learn about black seed from the Greeks, since no description or record of its use is found before

Islām. He also claims that it was only with the advent of Islām that the Prophet Muḥammad mentioned its therapeutic value and curative potentials, a view which must be called into question. As Said has explained, black seed or *Nigella sativa* is the same plant mentioned in the Bible as well as the writings of Dioscorides, and Pliny.[23] Rachel Albert-Matesz reports,

> Cultivation of black seed has been traced back more than 3,000 years to the kingdom of the Assyrians and ancient Egyptians. A bottle of black cumin oil was found in the tomb of King Tutankhamun, perhaps to protect the ruler in the afterlife. Black cumin was a vital ingredient in many Egyptian dishes. Physicians of the pharaohs used the seeds as a digestive aid after opulent feasts and as a remedy for colds, headaches, toothaches, infections, inflammatory disorders and allergies. Black seed oil has been a beauty secret of women since ancient times. Queen Nefertiti, praised for her exquisite complexion, was an avid user of black seed oil. Pliny the Elder crushed black seeds, mixed them with vinegar and honey, and applied the paste to snake bites and scorpion stings.[24]

According to Chaudhary, *Nigella sativa* is native to South West Asia. Elsewhere, it is cultivated as a crop. It is also known as *ḥabbah al-barakah* in Saudi Arabic.[25]

Properties and Uses: *Nigella sativa* is considered stimulant, antiphlegmatic, attenuant, suppurative, detergent, diuretic, emmenagogue, lactagogue, uterine stimulant, anthelmintic, expectorant, antiflatulent, antidyspeptic, antipyretic, carminative, tonic, and abortifacient. Internally, the seeds of *N. sativa* are used for painful menstruation, postpartum contractions, insufficient lactation, and bronchial complaints. It is to treat coughs, digestive and hepatic disorders, jaundice, tertian fever, paralysis, and piles. A decoction of the seed is given to promote contraction of the uterus after birth and also to secrete milk. It is also used to treat amenorrhea and dysmenorrhea, as well as eruptive skin diseases. Black seed and its oil have been used to purge parasites and worms, detoxify the body, to improve amoebic dysentery, shigellosis, and to treat abscesses, old tumors, ulcers of the mouth, and rhinitis. Recent research confirms these uses for humans, dogs, cats and horses. In aromatherapy, it is used to treat the common cold. The oil of *Nigella sativa* seeds is applied to treat alopecia, skin disorders, and earaches. More than 200 university studies conducted since 1959 attest to the effectiveness of traditional uses of black seed.[26]

Scientific Studies: *Antibacterial Activity* In a study conducted by Selcuk University in Turkey, a series of essential oils of 11 Turkish plant spices (black thyme, cumin, fennel [sweet], laurel, marjoram, mint, oregano, pickling herb, sage, savory, and thyme), were screened for antibacterial effects against six *Bacillus* species. All of the tested essential oils (except for cumin) showed antibacterial activity against one or more of the *Bacillus* species used in this study.[27] Generally, the essential oils at 1:50 and 1:100 levels were more effective. Based on the results of this study, it is likely that essential oils of some spices may be used as antimicrobial agents to prevent the spoilage of food products. Research has also concluded that *N. sativa* oil is active against standard as well as multi-drug resistant strains of *S. aureus* and *P. aerugenosa* and may be used therapeutically in susceptible cases.[28]

Antidiabetic Activity According to M. Laiq Ali Khan, Director of the Shah Faisal Institute of Ḥadīth and Medical Sciences, modern trials have proven that black seed alone or in combination with other drugs are highly effective in diabetes mellitus.[29]

Anticancer Activity In vitro studies in Jordan and the United States have shown the volatile oil of *N. sativa* is anti-leukemic. In a controlled 8-week animal trial conducted by Tanta University in Egypt, the chemopreventive effects of orally administered *N. sativa* oil were investigated.[30] Treatment with black seed oil in the initiation state did not exhibit significant inhibitory effects; however, it did have significant anti-proliferative activity in both initiation and post-initiation stages, especially the latter. According to an animal study conducted by Hamdard University in India, *N. sativa* seems to be a potent chemo-protective agent capable of suppressing tumor production.[31]

Black Seed Notes

1. Bukhārī M. *Ṣaḥīḥ al-Bukhārī*. al-Riyyāḍ: Bayt al-Afkār, 1998; Muslim. *Jāmi' al-ṣaḥīḥ*. al-Riyyāḍ: Bayt al-Afkār, 1998; Ibn Mājah M. *Sunan*. Trans. MT Anṣārī. Lahore: Kazi Publications, 1994; Ibn Ḥanbal A. *Musnad al-Imām Aḥmad ibn Ḥanbal*. Bayrūt: al-Maktabah al-Islāmiyyah, 1969; Chaghhaynī M. *Ṭibb al-nabī*. Trans. C Elgood. *Osiris* 1962; 14: 191.
2. Ibn Ḥabīb A. *Mujtaṣar fī al-ṭibb/Compendio de medicina*. Ed. C Álvarez de Morales and F Girón Irueste. Madrid: Consejo Superior de Investigaciones Científicas, 1992: 56.
3. This tradition is found, with slight differences, in Aḥmad, Ibn Mājah, Tirmidhī, and Nisābūrī.
4. Ibn Ḥanbal A. *Musnad al-Imām Aḥmad ibn Ḥanbal*. Bayrūt: al-Maktabah al-Islāmiyyah, 1969; Ibn Qayyim al-Jawziyyah M. *al-Ṭibb al-nabawī*. Bayrūt: Dār al-Kitāb, 1985; Tirmidhī M. *al-Jāmi' al-ṣaḥīḥ*. al-Qāhirah: Muṣṭafā al-Bābī al-Ḥalabī [1937–].
5. Ibn Ṭulūn S. *al-Manhal al-rawī fī al-ṭibb al-nabawī*. Ed. 'Azīz Bayk. Riyyāḍ: Dār 'ālam al-kutub, 1995.
6. Ibn Ḥabīb A. *Mujtaṣar fī al-ṭibb/Compendio de medicina*. Ed. C Álvarez de Morales and F Girón Irueste. Madrid: Consejo Superior de Investigaciones Científicas, 1992: 70/37.

7. Majlisī M. *Biḥār al-anwār*. Ṭihrān: Javad al-Alavi, 1956.
8. Majlisī M. *Biḥār al-anwār*. Ṭihrān: Javad al-Alavi, 1956
9. Nisābūrī A. *Ṭibb al-a'immah*. Bayrūt: Dār al-Maḥajjah al-Bayḍā', 1994.
10. Nisābūrī A. *Islamic Medical Wisdom: The Ṭibb al-a'immah*. Trans. B. Ispahany. Ed. AJ Newman. London: Muḥammadī Trust, 1991: 129; Majlisī M. *Biḥār al-anwār*. Ṭihrān: Javad al-Alavi, 1956.
11. Majlisī M. *Biḥār al-anwār*. Ṭihrān: Javad al-Alavi, 1956.
12. Riḍā 'A al-. *Risālah fī al-ṭibb al-nabawī*. Ed. MA Bār. Bayrūt: Dār al-Manāhil, 1991: 172.
13. Bīrūnī, AR al-. *al-Bīrūnī's Book on Pharmacy and Materia Medica*. Ed. and trans. HM Said. Karachi: Hamdard National Foundation, 1973.
14. Dīnawarī AH. *Kitāb al-nabāt: Le dictionaire botanique d'Abū Ḥanīfa al-Dīnawarī*. al-Qāhirah: Institut Français d'Archéologie Orientale du Caire, 1973; Ibn Qayyim al-Jawziyyah M. *al-Ṭibb al-nabawī*. Bayrūt: Dār al-Kitāb, 1985; Ibn Ḥabīb A. *Mujtaṣar fī al-ṭibb/Compendio de medicina*. Ed. C Álvarez de Morales and F Girón Irueste. Madrid: Consejo Superior de Investigaciones Científicas, 1992: 77/45; 66/33.
15. Johnstone P, trans. *Medicine of the Prophet*. Ibn Qayyim al-Jawziyyah. Cambridge: The Islamic Texts Society, 1998.
16. Iṣbahānī AN al-. *Mawsū'at al-ṭibb al-nabawī*. Ed. MKD al-Turkī. Bayrūt: Dār Ibn Ḥazm, 2006.
17. Ibn Qayyim al-Jawziyyah M. *al-Ṭibb al-nabawī*. Bayrūt: Dār al-Kitāb, 1985.
18. Ibn al-Qayyim al-Jawziyyah. *Natural Healing with the Medicine of the Prophet*. Pearl Publishing. Trans. M al-Akīlī. Philadelphia, 1993; Sūyūṭī J. *As-Sūyūṭī's Medicine of the Prophet*. Ed. A Thomson. London: Ṭā-Hā Publishers, 1994; Chishti SHM. *The Book of Sufi Healing*. Rochester, Vermont: Inner Traditions International, 1991: 57.
19. Iṣbahānī AN al-. *Mawsū'at al-ṭibb al-nabawī*. Ed. MKD al-Turkī. Bayrūt: Dār Ibn Ḥazm, 2006.
20. Chishti H. Letter to the author. October 8, 2007.
21. Chishti H. Letter to the author. October 8, 2007.
22. Ibn Ḥabīb A. *Mujtaṣar fī al-ṭibb/Compendio de medicina*. Ed. C Álvarez de Morales and F Girón Irueste. Madrid: Consejo Superior de Investigaciones Científicas, 1992: 77/45.
23. Bīrūnī, AR al-. *al-Bīrūnī's Book on Pharmacy and Materia Medica*. Ed. and trans. HM Said. Karachi: Hamdard National Foundation, 1973.
24. Albert-Matesz R. One of life's tiny treasures. http://www.herbcompanion.com/articles/10_11_03-tinytreasures
25. Chaudhary SA. *Flora of the Kingdom of Saudi Arabia*. al-Riyyāḍ: Ministry of Agriculture and Water, 1999.
26. Albert-Matesz R. One of life's tiny treasures. http://www.herbcompanion.com/articles/10_11_03-tinytreasures; Schleicher P, Saleh M. *Black Cumin: The Magical Egyptian Herb for Allergies, Asthma, and Immune Disorders*. Rochester, Vermont: Healing Arts Press, 2000.
27. *Ozcan, Sagdic, Ozkan*. Inhibitory effects of spice essential oils on the growth of *Bacillus* species. *J* 2006; 9(3): 418–421.
28. Salman MH; Khan RA, Shukla, I. Antimicrobial activity of Nigella sativa oil against Staphylococcus aureus obtained from clinical specimens, 38th Annual Conference of Indian Pharmacological Society (Dec 28–30, 2005); Chennai I, Salman, MT, Khan RA, Shukla I Antimicrobial activity of Nigella sativa oil against multi-drug resistant Pseudomonas aerugenosa from clinical specimens. XIV Annual Conference of Indian Association of Pathologists & Microbiologists (UP Chapter)— UP-PATHMICON (Nov. 23, 2005).
29. Khan MLA. Benefits of kalonji (black seed). http://www.crescentlife.com/ dietnutrition/kalonji.htm
30. Salim, Fukushima. Chemopreventive potential of volatile oil from black cumin (*Nigella sativa* L.) seeds against rat colon carcinogenesis. *Nutr* 2003; 45(2): 195–202.
31. Khan, Sharma, Sultana. *Nigella sativa* (black cumin) ameliorates potassium bromate-induced early events of carcinogenesis: diminution of oxidative stress. *Hum* 2003 Apr; 22(4): 193–203.

Bottle Gourd / *Qara', Dubbā', Yaqṭīn*

FAMILY: Cucurbitacea

BOTANICAL NAME: *Lagenaria vulgaris* (syn. *Lageneria siceraria)*

COMMON NAMES: *English* Bottle Gourd, White Gourd, Calabash; *French* Calebasse d'Europe, Cougourde; *Spanish* Calabaza de botella; *German* Echter Flaschenkürbis; *Urdu/Unānī* Kaddu, Qara, Kaddu-e-Daraz, Loki, Ghiya; *Modern Standard Arabic* Qara' ṭawīl, Qara' dubbā', Yaqṭīn

SAFETY RATING: GENERALLY SAFE TO DEADLY Although considered potentially toxic, the fruits, leaves, and flowers of bottle gourd are eaten on many continents. According to Duke, when the fresh flesh of bottle gourd is fed to rabbits it leads to restlessness and dyspnea, with paralysis and death from asphyxia. While it may be relatively safe for human consumption in small quantities, it should be consumed with caution. Other species of gourd, however, are entirely inedible because they contain a bitter substance which acts as a purgative. Some species of gourd are mildly toxic, and others are outright poisonous. Squash which have been cross-pollinated with gourds may also be poisonous. Overdose of certain species of gourd can be fatal.

PROPHETIC PRESCRIPTION: The Qur'ān says that *dubbā'* is a plant that God made grow to shade Prophet Yūnus (Jonah) when he washed up on the shore after being swallowed by a large fish or whale (37:146). The Messenger of Allāh was very fond of gourd and used to consume it regularly.[1] On one occasion, he said, "Let them have gourd (*qara'*) for they stimulate the intellect and the brain."[2] He also told his wife 'Ā'ishah "When you cook mixed vegetables with meat, add more bottle gourd (*dubbā'*) in it, for it is a tonic that revitalizes a sad heart."[3] While the Prophet was cutting some gourd, he was asked, "What shall be made of this?" He responded that "It will be added to our food."[4] He also said, "Add more gourd (*dubbā'*) to the stew. It strengthens the depressed heart."[5] In another tradition, the Prophet said, "If any of you make a gravy soup, let him put gourd into it, for verily this increases the mind and the brain."[6]

Anas bin Malik narrated that a tailor invited God's messenger to partake of a meal and offered him barley bread besides a dish made with gourd (*dubbā'*) and dried meat (*qadīd*). Anas added, "I saw the Messenger of Allāh picking pieces of *dubbā'* from around the dish; and I always liked *dubbā'* from that day onwards."[7] According to Bukharī and Muslim, Anas bin Malik used to eat cooked gourd and would say "What a blessed plant! I love it because the Messenger of Allāh loved it."[8]

In a tradition related by Tabarānī, the Prophet is reported to have said, "Take gourd (*qarā'*) for it increases the brain."[9] In a tradition reported by Bayhaqī, the Messenger of Allāh says, "Take gourd (*qarā'*) for it increases the brain and the intellect."[10] It is also reported that the Prophet said, "If Almighty Allāh had possessed a tree lighter than the gourd (*yaqṭīn*), then verily He would have made it for our brother Yūnus, the Prophet."[11] In the version related by Daylamī, the tradition commences with "Eat gourd (*yaqṭīn*)."[12]

Like the Prophet, the Imāms also spoke of the medicinal properties of the gourd. Imām 'Alī said, "Eat gourd (*dubbā'*) for it increases the brain."[13] Imām Ja'far al-Ṣādiq conveyed the same meaning, saying, "Gourd (*dubbā'*) increases the brain." He also said, "It is good for colic (*qawlanj*)."[14]

Issues in Identification: Yusuf 'Ali translates the Qur'ānic *dubbā'* as "a spreading plant of the gourd kind," while Picktall translates it as a "tree of gourd," and Aṣad prefers not to specify a species, describing it simply as a "creeping plant." In Dīnawarī, we read that *qara'* is the fruit of the *yaqṭīn*. It is also known as *dubbā'* and it grows on the ground. According to Ibn al-Jawziyyah, *yaqṭīn* is a general term embracing both *dubbā'* and *qara'*, and indicates any shrub that does not have an upright stalk, like the watermelon (*biṭṭīkh*) and cucumbers (*qithā'*, *khiyyār*). As he explains, the *yaqṭīn* mentioned in the Qur'ān is the plant of the *dubbā'*, and its fruit is called *dubbā'* and *qara'*, and shrub of *yaqṭīn*.[15] According to both Bīrūnī and Akīlī *dubbā'* is a dried bottle gourd.[16] Turkī says that *qara'* refers to gourd, without providing a scientific name.[17] Akīlī, Thomson, and Farooqi believe that *yaqṭīn*, *qara'*, and *duba'* refer to *Lagenaria vulgaris*, also known as *Lagenaria siceraria*.[18] As Chaudhary explains, *Lagenaria siceraria* is known as *habā*, and *yaqṭīn*, in the Saudi dialect.[19]

In his translation of *Sunan Abū Dāwūd*, Ahmad Hasan mistranslates the Prophetic *qara'* as pumpkin, giving the word its modern sense rather than the meaning it possessed at the time of the Prophet. In his note to chapter 1425 on "Eating Pumpkin," he states that "the Holy Prophet liked pumpkin very much. It is, therefore, recommended for every Muslim to like pumpkin. But it is not obligatory on him to eat it." Elgood translates *qara'* as pumpkin and *yaqṭīn* as gourd. He admits, however, that "Pumpkin is not quite correct as a translation for the Arabic word *yaqṭīn*. Strictly speaking, the word means any plant which has no stalk for its support, such as melons, marrows or pumpkins."[20] Turkī has also rendered *yaqṭīn* as pumpkin.[21] While the word *yaqṭīn* does embrace pumpkins in Modern Standard Arabic and colloquial Arabic dialects, it could not have referred to them during the time of the Prophet.

Although pumpkins are cultivated throughout Arabia, they are native to the Americas. It was only after 1492 that they started to spread throughout the rest of the world. In Europe, pumpkins were only first grown in 1550.[22] The Prophet Muḥammad, who lived in Arabia from A.D. 570 to 632, could never have consumed pumpkin. While it is true that pumpkin and squash are *qara'* (as well as *kūsāh*) in modern Arabic dialects, *qara'* did not refer to pumpkin or squash at the time of the Prophet. Ḥasan's mistranslation, however, has been cited in many articles and books, all encouraging Muslims to eat pumpkin. Basing himself on poor translations, Farooqi quotes traditions in which *qara'* is rendered at times as gourd, and at others, as pumpkin, causing a great deal of confusion. All evidence indicates that *ḥabā* and *yaqṭīn* is *Lagenaria vulgaris*, synonymous with *Lagenaria siceraria*.

Properties and Uses: The bottle gourd, calabash or white gourd is a vine grown for its fruit. When harvested young, it is used as a vegetable. It is considered nutritive, digestive, diuretic, emollient, antibilious, sedative, and febrifuge. When harvested mature and dried, it is used as a bottle, utensil, or pipe. According to Bakhru, the cooked vegetable is cooling, diuretic, and antibilious. The bottle gourd is valuable in treating urinary disorders, excessive thirst, and insomnia. Bottle gourds should never be eaten raw.

Scientific Studies: *Antihyperlipidemic and Hypolipidemic Activity* In an animal study conducted by the Institute of Pharmaceutical Education and Research in India, *Lagenaria siceraria* extracts dose-dependently inhibited the total cholesterol, triglycerides, low-density lipoproteins level, and significantly increased the high density lipoproteins level. The findings suggest that *L. siceraria* extracts possess marked and hypolipidemic activity of the extracts.[23]

Anticancer Activity According to an animal study conducted by Hyogo College of Medicine in Japan, dietary fiber from *Lagenaria siceraria* suppresses colonic carcinogenesis in mice.[24]

Bottle Gourd Notes

1. Abū Dāwūd S. *Ṣaḥīḥ Sunan Abū Dāwūd.* Riyyāḍ: Maktab al-Tarbiyyah, 1989; Ibn Anas M. *al-Muwaṭṭa'.* Bayrūt: Dār al-Gharb, 1999; Tirmidhī M. *al-Jāmi' al-ṣaḥīḥ.* al-Qāhirah: Muṣṭafā al-Bābī al-Ḥalabī [1937–]; Ibn Qayyim al-Jawziyyah M. *al-Ṭibb al-nabawī.* Bayrūt: Dār al-Kitāb, 1985.
2. Sūyūṭī J. *As-Sūyūṭī's Medicine of the Prophet.* Ed. A Thomson. London: Ṭā-Hā Publishers, 1994: 85; Muslim. *Jāmi' al-ṣaḥīḥ.* al-Riyyāḍ: Bayt al-Afkār, 1998.
3. Ibn Qayyim al-Jawziyyah M. *al-Ṭibb al-nabawī.* Bayrūt: Dār al-Kitāb, 1985.
4. Tirmidhī M. *al-Jāmi' al-ṣaḥīḥ.* al-Qāhirah: Muṣṭafā al-Bābī al-Ḥalabī [1937–].
5. Ibn Qayyim al-Jawziyyah M. *al-Ṭibb al-nabawī.* Bayrūt: Dār al-Kitāb, 1985.
6. Chaghhaynī M. *Ṭibb al-nabī.* Trans. C Elgood. *Osiris* 1962; 14: 190.
7. Bukhārī M. *Ṣaḥīḥ al-Bukhārī.* al-Riyyāḍ: Bayt al-Afkār, 1998; Ibn Qayyim al-Jawziyyah M. *al-Ṭibb al-nabawī.* Bayrūt: Dār al-Kitāb, 1985.
8. Ibn Qayyim al-Jawziyyah M. *al-Ṭibb al-nabawī.* Bayrūt: Dār al-Kitāb, 1985.
9. Ibn Ṭulūn S. *al-Manhal al-rawī fī al-ṭibb al-nabawī.* Ed. 'Azīz Bayk. Riyyāḍ: Dār 'ālam al-kutub, 1995.
10. Ibn Ṭulūn S. *al-Manhal al-rawī fī al-ṭibb al-nabawī.* Ed. 'Azīz Bayk. Riyyāḍ: Dār 'ālam al-kutub, 1995.
11. Chaghhaynī M. *Ṭibb al-nabī.* Trans. C Elgood. *Osiris* 1962; 14: 190.
12. Ibn Ṭulūn S. *al-Manhal al-rawī fī al-ṭibb al-nabawī.* Ed. 'Azīz Bayk. Riyyāḍ: Dār 'ālam al-kutub, 1995.
13. Majlisī M. *Biḥār al-anwār.* Ṭihrān: Javad al-Alavi, 1956.
14. Majlisī M. *Biḥār al-anwār.* Ṭihrān: Javad al-Alavi, 1956.
15. Ibn Qayyim al-Jawziyyah M. *al-Ṭibb al-nabawī.* Bayrūt: Dār al-Kitāb, 1985.
16. Bīrūnī, AR al-. *al-Bīrūnī's Book on Pharmacy and Materia Medica.* Ed. and trans. HM Said. Karachi: Hamdard National Foundation, 1973; Ibn al-Qayyim al-Jawziyyah. *Natural Healing with the Medicine of the Prophet.* Pearl Publishing. Trans. M al-Akīlī. Philadelphia, 1993.
17. Iṣbahānī AN al-. *Mawsū'at al-ṭibb al-nabawī.* Ed. MKD al-Turkī. Bayrūt: Dār Ibn Ḥazm, 2006.
18. Ibn al-Qayyim al-Jawziyyah. *Natural Healing with the Medicine of the Prophet.* Pearl Publishing. Trans. M al-Akīlī. Philadelphia, 1993: 266, 308.
19. Chaudhary SA. *Flora of the Kingdom of Saudi Arabia.* al-Riyyāḍ: Ministry of Agriculture and Water, 1999.
20. Elgood C. Trans. *Medicine of the Prophet.* J Sūyūṭī, M Chaghhaynī. *Osiris* 1962; 14: 181.
21. Iṣbahānī AN al-. *Mawsū'at al-ṭibb al-nabawī.* Ed. MKD al-Turkī. Bayrūt: Dār Ibn Ḥazm, 2006.
22. Toussaint-Samat M. *A History of Food.* Trans. Anthea Bell. West Sussex: Wiley-Blackwell, 2009: 689.
23. Ghule BV, Ghante MH, Saoji AN, Yeole PG. Hypolipidemic and antihyperlipidemic effects of Lagenaria siceraria (Mol.) fruit extracts. *Indian J Exp Biol.* 2006 Nov; 44(11): 905–909.
24. Furukawa. The effects of dietary fiber from *Lagenaria siceraria* (yugao-melon) on colonic carcinogenesis in mice. *Cancer.* 1995 Mar 15; 75(6 Suppl): 1508–1515.

Camphor/*Kāfūr*

FAMILY: Dipterocarpaceae
BOTANICAL NAME: *Dryobalanops aromatica*
COMMON NAMES: *English* Camphor; *French* Camphre; *Spanish* Alcanfor; *German* Flügeleichel, Kampfer, Kampferölbaum; *Urdu/Unānī* Kafoor, Kapoor; *Modern Standard Arabic* Kāfūr

SAFETY RATING: DANGEROUS TO DEADLY Camphor is potentially lethal and should only be used with expert supervision. A mere gram can be lethal to a child while twenty grams can be fatal in an adult. While camphor is used internally in traditional Chinese medicine, it is only the natural plant extract that is used. The commercially prepared camphor most people are familiar with contains other deadly chemicals. Ingestion of even a slight amount of camphor can cause seizures in susceptible individuals. As such, patients with epilepsy or Parkinson's disease should avoid its use. Due to its potential toxicity, and since alternative treatments exist, camphor should not be taken internally for upper respiratory tract infections. Camphor, in any form, must not be employed by women who are pregnant or lactating. The essential oil of camphor should never be applied directly to or near the nostrils of small children or asthmatics, as this can trigger bronchial spasms and convulsions, leading to respiratory arrest. In fact, camphor salves should never be used on infants and small children as external application can cause skin irritation and lead to poisoning through inhalation. Since camphor may be stored in fat, application of camphor to the skin can lead to systemic poisoning. Camphor oil should never be applied to burned, injured, or broken skin. When applied to the skin, camphor oil may cause irritation and contact eczema in sensitive persons. All products containing camphor should be kept away from children as even three to four teaspoons of Vicks VapoSteam or two teaspoons of Vicks VapoRub Cream can be toxic and even fatal if swallowed by an infant. In the event of accidental ingestion, call the nearest poison control center immediately. The symptoms of camphor overdose include delirium, intoxication, spasms, vomiting, heart palpitations, convulsions, and respiratory problems. Camphor is subject to legal restrictions in some countries.

Prophetic Prescription: When describing the delights of Paradise, the Qur'ān says that "the righteous shall drink a cup wherefrom the mixture is of water of *Kāfūr*" (76:5). Both Yusuf 'Ali and Picktall have preferred not to translate the term, while Aṣad has described it as a drink "flavored with the calyx of sweet-smelling flowers."

Issues in Identification: As Wilfred H. Schoff has explained, modern camphor and the camphor of earlier sea-trade are not the same product.[1] Modern camphor is obtained by passing steam over the leaves, wood, and bark of *Cinnamomum camphora*, the laurel tree of Southern China and Formosa. Its uses are mainly commercial. However, the original camphor was a natural accumulation in the light and fibrous wood of *Dryobalanops aromatica*, the camphor tree of Sumatra and Borneo. Its uses were mainly medicinal. True camphor should also not be confused with counterfeit Chinese camphor which is called *ngai* and which is made from *Blumea balsamifera*. The market price of true Sumatran camphor is about ten times that of the *ngai* camphor and fifty times that of the tree-laurel camphor.

According to Farooqi, "present day camphor was not known to Arabs during Prophet Muḥammad" and that the *kāfūr* of the Qur'ān and the Sunnah refers to henna.[2] According to Farooqi, the earliest reference to camphor comes from A.D. 637. He holds that only references to *kāfūr* from after this date refer to *Dryobalanops aromatica* or *Cinnamomun camphora*. Farooqi is mistaken.

Farooqi claims that camphor was unknown to the Arabs until the time of the Caliph 'Umar, and that the first reference to camphor in Arabic was made by the famous physician Isḥāq ibn 'Ammān in the late 9th century. However, as Schoff has shown, camphor does indeed appear in the writings of Symeon Seth, Aetius, Paulus Aegineta, and Leo Medicus, Hellenistic medical writers of the 4th to 6th centuries of our era. The plant also appears in the *Syrian Book of Medicine*, which is traced to the 3rd and 5th centuries C.E. Camphor also appears in the *Āyur-Veda* of Susruta, a Sanskrit medical work, believed to be at least as old as the 4th century. Imru al-Qays, an Arab prince who wrote before the time of Muḥammad, mentions camphor, and Weil, in his *History of the Caliphs*, relates that when the Arabs pillaged the palace of the last Sassanian King in 636 C.E., they took musk, amber, sandalwood, and other Eastern aromatics, and "much camphor."[3]

Farooqi would have us believe that the Arabs only discovered camphor through the spread of Islām and that the Muslims soldiers who first came across it did not know what it was. The fact that a foot-soldier did not know what camphor looks like does not mean that it did not exist. With the exception of those who use the product, most people who come across camphor today would be unable to identify it. Because the spread of Islām followed pre–Islamic trade routes, whatever circulated on those routes during the early days of Islām had circulated along them in pre–Islamic times. As Wilfred H. Schoff explains, "The rapid spread of Islām over the Indian Archipelago followed lines of trade established by Arab shipping long before the time of Muḥammad."[4]

As George F. Ḥouranī has shown in *Arab Seafaring: In the Indian Ocean in Ancient and Early Medieval Time*, the pre–Islamic Arabs had trade ties with camphor-producing regions since antiquity. Classical Arab botanists like Dīnawarī, however, explained that *kāfūr* was not a plant from the Arab world, debunking Farooqi's claim that the *kāfūr* of the ancient Arabs was *ḥinnā*, a plant well-known to the Arabs.[5] Dīnawarī says that *kāfūr* was like *ṣamgh* or gum arabic, a description of color and texture which cannot be applied to henna.[6]

According to Muhammad Ali, the Aḥmadiyyah translator of the Qur'ān, *kāfūr* derives from the stem *kfr*. Influenced by Ali, Farooqi attempts to derive *kāfūr* from the Hebrew *kopher* on the basis of their sounding the same. The Hebrew *kopher* literally means to cover over or to smear. The meaning extends to hiding and concealing, or even to suppressing, and was used figuratively to refer to henna. The vast majority of linguists, however, believe that the Arabic *kāfūr* derives from the Malay *kapur barus*. Malay traders called it *kapur*, which means "chalk," because of its white color.

According to Dīnawarī, *kāfūr* was originally *qaffūr* and the term was *mu'arrab* or *Arabized* as *kāfūr*, on the basis of the Arabic root *kfr*, which means to cover, as *kāfūr* refers to a bark.[7] If this is the case, the Arabic *kāfūr* may have been directly borrowed from the Sanskrit *karpūraḥ*. Upon entering Arabic, the phoneme /k/ would have been colored by the syllable /ar/ turning it into *qar*, the Sanskrit /p/ would have turned into /f/ and the final /aḥ/ would have been dropped in the following fashion: *karpūraḥ* > *qarffūrah* > *qaffūrah* > *qāffūr* >*qāfūr* >*kāfūr*. Whether the Arabic *kāfūr* is of Malay or Sanskrit origin, it seems relatively certain that it is not of Semitic origin. It appears to be a foreign word that was Arabized, as were the names of most new plants which were introduced to the Arabs. As we see in Dīnawarī, the foreign names of new plants were only briefly embraced in Arabic, in a slightly Arabized form, shortly to be supplanted when new Arabic names were coined for them. The fact that *qāffūr* or *kapūr* could easily be associated with the root *kfr*, both phonetically and semantically, facilitated the task of integrating the term into Arabic.

Although the *kāfūr* mentioned by the Prophet and the Imāms was likely derived from *Dryobalanops aromatica* or Borneo camphor, there is a remote possibility that it may have been derived from *Cinnamomum camphora*. According to Ghazanfar, although it is native to East Asia and the Far East, *Cinnamomum camphora* is cultivated in Arabia.[8] Farooqi excluded, it is the consensus of *ṭibb* practitioners and botanists that the Arabic *kāfūr* is indeed camphor.

Properties and Uses: *Dryobalanops aromatica* or Borneo camphor is a bitter, pungent, stimulant herb that relieves pain, lowers fever, relaxes spasms, and reduces inflammation. It also has antibacterial effects. Taken internally, camphor is used for fainting, convulsions associated with high fever, cholera, and pneumonia. It is used externally for rheumatism, ringworm, abscesses, boils, cold sores, mouth ulcers, sore throat, chest infections, and conjunctivitis. In aromatherapy, it is used internally and externally as an antiseptic, sedative, and tonic for the heart and adrenal cortex, mainly in skin problems, rheumatism, infectious diseases, depression, and convalescence.

Cinnamomum camphora, or modern camphor, is a bitter, strongly aromatic herb that stimulates the circulatory and nervous systems, reduces inflammation, and relieves pain and spasms. It is considered coolant, slightly expectorant, and antiseptic. Modern camphor is narcotic and an irritant in large doses, but an effective sedative, anodyne, and diaphoretic in small ones. It is analgesic, anthelmintic, antirheumatic, antispasmodic, cardiotonic, odontalgic, and tonic. It also benefits digestion and destroys parasites.

In Unānī medicine, modern camphor is considered antispasmodic, stimulant, carminative, stomachic, anaphrodisiac, antipyretic, nervine, sedative, diaphoretic, rubefacient, resolvent, and antiseptic. It dilates vessels, increases the flow of gastric juice and peristalsis. It is used as a refrigerant, and an anaphrodisiac.

Internally, modern camphor is used to treat hysteria, dysmenorrhea, nervousness, diarrhea, colic, flatulence, rheumatism, gout, tenesmus, asthma, cough, bronchitis, coryza, eye complaints, toothache, headache, spasms, chorea, epilepsy, painful menstruation, gout, rheumatism, insomnia, nausea, thyphoid condition, and mania. It is also used as an inhalant for bronchial and nasal congestion. In traditional Chinese medicine, it is use for skin diseases, wounds, and as a stimulant in cases of unconsciousness. In aromatherapy, it is used for digestive complaints and depression.

Externally, modern camphor is employed as a wash, in liniments for joint and muscle pain, in balms for chilblains, chapped lips, and cold sores. It is used as an ointment for ulcers, gangrene, scabies, sprains, bruises, and rheumatic pains. Although it is used as an inhalant for bronchial congestion, caution should be exercised as excessive use can cause vomiting, palpitations, convulsions, and death.

Camphor and ginger are both refrigerants and were widely used as ingredients in cooling drinks in medieval times. The French also used it in cookery. Camphor is poisonous in large quantities, and large doses can cause respiratory failure in children. It can be absorbed through the skin and cause systemic poisoning. It can cause seizures, confusion, irritability, and neuromuscular hyperactivity.

In 1980, the FDA set a limit of 11 percent allowable camphor in consumer products and totally banned products labeled as camphorated oil, camphor oil, camphor liniment, and camphorated liniment. It does, however, allow white camphor essential oil since it contains no significant amount of camphor. Since alternative treatments exist, medicinal use of camphor is discouraged by the FDA, except for skin-related uses, such as medicated powders, which contain only small amounts of camphor.

Scientific Studies: *Antifungal Activity* According to an in-vitro study conducted by Nanjing University in China, an *Acinetobacter* strain isolated from the stems of *Cinnamomum aromatica* is antibacterial.[9]

Anticandidal Activity According to an in-vitro study conducted by the Defense Research Laboratory in India, the essential oil of *Cinnamomum aromatica* exhibited higher anticandidial activity than the synthetic antibiotics miconazole and clotrimazole.[10]

Insect Repellant Activity According to a study conducted by Nanjing University in China, the essential oil from the seeds of *Cinnamomum aromatica* exhibit repellent and insecticidal activity, showing its potential for use in the control of storage pests.[11] Another study, conducted by Chonbuk National University in the Republic of Korea, showed that the repellant activity of the methanol extract of *C. aromatica* was 94 percent compared to 82 percent for deet, although the duration of the effect was shorter for camphor.[12]

Anti-inflammatory and Antioxidative Activity

In a study conducted by Cheju National University in South Korea, the anti-inflammatory effect of *Cinnamomum camphora* was confirmed.[13]

Anti–Demodex folliculorum *Infestation Activity* In a study conducted by Mansoura University in Egypt, 15 females suffering from *Erythematotelangiectatic rosacea* and 12 females free from other dermatological lesions were treated with 1/3 diluted camphor oil with glycerol and 500 mg metronidazole orally for fifteen days. The results were highly successful with no clinical side effects.[14]

Ophthalmic Aiding Activity In an open prospective multicenter clinical trial conducted by the All India Institute of Medical Sciences, patients suffering from various ophthalmic disorders were treated with the herbal drop preparation known as Ophthacare, which contains the following Ayurvedic herbs, reportedly possessing anti-infective and anti-inflammatory properties: *Carum copticum*, *Terminalia belerica*, *Emblica officinalis*, *Curcuma longa*, *Ocimum sanctum*, *Cinnamomum camphora*, and *Rosa damascena*. In most cases, an improvement was observed in the treatment with the herbal eye drop formula with no side effects observed during the course of the study. Researchers concluded that the herbal eye drop Ophthacare has a useful role in a variety of infective, inflammatory and degenerative ophthalmic disorders.[15]

Antiplasmodial Activity According to an in-vitro study conducted by the Institute for Medical Research in Malaysia, *Blumea balsamifera* was shown to possess antiplasmodial activity.[16]

Antifungal Activity According to a study conducted by De La Salle University in the Philippines, the leaves of *Blumea balsamifera* have moderate activity against certain types of fungi.[17]

Hepaprotective Activity According to study conducted by Sunyatsen University in China, blumeatin, isolated from *Blumea balsamifera*, may protect liver against chemically-induced liver damage.[18]

Camphor Notes

1. Schoff WH. Camphor. *Journal of the American Oriental Society* 1922; 42: 355.
2. Farooqi MIH. *Medicinal Plants in the Traditions of Prophet Muḥammad.* Lucknow: Sidrah Publishers, 1998: 206–213.
3. Schoff WH. Camphor. *Journal of the American Oriental Society* 1922; 42: 359–360.
4. Schoff WH. Camphor. *Journal of the American Oriental Society* 1922; 42: 366.
5. Dīnawarī AH. *Kitāb al-nabāt/The Book of Plants.* Ed. Bernhard Lewin. Bayrūt: Dār al-Qalam, 1974: 90; Dīnawarī AH. *Kitāb al-nabāt: Le dictionaire botanique d'Abū Ḥanīfa al-Dīnawarī.* al-Qāhirah: Institut Français d'Archéologie Orientale du Caire, 1973.
6. Dīnawarī AH. *Kitāb al-nabāt: Le dictionaire botanique d'Abū Ḥanīfa al-Dīnawarī.* al-Qāhirah: Institut Français d'Archéologie Orientale du Caire, 1973: 90.
7. Dīnawarī AH. *Kitāb al-nabāt/The Book of Plants.* Ed. Bernhard Lewin. Bayrūt: Dār al-Qalam, 1974: 90; Dīnawarī AH. *Kitāb al-nabāt: Le dictionaire botanique d'Abū Ḥanīfa al-Dīnawarī.* al-Qāhirah: Institut Français d'Archéologie Orientale du Caire, 1973.
8. Ghazanfar SA. *Handbook of Arabian Medicinal Plants.* Boca Raton: CRC Press, 1994.
9. Liu, Chen, Liu, Lian, Gu, Caer, Xue, Wang. Study of the antifungal activity of *Acinetobacter baumannii* LCH001 in vitro and identification of its antifungal components. *Appl* 2007; 76(2): 459–466.
10. Dutta, Karmakar, Naglot, Aich, Begam. Anticandidial activity of some essential oils of a mega biodiversity hotspot in India. *Mycoses.* 2007; 50(2): 121–124.
11. Liu, Mishra, Tan, Tang, Yang, Shen. Repellent and insecticidal activities of essential oils from *Artemisia princeps* and *Cinnamomum camphora* and their effect on seed germination of wheat and broad bean. *Bioresour* 2006; 97(15): 1969–1973.
12. Yang, Lee, Lee, Lee, Ahn. Repellency of aromatic medicinal plant extracts and a steam distillate to *Aedes aegypti. J* 2004; 20(2): 146–149.
13. Lee, Hyun, Yoon, Kim, Rhee, Kang, Cho, Yoo. In vitro anti-inflammatory and anti-oxidative effects of *Cinnamomum camphora* extracts. *J* 2006; 103(2): 208–216.
14. El-Shazly, Hassan, Soliman, Morsy, Morsy. Treatment of human *Demodex folliculorum* by camphor oil and metronidazole. *J* 2004; 34(1): 107–116.
15. Biswas, Gupta, Das, Kumar, Mongre, Haldar, Beri. Evaluation of Ophthacare eye drops — a herbal formulation in the management of various ophthalmic disorders. *Phytother* 2001; 15(7): 618–20.
16. Noor, Khozirah, Mohd, Ong, Rohaya, Rosilawati, Hamdino, Badrul, Zakiah. Antiplasmodial properties of some Malaysian medicinal plants. *Trop* 2007; 24(1): 29–35.
17. Ragasa, Co, Rideout. Antifungal metabolites from *Blumea balsamifera. Nat* 2005; 19(3): 231–237.
18. Xu, Chen, Liang, Lin, Deng, Long. [Protective action of blumeatin against experimental liver injuries]. *Zhongguo* 1993; 14(4): 376–378.

Caper / *Kabbār*

Family: Capparidaceae

Botanical Name: *Capparis spinosa*

Common Names: *English* Common caper bush; *French* Câprier, Câprier épineux, câpre; *Spanish* Alcaparra; *German* Echter Kapernstrauch, Kaper; *Urdu/Unānī* Kabbar; *Modern Standard Arabic* Kabbār, Qabbār, Shawku al-ḥamār

Safety Rating: Generally Safe Capers are generally considered safe for most people when used in quantities normally consumed as food. In overdose, the leaves and roots can cause problems.

Prophetic Prescription: According to the Messenger of Allāh, "The Fire laughed, and out came truffles (*kamā'*), and the Earth laughed, and out came capers (*kabr*)."[1] It is also reported that Ibn 'Abbās visited the Prophet while his face was pale. The Prophet asked him what was wrong with him and Ibn 'Abbās explained that he was suffering from hemorrhoids. The Prophet then asked him, "What prevents you from using spiny capers (*'asaf*) and capers (*kabr*). Take them, crush them, and eat them." He did so, and he was cured.[2]

Issues in Identification: It is the consensus that *kabr* is Arabic for caper. As Nehmé explains, both *kabr* and *kabbār* refer to *Capparis* while *kabr shā'ik* and *'aṣaf* refer to *Capparis spinosa*.[3] Mandaville notes that the plant is rare to occasional in eastern Saudi Arabia where it is known as *shafallāh*.[4] According to Ghazanfar, *Capparis spinosa* is known as *aṣaf* and *fakuha* in Oman, Qatar, and Saudi Arabia. The plant is found throughout Arabia, in wadis, and the lower foothills of mountains. There are approximately 40 species of Capparidaceae in Arabia, including *Capparis cartilaginea* and *Capparis decidua*, both of which have medicinal properties.[5]

As Duke has observed, both *Capparis spinosa* and *Capparis decidua* occur in the Holy Land. In all likelihood, the Prophet was referring to *Capparis spinosa* as this is the main commercial producer of capers. According to Chaudhary, *Capparis spinosa* is widespread from Africa through Southern Europe and the Middle East, Central Asia, and India. The species is quite variable in appearance and is represented by at least two varieties in Saudi Arabia: *spinosa* and *mucronifolia*. *Spinosa* is known in Saudi Arabic as *kabar*, *aṣaf*, and *laṣaf*.[6] According to Dīnawarī, *kabr*, also known as *laṣaf*, has a spine, and produces a fruit called *shafallāh*, which is white. When it becomes ripe, its extremities become red. One the basis of this description, the *kabr* mentioned by the Prophet is almost certainly *Capparis spinosa*.

Properties and Uses: The caper bush is an astringent, diuretic, expectorant herb that is regarded as a stimulating tonic. The root and root bark are considered deobstruent, detergent, astringent, resolvent, and expectorant. They are also viewed as anthelmintic, antiflatulent, carminative, diuretic, and emmenagogue. The fruit is considered a stomach tonic, appetitive, carminative, and aperient. Internally, the root bark is used for gastrointestinal infections, diarrhea, gout, rheumatism, numbness, dropsy, and sciatica, while the flower buds are used for coughs. A decoction of the bark is used to relieve toothaches. Leaf extracts are used to treat earaches, and the flower buds are used to treat eye infections. According to Ghazanfar, the leaves of the plant are used in Arabia to treat earache, coughs, and diabetes, as well as expelling stomach worms.[7]

Scientific Studies: *Anti-cirrhotic Activity* In a randomized, double-blind, placebo-controlled, trial conducted by the Institute of Medicinal Plants in Tehran, the efficacy of herbal medicine Liv-52 (consisting of *Mandur basma*, *Tamarix gallica* and herbal extracts of *Capparis spinosa*, *Cichorium intybus*, *Solanum nigrum*, *Terminalia arjuna* and *Achillea millefolium*) on liver cirrhosis outcomes was compared with the placebo for 6 months in 36 cirrhotic patients. The study concluded that Liv-52 produced a hepatoprotective effect in cirrhotic patients, the result of the diuretic, anti-inflammatory, anti-oxidative, and immunomodulating properties of the herbs.[8]

Anti-inflammatory Activity In a study conducted by the University of Catania in Italy, the lyophilized methanolic extract of the flowering buds of *Capparis spinosa* were found to counteract the harmful effects of induced inflammation. This protection actually appeared to be greater than that elicited by indomethacin, the allopathic medicine usually employed in joint diseases. Since capers possess a chondroprotective effect, the researchers concluded that they could be used in the management of cartilage damage during inflammatory processes.[9]

In a study of Saudi Arabian medicinal plants, researchers found that the aqueous extract of *Capparis spinosa* and *Capparis decidua* possessed significant anti-inflammatory activity. Although both were devoid of analgesic activity, *Capparis decidua* was found to possess significant antipyretic effect.[10]

Antiallergenic Activity In a controlled animal trial conducted by the University of Messina in Italy, two lyophilized extracts from *Capparis spinosa* flowering buds showed a good protective effect against histamine-induced bronchospasms. Researchers also performed a histamine prick test on humans, applying a gel formulation containing a 2 percent caper extract. The caper gel formulation possessed a marked inhibitory effect (46.07 percent) against histamine-induced skin erythema.[11]

Antidiabetic Activity According to a controlled animal trial conducted in Morocco, the aqueous extract of capers induced a significant decrease in plasma triglycerides in normal rats after one and two weeks of once-daily administration. A significant decrease of plasma cholesterol levels was also observed after four days and one week of repeated oral administration. In diabetic rats, caper treatment equally caused a decrease of plasma triglycerides levels after repeated oral administration. Four days after repeated oral administration of aqueous *Capparis spinosa* extract, the plasma cholesterol levels were significantly decreased and still dropped after two weeks. Researchers concluded that the aqueous extract of *C. spinosa* exhibits a potent lipid lowering activity.[12]

In an animal study conducted by the Laboratory of Endocrinian Physiology in Errachidia, Morocco, aqueous extracts of *Carum carvi* and *Capparis spinosa* produced a significant decrease in blood glucose levels, nearly normalizing them within two weeks of daily repeated administration. Researchers concluded that the aqueous extracts of *C. carvi* and *C. spinosa* exhibit a potent anti-hyperglycemic activity without affecting basal plasma insulin concentrations.[13]

Antioxidative Activity In a study conducted by the University of Catania in Italy, the lyophilized extract from the flowering buds of capers showed significant antioxidant effects.[14] According to a study conducted by the Pharmaco-Biological Department at the University of Messina, Italy, capers are not only highly nutritive, but also a strong antioxidant.[15]

Antifungal Activity In a study conducted by An-Najah National University in Palestine, capers were found to possess a high level of antimycotic activity, completely preventing the growth of *Microsporum canis* and *Trichophyton violaceum*.[16]

Antihepatoxic Activity In a study conducted by M.S. University of Baroda in India, capers were found to possess significant antihepatotoxic activity.[17]

Caper Notes

1. Sūyūṭī J. *As-Sūyūṭī's Medicine of the Prophet*. Ed. A Thomson. London: Ṭā-Hā Publishers, 1994: 88, Ibn Qayyim al-Jawziyyah M. *al-Ṭibb al-nabawī*. Bayrūt: Dār al-Kitāb, 1985.

2. Ibn al-Sunnī. *Ṭibb al-nabī*. Ed. Omer Recep. Philipps-Universität: Marburg/Lahn, 1969: 82.

3. Nehmé M. *Dictionnaire étymologique de la flore du Liban*. Bayrūt: Librairie du Liban, 2000.

4. Mandaville JP. *Flora of Eastern Saudi Arabia*. London: Kegan Paul, 1990.

5. Ghazanfar SA. *Handbook of Arabian Medicinal Plants*. Boca Raton: CRC Press, 1994.

6. Chaudhary SA. *Flora of the Kingdom of Saudi Arabia*. al-Riyyāḍ: Ministry of Agriculture and Water, 1999.

7. Ghazanfar SA. *Handbook of Arabian Medicinal Plants*. Boca Raton: CRC Press, 1994.

8. Huseini, Alavian, Heshmat, Heydari, Abolmaali. The efficacy of Liv-52 on liver cirrhotic patients: a randomized, double-blind, placebo-controlled first approach. *Phytomedicine*. 2005; 12(9): 619–624.

9. Panico, Cardile, Garufi, Puglia, Bonina, Ronsisvalle. Protective effect of *Capparis spinosa* on chondrocytes. *Life* 2005; 77(20): 2479–2488.

10. Ageel, Parmar, Mossa, Al-Yahya, Al-Said, Tariq. Anti-inflammatory activity of some Saudi Arabian medicinal plants. *Agents* 1986; 17(3–4): 383–384.

11. Trombetta, Occhiuto, Perri, Puglia, Santagati, De, Saija, Bonina. Antiallergic and antihistaminic effect of two extracts of *Capparis spinosa* L. flowering buds. *Phytother* 2005; 19(1): 29–33.

12. Eddouks, Lemhadri, Michel. Hypolipidemic activity of aqueous extract of *Capparis spinosa* L. in normal and diabetic rats. *J* 2005; 98(3): 345–350.

13. Eddouks, Lemhadri, Michel. Caraway and caper: potential anti-hyperglycemic plants in diabetic rats. *J* 2004; 94(1): 143–148.

14. Bonina, Puglia, Ventura, Aquino, Tortora, Sacchi, Saija, Tomaino, Pellegrino, de. In vitro antioxidant and in vivo photoprotective effects of a lyophilized extract of *Capparis spinosa* L buds. *J* 2002; 53(6): 321–335.

15. Germano, De, D'Angelo, Catania, Silvari, Costa. Evaluation of extracts and isolated fraction from *Capparis spinosa* L. buds as an antioxidant source. *J* 2002; 50(5): 1168–1171.

16. Ali-Shtayeh, Abū. Antifungal activity of plant extracts against dermatophytes. *Mycoses*. 1999; 42(11–12): 665–672.

17. Gadgoli, Mishra. Antihepatotoxic activity of p-methoxy benzoic acid from *Capparis spinosa*. *J* 1999; 66(2): 187–192.

Caraway / *Karawyah, Karawyā*

Family: Apiaceae

Botanical Name: *Carum carvi*

Common Names: *English* Caraway; *French* Carvi, Cumin des près, Kummel; *Spanish* Alcaravea; *German* Echter Kümmel, Kümmel, Feldkümmel; *Urdu/Unānī* Zeerah Siyah, Shah Zeerah, Kamoon-e-Kirmani, Kamoon-e-Aswad, Karowya, Qirdmana; *Modern Standard Arabic* Kammūn armānī, Karawyah, al-Niqr, al-Niqrah, al-Nighrid

Safety Rating: Generally Safe Caraway seeds are generally considered safe for most people in quantities of no more than six grams per day. The oil, however, is a mucous membrane irritant, and can cause kidney or liver damage if taken over an extended period of time.

Prophetic Prescription: In cases of an ant infestation, Imām Ja'far al-Ṣādiq recommended grinding caraway and throwing it into the ant hills.[1]

Issues in Identification: As Dīnawarī explains, *karawyā* is a well-known spice, also known as *taqrīd*, which is not of Arab origin.[2] It is the consensus that *karawyā* is Arabic for caraway. According to Bīrūnī, *karawyā* is also known as *karuyā*, *shāhzīrah*, *taqrad*, *naqd* and *naqdah*. As Said says, it is also known as *kūrūyā* and refers to *Carum carvi*.[3]

Properties and Uses: *Carum carvi* or caraway

is a pungently aromatic, stimulant herb that is carminative, diuretic, and stomachic, reduces gastrointestinal and uterine spasms, and encourages productive coughing. It is used internally for indigestion, flatulence, and colic, especially in children, as well as hiatal hernia, stomach ulcer, diarrhea, menstrual cramps, bronchitis and constipation.

Externally, caraway is used as a gargle for laryngitis. Having antibacterial properties, it is included in mouthwash and is used to treat toothaches. It is also added to laxatives as a corrective to reduce nausea and griping and to various products for digestive problems. The seeds are chewed for prompt relief from indigestion. It has been recently discovered that carvone, the largest constituent of the oil, has potential uses as an insect repellant.

SCIENTIFIC STUDIES: *Insect Repellant Activity* Various scientific studies confirm that some of the essential oils and terpenoids from caraway repel insects.[4]

Larvacidal Activity According to a study conducted by Chiang Mai University in Thailand, the volatile oil of *Carum carvi* exerts significant larvicidal activity against two mosquito species, *Anopheles dirus*, the major malaria vector, and *Aedes aegypti*, the main vector of dengue and dengue hemorrhagic fever in urban areas.[5]

*Anti–*Helicobacter pylori *Activity* In a study conducted by the University of Illinois at Chicago, the methanol extract of *Carum carvi* seed had an MIC of 100 microg/mL against 15 HP strains.[6]

Antiulcer Activity According to one study, a combination of caraway and peppermint oil decreased or eliminated pain in patients with nonulcer dyspepsia.[7]

Anti-Constipation Activity In a study evaluating the laxative effects of an herbal product containing caraway, all patients found relief from constipation within the first two days.[8]

Anticancer Activity According to one study, caraway oil inhibits certain types of skin tumors in mice.[9]

Caraway Notes

1. Nisābūrī A. *Ṭibb al-a'immah*. Bayrūt: Dār al-Maḥajjah al-Bayḍā', 1994: 186.

2. Dīnawarī AH. *Kitāb al-nabāt: Le dictionaire botanique d'Abū Ḥanīfa al-Dīnawarī*. al-Qāhirah: Institut Français d'Archéologie Orientale du Caire, 1973.

3. Bīrūnī, AR al-. *al-Bīrūnī's Book on Pharmacy and Materia Medica*. Ed. and trans. HM Said. Karachi: Hamdard National Foundation, 1973.

4. Sharma, Vartak. Vapor toxicity & repellence of some essential oils & terpenoids to adults of *Aedes aegypti* (L) (Diptera: Culicidae). *Indian* 1993; 97: 122-127; Barnard. Repellency of essential oils to mosquitoes Diptera: Culicidae. *J* 1999; 36(5): 625-629; Arun K. Tripathi, Veena Prajapati, Sushil Kumar. Bioactivities of l-Carvone, d-Carvone, and Dihydrocarvone Toward Three Stored Product Beetles. *J Economic Entomol.* 1594-1601.

5. Pitasawat, Champakaew, Choochote, Jitpakdi, Chaithong, Kanjanapothi, Rattanachanpichai, Tippawangkosol, Riyong, Tuetun, Chaiyasit. Aromatic plant-derived essential oil: An alternative larvicide for mosquito control. *Fitoterapia.* 2007; 78(3): 205-210.

6. Mahady, Pendland, Stoia, Hamill, Fabricant, Dietz, Chadwick. In vitro susceptibility of *Helicobacter pylori* to botanical extracts used traditionally for the treatment of gastrointestinal disorders. *Phytother* 2005; 19(11): 988-991.

7. May B, et al. Effectiveness of a fixed peppermint oil/caraway oil combination in non-ulcer dyspepsia. *Arzneimitell-forschung* 1996; 46: 1149-1153.

8. Fetrow CW, Avila JR. *The Complete Guide to Herbal Medicines*. Springhouse: Springhouse Corporation, 2000.

9. Schwaireb MH. Caraway oil inhibits skin tumors in female BALB/c mice. *Nutrition and Cancer* 19: 321-325.

Carob / *'Anam*

FAMILY: Fabaceae

BOTANICAL NAME: *Ceratonia siliqua*

COMMON NAMES: *English* Carob; *French* Caroube; *Spanish* algarroba; *German* Johannisbrot, Karobbaum, Karubenbaum, Johannisbrot, Dornigen Johannisbrotbaun; *Urdu/Unānī* Kharnub, Kharnub-e-Shami; *Modern Standard Arabic* Kharrūb, Kharnūb

SAFETY RATING: GENERALLY SAFE Carob is generally considered safe for most people. According to Duke, when carob is used to treat infant diarrhea, the child must be monitored by a professional to ensure proper hydration with high electrolyte fluid during acute cases. The use of carob should be avoided when intestinal obstructions or stenoses are present. Diabetics should also have their insulin monitored when using carob. It should also be remembered that carob can interfere with intestinal absorption of oral medicines.

PROPHETIC PRESCRIPTIONS: The Messenger of Allāh said, "There are three types of *miswāk*. If you do not have *arak*, then use *'anam* or *baṭm*."[1]

ISSUES IN IDENTIFICATION: According to Farooqi, *'anam* is the branch of the *Acacia nilotica* which is commonly used as a toothbrush in many countries, including India.[2] Although acacia is indeed used as *miswāk* in Arabia, we have been unable to find a single Arabic botanical source, either modern or classical, which identifies *'anam* with acacia, reason enough to dismiss this identification.

As Dīnawarī explains, there are many opinions regarding the identity of *'anam*. Some say that it has red flowers, some that it has red fruit, others that only its extremities are red, and yet others who say that its vines have blood red flowers. For the ancient Arabs, *'anam* was a small green plant with very red flowers.[3] As Said explains, "*'anam* is a species of Arabian tree producing red fruit to which a finger dyed with henna is often compared. It might also denote the extremities of the Syrian carob-tree. It also signifies, amongst other things, the tendrils of a vine twigging round an arbor."[4]

According to Aṣma'ī, *'anam* is a vine which has reddish fingers. He cites Abū Ubaydah who identifies *'anam* as the stems of *kharrūb shāmī* or carob, as well as Ibn al-Kalbī, who says that it refers to *kharrūb shāmī* as a whole, a plant whose pods start out green and become all red when they are ripe. Aṣma'ī cites Yasārī, who states that *'anam* is a parasitic vine which lives on other plants, and Abū 'Amru who holds that *'anam* are trees which grow on the *samrah* and which contain red worms. Aṣma'ī cites other opinions which hold that *'anam* is a vine with leaves like *rayḥān*, and red flowers like *nu'mān*, but only smaller. He also explains that the tribe of Banū Fazārah identifies *'anam* with *zahr diflah*, the flowers of the pink bay tree. On the basis of the usage described by the Prophet, namely, as a frayed toothbrush, flowers and parasitic vines can easily be discarded, leaving only carob as a suitable candidate. This is consistent with current dialectical Arabic usage which identifies carob as *kharnūb, kharnūb nubṭī, kharnīb shāmī, kharrūb, kharrūbah,* and *khirnūb*.

Properties and Uses: Carob is a nutritious, sweet-tasting herb, which is 8 percent protein and contains vitamins A, B, B2, B3, and D. It is also high in calcium, phosphorus, potassium, and magnesium. It also contains iron, manganese, barium, copper, and nickel. Since it contains no caffeine or theobromine, it is considered an excellent alternative to cocoa.

Carob is considered antacid, antibacterial, anticancer, anticarcinoma, anticoagulant, antiexudative, antioxidant, antiproliferant, and antiseptic. It is also considered antitoxic, antitussive, antiviral, apoptotic, astringent, bechic, a capsase-3 inducer, demulcent, digestive, diuretic, emollient, fungicide, and hemolytic. Finally, it is believed to be hypocholesterolemic, hypoglycemic, hypoinsulemic, hypolipidemic, laxative, and pancreatonic, as well as pectoral, purgative, and resolvent.

Carob is used for asthma, atherosclerosis, cancer, carcinoma, catarrh, celiac disease, childbirth, colitis, constipation, cough, and dehydration, as well as diabetes, diarrhea, duodenosis, dyspepsia, enterosis, and gastrosis. It is also used for heartburn, hepatosis, high cholesterol, hyperglycemia, hyperlipidemia, hyperperistalsis, induration, and infection. Finally, it is also employed in the treatment of mononucleosis, mycosis, obesity, sprue, steatorrhea, ulcers, vomiting, and warts.

Internally, the pulp of the seed pod is used as a mild laxative, and to treat coughs, while the flour made from the ripe seedpods is used to treat diarrhea. The flour is also used externally to treat skin problems. The bark is strongly astringent and used in a decoction to treat diarrhea. In South America, carob is traditionally used to treat syphilis and gonorrhea. In the United States, the leaves were used in the treatment of epilepsy.

Scientific Studies: *Rehydrating Activity* In a controlled study conducted by Ege University Medical Faculty in Turkey, the clinical antidiarrheal effect of carob bean juice was tested on 80 children aged 4 to 48 months, who were admitted to the hospital with acute diarrhea and mild or moderate dehydration. In children receiving an oral rehydration solution and carob bean juice, the duration of diarrhea was shortened by 45 percent, while stool output was reduced by 44 percent, and the oral rehydration solution requirement was decreased by 38 percent compared with children who only received oral hydration solution. Since the use of carob bean juice had no side effects and was highly effective, researchers concluded that it may have a role in the treatment of children's diarrhea, after it has been technologically processed.[5]

Anti-Proliferative Activity In an animal study conducted by Emilia University in Italy, the extract from pods and leaves of carob were shown to contain antiproliferative agents which could be of practical importance in the development of functional foods and/or chemopreventive drugs.[6]

Antioxidative Activity In an in-vitro study conducted by the University of Shizuoka in Japan, the polyphenols from carob pods were found to be antioxidant.[7] Since carob pods are presently discarded, these results suggest that they could be utilized as a functional food or food ingredient.

Antidiabetic Activity While presently unconfirmed by scientific studies, carob is one of the medicinal plants used in Israel for the treatment of hypoglycemia.[8]

Carob Notes

1. Iṣbahānī AN al-. *Mawsū'at al-ṭibb al-nabawī*. Ed. MKD al-Turkī. Bayrūt: Dār Ibn Ḥazm, 2006.

2. Farooqi MIH. *Medicinal Plants in the Traditions of Prophet Muḥammad*. Lucknow: Sidrah Publishers, 1998: 75.

3. Dīnawarī AH. *Kitāb al-nabāt: Le dictionaire botanique*

d'Abū Ḥanīfa al-Dīnawarī. al-Qāhirah: Institut Français d'Archéologie Orientale du Caire, 1973.
4. Bīrūnī, Abū Rayḥān al. *al-Bīrūnī's Book on Pharmacy and Materia Medica*. Ed. and trans. HM Said. Karachi: Hamdard National Foundation, 1973: 241.
5. Aksit, Caglayan S, Cukan, Yaprak. Carob bean juice: a powerful adjunct to oral rehydration solution treatment in diarrhea. *Paediatr* 1998; 12(2): 176–181.
6. Corsi, Avallone, Cosenza, Farina, Baraldi, Baraldi. *Fitoterapia*. 2002; 73(7–8): 674–684.
7. Kumazawa, Taniguchi, Suzuki, Shimura, Kwon, Nakayama. Antioxidative activity of polyphenols in carob pods. *J* 2002; 50(2): 373–377.
8. Yaniv, Dafni, Friedman, Palevitch. Plants used for the treatment of diabetes in Israel. *J* 1987; 19(2): 145–151.

Carrot/*Jazar*

FAMILY: Apiaceae

BOTANICAL NAME: *Daucus carota*

COMMON NAMES: *English* Carrot; *French* Carotte; *Spanish* Zanahoria; *German* Karotte, Möhre; *Urdu/Unānī* Gazar (cultivated), Gazar bari (wild); *Modern Standard Arabic* Jazar

SAFETY RATING: SAFE Cultivated carrots are considered safe. As Stobart warns, wild carrots, however, are somewhat poisonous.[1]

PROPHETIC PRESCRIPTION: Imām Ja'far al-Ṣādiq, "Order your servant to boil carrots so that you can eat them. Eat boiled carrots for they warm the kidneys, and give an erection." He also added, "Carrots are a protection against colic (*qawlanj*) and hemorrhoids, and encourage sexual intercourse."[2]

ISSUES IN IDENTIFICATION: It is the consensus that *jazar* is the Arabic word for carrot, both wild and cultivated. The carrots referred to by the Imām Ja'far al-Ṣādiq were of the wild variety. Although carrots have been consumed since Classical times, ancient carrots were cultivated for their aromatic leaves and seeds, and not their roots. Some of the relatives of the carrot, such as parsley, fennel, dill, and cumin, continue to be cultivated for their leaves and seeds. The root of the carrot was only mentioned for the first time in the 1st century C.E.

It was only in the 8th or 10th century that Eastern carrots were domesticated in Central Asia, likely in modern-day Afghanistan, which is the center of diversity of the wild carrot. Surviving specimens of the eastern carrot are commonly purple or yellow and typically have branched roots. These purple and yellow varieties moved westward through Iran and Syria, and were introduced into Spain by the Muslims in the 1100s.[3] Simeon Seth mentioned yellow and red carrots in the 11th century. In the 12th century, the Andalusian agriculturist Ibn al-'Awwām mentioned both yellow and red carrots in his treatise on agriculture, *Kitāb al-filāḥah*, which was one of the most important works on the subject during medieval times. He described the red carrot as juicy and tasty while the yellow one was coarser and of inferior flavor.[4] The orange colored carrots we are familiar with in the West today were only developed in the Netherlands in the 18th century.[5] As Biggs, McVicar, and Flowerdue explain,

> Though there are white, yellow, purple, and violet carrots, most of us are more familiar with orange carrots, which have been known only since the eighteenth century.... Moorish invaders took them to Spain in the twelfth century; they reached northwest Europe by the fourteenth and England in the fifteenth century. Gerard mentions only one yellow variety, purple ones being most popular.[6]

According to Bianchini and Lambert Ortiz, carrots only became popular in Europe during the Renaissance when the more modern varieties we are familiar with were developed.[7] In any event, the only carrots which existed in the Middle East during the time of the Sixth Shī'ite Imām were the wild, eastern, varieties which were purple carrots that verged on black, as well as yellow carrots, which appear to have been the product of mutation.

PROPERTIES AND USES: *Daucus carota* ssp. *sativa*, carrot, the domesticated is a highly nutritious herb, rich in beta carotene, which improves vision, encourages healthy skin, and has anticancer effects. *Daucus carota*, the wild carrot, is an aromatic herb that is diuretic, stimulates the uterus, and soothes the digestive tract. The whole plant is used internally to treat urinary stones, cystitis, and gout, while the seeds are used to treat edema, flatulent indigestion, and menstrual problems.

SCIENTIFIC STUDIES: *Antioxidative Activity* According to a lab study conducted by the University of Wisconsin, Madison, the carrots with the highest antioxidant capacity are those which are purple-yellow, followed by those which are purple-orange. After those two types, the antioxidative activity did not vary much among the other varieties of carrots.[8]

According to a study conducted by the Central Food Technological Research Institute in India, the anthocyanin obtained from carrot shows a stronger antioxidation activity than malvidin, peonidin and alpha-tocopherol, and weaker activity than delpinidin.[9]

Antithrombotic Activity According to an in vitro study and in vivo animal trial conducted by Kobe Gakuin University in Kobe, Japan, different carrot varieties demonstrate a variable effect on thrombosis. One particular variety, the SAKATA-0421, showed antithrombotic effect in vivo possibly due to antiplatelet reactivity and/or spontaneous thrombolytic activity. As a result of their findings, researchers were able to add this variety of carrot to the list of antithrombotic fruits and vegetables.[10]

Antifungal Activity According to an animal trial conducted by the Calçada Martim de Freitas, Universidade de Coimbra in Portugal, *Daucus carota* oil shows both antifungal activity, and exhibits a very low detrimental effect on mammalian cells.[11]

Anti-inflammatory Activity In a study conducted by the University of Wisconsin, Madison, the anti-inflammatory activity of extracts and phytochemicals from purple carrot were confirmed.[12]

Cognitive-Enhancing and Cholesterol-Lowering Activity In a controlled animal trial conducted by Guru Jambheshwar University (State Technical University) in India, the consumption of *Daucus carota* extract caused significantly increased memory scores. The mice who consumed *D. carota* extract also demonstrated a remarkable reduction in total cholesterol level, to the extent of 23 percent in the young, and 21 percent in the aged animals. As a result of these findings, researchers concluded that *D. carota* extract may prove to be a useful remedy for the management of cognitive dysfunctions and hypercholesterolemia.[13]

Antifungal Activity According to a study conducted by the University of Opole in Poland, carrot seed oil exhibits strong antifungal activity.[14]

Hypotensive Activity According to an in vitro study conducted by the Aga Khan University Medical College in Pakistan, two cumarin glycosides from the aerial parts of *D. carota* exhibited blood pressure–lowering activity.[15]

Hepaprotective Activity According to a study conducted by Jadavpur University in Calcutta, India, carrot extract exhibits significant hepaprotective activity.[16]

Antispasmodic Activity In a study conducted in India, the seeds of *Daucus carota* were found to exhibit nonspecific smooth muscle relaxant and spasmolytic activity which was approximately one-tenth that of papaverine.[17]

Antibacterial Activity According to a study conducted by the Université de Monastir in Tunisia, the essential oils from flowers and roots of *Daucus carota* ssp. *maritimum* exhibited antibacterial activity against a series of common human pathogenic bacteria, and of some clinically and environmentally isolated strains.[18]

Carrot Notes

1. Stobart T. *Herbs, Spices, and Flavoring.* Woodstock, NY: Overlook Press, 1982: 39.
2. Ţabarsī H. *Mustadrak al-Wasā'il.* Bayrūt: Mu'assasat Āl al-Bayt, 1987–1988.
3. Weaver, WW. *Heirloom Vegetable Gardening.* New York: Henry Holt, 1997: 121.
4. Davidson A. *The Oxford Companion to Food.* Oxford: Oxford University Press, 1999: 140.
5. Although the Codex of Dioscorides, which dates from 500–511 C.E., appears to show an orange carrot, somewhat branching in the root, some botanists argue that the codex actually depicts a yellow carrot. With rare exception, most botanists believe that orange carrots only appeared in the 18th century. See: Weaver, WW. *Heirloom Vegetable Gardening.* New York: Henry Holt, 1997: 120–21.
6. Biggs M, McVicar J, Flowerdew B. *Vegetables, Herbs, and Fruit: An Illustrated Encyclopedia.* Buffalo/Richmond Hill: Firefly Books, 2006: 100.
7. Bianchini F., and F. Corbetta. *The Complete Book of Fruits and Vegetables.* New York: Crown, 1976: 104; Lambert Ortiz E. *The Encyclopedia of Herbs, Spices, and Flavourings: A Cook's Compendium.* New York: DK, 1992.
8. Sun, Simon, Tanumihardjo. Antioxidant phytochemicals and antioxidant capacity of biofortified carrots (*Daucus carota* L.) of Various Colors. *J* 2009 Apr 9.
9. Ravindra, Narayan. Antioxidative activity of the anthocyanin from carrot (*Daucus carota*) callus culture. *Int* 2003 Sep; 54(5): 349–55.
10. Yamamoto, Naemura, Ijiri, Ogawa, Suzuki, Shimada, Giddings. The antithrombotic effects of carrot filtrates in rats and mice. *Blood* 2008 Dec; 19(8): 785–92.
11. Tavares, Gonçalves MJ, Cavaleiro, Cruz, Lopes, Canhoto, Salgueiro. Essential oil of *Daucus carota* subsp. *halophilus*: composition, antifungal activity and cytotoxicity. *J* 2008 Sep 2; 119(1): 129–34.
12. Metzger, Barnes, Reed. Purple carrot (*Daucus carota* L.) polyacetylenes decrease lipopolysaccharide-induced expression of inflammatory proteins in macrophage and endothelial cells. *J* 2008 May 28; 56(10): 3554–60.
13. Vasudevan, Parle. Pharmacological evidence for the potential of *Daucus carota* in the management of cognitive dysfunctions. *Biol* 2006 Jun; 29(6): 1154–61.
14. Jasicka-Misiak, Lipok, Nowakowska, Wieczorek, Mlynarz P, Kafarski. Antifungal activity of the carrot seed oil and its major sesquiterpene compounds. *Z* 2004 Nov-Dec; 59(11–12): 791–6.
15. Gilani, Shaheen, Saeed, Bibi, Irfanullah, Sadiq, Faizi. Hypotensive action of coumarin glycosides from *Daucus carota. Phytomedicine* 2000 Oct; 7(5): 423–6.
16. Bishayee, Sarkar, Chatterjee. Hepatoprotective activity of carrot (*Daucus carota* L.) against carbon tetrachloride intoxication in mouse liver. *J* 1995 Jul 7; 47(2): 69–74.
17. Gambhir, Sen, Sanyal, Das. Antispasmodic activity of the tertiary base of *Daucus carota*, Linn. Seeds. *Indian* 1979 Jul-Sep; 23(3): 225–8.
18. Jabrane, Jannet, Harzallah-Skhiri, Mastouri, Casanova, Mighri. Flower and root oils of the tunisian *Daucus carota* L. ssp. *maritimus* (*Apiaceae*): integrated analyses by GC, GC/MS, and 13C-NMR spectroscopy, and in vitro antibacterial activity. *Chem* 2009 Jun; 6(6): 881–9.

Cedar/*Arz*

FAMILY: Pinaceae

BOTANICAL NAME: *Cedrus libani*

COMMON NAMES: *English* Cedar of Lebanon; *French* Cedre; *Spanish* Cedro; *German* Zeder; *Urdu/Unānī* Dayaar, Azaad; *Modern Standard Arabic* Arz, Arz lubnān

SAFETY RATING: GENERALLY SAFE True cedar (*Cedrus*), which is native to North Africa and Asia, is safe when used externally and inhaled. As Duke notes, there are no known health hazards or side effects associated with proper therapeutic doses. True cedar must not be confused with white cedar (*Thuja occidentalis*), which is native to North America. In order to fight scurvy, Native Canadians used to make a tea from *Thuja occidentalis*, which has been shown to contain 50mg of vitamin C per 100 grams. *Thuja*, however, contains terpene thujone, which has potentially lethal properties. The leaves of the plant are toxic if eaten, while its oil is both abortifacient and convulsant. Hence, unless required to combat scurvy in a life-threatening situation, consuming *Thuja* should be avoided, and never considered a substitute for true cedar. Although it is traditionally used an inhalant, it must never be used by any-one suffering from a dry, irritating cough indicating a stagnant mucous pulmonary condition, nor should it be used in cases when diarrhea is present. In all cases, *Thuja* should not be used by pregnant women.

PROPHETIC PRESCRIPTION: According to the Messenger of Allāh said, "The hypocrite is likened to the cedar (*arz*). It remains standing until it is harvested."[1]

ISSUES IN IDENTIFICATION: According to Ibn Jawziyyah, *arz* is *ṣanawbar* or pine.[2] Dīnawarī is more precise, explaining that *arz* is the male tree, which produces no fruit, while *ṣanawbar* is the female, fruit-producing, tree.[3] According to Dīnawarī, the cedar is not a plant from the land of the Arabs.[4] In Duke's view, the biblical cedar refers to *Cedrus libani* which is known in Arabic as *arz*, *arz lubnān*, and *arz al-rabb*, among other colloquial Arabic names.

PROPERTIES AND USES: *Cedrus libani* is considered antiseptic, bactericide, diuretic, expectorant, fungicidal, and insecticidal. The leaves and wood are used to disinfect the respiratory tract, stimulate the circulatory system, and calm the nerves. Cedar of Lebanon is used to treat asthma, bacteria, bacillus, blennorrhagia, boils, bronchosis, burns, cancer, catarrh, cough, dermatosis, enterobacter, fungus, gastrosis, heliobacter and induration. It is also used to treat infections, klebsiella, listeria, mycobacterium, phthisis, proteus, pseudomonas, pulmonosis, and rash, as well as respirosis, staphylococcus, and tuberculosis. The odor repels insects. The oil is used in perfumery, notably in jasmine-scented soap. Externally, it is used for skin diseases, ulcers, and dandruff, and as an inhalation for bronchitis, tuberculosis, and nervous tension.

SCIENTIFIC STUDIES: *Alpha-amylase Inhibitory Activity* According to a study conducted by the University of Calabria in Italy, *Cedrus libani* wood oil inhibits activity of alpha-amylase, while the leaves and cones were devoid of any significant activity.[5]

Antiherpetic Activity According to a study conducted by the University of Calabria in Italy, the ethanol extracts and essential oil from *Cedrus libani* cones and leaves exhibit an interesting activity against herpes simplex virus type 1.[6]

Antimicrobial Activity According to a study conducted by the University of Dicle in Turkey, the ethanol extract of resins obtained from the roots and stems of *Cedrus libani* was shown to be highly effective against tested microorganisms by preventing their growth to a greater extent.[7] Another study, conducted by Sütçü Imām University in Turkey, confirmed the antimicrobial activity of *Cedrus libani*.[8]

Anti–Helicobacter pylori *Activity* According to a study conducted by Gazi University in Turkey, *Cedrus libani* was shown to possess anti–*Helicobacter pylori* activity.[9]

Cedar Notes

1. Muslim. *Jāmi' al-ṣaḥīḥ*. al-Riyyāḍ: Bayt al-Afkār, 1998; Bukhārī M. *Ṣaḥīḥ al-Bukhārī*. al-Riyyāḍ: Bayt al-Afkār, 1998; Iṣbahānī AN al-. *Mawsū'at al-ṭibb al-nabawī*. Ed. MKD al-Turkī. Bayrūt: Dār Ibn Ḥazm, 2006.
2. Ibn Qayyim al-Jawziyyah M. *al-Ṭibb al-nabawī*. Bayrūt: Dār al-Kitāb, 1985.
3. Dīnawarī AH. *Kitāb al-nabāt/The Book of Plants*. Ed. Bernhard Lewin. Bayrūt: Dār al-Qalam, 1974: 102.
4. Dīnawarī AH. *Kitāb al-nabāt/The Books of Plants*. Ed. Bernhard Lewin. Uppsala/Wiesbaden: A.-B. Lundequistska Bokhandeln and Otto Harrassowitz, 1953: 5.
5. Loizzo, Saab, Statti, Menichini. Composition and alpha-amylase inhibitory effect of essential oils from *Cedrus libani*. *Fitoterapia*. 2007; 78(4): 323–326.
6. Loizzo, Saab, Tundis, Statti, Lampronti, Menichini, Gambari, Cinatl, Doerr. Phytochemical analysis and in vitro evaluation of the biological activity against herpes simplex virus type 1 (HSV-1) of *Cedrus libani* A. Rich. *Phytomedicine*. 2007 May 3.
7. Kizil, Kizil, Yavuz, Aytekin. Antimicrobial activity of the resins obtained from the roots and stems of *Cedrus libani* and *Abies cilicica*. *Prikl Biokhim Mikrobiol*. 2002; 38(2): 166–168.
8. Digrak M, Ilçim A, Hakki. Antimicrobial activities of several parts of *Pinus brutia*, *Juniperus oxycedrus*, *Abies cilicia*,

Cedrus libani and *Pinus nigra*. *Phytother* 1999; 13(7): 584–587.
9. Yesilada E, Gürbüz, Shibata. Screening of Turkish anti-ulcerogenic folk remedies for anti-*Helicobacter pylori* activity. *J* 1999; 66(3): 289–293.

Celery / *Karafs*

FAMILY: Apiaceae

BOTANICAL NAME: *Apium graveolens*

COMMON NAMES: *English* wild celery; *French* Céleri, Ache, Ache des marais; *Spanish* Apio; *German* Echte Sellerie; *Urdu/Unānī* Karafs, Ajmod, Fatrasaliyun; *Modern Standard Arabic* Karafs, Karafs nabṭī, Karafs al-mā', Karafs barrī

SAFETY RATING: GENERALLY SAFE TO DEADLY Since garden celery was only developed in the 17th century, the only celery the Prophet could have referred to was wild celery, a member of the parsley family, which contains many poisonous plants. Wild celery contains apiol, which is a poisonous principle. In large amounts, wild celery is toxic in its own right and can even be fatal. Despite the claims of some traditional herbalists, wild celery is not a non-toxic abortive. As such, it should never be used to terminate unwanted pregnancies. Under wet conditions, wild celery can cause a rash similar to poison ivy. The oil also causes photosensitivity. Due to the dangers it poses, particularly for pregnant women and people with kidney problems, the consumption of wild celery should be avoided. Garden celery, the variety available in supermarkets, should always be preferred, as it is generally considered safe for most people.

PROPHETIC PRESCRIPTION: The Messenger of Allāh is reported to have said, "Whoever eats celery (*karafs*) before going to bed will have sweet breath, and he will be free from toothache."[1] It is also reported that he said, "Celery is the vegetable of the Prophets"[2]; and "Eat celery, for if there is anything that enlarges the mind, it is this."[3] According to Ibn Sunnī, it is told that the Prophet prescribed celery for Ḥabībah bint al-Jahsh to treat her irregular menstrual flow (*istiḥāḍah*).[4] In another spurious tradition, one falsified by 'Abd al-Rahīm ibn Ḥabīb al-Farābī, the Prophet says, "My brother al-Khiḍr is in the sea, and al-Yāsā' is on the earth. They meet and go to Makkah every year. They drink a mouthful of zamzam which lasts them, and their food is celery." Imām 'Alī al-Riḍā recommended the consumption of the comprehensive medication with a decoction of celery root (*uṣūl al-karafs*) for pain on the left side and with cumin for the right side.[5]

ISSUES IN IDENTIFICATION: With the exception of Elgood, who claims that *karafs* is parsley, it is the consensus that *karafs* is Arabic for celery.[6] As Nehmé explains, *Apium* is *karafs* or celery while *Apium graveolens* is *karafs 'abiq*, which is known as celery and smallage.[7] Said also identifies *karafs* with *Apium graveolens*.[8]

Modern cultivated celery (*Apium graveolens* var. *dulce*), with its pale, succulent stems and mild flavor, was only developed during the 17th century in Italy, becoming popular in the rest of the world in the 19th century. Any reference to celery in classical Islamic literature invariably refers to wild celery, known also known as smallage (*A. graveolens*). Celery was only consumed cooked until the 18th century.

Wild celery is rarely used for culinary purposes due to its bitterness and its toxicity in large amounts. The seeds, however, are used in small quantities to flavor soups and stews or mixed with salt as a condiment. According to Mandaville, *A. graveolens* is locally frequent in eastern Saudi Arabia, where it is a weed of wet shaded oasis fields, gardens, and lawns.[9]

PROPERTIES AND USES: Wild celery is an aromatic, bitter, tonic herb that reduces blood pressure, relieves indigestion, stimulates the uterus, and has diuretic and anti-inflammatory properties. The herb is carminative, deobstruent, diaphoretic, appetitive, antiphlegmatic, lithontriptic, diuretic, emmenagogue, ecbolic, and anthelmintic. It is also reported to have sedative and aphrodisiac effects.

Wild celery is used internally for osteoarthritis, rheumatoid arthritis, gout, inflammation of the urinary tract, asthma, bronchitis, cough, fever, hiccups, flatulence, fluid retention, headache, heartburn, hives, intestinal gas, amenorrhoea, liver disorders, chest pains and inflammations, muscle spasms, nervousness or hysteria, rheumatism, spleen disorders, tension headaches, toothache, and vomiting.

Although some traditional herbalists claim that wild celery is a non-toxic abortive, the ecbolic effect of the herb is the direct result of its toxicity. As such, it should not be given to pregnant women or used to terminate unwanted pregnancies through oral consumption or via a suppository placed and kept deep in the vaginal canal.

Externally, celery is used for fungal infections and its oil is used for tumors. It is often combined with *Menyanthes trifoliata* and *Guaiacum officinale* for rheumatic complaints, and with *Taraxacum officinale* to increase its potency.

Scientific Studies: *Antihypertensive, Anti-Jaundice, and Antidiabetic Activities* According to a study conducted by the University of Victoria in Canada, the use of celery in the treatment of hypertension, jaundice, and diabetes, seems to be safe, and deserves further evaluation.[10] According to another study, celery lowered the blood pressure of patients suffering from hypertension.[11]

Anticancer Activity According to an animal trial conducted by Hamdard University in India, the methanolic extract of celery seeds manifests potent chemopreventive activity.[12]

Antimicrobial Activity According to a study conducted by Punjab University in India, *Apium graveolens* shows moderate anti-microbial activity against multi-drug resistant *Salmonella*.[13]

Hepaprotective Activity In an animal trial conducted by Hamdard University in India, extracts of *Apium graveolens* were shown to possess significant hepaprotective activity comparable with the drug silymarin.[14] According to an animal trial conducted by Punjab University in India, the methanolic extract of *A. graveolens* seeds possesses significant hepaprotective activity.[15]

Mosquitocidal, Nematicidal, and Antifungal Activities In a study conducted by Michigan State University in the U.S., the methanolic extract of *A. graveolens* possesses mosquitocidal, nematicidal, and antifungal activities.[16]

Antihyperlipidemic Activities According to a controlled animal trial conducted by the National University of Singapore, the aqueous extract of celery possesses potent antihyperlipidemic properties, significantly reducing total serum cholesterol levels, LDL, and triglyceride concentrations.[17]

Anti-inflammatory Activity In a study conducted by the Jordan University of Science and Technology, the ethanolic extract *A. graveolens* demonstrated an antinociceptive effect, supporting its use for painful and inflammatory conditions.[18]

Larvacidal Activity According to a study conducted by Chiang Mai University in Thailand, *A. graveolens* volatile oil exerts significant larvicidal activity against the two mosquito species after 24-hour exposure, including, *Anopheles dirus*, the major malaria vector, and *Aedes aegypti*, the main vector of dengue and dengue hemorrhagic fever in urban areas.[19]

Celery Notes

1. Ibn Qayyim al-Jawziyyah M. *al-Ṭibb al-nabawī*. Bayrūt: Dār al-Kitāb, 1985.
2. Chaghhaynī M. *Ṭibb al-nabī*. Trans. C Elgood. *Osiris* 1962; 14: 190.
3. Chaghhaynī M. *Ṭibb al-nabī*. Trans. C Elgood. *Osiris* 1962; 14: 191.
4. Ibn Ṭulūn S. *al-Manhal al-rawī fī al-ṭibb al-nabawī*. Ed. 'Azīz Bayk. Riyyāḍ: Dār 'ālam al-kutub, 1995.
5. Nisābūrī A. *Islamic Medical Wisdom: The Ṭibb al-a'immah*. Trans. B. Ispahany. Ed. AJ Newman. London: Muḥammadī Trust, 1991: 114.
6. Elgood C. Trans. *Ṭibb al-nabī or Medicine of the Prophet*. Sūyūṭī J, M Chaghhaynī. *Osiris* 1962: 14.
7. Nehmé M. *Dictionnaire étymologique de la flore du Liban*. Bayrūt: Librairie du Liban, 2000.
8. Bīrūnī, AR al-. *al-Bīrūnī's Book on Pharmacy and Materia Medica*. Ed. and trans. HM Said. Karachi: Hamdard National Foundation, 1973.
9. Mandaville JP. *Flora of Eastern Saudi Arabia*. London: Kegan Paul, 1990.
10. Lans. Ethnomedicines used in Trinidad and Tobago for urinary problems and diabetes mellitus. *J* 2006; 2: 45.
11. Fetrow CW, Avila JR. *The Complete Guide to Herbal Medicines*. Springhouse: Springhouse Corporation, 2000.
12. Sultana, Ahmed, Jahangir, Sharma. Inhibitory effect of celery seeds extract on chemically induced hepatocarcinogenesis: modulation of cell proliferation, metabolism and altered hepatic foci development. *Cancer* 2005; 221(1): 11–20.
13. Rani, Khullar. Antimicrobial evaluation of some medicinal plants for their anti-enteric potential against multi-drug resistant *Salmonella typhi*. *Phytother* 2004; 18(8): 670–673.
14. Ahmed, Alam, Varshney, Khan. Hepatoprotective activity of two plants belonging to the Apiaceae and the Euphorbiaceae family. *J* 2002; 79(3): 313–316.
15. Singh, Handa. Hepatoprotective activity of *Apium graveolens* and *Hygrophila auriculata* against paracetamol and thioacetamide intoxication in rats. *J* 1995; 15; 49(3): 119–126.
16. Momin, Nair. Mosquitocidal, nematicidal, and antifungal compounds from *Apium graveolens* L. seeds. *J* 2001; 49(1): 142–145.
17. Tsi, Das, Tan. Effects of aqueous celery (*Apium graveolens*) extract on lipid parameters of rats fed a high fat diet. *Planta* 1995; 61(1): 18–21.
18. Atta, Alkofahi. Anti-nociceptive and anti-inflammatory effects of some Jordanian medicinal plant extracts. *J* 1998 Mar; 60(2): 117–124.
19. Pitasawat, Champakaew, Choochote, Jitpakdi, Chaithong, Kanjanapothi, Rattanachanpichai, Tippawangkosol, Riyong, Tuetun, Chaiyasit. Aromatic plant-derived essential oil: an alternative larvicide for mosquito control. *Fitoterapia*. 2007; 78(3): 205–210.

Chickpea/*Ḥummuṣ*

Family: Fabaceae

Botanical Name: *Cicer arietinum*

Common Names: *English* Chickpea; *French* Pois chiche, Cicérole; *Spanish* Garbanzo; *German* Echte Kicher, Kichererbse Römische Kicher; *Urdu/Unānī* Chana, Nakhud, Hummus; *Modern Standard Arabic* Ḥummuṣ

Safety Rating: Generally Safe Chickpeas are generally considered safe for most people. As Duke reports, the oxalic acid found in *Cicer ari-*

etinum may be contraindicated in people who suffer from calculus. He also cites Boulos who notes that inadequately cooked chickpeas can cause paralysis in the same fashion that lathyrus peas can cause lathyrism.

PROPHETIC PRESCRIPTION: According to Imām Jaʿfar al-Ṣādiq, roasted chickpea flour was made in accordance with a revelation from Allāh: it helps build weight, strengthens bones, and is the food of the prophets. According to the Imām, dry chickpea flour removes or diminishes white spots; when combined with olive oil, it increases weight, strengthens bones, and it helps to clear up one's complexion. The Imām explained that consuming three tablespoons of roasted chickpea flour helps cure phlegm and bile. In another tradition, he states that chickpea flour diminishes thirst, cures stomach problems, relieves nausea, cures seventy diseases, and lowers high blood pressure. When chickpeas were mentioned in his presence, the Imām said, "It is good for chest pain."[1] According to Imām Muḥammad al-Taqī, the consumption of roasted chickpea flour is a treatment for excessive menstruation.

ISSUES IN IDENTIFICATION: It is the consensus that the Arabic *ḥummuṣ* refers to chickpea, although there is debate regarding the particular type. As Nehmé explains, *ḥummuṣ* is *Cicer* or chickpea; *ḥummuṣ shā'ī'* is *Cicer arietinum* or common chickpea; *ḥummuṣ maqṣūṣ* is *Cicer incisum* or cut chickpea, and *ḥummuṣ rīshī al-takhrīm* is *Cicer pinnatifidum*.[2] As Duke relates, the biblical *hamitz*, the Arabic *ḥummuṣ*, and the Aramaic *himtza*, mean chickpea and refer to *Cicer arietinum*. Duke believes that the biblical chickpea also embraced *Pisum*, *Vicia*, and even *Trigonella*.

PROPERTIES AND USES: *Cicer arietinum* is considered highly nutritive. Chickpeas contain 23 percent protein, are a good source of zinc, and have levels of calcium similar to yogurt and close to that of milk. They are very high in dietary fiber and an especially good source of carbohydrates for persons with insulin sensitivity or diabetes. They also happen to be very low in fat.

Cicer arietinum is considered allergenic, anthelmintic, antianemic, antiatherogenic, antibilious, anticervisotic, anticheilitic, anticoronary, antidementic, antidepressant, antigingivitic, antiglossitic, antigout, and antihyperlipidemic. It is also viewed as antiinfertility, anti-inflammatory, antileukemic, antimetaplastic, antimyelotoxic, antineuropathic, antiperiodontotic, and antiplaque. It is considered antipolyp, antipsychotic, anti-spina-bifida, antistress, antiviral, aphrodisiac, astringent, bifidogenic, cardioprotective, dpuratie, diuretic, and estrogenic. It is equally viewed as flatugenic, fungicide, hematopoietic, hypocholesterolemic, hypolipidemic, immunostimulant, lactagogue, laxative, lipolytic, and mitogenic. Finally, it is seen as orexigenic, proteolytic, refrigerant, reverse-transciptase inhibitor, soporific, stimulant, stomachic, tonic, trypsin inhibitor, xanthine-oxidase inhibitor, and uricosuric.

Cicer arietinum is used to treat a wide host of ailments, including: alactea, anemia, anorexia, atherosclerosis, biliousness, bronchosis, calculus, cancer of the colon, cancer of the penis, cancer of the testicle, cardiopathy, catarrh, cervicosis, cheilosis, cholera, cirrhosis, constipation, cough, cutamenia, dandruff, dementia, depression, dermatosis, diarrhea, and dyspepsia. It is also used for edema, fever, fracture, fungus, gas, gingivosis, glossosis, gout, headache, hepatosis, high cholesterol, HIV, impotence, infection, infertility, inflammation, itch, obesity, orchosis, ozoena, pain, periodontosis, pharyngosis, plaque, polyp, and pulmonosis. Finally, it is employed in the treatment of smallpox, snakebite, sore throat, spina bifida, splenosis, sprain, stress, stroke, thirst, toothache, vomiting, warts, and worms.

SCIENTIFIC STUDIES: *Anticancer Activity* According to a study conducted by the University of Illinois at Chicago, epidemiological studies have reported a low incidence of colon cancer in countries with high legume consumption. Moreover, experimental studies have found that legumes, such as soybeans and pinto beans, have anticancer properties. In a controlled animal trial, researchers found a 64 percent suppression of azoxymethane-induced aberrant crypt foci in animals fed garbanzo flour, versus an inhibition of 58 and 55 percent for soy and mixed flour groups, respectively. These results demonstrate that garbanzo beans possess bioactive compounds capable of inhibiting the formation of pre-cancerous lesions in mice and suggest that, like soybeans, their consumption contributes to a reduction in colon cancer incidence.[3]

In a study conducted by the Instituto de la Grasa in Spain, pulses (edible seeds of legumes) should be part of a healthy diet, and it is also becoming clear that they have health-promoting effects. Nevertheless, most studies on the bioactive or health-promoting properties of pulses have been carried out using soybeans.[4] Chickpea seeds are a staple in the traditional diet of many Mediterranean, Asian, and South and Central American countries. Both cell growth-promoting and cell growth-inhibiting effects were found. Most interestingly, a fraction soluble in ethanol and acetone specifically and almost completely inhibited the growth of Caco-2 cells exhibiting a cancerous phenotype. It is concluded that chickpea seeds are a source of bioactive components and deserve further study for their possible anticancer effect.

Cholesterol-Lowering Activity In a study conducted by Punjab Agricultural University in India, Bengal gram seed coat appeared to be a potent hypocholesterolemic/hypolipidemic agent in rabbits. When fed to hypercholesterolemic rabbits, it lowered hepatic cholesterol/lipid much more than in the control group. Aortic lipid levels were rather marginally increased but the increase was less in Bengal gram seed coat-fed rabbits. Though the seed coat of Bengal gram (chickpea) failed to prevent the development of atherosclerosis in hypercholesterolemic rabbits, it certainly slowed down the process of its development. The hypocholesterolemic action of Bengal gram seed coat appeared to be due to the increased catabolism and excretion of cholesterol.[5]

Two isoflavones, biochanin-A and formononetin isolated from *Cicer arietinum*, have been shown to possess hypolipidemic properties for Triton WR-1339 induced hyperlipidemia in male albino rats, when administered as a crude extract or as individual compounds.[6] Isoflavones isolated from three commonly used pulses such as chickpea (*Cicer arietinum*), greengram (*Phaseolus aureus*) and blackgram (*Phaseolus mungo*) and p-coumaric acid were supplemented to the hypercholesterolemia-inducing diet of rats. Among isoflavones, biochanin A and formononetin showed hypolipidemic activity but diadzein did not; p-coumaric acid also produced a significant reduction in serum cholesterol levels.[7]

In a controlled trial conducted by the Postgraduate Institute of Basic Medical Sciences in India, animals which consumed chickpea flour showed a significant decrease in lipids.[8] In another controlled trial conducted by the University of Agriculture in Pakistan, researchers found that the consumption of chickpea flour assists in lowering blood cholesterol, blood glucose, and LDL-cholesterol, thus leading to a lesser risk of developed coronary heart disease and diabetes mellitus.[9]

Chickpea Notes

1. 'Amilī H. *Wasā'il al-shī'ah*. Bayrūt: al-Mu'assasah.
2. Nehmé M. *Dictionnaire étymologique de la flore du Liban*. Bayrūt: Librairie du Liban, 2000.
3. Murillo, Choi, Pan, Constantinou, Mehta. Efficacy of garbanzo and soybean flour in suppression of aberrant crypt foci in the colons of CF-1 mice. *Anticancer* 2004; 24(5A): 3049–3055.
4. Giron-Calle, Vioque, del, Pedroche, Alaiz, Millan. Effect of chickpea aqueous extracts, organic extracts, and protein concentrates on cell proliferation. *J* 2004; 7(2): 122–129.
5. Mand, Soni, Gupta, Vadhera, Singh. Role of Bengal gram (*Cicer arietinum*) seed coat as an antiatherogenic agent in rabbits. *Indian* 1991; 43(5): 347–350.
6. Siddiqui, Siddiqi. Hypolipidemic principles of *Cicer arietinum*: biochanin-A and formononetin. *Lipids*. 1976; 11(3): 243–246.
7. Sharma. Isoflavones and hypercholesterolemia in rats. *Lipids*. 1979; 14(6): 535–539.
8. Gopalan, Gracias, Madhavan. Serum lipid and lipoprotein fractions in bengal gram and biochanin A induced alterations in atherosclerosis. *Indian* 1991; 43(3): 185–189.
9. Habib, Ahsan. Comparative serum cholesterol and glucose responses of rats fed on wheat flour and chickpea composite flour. *Asia* 2004; 13(Suppl): S66.

Christ's Thorn/*Sidr, Nabaq*

FAMILY: Rhamnaceae

BOTANICAL NAME: *Ziziphus spina-christi*

COMMON NAMES: *English* Christ's thorn, Syrian Christ-thorn, Nabk tree, Jujube (fruit); *French* Épine du Christ, Nabca, Jujube (fruit); *Spanish* Azufaifo comestible, Espina de Cristo; *German* Gewöhnlicher Christdorn, Judendorn, Stechdorn, Jujube (fruit), Chinesische Dattel (fruit), Azufaifa (fruit), Azofaifo (fruit); *Urdu/Unānī* Unnab; *Modern Standard Arabic* Shajarat al-nabaq, al-Sidr, 'Anab, Zayzaf, Zayzafūn, Nabaq (fruit)

SAFETY RATING: GENERALLY SAFE *Ziziphus spina-christi* seems to be safe for most people when used as directed. Although studies have revealed no teratogenic or fetotoxic effects, it has been used in China as a form of birth control. As such, for the sake of caution, it should not be consumed medicinally by women who are pregnant or lactating.

PROPHETIC PRESCRIPTION: The Qur'ān speaks of *sidrah* and *sidrin* on several occasions (34:16; 53:14; 53:16; 56:28), which is translated by Yusuf 'Ali, Picktall, and Aṣad, as Lote-tree. In an apocryphal tradition related by Abū Nu'aym, the Messenger of Allāh said, "When Adam was sent down to earth, the first fruit that he ate was a *nabaq*."[1] The Prophet also said, "The jujube tree drives away intoxication, weakness of the eye, and purifies the heart."[2] During Islamic funeral rites, the Prophet instructed people to "Wash the deceased with water and *sidr*."[3] He also stated that "If anyone cuts down a *sidr*, Allāh will cast him headfirst into Hell."[4] According to traditions related by Muslim and Būkhārī, the Prophet is said to have seen a *sidr* during his Night Journey. It is also reported by Ibn Ḥabīb that the Prophet used to wash his face with *sidr* water.[5]

Issues in Identification: According to Bīrūnī, the fruit of the *sidr* is known as *nabaq*.[6] Dīnawarī says that *sidr* is the *nabaq* tree and that it has round leaves.[7] Akīlī identifies *sidr* as both *Ziziphus vulgaris* and *Rhamnus catharticus*, and *nabaq* as lote fruit or jujube.[8]

Due to the accuracy of the Arabic language, and the precision of the Prophet, it is seems highly unlikely the terms *sidr* and *nabaq* should be so vague. Although *Rhamnus* is known in Arabic as *nabaq* and *zafrīn*, *Rhamnus cathartica* is called *zafrīn mus-hil* and *shajarat al-dukn*. In fact, besides the generic name, none of the species of *Rhamnus* are known as *sidr* or *nabaq*. *Ziziphus jujuba* or common jujube is a more plausible proposal, however it is known in Arabic as *'unnāb shā'i'*.

The only plant which bears both the names of *sidr* and *nabaq* is *Ziziphus spina-christi*, which is known as both *sidr*, and *nabaq al-masīḥ*. Accordingly, the vast majority of commentators and translators of the Qur'ān have identified *sidrah* as a species of lote tree from the *Ziziphus* genus. Thomson says that *sidr* is the lote tree. The Hans Wehr Dictionary identifies *sidr* as the lotus tree or *Ziziphus lotus*. Elgood and Turkī identify *sidr* as the lote tree.[9] Said identifies *sidr* with *Ziziphus spina-christi*, as does Ghazanfar, Bashā, Johnstone.[10] According to Duke, *Ziziphus spina-christi* is known in Arabic as *sidr*.

Through a series of unconvincing and contradictory arguments, Farooqi claims that *sidr* is Arabic for cedar.[11] The author bases part of his argument on claims that the Arabic *sidr* is a derivation of the Greek *cedrus*. Farooqi, however, seems to ignore the fact that the letter /c/ did not have an /s/ sound in Greek and Latin: it was hard and pronounced like an English /k/. According to the rules of Arabic phonetics, the Greek and Latin *cedrus* would have entered the language as *kidrus*.

Farooqi's argument is also inconsistent from the point of view of *fiqh*. In Islamic jurisprudence, *sidr* is not an obscure plant whose true botanical origin was lost over the centuries. On the contrary, *sidr* has been employed on a daily basis in Muslim funeral ablutions for almost fifteen hundred years. According to the precepts for purifying a corpse for burial, the body of the deceased must first be washed with water mixed with *sidr* leaves. The exact identity of the leaves was specifically indicated: the leaves of a tree, sometimes called the lotus tree or Christ's thorn, whose scientific name is *Ziziphus spina-christi*. The corpse is then washed with water mixed with camphor, and then finally with pure water. The exact identity of *sidr* has been preserved, not only through writing, but by practice in the *ghusl al-mayyit* or ablution of the corpse.

According to Ghazanfar, *Ziziphus spina-christi* is found throughout Arabia, and is frequently cultivated.[12] Mandaville notes that it is commonly cultivated in eastern Arabia where it is a frequently planted around towns and villages. The fruit is known as *nabaq*, while the shrub is known as *nabiq*. The dried, powdered leaves or *sidr* have long been used as a hair wash in eastern Arabia, and is still sold for that use in traditional markets. It continues to be used to wash the dead. *Sidr* remains an important cultivated tree grown in towns and villages in Saudi Arabia.[13] The debate regarding its botanical identity is the result of researchers who are detached from the region and its reality. *Sidr* is *Ziziphus spina-christi* and its identity has never been lost by the Arabs.

Properties and Uses: *Ziziphus* is a mucilaginous, nutritive, astringent, pectoral, sedative herb, with a sweet and sour taste. It controls allergic responses, relieves coughing, soothes irritated or damaged tissues, protects the liver, prevents stress ulcer formation, and has a tonic effect on spleen and stomach energies. It also moderates the actions of other herbs. Jujube fruits contain 5 percent protein, 4 percent sugar, and a generous amount of vitamin C, and other minerals. They are used to gain weight, strengthen muscles, boost body strength, and stimulate the immune system.

Internally, *Ziziphus* fruits are used for chronic fatigue, loss of appetite, diarrhea, anemia, irritability, and hysteria. The seeds are used internally for palpitations, insomnia, nervous exhaustion, night sweats, and excessive perspiration. It is often combined with *Panax ginseng* or *Angelica sinensis*, and added to tonic prescriptions as a buffer to improve synergy and minimize side effects. Jujube fruits are antidote, diuretic, emollient, and expectorant. In Chinese medicine, jujube is used to activate the liver. It is used to treat coughs, asthma, and respiratory problems. The fruits are also used to regulate the heart beat, insomnia, nervous exhaustion, depression, night sweats, and excessive perspiration. Fruits are also used to sweeten and flavor medicines. Dried jujube fruits are anodyne, anticancer, pectoral, refrigerant, sedative, stomachic, styptic, and tonic. They are used internally to purify the blood and to treat chronic fatigue, loss of appetite, diarrhea, pharyngitis, bronchitis, anemia, irritability, and hysteria. They are considered effective tranquilizers, anticancer, and anti–respiratory problem agents, which relieve fever and pain, prevent bleeding, and help ease digestion. The seeds are also hypnotic, and narcotic. The leaves are used in an infusion for relaxation, diuresis, and purgation. Long-term use is reputed to improve the complexion.

SCIENTIFIC STUDIES: *Antidiabetic Activity* According to an animal study conducted by Assiut University in Egypt, *Ziziphus spina-christi* leaves appears to be a safe alternative to lower blood glucose.[14] In a four week animal study conducted by Bonn University in Germany, the butanol extract of *Z. spina-christi* leaves as well as christinin-A, its main saponin glycoside, significantly reduced serum glucose levels, liver phosphorylase and glucose-6-phosphatase activities, and significantly increased serum pyruvate level and liver glycogen content after four weeks of treatment in diabetic rats.[15]

Immune System Stimulating Activity According to a study conducted in Japan, jujube stimulates the immune system.[16]

Liver Stimulating Activity In one clinical trial in China 12 patients with liver complaints were given jujube, peanuts and brown sugar nightly. In four weeks their liver function had improved.[17]

Christ's Thorn Notes

1. Iṣbahānī AN al-. *Mawsū'at al-ṭibb al-nabawī.* Ed. MKD al-Turkī. Bayrūt: Dār Ibn Ḥazm, 2006.
2. Chaghhaynī M. *Ṭibb al-nabī.* Trans. C Elgood. *Osiris* 1962; 14: 190.
3. Bukhārī M. *Ṣaḥīḥ al-Bukhārī.* al-Riyyāḍ: Bayt al-Afkār, 1998.
4. Bukhārī M. *Ṣaḥīḥ al-Bukhārī.* al-Riyyāḍ: Bayt al-Afkār, 1998.
5. Ibn Ḥabīb A. *Mujtaṣar fī al-ṭibb/Compendio de medicina.* Ed. C Álvarez de Morales and F Girón Irueste. Madrid: Consejo Superior de Investigaciones Científicas, 1992: 56/23.
6. Bīrūnī, AR al-. *al-Bīrūnī's Book on Pharmacy and Materia Medica.* Ed. and trans. HM Said. Karachi: Hamdard National Foundation, 1973.
7. Dīnawarī AH. *Kitāb al-nabāt: Le dictionaire botanique d'Abū Ḥanīfa al-Dīnawarī.* al-Qāhirah: Institut Français d'Archéologie Orientale du Caire, 1973.
8. Ibn al-Qayyim al-Jawziyyah. *Natural Healing with the Medicine of the Prophet.* Pearl Publishing. Trans. M al-Akīlī. Philadelphia, 1993.
9. Elgood C. Trans. *Ṭibb al-nabī or Medicine of the Prophet.* Sūyūṭī J, M Chaghhaynī. *Osiris* 1962; 14; Iṣbahānī AN al-. *Mawsū'at al-ṭibb al-nabawī.* Ed. MKD al-Turkī. Bayrūt: Dār Ibn Ḥazm, 2006.
10. Bīrūnī, AR al-. *al-Bīrūnī's Book on Pharmacy and Materia Medica.* Ed. and trans. HM Said. Karachi: Hamdard National Foundation, 1973; Ghazanfar SA. *Handbook of Arabian Medicinal Plants.* Boca Raton: CRC Press, 1994; Johnstone P, trans. *Medicine of the Prophet.* Ibn Qayyim al-Jawziyyah. Cambridge: The Islamic Texts Society, 1998; Bāshā HS. *Qabasāt min al-Ṭibb al-nabawī wa-al-adillah al-'ilmīyah al-ḥadīthah.* Jiddah: Maktabat al-Sawādī lil-Tawzī', 1991.
11. Farooqi MIH. *Medicinal Plants in the Traditions of Prophet Muḥammad.* Lucknow: Sidrah Publishers, 1998: 193–205
12. Ghazanfar SA. *Handbook of Arabian Medicinal Plants.* Boca Raton: CRC Press, 1994.
13. Mandaville JP. *Flora of Eastern Saudi Arabia.* London: Kegan Paul, 1990.
14. Abdel-Zaher, Salim, Assaf, Abdel-Hady. Antidiabetic activity and toxicity of *Ziziphus spina-christi* leaves. *Ethnopharmacol.* 2005; 101(1–3): 129–138.
15. Glombitza, Mahran, Mirhom, Michel, Motawi. Hypoglycemic and anti-hyperglycemic effects of *Ziziphus spina-christi* in rats. *Planta* 1994; 60(3): 244–247.
16. Chevallier A. *The Encyclopedia of Medicinal Plants.* London: Dorling Kindersley, 1996.
17. Chevallier A. *The Encyclopedia of Medicinal Plants.* London: Dorling Kindersley, 1996.

Chrysanthemum / *Ghabīrā'*

FAMILY: Asteraceae

BOTANICAL NAME: *Chrysanthemum* spp.

COMMON NAMES: *English* Chrysanthemum; *French* Chrysanthème; *Spanish* Crisantemo; *German* Chrysantheme; *Urdu/Unānī* N.A.; *Modern Standard Arabic* Ghabīrā'

SAFETY RATING: Chrysanthemum is generally considered safe when used in the recommended doses. People suffering from diarrhea should observe caution when using chrysanthemum. Individuals who are allergic to daisies or asters should not use chrysanthemum. The safety of *Chrysanthemum* has not been established in young children, women who are pregnant or nursing, or those who suffer from severe kidney or liver disease.

PROPHETIC PRESCRIPTION: Imām Ja'far al-Ṣādiq said the following concerning chrysanthemum: "Its flesh produces flesh. Its bone produces bone. Its skin produces skin. Moreover, it warms the kidneys, it burnishes the stomach, and is a protection against hemorrhoids and incontinence (*taqṭī*). It strengthens the legs and it fights leprosy (*judhām*) with the help of Allah."[1]

ISSUES IN IDENTIFICATION: We have been unable to locate the term *ghabīrā'* in our Arabic sources. The word was translated by Ahmad Wahaj al-Siddiqui as "a flower tree with a fruit" which is most certainly incorrect.[2] Although we could not find a definition for *ghabīrā'* in Arabic sources, we did discover that the Nubian *toshka* means "the place of the *al-ghabīrā'* plant. If *toshka* signifies *ghabīrā'*, any issue regarding identification is settled as *toshka* stands for *Chrysanthemum*.

PROPERTIES AND USES: *Chrysanthemum* flowers considered antibacterial, antifungal, carminative, depurative, diaphoretic, febrifuge, ophthalmic, refrigerant, and sedative. Used for thousands of years in traditional Chinese medicine, the bitter aromatic *Chrysanthemum* flowers are made into a tea to improve vision, soothe sore eyes, relieve headaches, and to fight infections. Internally, the consumption of *Chrysanthemum* flowers is said to dilate the coronary artery. As a result, the flowers are used to treat hypertension, coronary heart disease, and angina. Externally, the leaf juice is applied onto wounds to help prevent infection.

SCIENTIFIC STUDIES: *Anti-HIV Activity* In a lab study conducted by the Korea Institute of Science and Technology in Seoul, an isolated compound from *Chrysanthemum morifolium* showed strong HIV-1 integrase inhibitory activity.[3] Further studies have also demonstrated the H1V-1 inhibitory activity of *Chrysanthemum morifolium*.[4]

Antimicrobial Activity According to a lab study conducted by Süleyman Demirel University in Isparta, Turkey,

Chrysanthemum indicum exhibits antimicrobial activities against both *Staphylococcus aureus* and *Escherichia coli*.[5] Further studies have also demonstrated the antimicrobial activity of the plant.[6]

Antimycotic Activity The supercritical extracts of chrysanthemums have been shown to possess antimycotic activity.[7]

Neuroprotective Activity Chrysanthemum morifolium extracts have been shown to possess neuroprotective activity.[8]

Antiarrhythmic Activity In an animal study conducted by Zhejiang University, *Chrysanthemum Morifolium* Ramat reduced myocardial vulnerability and exerted antiarrhythmic effects.[9]

Antibacterial Activity In a lab study conducted by Islamic Azad University in Khalkhal, Iran, the water-distilled essential oils from leaves, stems and roots of *Chrysanthemum parthenium* showed inhibitory effects on *Escherichia coli* and *Salmonella typhi*, but were not active against *Staphylococcus aureus*.[10] In another lab study, the essential oil of *Chrysanthemum boreale* Makino also exhibited antibacterial activity.[11]

Anti-inflammatory Activity In an animal study conducted by the Korea Institute of Oriental Medicine, *Chrysanthemum indicum* Linné was shown to be an effective anti-inflammatory agent in murine phorbol ester-induced dermatitis. The researchers concluded that the extract may have therapeutic potential in a variety of immune-related cutaneous diseases.[12]

Antiarthritic Activity In a controlled animal study conducted at Anhui Medical University in China, the extract of total flavonoids of *Chrysanthemum indicum* inhibited proliferation and induced apoptosis in synovial cells, exerting a therapeutic effect on rheumatoid arthritis.[13]

Antiherpetic Activity According to a study conducted by the Laboratoire des Maladies Transmissibles et Substances Biologiquement Actives in Monastir, France, *Chrysanthemum* extracts exhibit antimicrobial and/or anti–HSV-1 activities.[14]

Antioxidative Activity According to a lab study conducted by the Korea Institute of Science and Technology, two compounds from *Chrysanthemum morifolium* Ramar show potent superoxide anion radical scavenging activity.[15]

Anti-inflammatory and Immunomodulatory Activity In an animal study conducted by the University of Science and Technology in Hefei, China, *Chrysanthemum indicum* L. demonstrated anti-inflammatory, humoral and cellular immunomodulatory and mononuclear phagocytic activities, probably due to the presence of flavonoids.[16]

Antimutagenic Activity In a study conducted the Kinki University in Osaka, Japan, a methanol extract from the flower heads of *Chrysanthemum morifolium* showed antimutagenic activity.[17]

Chrysanthemum Notes

1. Majlisī M. *Biḥār al-anwār*. Ṭihrān: Javad al-Alavi, 1956; 'Amilī H. *Wasā'il al-shī'ah*. Bayrūt: al-Mu'assasah, 1993.

2. Siddiqui AW. *The Qur'an and Science*. http://www.thequranandscience.com/display.php?book/39/4

3. Lee JS, Kim, Lee. A new anti–HIV flavonoid glucuronide from *Chrysanthemum morifolium*. *Planta Med*. 2003 Sep; 69(9): 859–61.

4. Collins RA, Ng TB, Fong WP, Wan CC, Yeung HW. A comparison of human immunodeficiency virus type 1 inhibition by partially purified aqueous extracts of Chinese medicinal herbs. *Life Sciences* 1997; 60(23): PL345-51; Hu CQ, Chen K, Shi Q, Kilkuskie RE, Cheng YC, Lee KH. Anti-AIDS agents, 10. Acacetin-7-O-beta-D-galactopyranoside, an anti-HIV principle from *Chrysanthemum morifolium* and a structure-activity correlation with some related flavonoids. *Journal of Natural Products* 1994; 57(1): 42–51.

5. Aridogan BC, Baydar, Kaya, Demirci, Ozbasar D, Mumcu Antimicrobial activity and chemical composition of some essential oils. *Arch* 2002 Dec; 25(6): 860–4.

6. Sassi AB, Harzallah-Skhiri F, Bourgougnon N, Aouni M. Antimicrobial. *The Indian Journal of Medical Research* 2008; 127 (2): 183–92.

7. Marongiu B, Piras A, Porcedda S, et al. Chemical and biological comparisons on supercritical extracts of *Tanacetum cinerariifolium* (Trevir) Sch. Bip. with three related species of chrysanthemums of Sardinia (Italy). *Natural Product Research* 2009; 23(2): 190–9.

8. Kim IS, Koppula S, Park PJ, Kim EH, Kim CG, Choi WS, Lee KH, Choi DK. *Chrysanthemum morifolium* Ramat (CM) extract protects human neuroblastoma SH-SY 5Y cells against MPP(+)— induced cytotoxicity. *J* 2009 Sep 18.

9. Zhang, Ye, Cui, Qiu, Xu, Wang, Qian, Jiang, Xia. [Antiarrhythmic effect of ethyl acetate extract from *Chrysanthemum morifolium* Ramat on rats]. *Zhejiang* 2009 Jul; 38(4): 377–82.

10. Shafaghat A, Sadeghi H, Oji K. Composition and antibacterial activity of essential oils from leaf, stem and root of *Chrysanthemum parthenium* (L.) Bernh. from Iran. *Nat Prod Commun*. 2009 Jun; 4(6): 859–60.

11. Kim KJ, Kim YH, Yu HH, Jeong SI, Cha JD, Kil BS, You YO. Antibacterial activity and chemical composition of

essential oil of *Chrysanthemum boreale*. *Planta Med.* 2003 Mar; 69(3): 274–7.

12. Lee do Y, Choi G, Yoon T, Cheon MS, Choo BK, Kim HK. Anti-inflammatory activity of Chrysanthemum indicum extract in acute and chronic cutaneous inflammation. *J Ethnopharmacol.* 2009 May 4; 123(1): 149–54.

13. Xie XF, Li J, Chen Z, Hu CM, Chen WW. Beneficial effect of total flavonoids of Chrysanthemum indicum on adjuvant arthritis by induction of apoptosis of synovial fibroblasts]. *Zhongguo Zhong Yao Za Zhi.* 2008 Dec; 33(23): 2838–41.

14. Sassi AB, Harzallah-Skhiri F, Bourgougnon N, Aouni M. Antimicrobial activities of four Tunisian Chrysanthemum species. *Indian* 2008 Feb; 127(2): 183–92.

15. Kim HJ, Lee YS. Identification of new dicaffeoylquinic acids from *Chrysanthemum morifolium* and their antioxidant activities. *Planta Med.* 2005 Sep; 71(9): 871–6.

16. Cheng W, Li J, You T, Hu C. Anti-inflammatory and immunomodulatory activities of the extracts from the inflorescence of Chrysanthemum indicum Linné. *J Ethnopharmacol.* 2005 Oct 3; 101(1–3): 334–7.

17. Miyazawa M, Hisama M. Antimutagenic activity of flavonoids from *Chrysanthemum morifolium*. *Biosci Biotechnol Biochem.* 2003 Oct; 67(10): 2091–9.

Citron / *Utruj*

FAMILY: Rutaceae

BOTANICAL NAME: *Citrus medica*

COMMON NAMES: *English* Adam's apple, Cedrat tree, Citron; *French* Cédratier, Cédrat (fruit); *Spanish* Cidro, Limonero; limón (fruit); *German* Echte Zitrone, Cedratbaum; *Urdu/Unānī* Turanj, Utraj, Bijorah; *Modern Standard Arabic* Turunj, Utruj

SAFETY RATING: GENERALLY SAFE *Citrus medica* is generally considered safe for most people. Although it was once believed to cause renal cancer in rats, sweet orange oil (oil of citron) is not carcinogenic. In fact, the limonene it contains is now known as a significant chemopreventive agent.

PROPHETIC PRESCRIPTION: According to the Prophet Muḥammad, "The believer who reads the Qur'ān is like the citron (*utruj*): good to taste, and good to smell."[1] He also said, "Citrus fruit is very useful. It is a stimulant for the heart."[2] According to Imām 'Alī ibn Abī Ṭālib, the Prophet was fond of looking at citron trees.[3] Imām Ja'far al-Ṣādiq once said to his companions, "Tell me; with what do your physicians instruct you to eat citron?" He replied, "O son of the Messenger of Allāh, they instruct us to eat it before meals." He said, "There is nothing more beneficial than it after a meal. Eat its preserves (*al-murabbā*), for its pit has a fragrance like the fragrance of musk."[4] In another narration, he said, "It is good before meals but even better after meals." He then said, "It causes harm before the meal and is beneficial after the meal. Dry cheese digests citron."[5]

ISSUES IN IDENTIFICATION: Although *utruj* is a type of citrus, there is debate regarding the exact type it represents. The *Larūs* Dictionary remains vague regarding the definition of *utruj*, saying that it is a citrus fruit which is tart like lemon. Farooqi points out that several species were introduced in the north of Arabia much before Islām and that their cultivation seems to have been quite common in Medina during the time of the Prophet. He identifies *utruj* as *Citrus* species like *C. aurantifolia*, *C. bergamia*, *C. limon*, *C. reticulata*, and *C. sinensis*. For Said and Ispahany, *utruj* is citron (*Citrus medica*) while Akīlī identifies it as the Cedrat tree (*Citrus medica*) or Shaddock (*Citris maxima*).[6] Turkī, Álvarez de Morales and Girón Irueste identify *utruj* as *Citrus medica*.[7] Said, however, applies the term *turunj* to *Citrus medica*. Elgood simply identifies *utruj* as citron.[8]

Since the oranges cultivated in the Middle East, Near East, and Mediterranean regions were predominantly bitter oranges, *Citrus sinensis* cannot be considered as it was only introduced in large numbers in the 15th century, brought from China or India by Portuguese traders. Although Dīnawarī was familiar with both sweet and sour oranges, sweet oranges do not seem to have grown in the *Hijāz* during the time of the Prophet. This contention is supported by a tradition related by Ibn Ṭūlūn which states that 'Ā'ishah used to combine *utruj* with honey. Whether it was citron or bitter orange, the citrus fruit cultivated in Arabia was tart, and needed to be sweetened in order to make it palatable.

Initially, we were inclined towards the bitter or Seville orange, known by the scientific name of *Citrus aurantium*. Bīrūnī, however, provides a solution to this confusion. According to Bīrūnī, the fruit in question is known as *utruj*, *utrunj*, *turunj*, and *mutakka'*.[9] Thanks to these synonyms, we can confidently identify the exact citrus fruit referred to by the Prophet and the Imāms.

The shaddock (*Citris maxima*) is the first fruit to be discarded. It is allied to the orange and the lemon and is presumably native to Malaysia and Polynesia. It has a pungent, tart, but agreeable flavor, and is highly prized in the Orient. It is also called pummelo or grape-fruit. The Arabic name for this fruit is *laymūn hindī* which bears no resemblance to the name used by the Prophet and the Imāms. The sour, bitter, or Seville orange, known as *Citrus aurantium*, can also be cast aside, as it is known in Arabic as *nārinj* and *kabād nafāsh*. According to Ghazanfar, it is also known in Arabia as *lumī*.[10]

The only variety of citrus known as *utruj* is *Citrus medica*, which is also known as *turunj*. This is a primitive citrus with less water and more phytochemicals. Known in English as Adam's apple, cedrat tree, or citron, *utruj* is a small citrus tree bearing fruit similar to a lemon, but larger, and without a terminal nipple. It is the parent species of many varieties of citrus, including lemon, lime, and sweet lime. The fact that *ethrog* is the Hebrew name for *Citrus medica* also supports our argument. Most translators and exegetes of the Bible, along with botanists like Duke, Moldenke, and Zohary, agree that *utruj* and *turanj* refer to *Citrus medica*. Johnstone has likewise identified *utruj* as *Citrus medica*.[11] *Citrus medica* or citron should not be confused with *Citrus limon*, lemon, which only reached Egypt and Palestine in the tenth century, and which was cultivated in Genoa by the mid-fifteenth century.[12]

PROPERTIES AND USES: *Citrus medica* is considered analgesic, antibilious, antidote, anti-inflammatory, antiscorbutic, antiseptic, antispasmodic, aromatic, aphrodisiac, astringent, bronchoprotective, cardiotonic, carminative, digestive, hypotensive, laxative, orexigenic, refrigerant, sedative, stimulant, stomachic, tonic, and vermifuge. Its seeds are antipyretic, and anthelmintic, while its juice is acid.

Citron is used to treat anorexia, asthma, biliousness, bronchosis, calculus, cancer, caries, colds, colic, constipation, cough, cramp, diarrhea, dysentery, dyspepsia, dysuria, earache, enterosis, fever, gastrosis, halitosis, headache, hemorrhoid, hiccough, high blood pressure, impotence, infection, inflammation, intoxication, jaundice, leprosy, lumbago, and nausea. It is also used for odontosis, opththalmia, otosis, palpitation, pharyngosis, rheumatism, sclerosis, seasickness, snakebite, sore throat, splenosis, stomatosis, stomach ache, syphilis, teeth and gum problems, thirst, tumor, sexually transmitted disease, vomiting, and worms. Externally, it is used as a hair rinse, a facial astringent, and for sunburn, warts, and corns.

As Ghazanfar explains, a variety of sweet orange, known as *safargal*, is eaten in Oman as a general tonic to improve the stomach, and to treat jaundice. It is also believed that smelling the plant or fruit as an aromatherapeutic measure is good for the heart. In Yemen, orange rind is believed to make the stomach strong and enhance appetite. The pulp is also believed to be beneficial in strengthening the heart.[13]

SCIENTIFIC STUDIES: *Citraturic Activity* According to a human trial of 32 patients with hypocitraturic nephrolithiasis conducted by the Duke University Medical Center, lemonade therapy appeared to be a reasonable alternative for patients with hypocitraturia who cannot tolerate first line therapy.[14]

Antibacterial and Anti-inflammatory Activity According to a study conducted by the Hebrew University in Israel, a mixture of citrus oil and Dead Sea magnesium chloride could be used as a natural antibacterial and anti-inflammatory agent.[15]

Antifertility Activity According to an animal study conducted by SRTR Medical College in India, the ethyl-acetate fraction of Citrus limon seeds showed most encouraging antifertility activity. They ethyl-acetate fraction was found to be an anti-zygotic agent. When the test drug was withdrawn, fertility was completely restored.[16]

Antiarthritic Activity According to an animal study conducted by Kitasato University in Japan, the oral administration of the citrus flavonoid hesperidin has a preventive and therapeutic effect against induced arthritis. These results suggest that hesperidin could be effective in treating human rheumatoid arthritis patients.[17]

Radioprotective Activity According to an in-vitro study conducted by Mazandaran University of Medical Sciences in Iran, hesperidin has powerful effects on radiation-induced DNA damage and on the decline in cell proliferation in mouse bone marrow.[18]

Citron Notes

1. Bukhārī M. *Ṣaḥīḥ al-Bukhārī*. al-Riyyāḍ: Bayt al-Afkār, 1998; Muslim. *Jāmi' al-ṣaḥīḥ*. al-Riyyāḍ: Bayt al-Afkār, 1998; Ibn Qayyim al-Jawziyyah M. *al-Ṭibb al-nabawī*. Bayrūt: Dār al-Kitāb, 1985; Ibn Ṭulūn S. *al-Manhal al-rawī fī al-ṭibb al-nabawī*. Ed. 'Azīz Bayk. Riyyāḍ: Dār 'ālam al-kutub, 1995.

2. Farooqi MIH. *Medicinal Plants in the Traditions of Prophet Muḥammad*. Lucknow: Sidrah Publishers, 1998: 125

3. Ibn Ṭulūn S. *al-Manhal al-rawī fī al-ṭibb al-nabawī*. Ed. 'Azīz Bayk. Riyyāḍ: Dār 'ālam al-kutub, 1995; Muttaqī. *Kanz al-'ummāl*. Bridgeview, Il: Bayt al-Afkār al-Dawliyyah, 1999.

4. Nisābūrī A. *Islamic Medical Wisdom: The Ṭibb al-a'immah*. Trans. B. Ispahany. Ed. AJ Newman. London: Muḥammadī Trust, 1991: 179.

5. Nisābūrī A. *Islamic Medical Wisdom: The Ṭibb al-a'immah*. Trans. B. Ispahany. Ed. AJ Newman. London: Muḥammadī Trust, 1991: 180.

6. Bīrūnī, AR al-. *al-Bīrūnī's Book on Pharmacy and Materia Medica*. Ed. and trans. HM Said. Karachi: Hamdard National Foundation, 1973; Ibn al-Qayyim al-Jawziyyah. *Natural Healing with the Medicine of the Prophet*. Pearl Publishing. Trans. M al-Akīlī. Philadelphia, 1993.

7. Iṣbahānī AN al-. *Mawsū'at al-ṭibb al-nabawī*. Ed. MKD al-Turkī. Bayrūt: Dār Ibn Ḥazm, 2006; Ibn Ḥabīb A. *Mujtaṣar fī al-ṭibb/Compendio de medicina*. Ed. C Álvarez de Morales and F Girón Irueste. Madrid: Consejo Superior de Investigaciones Científicas, 1992.

8. Elgood C. Trans. *Ṭibb al-nabī or Medicine of the Prophet*. Sūyūṭī J, M Chaghhaynī. *Osiris* 1962; 14.
9. Bīrūnī, AR al-. *al-Bīrūnī's Book on Pharmacy and Materia Medica*. Ed. and trans. HM Said. Karachi: Hamdard National Foundation, 1973.
10. Ghazanfar SA. *Handbook of Arabian Medicinal Plants*. Boca Raton: CRC Press, 1994.
11. Johnstone P, trans. *Medicine of the Prophet*. Ibn Qayyim al-Jawziyyah. Cambridge: The Islamic Texts Society, 1998.
12. Biggs M, McVicar J, Flowerdew B. *Vegetables, Herbs, and Fruit: An Illustrated Encyclopedia*. Buffalo/Richmond Hill: Firefly Books, 2006: 482.
13. Ghazanfar SA. *Handbook of Arabian Medicinal Plants*. Boca Raton: CRC Press, 1994.
14. Kang Long-term lemonade based dietary manipulation in patients with hypocitraturic nephrolithiasis. *J Urol.* 2007; 177(4): 1358–1362.
15. Mizrahi, Shapira, Domb, Houri-Haddad. Citrus oil and MgCl2 as antibacterial and anti-inflammatory agents. *J* 2006; 77(6): 963–968.
16. Kulkarni, Kothekar, Mateenuddin. Study of anti-fertility effect of lemon seeds (*Citrus limonum*) in female albino mice. *Indian* 2005; 49(3): 305–312.
17. Kawaguchi, Maruyama, Kometani, Kumazawa. Suppression of collagen-induced arthritis by oral administration of the citrus flavonoid hesperidin. *Planta* 2006; 72(5): 477–479.
18. Hosseinimehr, Nemati. Radioprotective effects of hesperidin against gamma irradiation in mouse bone marrow cells. *Br* 2006; 79(941): 415–418.

Clove/*Qaranful*

FAMILY: Myrtaceae

BOTANICAL NAME: *Syzygium aromaticum*

COMMON NAMES: *English* Clove; *French* Clou; *Spanish* Clavo de olor; *German* Gewürznelke, Nelke, Brutzwiebel, Gewürznelkenbaum, Nebenzwiebel (des Knoblauchs, Schnittlauchs), Knoblauchzehe; *Urdu/Unānī* Qaranful, Laung; *Modern Standard Arabic* al-Qaranful

SAFETY RATING: GENERALLY SAFE Cloves are generally considered safe when used as directed. They should not, however, be taken in combination with anticoagulants or with aminopyrine. Cloves should not be used when constipation is present, nor should they be consumed during pregnancy.

PROPHETIC PRESCRIPTION: A man was struck with the bad wind (*al-rīḥ al-khabīthah*) which pulled down his face and eyes to one side, symptoms which arise with Bells' palsy, a condition caused by brain tumors, strokes, and Lyme disease. When it was mentioned to Imām Muḥammad al-Taqī, he said,

> Take five *mithqāl* [4.25 grams] of cloves and put it in a dry bottle. Close the lid tightly and coat it with clay and place it in the sun for one day in the summer or two days in the winter. Then take out the cloves and grind it until fine. Mix it with rainwater until it becomes a thick liquid. Let him lie on his back and coat the ground clove on the side of the face that is pulled down. Let him remain lying down until the clove mixture dries. When it dries, Allāh will remove it from him and restore him to his best condition, Allāh, the Exalted, willing.

The stricken man was treated as instructed and was restored to the best of health.[1]

ISSUES IN IDENTIFICATION: It is the consensus that *qaranful* is the Arabic for cloves. For Said, the term refers to *Syzygium aromaticum*.[2] Hans Wehr identifies it simply as clove. According to Ghazanfar, *Syzygium aromaticum* is known in Yemeni as *zīrr*.[3] Although they are commonly used in Arabia for medicinal purposes and for cookery, cloves do not grow in Arabia. They have been imported to Arabia from Zanzibar and India since ancient times. According to Dīnawarī, *qaranful* came from China, as it does not grow in Arabia.

PROPERTIES AND USES: *Syzgium aromaticum*, known commonly as black cloves, are the aromatic dried flower buds of a tree in the family Myrtaceae. They are stimulant, stomachic, carminative, antiemetic, aromatic, antispasmodic, anti-inflammatory, antimicrobial, antifungal, rubefacient, germicide, analgesic and antiseptic. The main component in the essential oil extracted from cloves is eugeneol, responsible for the clove's aroma, and having pronounced antiseptic and anesthetic properties. Black cloves increase temperature, circulation, digestion, and nutrition, and are used to stimulate and disinfect the kidneys, skin, liver, and bronchi. Internally, black cloves are used to treat nausea, vomiting, flatulence, colic, and indigestion. They are also combined with other herbs as a stomachic, and carminative. Externally, they are used for rheumatism and neuralgia. The essential oil of black cloves is used locally to treat toothaches, inflammations of the mouth, throat, and pharyngeal mucosa. In dentistry, it is used as a local analgesic and antiseptic. As a poultice, cloves are applied to the nape of the neck for infantile convulsions. According to Ghazanfar, Arabs employ cloves for coughs, as a digestive, carminative, to regulate menstruation, and for treating toothache.[4]

SCIENTIFIC STUDIES: *Antileishmanial and antifungal activity* In a study conducted by the Universidade Federal de Juiz de Fora in Brazil, the antileishmanial and antifungal activity of 24 methanol extracts from 20 plants were evaluated against promastigotes forms of two species of Leishmania (*L. amazonensis* and *L. chagasi*) and two yeasts (*Candida albicans* and *Cryptococcus neoformans*). Among the 20 tested methanolic extracts, *Syzygium cumini* exhibited the best activity against *C. neoformans.*[5]

Antiallergenic Activity In a study conducted by the Instituto de Tecnologia em Farmacos, the aqueous leaf extract of *Syzygium cumini* skeels was found to be antiallergic, and antiedematogenic.[6]

Antimicrobial Activity According to a study conducted by Loyola College in India, the antimicrobial activity of 18 ethnomedicinal plant extracts were evaluated against nine bacterial strains (*Bacillus subtilis, Staphylococcus aureus, Staphylococcus epidermidis, Enterococcus faecalis, Escherichia coli, Klebsiella pneumonia, Pseudomonas aeruginosa, Ervinia* spp., *Proteus vulgaris*) and one fungal strain (*Candida albicans*). The results indicated that out of 18 plants, 10 plants exhibited antimicrobial activity against one or more of the tested microorganisms. Among the plants tested, *Syzygium lineare* was one of the most active, showing its potential as a new source for antimicrobial agents.[7] Further studies have also demonstrated the antimicrobial activity of clove oil.[8]

Antioxidative Activity In a study conducted by the University of Vienna, the antioxidative activity of a commercial rectified clove leaf essential oil and its main constituent eugenol was tested. The essential oil from clove demonstrated scavenging activity as well as a significant inhibitory effect against hydroxyl radicals and acted as an iron chelator. With respect to the lipid peroxidation, the inhibitory activity of clove oil determined using a linoleic acid emulsion system indicated a higher antioxidative activity than the standard BHT.[9]

Chemopreventive Activity In a 26-week controlled animal trial conducted by the Chittarajan National Cancer Institute in India, the chemopreventive potential of aqueous infusion of clove was examined in induced lung carcinogenesis. Significant reduction in the number of proliferating cells and an increased number of apoptotic cells was also noted in lung lesions following clove treatment. The observations signify the chemopreventive potential of clove in view of its apoptogenic and antiproliferative properties.[10]

Antidiabetic Activity In a 28-day double-blind, double-dummy, randomized human clinical trial conducted by the Universidade Federal do Rio Grande do Sul in Brazil, a tea prepared from the leaves of *Syzygium cumini* skeels was found to have no hypoglycemic effect.[11]

Anti-Hyperglycemic Activity According to an animal trial conducted by the University of the Philippines, *Syzygium cumini* exhibits anti-hyperglycemic activity when fed simultaneously with glucose. At the same dosages of 5 mg/20 g per mouse, *Syzygium cumini*–treated mice showed a significant decrease in blood glucose levels.[12]

Anticarcinogenic Activity In an animal study conducted by Chittarajan National Cancer Institute in India, the chemopreventive action of aqueous infusion of cloves on induced skin carcinogenesis was assessed. The results indicated protection against skin papilloma formation in a dose dependent manner. It was shown that oral administration of aqueous infusions of clove not only delays the formation of papilloma but also reduces the incidence of papilloma as well as the cumulative number of papillomas per papilloma bearing mouse. These observations suggest a promising role for cloves in restriction of the carcinogenesis process.[13]

Antibacterial Activity In a study conducted by S & B Foods Inc., in Japan, the effect of a clove (*Syzygium aromaticum*) on *Candida albicans* growth was examined. When the clove preparation was administered into the oral cavity of candida-infected mice, their oral symptoms were improved and the number of viable candida cells in the cavity was reduced. In contrast, when the clove preparation was administered intragastrically, oral symptoms were not improved, but viable cell numbers of candida in the stomach and feces were decreased. These findings demonstrate that oral intake of clove may suppress candida cells.[14]

Antibacterial Activity According to a study conducted by Calicut University in India, the leaf essential oils of *Syzygium cumini* was shown to have a good antibacterial effect, while that of *Syzygium travancoricum* was moderate.[15]

Aphrodisiacal Activity In a controlled animal study conducted by Aligarh Muslim University in India, 50 percent ethanolic extract of clove produced a significant and sustained increase in the sexual activity of normal male rats, without any conspicuous gastric ulceration and adverse effects. The resultant aphrodisiac effectiveness of the extract lends support to the claims for its traditional usage in sexual disorders.[16]

Anticarcinogenic Activity According to an in-vitro study conducted by Mahidol University in Thailand, *Syzygium aromaticum* (leaf) inhibits the growth of *Helicobacter pylori*. This data indicates that the plant may have chemopreventative activities and may partly explain the reduced incidence of gastric cancer in Thailand.[17]

Anti-inflammatory Activity In an animal study conducted by the Indian Veterinary Research Institute in India, the ethanolic extract of the bark of *Syzygium cumini* showed potent anti-inflammatory action against different phases of inflammation without any side effect on gastric mucosa.[18]

Antihepatitic Activity In an in vitro study conducted by the Toyama Medical and Pharmaceutical University in Japan, water extracts of *Syzygium aromaticum* were the most active in inhibiting the hepatitis C virus.[19]

Antiparasitic Activity According to a study conducted by the Instituto Oswaldo Cruz in Brazil, the essential oil of clove (*Syzygium aromaticum* L.) is most effective in inhibiting parasite growth.[20]

Antiherpetic Activity Clove oil increases the effectiveness of acyclovir, a drug used to treat herpes.[21]

Anti-HIV Activity According to a study conducted by the University of North Carolina at Chapel Hill, oleanolic acid from *Syzygium claviflorum* (leaves) inhibits HIV-1 replication in acutely infected H9 cells, as well as H9 cell growth. The study demonstrated that derivatives of betulinic acid, isolated from the leaves of *S. claviflorum* as an anti–HIV principle, exhibited extremely potent anti–HIV activity. Among the oleanolic acid derivatives, 18 demonstrated the most potent anti–HIV activity.[22]

Clove Notes

1. Nisābūrī A. *Islamic Medical Wisdom: The Ṭibb al-a'immah*. Trans. B. Ispahany. Ed. AJ Newman. London: Muḥammadī Trust, 1991: 85–86.
2. Bīrūnī, AR al-. *al-Bīrūnī's Book on Pharmacy and Materia Medica*. Ed. and trans. HM Said. Karachi: Hamdard National Foundation, 1973.
3. Ghazanfar SA. *Handbook of Arabian Medicinal Plants*. Boca Raton: CRC Press, 1994.
4. Ghazanfar SA. *Handbook of Arabian Medicinal Plants*. Boca Raton: CRC Press, 1994.
5. Braga, Bouzada, Fabri, de, Moreira, Scio, Coimbra. Antileishmanial and antifungal activity of plants used in traditional medicine in Brazil. *J Ethnopharmacol.* 2007; 111(2): 396–402.
6. Brito, Lima, Ramos, Nakamura, Cavalher-Machado, Siani, Henriques, Sampaio. Pharmacological study of anti-allergenic activity of *Syzygium cumini* (L.) Skeels. *Braz J Med Biol Res.* 2007; 40(1): 105–115.
7. Duraipandiyan, Ayyanar, Ignacimuthu. Antimicrobial activity of some ethnomedicinal plants used by Paliyar tribe from Tamil Nadu, India. *BMC Complement Altern Med.* 2006; 6: 35.
8. Briozzo J, et al. Antimicrobial activity of clove oil dispersed in a concentrated sugar solution. *Journal of Applied Bacteriology* 1989; 66: 69–75.
9. Jirovetz, Buchbauer, Stoilova, Stoyanova, Krastanov, Schmidt. Chemical composition and antioxidant properties of clove leaf essential oil. *J Agric Food Chem.* 2006; 54(17): 6303–6307.
10. Banerjee, Panda, Das. Clove (*Syzygium aromaticum* L.), a potential chemopreventive agent for lung cancer. *Carcinogenesis.* 2006; 27(8): 1645–1654.
11. Teixeira, Fuchs, Weinert, Esteves. The efficacy of folk medicines in the management of type 2 diabetes mellitus: results of a randomized controlled trial of *Syzygium cumini* (L.) Skeels. *J Clin Pharm Ther.* 2006; 31(1): 1–5.
12. Villasenor, Lamadrid. Comparative anti-hyperglycemic potentials of medicinal plants. *J Ethnopharmacol.* 2006; 104(1–2): 129–131.
13. Banerjee, Das. Anticarcinogenic effects of an aqueous infusion of cloves on skin carcinogenesis. *Asian* 2005; 6(3): 304–308.
14. Taguchi, Ishibashi, Takizawa, Inoue, Yamaguchi, Abe. Protection of oral or intestinal candidiasis in mice by oral or intragastric administration of herbal food, clove (*Syzygium aromaticum*). *Nippon* 2005; 46(1): 27–33.
15. Shafi, Rosamma, Jamil, Reddy. Antibacterial activity of *Syzygium cumini* and *Syzygium travancoricum* leaf essential oils. *Fitoterapia.* 2002; 73(5): 414–416.
16. Tajuddin, Ahmad S, Latif, Qasmi. Effect of 50 percent ethanolic extract of *Syzygium aromaticum* (L.) Merr. & Perry. (clove) on sexual behavior of normal male rats. *BMC Complement Altern Med.* 2004; 4: 17.
17. Bhamarapravati, Pendland, Mahady. Extracts of spice and food plants from Thai traditional medicine inhibit the growth of the human carcinogen *Helicobacter pylori*. *In* 2003; 17(6): 541–544.
18. Muruganandan, Srinivasan, Chandra, Tandan, Lal, Raviprakash. Anti-inflammatory activity of *Syzygium cumini* bark. *Fitoterapia.* 2001; 72(4): 369–375.
19. Hussein, Miyashiro, Nakamura, Hattori, Kakiuchi, Shimotohno. Inhibitory effects of Sudanese medicinal plant extracts on hepatitis C virus (HCV) protease. *Phytother* 2000; 14(7): 510–516.
20. Santoro, Cardoso, Guimaraes, Mendonca, Soares. *Trypanosoma cruzi*: Activity of essential oils from *Achillea millefolium* L., *Syzygium aromaticum* L. and *Ocimum basilicum* L. on epimastigotes and trypomastigotes. *Exp* 2007; 116(3): 283–290.
21. Balch PA. *Prescription for herbal healing*. New York: Avery, 2002; Kurokawa M, Nagasaka K, Hirabayashi T, et al. Efficacy of traditional herbal medicines in combination with Acyclovir against herpes simplex virus type I infection in vitro and in vivo. *Antiviral Research* 1995; 27(1–2): 19–37.
22. Kashiwada, Wang, Nagao, Kitanaka, Yasuda, Fujioka, Yamagishi, Cosentino, Kozuka, Okabe, Ikeshiro, Hu, Yeh, Lee. Anti-AIDS agents. 30. Anti-HIV activity of oleanolic acid, pomolic acid, and structurally related triterpenoids. *J* 1998; 61(9): 1090–1095.

Colocynth/*Ḥanẓal*

Family: Cucurbitaceae

Botanical Name: *Citrullus colocynthis*

Common Names: *English* Colocynth, Bitter apple, Bitter gourd, Bitter cucumber, Egusi, Vine of Sodom; *French* Coloquinte, Chicotin; *Spanish* Manzana silvestre, Sandía amarga, Coloquíntida; *German* Bitterzitrulle, Bitterapfel, Koloquinthe; *Urdu/Unānī* Hanzal, Indrayin, Kharpaza talkh, Tumma; *Modern Standard Arabic* Ḥanẓal, Marāratu al-ṣaḥārī, Ḥadaj, 'Alqam

SAFETY RATING: DANGEROUS TO DEADLY A traditional food plant in Africa, it is claimed that colocynth is safe when consumed in moderation. In reality, colocynth is a poisonous gourd which is unsafe for use and was banned by the Food and Drug Administration in 1991. Even when consumed in very small amounts, colocynth can cause severe irritation of the stomach and intestinal lining, bloody diarrhea, kidney damage, bloody urine, and inability to urinate. In toxic amounts (600–1000 mg), it can cause sharp, violent pain in the bowels, toxic acute colitis, hematochezia, and dangerous inflammation. Lethal doses (as low as 2 mg) lead to convulsions, paralysis, and possibly death due to circulatory collapse. As both food and medicine, the seed, and particularly the poisonous pulp of colocynth, should be strongly discouraged if not prohibited. It should never be administered to pregnant women, nor should it be used as a vaginal suppository to induce an abortion.

PROPHETIC PRESCRIPTION: The Messenger of Allāh said, "The sinner (*fājir*) who does not read the Qur'ān resembles the colocynth (*ḥanẓal*). It has no smell, and tastes bitter."[1]

ISSUES IN IDENTIFICATION: It is the consensus that *ḥanẓal* is Arabic for colocynth. According to Abū Nu'aym al-Iṣbahānī, the plant is also known as *shariyān*.[2] Bīrūnī mentions that *ḥanẓal* is also known as *qūlūfunṭās, qara', ḥadaj, al-sharā, 'alqam,* and *ṣāb*. Said identifies the plant as *Citrullus colocynthis*.[3] As Nehmé explains, *Citrullus* is *sitrullūs* and *Citrullus colocynthis* is *ḥanẓal* and *'alqam* in Modern Standard Arabic.[4] The fruit of this very bitter plant is known as *tuffāḥ murr* or "bitter apple."

As Ghazanfar explains, *Citrullus colocynthis* is found throughout Arabia on sandy, silty, and gravelly grounds.[5] According to Mandaville, *Citrullus colocynthis* is common in the same type of terrain in eastern Saudi Arabia, especially in wadis. It is known as *sharī* in the south and as *ḥanẓal* in the north. According to Chaudhary, *Citrullus colocynthis* is known as *ḥanẓal* and *sharī* in Saudi Arabic. It is native to tropical and subtropical Africa, the Middle East, Pakistan, and India. In Australia and elsewhere, it was nonnative and was introduced. In its native Saudi Arabian soil, it is widely distributed, especially in wadis and areas receiving rainwater run-off.[6]

PROPERTIES AND USES: *Citrullus colocynthis* is a drastic hydragogue, cathartic, hepatic stimulant, diuretic, and abortifacient. It is considered a bitter in small doses, and an emetic in large doses. Colocynth is an irritant and cathartic poison which causes violent episodes of the gripe, and dangerous bowel movements producing copious watery evacuations. The pulp and seeds of the fruit are strongly laxative and, in excessive doses, poisonous.[7] Even moderate doses can inflame the mucous membranes of the intestines, causing vomiting, severe tormina, and bloody stools. Except in minute doses, it is never used alone, being combined with other herbs to counter its harsh and griping effects. The purgative action is so drastic that it has caused fatalities. Colocynth was used to treat gonorrhea, stomach and intestinal disorders, neuralgic pains of the viscera, dyspepsia, chronic diarrhea, dysentery, constipation, headaches, as well as many other ailments. According to Ghazanfar, Arabs employ colocynth leaves, seeds, roots, and dried fruits, to treat dog, insect, and snake bites, as a laxative, to relieve pain in joints, and as a hair colorant.[8] In the event of poisoning, the stomach should be evacuated, followed by oral or rectal administration of opium tincture, followed by the administration of stimulating and mucilaginous beverages.

SCIENTIFIC STUDIES: *Anticancer Activity* According to research conducted by Bar-Ilan University in Israel, cucurbitacin glucosides isolated from *C. colocynthis* might have therapeutic value against breast cancer cells.[9]

Antidiabetic Activity According to an animal study conducted by the United Arab Emirates University, the oral administration of the aqueous extract of the *C. colocynthis* can ameliorate some of the toxic effects of streptozotocin.[10] According to an animal study conducted by the University of Basra in Iraq, the aqueous extract of *C. colocynthis* rind possesses a hypoglycaemic effect and its hypoglycaemic action could be attributed to the presence of saponin in addition to the presence of glycosidic components.[11]

Colocynth Notes

1. Bukhārī M. *Ṣaḥīḥ al-Bukhārī*. al-Riyyāḍ: Bayt al-Afkār, 1998; Iṣbahānī AN al-. *Mawsū'at al-ṭibb al-nabawī*. Ed. MKD al-Turkī. Bayrūt, Lubnān: Dār Ibn Ḥazm, 2006.
2. Iṣbahānī AN al-. *Mawsū'at al-ṭibb al-nabawī*. Ed. MKD al-Turkī. Bayrūt, Lubnān: Dār Ibn Ḥazm, 2006.
3. Bīrūnī, AR al-. *al-Bīrūnī's Book on Pharmacy and Materia Medica*. Ed. and trans. HM Said. Karachi: Hamdard National Foundation, 1973.
4. Nehmé M. *Dictionnaire étymologique de la flore du Liban*. Bayrūt: Librairie du Liban, 2000.
5. Ghazanfar SA. *Handbook of Arabian Medicinal Plants*. Boca Raton: CRC Press, 1994.
6. Chaudhary SA. *Flora of the Kingdom of Saudi Arabia*. al-Riyyāḍ: Ministry of Agriculture and Water, 1999.
7. Mandaville JP. *Flora of Eastern Saudi Arabia*. London: Kegan Paul, 1990.
8. Ghazanfar SA. *Handbook of Arabian Medicinal Plants*. Boca Raton: CRC Press, 1994.
9. Tannin-Spitz, Grossman, Dovrat, Gottlieb, Bergman. Growth inhibitory activity of cucurbitacin glucosides isolated

from *Citrullus colocynthis* on human breast cancer cells. *Biochem* 2007; 73(1): 56–67.

10. Al-Ghaithi, El-Ridi, Adeghate, Amiri. Biochemical effects of Citrullus colocynthis in normal and diabetic rats. *Mol* 2004; 261(1–2): 143–149.

11. Abdel-Hassan, Abdel-Barry, Tariq. The hypoglycaemic and antihyperglycaemic effect of *Citrullus colocynthis* fruit aqueous extract in normal and alloxan diabetic rabbits *J* 2000; 71(1–2): 325–330.

Coriander / *Kuzbarah*

Family: Apiaceae

Botanical Name: *Coriandrum sativum*

Common Names: *English* Coriander, cilantro, Chinese parsley; *French* Coriandre; *Spanish* Culantro, Cilandro; *German* Echter Koriander; *Urdu/Unānī* Kashneez, Dhaniya, Kuzbarah; *Modern Standard Arabic* Kuzbarah, Kusburah, Qalantarah, al-Nakud, al-Naqrah

Safety Rating: Generally Safe Coriander is generally considered safe for most people. The juice of the plant, however, is considered an intoxicant. According to some herbalists, the continuous use of the herb can cause temporary sexual insufficiency. In moist situations, the leaves may harbor *Listeria*.

Prophetic Prescription: A woman wrote to Imām 'Alī al-Riḍā complaining of the continuous flow of blood. He wrote to her, "Take one handful of coriander (*kuzbarah*) and one of sumac (*summāq*) and soak it for one night in the open air. Then put it on the fire and sieve it. Drink a saucer of it and the blood will cease, Allāh, the Exalted, willing."[1]

Issues in Identification: It is the consensus that *kuzbarah* is Arabic for coriander. According to Bīrūnī, the word is spelled both *kuzbarah* and *kusbarah*. As Said says, it refers to *Coriandrum sativum* L.[2] As Nehmé explains, *Coriandrum* is *kuzbarah* in Arabic, and *C. sativum* is *kuzbarah zirā'iyyah*.[3] According to Hans Wehr, *tabal* is the botanical term for coriander and also has the general sense of spice, condiment, and seasoning.

Coriander does not grow in the desert. It does, however, grow in irrigated deserts in Egypt. As Mandaville explains, coriander is only found as a rare escape along roadsides or on other disturbed ground in eastern Saudi Arabia. It is known as *kuzbarah* in Saudi Arabic. It is also pronounced as *kozbrah*, *kazbarah*, and *khazbarah*, and is sometimes cultivated in oasis gardens.[4]

Properties and Uses: *Coriandrum sativum*, known commonly as coriander and cilantro, is an aromatic, expectorant, carminative, stimulant, stomachic, antibilious, tonic, diuretic, antiseptic, and stomachic herb which is rich in volatile oils. Coriander seeds act mainly on the digestive system, stimulating the appetite by increasing the secretion of gastric juices, relieving irritation, flatulence and indigestion. The seeds reduce griping in laxative preparations. Coriander is used to treat arthritis, dyspepsia, flatulence, vomiting, rheumatism, neuralgia, bleeding piles, pinworms, tapeworms, and other worm infections. It is also used as an ingredient in some creams, lotions, and perfumes. A poultice of bruised seeds relieves painful joints, ulcers, carbuncles, rheumatism and neuralgia. An infusion of the seeds is also used as an eye-wash.

Scientific Studies: *Antibacterial Activity* Research has confirmed that coriander seed oil is both fungicidal and bactericidal.[5]

Anxiolytic Activity Research has confirmed that coriander acts as an anxiolytic.[6] Coriander may therefore prove useful in the treatment of anxiety, or anxiety disorders.

Coriander Notes

1. Nisābūrī A. *Islamic Medical Wisdom: The Ṭibb al-a'immah*. Trans. B. Ispahany. Ed. AJ Newman. London: Muḥammadī Trust, 1991: 130.

2. Bīrūnī, AR al-. *al-Bīrūnī's Book on Pharmacy and Materia Medica*. Ed. and trans. HM Said. Karachi: Hamdard National Foundation, 1973.

3. Nehmé M. *Dictionnaire étymologique de la flore du Liban*. Bayrūt: Librairie du Liban, 2000.

4. Mandaville JP. *Flora of Eastern Saudi Arabia*. London: Kegan Paul, 1990.

5. Lo, Iacobellis, De, Capasso, Senatore. Antibacterial activity of *Coriandrum sativum* L. and *Foeniculum vulgare* Miller var. *vulgare* essential oils. *J* 2004; 52(26): 7862–7866.

6. Emamghoreishi, Khasaki M, Aazam. *Coriandrum sativum*: an evaluation of its anxiolytic effect in the elevated plus-maze. *J* 2005; 96(3): 365–370.

Costus / *Qusṭ, Kust*

Family: Asteraceae

Botanical Name: *Saussurea lappa*

Common Names: *English* Costus; *French* Costus; *Spanish* Costus, Costo; *German* Costus, Kostwurz; *Urdu/Unānī* Qust, Koth, Kuth; *Modern Standard Arabic* Qusṭ, Kusṭ, Kust

Safety Rating: Generally Safe to Dangerous *Saussurea lappa* is generally considered safe when used as directed under the supervision of an expert. When smoked, however, it causes narcotic effects. It is imperative that the costus consumed be pure, as it often contains a contaminant called aristocholic acid, which damages the kidneys and causes cancer. Individuals who are allergic to plants and herbs in the Asteraceae family, which includes daisies, ragweed, chrysanthemums, marigolds, and many others, should not consume costus.

Prophetic Prescription: During his ascent into Heaven (*mi'rāj*), the Prophet Muḥammad was told by the angels, "The best treatment you have is cupping and sea costus (*qusṭ al-baḥrī*)."[1] In the version related by Chaghhaynī, black seed is also included.[2] The Messenger of Allāh also said, "It is very good to be treated with ... costus (*qusṭ*)."[3] He also said, "Accept being treated with costus (*qusṭ*) because it has many benefits."[4] According to Imām 'Alī ibn Abī Ṭālib, the Messenger of Allāh said, "You have costus (*kust*) which contains seven remedies: administered by mouth it is useful against pleurisy and heart pain; administered by nose, it is effective against *al-'udra* and headaches; and as an incense it is effective against the cold." Imām 'Alī allegedly did not remember the two other diseases.[5] It is also reported that the Messenger of Allāh allowed women to use a little costus (*qusṭ*) when they did their ritual ablutions after menstruation.[6]

Issues in Identification: According to Bīrūnī, the plant is known as *qusṭ*, *kust*, and *kusṭ*. As Said says, it refers to *Saussurea lappa*.[7] Abū Dawūd, Sūyūṭī, Ibn Ḥabīb, Thomson, Farooqi, and Akīlī all assert that *'ūd al-hindī* is also known as *kust al-hindī* and *qusṭ al-hindī*.[8] As we have explained in the section on aloeswood, it is important to distinguish between *'ūd al-hindī*, which is aloeswood, and *qusṭ*, which is costus. As Miki explains in *Index of the Arab Herbalist's Materials*, white or sea-costus is *Hyacinthus* while Indian costus is *Saussurea lappa*.[9] According to modern incense traders, there are two types of costus root: *Costus arabicus*, and *Saussurea lappa*. Álvarez de Morales and Girón Irueste are correct in identifying *kust* as *Aucklandia costus* Falc., which is the same as *Saussurea Lappa* L.[10]

Properties and Uses: *Saussurea lappa*, known commonly as costus, is a bitter, pungent, anthelmintic, antiseptic, aphrodisiac, astringent, antispasmodic, alterative, aromatic, anodyne, bronchodilator, carminative, diuretic, expectorant, prophylactic, stimulant warming herb that relaxes spasms, lowers blood pressure, relieves pain, and has antibacterial and antifungal effects.[11]

Costus is used as a treatment for numerous diseases, including pleurisy, the swelling and inflammation of the pleura, which is the moist, double-layered membrane that surrounds the lungs and lines the rib cage. Costus also acts to dilate the lungs, assist expectoration, relax spasms, and relieve pain while exerting a general mild tonic effect. Internally, *Saussurea lappa* is indicated for abdominal distention and pain, chest pains due to liver problems and jaundice, gall bladder pain, constipation associated with energy stagnation, and asthma. It is also used for digestive problems, cough, asthma, cholera, dyspepsia, edema, skin diseases, jaundice, rheumatism, fever, gout, sciatica, malaria, hiccup, bronchitis, and leprosy. The Ethiopians have used costus since ancient times to destroy both types of tapeworm: the *Taenia solium* and *Bothriocephalus latus*. However, as it possesses little cathartic power, the subsequent administration of a purgative is generally necessary to bring away the destroyed entozoan. *Saussurea lappa* is also used as an alterative in wounds, skin diseases, tumors and rheumatism. Al-Kindī used costus to treat the kidney and the bladder.[12]

Scientific Studies: *Antifungal and Antibacterial Activity* In a study conducted by the Universiti Putra Malaysia, dichloromethane and methanol extracts of several species of costus were screened for antimicrobial and antioxidant activities.[13] Most of the extracts were found to be antibacterial, with *Costus discolor* showing very potent antifungal activity against only *Aspergillus ochraceous*.

Antioxidative Activity A recent study conducted by the National Botanical Research Institute in India seems to confirm the antioxidative activity of *Saussurea costus* and its ability to scavenge DPPH, nitric oxide, and superoxide radicals along with its ability to inhibit lipid peroxidation and GSH oxidation.[14] According to a study conducted by the Universiti Putra Malaysia in Selangor, the antioxidative activity of *Costus discolor* is comparable to that of alpha-tocopherol.[15]

Antidiabetic Activity In an animal study conducted by the University of Dhaka in Bangladesh, the rhizome of *Costus speciosus* was found to have interesting possibilities as a source of oral hypoglycemic agents.[16]

Antiurolithiatic Activity In Brazilian folk medicine, *Costus spiralis* is used in urinary affections and for expelling urinary stones, uses which have been scientifically corroborated by the Universidade Federal de Sao Paulo, where antiurolithiatic activity of the water extract of *Costus spiralis* Roscoe was tested on formation of calculi on implants of calcium oxalate crystals or zinc disc in the urinary bladder of rats.[17] Implantation of the foreign body in the urinary bladder of adult rats induced formation of urinary stones and hypertrophy of the smooth musculature. The oral treatment with the extract of *Costus spiralis* Roscoe four weeks after surgery reduced the growth of calculi. It did not, however, prevent hypertrophy of the organ's smooth musculature. The results indicate that the extract of *Costus spiralis* Roscoe is endowed with antiurolithiatic activity, thus confirming the folk information. The effect, however, was unrelated to increased diuresis or to a change of the muscarinic receptor affinity of the bladder's smooth musculature to cholinergic ligands.

Anticancer Activity Pharmacological and clinical research has shown that alkaloids from *Radix saussurea* have antispasmodic, bronchodilatory, and blood pressure-lowering effects. Extracts of *Saussurea laniceps*, commonly known as snow lotus, a rare plant found only above the 3,500 meter altitude region in the Himalaya and southwest China, have recently been studied as a possible cancer-fighting agents. In a Japanese study, an injection of 3 percent of costus root oil was found to inhibit tumor growth in mice.[18] Histological findings of the skin indicated that the costus root oil caused an accumulation of lymphoid cells. In theory, if the delayed hypersensitivity reaction caused by the costus root oil were to be used as a means of aggregating lymphoid cells, these cells would attack cancer cells in a nonspecific manner. Consequently it is anticipated that costus root oil will be quite promising as a non-specific agent for cancer immunotherapy.

Costus Notes

1. Bukhārī M. *Ṣaḥīḥ al-Bukhārī*. al-Riyyāḍ: Bayt al-Afkār, 1998; Tirmidhī M. *al-Jāmi' al-ṣaḥīḥ*. al-Qāhirah: Muṣṭafā al-Bābī al-Ḥalabī, [1937-]; Nasā'ī A. *Sunan al-Nisā'ī*. al-Qāhirah: Muṣṭafā al-Bābī al-Ḥalabī, 1964-65; Ibn Anas M. *al-Muwaṭṭa'*. Bayrūt: Dār al-Gharb, 1999.
2. Chaghhaynī M. *Ṭibb al-nabī*. Trans. C Elgood. *Osiris* 1962; 14: 191.
3. Bukhārī M. *Ṣaḥīḥ al-Bukhārī*. al-Riyyāḍ: Bayt al-Afkār, 1998.
4. Sūyūṭī J. *As-Sūyūṭī's Medicine of the Prophet*. Ed. A Thomson. London: Ṭā-Hā Publishers, 1994: 86.
5. Ibn Ḥabīb A. *Mujtaṣar fī al-ṭibb/Compendio de medicina*. Ed. C Álvarez de Morales and F Girón Irueste. Madrid: Consejo Superior de Investigaciones Científicas, 1992: 78/45.
6. Sūyūṭī J. *As-Sūyūṭī's Medicine of the Prophet*. Ed. A Thomson. London: Ṭā-Hā Publishers, 1994: 77.
7. Bīrūnī, AR al-. *al-Bīrūnī's Book on Pharmacy and Materia Medica*. Ed. and trans. HM Said. Karachi: Hamdard National Foundation, 1973.
8. Abū Dāwūd S. *Ṣaḥīḥ Sunan Abū Dāwūd*. Riyyāḍ: Maktab al-Tarbiyyah, 1989; Sūyūṭī J. *As-Sūyūṭī's Medicine of the Prophet*. Ed. A Thomson. London: Ṭā-Hā Publishers, 1994; Ibn Ḥabīb A. *Mujtaṣar fī al-ṭibb/Compendio de medicina*. Ed. C Álvarez de Morales and F Girón Irueste. Madrid: Consejo Superior de Investigaciones Científicas, 1992; Ibn al-Qayyim al-Jawziyyah. *Natural Healing with the Medicine of the Prophet*. Pearl Publishing. Trans. M al-Akīlī. Philadelphia, 1993; Farooqi MIH. *Medicinal Plants in the Traditions of Prophet Muḥammad*. Lucknow: Sidrah Publishers, 1998.
9. Miki W. *Index of the Arab Herbalist's Materials*. Tokyo: Institute for the Study of Languages and Cultures of Asia and Africa, 1976.
10. Ibn Ḥabīb A. *Mujtaṣar fī al-ṭibb/Compendio de medicina*. Ed. C Álvarez de Morales and F Girón Irueste. Madrid: Consejo Superior de Investigaciones Científicas, 1992.
11. Bown D. *Encyclopedia of Herbs and Their Uses*. Westmount: RD Press, 1995: 350.
12. Levey M, al-Khaledy N, eds. *The Medical Formulary of al-Samarqandī*. Philadelphia: University of Pennsylvania Press, 1967: 199, note 223.
13. Habsah, Amran M, Mackeen, Lajis, Kikuzaki, Nakatani, Rahman, Ghafar, Ali. Screening of *Zingiberaceae* extracts for antimicrobial and antioxidant activities. *J* 2000; 72(3): 403–410.
14. Pandey, Govindarajan, Rawat, Pushpangadan. Free radical scavenging potential of *Saussurea costus*. *Acta Pharm*. 2005; 55(3): 297–304.
15. Habsah, Amran, Mackeen, Lajis, Kikuzaki, Nakatani, Rahman, Ghafar, Ali. Screening of *Zingiberaceae* extracts for antimicrobial and antioxidant activities. *J* 2000; 72(3): 403–10.
16. Nandi. Hypoglycemic effects of three plants from eastern Himalayan belt. *Diabetes* 1994; 26(3): 127–38.
17. Araujo, Diogo, da, Riggio, Lapa, Souccar. Evaluation of the antiurolithiatic activity of the extract of *Costus spiralis* Roscoe in rats. *J* 1999; 66(2): 193–8.
18. Takanami, Ikeda, Nakayama. [Effects of costus oil in murine tumors]. *Gan* 1987; 14(7): 2276–2279.

Cucumber/*Khiyyār, Qithā'*

Family: Cucurbitaceae

Botanical Name: *Cucumis sativus*

Common Names: *English* Cucumber, Garden cucumber; *French* Concombre, concombre; *Spanish* Pepino; *German* Schlangengurke; *Urdu/Unānī* Khiyar, Khira; *Modern Standard Arabic* Qithā', Faqqūṣ, Khiyyār

Safety Rating: Generally Safe Cucumbers are generally considered safe for most people.

Prophetic Prescription: The *qithā'* or cucumber is mentioned in the Qur'ān in the context of the Exodus (2:61). It is reported that the Messenger of Allāh used to eat cucumber (*qithā'*) with fresh ripe dates (*ruṭab*).[1] It is related that he said, "When you eat cucumber, begin to eat from the end."[2]

Imām Ja'far al-Ṣādiq prescribed cucumber for pain of the bladder and urethra, saying "Take cucumber and peel it. Cook its peel in water with the roots of endive (*al-hindibā'*). Then strain it and pour lump sugar over it. Drink one *raṭl* [approximately 14.3 ounces] of it every day before breakfast for three days. It is good, tried, and beneficial, Allāh, the Exalted, willing."[3]

It is related that Imām 'Alī al-Riḍā prescribed cucumber for the treatment of jaundice saying, "Take cucumber and peel it. Cook the peel in water and drink one *raṭl* of it every day for three days, on an empty stomach."[4] In another tradition, Imām 'Alī al-Riḍā recommended cucumber to treat the cold. As he explained, "He who fears the cold (*zukkām*) in summer, let him eat cucumber everyday and not sit under the sun."[5]

ISSUES IN IDENTIFICATION: It is the consensus that *khiyyār* and *qithā'* are Arabic for cucumber. In what must certainly be a mistake, Turkī's index indicates that *qithā'* is *Lepidium sativum*.[6] According to Bīrūnī, *khiyyār* is also known as *al-qithā'*. Said identifies it as *Cucumis melo* and *Cucumis sativis*.[7] The Prophet may have been referring to *Cucumis sativus*, the common cucumber, known in Arabic as *khiyyār* and *quithd*. Cucumbers are cultivated throughout Arabia.

The Prophet and the Imāms certainly did not mean *Cucumis melo*, as some authors have suggested, which is melon or muskmelon, known as *qāwūn* in Arabic. As Weaver explains, Medieval and Renaissance sources often equated melons with cucumbers and watermelons and, even later, with New World squash (191). In this particular case, it does not seem sensible that the Prophet and the Imāms could have prescribed people to peel, cook, and eat melon or watermelon skin.

It should be stressed that cucumbers originated in India some three thousand years ago. As Duke explains, Zohary argues that cucumbers did not exist in biblical Egypt, a claim which is hard to digest. Cucumbers were clearly mentioned by the Prophet in the 7th century. They were being cultivated in France in the 9th century, had reached England by the 14th century, and were introduced into North America in the mid–16th century. As a result, the varieties of cucumbers we are familiar with in the West are modern varieties. The cucumbers which existed in the time of the Prophet must have more closely resembled some of the Asian heirloom varieties.

PROPERTIES AND USES: *Cucumis sativus* is a cooling, diuretic, sedative, aperient, antipyretic, nutrient, and alterative herb that clears and softens the skin while its seeds expel intestinal parasites. Internally, the fruit is used for blemished skin, heat rashes, thirst, insomnia, and overheating in hot weather. It is also used to treat high and low blood pressure. The ground seeds are used to treat tapeworm. Externally, it is applied for sunburn, scalds, sore eyes, and conjunctivitis. As Ghazanfar explains, Arabs use the seeds and roots of cucumbers as an emetic, emulcent, diuretic, purgative, and as a vermifuge.[8]

Cucumbers are very good sources of vitamin C and molybdenum, and a good source of vitamin A, potassium, manganese, folate, dietary fiber, tryptophan, and magnesium. Although the flesh of cucumbers is primarily composed of water, it also contains ascorbic acid and caffeic acid, both of which help soothe skin irritations and reduce swelling. The skin of the cucumber contains silica, an essential component for the health of connective tissue, which includes muscles, tendons, ligaments, cartilage, and bone. Cucumber juice is often recommended as a source of silica to improve the complexion and health of the skin. Cucumber's high water content makes it naturally hydrating. Ascorbic acid and caffeic acid prevent water retention, which may explain why cucumbers applied topically are often helpful for swollen eyes, burns, and dermatitis.

Cucumber juice is an ingredient of many natural beauty creams, cosmetics and lotions. The seeds, like celery and pumpkin seeds, are diuretic; they also have the ability to expel tapeworms from the body. According to Ibn Buṭlān, cucumbers help provoke urination.[9] As a beauty aid, slices of cucumber can be applied directly to the skin. As a diuretic, the juice is indicated in kidney ailments and rheumatic conditions. Cucumber has a long history of use in Islamic medicine. Ibn Buṭlān used cucumbers for burning fevers.[10] Samarqandī used a combination of cucumber and muskmelon to treat fever.[11] Ibn Sīnā treated tetanus in children with water in which cucumber was boiled.[12]

SCIENTIFIC STUDIES: *Antihypertensive Activity* Studies suggest that cucumbers can help people who have high blood pressure to cool down.[13] When people who participated in the "Dietary Approaches to Stop Hypertension Study" added foods high in potassium, magnesium, and fiber, their blood pressure dropped to healthier levels.[14] Those who ate a diet rich in these compounds in addition to other foods on this diet (low-fat dairy foods, seafood, lean meat, and poultry), lowered their blood pressure by 5.5 points (systolic) over 3.0 points (diastolic).

Cucumber Notes

1. Bukhārī M. *Ṣaḥīḥ al-Bukhārī*. al-Riyyāḍ: Bayt al-Afkār, 1998; Muslim. *Jāmi' al-ṣaḥīḥ*. al-Riyyāḍ: Bayt al-Afkār, 1998; Ibn Mājah M. *Sunan*. Trans. MT Anṣārī. Lahore: Kazi Publications, 1994; Tirmidhī M. *al-Jāmi' al-ṣaḥīḥ*. al-Qāhirah: Muṣṭafā al-Bābī al-Ḥalabī, [1937-].
2. Chaghhaynī M. *Ṭibb al-nabī*. Trans. C Elgood. *Osiris* 1962; 14: 190.
3. Nisābūrī A. *Islamic Medical Wisdom: The Ṭibb al-a'immah*. Trans. B. Ispahany. Ed. AJ Newman. London: Muḥammadī Trust, 1991: 93.

4. Nisābūrī A. *Islamic Medical Wisdom: The Ṭibb al-a'immah*. Trans. B. Ispahany. Ed. AJ Newman. London: Muḥammadī Trust, 1991: 88.
5. Riḍā 'A al-. *Risālah fī al-ṭibb al-nabawī*. Ed. MA Bār. Bayrūt: Dār al-Manāhil, 1991: 173.
6. Iṣbahānī AN al-. *Mawsū'at al-ṭibb al-nabawī*. Ed. MKD al-Turkī. Bayrūt: Dār Ibn Ḥazm, 2006.
7. Bīrūnī, AR al-. *al-Bīrūnī's Book on Pharmacy and Materia Medica*. Ed. and trans. HM Said. Karachi: Hamdard National Foundation, 1973.
8. Ghazanfar SA. *Handbook of Arabian Medicinal Plants*. Boca Raton: CRC Press, 1994.
9. Ibn Buṭlān, *The Medieval Health Handbook: Tacuinum sanitatis*. Ed. L Cogliati Arano. Trans. O Ratti and A Westbrook. New York: George Braziller, 1976: 141.
10. Ibn Buṭlān, *The Medieval Health Handbook: Tacuinum sanitatis*. Ed. L Cogliati Arano. Trans. O Ratti and A Westbrook. New York: George Braziller, 1976: 141.
11. Levey M, al-Khaledy N, eds. *The Medical Formulary of al-Samarqandī*. Philadelphia: University of Pennsylvania Press, 1967: 63; 173, note 31.
12. Ibn Sīnā. *The Canon of Medicine*. Ed. O. Cameron Gruner. London: Luzaz, 1930: 373.
13. Appel LJ, Moore TJ, Obarzanek E, et al. A clinical trial of the effects of dietary patterns on blood pressure. DASH Collaborative Research Group. *N Engl J Med*. 1997; 17; 336(16): 1117–1124, 1997.
14. The George Mateljan Foundation. *The World's Healthiest Foods*. http://www.whfoods.com/genpage.php?tname=foodspice&dbid=42#nutritionalprofile

Cumin / *Kammūn*

Family: Apiaceae

Botanical Name: *Cuminum cyminum*

Common Names: *English* Cumin; *French* Cumin des près, Cumin officinale; *Spanish* Comino; *German* Kreuzkümmel, Mutterkümmel, Weißer Kümmel, Kumin, Cumin; *Urdu/Unānī* Zeerah Safaid, Kammun-e-Abyaz; *Modern Standard Arabic* Kammūn

Safety Rating: Generally Safe Cumin is generally considered safe for most people. It should not, however, be consumed by pregnant women.

Prophetic Prescription: According to the Messenger of Allāh, "If there was anything that could stave off death, it would have been cumin (*sannūt*) and ghee."[1]

Issues in Identification: According to Bīrūnī "It is said that it is *sannūt* and *sinnūt* and both mean cumin."[2] Dīnawarī says that *kammūn* is a well-known herb and that some people call it *sannūt*. He says that the Arabs would obtain it from Oman, where it was not grown, but imported from Kirman. Other Arabs say that *kammūn* is *al-rāzyānj*, which is grown in Arabia.[3] Ibn al-Ārabī says that *sannūt* is a seed that resembles the *kammūn* but it is not *kammūn*. The general view among both classical and modern Arab botanists is that *kammūn* is Arabic for cumin. As Ghazanfar explains, *Cuminum cyminum* is probably a native of Egypt. It is known in Arabia as *kimmūn* and *sanūt*, where it exists as a cultivated plant.[4] *Kammūn* is also known as *sannūt* in Syria.

Properties and Uses: *Cuminum cyminum*, known commonly as cumin, is one of the most ancient of medicinal herbs and has been cultivated since early times in Arabia, India, China, and the Mediterranean. It is an aromatic, astringent herb that benefits the digestive system and acts as a stimulant to the sexual organs. A highly stimulant, antispasmodic, and carminative herb, it is also considered astringent, pectoral, diuretic, anthelmintic, antidyspeptic, desiccant, detersive, stomachic, antidiarrheal, antiphlegmatic, emmenagogue, and anti-flatulent. Internally, cumin it is used for minor digestive problems, flatulence, colic, hiccup, indigestion, loss of appetite, diarrhea, as well as migraines of digestive origin. The oil is antiseptic, antibacterial, and larvicidal. Externally, an infusion of cumin seeds is used as an eye-wash and to improve the complexion of the face. As Ghazanfar explains, Gulf Arabs used its dried seeds and leaves as a carminative, for digestive problems, for swellings, cloudy eyes, and as a general tonic.[5]

Scientific Studies: *Antidiabetic Activity* In an animal study conducted by Annamalai University in India, the oral administration of *Cuminum cyminum* for 6 weeks caused a significant reduction in blood glucose and an increase in total hemoglobin and glycosylated hemoglobin. It also prevented a decrease in body weight. *Cuminum cyminum* treatment also resulted in a significant reduction in plasma and tissue cholesterol, phospholipids, free fatty acids and triglycerides. Histological observations demonstrated significant fatty changes and inflammatory cell infiltrates in diabetic rat pancreas. But supplementation with *Cuminum cyminum* to diabetic rats significantly reduced the fatty changes and inflammatory cell infiltrates. Moreover, *Cuminum cyminum* supplementation was found to be more effective than glibenclamide in the treatment of diabetes mellitus.[6]

Anticancer Activity In a study conducted by Annamalai University in India, chili (*Capsicum annuum* L.) supplementation slightly promoted colon carcinogenesis in rats, while cumin (*Cuminum cyminum*) or black pepper (*Piper nigrum* L.) suppressed it.[7] Considering that colon cancer is the second most common cancer among men and women worldwide, the potential anticancer properties of cumin (*Cuminum cyminum*) seem quite promising, though double-blind clinical trials on human subjects are essential.

In a study conducted by Jawaharlal Nehru University in India, cumin was shown to significantly inhibit stomach tumors in mice.[8]

In a study conducted at Annamalai University in India, the administration of chili (*Capsicum annuum*) to rats showed an increase of beta-glucuronidase activity in the distal colon, distal intestine, liver and colon contents and the activity of mucinase was increased in both the colon and fecal contents when compared to control rats, the same increase found in the presence of DMH, a known colon carcinogen.[9] Supplementation with cumin (*Cuminum cyminum*) and black pepper (*Piper nigrum*) in the presence of DMH, however, showed more or less similar values as that of the control rats. The increase in beta-glucuronidase activity may increase the hydrolysis of glucuronide conjugates, liberating the toxins, while the increase in mucinase activity may enhance the hydrolysis of the protective mucins in the colon. Thus cumin and black pepper may protect the colon by decreasing the activity of beta-glucuronidase and mucinase.

In an animal study conducted by the Isotope Division of the Cancer Institute in India, cumin seeds (*Cuminum cyminum* Linn.) significantly decreased the incidence of induced neoplasia and hepatomas.[10] These results suggest that cumin seeds may prove to be valuable anticarcinogenic agents.

In a study conducted by Annamalai University in India the effect of red chili (*Capsicum annuum*), cumin (*Cuminum cyminum*), and black pepper (*Piper nigrum*) on colon cancer induced in rats by a colon-specific carcinogen was examined.[11] The results indicated that chili supplementation promotes colon carcinogenesis, whereas cumin or black pepper suppresses colon carcinogensis in the presence of the procarcinogen DMH.

Antibacterial Activity According to a study conducted by DDU Gorakhpur University in India, the essential oil of *Cuminum cyminum* was very effective against eight pathogenic bacteria which cause infections in the human body. In fact, the essential oil of cumin was equal or more effective when compared with standard antibiotics, at a very low concentration.[12]

Cumin Notes

1. Bīrūnī, AR al-. *al-Bīrūnī's Book on Pharmacy and Materia Medica.* Ed. and trans. HM Said. Karachi: Hamdard National Foundation, 1973: 84–85, 283.

2. Bīrūnī, AR al-. *al-Bīrūnī's Book on Pharmacy and Materia Medica.* Ed. and trans. HM Said. Karachi: Hamdard National Foundation, 1973: 84–85, 283.

3. Dīnawarī AH. *Kitāb al-nabāt: Le dictionaire botanique d'Abū Ḥanīfa al-Dīnawarī.* al-Qāhirah: Institut Français d'Archéologie Orientale du Caire, 1973.

4. Ghazanfar SA. *Handbook of Arabian Medicinal Plants.* Boca Raton: CRC Press, 1994.

5. Ghazanfar SA. *Handbook of Arabian Medicinal Plants.* Boca Raton: CRC Press, 1994.

6. Dhandapani, Subramanian, Rajagopal, Namasivayam. Hypolipidemic effect of *Cuminum cyminum* L. on alloxan-induced diabetic rats. *Pharmacol* 2002; 46(3): 251–255.

7. Nalini, Manju, Menon. Effects of spices on lipid metabolism in 1, 2-dimethylhydrazine-induced rat colon carcinogenesis. *J* 2006; 9(2): 237–245.

8. Gagandeep, Dhanalakshmi, Mendiz, Rao, Kale. Chemopreventive effects of *Cuminum cyminum* in chemically induced forestomach and uterine cervix tumors in murine model systems. *Nutr* 2003; 47(2): 171–180.

9. Nalini, Sabitha, Viswanathan, Menon. Influence of spices on the bacterial (enzyme) activity in experimental colon cancer. *J* 1998; 62(1): 15–24.

10. Aruna, Sivaramakrishnan. Anticarcinogenic effects of some Indian plant products. *Food* 1992; 30(11): 953–956.

11. Nalini, Manju, Menon. Effects of spices on lipid metabolism in 1,2-dimethylhydrazine-induced rat colon carcinogenesis. *J* 2006; 9(2): 237–245.

12. Singh, Kapoor, Pandey, Singh, Singh. Studies on essential oils: part 10; antibacterial activity of volatile oils of some spices. *Phytother* 2002; 16(7): 680–682.

Cyclamen / *Bukhūr Maryam*

FAMILY: Primulaceae

BOTANICAL NAME: *Cyclamen europaeum*

COMMON NAMES: *English* Cyclamen, Bleeding gum, Sow-bread; *Spanish* Ciclamen; *French* Cyclame, Cyclamine, Pain de pourceau; *German* Europäisches Alpenveilchen, Cyclamen; *Urdu/Unānī* Bakhur-i-Miryam, Panja-e-Maryam, Keef-e-Maryam, Hatha Jodi, Hata Jodi; *Modern Standard Arabic* Būkhūr Maryam, 'Arṭanitā, Khubz al-mashāyikh, Walaf, Rakaf

BOTANICAL NAME: *Cyclamen hederiefolium*

COMMON NAMES: *English* Ivy-Leaved Cyclamen; *French* Cyclame, Cyclamine a fleurs de lièrre; *Spanish* Ciclamino, Artánita, Pan de puerco; *German* Alpenveilchen, Zyklame, Zyklamen; *Urdu/Unānī* Bakhur-i-Miryam; *Modern Standard Arabic* Būkhūr Maryam

SAFETY RATING: DANGEROUS TO DEADLY Cyclamen is a highly poisonous plant. As such, it must never be taken internally. Ingestion of even small amounts frequently results in death.

PROPHETIC PRESCRIPTION: Imām Muḥammad

al-Bāqir prescribed cyclamen for his bondmaid saying it was beneficial for everything caused by the spirits such as possession [*al-mass*], mental disorder, madness, the falling sickness, ensnarement, and so forth.[1]

Issues in Identification: It is the consensus that *bukhūr* is Arabic for incense, *Cyclamen* is *sakawka'*, and *Cylamen europaeum* is *bukhūr Maryam*. As Nehmé explains, Cyclamen is known in Modern Standard Arabic as *bukhūr Maryam*, *duwayk al-jabal*, *sīdū*, and *qarn al-ghazāl*.[2] *Cyclamen europaeum* and *Cyclamen hederifolium* are distributed over Southern Europe, North Africa, and Western Asia.

Properties and Uses: Cyclamen is a poisonous plant. It must only be used with extreme caution under the guidance of a trained professional. Internally, the rootstock is used as a drastic purgative and cathartic. Its effects are frequently severe, causing violent emesis, hypercatharsis, intestinal inflammation, cold sweats, tinnitus aurium, and spasmodic movements, which sometimes result in death.

The fresh root is also used in a homeopathic remedy. Externally, a cyclamen ointment made from the fresh tubers is applied to the bowels to expel worms in children, to cause enemis in adults, to cause purging, and to increase urinary discharge.

Scientific Studies: *Analgesic and Anti-inflammatory Activity* According to a study conducted by Bologna University, the anti-inflammatory and analgesic properties of *Cyclamen repandum* might be the result of its saponin content.[3]

Antispermatogenic Activity In a study of Yugoslav plants, the saponins of *Cyclamen persicum* were found to be spermicidal, suggesting their potential use as a natural spermicide.[4]

Anticancer Activity Cyclamen persicum also shows potential as a tumor inhibitor.[5]

Cyclamen Notes

1. Nisābūrī A. *Islamic Medical Wisdom: The Ṭibb al-a'immah*. Trans. B. Ispahany. Ed. AJ Newman. London: Muḥammadī Trust, 1991: 146.

2. Nehmé M. *Dictionnaire étymologique de la flore du Liban*. Bayrūt: Librairie du Liban, 2000.

3. Speroni, Cervellati, Costa, Dall'acqua, Guerra, Panizzolo, Utan, Innocenti. Analgesic and anti-inflammatory activity of *Cyclamen repandum* S. et S. *Phytother* 2007; 21(7): 684–689.

4. Primorac, Sekulovic, Antonic. In vitro determination of the spermicidal activity of plant saponins. *Pharmazie*. 1985; 40(8): 585.

5. Kupchan, Hemingway, Knox, Barboutis, Werner, Barboutis. Tumor inhibitors. XXI. Active principles of *Acer negundo* and *Cyclamen persicum*. *J* 1967; 56(5): 603–608.

Date / *Tamr, Ruṭb, 'Ajwah, Balaḥ, Nakhl*

Family: Palmaea

Botanical Name: *Phoenix dactylifera*

Common Names: *English* Date palm; *French* Dattier; *Spanish* Dátil; *German* Dattel; *Urdu/Unānī* Khurma, Khajur, Chuhara; *Modern Standard Arabic* Tamr, Ruṭb, 'Ajwah, Balaḥ

Safety Rating: Generally Safe Dates are generally considered safe for most people.

Prophetic Prescription: Dates and palms are mentioned over twenty times in the Qur'ān (2:269; 6:99; 6:141; 13:4; 16:11; 16:67; 18:32; 19:23; 19:25; 20:71; 23:19; 26:148; 36:34; 50:10; 54:13; 54:20; 55:11; 55:68; 59:5; 69:7; 80:29; 111:5). Consequently, the Prophet and the Imāms of *Ahl al-Bayt* held the date tree and its fruit in high esteem. The Messenger of Allāh said, "There is a tree which is similar to a Muslim [in goodness], and that is the palm tree."[1] He told his followers to, "Treat your aunts with honor: the palm tree and the dried grape."[2] He also said, "The palm tree and the pomegranate were created with what was left over from the dust of Adam."[3]

According to the Prophet, "The best of all your dates is that of *al-barnī*, which drives out disease."[4] Imām 'Alī ibn Abī Ṭālib said, "The best of dates are known as *al-barnī*."[5] In a similar tradition, Imām Ja'far al-Ṣādiq said, "The best of all your dates is *al-barnī*. It removes disease and there is no disease in it. It removes fatigue. It fills [the stomach]. It removes phlegm. There is goodness in each one [i.e., *barnī*]."[6]

Imām Mūsā al-Kāẓim prescribed eating *barnī* dates on an empty stomach and not drinking water for cases of dampness (*al-ruṭūbah*) and eating *barnī* dates on an empty stomach and drinking water after it in cases of excessive dryness (*al-yubs*).[7]

The Messenger of Allāh encouraged the consumption of dates as a staple. According to both Bukhārī and Aḥmad, dates and water were the basis of the Prophet's diet."[8] He said, "The date is the best breakfast for a believer."[9] He used to eat melon with fresh dates, saying that "One drives out heat, the other, cold."[10] It is also reported that he said, "When dates are in season, congratulate me: when they are out of season, sympathize."[11] He used to break his fast with fresh dates and, if there were none, with dried dates (*tamarāt*).[12] The Prophet also used to rub dates in the mouths of newborn babies.[13] He said, "He who finds a date, let him break his fast with it. And he who finds no date, let him break his fast with water. For verily, that is purity."[14]

The Prophet Muḥammad said that the "'*Ajwah* date is an excellent remedy."[15] The Prophet said, "Whoever starts his day with seven '*Ajwah dates*, will not be harmed that day by poison or witchcraft."[16] He said that the "'*Ajwah* is from Paradise, and it contains an antidote against poison (*al-samm*)."[17] He also explained that "The best part of the date is its tip."[18] According to Sūyūṭī, the '*ajwah* is a type of date from Medina which is larger than the Sihānī, dark in color, and which was planted by the Prophet himself.[19]

The Prophet also prescribed dates for his companion Sa'd, who suffered from "coolness of the heart." The Prophet told him that he was suffering from heart sickness, told him to see al-Ḥārith b. Kaladah, who was a physician, telling him to take seven '*ajwah* dates from Medina and grind them with their kernels and then put them into his mouth.[20]

The Messenger of Allāh recommended dates for a host of medical reasons. He said, "Dates are a fruit which seed came from Paradise. They are an antidote for poison, a rich source for increasing semen, and drinking the water of soaked Madīnah dates breaks the spell of witchcraft."[21] He recommended people to "Eat fresh dates (*balaḥ*), with dried dates (*tamr*), for when Satan regards the son of Adam eating these two, he says: the son of Adam remained until he has eaten the new with the old."[22]

The Messenger of Allāh recommended the consumption of dates by pregnant women, saying, "Your women-folk should eat dates, for whoever makes dates their food will produce children with ease."[23] He stated, "Fresh dates are the best food for a woman after she gives birth."[24] Imām al-Ṣādiq explained that "Feed your women *barnī* dates after they give birth so that they can produce more milk for your children."[25] He also said that "There is no better medicine for a woman who has just delivered than fresh dates [*ruṭb*]."[26] The Prophet is also reported to have said, "If one of your women has given birth to a child, see that the first thing that she eats are fresh dates [*ruṭb*]. Verily, Maryam [Mary] did not eat anything better than these when she gave birth to 'Isā [Jesus]."[27]

Imām 'Alī al-Riḍā said, "He who wishes to prevent pain in his lower parts as well as the wind of hemorrhoids, he should eat seven dates covered in cow butter every night."[28] Imām Ja'far al-Ṣādiq recommended abstaining from dates because the Prophet made Imām 'Alī abstain from eating them when he was ill.[29] The Prophet also recommended abstaining from dates when suffering from inflammation of the eyes.[30]

The Messenger of Allāh recommended the use of dates to treat parasitic infections, saying, "Every date on an empty stomach means the death of a worm."[31] Imām 'Alī ibn Abī Ṭālib said and Imām Ja'far al-Ṣādiq said, "Whoever eats seven '*ajwah* dates before sleeping will kill the worms in his belly."[32] "Eat '*ajwah*" he said, "for the dried date of the '*ajwah* will cause them to die — and eat it on an empty stomach."[33] He has taken these instructions from the Prophet who had said, "Take dates early in the morning. They kill worms."[34]

ISSUES IN IDENTIFICATION: It is the consensus that *nakhl* means date palm, *bisr* means unfertilized female date, *balaḥ* means fertilized unripe date, *ruṭab* mean fresh dates, *tamr* means dried dates, and '*ajwah* means mashed dates in Arabic. Dates have been widely cultivated in Arabia since antiquity.

PROPERTIES AND USES: Dates have numerous medicinal properties. They are high in natural aspirin and they have a laxative effect. The regular consumption of dates is linked to lower rates of certain cancers, particularly pancreatic cancer. Dates have the best nutrient score among fresh fruits as well as the highest concentration of polyphenols among the dried fruits.[35]

Dates are fat free, sodium free, cholesterol free, and are one of the best sources of fiber. It comes as no surprise, then, that Ibn Buṭlān would state that sweet, fresh dates help the intestines.[36] One serving of dates provides 240 mg of potassium, which is even more than bananas. Furthermore, dates are packed with vitamin B-complex and magnesium. Research suggests that this combination of nutrients may reduce the risk of heart disease, cancer, hypertension, diabetes and help reduce LDL cholesterol.

Dates are used to treat intestinal disturbances, children's diarrhea, dysentery, as a laxative, and as an aphrodisiac. They contain stimulants that strengthen the muscles of the uterus in the last months of pregnancy, helping with the dilation of the uterus at the time of delivery and reducing bleeding after delivery. The Prophet has emphasized the nutritional value of dates and their effectiveness in the growth of the fetus. Dates are particularly suited for women who are breast-feeding as they contain elements which alleviate depression, and enrich breast milk.

SCIENTIFIC STUDIES: *Antioxidative Activity* In a study conducted by Kuwait University, the antioxidant and antimutagenic properties of fruits of the date palm were studied for the first time in vitro.[37] According to the study, there was a dose-dependent inhibition of superoxide and hydroxyl radicals by an aqueous extract of date fruit. These results indicate that antioxidant and antimutagenic activity in date fruit is quite potent and implicates the presence of compounds with potent free-radical-scavenging activity.

Date Notes

1. Bukhārī M. *Ṣaḥīḥ al-Bukhārī.* al-Riyyāḍ: Bayt al-Afkār, 1998; Muslim. *Jāmi' al-ṣaḥīḥ.* al-Riyyāḍ: Bayt al-Afkār, 1998.
2. Chaghhaynī M. *Ṭibb al-nabī.* Trans. C Elgood. *Osiris* 1962; 14: 189.
3. Chaghhaynī M. *Ṭibb al-nabī.* Trans. C Elgood. *Osiris* 1962; 14: 189.
4. Sūyūṭī J. *As-Sūyūṭī's Medicine of the Prophet.* Ed. A Thomson. London: Ṭā-Hā Publishers, 1994: 44
5. Sūyūṭī J. *As-Sūyūṭī's Medicine of the Prophet.* Ed. A Thomson. London: Ṭā-Hā Publishers, 1994: 44.
6. Majlisī M. *Biḥār al-anwār.* Ṭihrān: Javad al-Alavi, 1956.
7. Nisābūrī A. *Islamic Medical Wisdom: The Ṭibb al-a'immah.* Trans. B. Ispahany. Ed. AJ Newman. London: Muḥammadī Trust, 1991: 79.
8. Nasā'ī A. *Sunan al-Nisā'ī.* al-Qāhirah: Muṣṭafā al-Bābī al-Ḥalabī, 1964–65; Chaghhaynī M. *Ṭibb al-nabī.* Trans. C Elgood. *Osiris* 1962; 14: 189.
9. Chaghhaynī M. *Ṭibb al-nabī.* Trans. C Elgood. *Osiris* 1962; 14: 189.
10. Tirmidhī M. *al-Jāmi' al-ṣaḥīḥ.* al-Qāhirah: Muṣṭafā al-Bābī al-Ḥalabī, [1937-].
11. Chaghhaynī M. *Ṭibb al-nabī.* Trans. C Elgood. *Osiris* 1962; 14: 189.
12. Ibn Ḥanbal A. *Musnad al-Imām Aḥmad ibn Ḥanbal.* Bayrūt: Mu'assasat al-Risālah, 1993.
13. Bukhārī M. *Ṣaḥīḥ al-Bukhārī.* al-Riyyāḍ: Bayt al-Afkār, 1998.
14. Chaghhaynī M. *Ṭibb al-nabī.* Trans. C Elgood. *Osiris* 1962; 14: 189.
15. Bukhārī M. *Ṣaḥīḥ al-Bukhārī.* al-Riyyāḍ: Bayt al-Afkār, 1998; Muslim. *Jāmi' al-ṣaḥīḥ.* al-Riyyāḍ: Bayt al-Afkār, 1998.
16. Bukhārī M. *Ṣaḥīḥ al-Bukhārī.* al-Riyyāḍ: Bayt al-Afkār, 1998; Muslim. *Jāmi' al-ṣaḥīḥ.* al-Riyyāḍ: Bayt al-Afkār, 1998.
17. Tirmidhī M. *al-Jāmi' al-ṣaḥīḥ.* al-Qāhirah: Muṣṭafā al-Bābī al-Ḥalabī, [1937-]; Nisābūrī A. *Islamic Medical Wisdom: The Ṭibb al-a'immah.* Trans. B. Ispahany. Ed. AJ Newman. London: Muḥammadī Trust, 1991: 103; Nasā'ī A. *Sunan al-Nisā'ī.* al-Qāhirah: Muṣṭafā al-Bābī al-Ḥalabī, 1964–65; Ibn Mājah M. *Sunan.* Trans. MT Anṣārī. Lahore: Kazi Publications, 1994.
18. Ibn Ḥabīb A. *Mujtaṣar fī al-ṭibb/Compendio de medicina.* Ed. C Álvarez de Morales and F Girón Irueste. Madrid: Consejo Superior de Investigaciones Científicas, 1992: 72.
19. Sūyūṭī J. *As-Sūyūṭī's Medicine of the Prophet.* Ed. A Thomson. London: Ṭā-Hā Publishers, 1994: 45.
20. Abū Dāwūd S. *Ṣaḥīḥ Sunan Abū Dāwūd.* Riyyāḍ: Maktab al-Tarbiyyah, 1989; Ibn Mājah M. *Sunan.* Trans. MT Anṣārī. Lahore: Kazi Publications, 1994; Ibn Ḥanbal A. *Musnad al-Imām Aḥmad ibn Ḥanbal.* Bayrūt: al-Maktabah al-Islāmiyyah, 1969; Iṣbahānī AN al-. *Mawsū'at al-ṭibb al-nabawī.* Ed. MKD al-Turkī. Bayrūt: Dār Ibn Ḥazm, 2006.
21. Nasā'ī A. *Sunan al-Nisā'ī.* al-Qāhirah: Muṣṭafā al-Bābī al-Ḥalabī, 1964–65; Ibn Mājah M. Sunan. Trans. MT Anṣārī. Lahore: Kazi Publications, 1994.
22. Ibn Mājah M. *Sunan.* Trans. MT Ansari. Lahore: Kazi Publications, 1994; Nasā'ī A. *Sunan al-Nisā'ī.* al-Qāhirah: Muṣṭafā al-Bābī al-Ḥalabī, 1964–65.
23. Sūyūṭī J. *As-Sūyūṭī's Medicine of the Prophet.* Ed. A Thomson. London: Ṭā-Hā Publishers, 1994: 45.
24. Ibn Ḥabīb A. *Mujtaṣar fī al-ṭibb/Compendio de medicina.* Ed. C Álvarez de Morales and F Girón Irueste. Madrid: Consejo Superior de Investigaciones Científicas, 1992: 71.
25. Majlisī M. *Biḥār al-anwār.* Ṭihrān: Javad al-Alavi, 1956.
26. Majlisī M. *Biḥār al-anwār.* Ṭihrān: Javad al-Alavi, 1956.
27. Chaghhaynī M. *Ṭibb al-nabī.* Trans. C Elgood. *Osiris* 1962; 14: 189.
28. Riḍā 'A al-. *Risālah fī al-ṭibb al-nabawī.* Ed. MA Bār. Bayrūt: Dār al-Manāhil, 1991: 166.
29. Nisābūrī A. *Islamic Medical Wisdom: The Ṭibb al-a'immah.* Trans. B. Ispahany. Ed. AJ Newman. London: Muḥammadī Trust, 1991: 69.
30. Nisābūrī A. *Islamic Medical Wisdom: The Ṭibb al-a'immah.* Trans. B. Ispahany. Ed. AJ Newman. London: Muḥammadī Trust, 1991: 106; Sūyūṭī J. *As-Sūyūṭī's Medicine of the Prophet.* Ed. A Thomson. London: Ṭā-Hā Publishers, 1994.
31. Chaghhaynī M. *Ṭibb al-nabī.* Trans. C Elgood. *Osiris* 1962; 14: 189.
32. Nisābūrī A. *Ṭibb al-a'immah.* Bayrūt: Dār al-Maḥajjah al-Bayḍā', 1994: 78; Majlisī M. *Biḥār al-anwār.* Ṭihrān: Javad al-Alavi, 1956.
33. Nisābūrī A. *Ṭibb al-a'immah.* Bayrūt: Dār al-Maḥajjah al-Bayḍā', 1994: 78.
34. Farooqi, MIH. *Medicinal Plants in the Traditions of Prophet Muḥammad.* Lucknow: Sidrah Publishers, 1998: 111.
35. Vinson, JA, Zubik L, Bose P, Samman N., Proch J. Dried fruits: excellent in vitro an in vivo antioxidants. *J Am Coll Nutr.* 2005; 24(1): 44–50.
36. Ibn Buṭlān, *The Medieval Health Handbook: Tacuinum sanitatis.* Ed. L Cogliati Arano. Trans. O Ratti and A Westbrook. New York: George Braziller, 1976: 132.
37. Vayalil. Antioxidant and antimutagenic properties of aqueous extract of date fruit (*Phoenix dactylifera* L. *Arecaceae*). *J* 2002; 50(3): 610–617.

Dill/*Shabath, Sanūt*

Family: Apiaceae

Botanical Name: *Anethum graveolens*

Common Names: *English* Dill, Dill-seed, dill weed; *French* Aneth, Fenouil bâtard, Fenouil puant; *Spanish* Eneldo; *German* Dill, Kümmerlingskraut, Dillfenchel, Gurkenkraut; *Urdu/Unānī* Shibt, Soya, Shabbat; *Modern Standard Arabic* Shibith, Sadhāb al-barrī

Safety Rating: Generally Safe Dill is generally considered safe for most people. It should not, however, be taken medicinally by pregnant women. The juice of the plant may make the skin photosensitive.

Prophetic Prescription: According to the

Prophet Muḥammad, "You have senna (*sanā*) and *sannūt* in which there is a cure for every disease except death."[1] He also said, "There are three things which are a cure for every disease except death. There is senna (*sanā*) and there is *sannūt*."[2] (The third element is not named.) Imām Ja'far al-Ṣādiq prescribed dill (*shibith*) water cooked with honey to drink for three days to treat a woman who suffered from severe panic during sleep, to the point that it was believed that she had been touched by the jinn.[3]

Issues in Identification: It is the general consensus that *Anethum graveolens* is *shibth*, *shibitt*, and *sannūt*, which is known as dill or false fennel. Common dill is known in Arabic as *shibth 'abiq*, *sadhāb al-barrī*, and *ḥulwah*. Hans Wehr says that *Anethum graveolens* is *shbītt*. Bīrūnī has recorded it as *shibth* and *shabth*, which Said identifies as *Anethum graveolens*. Bīrūnī also speaks of *ḥazā'*, which Said identifies as either *Anethum graveolens* or *Selinum anethum*.[4] According to Duke, the post-biblical *shiveth* is identical to the Arabic *shibth*, both of which refer to *Anethum graveolens*.

As for the meaning of *sannūt*, scholars are divided on the issue, some suggesting that it means honey, a mixture of Makkan fat, a seed similar to cumin or dates.[5] According to Farooqi, "*sannūt* seems to be the Arabic name of dill."[6] This is also the opinion of Ibn Ṭūlūn, Abū Nu'aym al-Iṣbahānī, and Turkī.[7] This is certainly the case as *sannūt* remains the name for *Anethum* in Arabic. It seems clear that the scholars were unfamiliar with the Prophet's saying, *Al-thufā' al-ḥurf wa al-sannūt shbit* or "*Thufā'* is garden-cress and *sannūt* is dill."[8]

According to Ghazanfar, *Anethum graveolens* is found throughout Arabia, wild or cultivated.[9] According to Mandaville, *Anethum graveolens* is infrequent in eastern Saudi Arabia, found only as a weed or escape from cultivation in oases. It is known in Saudi Arabic as *ḥulwah*.[10] According to Ghazanfar, it is known in Oman as *ḥulwa*, *sbinet*, *shibith*, and *sadhāb al-barr*, while it is known in Qatar as *shabāt*.[11]

Properties and Uses: Dill is a pungent, cooling, aromatic, carminative herb that is digestive, febrifuge, diuretic, resolvent, emmenagogue, galactagogue and sialagogue. It is a cardiac tonic, soporific, stomachic, and stimulant. An antispasmodic and a calmative, it is used internally for digestive disorders, including indigestion, colic, hiccup, flatulence, especially as an ingredient of gripe water for babies, and hiatus hernia. Dill is used to treat bad breath, hiccups, insomnia, intestinal gas, muscle spasms, stomach pain, to stimulate the appetite, to strengthen nails, and to promote the flow of milk in nursing mothers. In Unānī medicine, dill is used externally as an eye wash.

Scientific Studies: *Antioxidative Activity* Dill has been shown to have antioxidative activity comparable to dl-alpha-tocopherol and quercetin.[12]

Anticancer Activity Anethofuran, carvone, and limonene from dill weed oil are considered potential cancer chemopreventive agents.[13]

Antifertility Activity In a controlled animal trial conducted by Shiraz University in Iran, *Anethum graveolens* extract was shown to possess menstrual cycle regulatory and anti-fertility properties.[14]

Antibacterial Activity In a study conducted by the University of London, extracts from *Anethum graveolens* were shown to possess antibacterial activity against a panel of rapidly growing mycobacteria with minimum inhibitory concentration.[15]

In an animal trial conducted by Mashhad University of Medical Sciences in Iran, *Anethum graveolens* seed extracts were shown to possess significant mucosal protective and antisecretory effects of the gastric mucosa.[16] In a study conducted by DDU Gorakhpur University in India, the essential oil of dill was very effective against eight pathogenic bacteria which cause infections in the human body.[17]

Antihyperlipidemic and Cholesterol-Lowering Activity In an animal trial conducted by the University of Tehran, the oral administration of the essential oil of dill seeds for 14 days reduced tricylglycerides and total cholesterol levels by almost 50 and 20 percent, respectively. Oral administration of the essential oil of *Anethum graveolens* seeds, at two different doses, also reduced the tricylglyceride levels by almost 42 percent.[18]

Dill Notes

1. Sūyūṭī J. *As-Sūyūṭī's Medicine of the Prophet.* Ed. A Thomson. London: Ṭā-Hā Publishers, 1994: 70; Ibn Mājah M. *Sunan.* Trans. MT Anṣārī. Lahore: Kazi Publications, 1994; Ibn 'Asākir.

2. Sūyūṭī J. *As-Sūyūṭī's Medicine of the Prophet.* Ed. A Thomson. London: Ṭā-Hā Publishers, 1994: 71.

3. Nisābūrī A. *Islamic Medical Wisdom: The Ṭibb al-a'immah.* Trans. B. Ispahany. Ed. AJ Newman. London: Muḥammadī Trust, 1991: 143.

4. Bīrūnī, AR al-. *al-Bīrūnī's Book on Pharmacy and Materia Medica.* Ed. and trans. HM Said. Karachi: Hamdard National Foundation, 1973.

5. Sūyūṭī J. *As-Sūyūṭī's Medicine of the Prophet.* Ed. A Thomson. London: Ṭā-Hā Publishers, 1994: 71.

6. Farooqi MIH. *Medicinal Plants in the Traditions of Prophet Muḥammad.* Lucknow: Sidrah Publishers, 1998: 94

7. Ibn Ṭulūn S. *al-Manhal al-rawī fī al-ṭibb al-nabawī.* Ed. 'Azīz Bayk. Riyyāḍ: Dār 'ālam al-kutub, 1995.

8. Ibn Ḥabīb A. *Mujtaṣar fī al-ṭibb/Compendio de medi-*

cina. Ed. C Álvarez de Morales and F Girón Irueste. Madrid: Consejo Superior de Investigaciones Científicas, 1992: 78/46.

9. Ghazanfar SA. *Handbook of Arabian Medicinal Plants*. Boca Raton: CRC Press, 1994.

10. Mandaville JP. *Flora of Eastern Saudi Arabia*. London: Kegan Paul, 1990.

11. Ghazanfar SA. *Handbook of Arabian Medicinal Plants*. Boca Raton: CRC Press, 1994.

12. Souri E, Amin G, Farsam H, Andaji S. The antioxidative activity of some commonly used vegetables in Iranian diet. *Fitoterapia* 2004; 75(6): 585–588.

13. Zheng GQ, Kenney PM, Lam LK. Anethofuran, carvone, and limonene: potential chemopreventive agents from dill weed oil and caraway oil. *Plant Med.* 1992; 58(4): 338–341.

14. Monsefi, Ghasemi, Bahaoddini. The effects of *Anethum graveolens* L. on female reproductive system. *Phytother* 2006; 20(10): 865–868.

15. Stavri, Gibbons. The antimycobacterial constituents of dill (*Anethum graveolens*). *Phytother* 2005; 19(11): 938–941.

16. Hosseinzadeh, Karimi, Ameri. Effects of *Anethum graveolens* L. seed extracts on experimental gastric irritation models in mice. *BMC* 2002; 2: 21.

17. Singh, Kapoor, Pandey, Singh, Singh. Studies on essential oils: part 10; antibacterial activity of volatile oils of some spices. *Phytother* 2002; 16(7): 680–682.

18. Yazdanparast, Alavi. Antihyperlipidaemic and antihypercholesterolaemic effects of *Anethum graveolens* leaves after the removal of furocoumarins. *Cytobios.* 2001; 105(410): 185–191.

Eggplant/*Bādhinjān*

Family: Solanaceae

Botanical Name: *Solanum melongena*

Common Names: *English* Eggplant, Aubergine; *French* Mélongèn, Aubergine, Plante aux oeufs; *Spanish* Berenjena; *German* Eierfrucht, Eierpflanze, Aubergine, Nachtschatten; *Urdu/Unānī* Baigan, Badanjan, Badangan; *Modern Standard Arabic* Bādhinjān

Safety Rating: Generally Safe Eggplant is generally considered safe for most people. Since eggplant contains oxalates, which may interfere with the absorption of calcium, excessive consumption should be avoided. Eggplants also contain solanine, a calcium inhibitor. Consequently, they should be avoided by persons suffering from arthritis.

Prophetic Prescription: It is reported that the Messenger of Allāh said, "Eggplant is useful, taken for whatever purpose (as food or medicine)."[1] It is also related that he said, "Eat eggplant, and much of it, for verily it is a plant that I saw in Paradise. Whoever eats of it as a disease, for him it is a disease. And whoever eats of it as a medicine, for him it is a medicine."[2] Imām Ja'far al-Ṣādiq told his followers to "Eat eggplant. It is a cure for every illness."[3] He also said, "Eggplant is good for the black bile, and is not harmful for the yellow bile."[4] Imām 'Alī al-Riḍā used to say, "Give us eggplant, for it is hot in the cold and cool in the heat, suitable at all times and good in every condition."[5]

Issues in Identification: It is the consensus that *bādhinjān* is Arabic for *Solanum melongena.* Although it is native to India, eggplant spread into the Islamic world. From North Africa, it was taken to al-Andalus by the Muslims, and to the Americas by the Spaniards. Eggplant is currently cultivated throughout Arabia. Sūyūṭī mentions black and white varieties.[6] Since the eggplant has been developed into so many varieties, the original varieties consumed by the Prophet have most certainly been lost.

Properties and Uses: Eggplant possesses antibacterial properties, aids in the excretion of bile by the liver, promotes the flow of bile into the duodenum from the gall bladder, lowers cholesterol, and acts as a diuretic. Eggplant contains various caffeic substances, an alkaloidal glycoside called solanine, anthocyanins, and some vitamins. Because there are a few documented reports concerning the effects of *Solanum melongena* on cholesterol metabolism, its possible hypocholesterolemic activity has not been proven by well-controlled studies or in human trials.

Scientific Studies: *Antioxidative Activity* According to a study conducted at Okayama Prefectural University in Japan, eggplant peels contain an antioxidant which acts as an angiogenesis inhibitor. According to a study conducted at the University of Kerala in India, isolated flavanoids from *Solanum melongena* showed potent antioxidative activity.[7]

Anticancer Activity As a topical cream, the glycoalkaloids in eggplant have been used to treat skin cancers such as basal cell carcinoma, according to Australian researchers.[8]

Hypolipidemic Activity The anti-diabetic properties of eggplant have been known for centuries in India. An anti-diabetic remedy based on eggplant, bitter gourd and jamun, the fruit of the rose apple tree, was patented in 1999 by Cromak Research Inc.[9]

According to another study conducted in India, flavanoids extracted from the fruits of *Solanum melongena*, and orally administered at a dose of 1mg/100g BW/day, showed significant hypolipidemic action in normal and cholesterol fed rats.[10]

In a 6-week controlled trial of 21 individuals conducted at the Instituto do Coracao, Hospital das Clinicas, Brazil, the effect of eggplant extract on serum lipid levels was compared to that of lovastatin. No significant variation was observed in the HDL-cholesterol and triglyceride levels in the 3 groups during the study. As a result of this study, its authors concluded that eggplant extract with orange juice could not be considered an alternative to statins in reducing serum cholesterol levels.[11]

In a 5-week controlled trial of 38 hypercholesterolemic human volunteers conducted by the Instituto de Ciencias Biologicas in Belo Horizonte, Brazil, the ingestion of *Solanum melongena* had a modest and transitory effect on serum cholesterol and triglycerides which was not different from that obtained with standard orientation for dyslipidemia patients, namely, diet and exercise.[12] In a 3-month, double-blind, placebo-controlled, human trial of over 41 hyperlipidemic volunteers, conducted by the Universidade Estadual de Maringa in Portugal, the daily intake of dried powdered *Solanum melongena* had no significant effect on cholesterol.[13]

Eggplant Notes

1. Ibn al-Jawziyyah says it is unauthenticated. Ibn Qayyim al-Jawziyyah M. *al-Ṭibb al-nabawī.* Bayrūt: Dār al-Kitāb, 1985.
2. Chaghhaynī M. *Ṭibb al-nabī.* Trans. C Elgood. *Osiris* 1962; 14: 190.
3. Nisābūrī A. *Ṭibb al-a'immah.* Bayrūt: Dār al-Maḥajjah al-Bayḍā', 1994: 184.
4. Nisābūrī A. *Ṭibb al-a'immah.* Bayrūt: Dār al-Maḥajjah al-Bayḍā', 1994: 184.
5. Nisābūrī A. *Islamic Medical Wisdom: The Ṭibb al-a'immah.* Trans. B. Ispahany. Ed. AJ Newman. London: Muḥammadī Trust, 1991: 184–85.
6. Sūyūṭī J. *As-Sūyūṭī's Medicine of the Prophet.* Ed. A Thomson. London: Ṭā-Hā Publishers, 1994.
7. Sudheesh S, Sandhya C, Sarah Koshy A, Vijayalakshmi NR. Antioxidative activity of flavonoids from *Solanum melongena. Phytother Res.* 1999; (5): 393–396.
8. *Medicinal Benefits of Whole Foods.* www.naturalways.com/medValFd.htm.
9. *Medicinal Benefits of Whole Foods.* www.naturalways.com/medValFd.htm.
10. Presannakumar, Vijayakumar, Vijayalakshmi. Hypolipidemic effect of flavonoids from *Solanum melongena. Sudheesh. Plant Foods Hum Nutr* 1997; 51(4): 321–330.
11. Praca JM, Thomas A, Caramelli B. Eggplant (*Solanum melongena*) extract does not alter serum lip levels. *Arq Bras Cardiol* 2004; 82(3): 269–276.
12. Guimaraes, Galvao, Batista, Azevedo, Oliveira, Lamounier, Freire, Barros, Sakurai, Oliveira, Vieira, Alvarez-Leite. Eggplant (*Solanum melongena*) infusion has a modest and transitory effect on hypercholesterolemic subjects. *Braz J Med Biol Res.* 2000; 33(9): 1027–1036.
13. Silva, Takahashi, Eik, Albino, Tasim, Serri, Assef, Cortez, Bazotte. Absence of hypolipidemic effect of *Solanum melongena* L. (eggplant) on hyperlipidemic patients. *Arq Bras Endocrinol Metabol.* 2004; 48(3): 368–373.

Endive/*Hindibā'*

FAMILY: Asteraceae

BOTANICAL NAME: *Cichorium endivia*

COMMON NAMES: *English* Endive, chicory, escarole; *French* Chicorée endive, Endive, Scarole; *Spanish* Endibia, Chicoria, Achicoria, Escarola; *German* Endivienwegwarte, Endivie, Escariol; *Urdu/Unānī* Kasni, Hindiba; *Modern Standard Arabic* Kasnīsah, Hindibā'

SAFETY RATING: GENERALLY SAFE Endive and chicory are generally considered safe for most people in food quantities and in proper therapeutic dosages. People who are hypersensitive to chicory or plants from the Asteraceae family should avoid the plant to prevent possible allergic reactions.

PROPHETIC PRESCRIPTION: The Messenger of Allāh said, "Eat endives (*hindibā'*) ... for verily there is not one day that drops of water of Paradise do not fall upon them."[1] He also said, "Take endive (*hindibā'*), but do not wash it."[2] Both the Prophet and Imām 'Alī ibn Abī Ṭālib said "Eat endive (*hindibā'*), for there is not a morning when drops of heaven do not fall on it."[3] Imām Ja'far al-Ṣādiq said, "Take endive (*hindibā'*), for it increases semen and improves one's progeniture. It is hot and increases the number of male children."[4] The Imām also said, "He who wants more money and more male offspring should increase his consumption of endive (*hindibā'*)."[5] Likewise, he said, "Use endive (*hindibā'*) for it increases semen (*al-mā'*) and beautifies the face."[6] The Imām explained that "He who spends the night with seven portions of endive (*hindibā'*) in his inside is protected from colic for the entire night, Allāh willing."[7] On one occasion, a man came to Imām Ja'far al-Ṣādiq complaining of a disturbance of the head and teeth and a throbbing in the eye, and a swollen face. The Imām said, "Take this endive (*hindibā'*) and extract its juice. Take the juice and pour it over a lot of lump sugar. It will relieve it and drive away its harm."[8] The patient went home, drank the preparation and in the morning he was cured.

ISSUES IN IDENTIFICATION: According to Dīnawarī, endive is known as *hindibā'*, and *hindabā'*.[9] As Nehmé explains, *Cichorium* is *hindibā'*, known as chicory and succory, while *Cichorium intybus* is *hindibā' barriyah* or common chicory. Bīrūnī says that *hindibā'* is also known as *hundubā'* and Said identifies it as *Cichorium endivia* L. (wild chicory, endive), also known as *hummad al-bustānī*, which is endemic to Egypt and East India.[10] Ibn

Ḥabīb says that *hindibā'* is also known as *al-sarīs.*[11] Akīlī, Johnstone, Álvarez de Morales, and Girón Irueste, among others, identify *hindibā'* as *Cichorium intybus.*[12] *Cichorium intybus* is found in sandy habitats in Saudi Arabia where it is also cultivated and used commonly.

According to Duke, the bitter herbs of Moses may have included any or all the nine Mediterranean species of *Cichorium*, including *C. endivia* which he identifies as the Arabic *hindibā'*. As the author notes, the Arabic term *hindibā'* also applies to *C. intybus.*

It is important to note that the *hindibā'* mentioned by the Prophet and the Imāms referred to chicory and not Belgian or French endive, which was only discovered in the early to mid–1800s when a Belgian accidently dug up wild chicory roots. The plant was further developed by M. Brézier, a Belgian botanist, resulting in the variety we are familiar with today.[13]

Properties and Uses: Endive belongs to the *Cichorium* genus, known for its diuretic, stomachic, tonic, digestive, cholagogue, laxative, anti-inflammatory properties and tonic effect on the liver and gall bladder. *C. endivia* in particular is considered allergenic, antibilious, antioxidant, antiradicular, aphrodisiac, bitter, carminative, choleretic, decongestant, and emetic. It is also viewed as demulcent, depurative, digestive, diuretic, febrifuge, laxative, orexigenic, refrigerant, resolvent, and sedative. Finally, it is also considered stimulant, tonic, vermifuge, and vulnerary.

Internally, *C. endivia* is used to treat anorexia, biliousness, cancer of the liver, spleen, throat, and uterus, catarrh, constipation, cramp, diarrhea, dropsy and dyspepsia. It is also employed in the treatment of enterosis, fever, fluid retention, gastrosis, gallstones, gout, headache, hemorrhoid, hepatosis, impotence, induration, inflammation, jaundice and pharyngosis. Finally, it is used for pulmonosis, splenosis, swelling, toothache, uterosis, wart, worms, and the treatment of wounds.

Cichorium intybus has a long list of activities. It is considered alexiteric, allergenic, alterative, analgesic, antibilious, antiexudative, antifeedant, anti-inflammatory, antilipogenic, antimalarial, antimetastatic, antimutagenic, antioxidant, antiradicular, antiseptic, antispermatogenic, and antisteatotic. It is also viewed as bactericide, bifidogenic, bitter, bradycardic, cerebroprotective, cardiodepressant, cardiotonic, carminative, cerebrotonic, chemopreventive, cholagogue, choleretic, COX-2 inhibitor, decongestant, demulcent, depurative, digestive, and diuretic. It is equally considered emmenagogue, febrifuge, hepatoprotective, hypocholesterolemic, hypoglycemic, hypotensive, laxative, lipolytic, negative chronotropic, negative inotropic, nervice, and neuroprotective. Finally, it is seen as orexigenic, presistaltic, phytoalexin, prebiotic, refrigerant, sedative, stomachic, and tonic.

Cichorium intybus is used to treat a long host of ailments and conditions, including acne, adenopathy, ague, Alzheimer's, Amenorrhea, anorexia, arrhythmia, arthrosis, asthma, atony, bacterial infection, biliousness, and cancers of the breast, uterus, colon, gums, liver, lung, mouth, spleen, stomach, and tongue. It is used for catarrh, chancre, conjunctivosis, constipation, cramps, cystosis, deafness, dermatosis, diabetes, diarrhea, dropsy, dysmenorrhea, dyspepsia, edema, enterosis, epilepsy, fever, gallstone, gastrosis, gingivosis, glossosis, gout, gravel, headache, heartburn, hemorrhoid, hepatosis, high blood pressure, hypercholesterolemia, and hyperglycemia. It is employed in the treatment of induration, infection, inflammation, insomnia, jaundice, lachrymosis, lumbago, malaria, melancholy, nausea, nephrosis, obesity, oliguria, ophthalmia, pain, pharyngosis, pseudomonas, pulmonosis, pyelonephrosis, respirosis, rash, rheumatism, sclerosi, sore, and sore throat. Finally, it is used for splenomegaly, splenosis, stone, swelling, tachycardia, toothache, tuberculosis, urethrosis, urolithiasis, uterosis, vomiting, worms, and wounds.

Scientific Studies: *Anticancer Activity* According to the Cancer Prevention Research Program, Fred Hutchinson Cancer Research Center in Seattle, the review of the epidemiological data, including both cohort and case-control studies, of all cancer sites, strongly suggests that plant foods like endives have preventive potential and that people who consume fewer vegetable and fruits have higher rates of cancer.[14]

Cardioregulating Activity Although more research needs to be conducted on the issue, chicory may have some use in treating irregular heartbeats.[15]

Endive Notes

1. Iṣbahānī AN al-. *Mawsū'at al-ṭibb al-nabawī.* Ed. MKD al-Turkī. Bayrūt: Dār Ibn Ḥazm, 2006.

2. Farooqi MIH. *Medicinal Plants in the Traditions of Prophet Muḥammad.* Lucknow: Sidrah Publishers, 1998: 64.

3. Chaghhaynī M. *Ṭibb al-nabī.* Trans. C Elgood. *Osiris* 1962; 14: 189; Nisābūrī A. *Islamic Medical Wisdom: The Ṭibb al-a'immah.* Trans. B. Ispahany. Ed. AJ Newman. London: Muḥammadī Trust, 1991: 182.

4. Nisābūrī A. *Islamic Medical Wisdom: The Ṭibb al-a'immah.* Trans. B. Ispahany. Ed. AJ Newman. London: Muḥammadī Trust, 1991: 172; Ṭabarsī H. *Mustadrak al-Wasā'il.* Bayrūt: Mu'assasat Āl al-Bayt, 1987–1988.

5. Majlisī M. *Biḥār al-anwār.* Ṭihrān: Javad al-Alavi, 1956.

6. Majlisī M. *Biḥār al-anwār.* Ṭihrān: Javad al-Alavi, 1956.
7. Majlisī M. *Biḥār al-anwār.* Ṭihrān: Javad al-Alavi, 1956.
8. Nisābūrī A. *Islamic Medical Wisdom: The Ṭibb al-a'immah.* Trans. B. Ispahany. Ed. AJ Newman. London: Muḥammadī Trust, 1991: 182; Ṭabarsī H. *Mustadrak al-Wasā'il.* Bayrūt: Mu'assasat Āl al-Bayt, 1987–1988.
9. Dīnawarī AH. *Kitāb al-nabāt: Le dictionaire botanique d'Abū Ḥanīfah al-Dīnawarī.* al-Qāhirah: Institut Français d'Archéologie Orientale du Caire, 1973.
10. Bīrūnī, AR al-. *al-Bīrūnī's Book on Pharmacy and Materia Medica.* Ed. and trans. HM Said. Karachi: Hamdard National Foundation, 1973.
11. Ibn Ḥabīb A. *Mujtaṣar fī al-ṭibb/Compendio de medicina.* Ed. C Álvarez de Morales and F Girón Irueste. Madrid: Consejo Superior de Investigaciones Científicas, 1992: 98/69.
12. Ibn al-Qayyim al-Jawziyyah. *Natural Healing with the Medicine of the Prophet.* Pearl Publishing. Trans. M al-Akīlī. Philadelphia, 1993; Johnstone P, trans. *Medicine of the Prophet.* Ibn Qayyim al-Jawziyyah. Cambridge: The Islamic Texts Society, 1998; Ibn Ḥabīb A. *Mujtaṣar fī al-ṭibb/Compendio de medicina.* Ed. C Álvarez de Morales and F Girón Irueste. Madrid: Consejo Superior de Investigaciones Científicas, 1992.
13. Fortin F. *The Visual Food Encyclopedia.* New York: Macmillan, 1996: 92; Murray MT, Pizzorno L. *The Encyclopedia of Healing Foods.* New York: Simon & Schuster, 2005: 197; Toussaint-Samat M. *A History of Food.* Trans. Anthea Bell. West Sussex: Wiley-Blackwell, 2009: 689.
14. Potter, Steinmetz. Vegetables, fruit and phytoestrogens as preventive agents. *IARC* 1996; (139): 61–90.
15. Fetrow CW, Avila JR. *The Complete Guide to Herbal Medicines.* Springhouse: Springhouse Corporation, 2000.

Fennel/*Rāziyānaj*

Family: Apiaceae

Botanical Name: *Foeniculum vulgare*

Common Names: *English* Common fennel, bitter fennel; *French* Fenouil, Aneth doux; *German* Echter Fenchel, Süßfenchel; *Spanish* Hinojo; *Urdu/Unānī* Saunf, Saunph, Badiyan, Raziyanah, Raziyanaj; *Modern Standard Arabic* Shumrah, Shamār, Shamar

Safety Rating: Generally Safe All part of the fennel plant are generally considered safe for most people when used in moderation. The seeds, however, should be avoided by those with a history of allergies or skin sensitivities. They should also be avoided by pregnant women due to their hormonal action.

Prophetic Prescription: Imām Mūsā al-Kāẓim told a group of physicians, "Confine yourselves to the chief of these medicines: myrobalan (*al-ihlīlaj*), fennel (*al-rāziyānaj*), and sugar. [Take it] at the beginning of the summer for three months, three times a month, and at the beginning of the winter for three months, three days a month, three times. Let the place of the fennel be from near the gummastic (*maṣṭakā*) and one will not fall ill except for the illness of death."[1]

Issues in Identification: The tradition below may cause confusion as Imām Mūsā al-Kāẓim has referred to fennel by its Persian name *rāziyānaj*. The herb is also known as *rāziyanah*, and is the Persian equivalent of the Arabic *shumrah* and *shamār*. According to Ghazanfar, it is also known as *shīḥ* is Saudi Arabia, and as *samār* in Yemen. In al-Andalus and the Maghreb, it is known as *basbās*. It is found in cosmopolitan areas in Saudi Arabia where it is cultivated.[2]

Properties and Uses: *Foeniculum vulgare*, commonly known as fennel, is a sweet, aromatic, mildly diuretic herb that relieves digestive problems, increases milk flow, relaxes spasms, and reduces inflammation. It is also a carminative, stimulant, galactogogue, decongestant, diuretic, diaphoretic, pain-reducer, and fever-reducer, with anti-microbial properties. In Unānī medicine, it is considered sedative, stomachic, anthelmintic, expectorant, restorative, and aphrodisiac.

Internally, fennel seeds are used for indigestion, flatulence, colic, Crohn's disease, food poisoning, motion sickness, vomiting, coughs, tuberculosis, bronchitis, fevers, sore throat, neuralgia, sciatica, swollen glands, skin eruptions, wounds, tumors, sores, furuncles, asthma, bronchitis, emphysema, tuberculosis, and insufficient lactation. The roots are used for urinary disorders. The herb is also used to stimulate menstruation and to promote childbirth and delivery.

Externally, fennel seed is used to treat conjunctivitis and dermatitis. It is also used as mouthwash and to treat sore throat. It is combined with *Chamaemelum nobile*, *Filipendula ulmaria*, *Mentha x piperita*, and *Geranium maculatum* for digestive disorders. Fennel oil is combined with oils of *Thymus vulgaris* and *Eucaplytis globulus* and diluted with vegetable oil as a rub for bronchial congestion. Fennel is also added to laxative preparations to prevent griping, and to "gripe water" for babies. Fennel oil is not given to pregnant women.

Scientific Studies: *Larvacidal Activity* According to a study conducted by Chiang Mai University in Thailand, *Foeniculum vulgare* exerts significant larvicidal activity against the two mosquito species after 24-hour exposure, including *Anopheles dirus*, the major malaria vector, and *Aedes aegypti*, the main vector of dengue and dengue hemorrhagic fever in urban areas.[3]

Antiulcer and Antioxidative Activity According to a study conducted by Afyon Kocatepe University in Turkey, *Foeniculum vulgare* has clearly a protective effect against gastric mucosal lesions, and this effect, at least in part, depends upon the reduction in lipid peroxidation and augmentation in the antioxidative activity.[4]

According to a study conducted by Yonsei University in South Korea, the oral administration of *Foeniculum vulgare* fruit methanolic extract exhibits inhibitory effects against acute and subacute inflammatory diseases and type 4 allergic reactions. They found it also possesses a central analgesic effect. These results seem to support the use of fennel fruit methanolic extract in relieving inflammation.[5]

Antifungal Activity According to a study conducted by the University of Selcuk in Turkey, fennel oils exhibit different degrees of fungistatic activity, depending on doses.[6]

Anti-Constipation Activity According to a double-blind, placebo-controlled, 2-armed, parallel-group clinical trial of 86 nursing home residents conducted by Cedarbrook Nursing Home in the U.S., Smooth Move herbal tea, which contains fennel, increased the average number of bowel movements of residents, confirming its efficacy as a treatment for chronic constipation.[7]

Memory-Enhancing Activity According to an animal study conducted by SET's College of Pharmacy in India, *Foeniculum vulgare* extract significantly increases step-down latency and acetylcholinesterase inhibition. It was concluded that *F. vulgare* could be employed in the treatment of cognitive disorders such as dementia and Alzheimer's disease.[8]

Gastro-Intestinal Activity According to an ongoing screening program conducted by the University of Illinois at Chicago, the methanol extract of *Foeniculum vulgare* seeds has an MIC of 25 microg/mL against 15 HP strains.[9]

Anticolic Activity According to a randomized, double-blind, placebo-controlled trial conducted by the Universita di Torino, the effectiveness and side effects of a phytotherapeutic agent with *Matricariae recutita*, *Foeniculum vulgare* and *Melissa officinalis* was examined in the treatment of infantile colic. Ninety-three breastfed colicky infants were enrolled, while 88 infants completed the trial: 41 in the phytotherapeutic agent group and 47 in the control. Crying time reduction was observed in 85.4 percent subjects for the phytotherapeutic agent and in 48.9 percent subjects for the placebo. No side effects were reported. The study showed that colic in breastfed infants improved within one week of treatment with an extract based on *Matricariae recutita*, *Foeniculum vulgare* and *Melissa officinalis.*[10]

In a randomized placebo-controlled trial of 125 colicky infants aged 2 to 12 weeks conducted by St. Petersburg Medical Academy of Postdoctoral Education in Russia, the use of fennel oil emulsion eliminated colic in 65 percent of infants in the treatment group, which was significantly better than 23.7 percent of infants in the control group. There was a significant improvement of colic in the treatment group compared with the control group. Side effects were not reported for infants in either group during the trial. The study suggests that fennel seed oil is superior to placebo in decreasing intensity of infantile colic.[11]

Anti-hirsutism Activity In a double-blind study conducted by Shiraz University of Medical Sciences in Iran, 38 patients suffering from idiopathic hirsutism, namely, the occurrence of excessive male-pattern hair growth in women, were treated with creams containing 1 percent and 2 percent of fennel extract and placebo. After hair diameter was measured and rate of growth was considered, the cream containing 2 percent fennel was found to be better than the one containing 1 percent and both were more potent than placebo. The mean values of hair diameter reduction was 7.8 percent, 18.3 percent and -0.5 percent for patients receiving the creams containing 1 percent, 2 percent and 0 percent (placebo) respectively.[12] The effectiveness of the fennel cream confirms its use as an estrogenic agent in treating idiopathic hirsutism which is a disorder of peripheral androgen metabolism.

Hepaprotective Activity In an animal study conducted by Yuzuncu Yil University in Turkey, the essential oil of *Foeniculum vulgare* was shown to have a potent hepaprotective action against hepatic damage.[13]

Insect Repellent Activity According to a study conducted by Seoul National University, the repellent activity of materials derived from the methanol extract of fruits from *Foeniculum vulgare* was compared to that of deet. The fennel extract exhibited a moderate repellent activity at 30 minutes after treatment, whereas deet provided less than an hour of protection against mosquitoes. It was concluded that two components of fennel merited further study as potential mosquito repellent agents or as lead compounds.[14]

Antimicrobial and Antioxidative Activity According to a study conducted by Kangwon National University in Korea, the stems of *Foeniculum vulgare* contain an antimicrobial principle against *Bacillus subtilis*, *Aspergillus niger*, and *Cladosporium cladosporioides.*[15]

According to an in-vitro study conducted by the Istituto del C.N.R. per lo Studio delle Sostanze Naturali di Interesse Alimentare e Chimico–Farmaceutico in Italy, the essential oil of *Crithmum maritimum* L. (marine fennel) and two samples of *Foeniculum vulgare* Miller (common fennel) demonstrated antioxidant capacities, comparable in some cases to that of alpha-tocopherol and butylated hydroxytoluene (BHT), used as reference antioxidants. The essential oils were assayed against twenty-five genera of bacteria, including animal and plant pathogens, food poisoning and spoilage bacteria. Oils from the two samples of *F. vulgare* showed a higher and broader degree of inhibition than that of *Crithmum maritimum*.[16]

Cardiostimulating Activity According to a study conducted by Birzeit University in the Occupied West Bank of Palestine, the intravenous administration of the lyophilized boiled water extract of *Foeniculum vulgare* leaves produces a significant dose-related reduction in arterial blood pressure, without affecting the heart rate or respiratory rate. In contrast, the non-boiled aqueous extract showed very little hypotensive activity.[17]

Estrogenic Activity Fennel, *Foeniculum vulgare*, and anise, *Pimpinella anisum*, are plants which have been used as estrogenic agents for millennia. Specifically, they have been reputed to increase milk secretion, promote menstruation, facilitate birth, alleviate the symptoms of the male climacteric, and increase libido. In the 1930s, some interest was shown in these plants in the development of synthetic estrogens. The main constituent of the essential oils of fennel and anise, anethole, has been considered to be the active estrogenic agent. However, further research suggests that the actual pharmacologically active agents are polymers of anethole, such as dianethole and photoanethole.[18]

According to an animal trial, the oral administration of acetone extract of *Foeniculum vulgare* seeds for 15 days significantly decreased total protein concentration in testes and increased concentration in seminal vesicles and prostate gland. There was a decrease in activities of acid and alkaline phosphatase in all these regions, except that alkaline phosphatase was unchanged in vasa (vessel or duct). In female rats, oral administration of the extract for 10 days led to vaginal cornification and oestrus cycle. While moderate doses caused increase in weight of mammary glands, higher doses increased the weight of oviduct, endometrium, myometrium, cervix and vagina also. The results confirm the oestrogenic activity of the seed extract.[19]

Fennel Notes

1. Nisābūrī A. *Islamic Medical Wisdom: The Ṭibb al-a'immah*. Trans. B. Ispahany. Ed. AJ Newman. London: Muḥammadī Trust, 1991: 157.

2. Ghazanfar SA. *Handbook of Arabian Medicinal Plants*. Boca Raton: CRC Press, 1994.

3. Pitasawat, Champakaew, Choochote, Jitpakdi, Chaithong, Kanjanapothi, Rattanachanpichai, Tippawangkosol, Riyong, Tuetun, Chaiyasit. Aromatic plant-derived essential oil: An alternative larvicide for mosquito control. *Fitoterapia*. 2007; 78(3): 205–210.

4. Birdane, Cemek, Birdane, Gulcin, Buyukokuroglu. Beneficial effects of *Foeniculum vulgare* on ethanol-induced acute gastric mucosal injury in rats. *World* 2007; 13(4): 607–611.

5. Choi, Hwang. Anti-inflammatory, analgesic and antioxidant activities of the fruit of *Foeniculum vulgare*. *Fitoterapia*. 2004; 75(6): 557–565.

6. Ozcan, Chalchat, Arslan, Ates, Unver. Comparative essential oil composition and antifungal effect of bitter fennel (*Foeniculum vulgare* ssp. *piperitum*) fruit oils obtained during different vegetation. *J* 2006; 9(4): 552–561.

7. Bub, Brinckmann, Cicconetti, Valentine. Efficacy of an herbal dietary supplement (Smooth Move) in the management of constipation in nursing home residents: A randomized, double-blind, placebo-controlled study. *J* 2006; 7(9): 556–561.

8. Joshi, Parle. Cholinergic basis of memory-strengthening effect of *Foeniculum vulgare* Linn. *J* 2006; 9(3): 413–417.

9. Mahady, Pendland, Stoia, Hamill, Fabricant, Dietz, Chadwick. In vitro susceptibility of *Helicobacter pylori* to botanical extracts used traditionally for the treatment of gastrointestinal disorders. *Phytother* 2005; 19(11): 988–991.

10. Savino, Cresi, Castagno, Silvestro, Oggero. A randomized double-blind placebo-controlled trial of a standardized extract of *Matricariae recutita*, *Foeniculum vulgare* and *Melissa officinalis* (ColiMil) in the treatment of breastfed colicky infants. *Phytother* 2005; 19(4): 335–340.

11. Alexandrovich, Rakovitskaya, Kolmo, Sidorova, Shushunov. The effect of fennel (*Foeniculum vulgare*) seed oil emulsion in infantile colic: a randomized, placebo-controlled study. *Altern* 2003; 9(4): 58–61.

12. Javidnia, Dastgheib, Mohammadi, Nasiri. Antihirsutism activity of fennel (fruits of *Foeniculum vulgare*) extract. A double-blind placebo controlled study. *Phytomedicine*. 2003; 10(6–7): 455–458.

13. Ozbek, Ugras, Dulger, Bayram, Tuncer, Ozturk, Ozturk. Hepatoprotective effect of *Foeniculum vulgare* essential oil. *Fitoterapia*. 2003; 74(3): 317–319.

14. Kim, Kim, Chang, Ahn. Repellent activity of constituents identified in *Foeniculum vulgare* fruit against *Aedes aegypti* (Diptera: Culicidae). *J* 2002; 50(24): 6993–6996.

15. Kwon, Choi, Kim, Kim, Kim, Kang, Kim. Antimicrobial constituents of *Foeniculum vulgare*. *Arch* 2002; 25(2): 154–157.

16. Ruberto, Baratta, Deans, Dorman. Antioxidant and antimicrobial activity of *Foeniculum vulgare* and *Crithmum maritimum* essential oils. *Planta* 2000; 66(8): 687–693.

17. Abdul-Ghani, Amin. The vascular action of aqueous extracts of *Foeniculum vulgare* leaves. *J* 1988; 24(2–3): 213–218.

18. Albert-Puleo. Fennel and anise as estrogenic agents. *J* 1980; 2(4): 337–344.

19. Malini, Vanithakumari, Megala, Anusya, Devi, Elango. Effect of *Foeniculum vulgare* Mill. seed extract on the genital organs of male and female rats. *Indian* 1985; 29(1): 21–26.

Fenugreek/*Ḥulbah*

Family: Fabaceae

Botanical Name: *Trigonella foenum-graecum*

Common Names: *English* Fenugreek; *French* Fénugrec, Sénegrain; *Spanish* Alholva, Fenogreco; *German* Griechisches Bockshorn, Bockshornklee, Kuhhornklee, Ziegenhorn, Hirschwundkraut, Rehkörner, Fenugreek, feine Grete, Filigrazie, Schöne Margreth, Siebenzeiten, Stundenkraut, Methika, Philosophenklee; *Urdu/Unānī* Meythi, Hulba; *Modern Standard Arabic* Ḥulbah, Ḥalbah, Farīqah

Safety Rating: Generally Safe Fenugreek is generally considered safe in moderation. It should not, however, be consumed by pregnant women. It also prevents the absorption of oral drugs.

Prophetic Prescription: According to the Messenger of Allāh "If people knew the benefits of fenugreek, they would pay its weight in gold."[1] He said, "Seek a cure with fenugreek (*ḥulbah*)."[2] He recommended herbalists to "Mix fenugreek (*ḥulbah*) in your medicines."[3] Once, when Sa'd ibn Abī Waqqāṣ fell ill, the herbalist Ḥārith ibn Kaladah told him to consume a medicine consisting of dates, barley, and fenugreek (*ḥulbah*) boiled in water with honey once per day. The Prophet approved the preparation and the patient was relieved.[4]

Issues in Identification: It is the consensus that *ḥulbah* is Arabic for fenugreek. As Nehmé has explained, *Trigonella* or fenugreek is known in Arabic as *ḥulbah* and *ḥalbah*, and *Trigonella foenum-graecum* is known as *ḥulbah shā'i'ah* and *ḥulbah zirā'iyyah*.[5] According to both Ghazanfar and Mandaville, *Trigonella foenum-graecum* is almost an exclusively cultivated herb in eastern Saudi Arabia, rarely found as an escapee. It is known as *ḥulbah* in Saudi Arabic, as well as *ḥelbah* and *ḥilbah*.[6]

Properties and Uses: Fenugreek is a bitter, pungent, warming herb that increases milk flow, stimulates the uterus, soothes irritated tissues, lowers fever, improves digestion, promotes healing, and has laxative, expectorant, diuretic, antiparasitic, and antitumor effects. Seeds are eaten as a tonic for the liver, kidneys and male sexual organs.

Fenugreek is used internally for late-onset diabetes, poor digestion (especially in convalescence), gastric inflammation, digestive disorders, tuberculosis, painful menstruation, labor pains, and insufficient lactation. Fenugreek acts as a bulk laxative, lubricates the intestines, and reduces fever. It helps asthma and sinus problems by reducing mucus. It is used in the treatment of diabetes, inflamed lymph glands, leg ulcers, muscle pain, poor appetite, tuberculosis, and wounds. In Chinese medicine, fenugreek is used for kidney-related disorders. In Ayurvedic medicine, it is used mainly to treat digestive and bronchial complaints, debility, allergies, neurasthenia, gout and arthritis. Fenugreek is approved in Germany as an internal treatment for gastritis, loss of appetite, and as a poultice for inflammations.[7] Arab women used it to gain weight.[8] Externally, it is used for local inflammation and to soften the skin.[9] The herb is never given to pregnant women.

Scientific Studies: *Cholesterol-Lowering, Antidiabetic, Anti-inflammatory, Antimicrobial, Antifungal, and Antiulcer Activity* Small animal studies have revealed a large number of potential therapeutic applications of the seed. These include its use in treating baldness, cancer, elevated cholesterol levels, diabetes, inflammations, microbial and fungal infections, and stomach ulcers.[10]

Antidiabetic Activity Preliminary animal and human trials suggest possible hypoglycemic and antihyperlipidemic properties of fenugreek seed powder taken orally.[11] Studies have identified hypoglycemic activity of various fenugreek seed extracts in rabbits, rats, and dogs. Several small and mostly uncontrolled human studies have shown a reduction in plasma glucose concentration and insulin responses in non–insulin-dependent diabetics. Used to treat diabetes in the Middle East, some experimental date suggests that extracts of the seed do lower blood sugar levels. Small double-blind studies suggest that fenugreek can be helpful for both type 1 and type 2 diabetes. In one study of 60 people with type 2 diabetes, 25 mg per day of fenugreek led to significant improvements in overall blood sugar control, blood sugar elevations in response to a meal, and cholesterol levels.[12] Another study found benefits with only 15 mg of fenugreek per day.[13] In a small double-blind, controlled study, people with type 1 diabetes were randomly prescribed either fenugreek at a dose of 50 mg daily as part of their lunch and dinner, or the same meals without the powder, each for 10 days. Those on the fenugreek diet had significant decreases in their fasting blood sugar.[14] It may also interfere with certain drugs for diabetes. Its high mucilage coats the stomach and may prevent absorption of other drugs.[15]

According to a report published by the Indian Council of Medical Research, daily doses of fenugreek seeds, ranging from 25 to 100 grams, diminish reactive hyperglycemia in diabetic patients. Levels of glucose, serum cholesterol and triglycerides are also significantly reduced in the diabetes patients when the seeds were consumed. The report said that the effect of taking fenugreek seeds could be quite dramatic, when consumed with a 1200 to 1400 calories-per-day diet, which is usually recommended for diabetic patients.

In an animal study conducted by Satsang Herbal Research and Analytical Laboratories in India, the oral administration of 95 percent ethanolic extract of *Foenum-graecum* was confirmed to possess blood glucose-lowering effects.[16]

According to a review of scientific studies on traditional anti-diabetic herbs conducted by the Department of Chemistry, Yonsei University, Seoul, Korea, *Momordica charantia* L. (Cucurbitaceae), *Pterocarpus marsupium* Roxb. (Fabaceae), and *Trigonella foenum graecum* L. (Fabaceae), have been reported as beneficial for treatment of type 2 diabetes.[17]

In a 3-month controlled human trial conducted by Punjab Agricultural University in India, the effect of supplementation of a powdered mixture of three traditional medicinal plants — bitter gourd, jamun seeds, and fenugreek seeds, in raw and cooked form — on blood glucose was studied in 60 non-insulin-dependent male diabetics.[18] Daily supplementation of 1 g of this powered mixture for a 1.5-month period and then a further increase to 2 g for another 1.5 months significantly reduced the fasting as well as the postprandial glucose level of the diabetic patients. A significant decrease in oral hypoglycemic drug intake and decline in percentage of the subjects who were on hypoglycemic drugs were found after the 3-month feeding trial. It was concluded that 2 g of a powdered mixture of traditional medicinal plants in either raw or cooked form can be successfully used for lowering blood glucose in diabetics.

In a study conducted by the Central Food Technological Research Institute in India, fenugreek seeds (*Trigonella foenum-graecum*), garlic (*Allium sativum*), onion (*Allium cepa*), and turmeric (*Curcuma longa*) have been experimentally documented to possess antidiabetic potential. In a limited number of studies, cumin seeds (*Cuminum cyminum*), ginger (*Zingiber officinale*), mustard (*Brassica nigra*), curry leaves (*Murraya koenigii*) and coriander (*Coriandrum sativum*) have been reported to be hypoglycemic.[19]

In a 21-day animal study conducted by Ain Shams University in Egypt, oral administration of fenugreek seed reduced blood glucose level by 58 percent, restored liver glycogen content and significantly decreased kidney glycogen as well as liver glucose-6-phosphatase activity. Meanwhile, *Balanites aegyptiaca* extract reduced blood glucose level by 24 percent and significantly decreased liver glucose-6-phosphatase activity in diabetic rats. The results demonstrated that both the fenugreek and balanites extracts were able to in vitro inhibit alpha-amylase activity in dose-dependent manner. Fenugreek was a more potent inhibitor than balanites. These findings suggest that the hypoglycemic effect of fenugreek and balanites is mediated through insulinomimetic effect as well as inhibition of intestinal alpha-amylase activity.[20]

In a study conducted by the National Centre for Cell Science in India, the in vivo hypoglycemic activity of a dialyzed fenugreek seed extract was studied in alloxan-induced diabetic mice and found to be comparable to that of insulin.[21] Fenugreek seed extract also improved intraperitoneal glucose tolerance in normal mice. These results suggest that in vivo the hypoglycemic effect of fenugreek seed extract is mediated, at least in part, by the activation of an insulin signaling pathway in adipocytes and liver cells.

According to a study conducted by Jawaharlal Nehru University in India, oral administration of fenugreek seed powder for 3 weeks to alloxan diabetic rats stabilized glucose homeostasis and free radical metabolism in liver and kidney. This second study suggests that fenugreek seed power has a protective effect on the liver and kidney of diabetic rats, proving its potential as an anti-diabetic agent.[22]

In an animal trial conducted by Khulna Medical College, the effectiveness of defatted fenugreek seeds as an antidiabetogenic herb was examined.[23] The experiment was carried out in Bangabandhu Sheikh Mujib Medical University and BIRDEM from 1996 to 1998 on a total of 58 Long Evans rats of either sex. The experiment concluded that fenugreek decreases the fasting blood glucose level considerably by improving diabetes mellitus.

In an animal trial conducted by Annamalai University in India, supplementation with fenugreek leaves showed a significant effect on hyperglycemia, hypoinsulinemia and glycosylated hemoglobin in streptozotocin diabetic rats. Fenugreek leaves improved the body weight and liver glycogen. Fenugreek leaves also showed a significant effect on key carbohydrate metabolic enzymes in diabetic rats. The effect of fenugreek leaves was found to be similar to that of glibenclamide. Thus, fenugreek leaves exhibited antidiabetic action in streptozotocin-induced diabetic rats. Insulin restored all the parameters to near normal levels in diabetic rats.[24]

In a human trial conducted by the National Institute of Nutrition in India, fenugreek significantly reduced fasting blood sugar and improved the glucose tolerance test.[25] There was a 54 percent reduction in 24-h urinary glucose excretion. Serum total cholesterol, LDL and VLDL cholesterol and triglycerides were also significantly reduced. The HDL cholesterol fraction, however, remained unchanged. These results are further indicators of the usefulness of fenugreek seeds in the management of diabetes.

In a study conducted in Israel, the effect of fenugreek on postprandial glucose and insulin levels following the meal tolerance test was studied in non–insulin-dependent diabetics.[26] The addition of powdered fenugreek seed (15 g) soaked in water significantly reduced the subsequent postprandial glucose levels. The plasma insulin also tended to be lower in non–insulin-dependent diabetics given fenugreek but without a statistical difference. Fenugreek had no effect on lipid levels 3 h following the meal tolerance test. Fenugreek may have a potential benefit in the treatment of non–insulin-dependent diabetics.

In another study, fractions of fenugreek seed were added to the diet of normal or diabetic hypercholesterolemic dogs for 8 days.[27] The effects on levels of blood glucose, plasma glucagon and plasma cholesterol were investigated. The lipid extract had no effect. The defatted fraction, which is rich in fibers (53.9 percent) and contains 4.8 percent of steroid saponins, significantly lowered basal blood glucose, plasma glucagon, and plasma cholesterol levels in normal dogs. The addition of this fraction to the food of diabetic hypercholesterolemic dogs caused a decrease of cholesterolemia and reduced hyperglycemia. The study concluded that the defatted portion of fenugreek seed induces a hypocholesterolemic effect.

Uterine Stimulating Activity Extracts from fenugreek have been shown to stimulate uterine contractions in guinea pigs.[28]

Cholesterol-Lowering Activity A recent study showed that fenugreek seeds significantly lowered serum cholesterol levels (14 percent reduction) in a 24-week study with sixty non–insulin-dependent diabetics.[29]

The Peninsula Medical School, Universities of Exeter and Plymouth in the UK systematically reviewed the clinical evidence for herbal medicinal products in the treatment of hypercholesterolemia.[30] Systematic literature searches were conducted in 6 electronic databases. Twenty-five randomized clinical trials involving 11 herbal medicinal products were identified. Guggul (*Commiphora mukul*), fenugreek (*Trigonella foenum-graecum*), red yeast rice, and artichoke (*Cynara scolymus*) have been most extensively studied and have demonstrated reductions in total serum cholesterol levels of between 10 percent and 33 percent. The methodological quality as assessed by the Jadad score was less than 3 (maximum, 5) for 13 of the 25 trials. Many herbal medicinal products have potential hypocholesterolemic activity and encouraging safety profiles. However, only a limited amount of clinical research exists to support their efficacy. Further research is warranted to establish the value of these extracts in the treatment of hypercholesterolemia.

Cytoprotective Activity In a study conducted by Annamalai University in India, the cytoprotective effects of fenugreek polyphenolic extract were comparable with those of a positive control silymarin, a known hepatoprotective agent. The findings suggest that the polyphenolic compounds of fenugreek seeds can be considered cytoprotective during ethanol-induced liver damage.[31]

Antihypertriglyceridemic Activity In a study conducted by Tokyo University of Marine Science and Technology, researchers found that fenugreek seed extract reduced the body weight gain induced by a high-fat diet in obese mice.[32] The extract decreased plasma triglyceride gain induced by oil administration. The major component of the extract, 4-hydroxyisoleucine, also decreased plasma triglyceride gain. Fenugreek seed extract is a potentially positive component in the prevention of obesity induced by a high-fat diet.

Antioxidative Activity In a study conducted by Annamalai University in India, fenugreek seeds were found to possess potent antioxidant properties.[33]

In a study conducted by the University of Pune in India, the antioxidant properties of germinated fenugreek seeds were studied in comparison to those of dried seeds.[34] This study reveals significant antioxidative activity in germinated fenugreek seeds which may be due partly to the presence of flavonoids and polyphenols.

Anticancer Activity According to a study conducted by the United Arab Emirates University, fenugreek seeds show a potential protective effect against chemically induced breast cancer in rats.[35] At 200 mg/kg body weight, fenugreek seed extract significantly inhibited the induced mammary hyperplasia and decreased its incidence. Epidemiological studies also implicate apoptosis as a mechanism that might mediate the fenugreek's anti–breast cancer protective effects. This was apparently the first study which suggested significant chemopreventive effects of fenugreek seeds against breast cancer.

In a 15-week animal study conducted by Annamalai University in India, supplementation of fenugreek seeds inhibited colon carcinogenesis by modulating the activities of beta-glucuronidase and mucinase. According to researchers, the beneficial effect may be attributed to the presence of fiber, flavonoids and/or saponins.[36]

Antihyperthyroidic Activity According to an animal trial conducted by Devi Ahilya University in India, *Trigonella foenum-graecum* and *Allium sativum* extracts may be used individually but not together in the regulation of hyperthyroidism as they do not prove to be synergistic.[37]

Breast-Enhancing Activity George Washington University School of Medicine claims that no clinical trials have been published on breast-enhancing herbs like fenugreek. According to these researchers, the use of bust-enhancing products should be discouraged because of lack of evidence for efficacy and long-term safety concerns.[38] However, according to the Drug Information and Medication Use Outcomes Section, University of Illinois at Chicago, the use of fenugreek has been purported to be effective in anecdotal reports. Use of this agent may be warranted after considering risks versus benefits.[39]

Antiulcer Activity In a study conducted by Annamalai University in India, the aqueous extract and a gel fraction isolated from fenugreek seeds showed significant ulcer protective effects. The cytoprotective effect of the seeds seemed to be not only due to the anti-secretory action but also to the effects on mucosal glycoproteins. The fenugreek seeds also prevented the rise in lipid peroxidation induced by ethanol, presumably by enhancing antioxidant potential of the gastric mucosa thereby lowering mucosal injury. Histological studies revealed that the soluble gel fraction derived from the seeds was more effective than omeprazole in preventing lesion formation. These observations show that fenugreek seeds possess antiulcer potential.[40]

Fenugreek Notes

1. Nisābūrī A. *Ṭibb al-a'immah*. Bayrūt: Dār al-Maḥajjah al-Bayḍā', 1994: 255; Sūyūṭī J. *As-Sūyūṭī's Medicine of the Prophet*. Ed. A Thomson. London: Ṭā-Hā Publishers, 1994: 54; Farooqi, MIH. *Medicinal Plants in the Traditions of Prophet Muḥammad*. Lucknow: Sidrah Publishers, 1998: 72; Ibn Qayyim al-Jawziyyah M. *al-Ṭibb al-nabawī*. Bayrūt: Dār al-Kitāb, 1985. Ibn al-Jawziyyah says that this tradition is fabricated.

2. Ibn Qayyim al-Jawziyyah M. *al-Ṭibb al-nabawī*. Bayrūt: Dār al-Kitāb, 1985.

3. Nisābūrī A. *Ṭibb al-a'immah*. Bayrūt: Dār al-Maḥajjah al-Bayḍā', 1994: 256.

4. Ibn Qayyim al-Jawziyyah M. *al-Ṭibb al-nabawī*. Bayrūt: Dār al-Kitāb, 1985.

5. Nehmé M. *Dictionnaire étymologique de la flore du Liban*. Bayrūt: Librairie du Liban, 2000.

6. Ghazanfar SA. *Handbook of Arabian Medicinal Plants*. Boca Raton: CRC Press, 1994; Mandaville JP. *Flora of Eastern Saudi Arabia*. London: Kegan Paul, 1990.

7. White LB, Foster S. *The Herbal Drugstore*. N.p.: Rodale, 2000: 558.

8. Compton MS. *Herbal Gold*. St. Paul: Llewellyn, 2000: 193.

9. Gehrmann B, Koch WG, Tshirch CO, Brinkmann H. *Medicinal Herbs: A Compendium*. New York: Haworth Press, 2005: 81.

10. Tyler VE, Foster S. *Tyler's Honest Herbal*. 4th ed. New York: Haworth Press, 1999: 159.

11. Basch, Ulbricht, Kuo, Szapary P, Smith. Therapeutic applications of fenugreek. *Altern* 2003; 8(1): 20–7.

12. Sharma, RD, et al. Use of fenugreek seed powder in the management of non-insulin-dependent diabetes mellitus. *Nutr Res* 1996; 16: 1331–1339.

13. Madar Z, et al. Glucose-lowering effect of fenugreek in non-insulin-dependent diabetics. *Eur J Clin Nutr* 1988; 42: 51–54.

14. Sharma RD, Raghuram TC, and Rao NS. Effect of fenugreek seeds on blood glucose and serum lipids in type 1 diabetes. *Eur J Clin Nutr* 1990; 44: 301–306.

15. Gehrmann B, Koch WG, Tshirch CO, Brinkmann H. *Medicinal Herbs: A Compendium*. New York: Haworth Press, 2005: 81.

16. Kar, Choudhary, Bandyopadhyay. Comparative evaluation of hypoglycaemic activity of some Indian medicinal plants in alloxan diabetic rats. *J* 2003; 84(1): 105–108.

17. Jung, Park, Lee, Kang, Kang, Kim. Antidiabetic agents from medicinal plants. *Curr* 2006; 13(10): 1203–1218.

18. Kochhar, Nagi. Effect of supplementation of traditional medicinal plants on blood glucose in non-insulin-dependent diabetics: a pilot study. *J* 2005; 8(4): 545–549.

19. Srinivasan. Plant foods in the management of diabetis mellitus: spices as beneficial antidiabetic food adjuncts. *Int* 2005; 56(6): 399–414.

20. Gad MZ, El-Sawalhi, Ismail, El-Tanbouly. Biochemical study of the anti-diabetic action of the Egyptian plants fenugreek and balanites. *Mol* 2006; 281(1–2): 173–183.

21. Vijayakumar MV, Singh, Chhipa, Bhat. The hypoglycaemic activity of fenugreek seed extract is mediated through the stimulation of an insulin signaling pathway. *Br* 2005; 146(1): 41–48.

22. Thakran, Siddiqui, Baquer. *Trigonella foenum graecum* seed powder protects against histopathological abnormalities in tissues of diabetic rats. *Mol* 2004; 266(1–2): 151–159.

23. Mondal, Yousuf, Banu, Ferdousi, Khalil, Shamim. Effect of fenugreek seeds on the fasting blood glucose level in the streptozotocin induced diabetic rats. *Mymensingh* 2004; 13(2): 161–164.

24. Devi, Kamalakkannan, Prince. Supplementation of fenugreek leaves to diabetic rats. Effect on carbohydrate metabolic enzymes in diabetic liver and kidney. *Phytother* 2003; 17(10): 1231–1233.

25. Sharma, Raghuram, Rao. Effect of fenugreek seeds on blood glucose and serum lipids in type 1 diabetes. *Eur* 1990; 44(4): 301–306.

26. Madar, Abel, Samish, Arad. Glucose-lowering effect of fenugreek in non-insulin-dependent diabetics. *Eur* 1988; 42(1): 51–4.

27. Valette, Sauvaire, Baccou JC, Ribes. Hypocholesterolaemic effect of fenugreek seeds in dogs. *Atherosclerosis*. 1984; 50(1): 105–111.

28. Leung A, et al. *Encyclopedia of Common and Natural Ingredients used in Food, Drugs, and Cosmetics*. New York: John Wiley and Sons, 1996: 243–244.

29. Sharma RD, Sarkar A, Hazra DK, Misra B, Singh JB, Maheshwari BB, Sharma SK. *Nutrition Research*, 1996; 16(8): 1331–1339(9).

30. Thompson, Ernst. Herbs for serum cholesterol reduction: a systematic view. *J* 2003; 52(6): 468–478.
31. Kaviarasan, Ramamurty, Gunasekaran, Varalakshmi, Anuradha. Fenugreek (*Trigonella foenum graecum*) seed extract prevents ethanol-induced toxicity and apoptosis in Chang liver cells. *Alcohol* 2006; 41(3): 267–273.
32. Handa, Yamaguchi K, Sono, Yazawa. Effects of fenugreek seed extract in obese mice fed a high-fat diet. *Biosci* 2005; 69(6): 1186–1188.
33. Kaviarasan, Vijayalakshmi, Anuradha. Polyphenol-rich extract of fenugreek seeds protect erythrocytes from oxidative damage. *Plant* 2004; 59(4): 143–147.
34. Dixit, Ghaskadbi, Mohan, Devasagayam. Antioxidant properties of germinated fenugreek seeds. *Phytother* 2005; 19(11): 977–983.
35. Amin, Alkaabi, Al-Falasi, Daoud. Chemopreventive activities of *Trigonella foenum graecum* (fenugreek) against breast cancer. *Cell* 2005; 29(8): 687–694.
36. Devasena, Menon. Fenugreek affects the activity of beta-glucuronidase and mucinase in the colon. *Phytother* 2003; 17(9): 1088–1091.
37. Tahiliani, Kar. The combined effects of *Trigonella* and *Allium* extracts in the regulation of hyperthyroidism in rats. *Phytomedicine.* 2003; 10(8): 665–668.
38. Fugh-Berman. 'Bust enhancing' herbal products. *Obstet* 2003; 101(6): 1345–1349.
39. Gabay. Galactogogues: medications that induce lactation. *J* 2002; 18(3): 274–279.
40. Pandian, Anuradha, Viswanathan. Gastroprotective effect of fenugreek seeds (*Trigonella foenum graecum*) on experimental gastric ulcer in rats. *J* 2002; 81(3): 393–397.

Fig / *Tīn*

Family: Moraceae

Botanical Name: *Ficus carica*

Common Names: *English* Common fig tree; *French* Figuier, Carique; *Spanish* Higuera; *German* Echter Feigenbaum; *Urdu/Unānī* Teen, Anjeer; *Modern Standard Arabic* Tīn

Safety Rating: Generally Safe Figs are generally considered safe for most people.

Prophetic Prescription: Not only is the fig mentioned in the Qur'ān, it is the name of one of its chapters (95:1). The Prophet Muḥammad said, "If I were to say that any fruit descended from Paradise, I should say these, for the fruit of Paradise has no stones. So eat from them: for they put an end to hemorrhoids, and are beneficial for gout."[1] He also stated, "Eat figs for they help hemorrhoids and gout."[2] Both the Prophet and Imām 'Alī ibn Abī Ṭālib recommended to people that "To eat figs protects against colic."[3] The Imām also said, "[e]ating figs relaxes obstructions [in the body] and is beneficial for the wind of colic."[4]

Issues in Identification: It is the consensus that *tīn* is Arabic for fig. As Nehmé has explained, *Ficus* is known in Arabic as *tīn*, while *Ficus carica* is known as *tīn shā'ī'*.[5] According to Bīrūnī, *tīn* is also known as *balas*.[6] As Ghazanfar notes, *Ficus carica* is known as *balas 'arabī* in Yemeni Arabic.[7] Although there were no figs in the Ḥijāz and Medina during the time of the Prophet, they are now widely cultivated in all parts of Saudi Arabia. They are cultivated throughout South West Asia, North Africa, and Southern Europe. In all likelihood, the figs consumed by the Prophet were brought by caravan to Arabia from Mosul in what is now the Kurdish region of Iraq.

Properties and Uses: *Ficus carica*, known commonly as fig, is a sweet, laxative herb that soothes irritated tissues and is used internally for constipation and externally for hemorrhoids. Figs are nutritive, concoctive, laxative, emollient, expectorant, diaphoretic, digestive, diuretic, febrifuge, deobstruent, demulcent, and aperient, and contain the best nutrient score among dried fruits.[8] They contain gentle laxative substances and are thus well-suited for the treatment of constipation in children and individuals with a delicate constitution. Figs are in fact employed in the preparation of laxatives, usually in combination with senna and carminatives. Figs also contain antiulcer, antibacterial and antiparasitic properties and are beneficial in the treatment of asthma and sexual debility. The leaves, fruit, and latex of figs are effective in removing warts and corns. The soft interior pulp of roasted figs can be applied as a poultice to boils and carbuncles. A syrup made of the leaves of green fruits is excellent for coughs, hoarseness or shortness of breath and all diseases of the chest and lungs. According to Ibn Buṭlān, white, peeled figs purify the kidneys.[9]

Scientific Studies: *Antioxidative Activity* Figs are particularly elevated in antioxidants. According to one study, fig antioxidants can enrich lipoproteins in plasma and protect them from subsequent oxidation.[10]

Antimutagenic Activity In a study of the antimutagenic action of plants extracts of *Armoracia rusticana*, *Ficus carica*, *Zea mays*, and their mixture on environmental xenobiotics, researchers found that they decreased the genotoxicity of environmental mutagens.[11]

Anticancer Activity Figs are rich in flavonoids and polyphenols both of which are believed to reduce the risk of cancer and heart disease.[12] Both extract of figs and the fig compound, benzaidehyde, have helped shrink tumors in humans according to Japanese tests. In a study conducted by the Hebrew University in Jerusalem, figs were found to contain compounds which inhibit the proliferation of various cancer cells lines.[13]

Antidiabetic Activity In a controlled animal trial conducted by the University of Extremadura in Spain, researchers found that *Ficus carica* extract tends to normalize the antioxidant values in diabetic animals.[14] In a controlled, double-blind, human trial of insulin-dependent diabetes mellitus patients conducted by the Faculty of Medicine in Madrid, researchers found that a decoction of fig leaves, as a supplement to breakfast, lowered insulin levels by 12 percent while helping to control postprandial glycemia.[15]

Antiherpetic Activity In a study conducted by Shandong University in Jinan, *Ficus carica* leaf extract was found to possess a distinct anti–HSV-1 effect. It possessed low toxicity and had a direct killing-virus effect on HSV-1. Researchers concluded that the leaves of *Ficus carica* possess anti–HSV-1 effect, and their application on the area of medicine, food and drugs has expansive foreground.[16]

Anti-Hypoglycemic Activity In an animal study conducted by Satsang Herbal Research and Analytical Laboratories in India, the oral administration of 95 percent ethanolic extract of *Ficus glomerata* and *Ficus benghalensis* was confirmed to possess blood glucose lowering effects.[17]

Fig Notes

1. Nisābūrī A. *Ṭibb al-a'immah.* Bayrūt: Dār al-Maḥajjah al-Bayḍā', 1994: 256; Iṣbahānī AN al-. *Mawsū'at al-ṭibb al-nabawī.* Ed. MKD al-Turkī. Bayrūt: Dār Ibn Ḥazm, 2006; Sūyūṭī J. *As-Sūyūṭī's Medicine of the Prophet.* Ed. A Thomson. London: Ṭā-Hā Publishers, 1994.

2. Chaghhaynī M. *Ṭibb al-nabī.* Trans. C Elgood. *Osiris* 1962; 14: 190.

3. Chaghhaynī M. *Ṭibb al-nabī.* Trans. C Elgood. *Osiris* 1962; 14: 189; Nisābūrī A. *Ṭibb al-a'immah.* Bayrūt: Dār al-Maḥajjah al-Bayḍā', 1994: 182.

4. Nisābūrī A. *Ṭibb al-a'immah.* Bayrūt: Dār al-Maḥajjah al-Bayḍā', 1994: 182.

5. Nehmé M. *Dictionnaire étymologique de la flore du Liban.* Bayrūt: Librairie du Liban, 2000.

6. Bīrūnī, AR al-. *al-Bīrūnī's Book on Pharmacy and Materia Medica.* Ed. and trans. HM Said. Karachi: Hamdard National Foundation, 1973.

7. Ghazanfar SA. *Handbook of Arabian Medicinal Plants.* Boca Raton: CRC Press, 1994.

8. Vinson, JA, Zubik L, Bose P, Samman N., Proch J. Dried fruits: excellent in vitro an in vivo antioxidants. *J Am Coll Nutr.* 2005; 1: 44–50.

9. Ibn Buṭlān, *The Medieval Health Handbook: Tacuinum sanitatis.* Ed. L Cogliati Arano. Trans. O Ratti and A Westbrook. New York: George Braziller, 1976: 2.

10. Vinson, JA, Zubik L, Bose P, Samman N., Proch J. Dried fruits: excellent in vitro an in vivo antioxidants. *J Am Coll Nutr.* 2005; 1: 44–50.

11. Agabeili, Kasimova. Antimutagenic activity of *Armoracia rusticana, Zea mays,* and *Ficus carica* plant extracts and their mixture. *Tsitol* 2005; 39(3): 75–79.

12. Vison JA. The functional food properties of figs. *Cereal Foods World.* 1999; 44: 2: 82–87. http://www.aaccnet.org/funcfood/pdfs/99-0122-01f.pdf

13. Rubnov, Kashman, Rabinowitz, Schlesinger, Mechoulam R. Suppressors of cancer cell proliferation from fig (*ficus carica*) resin: isolation and structure elucidation. *J* 2001; 64(7): 993–996.

14. Perez, Canal, Torres. Experimental diabetes treated with *ficus carica* extract: effect on oxidative stress parameters. *Acta* 2003; 40(1): 3–8.

15. Serraclara, Hawkins, Perez, Dominguez, Campillo, Torres. Hypoglycemic action of an oral fig-leaf decoction in type-1 diabetic patients. *Diabetes* 1998; 39(1): 19–22.

16. Wang, Wang, Song, Jia, Wang, Xu. [Studies on antiherpetic effect of Ficus carica leaves]. *Zhong* 2004; 27(10): 754–756.

17. Kar, Choudhary, Bandyopadhyay. Comparative evaluation of hypoglycaemic activity of some Indian medicinal plants in alloxan diabetic rats. *J* 2003; 84(1): 105–108.

Fleawort / *Bizr Qaṭūnā, Ashbiyūsh*

FAMILY: Plantaginaceae

BOTANICAL NAME: *Plantago psyllium*

COMMON NAMES: *English* Flea-wort; *French* Psyllium, Herbe aux puces, Pucière; *Spanish* Zaragatona, Plantago ovata; *German* Flohwegerich, Flohsamen; *Urdu/Unānī* Ispaghul, Asapaghol, Bazr Qutuna; *Modern Standard Arabic* Ḥashīshat al-baswāghiyyah, Ḥashīshat al-barāghīth, Bizr qaṭūnā, Burghūṯī, Fasiliyyūn

SAFETY RATING: GENERALLY SAFE Used as herbal remedies since prehistoric times, *Plantago* species are generally considered safe for most people.

PROPHETIC PRESCRIPTION: According to the Messenger of Allāh, "You have *ashbiyūsh* which is used as a balm for the stomach." He added, "*Ashbiyūsh* is *bizr qaṭūnā* [*Plantago psyllium*]."[1] A man complained to Imām Muḥammad al-Bāqir about diarrhea. The Imām told him "Take one part of white clay, one part of fleawort seeds, one part of gum arabic (*ṣamgh 'arabī*), and one part of Armenian clay. Boil it over a low fire, and eat of it."[2] According to Imām Ja'far al-Ṣādiq, "He who had a fever, and drank the weight of two or three dirhams of fleawort [*bizr qaṭūnā*] that night, he is protected from pleurisy [*birsām*]."[3]

ISSUES IN IDENTIFICATION: According to Mandaville, *Plantago* is a very important genus in the desert annual flora with several species assuming vernal dominance over extensive areas. The main representatives of the genus include *Pantago amplexicaulis*, *Plantago boissieri*, *Plantago ciliate*,

Plantago coronopus, *Plantago lanceolata*, *Plantago major*, *Plantago ovata*, and *Plantago psammophila*.[4]

According to Bīrūnī, the plant is also known as *qaṭūna* and Said has identified it as *Plantago psyllium*.[5] According to Ghazanfar, psyllium is the dried seeds of *Plantago afra*, *Plantago indica*, and *Plantato ovata*, which is used as demulcents in the treatment of chronic constipation.[6]

There are only two types of *Plantago* with names that resemble the *bizr qaṭūnā* mentioned by Imām Muḥammad al-Bāqir: *Plantago afra* or African plantain, which is known as *lisān al-ḥamal al-ifrīqī*, *ʿushbat al-barāghīth*, and *bizirqaṭūnā*, as well as *Plantago ovata*, known in Omani and Saudi as *ḥabbah zargah*, *quraytah*, and *rebal*, and as *biḍr qūṭnū* in Yemeni.

The Imām could not have been referring to *Plantago asiatica*, as the plant is not used for diarrhea. Besides *Plantago psyllium* and *Plantago afra*, *Plantago major* is also used for diarrhea. This latter, however, is a rare plant in the region. According to Hakim Chishti, *Plantago major* is known as *lisān* and *al-ḥamal*. According to Álvarez de Morales and Girón Irueste, *ashbiyūsh* is a synonym for *bizr qaṭunah*.[7]

PROPERTIES AND USES: *Plantago psyllium*, known as Spanish psyllium, fleaseed, and fleawort, is a sweet, astringent, cooling herb that moistens the membranes, soothes irritation, and absorbs digestive toxins. It is used internally for constipation and diarrhea and externally for skin irritation and inflamed eyelids. In Ayurvedic medicine, it is used with buttermilk to treat diarrhea and with warm milk for constipation.

Plantago major, known as greater plantain, and rat-tail plantain, is an astringent and demulcent herb that is a diuretic and an expectorant. It promotes healing, and is effective against bacterial infections. Roots and leaves are hemostatic, refrigerant and diuretic. *Plantago major* is used internally for diarrhea, hemorrhage, hemorrhoids, cystitis, bronchitis, excess mucus, catarrh, sinusitis, asthma, hay fever, ear infections, dry coughs, irritated throat, respiratory problems, and gastric ulcers. Externally, fresh leaves are crushed and applied to wounds, insect bites, sores, bruises, ulcers, eye inflammations, shingles, hemorrhoids, and varicose ulcers. It is often used to moderate the irritant effect of herbs containing volatile oils.

Psyllium, in general, is used to treat burns, cancer, chronic bronchitis, chronic diarrhea, constipation, cough, dysentery, fluid retention, hemorrhoids, high cholesterol, immune system problems, poison ivy, skin and mucous membrane inflammation, throat irritation, urinary tract disorders, and wounds.

SCIENTIFIC STUDIES: *Safety of Psyllium Supplement* According to the Food and Drug Administration laxative drug products in granular dosage form containing the bulk-forming psyllium ingredients (psyllium hemicellulose, psyllium hydrophilic mucilloid, psyllium seed, psyllium seed [blond], psyllium seed husks, plantago ovata husks, and plantago seed) are not generally recognized as safe and effective and are misbranded. In fact, they have resulted in esophageal obstruction. This caution does not apply to psyllium laxatives in nongranular dosage forms, such as powders, tablets, or wafers. This final rule is part of FDA's ongoing review of OTC drug products.[8]

Cholesterol-Lowering Activity According to the U.S. Food and Drug Administration, "Eating soluble fiber from foods such as psyllium as part of a diet low in saturated fat and cholesterol may reduce the risk of heart disease."[9]

Antidiabetic Activity According to an 8-week, randomized, double-blind, placebo-controlled study conducted by the Institute of Medicinal Plants in Tehran, Iran, 49 subjects with type 2 diabetes were given *Plantato ovata* or a placebo in combination with their anti-diabetic drugs. Fasting blood glucose, and HbA1c, showed a significant reduction, whereas HDL-C increased significantly following psyllium treatment. LDL/HDL ratio was significantly decreased. The results showed that 5.1 g b.i.d. of psyllium for persons with type 2 diabetes is safe, well-tolerated, and improves glycemic control.[10]

Anti-inflammatory Activity In an animal trial conducted by the University of Granada, Spain, dietary fiber supplementation with 5 percent *Plantago ovata* seeds ameliorated the development of colonic inflammation. This effect was associated with an increased production of short-chain fatty acids which can act synergistically in inhibiting the production of pro-inflammatory mediators.[11]

Anticancer Activity In a paired case-control study of 424 people diagnosed with colon cancer conducted by the Community Health Center of Area 4 in Madrid, the consumption of *Plantago ovata* was associated with a reduced risk of colon cancer.[12]

In a 12 month, open label, parallel-group, multicenter, randomized clinical trial of 105 patients with ulcerative colitis, the consumption of *Plantago ovata* seeds appeared to be as effective as mesalamine in maintaining remission. The active compound appears to be butyrate, which is released by *Plantago ovata* seeds during colonic fermentation.[13]

Hypolipidemic Activity According to a study conducted by the University of Sonora in Mexico, Plantago ovata husks is recognized as a potent agent in lowering plasma cholesterol. The study suggests that *Plantago ovata* exerts its hypolipidemic effect by affecting bile acid absorption and altering hepatic cholesterol metabolism.[14]

According to a 6-week, randomized, double-blind, placebo-controlled study of 125 subjects conducted by the Mexican Social Security Institute and Research Group on Diabetes and Chronic Illnesses, with the daily consumption of 5 g t.i.d. of *Plantago psyllium*, fasting plasma glucose, total cholesterol, LDL cholesterol, and triglycerides levels, showed a significant reduction, whereas HDL cholesterol increased significantly following psyllium treatment. The results of the study indicate that 5 g t.i.d. of psyllium is useful, as an adjunct to dietary therapy, in patients with type 2 diabetes, to reduce plasma lipid and glucose levels.[15]

According to a study of 12 patients with non-insulin-dependent diabetes mellitus and ten healthy volunteers, adding *Plantago psyllium* to meals may reduce glycemic index of carbohydrate foods and may help diabetic control.[16]

According to an animal study conducted by the Wistar Institute in the United States, defatted psyllium husk feeding virtually normalized liver size and serum triglyceride levels and produced lower serum total cholesterol levels and higher HDL-cholesterol than observed in normal controls. Defatted psyllium husk feeding also yielded liver lipid values which were in the normal range.[17]

Antioxidative Activity According to a study conducted by the University of Seville, the methanol extracts from five *Plantago* species (*Plantago afra*, *Plantago coronopus*, *Plantago lagopus*, *Plantago lanceolata*, and *Plantago serraria*) all showed antioxidative activity. *Plantago serraria* exhibited the strongest activity as a DPPH scavenger. *Plantago lanceolata* and *Plantago serraria* were found to be the most active in the lipid peroxidation inhibition assay. The study concludes that *Plantago serraria*, in particular, is a possible new source of natural antioxidants.[18]

Fleawort Notes

1. Ibn Ḥabīb A. *Mujtaṣar fī al-ṭibb/Compendio de medicina*. Ed. C Álvarez de Morales and F Girón Irueste. Madrid: Consejo Superior de Investigaciones Científicas, 1992: 67/34.

2. Nisābūrī A. *Islamic Medical Wisdom: The Ṭibb al-a'immah*. Trans. B. Ispahany. Ed. AJ Newman. London: Muḥammadī Trust, 1991: 79.

3. Majlisī M. *Biḥār al-anwār*. Ṭihrān: Javad al-Alavi, 1956.

4. Mandaville JP. *Flora of Eastern Saudi Arabia*. London: Kegan Paul, 1990.

5. Bīrūnī, AR al-. *al-Bīrūnī's Book on Pharmacy and Materia Medica*. Ed. and trans. HM Said. Karachi: Hamdard National Foundation, 1973.

6. Ghazanfar SA. *Handbook of Arabian Medicinal Plants*. Boca Raton: CRC Press, 1994.

7. Ibn Ḥabīb A. *Mujtaṣar fī al-ṭibb/Compendio de medicina*. Ed. C Álvarez de Morales and F Girón Irueste. Madrid: Consejo Superior de Investigaciones Científicas, 1992.

8. Food. Laxative drug products for over-the-counter human use; psyllium ingredients in granular dosage forms. Final rule. *Fed* 2007; 72(60): 14669–14674.

9. Balch PA. *Prescription for Herbal Healing*. New York: Avery, 2002.

10. Ziai, Larijani, Akhoondzadeh, Fakhrzadeh, Dastpak, BanDārian, Rezai, Badi, Emami. Psyllium decreased serum glucose and glycosylated hemoglobin significantly in diabetic outpatients. *J* 2005; 102(2): 202–207.

11. Rodriguez-Cabezas, Galvez, Camuesco, Lorente, Concha, Martinez-Augustin, Redondo, Zarzuelo. Intestinal anti-inflammatory activity of dietary fiber (*Plantago ovata* seeds) in HLA-B27 transgenic rats. *Clin* 2003; 22(5): 463–471.

12. Juarranz, Calle-Puron, Gonzalez-Navarro, Regidor-Poyatos, Soriano, Martinez-Hernandez, Rojas, Guinee. Physical exercise, use of *Plantago ovata* and aspirin, and reduced risk of colon cancer. *Eur* 2002; 11(5): 465–472.

13. Fernandez-Banares, Hinojosa, Sanchez-Lombrana, Navarro, Martinez-Salmeron, Garcia-Puges, Gonzalez-Huix, Riera, Gonzalez-Lara, Dominguez-Abascal, Gine, Moles, Gomollon, Gassull. Randomized clinical trial of *Plantago ovata* seeds (dietary fiber) as compared with mesalamine in maintaining remission in ulcerative colitis. Spanish Group for the Study of Crohn's Disease and Ulcerative Colitis (GETECCU). *Am* 1999; 94(2): 427–433.

14. Romero, West, Zern, Fernandez. The seeds from *Plantago ovata* lower plasma lipids by altering hepatic and bile acid metabolism in guinea pigs. *J* 2002; 132(6): 1194–1198.

15. Rodriguez-Moran, Guerrero-Romero, Lazcano-Burciaga. Lipid- and glucose-lowering efficacy of *Plantago psyllium* in type 2 diabetes. *J* 1998; 12(5): 273–278.

16. Frati, Benítez Pinto W, Raul, Casarrubias. Lowering glycemic index of food by acarbose and *Plantago psyllium* mucilage. *Arch* 1998; 29(2): 137–141.

17. Kritchevsky, Tepper, Klurfeld. Influence of psyllium preparations on plasma and liver lipids of cholesterol-fed rats. *Artery*. 1995; 21(6): 303–311.

18. Galvez, Martin-Cordero, Houghton, Ayuso. Antioxidative activity of methanol extracts obtained from Plantago species. *J* 2005; 53(6): 1927–1933.

Frankincense/ *Kundur, Lubān*

FAMILY: Burseraceae

BOTANICAL NAME: *Boswellia carteri*

COMMON NAMES: *English* Frankincense, Olibanum tree; *French* Oliban, Arbre à l'encens; *Spanish* Incienso, Olíbano; *German* Echter Weihrauchbaum, Olibanum; *Urdu/Unānī* Luban,

Luban-e-Hindi; *Modern Standard Arabic* Lubān, Lubān dhakr

BOTANICAL NAME: *Boswellia serrata*
COMMON NAMES: *English* Frankincense, Olibanum tree; *French* Oliban, Arbre à l'encens; *Spanish* No common name; *German* Indischer Weihrauch; *Urdu/Unānī* Kundar, Luban-e-Hindi; *Modern Standard Arabic* Kundur, Lubān

SAFETY RATING: GENERALLY SAFE TO POTENTIALLY DEADLY Internally, true frankincense is only edible if it is pure, translucent, and free of black or brown impurities. The edible product is often light yellow with a very slight greenish tint. Frankincense poses no known health hazards or side effects when consumed in proper therapeutic doses. Some essential oils, however, can be poisonous, and should never be taken internally or applied to the skin. Extreme caution should be taken before consuming or applying the essential oil of frankincense. When non-toxic, and non-irritant, the essential oil of frankincense seems safe for use by most adults. In sensitive people, however, it may cause irritation when applied to the skin. When burned, frankincense may cause respiratory problems in sensitive individuals. Internally or externally, frankincense should not be used during pregnancy or lactation.

PROPHETIC PRESCRIPTION: Frankincense has been used for cosmetic and medicinal purposes since the earliest of times. It was associated with longevity and memory in Classical times.[1] The Prophet Muḥammad endorsed the use of the herb, advising people to, "Use frankincense (*kundur*), for it invigorates the heart with courage, and it is a remedy for forgetfulness."[2] He encouraged people to "Fill your homes with the smoke of frankincense (*lubān*) and wormwood (*shīḥ*)"[3] and "Fill your home with incense from frankincense (*lubān*), Syrian rue (*ḥarmal*), wormwood (*shīḥ*), myrrh (*marr*), and thyme (*sa'tar*)."[4] He also said,

> Use incense, which is frankincense, as medicine for it is an incense for all things and all persons which are in a home. Just like God expelled from seventy-two homes every type of demon (*'ifrīt*) which came with open mouths and outstretched hands, they shall also be expelled from every house in which incense is used.[5]

The Prophet allegedly encouraged exposing women to incense while they were pregnant, saying, "Let your women-folk use incense when they are pregnant for verily, the child in the womb will turn out to be a man with a strong heart, and should it be a girl, she will have a beautiful figure and wide hips."[6] He also said, "The best incense is frankincense. It was the incense used by Mary when she was giving birth. The house in which frankincense is used shall never be approached by an envious person, a sorcerer (*kāhin*), a devil or a witch."[7]

The Messenger of Allāh is reported to have mixed water with frankincense (*kundur*), keeping it over night, sweetening it in the morning and drinking it, saying, "It is a good remedy for urinary diseases and loss of memory."[8] A man came to the Messenger of Allāh complaining of memory loss. The Prophet advised him to, "Soak *kundur* in water, take it early in the morning because it helps neurosis."[9]

According to Imām 'Alī, "The recitation of Qur'ān, *al-siwāk* [twig of *miswāk*], and storax are purifiers of phlegm."[10] He also said, "Use frankincense, for it fortifies the heart, and drives out forgetfulness."[11] According to many sources, Imām 'Alī ibn Abī Ṭālib advised reciting the Qur'ān and chewing *kundur* to clear phlegm and to sharpen the memory.

ISSUES IN IDENTIFICATION: According to Bīrūnī, *lubān* is frankincense, and *mā' sā'il* is storax. As Ibn Ḥabīb explains, "*Kundur* is *labān* and *al-ḥaḍḍ* is *kuḥl jawlān*."[12] As Said explains, *lubnah lubnī* is liquid storax obtained from *Liquidambar orientalis.* He further offers that *lubān* is *Olibamum*, especially *Boswellia carteri*, although *Boswellia serrata* and *Boswellia glabra* may also have been meant, while *kundur* and *lubān* are frankincense or *Boswellia serrata.* As Bīrūnī explains, *kundur* is a word of Persian provenance which means frankincense. *Kundur* is the frankincense tree and *nard* is its gum resin.[13] According to Duke, the frankincense of the Bible refers to *Boswellia sacra*, which is synonymous with *Boswellia carteri* (*B. sacra* being the more common descriptor in current usage). According to Ghazanfar, *Boswellia sacra* is found in southern Arabia. In Dhofar, it is found in dry zones, and in wadis extending to the coast on the lower slopes of gullies and runoffs.[14]

PROPERTIES AND USES: The oleo-resin of *Boswellia carteri* is called *labān*, whereas that of *B. serrata* is called *Kundur.*

Boswellia (Burseraceae) is a bitter, pungent herb that stimulates the circulation, calms the nerves, and has anti-inflammatory, anti-arthritic, and pain-relieving effects. It is considered demulcent, emollient, aphrodisiac, exhilarant, emmenagogue, stimulant-expectorant, abortifacient, antidiarrhoeal, detersive and resolvent, antiseptic, and tonic. The gum resin of the trunk, exuded when incisions are made and hardened in the open air, is used to treat chronic inflammatory intestinal illnesses (colitic ulcerosa, Crohn's disease), asthma, bronchitis, diarrhea, obesity, amenorrhea, menor-rhagia, polyuria, rheumatism, ulcers, bad breath, scrofulous, syphilis, gonorrhea, sores, ringworm, jaundice, dysentery, dyspepsia, piles, and nervous diseases. Externally, it is used to treat pterygium, epiphora, conjunctivitis, and skin problems. Frankincense is frequently used as a fumigant.

SCIENTIFIC STUDIES: *Anticancer Activity* In a study conducted by the Foundation for Collaborative Medicine and Research in Greenwich in the U.K., *Boswellia serrata*, a lipoxygenase inhibitor, was shown to successfully reverse multiple brain metastases in a breast cancer patient who had not shown improvement after standard therapy. The results suggest a potential new area of therapy for breast cancer patients with brain metastases that may be useful as an adjuvant to our standard therapy.[15] In a study conducted by Nihon University in Japan, fifteen compounds exhibited potent cytotoxic activities against all of the three human neuroblastoma cells tested.[16]

Antidiarrheic Activity In an animal study conducted by the University of Naples Federico II in Italy, *Boswellia serrata* gum resin extract was shown to prevent diarrhea, normalizing intestinal motility in pathophysiological states without slowing the rate of transit.[17] These results could explain, at least in part, the clinical efficacy of this Ayurvedic remedy in reducing diarrhea in patients with inflammatory bowel disease.

Anti-inflammatory Activity According to a study conducted by the Ichimaru Pharcos Company in Japan, 16 compounds from *Boswellia carteri* resin exhibit marked anti-inflammatory activity with a 50 percent inhibitory dose.[18] This discovery supports the ethnomedical use of *Boswellia carteri* in the treatment of rheumatoid arthritis and other inflammatory diseases.

In a random, blinded animal study, conducted by University of Maryland, Ruxiang (*Gummi olibanum*), the dried gum resin of *Boswellia carteri*, showed significant anti-arthritic and anti-inflammation effects.[19] The study confirmed the traditional use of Chinese medicine in alleviating pain and inflammation for thousands of years.

Immunostimulating Activity In a study conducted by Mansoura University in Egypt, the essential oil of frankincense was shown to possess strong immunostimulant activity (90 percent lymphocyte transformation) when assessed by a lymphocyte proliferation assay.[20]

Antiarthritic Activity In an 8-week randomized double-blind, placebo-controlled crossover study of 30 patients conducted by Indira Gandhi Medical College in India, *Boswellia serrata* extract was shown to be effective and safe in the treatment

of osteoarthritis of the knee.[21] All patients receiving *Boswellia serrrata* extract reported decrease in knee pain, increased knee flexion, increased walking, and a decrease in the frequency of swelling. The differences between *Boswellia serrata* and placebo were statistically significant, and clinically relevant. With the exception of minor gastrointestinal issues, the treatment was well tolerated. According to researchers, *Boswellia serrata* extract may also find therapeutic use in other forms of arthritis.

Anti-inflammatory Activity In a study conducted by Universitat Tubingen in Germany, the anti-inflammatory properties of *Boswellia serrata* resin were confirmed.[22] In clinical trials, promising results were observed in patients with rheumatoid arthritis, chronic colitis, ulcerative colitis, Crohn's disease, bronchial asthma, and peritumoral brain edemas.

In a study conducted by the University of the West Indies in Jamaica, two cases of therapy with frankincense and myrrh in children are presented.[23] The long history of this unusual treatment is outlined, demonstrating that for several millennia such agents have been employed in a number of medical contexts, as well as in the perfume and incense industries.

Antiulcer Activity According to a double-blind study, 400 milligrams of *Boswellia*, containing 37.5 percent of gum resins, three times a day for four to eight weeks, may be useful in the treatment of ulcerative colitis.[24]

Frankincense Notes

1. Bown D. *Encyclopedia of Herbs & their Uses*. Westmount: RD Press, 1995: 250.

2. Nisābūrī A. *Ṭibb al-a'immah*. Bayrūt: Dār al-Maḥajjah al-Baydā', 1994: 259; Sūyūṭī J. *As-Sūyūṭī's Medicine of the Prophet*. Ed. A Thomson. London: Ṭā-Hā Publishers, 1994.

3. Sūyūṭī J. *As-Sūyūṭī's Medicine of the Prophet*. Ed. A Thomson. London: Ṭā-Hā Publishers, 1994: 91; Bayhaqī A. al-Sunan al-kubrā. Bayrūt: Dār Ṣadīr, 1968.

4. Ibn Ḥabīb A. *Mujtaṣar fī al-ṭibb/Compendio de medicina*. Ed. C Álvarez de Morales and F Girón Irueste. Madrid: Consejo Superior de Investigaciones Científicas, 1992: 75/43.

5. Ibn Ḥabīb A. *Mujtaṣar fī al-ṭibb/Compendio de medicina*. Ed. C Álvarez de Morales and F Girón Irueste. Madrid: Consejo Superior de Investigaciones Científicas, 1992: 75/43.

6. Iṣbahānī AN al-. *Mawsū'at al-ṭibb al-nabawī*. Ed. MKD al-Turkī. Bayrūt: Dār Ibn Ḥazm, 2006.

7. Ibn Ḥabīb A. *Mujtaṣar fī al-ṭibb/Compendio de medicina*. Ed. C Álvarez de Morales and F Girón Irueste. Madrid: Consejo Superior de Investigaciones Científicas, 1992: 75/43.

8. Iṣbahānī AN al-. *Mawsū'at al-ṭibb al-nabawī*. Ed. MKD al-Turkī. Bayrūt: Dār Ibn Ḥazm, 2006.

9. Ibn Qayyim al-Jawziyyah M. *al-Ṭibb al-nabawī*. Bayrūt: Dār al-Kitāb, 1985.

10. Nisābūrī A. *Ṭibb al-a'immah*. Bayrūt: Dār al-Maḥajjah al-Baydā', 1994: 79.

11. Sūyūṭī J. *As-Sūyūṭī's Medicine of the Prophet*. Ed. A Thomson. London: Ṭā-Hā Publishers, 1994: 91.

12. Ibn Ḥabīb A. *Mujtaṣar fī al-ṭibb/Compendio de medicina*. Ed. C Álvarez de Morales and F Girón Irueste. Madrid: Consejo Superior de Investigaciones Científicas, 1992: 56/22.

13. Bīrūnī, AR al-. *al-Bīrūnī's Book on Pharmacy and Materia Medica*. Ed. and trans. HM Said. Karachi: Hamdard National Foundation, 1973.

14. Ghazanfar SA. *Handbook of Arabian Medicinal Plants*. Boca Raton: CRC Press, 1994.

15. Flavin. A lipoxygenase inhibitor in breast cancer brain metastases. *J* 2007 Mar; 82(1): 91–93.

16. Akihisa, Tabata, Banno, Tokuda, Nishihara, Nakamura, Kimura, Yasukawa, Suzuki. Cancer chemopreventive effects and cytotoxic activities of the triterpene acids from the resin of *Boswellia carteri*. *Biol* 2006; 29(9): 1976–1979.

17. Borrelli, Capasso, Capasso, Ascione, Aviello, Longo, Izzo. Effects of *Boswellis serrata* on intestinal motility in rodents: inhibition of diarrhea without constipation. *Br* 2006; 148(4): 553–560.

18. Banno, Akihisa, Yasukawa, Tokuda, Tabata, Nakamura, Nishimura, Kimura, Suzuki. Anti-inflammatory activities of the triterpene acids from the resin of *Boswellia carteri*. *J* 2006; 107(2): 249–253.

19. Fan, Lao, Zhang, Zhou, Wang, Moudgil, Lee, Ma, Zhang, Berman. Effects of an acetone extract of *Boswellia carteri* Birdw. (*Burseraceae*) gum resin on adjuvant-induced arthritis in lewis rats. *J* 2005; 101(1–3): 104–109.

20. Mikhaeil, Maatooq, Badria, Amer. Chemistry and immunomodulatory activity of frankincense oil. *Z* 2003; 58(3–4): 230–238.

21. Kimmatkar, Thawani, Hingorani, Khiyani. Efficacy and tolerability of *Boswellia serrata* extract in treatment of osteoarthritis of knee — a randomized double blind placebo controlled trial. *Phytomedicine*. 2003; 10(1): 3–7.

22. Ammon HP. [Boswellic acids (components of frankincense) as the active principle in treatment of chronic inflammatory diseases]. *Wien* 2002; 152(15–16): 373–8.

23. Michie, Cooper. Frankincense and myrrh as remedies in children. *J* 1991 Oct; 84(10): 602–5.

24. Balch PA. *Prescription for Herbal Healing*. New York: Avery, 2002.

Garden Cress / *Thufā'*

Family: Brassicaceae

Botanical Name: *Lepidium sativum*

Common Names: *English* Garden cress, Peppergrass; *French* Passerage cultivée, Cresson alénois; *Spanish* Mastuerzo, Lepido; *German* Gartenkresse; *Urdu/Unānī* Habb-ul-Rashaad, Hurf, Haloon; *Modern Standard Arabic* 'Uṣāb zirā'ī, Rashād, Ḥurf

Safety Rating: Generally Safe Garden cress is generally considered safe when consumed in food quantities. Large consumption, however, can cause irritation of the gut. As it can accumulate heavy metals, it is important to only consume garden cress grown in fresh, clean water. Garden cress should not be consumed during pregnancy or lactation.

Prophetic Prescription: The Prophet Muḥammad stated that "[a]loe (*ṣabir*) and garden cress (*thufā'*) are both cures for an illness."[1] He also said, "You have garden cress (*thufā'*) seed. Allāh made it a cure for every disease."[2]

Issues in Identification: The identity of *thufā'* has been a great source of confusion for translators. Both Akīlī and Johnstone claim that the term embraces both *Lepidium sativum* (garden cress) and *Nasturtium officinale* (water cress).[3] Botanical and linguistic sources, however, seem to suggest otherwise. According to Bīrūnī, *thufā'* is a synonym for *ḥurf*, or *ḥurf al-suṭūḥ*, which Said identifies as *Lepidium sativum* (garden cress). As Bīrūnī explains, the best kind was grown in Iraq, had a pungent taste, and was known to the public as *ḥabb al-rashād*.[4] Ibn Ṭūlūn also identifies *thufā'* as *ḥabb al-rashād*.[5] Abū Nu'aym al-Iṣbahānī says that it is also known as *banḥūlah* and Turkī identifies it as garden cress.[6] Álvarez de Morales and Girón Irueste also specify that *thufā'* is *Lepidium sativum*.[7] According to Omer Recep, garden cress is also known as *ḥurf bābilī*.[8]

According to Hans Wehr, *ḥabb al-rashād* is *Lepidium sativum*. According to Mandaville, *Lepidium sativum* is rare in eastern Arabia, recorded there only as a weed of farms and gardens, but which might be found on old desert camp sites. It is known in Saudi Arabic as *rashād*.[9] According to Ghazanfar, *Lepidium sativum* is known in Omani Arabic as *rashād* and *rishād*, as *ḥilf* in Yemeni, and as *thufa* in Saudi Arabian. It is native to Egypt and Western Asia.[10] According to Chaudhary, *Lepidium sativum* is a common, widely-distributed, wild and cultivated herb of medicinal importance in Saudi Arabia. It is native to the northern hemisphere.[11]

Properties and Uses: *Lepidium sativum*, known commonly as garden cress, is antiscorbutic, diuretic, and stimulant. The plant is administered in cases of asthma, cough with expectoration, and bleeding hemorrhoids. The root is used to treat secondary syphilis and tenesmus. The seeds are galactogogue, and have been used to induce abortion. Applied as a poultice, the seeds are used to treat pains, and have also been used as an aperient.

Scientific Studies: *Heavy Metal Accumulating Activity* *Lepidium sativum* has been shown to be a micro-accumulator of heavy metals and is proposed as a biological method to treat sewage. In an experiment conducted by the Technical University of Lodz in Poland, *Lepidium sativum* absorbed 20 percent of the total mercury concentrated in contaminated soil.[12] Another study, conducted by Hort Research in New Zealand, confirmed that *Lepidium sativum* has the ability to accumulate arsenic present in polluted water. Researchers recommended that the *Lepidium sativum* grown in areas with elevated arsenic should not be consumed.[13]

Antidiabetic Activity *Lepidum sativum* is one of the most common herbs used in Errachidia province in southeastern Morocco to treat diabetes.[14]

Chemopreventive Activity According to an animal trial conducted by the University of Vienna, *Lepidium sativum* possesses chemopreventive activity. Pretreatment with either fresh garden cress juice, or its constituents, glucotropaeolin and benzylisothiocyanate, a breakdown product of glucotropaeolin, for three consecutive days caused a significant reduction in induced DNU damage in colon and liver cells in the range of 75–92 percent.[15]

Antihypertensive and Diuretic Activity According to an animal study conducted in Morocco, the daily oral administration of the aqueous *Lepidium sativum* extract for three weeks exhibited a significant antihypertensive and diuretic activity.[16]

Hypoglycemic Activity In another animal study conducted in Morocco, the aqueous extract of *Lepidium sativum* produced a significant decrease on blood glucose levels in diabetic rats after both a single dose and chronic 15 day repeated administration. Within two weeks of regular treatment, the blood glucose levels were normalized. Researchers concluded that *Lepidium sativum* exhibits potent hypoglycemic activity.[17]

DNA Protective Activity According to a study conducted by the University of Vienna, garden and water cress juices are highly protective against induced DNA damage in human derived cells.[18]

Garden Cress Notes

1. Abū Dāwūd S. *Sunan Abū Dāwūd.* Bayrūt: Dār Ibn Ḥazm, 1998.
2. Abū Dāwūd S. *Sunan Abū Dāwūd.* Bayrūt: Dār Ibn Ḥazm, 1998.
3. Ibn al-Qayyim al-Jawziyyah. *Natural Healing with the Medicine of the Prophet.* Pearl Publishing. Trans. M al-Akīlī. Philadelphia, 1993; Johnstone P, trans. *Medicine of the Prophet.* Ibn Qayyim al-Jawziyyah. Cambridge: The Islamic Texts Society, 1998.
4. Bīrūnī, AR al-. *al-Bīrūnī's Book on Pharmacy and Materia Medica.* Ed. and trans. HM Said. Karachi: Hamdard National Foundation, 1973.
5. Ibn Ṭulūn S. *al-Manhal al-rawī fī al-ṭibb al-nabawī.* Ed. 'Azīz Bayk. Riyyāḍ: Dār 'ālam al-kutub, 1995.
6. Iṣbahānī AN al-. *Mawsū'at al-ṭibb al-nabawī.* Ed. MKD al-Turkī. Bayrūt: Dār Ibn Ḥazm, 2006.
7. Ibn Ḥabīb A. *Mujtaṣar fī al-ṭibb/Compendio de medicina.* Ed. C Álvarez de Morales and F Giròn Irueste. Madrid: Consejo Superior de Investigaciones Científicas, 1992.
8. Dīnawarī AH. *Kitāb al-nabāt/The Book of Plants.* Ed. Bernhard Lewin. Uppsala/Wiesbaden: A.-B. Lundequistska Bokhandeln and Otto Harrassowitz, 1953: 95.
9. Mandaville JP. *Flora of Eastern Saudi Arabia.* London: Kegan Paul, 1990.
10. Ghazanfar SA. *Handbook of Arabian Medicinal Plants.* Boca Raton: CRC Press, 1994.
11. Chaudhary SA. *Flora of the Kingdom of Saudi Arabia.* al-Riyyāḍ: Ministry of Agriculture and Water, 1999.
12. Smolinska B, Cedzynska K. EDTA and urease effects on Hg accumulation by *Lepidium sativum. Chemosphere.* 2007 June 13.
13. Robinson B, Duwig C, Bolan N, Kannathasan M, Saravanan A. Uptake of arsenic by New Zealand watercress (*Lepidium sativum*). *Sci* 2003; 301(1–3): 67–73.
14. Tahraoui, El-Hilaly, Israili, Lyoussi. Ethnopharmacological survey of plants used in the traditional treatment of hypertension and diabetes in southeastern Morocco (Errachidia province). *J* 2007; 110(1): 105–117.
15. Kassie F, Rabot S, Uhl M, Huber W, Qin HM, Helma C, Schulte-Hermann R, Knasmüller S. Chemoprotective effects of garden cress (*Lepidium sativum*) and its constituents towards 2-amino-3-methyl-imidazo[4,5-f]quinoline (IQ)-induced genotoxic effects and colonic preneoplastic lesions. *Carcinogenesis.* 2002; 23(7): 1155–1161.
16. Maghrani M, Zeggwagh NA, Michel JB, Eddouks M. Antihypertensive effect of *Lepidium sativum* L. in spontaneously hypertensive rats. *J* 2005; 100(1–2): 193–197.
17. Eddouks M, Maghrani M, Zeggwagh NA, Michel JB. Study of the hypoglycaemic activity of *Lepidium sativum* L. aqueous extract in normal and diabetic rats. *J* 2005; 97(2): 391–395.
18. Kassie, Laky, Gminski, Mersch-Sundermann, Scharf, Lhoste, Kansmüller S. Effects of garden and water cress juices and their constituents, benzyl and phenethyl isothiocyanates, towards benzo(a)pyrene-induced DNA damage: a model study with the single cell gel electrophoresis/Hep G2 assay. *Chem* 2003; 142(3): 285–296.

Garlic / *Thawm, Fūm, Thūm*

FAMILY: Liliaceae

BOTANICAL NAME: *Allium sativum*

COMMON NAMES: *English* Garlic; *French* Ail; *Spanish* Ajo; *German* Knoblauch; *Urdu/Unānī* Lehsun, Saum, Seer; *Modern Standard Arabic* Thawm, Thūm

SAFETY RATING: GENERALLY SAFE Although garlic is generally safe for most people, it can cause bad breath, a burning sensation in the mouth or stomach, heartburn, gas, nausea, vomiting, body odor, and diarrhea. Negative side effects are often worse with raw garlic. Garlic should not be consumed in large amount for at least two weeks prior to surgery as it may interfere with normal blood clotting and increase bleeding time. For this reason, it should not be used in large amounts by persons with bleeding disorders, such as hemophiliacs. Likewise, garlic must not be combined with herbs that interfere with blood clotting, such as cat's claw, ginger, ginkgo, ginseng or feverfew. It should not be used by people suffering from stomach or digestive disorders such as gastritis due to potential gastric irritation. Since garlic can lower blood glucose levels, it should be used with caution in diabetic patients. As it can interfere with iodine metabolism, garlic should not be used in large quantities by patients suffering from thyroid dysfunction. Since large amounts of garlic can induce labor, large quantities should not be consumed during pregnancy. Garlic should also be avoided during lactation. It should not be consumed by patients being treated for HIV/AIDS.

Externally, garlic cloves or preparations should not be applied directly to the skin for periods longer than a few hours as this may result in a severe burn, particularly in small children. In hypersensitive persons, the application or garlic to the skin can cause contact dermatitis. As it may cause serious irritation, garlic oil should not be used to treat inner ear infections in children Finally, chopped garlic and garlic oil preparations are an ideal growth medium for dangerous bacteria like *Clostridium botulinum* when left to stand at room temperature for long hours.

Prophetic Prescription: Garlic and onion, known as *fūm*, *thūm*, *thawm*, and *baṣal*, are mentioned in the Qur'ān in the context of the Exodus (2:61). When garlic and onions were mentioned to the Prophet, he said, "The strongest is garlic." When asked whether it should be forbidden, he responded: "Eat it. And he who eats it should not come near this mosque until its odor goes away."[1] It is reported that the Messenger of Allāh forbade the consumption of fresh garlic and onions prior to interacting with people in the public sphere. As he explained, "He who eats them (garlic and onions) should not come near our mosque. If it is necessary to eat them, make them dead by cooking, that is, onions and garlic."[2] In another tradition, he included leek (*kurrāth*).[3] When Imām Ja'far al-Ṣādiq was asked about eating garlic and onion, he responded that "It is alright to eat them uncooked."[4]

The Prophet was opposed to eating fresh garlic and then mingling with people. He certainly did not oppose its consumption. On the contrary, the Prophet recommended garlic. He said, "Eat garlic. If it were not for the fact that I speak to the Angel, I would eat it myself[5]; "Eat garlic, O people! And treat yourself with it, for it contains a cure for many illnesses"[6]; and "Eat garlic for in it lies the cure for seventy diseases."[7] According to Imām 'Alī al-Riḍā, "He who wants to prevent wind in his body, let him eat garlic once every seven days."[8]

Issues in Identification: It is the consensus that *thawm* is the Arabic term for garlic. Although garlic is generally known as *thawm* in Arabic, the Qur'ānic name is *fūm*. Cultivated garlic is known as *thawm zirā'ī* and several dozen varieties exist.

Properties and Uses: Garlic is a stimulant, carminative, emmenagogue, antirheumatic, anthelmintic, alterative, expectorant, diaphoretic, disinfectant, and diuretic herb. Garlic is also antibacterial and anti-viral, discouraging the growth of Candida, trichomonas, staph, and *E. coli*, as well as intestinal worms. It is used to treat bladder infection, strep throat, vaginosis, yeast infections, and ear infections. It is also used to treat pulmonary problems, high blood pressure, rheumatism, asthma, chronic bronchial catarrh, loss of appetite, and constipation. It is used externally as a liniment or poultice for diseases of the lungs and ringworm. Over 250 studies have been conducted on the impact of garlic on cancer. Garlic use has been associated with lower rates of breast, colon, larynx, esophagus, and stomach cancer. It is also used to treat peptic ulcers. Although a few studies suggest otherwise, over 1,800 scientific studies support the use of garlic in lowering cholesterol and blood sugar levels, preventing heart attack and stroke, and treating infections and cancer.[9]

Scientific Studies: *Antithrombotic, Antitumor, Antifungal, and Antiparasitic Activity* Ajoene, a compound found in garlic, has been shown to possess antithrombotic, antitumor, antifungal, and antiparasitic effects.[10]

Antibacterial Activity The famous microbiologist, Louis Pasteur, performed some of the original work showing that garlic could kill bacteria.[11] Although there is no evidence that taking garlic orally can kill organisms throughout the body,[12] its action outside the body is similar to Bacitracin ointment.[13] From Roman antiquity to World War I it was used in poultices to prevent wound infections.[14]

In 1926, the British government issued a general plea for the public to supply it with garlic in order to meet wartime needs. Garlic was called "Russian penicillin" during World War II because, after running out of antibiotics, the Russian government turned to this ancient treatment for its soldiers.[15]

Both onion and garlic have been shown to inhibit the growth of various types of fungi, thus showing promise in treatment of fungal-associated diseases.[16] As an oil or vinegar, it is used to treat ear and mouth infections. Al-Kindī used garlic for ear pains and for its suppuration, pulsation, fistulas.[17] In clinical trials conducted in China, garlic cured 67 percent of a group of patients with intestinal bacterial infections and 88 percent who had amoebic dysentery.[18] Their blood cholesterol and lipid levels were also lowered. Researchers noted some success in treating deep fungal infections, whooping cough, lead poisoning, and some carcinomas. Even appendicitis was improved in a number of studies.[19] Low concentrations, approximately one clove per day, have been found to improve digestion, while larger quantities slows the process down.

Cholesterol-Lowering Activity Subjects who ate garlic for six months found that their LDL cholesterol and triglyceride levels went down, while their HDL cholesterol levels increased.[20] As far back as the 1st century A.D. Dioscorides wrote of garlic's ability to "clear the arteries."[21] According to Bratman,

> moderately good studies have found that certain forms of garlic can lower total cholesterol levels by about 9 to 12 percent, as well as possibly improve the ratio of good cholesterol and bad cholesterol. Garlic also appears to slightly improve hypertension, protect against free radicals, and slow blood coagulation. Putting all these benefits together, garlic may be a broad-spectrum treatment for arterial disease.[22]

Over 28 controlled clinical studies of using garlic to treat elevated cholesterol were published between 1985 and 1995. Together, they suggest that garlic can lower cholesterol by about 9 to 12 percent.[23] Virtually all these studies used garlic standardized to alliin content. A recent observational study of 200 individuals suggests that garlic can affect the hardening of the arteries by some unidentified means other than lowering cholesterol or blood pressure.[24] In a multicentric placebo-controlled randomized study involving 261 patients, standardized garlic tablets were shown to be effective in the treatment of hyperlipidemia, lowering total cholesterol values by an average of 12 percent, and triglyceride values by an average of 17 percent.[25] In a 12-week controlled animal study, the administration of *Allium porrum* bulb extract decreased total plasma total cholesterol, indicating that the plant may be useful for the treatment of hypercholesterolemia.[26] In a controlled clinical study of forty-two healthy adults with high cholesterol, LDL cholesterol was reduced by 11 percent by garlic treatment of 300 mg, three times per day, and 3 percent by placebo.[27] One study showed that garlic oil is ineffective.[28]

Antihypertensive Activity Numerous studies have found that garlic lowers blood pressure slightly, typically in the neighborhood of 5 to 10 percent more than placebo.[29] One the best studies showed a statistically significant drop of 11 percent in the systolic blood pressure in the diastolic pressure.[30] Over a period of 12 weeks, half were treated with 600 mg of garlic powder daily standardized to 1.3 percent alliin, the other half were given placebo. Another study suggests that garlic's effects increase if it given a longer time to act.[31] In a 16-week open trial of approximately 40 subjects with mild hypertension, the group treated with standardized garlic experienced a 10 percent drop in systolic blood pressure after four weeks, and a decrease of 19 percent after 16 weeks. Garlic has also been shown to normalize systolic blood pressure levels and can sustain them up to 24 hours.

Cardioprotective Activity In one study, 432 individuals who had suffered a heart attack were given either garlic juice in milk daily or no treatment at all over a period of 3 years.[32] The results showed a significant reduction of second heart attacks and about a 50 percent reduction in death rate among those taking garlic. A study conducted by the Centre for Cardiovascular Pharmacology in Germany, strongly supports the hypothesis that garlic intake has a protective effect on the elastic properties of the aorta related to aging in humans.[33] A study conducted by the University of Queensland concluded that "Kyolic" treatment reduces fatty streak development, vessel wall cholesterol accumulation and the development of fibro fatty plaques in neointimas of cholesterol-fed rabbits, thus providing protection against the onset of atherosclerosis.[34] According to a study conducted by East Carolina University School of Medicine, the effect of garlic preparations on lipids and blood pressure extend also to platelet function, offering wider protection of the cardiovascular system.[35]

Anticancer Activity The natural killer cells of the immune system are dramatically activated by garlic. Many studies point to garlic's antitumor effects. For example, residents in one region of China who do not eat garlic have about 1,000 times higher rates of stomach cancer than those in a neighboring garlic-eating region.[36] Several large studies strongly suggest that a diet high in garlic can prevent cancer. In one of the best studies, the Iowa Women's Study, a group of 41,837 women were questioned as to their lifestyle habits in 1986, and then followed continuously in subsequent years. At the 4-year follow-up, questionnaires showed that women whose diets included significant quantities of garlic were approximately 30 percent less likely to develop colon cancer.[37]

Anti-Viral Activity Recent research suggests that garlic may be able to prevent the common cold.[38]

Heavy Metal Protective Activity Studies of factory workers found that garlic not only detoxified harmful levels of lead from the blood, but seemed to prevent its accumulation in the first place.[39]

Antidiabetic Activity Many cultures turn to garlic to control mild diabetes. Conflicting clinical studies show it both lowers and raises blood sugar, suggesting that it may regulate insulin.

Antidiabetic Activity Studies have shown that garlic juices exert antioxidant and anti-hyperglycemic effects in diabetic rats, showing potential to alleviate liver and renal damage caused by diabetes.[40] Garlic has been experimentally documented to possess antidiabetic properties.[41] One study showed that only garlic, and not onion or fenugreek, is able to lower blood glucose levels significantly in diabetic rats.[42]

Antimutagenic and Anticarcinogenic Activity According to Justus-Liebig-University in Germany, diallyl disulfide, an oil soluble constituent of garlic, has been reported to cause antimutagenic and anticarcinogenic effects in vitro and in vivo. Garlic has been shown to prevent colon cancer in rats.[43]

Garlic Notes

1. Abū Dāwūd S. *Ṣaḥīḥ Sunan Abū Dāwūd.* Riyyāḍ: Maktab al-Tarbiyyah, 1989.

2. Abū Dāwūd S. *Ṣaḥīḥ Sunan Abū Dāwūd.* Riyyāḍ: Maktab al-Tarbiyyah, 1989.

3. Tiflis, qtd. Farooqi, MIH. *Medicinal Plants in the Traditions of Prophet Muḥammad.* Lucknow: Sidrah Publishers, 1998: 144

4. Majlisī M. *Biḥār al-anwār.* Ṭihrān: Javad al-Alavi, 1956.

5. Albānī M al-. *Ṣaḥīḥ al-Jāmiʿ.* Dimashq: al-Maktab al-Islāmī, 1970.

6. Dilmi, qtd. Farooqi MIH. *Medicinal Plants in the Traditions of Prophet Muḥammad.* Lucknow: Sidrah Publishers, 1998: 143

7. Chaghhaynī M. *Ṭibb al-nabī.* Trans. C Elgood. *Osiris* 1962; 14: 191.

8. Riḍā ʿA al-. *Risālah fī al-ṭibb al-nabawī.* Ed. MA Bār. Bayrūt: Dār al-Manāhil, 1991: 176.

9. Balch PA. *Prescription for Herbal Healing.* New York: Avery, 2002.

10. Ledezma, Apitz-Castro. [Ajoene the main active compound of garlic (*Allium sativum*): a new antifungal agent.] *Rev* 2006; 23(2): 75–80.

11. Bratman MD, Kroll D. *The Natural Pharmacist: Natural Health Bible.* USA: Prima, 1999: 197.

12. Nagai K. Experimental studies on the preventive effect of garlic extract against infection with influenza virus. *Jpn J Infect Dis* 1973; 47: 321; Chowdhury AK, et al. Efficacy of aqueous extract of garlic and allicin in experimental shigellosis in rabbits. *Indian J Med Res* 1991; 9333–36; Sharma VD, et al. Antibacterial property of *Allium sativum* Linn.: In vivo and in vitro studies. *Indian J Exp Biol* 1977; 15(6): 466–468; Hunan Hospital. Garlic in cryptococcal meningitis. A preliminary report of 21 cases. *Chin Med J* 1980; 93: 123–126; Caparaso N, et al. Antifungal activity in human urine and serum after ingestion of garlic (*Allium sativum*). *Antimocrob Agents Chemother* 1983; 23(5): 700–702.

13. Bratman MD, Kroll D. *The Natural Pharmacist: Natural Health Bible.* USA: Prima, 1999: 197: 200.

14. Bratman MD, Kroll D. *The Natural Pharmacist: Natural Health Bible.* USA: Prima, 1999: 197.

15. Bratman MD, Kroll D. *The Natural Pharmacist: Natural Health Bible.* USA: Prima, 1999: 198.

16. Shams-Ghahfarokhi, Shokoohamiri, Amirrajab, Moghadasi, Ghajari, Zeini, Sadeghi, Razzaghi-Abyaneh. In vitro antifungal activities of *Allium cepa, Allium sativum* and ketoconazole against some pathogenic yeasts and dermatophytes. *Fitoterapia.* 2006 Jun; 77(4): 321–323.

17. Levey M, al-Khaledy N, eds. *The Medical Formulary of al-Samarqandī.* Philadelphia: University of Pennsylvania Press, 1967: 242, note 539.

18. Keville K. *Herbs: an Illustrated Encyclopedia.* New York: Friedman/Fairfax, 1994: 30.

19. Chan H. But P. Eds. *Pharmacology and Applications of Chinese Materia Medica.* Vol. 1. Singapore: World Scientific, 1986.

20. Bordia A. Effect of garlic on blood lipids in patients with coronary heart disease. *Am J Clin Nutr.* 1981; 33(10): 2100–2103.

21. Bratman MD, Kroll D. *The Natural Pharmacist: Natural Health Bible.* USA: Prima, 1999: 197.

22. Bratman MD, Kroll D. *The Natural Pharmacist: Natural Health Bible.* USA: Prima, 1999: 198.

23. Silagy CA, et al. A meta-analysis of the effect of garlic on blood pressure. *J Hypertens* 1994; 12 (4): 463–468; Warshafsky, S, et al. Effect of garlic on total serum cholesterol. A meta-analysis. *Ann Intern Med* 1993, 119(7): 599–605; Mader FH. Treatment of hyperlipidaemia with garlic-powder tablets. Evidence from the German Association of General Practitioner's multicentric placebo-controlled double-blind study. *Arzneimittelforschung* 1990; 40(10): 1111–1116; Steiner M, et al. A double-blind crossover study in moderately hypercholesterolemic men that compared the effect of aged garlic extract and placebo administration on blood lipids. *Am J Clin Nutr* 1996; 64(6): 866–870.

24. Breithaupt-Grogler K, et al. Protective effect of chronic garlic intake on the elastic properties of the aorta in the elderly. *Circulation* 1997; 96(7): 2649–2655.

25. Mader. Treatment of hyperlipidaemia with garlic-powder tablets. Evidence from the German Association of General Practitioners' multicentric placebo-controlled double-blind study. *Arzneimittelforschung.* 1990; 40(10): 1111–1116.

26. Movahedian, Sadeghi, Ghannadi, Gharavi, Azarpajooh. Hypolipidemic activity of *Allium porrum* L. in cholesterol-fed rabbits. *J* 2006; 9(1): 98–101.

27. Can garlic reduce levels of serum lipids? A controlled clinical study. Jain, Vargas, Gotzkowsky, McMahon. *Am* 1993; 94(6): 632–635.

28. Santos OS de A, et al. Effects of garlic powder and garlic oil preparations on blood lipids, blood pressure and well being. *Br J Clin Res* 1995; 6: 91–100.

29. Silagy CA, et al. A meta-analysis of the effect of garlic on blood pressure. *J Hypertens* 1994; 12 (4): 463–468; Schulz V, et al. *Rational Phytotherapy.* New York: Springer-Verlag, 1998: 119.

30. Auer W, et al. Hypertension and hyperlipidemia: garlic helps in mild cases. *Br J Clin Pract Symp* 1990; 69(Suppl.): 3–6.

31. Santos OS de A, et al. Effects of garlic powder and garlic oil preparations on blood lipids, blood pressure and well being. *Br J Clin Res* 1995; 6: 91–100.

32. Bordia A. Knoblauch und koronare Herzkrankheit: Wirkungen einer Dreijahrigen Behandlung mit Knoblauchextrakt auf die Reinfarkt-und Mortalitatsrate. *Dtsch Apoth Ztg* 129(Suppl. 15): 16–17. As reported in the ESCOP monographs. Fascicule 3: *Allii sativi bulbus* (garlic). Exeter, UK: European Scientific Cooperative on Phytotherapy, 1997: 4.

33. Breithaupt-Grogler, Ling, Boudoulas, Belz. Protective effect of chronic garlic intake on elastic properties of aorta in the elderly. *Circulation.* 1997; 96(8): 2649–2655.
34. Efendy, Simmons, Campbell, Campbell. The effect of the aged garlic extract, "Kyolic," on the development of experimental atherosclerosis. *Atherosclerosis.* 1997; 11; 132(1): 37–42
35. Steiner, Lin. Changes in platelet function and susceptibility of lipoproteins to oxidation associated with administration of aged garlic extract. *J* 1998; 31(6): 904–908.
36. Brahmachari MD, Augusti KT. 1962. *J. Pharm. Pharmacol* 14: 254: 616; Jain RC, Vyas CR. *Brit Med J.* 1974; 2: 730.
37. Steinmetz KA, et al. Vegetables, fruit, and colon cancer in the Iowa Women's Health Study. *Am J Epidemiol* 1994: 139(1): 1–13.
38. "Garlic 'prevents common cold.'" *BBC News* Oct. 3, 2001. http://news.bbc.co.uk/2/hi/health/1575505.stm
39. Petkov, Stoev, Bakalov, Petev. *[The Bulgarian drug Satal as a therapeutic agent in industrial lead poisoning].* Gig *1965; 9(4): 42–49;* Petkov, V., V. Stoev, D. Bakalov & L. Petev. [Satal, a bulgarian drug to be used as a medicamentous agent in industrial lead poisoning.] Gigiena Truda I Professionalyne Zabolevaniya 1965; 9(4): 42–49.
40. El-Demerdash, Yousef, El-Naga. Biochemical study on the hypoglycemic effects of onion and garlic in alloxan-induced diabetic rats. *Food* 2005; 43(1): 57–63.
41. Srinivasan. Plant foods in the management of diabetes mellitus: spices as beneficial antidiabetic food adjuncts. *Int* 2005; 56(6): 399–414.
42. Jelodar, Maleki, Motadayen, Sirus. [Effect of fenugreek, onion and garlic on blood glucose and histopathology of pancreas of alloxan-induced diabetic rats. *Indian* 2005; 59(2): 64–69.
43. Sengupta, Ghosh, Das. Tomato and garlic can modulate azoxymethane-induced colon carcinogenesis in rats. *Eur* 2003; 12(3): 195–200.

Ginger / *Zanjabīl*

FAMILY: Zingiberacea

BOTANICAL NAME: *Zingiber officinale*

COMMON NAMES: *English* Common ginger; *French* Gingembre; *Spanish* Jengibre, Jenjibre; *German* Ingwer, Ingber; *Urdu/Unānī* Zanjabeel, Adrak, Sonth; *Modern Standard Arabic* Zanjabīl

SAFETY RATING: GENERALLY SAFE TO DANGEROUS In small amounts, up to four grams per day, ginger is generally safe for most people. Minor side effects occurring in some people include heartburn, diarrhea, and general stomach discomfort. Although it is used to treat morning sickness in early pregnancy, professional advice should be sought before taking large amounts as the effects on the fetus require more study. The consumption of dry ginger, which has different properties and effects than fresh ginger root, should be avoided during pregnancy. Since ginger may stimulate the gall bladder, it should not be used in large doses by patients suffering from gallstones.

As ginger may interfere with normal blood clotting, the herb should not be used at least one week prior to surgery. It should also be avoided by people suffering from a heart condition. Ginger should not be used concurrently with herbal products such as garlic, ginseng or ginkgo which interfere with the normal process of blood-clotting or with pharmaceuticals like aspirin, heparin or warfarin.

Large doses of ginger can be dangerous, causing cardiac effects, and depression of the central nervous system. While ginger is used to treat motion sickness, it should not be combined with medications to treat the same symptoms, such as dimenhydrinate (Dramamine) for example, since their possible interactions are currently unknown. Since ginger can lower blood glucose levels, it should not be used concurrently with medication used to lower blood sugar. When applied to the skin, ginger can cause irritation.

PROPHETIC PRESCRIPTION: Although the Qur'ān refers to ginger wine when describing Paradise (76:17), the vast majority of commentators interpret the term *zanjabīl* allegorically. According to Abū Sa'īd al-Khudrī, the Roman Emperor sent a jar of ginger jam to the Messenger of Allāh.[1] As a present, the Prophet gave some to his companions. In *Tafsīr-e-Mazharī*, it is stated that the Arabs were fond of ginger. Mawdudī has also written that the Arabs used to mix ginger with their drinking water.[2] According to Imām 'Alī al-Riḍā, "He who wishes to reduce forgetfulness and increase his memory, let him eat three portions of ginger with honey and *khardal* with his meal every day."[3] The Imām also states that "He who wants to increase in intellect ['*aql*], let him eat three grains of myrobalan (*halīlajāt*) with sugar (*sukkar ublūj*) every day."[4]

ISSUES IN IDENTIFICATION: It is the consensus that *zanjabīl* is the Arabic term for ginger. It is cultivated in some parts of Arabia.

PROPERTIES AND USES: *Zingiber officinale*, known commonly as ginger, is a sweet, pungent, aromatic, carminative, sternutatory, stimulant, sialogogue, laxative, antiflatulent, appetitive, rubefacient, anodyne, errhine, sialogogue, warming herb that is expectorant, increases perspiration, improves digestion and liver function, controls nausea, vomiting, and coughing, stimulates circulation, relaxes spasms, and relieves pain.

Internally, ginger is used to treat allergies, asthma, arthritis, bursitis, fibrocystic breasts, lymphedema, pain, atherosclerosis, high cholesterol, cancer, motion sickness, morning sickness, nausea, vomiting, indigestion, colic, abdominal chills, colds, coughs, strep throat, influenza, and peripheral circulatory complaints. It is used for antonic dyspepsia, flatulent colic, atonic gout, diarrhea, cholera, chronic bronchitis, alcoholic gastritis, corrective to nauseous medicines, condiment. It is also used to treat bacterial infections, parasitic infestation, as well as tumors. It aids digestion, relieves congestion and relieves fever, and soothes sore muscles. Externally, it is used for spasmodic pain, rheumatism, lumbago, menstrual cramps, and sprains.

SCIENTIFIC STUDIES: *Renoprotective Activity* According to a study conducted by the Amala Institute of Medical Sciences in India, the use of *Zingiber officinale* alone and in combination with alpha-tocopherol protect the kidney against cisplatin-induced acute renal failure.[5]

Myocardial Necrosis Alleviating Activity According to an animal study conducted by Hamdard University in India, pretreatment with ethanolic *Zingiber officinale* extract alleviates isoproterenol-induced oxidative myocardial necrosis in rats and exhibits cardioprotective properties.[6]

Anticancer Activity According to a paper published by the Industrial Toxicology Research Centre in India, some pungent constituents of ginger have potent antioxidant and anti-inflammatory activities, and some of them exhibit cancer preventive activity in experimental carcinogenesis.[7] According to one review, *Zingiber officinale* is an antiangiogenic through multiple processes that include effects on gene expression, signal processing, and enzyme activities.[8]

Antitumor Activity According to a study conducted by Seoul National University, the rhizome of ginger contains anti–tumor-promoting properties. Another study found that the pungent vanilloids found in ginger possess potential chemopreventive activities.[9] According to an animal trial conducted by CSIRO Health Sciences and Nutrition in Australia, zerumbone from *Zingiber aromaticum* is effective as an anticancer agent, possibly by its apoptosis-inducing and antiproliferative influences.[10]

Antidiabetic Activity According to a 6-week animal trial conducted by L.M. College of Pharmacy in India, the potential antidiabetic activity ginger juice was demonstrated on type 1 diabetic rats.[11] In an animal study conducted by Kuwait University, the hypoglycemic, hypocholesterolemic, and hypolipidemic potential of raw ginger was demonstrated, suggesting its great value in managing the effects of diabetic complications in human subjects.[12]

In a 20-day animal study conducted by Hamdard University in India, the oral administration of *Zingiber* ethanolic extract produced a significant anti-hyperglycemic effect in diabetic rats. The extract also lowered serum total cholesterol, triglycerides, and increased the HDL-cholesterol levels when compared with pathogenic diabetic rats. *Zingiber officinale* extract treatment lowered the liver and pancreas thiobarbituric acid reactive substances values as compared to pathogenic diabetic rats. The results of test drug were comparable to gliclazide, a standard anti-hyperglycemic agent. The results indicate that ethanolic extract of *Zingiber officinale* Roscoe can protect the tissues from lipid peroxidation. The extract also exhibits significant lipid lowering activity in diabetic rats. The study was the first pilot study to assess the potential of *Zingiber officinale* in diabetic dyslipidaemia.[13]

Antiarthritic Activity In a joint U.S./Indian study, a standardized multi-plant Ayurvedic drug (*Withania somnifera, Boswellia serrata, Zingiber officinale,* and *Curcuma longa*) was evaluated for its efficacy and safety in patients with symptomatic osteoarthritis of the knees. Out of 358 patients with chronic knee pain, ninety were found eligible to enroll in the randomized, double-blind, placebo-controlled, parallel efficacy, single-center, 32-week drug trial. Compared with placebo, the mean reduction in pain in the active group was significantly better. Similarly, the improvement in the scores at week 16 and week 32 were also significantly superior in the active group. This controlled drug trial demonstrated the potential efficacy and safety of an Ayurvedic drug containing ginger in the symptomatic treatment of osteoarthritis of the knees.[14]

Antiallergenic Activity According to a study conducted by the Prince of Songkla University in Thailand, the ethanolic extract of *Zingiber cassumunar* exhibited an antiallergenic effect. These findings support the use in Thai medicine of *Zingiber cassumunar* for treatment of allergy and allergic-related diseases.[15]

Hepaprotective Activity According to an animal study conducted by Lagos State University College of Medicine in Nigeria, the ethanol extract of the rhizome of *Zingiber officinale* provides a protective effect on carbon tetrachloride and acetaminophen-induced liver damage. These results indicate that the oil from the rhizome of *Zingiber officinale* could be useful in preventing chemically induced acute liver injury.[16]

Anti-inflammatory and Hypoglycemic Activity According to an in vitro and in vivo animal study conducted by the University of Durban, the ethanol extract of *Zingiber officinale* rhizomes possesses analgesic, anti-inflammatory and hypoglycaemic properties. These results lend pharmacological support to the traditional use of ginger in the treatment and/or management of painful, arthritic inflammatory conditions, as well as in the management and/or control of type 2 diabetes mellitus.[17] RMG Biosciences, Inc. has reported that during the past 25 years, many laboratories have provided scientific support for the long-held belief that ginger contains constituents with anti-inflammatory properties.[18]

Radioprotective Activity According to a study conducted by the Institute of Nuclear Medicine and Allied Sciences in India, *Zingiber officinale* possesses antioxidant, radioprotective, and neuromodulatory properties that can be effectively utilized for behavioral radioprotection, efficiently mitigating radiation-induced CTA in both males and females species.[19]

In a 30-day controlled animal study conducted by Kasturba Medical College in India, the hydroalcoholic extract of ginger rhizome was shown to be radioprotective. Pretreatment of mice with *Zingiber officinale* extract reduced the severity of symptoms of radiation sickness and mortality at all the exposure doses. The *Zingiber officinale* extract treatment protected mice against gastrointestinal-related deaths as well as bone marrow–related deaths. Ginger was found to scavenge radicals in a dose-dependent manner in vitro. The drug was nontoxic up to a dose of 1500 mg/kg body weight, the highest drug dose that could be tested for acute toxicity.[20]

Wrinkle-Inhibiting Activity According to an animal study conducted by Jichi Medical School, and Kao Biological Science Laboratories, in Japan, the topical application of an extract of *Zingiber officinale* significantly inhibits wrinkle formation induced by chronic UV-B irradiation, accompanied by a significant prevention of the decrease in skin elasticity. Results indicate that ginger extract has an ability to inhibit fibroblast-derived elastase, proving it potential as an anti-wrinkling agent.[21]

Weight Loss Promoting Activity According to a study conducted by L.M. College of Pharmacy in India, treatment with 250 mg/kg of methanol and ethyl acetate extracts of *Zingiber officinale* for 8 weeks produces significant reduction in body weight, glucose, insulin, and lipid levels as compared to obese control mice. The reduction in elevated glucose along with elevated insulin levels indicates that the treatment with *Zingiber officinale* improves insulin sensitivity.[22]

Anthelmintic Activity In a study conducted by the University of Agriculture in Pakistan, crude ginger powder and crude aqueous extract of dried ginger (1–3 g/kg) were administered to sheep naturally infected with mixed species of gastrointestinal nematodes. Both exhibited a dose- and a time-dependent anthelmintic effect with respective maximum reduction of 25.6 percent and 66.6 percent in eggs per gram of feces on day 10 of post-treatment. Levamisole (7.5 mg/kg), a standard anthelmintic agent, exhibited 99.2 percent reduction in eggs per gram. This study shows that ginger possesses in vivo anthelmintic activity in sheep, thus justifying the traditional use of this plant in helminth infestation.[23]

In an in-vitro study conducted by the Natural Products Research Unit and Prince of Songkla University in Thailand, the anti-giardial activity of chloroform, methanol and water extracts of 12 medicinal plants (39 extracts) was examined. The chloroform extracts from *Zingiber zerumbet* were classified as "active," with an IC50 of <100 microg/ml. This study shows that extracts from some medicinal plants have potential for use as therapeutic agents against *Giardia intestinalis* infections.[24]

Antihyperlipidemic and Antihyperinsulinemic Activity In an animal study conducted by Satsang Herbal Research and Analytical Laboratories in India, the oral administration of 95 percent ethanolic extract of *Zingiber officinale* was confirmed to possess blood glucose lowering effects.[25]

According to a study conducted by L.M. College of Pharmacy in India, methanolic extract of dried rhizomes of *Zingiber officinale* produces a significant reduction in fructose induced elevation in lipid levels, bodyweight, hyperglycemia and hyperinsulinemia. Although treatment with ethyl acetate extract of *Zingiber officinale* does not produce any significant change in either of the last two parameters, it produces a significant reduction in elevated lipid levels and body weight.[26]

Prokinetic and Spasmogenic Activity In a study conducted by the Aga Khan University Medical College in Pakistan, the prokinetic activity of ginger extract was confirmed in an in vivo test. Ginger extract was also shown to contain a cholinergic, a spasmogenic component which provides a sound mechanistic insight for the prokinetic action of ginger.[27]

Antiangiogenesis Activity According to an animal study conducted by Yonsei University in Korea, [6]-gingerol inhibits angiogenesis and may be useful in the treatment of tumors and other angiogenesis-dependent diseases.[28]

Chemopreventive Activity In a 15-week animal trial conducted by Annamalai University in India, administration of ginger significantly decreased the incidence of chemically-induced colon cancer.[29]

Anti-Atherosclerosis Activity In an animal trial conducted by RNT Medical College in India, dried ginger power significantly inhibited (50 percent) the development of atheroma in the aorta and coronary arteries caused by 75 days of cholesterol feeding. There was distinct decrease in lipid peroxidation, and enhancement of fibrinolytic activity in ginger treated animals. Ginger, however, did not lower blood lipids to any significant extent. According to the researchers, the distinct protection against atherosclerosis provided by ginger is probably the result of its free radical scavenging, prostaglandin inhibitory, and fibri properties.[30]

Anti-inflammatory and Anti-thrombotic Activity According to an animal study conducted by the Department of Biological Sciences, Faculty of Science in Kuwait, ginger could be used as a cholesterol-lowering, antithrombotic, and anti-inflammatory agent.[31]

Antiemetic Activity According to a randomized, double-blind study of 180 patients undergoing gynecologic laparoscopy conducted by Philipps-University of Marburg in Germany, ginger failed to reduce the incidence of postoperative nausea and vomiting after these procedures.[32] This study, of course, merely demonstrates that ginger does not combat chemically induced nausea. As has been proven in other studies, ginger is indeed effective in preventing nausea caused by motion sickness and early pregnancy.

Anxiolytic and Antiemetic Activity According to an animal study conducted by Samaj's College of Pharmacy in India, the benzene fraction of a petroleum ether extract of dried rhizomes of ginger possesses anticonvulsant, anxiolytic, and antiemetic activities.[33]

In a double blind, placebo-controlled, randomized clinical trial conducted by the University of South Florida, 26 subjects in the first trimester of pregnancy ingested 1 tablespoon of commercially prepared study syrup (or placebo) in 4 to 8 ounces of hot or cold water 4 times daily over a two week period. After 9 days, 10 of the 13 (77 percent) subjects receiving ginger had at least a 4-point improvement on the nausea scale. Only 2 of the 10 (20 percent) remaining subjects in the placebo group had the same improvement. Conversely, no woman in the ginger group, but 7 (70 percent) of the women in the placebo group, had a 2-point or less improvement on the nausea scale. Eight of the 12 (67 percent) women in the ginger group who were vomiting daily at the beginning of the treatment stopped vomiting by day 6. Only 2 of the 10 (20 percent) women in the placebo group who were vomiting stopped by day 6. It was concluded that the ingestion of 1 g of ginger in syrup in a divided dose daily may be useful for some patients experiencing nausea and vomiting in the first trimester of pregnancy.[34]

Antitumor Activity According to a study conducted by Seoul National University, the phenolic substances in *Zingiber officinale* possess potent antimutagenic and anticarcinogenic activities. The chemopreventive effects exerted by these phytochemicals are often associated with their antioxidative and anti-inflammatory activities.[35]

Aphrodisiacal Activity In controlled toxicity studies on animals conducted by King Saud University in Saudi Arabia on traditional Arab aphrodisiacs, *Zingiber officinale* showed no toxicity and significantly increased the sperm motility and sperm contents without producing a spermotoxic effect.[36]

*Anti-*Helicobacter pylori *Activity* According to an ongoing screening program conducted by the University of Illinois at Chicago, methanol extract of *Zingiber officinale* (ginger rhizome/root) had an MIC of 25 microg/mL against 15 HP strains while a combination of *Curcuma longa* root and ginger rhizome had a minimum inhibitory concentration of 50 microg/mL.[37]

Ginger Notes

1. Sūyūṭī J. *As-Sūyūṭī's Medicine of the Prophet*. Ed. A Thomson. London: Ṭā-Hā Publishers, 1994; Iṣbahānī AN al-. *Mawsū'at al-ṭibb al-nabawī*. Ed. MKD al-Turkī. Bayrūt: Dār Ibn Ḥazm, 2006; Ḥākim al-Nīsābūrī M. *al-Mustadrak 'alā al-ṣaḥīḥayn*. N.p.: n.p., n.d.
2. Farooqi MIH. *Plants of the Qur'ān*. Sidrah Publishers, Lucknow, 2000. 5th ed. 1989: 117.
3. Riḍā 'A al-. *Risālah fī al-ṭibb al-nabawī*. Ed. MA Bār. Bayrūt: Dār al-Manāhil, 1991: 168.
4. Riḍā, 'A al-. *Risālah fī al-ṭibb al-nabawī*. Ed. MA Bār. Bayrūt: Dār al-Manāhil, 1991: 168.
5. Ajith, Nivitha, Usha. *Zingiber officinale* Roscoe alone and in combination with alpha-tocopherol protect the kidney against cisplatin-induced acute renal failure. *Food* 2007; 45(6): 921–927.
6. Ansari, BhanDāri, Pillai. Ethanolic *Zingiber officinale* R. extract pretreatment alleviates isoproterenol-induced oxidative myocardial necrosis in rats. *Indian* 2006; 44(11): 892–897.
7. Shukla, Singh. Cancer preventive properties of ginger: A brief review. *Food* 2007 May; 45(5): 683–690.
8. Yance, Sagar. Targeting angiogenesis with integrative cancer therapies. *Integr* 2006; 5(1): 9–29.
9. Surh, Park, Chun, Lee, Lee, Lee. Anti-tumor-promoting activities of selected pungent phenolic substances present in ginger. *J* 1999; 18(2): 131–139.
10. Kirana, McIntosh, Record, Jones. Antitumor activity of extract of *Zingiber aromaticum* and its bioactive sesquiterpenoid zerumbone. *Nutr* 2003; 45(2): 218–225.
11. Akhani, Vishwakarma, Goyal. Anti-diabetic activity of *Zingiber officinale* in streptozotocin-induced type 1 diabetic rats. *J* 2004; 56(1): 101–105.
12. Al-Amin, Thomson, Al-Qattan, Peltonen-Shalaby, Ali. Anti-diabetic and hypolipidaemic properties of ginger (*Zingiber officinale*) in streptozotocin-induced diabetic rats. *Br* 2006; 96(4): 660–666.

13. Bhandari, Kanojia, Pillai. Effect of ethanolic extract of *Zingiber officinale* on dyslipidaemia in diabetic rats. *J* 2005; 97(2): 227–230.

14. Chopra, Lavin, Patwardhan, Chitre. A 32-Week Randomized, Placebo-Controlled Clinical Evaluation of RA-11, an Ayurvedic Drug, on Osteoarthritis of the Knees. *J* 2004; 10(5): 236–245.

15. Tewtrakul, Subhadhirasakul. Antiallergenic activity of some selected plants in the Zingiberaceae family. *J* 2007; 109(3): 535–538.

16. Yemitan, Izegbu. Protective effects of *Zingiber officinale* (Zingiberaceae) against carbon tetrachloride and acetaminophen-induced hepatotoxicity in rats. *Phytother* 2006; 20(11): 997–1002.

17. Ojewole. Analgesic, anti-inflammatory and hypoglycaemic effects of ethanol extract of *Zingiber officinale* (Roscoe) rhizomes (Zingiberaceae) in mice and rats. *Phytother* 2006; 20(9): 764–772.

18. Grzanna, Lindmark, Frondoza. Ginger — an herbal medicinal product with broad anti-inflammatory actions. *J* 2005; 8(2): 125–132.

19. Haksar, Sharma, Chawla, Kumar, Arora, Singh, Prasad, Gupta, Tripathi, Arora, Islam, Sharma. *Zingiber officinale* exhibits behavioral radioprotection against radiation-induced CTA in a gender-specific manner. *Pharmacol* 2006; 84(2): 179–188.

20. Jagetia, Baliga, Venkatesh. Ginger (*Zingiber officinale* Rosc.), a dietary supplement, protects mice against radiation-induced lethality: mechanism of action. *Cancer* 2004; 19(4): 422–435.

21. Tsukahara, Nakagawa, Moriwaki, Takema, Fujimura, Imokawa. Inhibition of ultraviolet-B-induced wrinkle formation by an elastase-inhibiting herbal extract: implication for the mechanism underlying elastase-associated wrinkles. *Int* 2006; 45(4): 460–468.

22. Goyal, Kadnur. Beneficial effects of *Zingiber officinale* on goldthioglucose induced obesity. *Fitoterapia.* 2006; 77(3): 160–163.

23. Iqbal, Lateef, Akhtar, Ghayur, Gilani. In vivo anthelmintic activity of ginger against gastrointestinal nematodes of sheep. *J* 2006; 106(2): 285–287.

24. Sawangjaroen, Subhadhirasakul, Phongpaichit, Siripanth, Jamjaroen, Sawangjaroen. The in vitro anti-giardial activity of extracts from plants that are used for self-medication by AIDS patients in southern Thailand. *Parasitol* 2005; 95(1): 17–21.

25. Kar, Choudhary, Bandyopadhyay. Comparative evaluation of hypoglycaemic activity of some Indian medicinal plants in alloxan diabetic rats. *J* 2003; 84(1): 105–108.

26. Kadnur, Goyal. Beneficial effects of *Zingiber officinale* Roscoe on fructose induced hyperlipidemia and hyperinsulinemia in rats. *Indian* 2005; 43(12): 1161–1164.

27. Ghayur, Gilani. Pharmacological basis for the medicinal use of ginger in gastrointestinal disorders. *Dig* 2005; 50(10): 1889–1197.

28. Kim, Min, Kim, Lee, Yang, Han, Kim, Kwon. [6]-Gingerol, a pungent ingredient of ginger, inhibits angiogenesis in vitro and in vivo. *Biochem* 2005; 335(2): 300–308.

29. Manju, Nalini. Chemopreventive efficacy of ginger, a naturally occurring anticarcinogen during the initiation, post-initiation stages of 1, 2 dimethylhydrazine-induced colon cancer. *Clin* 2005; 358(1–2): 60–67.

30. Verma, Singh, Jain, Bordia. Protective effect of ginger, *Zingiber officinale* Rosc on experimental atherosclerosis in rabbits. *Indian* 2004; 42(7): 736–738.

31. Thomson, Al-Qattan, Al-Sawan, Alnaqeeb, Khan, Ali. The use of ginger (*Zingiber officinale* Rosc.) as a potential anti-inflammatory and antithrombotic agent. *Prostaglandins* 2002; 67(6): 475–478.

32. Eberhart, Mayer, Betz, Tsolakidis, Hilpert, Morin, Geldner, Wulf, Seeling. Ginger does not prevent postoperative nausea and vomiting after laparoscopic surgery. *Anesth* 2003; 96(4): 995–998.

33. Vishwakarma, Pal, Kasture, Kasture. Anxiolytic and antiemetic activity of *Zingiber officinale. Phytother* 2002; 16(7): 621–626.

34. Keating, Chez. Ginger syrup as an antiemetic in early pregnancy. *Altern* 2002; 8(5): 89–91.

35. Surh. Anti-tumor promoting potential of selected spice ingredients with antioxidative and anti-inflammatory activities: a short review. *Food* 200240(8): 1091–1097.

36. Qureshi, Shah, Tariq, Ageel. Studies on herbal aphrodisiacs used in Arab system of medicine. *Am* 1989; 17(1–2): 57–63.

37. Mahady, Pendland, Stoia, Hamill, Fabricant, Dietz, Chadwick. In vitro susceptibility of *Helicobacter pylori* to botanical extracts used traditionally for the treatment of gastrointestinal disorders. *Phytother* 2005; 19(11): 988–991.

Grape / *'Inab, Karam*

FAMILY: Vitacea

BOTANICAL NAME: *Vitis vinifera*

COMMON NAMES: *English* Grape vine, Grape (fruit); *French* Vigne, Vigne noble (fruit); *Spanish* Vid, Parra; Uva (fruit); *German* Weinrebe; Rosine (fruit); *Urdu/Unānī* Angoor, Anab (fruit), Angur, Anb, Kishmish, Saongi, Maveez, Kishmish; *Modern Standard Arabic* 'Inab, Karam

SAFETY RATING: GENERALLY SAFE With the exception of allergic individuals, grapes and grape juice are generally considered to be safe for most people. When consumed in large quantities, however, grapes can cause diarrhea. Other potential side effects of excessive use include stomach upset, indigestion, nausea, vomiting, cough, dry mouth, sore throat, infections, headache, and muscular problems. Grapes or grape juice should not be consumed in medicinal amounts by women who are pregnant or lactating.

PROPHETIC PRESCRIPTION: The Holy Qur'ān mentions grapes on six occasions (2:266; 6:100; 13:4; 14:11; 16:67; 17:91; 18:32; 23:19; 36:34; 78:31–32, 80:28).[1] The Messenger of Allāh asked, "Let none of you call grapes (*'inab*) *karam*; *karam* signifies the Muslim."[2] He also said, "The word *karam* is only used for the heart of the believer."[3] And again, "Do not say *karam*, but say *'inab* (grapes), and *ḥabalah*."[4]

According to Abū Dāwūd, the Prophet was fond of grapes and melons.[5] He said, "The springtime of my Ummah is grapes and melons."[6] It is reported that he gave raisins to his companions, saying "Eat."[7] The Prophet is also reported to have said, "The best of food is bread, and the best of fruit is grapes."[8] He recommended people to, "Eat grapes one by one for thus they are more nourishing."[9] It is also reported that he said, "Noah complained to Allāh about his sorrow. So Allāh revealed to him that he should eat grapes. Then verily his sorrow departed."

Imām Ja'far al-Ṣādiq related that "One of the prophets complained to Allāh out of distress and He ordered him to eat grapes (*'inab*)."[10] In another tradition, he specified that the prophet in question was Nūḥ [Noah].[11]

Issues in Identification: It is the consensus that *'inab* is Arabic for grapes. Akīlī, however, claims that it refers to jujube,[12] and Turkī alleges that it refers to dried pomegranate seeds.[13] As Ghazanfar explains, *Vitis vinifera* is currently cultivated in Arabia in the lower hills.[14] During the early days of Islām, grapes were brought by caravan to Arabia from Bactria, the ancient name for a historical region in Central Asia.[15]

Properties and Uses: *Vitis vinifera* or grape is a sour, astringent, cooling herb that is diuretic, reduces inflammation, controls bleeding, improves circulation, and clears toxins. Grape is considered nutritive, concoctive, tonic, diuretic, deobstruent, resolvent, detersive, stimulant, astringent, diaphoretic, and laxative.

Internally, grape is used for varicose veins, excessive menstruation, menopausal syndrome, hemorrhage, urinary complaints, hypertension, high blood cholesterol, bronchitis, fevers, general debility, irritable stomach, ulceration, gangrene, tetanus, skin rashes, torpor and cellulite. Internally and externally, grape is used for inflammations of the mouth, gums, throat, and eyes. Fruits are the basis of a cure for poor liver function. According to Ibn Buṭlān, grape juice is indicated for "intestinal suffering."

Scientific Studies: *Anticarcinogenic Activity* In a study conducted by the Purdue University, grapes and grape extracts were shown to interact, often synergistically, with decaffeinated green tea extracts in the inhibition of cancer cell growth. Intratumoral injections of a 25:1 mixture of a green tea extract plus ground freeze-dried pomace was nearly as effective as standard synergistic green tea–Capsicum mixtures in inhibiting growth of mammary tumors in mice.[16] In a study conducted by the Ankara University School of Medicine in Turkey, black grape seed extract significantly inhibited the growth of cancerous colon tissues.[17] The study attempts to understand the basis for the beneficial effect of black grape in some kinds of human cancers.

Grape Notes

1. It is important to note that Islām categorically prohibits the consumption of wine and all intoxicant substances. Although wine has some medicinal properties when consumed in moderation, its harmful effects on health, its addictive nature, and the social problems it engenders greatly outway its potential benefits. This is precisely the Qur'ānic position, "They ask thee concerning wine and gambling. Say: 'In them is great sin, and some benefit, for men; but the sin is greater than the benefit'" (2: 219).

2. Abū Dāwūd S. *Ṣaḥīḥ Sunan Abū Dāwūd.* Riyyāḍ: Maktab al-Tarbiyyah, 1989.
3. Muslim. *Jāmi' al-ṣaḥīḥ.* al-Riyyāḍ: Bayt al-Afkār, 1998.
4. Muslim. *Jāmi' al-ṣaḥīḥ.* al-Riyyāḍ: Bayt al-Afkār, 1998
5. Abū Dāwūd S. *Ṣaḥīḥ Sunan Abū Dāwūd.* Riyyāḍ: Maktab al-Tarbiyyah, 1989.
6. Chaghhaynī M. *Ṭibb al-nabī.* Trans. C Elgood. *Osiris* 1962; 14: 189.
7. Sūyūṭī J. *As-Sūyūṭī's Medicine of the Prophet.* Ed. A Thomson. London: Ṭā-Hā Publishers, 1994: 65.
8. Chaghhaynī M. *Ṭibb al-nabī.* Trans. C Elgood. *Osiris* 1962; 14: 187.
9. Chaghhaynī M. *Ṭibb al-nabī.* Trans. C Elgood. *Osiris* 1962; 14: 190.
10. Majlisī M. *Biḥār al-anwār.* Ṭihrān: Javad al-Alavi, 1956.
11. Majlisī M. *Biḥār al-anwār.* Ṭihrān: Javad al-Alavi, 1956.
12. Ibn al-Qayyim al-Jawziyyah. *Natural Healing with the Medicine of the Prophet.* Pearl Publishing. Trans. M al-Akīlī. Philadelphia, 1993.
13. Iṣbahānī AN al-. *Mawsū'at al-ṭibb al-nabawī.* Ed. MKD al-Turkī. Bayrūt: Dār Ibn Ḥazm, 2006.
14. Ghazanfar SA. *Handbook of Arabian Medicinal Plants.* Boca Raton: CRC Press, 1994.
15. Tannahill R. *Food in History.* New York: Stein and Day, 1973: 126.
16. Morre, Morre. Anticancer activity of grape and grape skin extracts alone and combined with green tea infusions. *Cancer* 2006; 238(2): 202–209.
17. Durak, Cetin, Devrim, Erguder. Effects of black grape extract on activities of DNA turn-over enzymes in cancerous and non-cancerous human colon tissues. *Life* 2005; 76(25): 2995–3000.

Gum Arabic/*Ṣamgh 'Arabī*

Botanical Identity: *Acacia nilotica* (syn. *Acacia arabica*)

Family: Fabaceae

Common Names: *English* Gum arabic, gum-arabic; *French* Gomme arabe; *Spanish* Goma arábiga; *German* Gummi Arabicum, Gummiarabikum, Ägyptischer Schotendorn; *Urdu/Unānī* Samagh-e-Arabic, Gond Babool; *Modern Standard Arabic* Ṣamgh 'arabī, Umm ghīlān, Ṭalḥ, Aqāqiyā, Samar, Shittim

Safety Rating: Generally Safe Although it can cause gas, bloating, and loose stools, gum arabic is generally considered safe for most adults when used as directed. In individual who are allergic to acacia, gum arabic can cause skin reactions or asthma attacks. Acacia, in any form, should not be consumed during pregnancy or lactation.

Prophetic Prescription: A man complained to Imām Muḥammad al-Bāqir about diarrhea. The Imām told him, "Take one part of white clay, one part of fleawort seeds, one part of gum arabic (*ṣamgh 'arabī*), and one part of Armenian clay. Boil it over a low fire, and eat of it."[1]

Issues in Identification: According to Chaudhary, there are currently sixteen species of acacia in Saudi Arabia, including the common introductions.[2] The species used for their gum resin include *Acacia gerrardii*, *Acacia nilotica*, and *Acacia senegal*. According to Mandaville, *Acacia gerrardii* is a copious producer of gum arabic (*ṣamgh*). It is known in the colloquial dialect as *ṭalḥ*.[3] As Chaudhary explains, *Acacia gerrardii* has a wide distribution in Saudi Arabia. Its distribution in Saudi Arabia, Kuwait, Iraq, and Palestine follows ancient caravan routes.[4] The map of vegetation communities prepared by the Saudi Ministry of Agriculture and Water does not show *Acacia nilotica*. It does show *Acacia gerrardii*, *Acacia tortilis*, and *Acacia ehrenbergiana* around Medina. *Acacia gerrardii* is also shown in central Arabia. Around Mecca, *Acacia tortilis*, *Acacia ehrenbergiana*, and *Acacia commiphra* are also indicated. According to Chaudhary, *Acacia mellifera*, known also as *Acacia Senegal*, is widely distributed on the lower western slopes of the mountains and the submontane level areas in southwestern Saudi Arabia, known in Saudi as *katar*, and *ẓabah*.[5]

Properties and Uses: *Acacia* is a demulcent, emollient, protective, styptic, tonic, astringent, and nutritive herb. Acacia gum forms a protective coating over inflamed tissues, reducing irritation, and encouraging healing. It is used in coughs, laryngitis, gastritis, typhoid fever, dysentery, diarrhea, and diabetes mellitus. Acacia gum is also used to treat burns, sores, leprosy, the common cold, high cholesterol, infections, inflammation, kidney failure, sore nipples, and sore throat. A decoction of acacia bark is used as a gargle and mouth wash while acacia twigs are used to for brushing and flossing one's teeth, particularly for preventing plaque. As a douche, the decoction is used to treat gonorrhea, cystitis, vaginitis, and leucorrhoea. According to Ghazanfar, the resin, leaves, and seeds of *Acacia nilotica* are used for cataracts, as a demulcent, for treating diarrhea, diabetes, and toothache.[6]

As Ghazanfar explains, *Acacia gerardii* resin gum and pods are used for treating sore gums, loose teeth, burns and fevers, while *Acacia nilotica* resin, leaves and seeds are used for cataracts, as a demulcent, for treating diarrhea, diabetes, and toothache. *Acacia senegal* is also widely used to produce gum arabic. It is a soothing herb that forms a protective coating over inflamed tissues, reducing irritation, and encouraging healing. Internally, it is used in lozenges for sore throats, coughs, and mucus, and in commercial mixtures for diarrhea and dysentery. Externally, it is used for burns, sores, and leprosy. As Ghazanfar explains, the bark and resin are believed to be antiseptic. As Maude Grieve clarifies, *Acacia senegal* is not, strictly speaking, synonymous with acacia gum, which originally referred to Sudan, Kordofan or Egyptian Gum. The Prophet was clearly referring to the plant known as both *Acacia nilotica* and *Acacia arabica*.

Scientific Studies: *Demulcent Activity* According to Maude Grieve, the British and American Pharmacopoeia included acacia gum as a demulcent. It was employed as a soothing agent in inflammatory conditions of the respiratory, digestive, and urinary tract, and was useful in diarrhea and dysentery.

Nutritional Activity According to Maude Grieve, acacia gum is highly nutritious. She reports that some Bedouins lived almost entirely on it while they were in the desert, and that it has been proven that 6 ounces is sufficient to support an adult for twenty-four hours.[7]

Nephroprotective Activity Gum arabic is a complex polysaccharide used as suspending agent. It has been widely used by eastern folk medicine practitioners as a restorative agent and is thought to be an excellent curative for renal failure patients. According to an animal study conducted by King Saud University, oral administration of gum arabic appears to protect against nephrotoxicity, partly through the inhibition of the production of oxygen free radicals that cause lipid peroxidation.[8]

Rehydrating Activity According to North Shore University Hospital and New York University School of Medicine, gum arabic is a soluble fiber which enhances water, electrolyte, and glucose absorption. In an animal study, researchers confirmed that oral rehydration solutions supplemented with gum arabic results in optimal recovery from diarrhea. Gum arabic-supplemented rehydration solution had positive effects on fluid and electrolyte absorption.[9]

According to an animal study conducted by North Shore University Hospital and New York

University School of Medicine, gum arabic appears to be an effective enhancer of sodium absorption from oral rehydration solutions when tested in experimental animals. Since gum arabic does not affect viscosity, an alteration of solute diffusibility through the brush border membrane and changes in intercellular compartments may underlie the observed improvement of sodium absorption.[10]

Anti-Plaque Activity According to one study, chewing gum arabic may be useful in fighting dental plaque.[11]

Renoprotective Activity According to a case which took place at the University Hospital in al-Kadhimiya in Iraq, the parents of an 11-year-old girl with end-stage renal failure refused to continue her treatment by dialysis. She was then managed by a new regimen which combined traditional conservative management of chronic renal failure with addition of 1 g/kg per day of acacia gum. After four years of treatment, the patient experienced improved well-being, a good participation in outdoor activities, had never been acidotic, and had never experienced significant uremic symptoms. In short, this is the longest period of dialysis freedom ever reported in children with end-stage renal failure.[12]

Gum Arabic Notes

1. Nisābūrī A. *Islamic Medical Wisdom: The Ṭibb al-a'immah*. Trans. B. Ispahany. Ed. AJ Newman. London: Muḥammadī Trust, 1991: 79.
2. Chaudhary SA. *Flora of the Kingdom of Saudi Arabia*. al-Riyyāḍ: Ministry of Agriculture and Water, 1999.
3. Mandaville JP. *Flora of Eastern Saudi Arabia*. London: Kegan Paul, 1990.
4. Chaudhary SA. *Flora of the Kingdom of Saudi Arabia*. al-Riyyāḍ: Ministry of Agriculture and Water, 1999.
5. Chaudhary SA. *Flora of the Kingdom of Saudi Arabia*. al-Riyyāḍ: Ministry of Agriculture and Water, 1999.
6. Ghazanfar SA. *Handbook of Arabian Medicinal Plants*. Boca Raton: CRC Press, 1994.
7. Grieve M. Grieve M. *A Modern Herbal*. Ed. C.F. Leyel. Middlesex, England: Penguin, 1980.
8. Al-Majed, Mostafa, Al-Rikabi, Al-Shabanah. Protective effects of oral gum arabic administration on gentamicin-induced nephrotoxicity in rats. *Pharmacol* 2002; 46(5): 445–451.
9. Teichberg, Wingertzahn, Moyse, Wapnir. Effect of gum arabic in an oral rehydration solution on recovery from diarrhea in rats. *J* 1999; 29(4): 411–417.
10. Wapnir, Teichberg, Go, Wingertzahn, Harper. Oral rehydration solutions: enhanced sodium absorption with gum arabic. *J* 1996; 15(4): 377–382.
11. Clar DT, et al. The effects of *Acacia arabica* gum on the in-vitro growth and protease activities of periodontopathic bacteria. *J Clinical Periodontology* 1993; 20: 238–243.
12. Mosawi AJ. The use of acacia gum in end stage renal failure. *J Trop Pediatr.* May 2007.

Harmal (Syrian Rue)/*Ḥarmal*

Family: Nitrariaceae

Botanical Name: *Peganum harmala*

Common Names: *English* Harmel, Wild rue, Syrian rue, African rue; *French* Hermale, Harmel, Rue sauvage; *Spanish* Ruda siria, Alharma; *German* Syrische Raute, Harmalkraut, Harmelraute, Steppenraute, Wilde Raute; *Urdu/Unānī* Harmal, Hurmul, Ispand; *Modern Standard Arabic* Ḥarmal, Sadhāb barrī

Safety Rating: Generally Safe to Deadly Syrian rue is generally considered safe when consumed in food amounts. In medicinal amounts, it is considered unsafe as it can cause stomach irritation, changes in mood, sleep problems, dizziness, spasms, skin disorders, sensitivity to the sun, and kidney and liver problems. If consumed in excess, Syrian rue causes hallucinations, vomiting, and occasionally death. As such, its consumption should be avoided and, if used, should only be done with expert supervision. In all cases, Syrian rue must not be consumed by women who are pregnant or breast-feeding, as well as people suffering from kidney, liver, stomach, intestinal, or urinary tract problems. The essential oil of Syrian rue is a dangerous abortifacient. Syrian rue should not be applied externally as it is an irritant. Simply handling the foliage, flowers or fruit can cause burning, erythema, itching, and vesication.

Prophetic Prescription: The mystical and medicinal properties of harmal were expounded upon by the Prophet Muḥammad:

> That which grows from harmel (*ḥarmal*), its root, its branches, its leaves, and its flowers, have an angel which protects them until it reaches the end of its growth or dries up. Its root and stem possess the power of a spell. Its seed are a cure for seventy diseases. So treat yourselves with it and with frankincense.[1]

In a variant of this tradition, the Messenger of Allāh says:

> That which grows from harmel (*ḥarmal*), its root, its branches, its leaves, and its flowers, have an angel which protects them until it reaches the end of its growth or dries up. Its root and stem possess the power of a spell. Its seed are a cure for seventy diseases. So treat yourselves with it and with frankincense, making it reach all things and all people in your house. This is the way that all kinds of demons (*'ifrīt*) without open mouths and outstretched hands were expelled from seventy two houses. They will

> be expelled in the same way from the house in which incense is used.[2]

Imām Ja'far al-Ṣādiq further elaborated upon the benefits of wild rue:

> As for harmel, neither its root in the Earth nor its branch in the sky is shaken without there being an angel in charge of it until it becomes debris and becomes what it becomes. For Satan avoids seventy houses in which it is, and it is a healing for seventy illnesses, the least of which is leprosy. So do not be heedless of it.[3]

Imām Muḥammad al-Bāqir prescribed wild rue for bladder infections, "Take harmal and wash it six times in cold water and once in hot water. Then dry it in the shade and mix it with pure and clear oil. Eat it on an empty stomach and it will stop the dripping. Allāh, the Exalted, willing."[4]

The Prophet and the Imāms were referring to *Peganum harmala* (*ḥarmal*), a plant of the Nitrariaceae family. It is sometimes known as Syrian rue, a confusing name, as it is not related to rue (*Ruta graveolens*) from the Rutaceae family. Harmal has a long history of use in European and Middle Eastern herbalism. In fact, rue was an essential ingredient in many antidotes and cure-alls from Greco-Roman times to the mid 19th century. In al-Kindī, rue is used to treat phlegm, rheumatism, and nervous conditions.[5] He also uses it for insanity, epilepsy, and as an antidote to all kinds of poisons.[6] In Egypt, the seeds are used as a diuretic and vomitive while in Iran they are considered an aphrodisiac.[7]

ISSUES IN IDENTIFICATION: According to Hans Wehr, *ḥarmal* is Arabic for *Peganum harmala*, known in English as wild rue, Syrian rue, and African rue. As Nehmé explains, *ḥarmal* or common peganum is known as *ḥarmal* and *ghalqat al-dhi'b*.[8] According to Bīrūnī, *ḥarmal* is also known as *ghalqah* and *iẓlam*, which Said identifies as *Peganum harmala*. Bīrūnī also speaks of *ḥarmal abyaḍ*, *ḥurmal*, *ghalqat al-dhi'b*, and *sadhāb barrī*, which are all equally identified by Said as *Peganum harmala*.[9]

According to Mandaville, *Peganum harmala* is rare in eastern Arabia, found only as a weed or ruderal, nearly always on disturbed ground. It is well known in central and northern Arabia and Iraq. It is known in the Saudi dialect Arabic as *khiyyās* (stinkweed), *shajarat al-khunayzir*, as well as *ḥarmal*. The herb is found in sandy areas in Saudi Arabia. It is important to note that in the Saudi and Omani Dhofari dialects, *ḥarmal* is also the name given to *Rhazya stricta*. Although somewhat toxic, some elder Bedouins consider that smoking its dry leaves is an effective treatment for rheumatism. It is used for improving bad breath, chest pain, for conjunctivitis, constipation, and diabetes. It is also employed to lower fevers, to treat skin rash, as an anthelmintic, and to increase lactation.[10]

PROPERTIES AND USES: *Peganum harmala*, known commonly as harmal or Syrian rue, is much used in Arab medicine and is mentioned in early Muslim medical literature. It is a bitter, spicy, diuretic herb that stimulates the uterus and digestive system, and is reputedly aphrodisiac. It is considered hypnotic, sedative, alterative, antiperiodic, emmenagogue, lactagogue, expectorant, antiflatulent, anthelmintic, and abortifacient.

Peganum harmala is used internally for stomach complaints, urinary and sexual disorders, epilepsy, menstrual problems, nervous and mental illnesses, amnesia, sciatica, colic, and jaundice. It is used externally for hemorrhoids and baldness.[11] Dental cavities are fumigated by burning the seeds while the powdered seeds are used to treat tape worms, as well as intermittent and remittent fevers.

SCIENTIFIC STUDIES: *Antioxidative Activity* In a study conducted by the University of Sherbrooke in Canada, the protective effect of *Peganum harmala* extract and the two major alkaloids (harmine and harmaline) from the seeds of *Peganum harmala* were investigated for their protective effect against induced LDL oxidation, which has been implicated in the process of atherogenesis.[12] Harmaline and harmine reduced the rate of vitamin E disappearance and exhibited a significant free radical scavenging capacity. However, harmaline had a markedly higher antioxidant capacity than harmine in scavenging or preventive capacity against free radicals as well as inhibiting the aggregation of the LDL protein moiety (apolipoprotein B) induced by oxidation. The results suggested that *Peganum harmala* compounds could be a major source of compounds that inhibit LDL oxidative modification induced by copper.

Antitumor Activity In an animal study conducted by Sun Yat-sen University in China, administration of harmine derivatives resulted in tumor inhibition rates of 15.3–49.5 percent. While most of these compounds showed remarkable acute neurotoxicities, two of them had high antitumor activity and low toxicity, and might be chosen as lead molecules for further development. On the basis of these results, the researchers called for more studies on the effects of harmine derivatives on key regulators for tumor cell apoptosis.[13] In a study conducted by Faculté de médecine et de Pharmacie de Rabat in Morocco, the alkaloids of *Peganum harmala* were found to have significant antitumor activity. The study supports the Moroccan use of *Peganum harmala* to treat subcutaneous tumors, and suggests that the herb could prove useful as a novel anticancer therapy.[14]

Toxic Activity Harmaline, the active principle of the plant seeds, and its derivatives, cause visual troubles, loss of coordination, agitation and delirium, and, at high doses, it can produce paralysis. The Laboratoire de Pharmacologie et Toxicologie of the Faculté de Medecine et de Pharmacie de Rabat in Morocco assessed the toxicity of *Peganum harmala* seeds. The study evaluated the use and manipulation of therapeutic doses of aqueous extract of *Peganum harmala* in animal subjects. It found that therapeutic doses of *Peganum harmala.* Histologic study showed liver degeneration and spongiform changes in the central nervous system in rats treated with 2g/kg dose but not at the therapeutic dose of 1g/kg. The study confirmed that *Peganum harmala* can be used safely according to therapeutic doses and warms of the dangers of exceeding the recommended dosage.[15]

Anti-Parkinsonian Activity Historically, the use of alkaloids of the belladonna, harmala, and aporphine families were used in the treatment of Parkinson's disease since the original description of the malady in 1817.[16] In his 1991 article on Banisterine and Parkinson's disease, Sanchez-Ramos observed that 63 years had passed since Louis Lewin reported the use of a hallucinogenic compound prepared from the South American vine, *Banisteria caapi*, to treat Parkinson's disease.[17] This psychoactive compound, named banisterine, proved to be identical to harmine, but 30 years were to pass before it was shown to be a reversible monoamine oxidase inhibitor. The first reports of the use of banisterine to treat postencephalitic Parkinsonism in 1929 created a stir in the popular press and banisterine was hailed as a "magic drug." Despite continued studies of the harmala alkaloids by other researchers, interest in the therapeutic value of these compounds vanished during the 1930's. The story of banisterine is reviewed in this paper as it was the first MAO inhibitor to be used in Parkinsonism, and illustrates the historical role of psychoactive drugs in the development of effective therapies, and in elucidating the pathophysiology of Parkinson's disease.

Harmal Notes

1. Nisābūrī A. *Islamic Medical Wisdom: The Ṭibb al-a'immah.* Trans. B. Ispahany. Ed. AJ Newman. London: Muḥammadī Trust, 1991: 81.

2. Ibn Ḥabīb A. *Mujtaṣar fī al-ṭibb/Compendio de medicina.* Ed. C Álvarez de Morales and F Girón Irueste. Madrid: Consejo Superior de Investigaciones Científicas, 1992: 76/44.

3. Nisābūrī A. *Islamic Medical Wisdom: The Ṭibb al-a'immah.* Trans. B. Ispahany. Ed. AJ Newman. London: Muḥammadī Trust, 1991: 81–82; Majlisī M. *Biḥār al-anwār.* Ṭihrān: Javad al-Alavi, 1956.

4. Nisābūrī A. *Islamic Medical Wisdom: The Ṭibb al-a'immah.* Trans. B. Ispahany. Ed. AJ Newman. London: Muḥammadī Trust, 1991: 83.

5. Levey M, al-Khaledy N, eds. *The Medical Formulary of al-Samarqandī.* Philadelphia: University of Pennsylvania Press, 1967: 195, note 174.

6. Levey M, al-Khaledy N, eds. *The Medical Formulary of al-Samarqandī.* Philadelphia: University of Pennsylvania Press, 1967: 195, note 174.

7. Levey M, al-Khaledy N, eds. *The Medical Formulary of al-Samarqandī.* Philadelphia: University of Pennsylvania Press, 1967: 206, note 273.

8. Nehmé M. *Dictionnaire étymologique de la flore du Liban.* Bayrūt: Librairie du Liban, 2000.

9. Bīrūnī, AR al-. *al-Bīrūnī's Book on Pharmacy and Materia Medica.* Ed. and trans. HM Said. Karachi: Hamdard National Foundation, 1973.

10. Mandaville JP. *Flora of Eastern Saudi Arabia.* London: Kegan Paul, 1990.

11. Bown D. *Encyclopedia of Herbs and their Uses.* Westmount: RD Press, 1995: 323.

12. Berrougui, Isabelle, Cloutier, Hmamouchi, Khalil. Protective effects of *Peganum harmala* L. extract, harmine and harmaline against human low-density lipoprotein oxidation. *J Pharm Pharmacol.* 2006; 58(7): 967–974.

13. Chen, Chao, Chen, Hou, Yan, Zhou, Peng, Xu. Antitumor and neurotoxic effects of novel harmine derivatives and structure-activity relationship analysis. *Int* 2005; 114(5): 675–82.

14. Lamchouri, Settaf, Cherrah, Zemzami, Lyoussi, Zaid, Atif, Hassar. Antitumor principles from *Peganum harmala* seeds. *Therapie.* 199954(6): 753–758.

15. Lamchouri, Settaf, Cherrah, El, Tligui, Lyoussi, Hassar. Experimental toxicity of *Peganum harmala* seeds. *Ann* 2002; 60(2): 123–129.

16. Sourkes. "Rational hope" in the early treatment of Parkinson's disease. *Can* 1999; 77(6): 375–382.

17. Sanchez-Ramos. Banisterine and Parkinson's disease. *Clin* 1991; 14(5): 391–402.

Henna / *Ḥinnā'*

FAMILY: Lythraceae

BOTANICAL NAME: *Lawsonia inermis* (syn. *Lawsonia alba*)

COMMON NAMES: *English* Henna plant, Egyptian privet; *French* Henné, Henneh; *Spanish* Henna, Alheña; *German* Hennastrauch, Ägyptischer Hennastrauch; *Urdu/Unānī* Mehandi, Hina; *Modern Standard Arabic* Ḥinnā', al-Qaṭab

SAFETY RATING: GENERALLY SAFE TO DEADLY Pure henna is generally safe, but henna preparations are potentially lethal and consequently henna should only be used internally with expert supervision. It is only safe as a hair dye. Commercial preparations of henna paste, which are used for body decoration, are poisonous. They often contain other ingredients, including para-phenylenediamine or PPD, which can cause allergic reactions, such as red rash, contact dermatitis, itching, blisters, open sores, scarring of the skin, and other potentially harmful effects. Other allergic reactions to PPD include sensitivity to hair dye, sun block, and some types of black clothing. Sensitivity to PPD is lifelong. Once sensitized, the use of synthetic hair dye can be life-threatening. Some pastes include silver nitrate, carmine, pyrogallol, disperse orange dye, and chromium, which can cause allergic reactions, chronic inflammation, or late on-set allergic reactions to hairdressing products and dyes used in textiles. Some medical studies found heavy metals such as nickel, cobalt, lead, and mercury in henna tattoos. In people with glucose-6-phosphate dehydrogenase deficiency, the application of henna to the skin can cause life-threatening haemolysis. As such, henna must never be used internally, and it should be used externally with the greatest of caution. Due to the dangerous chemicals it contains, henna paste should not be applied externally to the skin of women who are pregnant or lactating. Even pure henna exhibits antifertility activity in animals, and may induce menstruation. It is ironic that a plant that prevents fertility is considered the symbol of fertility in the Arab world and India.

Prophetic Prescription: The Messenger of Allāh said, "Allāh created no plant more pleasing to Him than henna."[1] According to Anas ibn Malik, the herb most beloved by the Messenger of Allāh was henna blossom.[2] He said, "The lord of sweet smelling blossoms, in this world and the next, is henna blossom (*fāghiyyah*)."[3] Showing the great value of henna, the Prophet said, "Giving one dirham in the path of Allāh is the equivalent of seven hundred for another purpose, and giving one dirham's worth of henna is equal to nine thousand."[4] He also said, "There are five things taken from the books of the Prophets: cupping, perfume, *miswāk*, henna, and having multiple wives."[5]

The Messenger of Allāh recommended henna as a dye, saying, "The best way to hide old age (grey hair) is through henna (*ḥinnā'*) and indigo (*katam*)."[6] When he saw a man who had dyed his hair with henna, the Prophet said, "That is good." He then saw a man who had dyed his hair with both henna and indigo and said "That is better."[7]

The Messenger of Allāh prescribed henna for various ailments. According to Umm Salamah, "The Prophet, may Allāh bless him and grant him peace, never suffered from a wound or a thorn without putting henna on it."[8] He also told a man who complained of pain in his legs to dye them with henna.[9] According to Abū Hurayrah, when the Prophet suffered from migraines as a result of the receiving revelation, he would apply henna to his head.[10] According to Ibn Ḥabīb, the Prophet used to apply henna to scratches, wounds, ulcers, and would apply henna to his head for headaches.[11]

The Messenger of Allāh said, "Dye your hair with henna for it increases youth and virility" and "Dye your hair with henna for it has a pleasant smell and removes vitiligo."[12] He also said, "Make use of henna, the best of all dyes, for henna strengthens the skin and increases virility."[13] He is also reported to have said, "Henna is the dye of Islām. The use of it increases the good deeds of the faithful. It drives away headache, sharpens vision, and increases sexual powers. It is the master of all perfumes in this world and the next."[14] Finally, the Prophet is reported to have said, "Verily, if a cure resides in anything, it resides in henna."[15]

Imām Ja'far al-Ṣādiq recommended the use of henna for cases of leprosy and vitiligo. He instructed a patient to "Enter the steam bath and mix henna [*al-ḥinnā'*] with lime and coat your body with it. You will not be cured by anything else after that." The man said, "By Allāh, I did that only once and Allāh cured me, and it did not recur after that"[16] Imām Ja'far al-Ṣādiq "Do not have intercourse with your wife while you have your hair dyed, for if you are blessed with a child, it will be effeminate or a hermaphrodite (*mukhannath*)."[17]

Issues in Identification: It is the consensus that *hinna* is Arabic for *Lawsonia* and that *fāghiyyah al-ḥinna'* refers to henna blossom. Although it is true that some classical authors have referred to henna as *kāfūr*, Farooqi's claim that the camphor of the Qur'ān and the Sunnah is actually henna has been proven false through peer-review. As Duke points out, the dye of *Lawsonia alba* was known as puker by ancient Egyptians, *kupr* or *kuder* by the Copts, *kufra* in Aramaic and Accadian, *kopfer* in Hebrew, and *kaffūr* in Arabic.

While the identity of *ḥinnā'* is clear, there are differences of opinion regarding that of *fāghiyyah*. For Elgood and Turkī, it refers to henna blossom.[18] According to Akīlī *fāghiyyah* is Costmary, known as *chrysanthemum balsamita*.[19] Costmary, of course, is a European aromatic plant, smelling of tansy and used as a potherb and for salads. Costmary is not henna blossom. Furthermore, there is not a single chrysanthemum which bares an Arabic name remotely resembling *fāghiyyah*. As Said explains, *fāghiyyah* means privet-flower and it refers to *Zanthoxylum rhetsa*. *Z. alatum Roxb. Z. acanthopodium*, and *Z. Oxyphyllum*.[20] For all intents and purposes, the Prophet must have been referring to *fāghiyyat al-ḥinnā'* which are Meccan henna buds.

According to Ghazanfar, *Lawsonia inermis* is found throughout Arabia in disturbed soil and waste places. It is also widely cultivated in Arabia.[21] According to Mandaville, *Lawsonia inermis* is not infrequently cultivated as an ornamental in eastern Arabia and is sometimes found apparently spontaneous on waste ground or along roadsides in oasis areas. Its ability to self-propagate in eastern Arabia is questionable. It is known in Saudi Arabic as *ḥenna, hinnā, and hinā.*[22]

PROPERTIES AND USES: *Lawsonia inermis*, known commonly as henna, is considered astringent, antihemmorrhagic, cardio-inhibitory, hypotensive, detergent, alternative, refrigerant, tonic, antibacterial, and sedative. It is used for amebic dysentery, leprosy, wounds, ulcers, itching, scabies, pruritis, syphilis, jaundice, and herpes. As a folk medicine, it has been used as a remedy against amoebiasis, and headache. Henna extract shows antibacterial, antifungal, and ultraviolet light screening activity.

Antioxidative Activity In a study conducted by Mansoura University in Egypt, isolated compounds from the methanolic extract of henna leaves were found to possess an antioxidative activity comparable to that of ascorbic acid.[23]

Antimicrobial and Antibacterial Activity In an in vitro study conducted by Sultan Qaboos University in Oman, crude extracts of fresh and dry leaves and seeds were investigated for their antimicrobial activity against 3 standard bacterial strains namely: *Staphylococcus aureus*, *Escherichia coli* and *Pseudomonas aeruginosa*. All fresh and dry leaves and seeds of the Omani henna demonstrated antibacterial activity against all 3 standard strains and the 11 patients' isolated strains. Henna dry leaves demonstrated the best in-vitro antimicrobial activity and in particular against *Shigella sonnei*. However, henna fresh and dry seeds failed to show any activity against *Candida albicans*. Omani henna, however, does possess in-vitro antibacterial activity against a wide spectrum of bacterial strains and *Candida albicans*.[24]

Hepaprotective Activity In an animal study conducted by Nagpur University in India, the aqueous extract of *Lawsonia alba* bark was shown to possess hepaprotective and antioxidative activity.[25]

Anti-inflammatory, Antipyretic and Analgesic Activity In a study conducted by the United Arab Emirates University, crude ethanolic extract of *Lawsonia inermis* L. (0.25–2.0 g/kg) produced significant and dose-dependent anti-inflammatory, analgesic, and antipyretic effects in rats. The anti-inflammatory effect of lawsone (500 mg/kg) was not significantly different from that of the reference drug phenylbutazone (100 mg/kg).[26]

Tuberulostatic Activity In in-vivo animal studies conducted by S. M. S. Medical College in India, a dose of 5 mg/kg body weight of *Lawsonia inermis* led to significant resolution of experimental tuberculosis.[27]

Antifertility Activity According to an animal study, a daily dose of 3, 30, or 300 mg of *Lawsonia inermis* showed a 40–60 percent inhibition of pregnancy. The infertility produced by the powdered leaves of *Lawsonia inermis* appeared to be permanent.[28]

Henna Notes

1. Chaghhaynī M. *Ṭibb al-nabī.* Trans. C Elgood. *Osiris* 1962; 14: 191.
2. Bayhaqī A. *al-Sunan al-kubrā.* Bayrūt: Dār Ṣadīr, 1968.
3. Sūyūṭī J. *As-Sūyūṭī's Medicine of the Prophet.* Ed. A Thomson. London: Ṭā-Hā Publishers, 1994. This tradition is said to be apocryphal.
4. Chaghhaynī M. *Ṭibb al-nabī.* Trans. C Elgood. *Osiris* 1962; 14: 191.
5. Ibn Ḥabīb A. *Mujtaṣar fī al-ṭibb/Compendio de medicina.* Ed. C Álvarez de Morales and F Girón Irueste. Madrid: Consejo Superior de Investigaciones Científicas, 1992: 48.
6. Abū Dāwūd S. *Ṣaḥīḥ Sunan Abū Dāwūd.* Riyyāḍ: Maktab al-Tarbiyyah, 1989; Tirmidhī M. *al-Jāmi' al-ṣaḥīḥ.* al-Qāhirah: Muṣṭafā al-Bābī al-Ḥalabī, [1937-]; Nasā'ī A. *Sunan al-Nisā'ī.* al-Qāhirah: Muṣṭafā al-Bābī al-Ḥalabī, 1964–65; Ibn Mājah, M. *Sunan.* Trans. MT Anṣārī. Lahore: Kazi Publications, 1994; Iṣbahānī AN al-. *Mawsū'at al-ṭibb al-nabawī.* Ed. MKD al-Turkī. Bayrūt: Dār Ibn Ḥazm, 2006.
7. Farooqi MIH. *Medicinal Plants in the Traditions of Prophet Muḥammad.* Lucknow: Sidrah Publishers, 1998: 63.
8. Sūyūṭī J. *As-Sūyūṭī's Medicine of the Prophet.* Ed. A Thomson. London: Ṭā-Hā Publishers, 1994: 55–56.
9. Abū Dāwūd S. *Ṣaḥīḥ Sunan Abū Dāwūd.* Riyyāḍ: Maktab al-Tarbiyyah, 1989.
10. Ibn al-Sunnī. *Ṭibb al-nabī.* Ed. Omer Recep. Philipps-Universität: Marburg/Lahn, 1969: 33; Ibn Ḥabīb A. *Mujtaṣar fī al-ṭibb/Compendio de medicina.* Ed. C Álvarez de Morales and F Girón Irueste. Madrid: Consejo Superior de Investigaciones Científicas, 1992: 56/23.
11. Ibn Ḥabīb A. *Mujtaṣar fī al-ṭibb/Compendio de medicina.* Ed. C Álvarez de Morales and F Girón Irueste. Madrid: Consejo Superior de Investigaciones Científicas, 1992: 78/45.
12. Ibn Ṭulūn S. *al-Manhal al-rawī fī al-ṭibb al-nabawī.* Ed. 'Azīz Bayk. Riyyāḍ: Dār 'ālam al-kutub, 1995.
13. Sūyūṭī J. *As-Sūyūṭī's Medicine of the Prophet.* Ed. A Thomson. London: Ṭā-Hā Publishers, 1994: 19.
14. Chaghhaynī M. *Ṭibb al-nabī.* Trans. C Elgood. *Osiris* 1962; 14: 191.
15. Chaghhaynī M. *Ṭibb al-nabī.* Trans. C Elgood. *Osiris* 1962; 14: 191.
16. Nisābūrī A. *Islamic Medical Wisdom: The Ṭibb al-a'immah.* Trans. B. Ispahany. Ed. AJ Newman. London: Muḥammadī Trust, 1991: 86.
17. Nisābūrī A. *Islamic Medical Wisdom: The Ṭibb al-a'immah.* Trans. B. Ispahany. Ed. AJ Newman. London: Muḥammadī Trust, 1991: 175.
18. Elgood C. Trans. *Ṭibb al-nabī or Medicine of the Prophet.* Sūyūṭī J, M Chaghhaynī. *Osiris* 1962; 14; Iṣbahānī

AN al-. *Mawsū'at al-ṭibb al-nabawī*. Ed. MKD al-Turkī. Bayrūt: Dār Ibn Ḥazm, 2006.
19. Ibn al-Qayyim al-Jawziyyah. *Natural Healing with the Medicine of the Prophet*. Pearl Publishing. Trans. M al-Akīlī. Philadelphia, 1993.
20. Bīrūnī, AR al-. *al-Bīrūnī's Book on Pharmacy and Materia Medica*. Ed. and trans. HM Said. Karachi: Hamdard National Foundation, 1973.
21. Ghazanfar SA. *Handbook of Arabian Medicinal Plants*. Boca Raton: CRC Press, 1994.
22. Mandaville JP. *Flora of Eastern Saudi Arabia*. London: Kegan Paul, 1990.
23. Mikhaeil, Badria, Maatooq, Amer. Antioxidant and immunomodulatory constituents of henna leaves. *Z* 2004; 59(7–8): 468–476.
24. Habbal, Al-Jabri, El-Hag, Al-Mahrooqi, Al-Hashmi. In-vitro antimicrobial activity of *Lawsonia inermis* L. (henna). A pilot study on the Omani henna. *Saudi* 200; 26(1): 69–72.
25. Bhandarkar, Khan. Protective effect of *Lawsonia alba* Lam., against CCl4 induced hepatic damage in albino rats. *Indian* 2003 Jan; 41(1): 85–87.
26. Ali, Bashir, Tanira. Anti-inflammatory, antipyretic, and analgesic effects of *Lawsonia inermis* L. (henna) in rats. *Pharmacology* 1995; 51(6): 356–363.
27. Sharma. Tuberculostatic activity of henna (*Lawsonia inermis* Linn.). *Tubercle*. 1990; 71(4): 293–5.
28. Munshi, Shetye, Nair. Antifertility activity of three indigenous plant preparations. *Planta* 1977; 31(1): 73–75.

Indigo / *Kutm, Wasmah*

FAMILY: Fabaceae

BOTANICAL NAME: *Indigofera tinctoria*

COMMON NAMES: *English* Dyer's indigo plant, indigo plant; *French* Indigotier, Anil; *Spanish* Índigo; *German* Indigopflanze; *Urdu/Unānī* Neel, Wasmah, Katam; *Modern Standard Arabic* Nīl, Nīlnaj, wasmah, nīlah, naylaj, laylanj

SAFETY RATING: GENERALLY SAFE TO DEADLY *Indigo tinctoria* is generally considered safe as a hair dye. Besides occasional allergic reactions, it is generally considered safe for consumption for most people. However, since comprehensive tests have not been performed, it should not be used by pregnant or lactating women, young children, and individuals with severe kidney or liver disease. *Indigofera spicata*, and other species, are poisonous, and have been found to be lethal. For this reason, indigo should never be ingested internally unless one is absolutely certain that it has been harvested and processed by reliable experts.

PROPHETIC PRESCRIPTION: The Messenger of Allāh said, "The best you can use for changing the color of white hair are henna (*ḥinnā*) and indigo (*katam*)."[1] When he said a man who had dyed his hair with henna, the Prophet said, "That is great." He then saw a man who had dyed his hair with both henna (*ḥinnā*) and indigo (*kutm*) and said, "That is even better."[2] The Prophet himself used to die his hair with henna.[3]

ISSUES IN IDENTIFICATION: According to Bīrūnī, *wasmah* is also known as *khiṭr*. Said identifies the plant as indigo (*Indigofera tinctoria*) and stresses that the accepted orthography is *wasmā* and that the current orthography for *khiṭr* is *khaṭr*.[4] Álvarez Morales and Girón Irueste also translate *khaṭr* as *Isatis tinctoria*, L.[5] Johnstone and Turkī also identify *katam* as *Indigofera tinctoria*.[6] Turkī, however, holds that *wasmah* is *Memeceylon tinctorium*.[7] According to Bīrūnī, *'iẓlām* is indigo plant (*Indigofera tinctoria*) while *wasmah* is the leaf of indigo (either *Indigofera tinctoria* or *Isatis tinctoria*).[8] For Elgood, *kutm* and *wasmah* both refer to indigo leaf.[9] Bīrunī and Ibn al-Jawziyyah say that *nīl* and *ward al-nīl* is also *wasmah* (*Indigofera tinctoria*).[10] He says that *al-wasmah al-hindiyyah* is called *'iẓlim* in Arabic. Dīnawarī, says that *katam* leaves are dried, ground, and mixed with henna, as a hair dye, to make them thick and black. He says that the tree grows in the mountains and that its leaves are like those of *ās* (myrtle). Dīnawarī also explains that *'iẓlām* is the male *wasmah* plant, which grows a lot in India, that it is very green, and that its dried juice is called *nīlanj*.[11] On the basis of these descriptions, *katam* can be clearly identified as *Indigofera tinctoria*. Various species of *Indigofera* are found throughout Arabia.

PROPERTIES AND USES: *Indigofera tinctoria*, known commonly as indigo, is used to treat bleeding disorders, boils, carbuncles, diabetes, fever, hemorrhoids, inflammation, infant seizures, mumps, ovarian cancer, pain, scorpion bites, stomach cancer, toothaches, to reduce pain and to induce vomiting, as well as to detoxify the blood and to purify the liver. *Indigofera tinctoria* is believed to be the active ingredient in a traditional Chinese medicine used to treat chronic myelocytic leukemia. In large doses it can cause gastro-intestinal irritation, debility, and nervous derangements.

SCIENTIFIC STUDIES: *Antidyslipidemic Activity* In an animal study conducted by the Division of Medicinal and Process Chemistry in India, a diastereomeric flavonoid mixture from the aerial parts of *Indigofera tinctoria* were found to significantly reduced plasma triglycerides by 60 percent, total cholesterol by 19 percent, glycerol by 13 percent, and free fatty acid by 25 percent, along with an increase in HDL by 8 percent, and an HDL-C/TC ratio of 36 percent.[12]

Hepaprotective Activity In an animal trial conducted by the University of Madras in India,

Indigofera tinctoria extract was shown to possess hepaprotective effects in rats.[13] Treatment with diastereomeric flavonoid mixture 1 and 2 (80:20) significantly decreased the plasma triglycerides by 60 percent, total cholesterol 19 percent, glycerol 13 percent, and free fatty acid 25 percent accompanied with increase in high density lipoproteins-cholesterol (HDL-C) by 8 percent and HDL-C/TC ratio 36 percent in high fat diet fed dyslipidemic hamsters at the dose of 50 mg/kg body weight.

In a study conducted by the Regional Research Laboratory in India, a bioactive fraction, indigtone, obtained by fractionation of a petroleum ether extract of the aerial parts of *I. tinctoria*, showed significant dose related hepatoprotective activity against induced liver injury in rats and mice.[14]

Immunostimulating Activity Several studies suggest that wild indigo (*Baptisia tinctoria*), which is native to the central and eastern United States and Canada, may stimulate the immune system.[15]

Indigo Notes

1. Abū Dāwūd S. *Ṣaḥīḥ Sunan Abū Dāwūd*. Riyyāḍ: Maktab al-Tarbiyyah, 1989; Tirmidhī M. *al-Jāmi' al-ṣaḥīḥ*. al-Qāhirah: Muṣṭafā al-Bābī al-Ḥalabī, [1937-]; Nasā'ī A. *Sunan al-Nisā'ī*. al-Qāhirah: Muṣṭafā al-Bābī al-Ḥalabī, 1964–65; Ibn Mājah M. *Sunan*. Trans. MT Anṣārī. Lahore: Kazi Publications, 1994; Iṣbahānī AN al-. *Mawsū'at al-ṭibb al-nabawī*. Ed. MKD al-Turkī. Bayrūt: Dār Ibn Ḥazm, 2006.

2. Farooqi MIH. *Medicinal Plants in the Traditions of Prophet Muḥammad*. Lucknow: Sidrah Publishers, 1998: 63.

3. Bukhārī M. *Ṣaḥīḥ al-Bukhārī*. al-Riyyāḍ: Bayt al-Afkār, 1998.

4. Bīrūnī, AR al-. *al-Bīrūnī's Book on Pharmacy and Materia Medica*. Ed. and trans. HM Said. Karachi: Hamdard National Foundation, 1973.

5. Ibn Ḥabīb A. *Mujtaṣar fī al-ṭibb/Compendio de medicina*. Ed. C Álvarez de Morales and F Girón Irueste. Madrid: Consejo Superior de Investigaciones Científicas, 1992.

6. Johnstone P, trans. *Medicine of the Prophet*. Ibn Qayyim al-Jawziyyah. Cambridge: The Islamic Texts Society, 1998; Iṣbahānī AN al-. *Mawsū'at al-ṭibb al-nabawī*. Ed. MKD al-Turkī. Bayrūt: Dār Ibn Ḥazm, 2006.

7. Iṣbahānī AN al-. *Mawsū'at al-ṭibb al-nabawī*. Ed. MKD al-Turkī. Bayrūt: Dār Ibn Ḥazm, 2006.

8. Bīrūnī, AR al-. *al-Bīrūnī's Book on Pharmacy and Materia Medica*. Ed. and trans. HM Said. Karachi: Hamdard National Foundation, 1973.

9. Elgood C. Trans. *Ṭibb al-nabī or Medicine of the Prophet*. Sūyūṭī J, M Chaghhaynī. *Osiris* 1962: 14.

10. Ibn Qayyim al-Jawziyyah M. *al-Ṭibb al-nabawī*. Bayrūt: Dār al-Kitāb, 1985.

11. Dīnawarī AH. *Kitāb al-nabāt/The Book of Plants*. Ed. Bernhard Lewin. Bayrūt: Dār al-Qalam, 1974: 98.

12. Narender, Khaliq, Puri, Chander. Antidyslipidemic activity of furano-flavonoids isolated from *Indigofera tinctoria*. *Bioorg* 2006; 16(13): 3411–3414.

13. Sreepriya, Devaki, Nayeem. Protective effects of Indigofera tinctoria L. against D-Galactosamine and carbon tetrachloride challenge on 'in situ' perfused rat liver. *Indian* 2001; 45(4): 428–434.

14. Singh, Saxena, Chandan, Bhardwaj, Gupta, Suri, Handa. Hepatoprotective activity of indigtone: a bioactive fraction from *Indigofera tinctoria* Linn. *Phytother* 2001; 15(4): 294–297.

15. Beuscher N, Kopanski L. Stimulating of immunity by the contents of *Baptisia tinctoria*. Planta Medica 1995; (5): 381–384; Beuscher N, et al. Immunologically active ghlycoproteins of *Baptisia tinctoria*. *Planta Medica* 1989; 55: 358–363; Egert D, Beuscher N. Studies on antigen specificity of immunoreactive arabinogalactan proteins extracted from *Baptisia tinctoria* and *Echinacea purpurea*. *Planta Medica* 1992; 58: 163–165; Wagner H, Jurcic K. Immunologic studies on plant combination preparations. In-vitro and in-vivo studies on the stimulation of phagocystosis. *Arzneimittel-Forschung* 1991; 41: 1072–1076.

Jasmine/*Yāsamīn, Zanbaq*

FAMILY: Oleaceae

BOTANICAL NAME: *Jasminun officinale*

COMMON NAMES: *English* Poet's jasmine, white flowered jasmine, jessamine; *French* Jasmin commun, Jasmin blanc; *Spanish* Jazmín; *German* Echter Jasmin, Weißer Jasmin; *Urdu/Unānī* Chameli, Chanbeli, Yasmeen; *Modern Standard Arabic* yāsmīn, sajlāṭ

SAFETY RATING: GENERALLY SAFE Jasmine is generally considered safe for most people in quantities normally consumed as food. In some cases, however, it may cause allergic reactions. Since the safety of jasmine in medicinal doses has not been determined, it should not be consumed by women who are pregnant or lactating.

PROPHETIC PRESCRIPTION: The Prophet Muḥammad stressed the benefits and healing properties of jasmine. According to the Messenger of Allāh, "[t]here is no oil more beneficial for the body than the oil of jasmine. In it are numerous benefits and healing for seventy illnesses."[1] On one occasion, he said, "[t]here is nothing better for the body than *al-rāziqī*." He was asked "[w]hat is *al-rāziqī*?" and replied that it was "Jasmine."[2]

The Imāms from the Household of the Prophet also encouraged the use of jasmine. Imām Ja'far al-Ṣādiq stated that "Jasmine is the most excellent thing with which you oil your body."[3] He once told his followers to "[u]se *al-kays* and anoint yourselves with it, for in it is a healing for seventy illnesses." He was asked, "O son of the Messenger of Allāh, what is *al-kays*?" He replied, "Jasmine, that of the *al-rāziqī* variety."[4]

A patient came to Imām 'Alī al-Riḍā complaining from severe cold in the head. The Imām wrote to him saying "You must inhale ambergris and jasmine (*al-zanbaq*) after eating. You will be cured of it, Allāh, the Sublime and Majestic, willing."[5] A man complained to Imām al-Ṣādiq that he was detained by a wind penetrating (*rīḥ shabīkah*) penetrating him from head to feet. He told him to "Inhale ambergris (*al-'anbar*) and mercury (*al-zaybaq*) on an empty stomach and you will be cured of it, Allāh, the Exalted, willing."[6]

ISSUES IN IDENTIFICATION: It is the consensus that *yāsamīn* is Arabic for jasmine. According to Bīrūnī, the flower is also known as *samsiq*, *siḥlat*, *ysamūn*, and *yasam*. The *rāziqī* refers to the yellow variety which, in all likelihood, refers to *Jasminun fruticans*, known as yellow jasmine, which bares the Arabic names *yāsamīn daghalī*, *yāsamīn barrī*, and *yāsamīn aṣfar*.[7] The extracted oil or *duhn* is known as *zanbaq*. According to Ghazanfar, *Jasminum grandiflorum* occurs in South Western Arabia. Species of jasmine, such as *Jasminum sambuc*, are widely cultivated in Arabia for their fragrant flowers.[8] It is imperative that true yellow jasmine (*Jasminum odoratissimum*) not be confused with yellow jasmine, the common name given to *Gelsemium nitidum*, which is also known as false jasmine, wild woodbine, and Carolina jasmine. The latter is a powerful spinal depressant which is lethal in even moderate doses, causing respiratory failure.

PROPERTIES AND USES: *Jasminun officinale*, known as common jasmine, poet's jasmine, and jessamine, is aromatic, tonic, calmative, euphoric, aphrodisiac and antispasmodic herb, with aphrodisiac and antiseptic effects, that increases milk flow and stimulates the uterus. It is used to treat rheumatism, and gout. It is also used in aromatherapy for depression, nervous tension, impotence, frigidity, menstrual disorders, respiratory disorders of nervous origin, and weak digestion.

Jasminum grandiflorum, known as royal jasmine and Spanish jasmine, is a bitter astringent, cooling herb that calms the nerves, checks bleeding, and stimulates the uterus. Regarded as an aphrodisiac for women and an alterative, it is reputedly effective against various cancers, and bacterial and viral infections. Internally, it is used mainly in Ayurvedic medicine, for infectious illnesses with high fever, complaints involving bleeding, sunstroke, conjunctivitis, dermatitis, urethritis, cancer (especially Hodgkin's disease and cancers of the bone, lymph nodes, and breast), emotional upsets, and headaches. It is often combined with *Santalum album*.

SCIENTIFIC STUDIES: *Anticancer Activity* In an animal study conducted by Annamalai University in India, oral administration of ethanolic extract of *Jasminum grandiflorum* flowers for 14 weeks completely prevented the formation of tumors in the pre-initiation period. The ethanolic extract also exerted significant anti–lipid peroxidative effect, and improved the antioxidant defense system. The results of this study clearly indicate that *Jasminum grandiflorum* ethanolic extract has potent chemopreventive efficacy in experimental mammary carcinogenesis, warranting further studies to isolate and characterize the bioactive principle.[9]

In a study conducted by Annamali University in India, oral administration of ethanolic extract of *Jasminum grandiflorum* flowers for 14 weeks completely prevented the formation of chemically-induced mammary tumors in rats.[10] *Jasminum grandiflorum* also exerted significant anti–lipid peroxidative effect and improved the antioxidant defense system in the treated rats. The study concludes that *Jasminum grandiflorum* has potent chemopreventive efficacy in experimental mammary carcinogenesis and further studies are warranted to isolate and characterize the bioactive principle.

Anti-inflammatory and Anti-Nociceptive Activity In a study conducted by Jordan University of Science and Technology, the ethanolic extract of *Jasminum officinale* was found to possess anti-inflammatory effects which were dose dependent, confirming the plant's use for painful and inflammatory conditions.[11]

Lactation Suppressing Activity In a study conducted by the Christian Medical College in India, the application of *Jasminum sambac* flowers was shown to be an effective and inexpensive method of suppressing puerperal lactation which can be used as an alternative in situations where cost and nonavailability restrict the use of bromocriptine.[12]

Jasmine Notes

1. Nisābūrī A. *Islamic Medical Wisdom: The Ṭibb al-a'immah*. Trans. B. Ispahany. Ed. AJ Newman. London: Muḥammadī Trust, 1991: 119.

2. Nisābūrī A. *Islamic Medical Wisdom: The Ṭibb al-a'immah*. Trans. B. Ispahany. Ed. AJ Newman. London: Muḥammadī Trust, 1991: 108.

3. Nisābūrī A. *Islamic Medical Wisdom: The Ṭibb al-a'immah*. Trans. B. Ispahany. Ed. AJ Newman. London: Muḥammadī Trust, 1991: 108.

4. Nisābūrī A. *Islamic Medical Wisdom: The Ṭibb al-a'immah*. Trans. B. Ispahany. Ed. AJ Newman. London: Muḥammadī Trust, 1991: 120.

5. Nisābūrī A. *Islamic Medical Wisdom: The Ṭibb al-a'immah*. Trans. B. Ispahany. Ed. AJ Newman. London: Muḥammadī Trust, 1991: 110.

6. Nisābūrī A. *Islamic Medical Wisdom: The Ṭibb al-a'immah*. Trans. B. Ispahany. Ed. AJ Newman. London: Muḥammadī Trust, 1991: 85.

7. Bīrūnī, AR al-. *al-Bīrūnī's Book on Pharmacy and Materia Medica*. Ed. and trans. HM Said. Karachi: Hamdard National Foundation, 1973.

8. Ghazanfar SA. *Handbook of Arabian Medicinal Plants.* Boca Raton: CRC Press, 1994.

9. Kolanjiappan, Manoharan. Chemopreventive efficacy and anti-lipid peroxidative potential of *Jasminum grandiflorum* Linn. On 7,12-dimethylbenz(a)anthracene-induced rat mammary carcinogenesis. *Fundam* 2005; 19(6): 687–693.

10. Kolanjiappan, Manoharan. Chemopreventive efficacy and anti-lipid peroxidative potential of *Jasminum grandiflorum* Linn. On 7,12-dimethylbenz(a)anthracene-induced rat mammary carcinogenesis. *Fundam* 2005; 19(6): 687–693.

11. Atta, Alkofahi. Anti-nociceptive and anti-inflammatory effects of some Jordanian medicinal plant extracts. *J* 1998; 60(2): 117–124.

12. Shrivastav P, George, Balasubramaniam, Jasper, Thomas, Kanagasabhapathy. Suppression of puerperal lactation using jasmine flowers (*Jasminum sambac*). *Aust* 1988; 28(1): 68–71.

Leek / *Kurrāth*

Family: Alliaceae

Botanical Name: *Allium porrum*

Common Names: *English* Leek; *French* Poireau; *Spanish* Puerro; *German* Porree, Lauch, Breitlauch, Winterlauch, Borree, Welschzwiebel, Gemeiner Lauch, Spanischer Lauch, Aschlauch, Fleischlauch; *Urdu/Unānī* Piyaz; *Modern Standard Arabic* kurrāth

Safety Rating: Generally Safe

Prophetic Prescription: It is reported that the Messenger of Allāh forbade the consumption of fresh garlic and onions prior to interacting with people in the public sphere. As he explained, "He who eats them [garlic and onions] should not come near our mosque. If it is necessary to eat them, make them dead by cooking"[1] In another tradition, he included leek (*kurrāth*).[2] When Imām Ja'far al-Ṣādiq was asked about leek, he said, "Eat it for it has four benefits: it gives good taste, it chases the wind, it stops hemorrhoids, and it is a protection against leprosy (*al-judhām*) for the one who uses it regularly."[3]

Issues in Identification: It is the consensus that *kurrāth* is the Arabic term for leek. It is difficult to determine, however, the precise variety referred to by the Prophet and the Imāms. By *kurrāth*, they may have meant *Allium porrum* or leek, *Allium ampeloprasum* or Levant garlic (which includes elephant garlic), or perhaps *Allium ampeloprasum* of the kurrat group, which includes salad leek or *kurrāth nabātī*, which is believed to be the leek of ancient Egypt.

Scientific Studies: *Hypolipidemic Activity* According to a controlled 12-week animal trial conducted by Isfahan University of Medical Sciences in Iran, *Allium porrum* was shown to significantly decrease LDL cholesterol. As a results, the researchers suggest that leek may be useful for the treatment of hypercholesterolemia.[4]

Antioxidative Activity According to a lab study conducted by Tehran University of Medical Sciences in Iran, leek shows an antioxidative activity comparable with those of dl-alpha-tocopherol and quercetin.[5]

Leek Notes

1. Abū Dāwūd S. *Ṣaḥīḥ Sunan Abū Dāwūd.* Riyyāḍ: Maktab al-Tarbiyyah, 1989.

2. Tiflis, qtd Farooqi, MIH. *Medicinal Plants in the Traditions of Prophet Muḥammad.* Lucknow: Sidrah Publishers, 1998: 144

3. 'Amilī H. *Wasā'il al-shī'ah.* Bayrūt: al-Mu'assasah, 1993.

4. Movahedian, Sadeghi, Ghannadi, Gharavi, Azarpajooh. Hypolipidemic activity of *Allium porrum* L. in cholesterol-fed rabbits. *J* 2006 Spring; 9(1): 98–101.

5. Souri, Amin, Farsam, Andaji. The antioxidative activity of some commonly used vegetables in Iranian diet. *Fitoterapia.* 2004 Sep; 75(6): 585–8.

Lemon Balm / *Bādharūj*

Family: Lamiaceae

Botanical Name: *Melissa officinalis*

Common Names: *English* Lemon balm, Balm, Common balm, Bee-balm, Balm-leaf; *French* Mélisse, Citronelle, Piment-des-abeilles; *Spanish* Melisa, Toronjil; *German* Zitronenmelisse, Melisse, Citronenmelisse, Gartenmelisse, Herzkraut; *Urdu/Unānī* Badaranjboya, Badarangboya, Mufarrehul Quloob, Muffarehul Qalb, Billi Lotan; *Modern Standard Arabic* ḥashīshat al-naḥl, turunjān

Safety Rating: Generally Safe Lemon balm is generally considered safe for most people when used as directed. It should not, however, be consumed by patients taking thyroid medication such as thyroxine as it might inhibit the absorption of this medicine. Lemon balm may cause drowsiness, and should not be consumed by women who are pregnant or lactating. The International Fragrance Association's 42nd amendment prohibited the use of Melissa oil (essential oils are highly concentrated and therefore potentially more dangerous than the raw herb), though that prohibition was later relaxed.

Prophetic Prescription: Imām 'Alī al-Riḍā used to say "Lemon balm (*al-bādharūj*) for us and watercress (*al-jirjīr*) for the Banū Umayyah."[1]

Issues in Identification: According to Dīnawarī, *bādharūj* is also known as *ḥawk* and *ẓawmarān*.[2] Although it is most commonly known as *turunjān makhzanī, ḥashīshat al-naḥl* in Arabic, *Melissa officinalis* is also known as *bādharūj*. Ispahany should not have translated the term as "mountain balm" as this refers to *Eriodictyon californicum* L. and *Eriodictyon glutinosum*, known by its Spanish name of *Yerba santa*, a plant which is native only to the southwestern United States. *Melissa*, of course, is native to southern Europe, western Asia, and northern Africa. According to Ibn Ḥabīb, *bādharūj* is *al-ḥabaq al-'arīḍ*. He describes it as having broad aromatic leaves. He says that the leaves are edible, but in excess they cause loss of vision.[3] For Álvarez de Morales and Girón Irueste, the plant in question is *Ocimum basilicum*, L.

Properties and Uses: *Melissa officinalis*, known commonly as lemon balm, is an aromatic, cooling, mildly sedative herb that lowers fever, improves digestion, relaxes spasms and peripheral blood vessels, and inhibits thyroid activity. It has antiviral, antibacterial, and insect-repellant properties. Internally, it is used for attention deficit disorder, heart attack, insomnia, stress, nervous disorders, Grave's disease, herpes, insomnia, irritable bowel syndrome, indigestion caused by nervous tension and excitability, hyperthyroidism, depression, anxiety, palpitations, fever, febrile conditions, painful menstruation, and tension headaches. Externally, it is used for herpes, sores, gout, insect bites, and as an insect repellant. This herb is gentle enough for babies and children.

Scientific Studies: *Antidementic Activity* According to research conducted by Northumbria University in the UK, extensive research suggests that lemon balm possesses cognition-enhancing properties. *Melissa officinalis* extracts have been shown to bind directly to both nicotinic and muscarinic receptors in human brain tissue. Robust anxiolytic effects have also been demonstrated following acute administration to healthy humans, with mnemonic enhancement restricted to an extract with high cholinergic binding properties. Chronic regimes of aromatherapy and essential oil respectively have also been shown to reduce agitation and attenuate cognitive declines in sufferers of dementia. Given the side effect profile of prescribed cholinesterase inhibitors, and a current lack of a well tolerated nicotinic receptor agonist, these herbal treatments may well provide effective and well-tolerated treatments for dementia, either alone, in combination, or as an adjunct to conventional treatments.[4]

According to a systematic review of controlled studies of herbal medicines used in the treatment of behavioral and psychological symptoms of dementia in the elderly, two herbs and herbal formulations were found to be useful, one of which was *M. officinalis*. *Melissa officinalis* was found useful in treating cognitive impairment, as well as agitation, as it possesses sedative effects. Although the herb demonstrated good therapeutic effectiveness, the researchers insisted that it needs to be compared with the effectiveness of traditional drugs. Further large multicenter studies were recommended in order to test the cost-effectiveness of the herbs for adult dementia and its impact in the control of cognitive deterioration.[5]

Antiherpetic Activity In an in-vitro study conducted by the University of Heidelberg in Germany, the aqueous extracts from *Melissa officinalis* showed high antiviral activity against HSV-1, HSV-2 and an acyclovir-resistant strain. At maximum non-cytotoxic concentrations of the extracts, plaque formation was significantly reduced by > 90 percent for HSV-1 and HSV-2 and > 85 percent for the acyclovir-resistant strain. In time-response studies over a period of 2 hours, a clearly time-dependent activity was demonstrated. These results indicate that the extract affects HSV before absorption, but has no effect on the intracellular virus replication. Therefore, the extract exerts its antiviral effect on free HSV and offers a chance to use it for topical therapeutic application against recurrent herpes infections.[6]

In a study conducted by Cukurova University in Turkey, the volatile oil components of *M. officinalis* showed antiviral activity against herpes simplex 2. *M. officinalis* volatile oil was found to be non-toxic to HEp-2 cells up to a concentration of 100 microg/ml. It was, however, found to be slightly toxic at a concentration over of 100 microg/ml. The antiviral activity of non-toxic concentrations against HSV-2 was tested. The replication of HSV-2 was inhibited, indicating that the *M. officinalis* extract contains an anti–HSV-2 substance.[7]

In a study conducted by the Centre of Biogenic Stimulants in Bulgaria, *M. officinalis* extracts were shown to possess virucidal and antiviral effects against herpes simplex type 1. Virucidal effect was registered within 3 and 6 hours of treatment with one extract. The remaining extracts inactivated the virus at the 12th and 24th hour. The presence of caffeic, rosmarinic and ferulic acids was demonstrated by thin-layer chromatography. Their role in the antiviral activity of *M. officinalis* is discussed.[8]

In a double-blind, placebo-controlled, randomized, human trial conducted by the Cooperative

Clinical Drug Research and Development GmbH, Berlin, Germany, standardized balm mint cream (active ingredient: 1 percent Lo-701—dried extract from *Melissa officinalis* L. leaves [70:1]) was shown to be effective in the treatment of herpes simplex labialis. Sixty-six patients with a history of recurrent herpes labialis were treated topically; 34 of them with verum and 32 with placebo. The cream had to be smeared on the affected area four times daily over five days. The cream was found to be effective in shortening the healing period, preventing the spread of infection, and relieving the symptoms of herpes, including itching, tingling, burning, stabbing pains, swelling, tautness and erythema. The different mechanisms of action of the balm mint extract rules out the development of resistance of the herpes virus. Some indication was also found that lemon balm treatment might prolong the intervals between outbreaks.[9] Further studies have also shown the effectiveness of *Melissa officinalis* in the treatment of herpes simplex.[10]

Hepaprotective Activity In an animal trial conducted by Istanbul University, the administration of *Melissa officinalis* L. extract reduced total cholesterol, total lipid, ALT, AST and ALP levels in serum, and LPO levels in liver tissue, while increasing glutathione levels in the tissue. As a result, it was suggested that *M. officinalis* extract exerted a hypolipidemic effect and showed a protective effect on the liver of hyperlipidemic rats.[11]

In a study conducted by the Universidade Federal do Rio de Janeiro, the chemical composition and the biological activities of *Melissa officinalis* essential oil was examined. An in-vitro cytotoxicity assay using the essential oil indicated that it was very effective against a series of human cancer cell lines, and a mouse cancer cell line. The oil also possessed antioxidative activity. These results point to the potential use of *M. officinalis* essential oil as an antitumor agent.[12]

Antimicrobial Activity Research has shown that *M. officinalis* possesses antimicrobial activity.[13]

Antispasmodic Activity According to research, *M. officinalis* possesses antispasmodic activity.[14]

Anti–Helicobacter pylori *Activity* According to an ongoing screening program conducted by the University of Illinois at Chicago, the methanol extract of *M. officinalis* leaves had an MIC of 100 microg/mL against 15 HP strains.[15]

Anti-HIV Activity The greatest potential of *Melissa officinalis* seems to be in the area of AIDS research. In an in-vitro study conducted by the Osaka Prefectural Institute of Public Health, *Melissa officinalis* showed potent anti–HIV-1 activity.[16]

Lemon Balm Notes

1. Nisābūrī A. *Islamic Medical Wisdom: The Ṭibb al-a'immah*. Trans. B. Ispahany. Ed. AJ Newman. London: Muḥammadī Trust, 1991: 185.
2. Dīnawarī AH. *Kitāb al-nabāt/The Book of Plants*. Ed. Bernhard Lewin. Uppsala/Wiesbaden: A.-B. Lundequistska Bokhandeln and Otto Harrassowitz, 1953: 292.
3. Ibn Ḥabīb A. *Mujtaṣar fī al-ṭibb/Compendio de medicina*. Ed. C Álvarez de Morales and F Girón Irueste. Madrid: Consejo Superior de Investigaciones Científicas, 1992: 99/71.
4. Kennedy, Scholey. The psychopharmacology of European herbs with cognition-enhancing properties. *Curr* 2006; 12(35): 4613–4623.
5. Dos, de, Medeiros-Souza, de. The use of herbal medicine in Alzheimer's disease-a systematic review. *Evid* 2006; 3(4): 441–445.
6. Nolkemper, Reichling, Stintzing, Carle, Schnitzler. Antiviral effect of aqueous extracts from species of the *Lamiaceae* family against herpes simplex virus type 1 and type 2 in vitro. *Planta* 2006; 72(15): 1378–1382.
7. Allahverdiyev, Duran, Ozguven, Koltas. Antiviral activity of the volatile oils of *Melissa officinalis* L. against herpes simplex virus type-2. *Phytomedicine*. 2004; 11(7–8): 657–661.
8. Dimitrova, Dimov, Manolova, Pancheva, Ilieva, Shishkov. Antiherpes effect of *Melissa officinalis* L. extracts. *Acta* 1993; 29: 65–72.
9. Koytchev, Alken, Dundarov. Balm mint extract (Lo-701) for topical treatment of recurring herpes labialis. *Phytomedicine*. 1999; 6(4): 225–230.
10. Wöbling RH, Leonhardt K. Local therapy of herpes simplex with dried extract from *Melissa officinalis*. *Phytomedicine* 1994; 1: 25–31.
11. Bolkent, Yanardag, KarAbūlut-Bulan, Yesilyaprak. Protective role of *Melissa officinalis* L. extract on liver of hyperlipidemic rats: a morphological and biochemical study. *J* 2005; 99(3): 391–398.
12. de, Alviano, Blank, Alves, Alviano, Gattass. *Melissa officinalis* L. essential oil: antitumoral and antioxidant activities. *J* 2004; 56(5): 677–681.
13. Larrando JV, Agut M, Calvo-Torras MA. Anti-microbial activity of essences from Labiates. *Microbios* 1995; 82(332): 171–172.
14. Forster HB, Niklas H, Lutz S. Antispasmodic effect of some medicinal plants. *Planta Medica* 1980; 40: 309–319.
15. Mahady, Pendland, Stoia, Hamill, Fabricant, Dietz, Chadwick. In vitro susceptibility of *Helicobacter pylori* to botanical extracts used traditionally for the treatment of gastrointestinal disorders. *Phytother* 2005; 19(11): 988–991.
16. Yamasaki, Nakano, Kawahata, Mori, Otake, Ueba, Oishi, Inami, Yamane, Nakamura, Murata, Nakanishi. Anti-HIV-1 activity of herbs in *Labiatae*. *Biol* 1998; 21(8): 829–833.

Lemongrass / *Idhkhīr*

FAMILY: Poaceae

BOTANICAL NAME: *Cymbopogon citratus*

COMMON NAMES: *English* Lemongrass; *French* Andropogon, herbe citronée, verveine des Indes;

Spanish Limoncillo, pasto limón, hierba limon; *German* Zitronengras; *Urdu/Unānī* Izkhar, Kah Maki, Kah Makah, Alf Gorkhar; *Modern Standard Arabic* idhkhīr

Safety Rating: Generally Safe Lemongrass is generally considered to be safe for most people when consumed in food quantities. It also appears to be safe when used medicinally for short periods. Inhaling lemongrass, however, can cause lung problems. Lemongrass should not be consumed by women who are pregnant or lactating.

Prophetic Prescription: During the time of the Prophet, the Muslims used to cover corpses with lemongrass.[1] It is also reported that the Messenger of Allāh declared that the vegetation in Mecca could not be uprooted, with the exception of *idhkhīr* since people used it for their graves and their houses.[2]

Issues in Identification: According to Said and Barr, *idhkhīr* is Arabic for lemon or ginger grass (*Cymbopogon schoenanthus*).[3] Bīrūnī refers to it as *tibn makkah*, *ṭīb-al-'arab*, *khilāl ma'mūnī*, *al-najm*, and *ra'y al-'īr*, which Said identifies as Geranium grass, camel's hay, lemongrass, scenanth, aromatic, and rush.[4] Johnstone has also identified *idhkhīr* as *Cymbopogon schoenanthus*.[5] Akīlī and Elgood, however, say that it refers to *Cymbopogon nardus* or bog-rush.[6] According to Mandaville, *Cymbopogon commutatus* is occasional to locally frequent in eastern Saudi Arabia, where it is known as *sakhbar*, *idhkhīr*, *khaṣāb*, and *ḥamrā'*.[7]

Properties and Uses: *Cymbopogon citratus*, or lemongrass, is a bitter, aromatic, cooling herb that increases perspiration, and relieves spasms. It is also effective against fungal and bacterial infections. Internally, it is used for digestive problems in children, and minor feverish illnesses. Externally, it is used for ringworm, athlete's foot, and scabies.

Scientific Studies: *Insecticidal Activity* According to a study conducted by the University of Lome in Togo, *Cymbopogon schoenanthus* possesses insecticidal activity.[8] Its crude essential oil was toxic to *Callosobruchus maculatus* as adults, and inhibited the development of newly laid eggs and neonate larvae.

Lemongrass Notes

1. Bukhārī M. *Ṣaḥīḥ al-Bukhārī*. al-Riyyaḍ: Bayt al-Afkār, 1998; Muslim. *Jāmi' al-ṣaḥīḥ*. al-Riyyaḍ: Bayt al-Afkār, 1998.
2. Ibn Qayyim al-Jawziyyah M. *al-Ṭibb al-nabawī*. Bayrūt: Dār al-Kitāb, 1985.
3. Bīrūnī, AR al-. *al-Bīrūnī's Book on Pharmacy and Materia Medica*. Ed. and trans. HM Said. Karachi: Hamdard National Foundation, 1973; Ibn Ḥabīb A. *al-Ṭibb al-nabawī*. Ed. MA Barr. Dimashq: Dār al-Qalam, 1993.
4. Bīrūnī, AR al-. *al-Bīrūnī's Book on Pharmacy and Materia Medica*. Ed. and trans. HM Said. Karachi: Hamdard National Foundation, 1973.
5. Johnstone P, trans. *Medicine of the Prophet*. Ibn Qayyim al-Jawziyyah. Cambridge: The Islamic Texts Society, 1998.
6. Ibn al-Qayyim al-Jawziyyah. *Natural Healing with the Medicine of the Prophet*. Pearl Publishing. Trans. M al-Akīlī. Philadelphia, 1993; Elgood C. Trans. *Ṭibb al-nabī or Medicine of the Prophet*. Sūyūṭī J, M Chaghhaynī. *Osiris* 1962: 14.
7. Mandaville JP. *Flora of Eastern Saudi Arabia*. London: Kegan Paul, 1990.
8. Ketoh, Koumaglo, Glitho, Huignard. Comparative effects of *Cymbopogon schoenanthus* essential oil and piperitone on *Callosobruchus maculatus* development. *Fitoterapia*. 2006; 77(7–8): 506–510.

Lentils / *'Adas*

Family: Fabaceae

Botanical Name: *Lens culinaris*

Common Names: *English* Lentil; *French* Lentille; *Spanish* Lenteja; *German* Echte Linse; *Urdu/Unānī* Adas, Masoor; *Modern Standard Arabic* 'adas, 'alas, balas

Safety Rating: Generally Safe

Prophetic Prescription: Lentils or *'adas* are mentioned in the Qur'ān in the context of the Exodus (2:61). The Messenger of Allāh is reported to have said, "Eating lentils fills the heart with love, washes the eyes of tears, and takes away pride."[1] It is equally claimed that he said, "Lentils soften the heart" and that "The sanctity of lentils has been described by seventy prophets."[2] In a very weak tradition (*munkar*), the Prophet supposedly complained to Allāh that the hearts of his followers were hard. Upon doing so, it was revealed to him, "Order them to eat lentils for they make the heart tender, the eyes weep, remove arrogance, and are the food of the pious (*abrār*)."[3]

According to Imām Ja'far al-Ṣādiq, "Lentil porridge (*sawīq al-'adaṣ*) removes thirst, strengthens the stomach, contains the cure for seventy diseases, extinguishes yellow [bile], and cools down the inside." It is also related that the Imām never separated himself from lentil porridge (*sawīq al-'adas*) when he traveled. He also used to tell his servants who suffered hemorrhages (*hayajān al-dam*), "Drink lentil porridge (*sawīq al-'adas*) for it calms hemorrhages (*hayajān al-dam*), and extinguishes [high] temperature (*ḥarārah*)."[4]

Issues in Identification: It is the consensus that *'adas* is Arabic for lentils. According to Bīrūnī, *'adas* is also known as *bulsun*. Said identifies *'adas* as *Lens culinaris*.[5]

Properties and Uses: Lentils are very high in protein, folic acid, and potassium. They are fairly good sources of thiamin and niacin, and provide calcium, phosphorus, and iron. They are also rich in vitamin A, B, and C. Lentils are used in Chinese medicine to regulate the digestive system, to stop diarrhea, and to supplement the spleen and the stomach. In Indian medicine, they are used to remedy constipation and other intestinal afflictions. They are also used to treat ulcers and slow-healing sores.

Scientific Studies: *Anticancer Activity* In a case-control study of 186 men and women conducted by Howard University College of Medicine, the consumption of legumes such as lentils was negatively associated with risk of colorectal cancer. Legumes like lentils are a good source of dietary fiber and of phytochemical compounds that may play a role in reducing adenoma formation or growth, hence decreasing the risk of colorectal cancer. Since African Americans are at greater risk for developing colorectal cancer, researchers encouraged nurses working with African Americans to encourage consumption of legumes in order to decrease this risk.[6]

In a human study conducted by the Harvard School of Public Health, 90,630 women who were between 26 and 46 in 1991 were followed for 8 years in an attempt to determine whether dietary flavanols reduce breast cancer. Researchers found a significant inverse association with the intake of beans or lentils, both major food sources of flavanols. The inverse association did not apply to tea, onions, apples, string beans, broccoli, green pepper or blueberries, which are also major food sources of flavanols. While researchers did not find an overall association between the intake of flavanols and risk of breast cancer, there was an inverse association with the intake of beans or lentils that merits further evaluation.[7] Beans and lentils appear to reduce the risk of breast cancer, for a reason beyond their flavanol content.

Lentils Notes

1. Bayhaqī A. *al-Sunan al-kubrā*. Bayrūt: Dār Ṣadīr, 1968; Iṣbahānī AN al-. *Mawsū'at al-ṭibb al-nabawī*. Ed. MKD al-Turkī. Bayrūt: Dār Ibn Ḥazm, 2006; Ibn Qayyim al-Jawziyyah M. *al-Ṭibb al-nabawī*. Bayrūt: Dār al-Kitāb, 1985; Ibn al-Jawziyyah considers this tradition to be apocryphal.

2. Ibn Qayyim al-Jawziyyah M. *al-Ṭibb al-nabawī*. Bayrūt: Dār al-Kitāb, 1985.

3. Iṣbahānī AN al-. *Mawsū'at al-ṭibb al-nabawī*. Ed. MKD al-Turkī. Bayrūt: Dār Ibn Ḥazm, 2006.

4. 'Amilī H. *Wasā'il al-shī'ah*. Bayrūt: al-Mu'assasah, 1993.

5. Bīrūnī, AR al-. *al-Bīrūnī's Book on Pharmacy and Materia Medica*. Ed. and trans. HM Said. Karachi: Hamdard National Foundation, 1973.

6. Agurs-Collins, Smoot, Afful, Makambi, Adams-Campbell. Legume intake and reduced colorectal adenoma risk in African Americans. *J* 2006; 17(2): 6–12.

7. Adebamowo, Cho, Sampson, Katan, Spiegelman, Willett, Holmes. Dietary flavonols and flavonol-rich foods intake and the risk of breast cancer. *Int* 2005; 20; 114(4): 628–633.

Lettuce/*Al-khas*

Family: Asteraceae

Botanical Name: *Lactuca sativa*

Common Names: *English* Lettuce; *French* Laitue, Salade; *Spanish* Lechuga; *German* Kopf, Salat, Welk; *Urdu/Unānī* Salaad, Kaahu, Khas; *Modern Standard Arabic* Khas

Safety Rating: Generally Safe to Deadly All varieties of lettuce contain a narcotic fluid known as *lactucarium*. Consumption of lettuce may cause drowsiness even in small quantities, while excess may cause restlessness. Due to its narcotic property, which resembles that of mild doses of opium, lettuce tea made with *L. serriola, L. virosa, L. canadensis* or other varieties can be abused as a drug. While *L. sativa* and *L. serriola* are mildly toxic, *L. virosa*, the variety with the highest level of lactucarium, is considered poisonous. Besides lactucarium, it contains hyoscyamine, a powerful depressant of the parasympathetic nervous system. Overdose of any variety of lettuce can induce terror, dangerous hallucinations, and death through cardiac paralysis. For this reason, lettuce should never be consumed as a juice. As Duke notes, bolted lettuce eaten as a vegetable has been reported to cause coma. While safe in food quantities, lettuce should only be used medicinally under expert supervision.

Prophetic Prescription: Imām Ja'far al-Ṣādiq said, "Use lettuce for it cuts [or purifies] the blood."[1]

Issues in Identification: It is agreed upon that *khas* is the Arabic word for lettuce, both wild and cultivated. By "lettuce," the Prophet and the Imāms may have been referring to primitive wild edible bitter lettuces such as *L. serriola*, known as prickly lettuce, wild lettuce, and compass plant. Although *L. sativa* or common garden lettuce was known in China in the 5th century, and may have existed earlier, it is not certain whether this variety had reached Arabia by the 6th century. If it was not known to the Prophet, it may have been known to the middle to late Imāms. The Prophet and the Imāms were certainly unfamiliar with Romaine lettuce, which was common in Italy during the Middle Ages. The light-green, dark-green, and red-spotted varieties of Romaine lettuce were described in 1623. Romaine lettuce is said to have been brought from Italy to France by Rabelais in 1537. The firm-headed forms of lettuce we are familiar with in the Western world had become well-developed in Europe by the 16th century. Oak-leaved, curly-leaved, and the various colorful types we are familiar with today in were first described in Europe the 16th and 17th centuries.

PROPERTIES AND USES: *Lactuca serriola* or wild lettuce is a very bitter, unpleasant smelling, sedative, nutritive, narcotic, hypnotic, antipyretic, expectorant herb, which stimulates the appetite, lowers high blood pressure, relieves pain, and soothes the digestive tract. Internally, the leaves are used by lactating mothers as a galactalogue. Along with vinegar, the leaves are considered a tonic for the intestines and digestive system. The seeds are consumed to treat insomnia, anxiety, neuroses, and hyperactivity in children, as well as dry coughs, bronchitis, whooping cough, rheumatic pain, and biliousness. They are often combined with *Humulus lupulus, Passiflora incarnata, Valeriana officinalis, Scutellaria lateriflora*, and *Cypripedium parviflorum*, to treat insomnia. Wild lettuce seeds are also used as a sexual suppressant. Externally, lettuce seeds are made into a paste, and applied to the forehead to treat headaches. Lettuce seed oil is massaged into the head to induce sleep. It is also used as a nasal drop. The dry latex is considered sedative, antispasmodic, and anodyne, and is preferred over opium.

SCIENTIFIC STUDIES: *Antidiabetic Activity* According to a lab study conducted by Taipei Medical University in Taiwan, *Lactuca indica* contains compounds that show significant antidiabetic activity.[2]

Analgesic and Anti-inflammatory Activity According to an animal trial conducted by the Institut Pasteur in Iran, *Lactuca sativa* seed extract exhibited a time- and dose-dependent analgesic effect and dose-dependent anti-inflammatory activity.[3]

Free Radical Scavenging Activity According to a lab study conducted by the United States Department of Agriculture, lettuce leaf extracts contain compounds with high specific peroxyl radical scavenging activities.[4]

According to a study conducted by the Institute of BioAgricultural Sciences in Taiwan, an extract of *Lactuca indica* possesses significant free radical scavenging activity, effectively protecting DNA from leukemia cells.[5]

According to a study conducted by Woosuk University in Korea, the methanolic extract of the aerial parts of *Lactuca scariola* show strong radical scavenging activity.[6]

Lettuce Notes

1. Majlisī M. *Biḥār al-anwār*. Ṭihrān: Javad al-Alavi, 1956; 'Amilī H. *Wasā'il al-shī'ah*. Bayrūt: al-Mu'assasah, 1993.
2. Hou CC, Lin SJ, Cheng JT, Hsu FL. Antidiabetic dimeric guianolides and a lignan glycoside from *Lactuca indica*. *J* 2003 May; 66(5): 625–9.
3. Sayyah, Hadidi, Kamalinejad. Analgesic and anti-inflammatory activity of *Lactuca sativa* seed extract in rats. *J* 2004 Jun; 92(2–3): 325–9.
4. Caldwell CR. Alkylperoxyl radical scavenging activity of red leaf lettuce (*Lactuca sativa* L.) phenolics. *J* 2003 Jul 30; 51(16): 4589–95.
5. Wang SY, Chang HN, Lin KT, Lo, Yang, Shyur. Antioxidant properties and phytochemical characteristics of extracts from *Lactuca indica*. *J* 2003 Feb 26; 51(5): 1506–12
6. Kim. Antioxidative components from the aerial parts of *Lactuca scariola* L. *Arch* 2001 Oct; 24(5): 427–30.

Lovage/*Kāshin*

FAMILY: Apiaceae

BOTANICAL NAME: *Levisticum officinale*

COMMON NAMES: *English* Lovage, mountain hemlock; *French* Livèche, Ache de montagne; *Spanish* Apio de monte, Perejil silvestre, Levístico; *German* Echter Liebstöckel, Maggikraut; *Urdu/Unānī* Kashin, Anjadan-e-Rumi, Marva Khusha, Ashtar gax; *Modern Standard Arabic* Kāshin, Anjadān rūmī

SAFETY RATING: GENERALLY SAFE Lovage is generally considered to be safe for most people. Long-term use, however, can increase sensitivity to the sun, increasing risk of rashes, sunburns, and skin cancer. Lovage should not be consumed by those who are pregnant or lactating, suffer from high blood pressure, and who have kidney and heart problems.

PROPHETIC PRESCRIPTION: Imām Ja'far al-Ṣādiq said "Drink lovage (*kāshin*), for it is good for pain of the waist."[1]

ISSUES IN IDENTIFICATION: According to Bīrūnī, the plant is known as *nānakhwah*. It is also written as *nānkhwah*. Said identifies it as *Ammi copticum* L. or *Carum copticum* (*Trachyspermum ammi*), known as bishop's-weed or ajwain, and says that it is also known as *al-kammūn al-ḥabashī* and *kammūn al-malik* in Arabic. This seems problematic as *T. ammi* L. is known as *khillah* and the varieties of the plant do not have names similar to *kāshin*. Said cannot possibly be correct, as the only plant named *kāshin* in Arabic is *Levisticum officinale.* Although she has misspelled it as *kāshim* in her English transliteration, Ispahany is correct in identifying *kāshin* as lovage. Álvarez de Morales and Girón Irueste also identify *kāshin* as *Levisticum officinale* Koch.[2] The Indo-Pakistani *ajwain* is often confused for and mislabeled as lovage. Ajwain, however, is not *Levisticum officinale,* but rather *Trachyspermum ammi.*

PROPERTIES AND USES: *Levisticum officinale* is a bittersweet, sedative, pungently aromatic herb that benefits digestion, relaxes spasms, increases perspiration, and acts as a diuretic and expectorant. Internally, lovage is used for digestive difficulties, heartburn, flatulence, colic, poor appetite, cystitis, gastric catarrh, painful menstruation, and slow labor. It is used as a sedative, to dissolve phlegm, to treat fluid retention, relieve muscle spasms, and treat urinary tract infections. Lovage is also employed to reduce water retention, to treat rheumatism, malaria, and jaundice, and as a prophylaxis for kidney stones. Externally, it is used as an antiseptic for sore throat, aphthous ulcers, and skin problems.

SCIENTIFIC STUDIES: *Diuretic Activity* Lovage is a traditional botanical medicine for the treatment of the urinary tract.[3] Lovage root is used as a diuretic.

Antispasmodic and Sedative Activity Some evidence suggests that lovage can ease muscle spasms and cause sedation in animals.[4]

Lovage Notes

1. Nisābūrī A. *Islamic Medical Wisdom: The Ṭibb al-a'immah.* Trans. B. Ispahany. Ed. AJ Newman. London: Muḥammadī Trust, 1991: 71.
2. Ibn Ḥabīb A. *Mujtaṣar fī al-ṭibb/Compendio de medicina.* Ed. C Álvarez de Morales and F Girón Irueste. Madrid: Consejo Superior de Investigaciones Científicas, 1992.
3. Yarnell. Botanical medicines for the urinary tract. *World* 2002; 20(5): 285–293.
4. Fetrow CW, Avila JR. *The Complete Guide to Herbal Medicines.* Springhouse: Springhouse Corporation, 2000.

Marjoram/*Marzanjūsh, Mardaqūsh*

FAMILY: Lamiaceae

BOTANICAL NAME: *Origanum majorana*

COMMON NAMES: *English* Sweet marjoram, knotted marjoram; *French* Marjolaine; *Spanish* Mejorana; *German* Echter Majoran; *Urdu/Unānī* Mirzanjosh, Mirzangosh, Dona Marwa; *Modern Standard Arabic* marzanjūsh, mardaqūsh, bardaqūsh, ḥabaq al-fīl, 'abqar

SAFETY RATING: GENERALLY SAFE TO DEADLY Used in medicinal amounts for short periods of time, marjoram is generally considered to be safe for most adults when used appropriately. At least, this is the opinion of the *American Herbal Products Association Botanical Safety Handbook.* The German Commission E, however, considers both *O. vulgare* and *O. majorana* (oregano) as "unapproved." Since it contains arbutin and hydroxyquinone, the latter of which is carcinogenic, marjoram should not be used for extended periods of time. Marjoram and oregano should not be given to children in medicinal amounts nor should marjoram be consumed be women who are pregnant or lactating. Marjoram salves should not be applied to infants and young children. Patients allergic to plants in the Lamiaceae family, such as hyssop, lavender, mint, and sage, should not consume marjoram or oregano.

PROPHETIC PRESCRIPTION: The Messenger of Allāh said, "Smell marjoram."[1] He also said, "May you have sweet marjoram (*marzanjūsh*), for it is most excellent for a loss of sense of smell."[2] He also said, "Take marjoram (*marzanjūsh*) for it is good for the cold."[3] Imām 'Alī al-Riḍā also recommended the taking the "comprehensive medication" for semiparalysis and facial paralysis in marjoram water as well as inhaling it.[4]

ISSUES IN IDENTIFICATION: According to Bīrūnī, the plant is known as *marzanjūsh* and *maranzūsh*, as well as *fākhūr, marw,* and *rayḥān al-shūk.* In Dīnawarī, it is also called *al-marzajūsh*, and *mardaqūsh.* He says that although it is not grown in Arabia, it is mentioned often in Arab poetry. It is also known as *simsim, al-'iṭr, 'anqaz,* and *samsaq.*[5] He describes the plant as very green with reddish extremities, and says that women use it for their hair.[6] He says that *marū* is oregano of Egypt, namely, *Origanum majorana.* Said, Elgood, Álvarez de Morales and Girón Irueste identify the plant as *Origanum majorana* or sweet marjoram.[7] Turkī simply says that it is marjoram.[8] Bīrūnī says that marjoram is also known as *'unquz* and *samsaq.* Farooqi identifies it as *Majorana hortensis* (marjoram) and *Origanum vulgare* (oregano). Akīlī claims that it refers to *Majorana hortensis.*[9] Johnstone says it is *Origanum majorana.*[10]

In Arabic, *Origanum* is *mardaqūsh, Origanum syriacum* is *mardaqūsh sūrī, za'tar,* and *zūbā', Origanum majorana* is *rayḥān Dāwūd,* and *mardaqūsh, Origanum vulgare* is *fuwadnaj jabalī,* and *sa'tar,* and finally, *Majorana hortensis* is both *marzanjūsh,* and *mardaqdūsh.* Since *Majorana hortensis* is the only variety which bears both of the names used by the Prophet and the Imāms, it is, in all likelihood, the herb they referred to. This would make sense since *Origanum majorana* originates from North Africa while *Majorana hortensis* is native to Syria.

PROPERTIES AND USES: There are various types of marjoram, including hop marjoram or Cretan dittany (marjoram) (*Origanum dictamnus*), sweet or knotted marjoram (*Origanum majorana*), Italian oregano or hardy marjoram (*Origanum majoricum*), and pot or Greek oregano (*Origanum onites*), all of which are mainly aromatic herbs. For medicinal properties, we must look to *Origanum vulgare* and *Origanum majorana*.

Origanum vulgare, known commonly as oregano or wild marjoram, is a pungently aromatic, antiseptic, warming herb that relaxes spasms, increases perspiration, benefits the digestion, stimulates the uterus, and acts as a mild expectorant. It is considered carminative, antiflatulent, anodyne, anticatarrhal, lithontriptic, diuretic, emmenagogue, and anthelmintic.

Internally, wild marjoram is used for colds, influenza, minor feverish illnesses, indigestion, flatulence, stomach upsets, and painful menstruation. It is also used for its antioxidative activity and to induce sweating. Externally, it is used for bronchitis, asthma, arthritis, inflammation, and muscular pain. The herb is never administered to pregnant women.

Origanum majorana, known commonly as sweet marjoram, is demulcent, resolvent, deobstruent, detersive, absorbent, antispasmodic, carminative, stimulant, emmenagogue, diaphoretic, tonic, stomachic, and anti-inflammatory. It is used internally for dyspepsia, indigestion, nausea, colic, and flatulence, as well as loss of appetite, rheumatism, neuralgia, sneezing, cough, respiratory ailments, and menstrual cramps. It is traditionally used to treat bruises, certain cancers, conjunctivitis, cough, headache, insomnia, lack of menstruation, menstrual cramps, motion sickness, muscle and joint pain, sharp intestinal pains in infants, to prevent intestinal gas, as well as to stimulate digestion. Externally, the oil is used to treat rheumatism, digestive complaints, hemicranias, and earache.

SCIENTIFIC STUDIES: *Anti-Hyperglycemic Activity* In an animal trial conducted by the Laboratory of Endocrinian Physiology in Morocco, the aqueous extract of *Origanum vulgare* exhibited anti-hyperglycemic activity without affecting basal plasma insulin concentrations.[11]

Antibacterial Activity In a study conducted by Proyecto the Instituto Nacional de Antropología e Historia in Mexico, *Origanum vulgare* exhibited a high and broad level of antibacterial activity against locally prevalent pathogenic bacteria.[12] According to a study conducted by the Aromatic and Medicinal Plant Group, Scottish Agricultural College, in the UK, the volatile oil of *O. vulgare* exhibits considerable inhibitory effects against 25 different genera of bacteria.[13]

Antioxidative Activity In a study conducted by the Northern Advancement Center for Science & Technology, in Japan, the radical scavenging activities of dried oregano leaves were found to be almost the same as that of quertecin and rosmarinic acid.[14] Other studies have confirmed the antioxidative activity of oregano.[15]

Anticancer and Antithrombotic Activity According to a study conducted by the University of Central Florida, the aristolochic acid I and II from *Origanum vulgare* produced a high inhibition of thrombin activity. They were also confirmed to possess activity against cancer.[16]

*Anti–*Helicobacter pylori *Activity* As part of an ongoing screening program conducted by the University of Illinois at Chicago, methanol extract of *Origanum majorana* herb had a MIC of 50 microg/mL against 15 HP strains.[17]

Antispasmodic Activity Research has confirmed the antispasmodic activity of marjoram, which accounts for its use in treating nausea, sharp intestinal pains, and menstrual cramps.[18]

Marjoram Notes

1. Chaghhaynī M. *Ṭibb al-nabī*. Trans. C Elgood. *Osiris* 1962; 14: 191.
2. Sūyūṭī J. *As-Sūyūṭī's Medicine of the Prophet*. Ed. A Thomson. London: Ṭā-Hā Publishers, 1994: 102.
3. Ibn Qayyim al-Jawziyyah M. *al-Ṭibb al-nabawī*. Bayrūt: Dār al-Kitāb, 1985; Abū Nu'aym al-Iṣbahānī; Ibn Ṭulūn S. *al-Manhal al-rawī fī al-ṭibb al-nabawī*. Ed. 'Azīz Bayk. Riyyāḍ: Dār 'ālam al-kutub, 1995.
4. Nisābūrī A. *Ṭibb al-a'immah*. Bayrūt: Dār al-Maḥajjah al-Bayḍā', 1994: 113.
5. Dīnawarī AH. *Kitāb al-nabāt: Le dictionaire botanique d'Abū Ḥanīfa al-Dīnawarī*. al-Qāhirah: Institut Français d'Archéologie Orientale du Caire, 1973.
6. Dīnawarī AH. *Kitāb al-nabāt/The Book of Plants*. Ed. Bernhard Lewin. Bayrūt: Dār al-Qalam, 1974: 209.
7. Elgood C. Trans. *Ṭibb al-nabī or Medicine of the Prophet*. Sūyūṭī J, M Chaghhaynī. *Osiris* 1962, 14; Ibn Ḥabīb A. *Mujtaṣar fī al-ṭibb/Compendio de medicina*. Ed. C Álvarez de Morales and F Girón Irueste. Madrid: Consejo Superior de Investigaciones Científicas, 1992.
8. Iṣbahānī AN al-. *Mawsū'at al-ṭibb al-nabawī*. Ed. MKD al-Turkī. Bayrūt: Dār Ibn Ḥazm, 2006.
9. Ibn al-Qayyim al-Jawziyyah. *Natural Healing with the Medicine of the Prophet*. Pearl Publishing. Trans. M al-Akīlī. Philadelphia, 1993.
10. Johnstone P, trans. *Medicine of the Prophet*. Ibn Qayyim al-Jawziyyah. Cambridge: The Islamic Texts Society, 1998.
11. Lemhadri, Zeggwagh, Maghrani, Jouad, Eddouks. Anti-hyperglycaemic activity of the aqueous extract of *Origanum vulgare* growing wild in Tafilalet region. *J* 2004; 92(2–3): 251–256.
12. Hersch-Martinez, Leanos-Miranda, Solorzano-Santos.

Antibacterial effects of commercial essential oils over locally prevalent pathogenic strains in Mexico. *Fitoterapia.* 2005; 76(5): 453–457.

13. Dorman, Deans. Antimicrobial agents from plants: antibacterial activity of plant volatile oils. *J* 2000; 88(2): 308–316.

14. Matsuura, Chiji, Asakawa, Amano, Yoshihara, Mizutani. DPPH radical scavengers from dried leaves of oregano (*Origanum vulgare*). *Biosci* 2003; 67(11): 2311–2316.

15. Lagouri V, Boskou D. Nutrient antioxidants in Oregano. *Int J Food Sciences and Nutrition* 1996; 47: 493–497.

16. Goun, Cunningham, Solodnikov, Krasnykch, Miles. Antithrombin activity of some constituents from *Origanum vulgare. Fitoterapia.* 2002; 73(7–8): 692–694.

17. Mahady, Pendland, Stoia, Hamill, Fabricant, Dietz, Chadwick. In vitro susceptibility of *Helicobacter pylori* to botanical extracts used traditionally for the treatment of gastrointestinal disorders. *Phytother Res.* 2005; 19(11): 988–991.

18. Van Den Broucke CO, Lemli JA. Antispasmodic activity or *Origanum compactum. Planta Medica* 1980; 38: 317–331.

Marshmallow/ *al-Khayrī, al-Khaṭmī*

FAMILY: Malvaceae

BOTANICAL NAME: *Althaea officinalis*

COMMON NAMES: *English* Marshmallow, marsh mallow; *French* Guimauve, Bon Visclo; *Spanish* Malvavisco; *German* Echten Eibischs; *Urdu/Unānī* Khatmi; *Modern Standard Arabic* khaṭmī, khaṭmiyyah

SAFETY RATING: GENERALLY SAFE TO POTENTIALLY DANGEROUS Although Western literature does not describe *Althaea officinalis* as dangerous, Unānī herbalists consider the herb to be an abortifacient. As such, it should be used with caution, and avoided by women who are pregnant.

PROPHETIC PRESCRIPTION: Imām Ja'far al-Ṣādiq said, "Washing one's head with marshmallow (*khaṭmī*) protects from headache, is a healing against poverty, and it cleans the head from disputes (*al-ḥazāzah*)." The Imām also said, "Washing one's head with marshmallow (*khaṭmī*) every Friday protects against psoriasis (*baraṣ*) and madness."[1]

ISSUES IN IDENTIFICATION: It is the consensus that *khaṭmī* is the Arabic word for marshmallow or *Althaea officinalis*.

PROPERTIES AND USES: *Althaea officinalis* is a sweet, mucilaginous herb with highly emollient, skin-protectant, expectorant, antiseptic, alterative, vulnerary, antiasthmatic, antitussive, diuretic, gastric-protective, cicatrizant, slightly laxative, odontalgic, and antibacterial activity. Due to its demulcent properties, it is effective in treating inflammations of the mucous membranes.

Internally, an infusion of the whole plant is considered an abortifacient and emmenagogue. The roots, which counter excess stomach acid, are used to treat inflammation and ulceration of the digestive tract, as well as peptic ulcers, gastritis, hiatus hernia, bronchitis, excess mucus, asthma, cough, whooping cough, sore throat, constipation, and cystitis. The leaves are used to treat urinary tract infections, excess mucus, bronchitis, irritating coughs, cystitis, and frequent urination. Externally, *Althaea officinalis* roots are used to treat bruises, sprains, boils, abscesses, eye and skin inflammations, insect bites, splinters, minor injuries, aching muscles, gingivitis, mastitis, and gangrene. The roots are often combined with *Symphytum officinale* for digestive problems, with *Glycyrrhiza glabra, Marrubium vulgare* or *Lobelia inflata* for bronchial complaints, with *Piper nigrum* for asthma, and with *Ulmus rubra* for external use. Used as a toothbrush or chewed, the dried root has a mechanical effect on the gums and helps to ease pain. When dried and powdered, the root is used to bind the active ingredients when making medicinal pills.

SCIENTIFIC STUDIES: *Antittussive Activity* According to an animal trial conducted by Medizinische Fakultät Comenius Universität in Bratislava, Slovakia, the polysaccharide isolated from the roots of marshmallow shows significant cough-inhibiting activity.[2]

In an in vivo study conducted by the Comenius University in Slovakia, the antittussive activity of various plant polysaccharides from *Althaea officinalis* was confirmed. The polysaccharides exhibited statistically significant cough-suppressing activity, which was noticeably higher than that of the non-narcotic drug used in clinical practice to treat coughing. On the basis of these results, the researchers concluded that the *Althaea officinalis* polysaccharides they tested be included among prospective antitussive agents.[3]

Antibacterial Activity According to a study conducted by the Applied Research Centre for Health in Edinburgh in the United Kingdom, *Althaea officinalis* exhibits unexpected antimicrobial activity.[4]

According to a study conducted by the University of Catania in Italy, *A. officinalis* exhibits inhibiting activity against periodontopathic bacteria. The researchers concluded that extracts of *A. officinalis* be used as a topical medication in periodontal prophylactics.[5]

Antioxidative Activity According to a study conducted by the Slovak Academy of Sciences in Bratislava, Slovakia, the polysaccharides from the aerial parts of *Althaea officinalis* var. *robusta* and *P. lanceolata* exhibited strong antioxidative activity.[6]

Inhibitory Activity on Melanocyte Activation According to a study conducted by Kao Biological Science Laboratories in Japan, an extract of *Althaea officinalis* may be a useful ingredient for a skin whitening agent.[7]

Marshmallow Notes

1. Majlisī M. *Biḥār al-anwār*. Ṭihrān: Javad al-Alavi, 1956.

2. Nosalova G, Strapková A, Kardosova A, Capek, Zathurecky L, Bukovská E. [Antitussive action of extracts and polysaccharides of marsh mallow (*Althaea officinalis* L. var. *robusta*.] *Pharmazie*. 1992 Mar; 47(3): 224–6.

3. Sutovska, Nosalova, Franova, Kardosova. The antitussive activity of polysaccharides from *Althaea officinalis* L. var. *robusta*, *Arctium lappa* L. var. *Herkules*, and *Prunus persica* L., *Batsch. Bratisl* 2007; 108(2): 93–9.

4. Watt, Christofi, Young. The detection of antibacterial actions of whole herb tinctures using luminescent *Escherichia coli*. *Phytother* 2007 Dec; 21(12): 1193–9.

5. Iauk, Lo, Milazzo, Rapisarda, Blandino. Antibacterial activity of medicinal plant extracts against periodontopathic bacteria. *Phytother* 2003 Jun; 17(6): 599–604.

6. Kardosová A, Machová E. Antioxidative activity of medicinal plant polysaccharides. *Fitoterapia*. 2006 Jul; 77(5): 367–73.

7. Kobayashi, Hachiya, Ohuchi, Kitahara, Takema. Inhibitory mechanism of an extract of *Althaea officinalis* L. on endothelin-1-induced melanocyte activation. *Biol* 2002 Feb; 25(2): 229–34.

Melons / *Baṭṭīkh, Biṭṭīkh*

Family: Cucurbitaceae

Botanical Name: *Citrullus lanatus*

Common Names: *English* Watermelon; *French* Pastèque, Melon d'eau; *Spanish* Sandía; *German* Wasserzitrulle, Wassermelone; *Urdu/Unānī* Tarbooz, Bittikh-e Hindi, Hindwana; *Modern Standard Arabic* biṭṭīkh

Botanical Name: *Cucumis melo*

Common Names: *English* Melon, Muskmelon; *French* Melon; *Spanish* Melon; *German* Melone; *Urdu/Unānī* Bittikh, Kharpaza, Kharbooza; *Modern Standard Arabic* biṭṭīkh, kharbaẓ

Safety Rating: Generally Safe to Deadly Watermelon is generally considered to be safe for most people. The sprouting seed produces a toxic substance and should never be consumed. As Duke cites, eating unripe watermelons, however, can cause serious illness, even death.

Prophetic Prescription: It is reported that the Messenger of Allāh used to like watermelons.[1] It is also related that he use to eat yellow melons (*kharbaẓ*) and say "They are the best."[2] The Prophet used to eat watermelon with fresh dates saying "The heat in one repels the cold of the other."[3] In his *Ṭibb al-nabī*, Maḥmūd ibn Muḥammad al-Chaghhaynī reports that the Prophet used to eat watermelon with fresh fruit and cheese, and that he would often eat a whole melon with nothing else.[4] According to Imām Mūsā al-Kāẓim, the Messenger of Allāh used to eat watermelon with sugar.[5]

The Messenger of Allāh said, "Watermelon is a food as well as a drink. It washes the bladder and is an aphrodisiac."[6] He also said, "To eat watermelon before a meal cleanses the stomach and roots out disease."[7] The Prophet also said, "Whenever you eat fruit, eat watermelon, because it is the fruit of Paradise, and contains a thousand blessings and a thousand mercies. The eating of it cures every disease."[8] He also said, "None of your women who are pregnant and eat watermelon will fail to produce offspring who are good in countenance and good in character."[9]

The Prophet is reported to have said, "The spring-time of my 'Ummah' is grapes and melons."[10] It is also related that he said, "Verily, in the watermelon there are ten virtues."[11] The Prophet is also reported to have said, "Whenever you eat fruit, eat watermelon because it is the fruit of Paradise and contains a thousand blessings and a thousand mercies. The eating of it cures every disease."[12] It is also recorded that he said,

> Tear the watermelon with your teeth and do not cut it to pieces for it is a blessed fruit, good and purifying to the mouth, bringing a blessing to the heart, and whitening the teeth. It is acceptable to God. Its smell is of amber. Its juice comes from the Fountain of Kawthar. Its good taste comes from Heaven. The very eating of it is a religious act.[13]

According to Ibn 'Abbās, the Messenger of Allāh said, "Take watermelon for they have ten virtues: a food and a drink, a stimulant to growth of the teeth, a perfume, a cleansing of the bladder, an increase in the spinal fluid, an increase in venery, a destruction of cold, and a cleansing for the skin."[14]

It is also related that the Prophet said, "Eat the fruit of the melon, and tear it with your teeth. Its juice is a mercy, its sweetness is from faith, and faith is from Paradise. He who takes a mouthful of watermelon, Allāh will inscribe forty thousand merits, and will wipe away seventy thousand evil deeds."[15]

It is reported that the Prophet was among a group of companions and said, "Allāh gives mercy to the man who feeds us with these watermelons." Then 'Alī stood up and brought more melons. These too were eaten by the Prophet, and his companions. Then he said, "Allāh will show mercy on the man who has fed us with these, to us who eat them now, and to anyone who will eat them among the Muslims from now until the Day of Resurrection."[16] It is related that some melons from Ṭā'if were brought to the Messenger of Allāh as a gift. He smelled them, and kissed them, saying, "Eat these with your teeth for they are among the lawful things of the earth. Their juice is of the mercy of Allāh, and their sweetness is of Paradise."[17]

Imām Ja'far al-Ṣādiq said, "Eat watermelon (*baṭṭīkh*) for it has ten benefits: it is the flesh of the Earth, it is devoid of disease, it is both a food and a drink, it is a fruit, it has a pleasant fragrance, it freshens (*ashnān*) the breath, it is the main part of a meal, it hydrates, it cleans the bladder, and is diuretic."[18] Finally, he warned that "Consuming watermelon (*baṭṭīkh*) on an empty stomach engenders semi-paralysis (*fālij*)."[19]

Issues in Identification: There is a great deal of confusion between melons and watermelons in both Hebrew and Arabic. Some translators believe that the biblical melon was *Cucumis melo*, while others believe that it was *Citrullus lanatus* (*C. vulgaris*). In any event, both fruits are perfectly suited to the climate of the Holy Land.

According to Hans Wehr, *baṭṭīkh* is melon or watermelon. Turkī renders it simply as melon.[20] In Arabic, however, melon or *Cucumis melo* is typically known as *shammām* or *qāwwūn*. When describing *baṭṭīkh,* Ṣuyutī spoke of the green and yellow varieties, which are immediately reminiscent of musk melons (a cultivar group of *C. melo*).[21] These are known as *baṭṭīkh aṣfar* and *baṭṭīkh akhḍar*.

Unless qualified by *aṣfar* or *akhḍar*, *baṭṭīkh* generally refers to watermelon, known in Saudi Arabian Arabic as *baṭṭīkh* and *joh*. This is the species which has been identified by Johnstone since Ibn al-Jawziyyah says that the kind of watermelon meant by the Prophet is the green variety.[22] In Ibn Ṭūlūn, we see that Abū Mashar described *baṭṭīkh* as being sweet and having stripes.[23] Since only watermelons have stripes, it might be best to discard musk melons when interpreting the words of the Prophet. As Chaudhary explains, variants of *Cucumis melo*, known as *kharsh* and *shammām* in Saudi Arabic, are wild and cultivated melons, found in the Western region of Saudi Arabia. Watermelon is known as *ḥabḥab* in the Saudi dialect.[24]

Although native to tropical Africa and India, watermelon is cultivated throughout Arabia, where they have long been naturalized. According to Biggs, McVicar, and Flowerdew, watermelons were first mentioned by Western botanists and travelers in the sixteenth century, but were little improved until they reached North America, where examples weighing over 100 pounds, and many varieties of colored flesh, rind, and seed, were developed.[25]

As for the melon, Weaver explains that Medieval and Renaissance sources often equated melons with cucumbers and watermelons and, even later, with New World squash (191). Pliny described the melon as a type of cucumber the size of a quince.[26] As Biggs, McVicar, and Flowerdew explains,

> The tasty, sweet, aromatic melons we know were apparently unknown to the ancients. They certainly grew similar fruits, but these seem to have been more reminiscent of the cucumber. Pliny, in the first century A.D., refers to the fruits dropping off the stalk when ripe, which is typical of melons, but they were still not generally considered very palatable. To quote Galen, the philosopher-physician, writing in the second century A.D., "the autumn (ripe) fruits do not excite vomiting as do the unripe." By the third century A.D., they had become sweeter and aromatic enough to be eaten with spices, and by the sixth and seventh centuries they were distinguished from cucumbers. The first reference to really delicious, aromatic melons comes in the fifteenth and sixteenth centuries, probably as the result of hybridization between many different strains.[27]

In Europe, melons were not cultivated until the Middle Ages, with the possible exception of al-Andalus.[28] These melons, of course, were viewed not as fruit, but as green vegetables, and were usually eaten as a kind of salad, with pepper and vinegar, and well seasoned with garum and silphium. In Toussaint-Samat's estimation, gardeners had to taste 50 melons before they found a good, sweet one, to perpetuate. It was only through careful selection over the centuries that the melon increased in size and sweetness and was no longer considered a green vegetable.[29]

If by *baṭṭīkh* the Prophet meant one of the ancient cultivated varieties of watermelon, that variety of *Citrullus vulgaris* probably no longer exists. If he was referring to wild or semiwild African watermelons, the fruit in question would be *Citrullus lanatus*. If by *baṭṭīkh*, Muḥammad meant melon or *Cucumis melo*, he must have been referring to the sweeter, more aromatic varieties which had been recently developed, and which could be eaten plain or made into juice. Such melons must not have been very sweet if they were commonly sweetened with sugar or other fresh fruit. They must also have been rather small if an entire melon was considered a single serving. As Toussaint-Samat observes, "melons and watermelons not much larger than apples still grow in the wild state around watering-holes in sub-Saharan savannas and in desert oases in the southern part of the African continent."[30]

PROPERTIES AND USES: *Citrullus lanatus* is a fruit which is primarily consumed as a cooling food in the summertime. It is also eaten as a coolant in hot weather and if one is suffering from a heat stroke.[31] Watermelon seeds are cardiac, demulcent, diuretic, enuresis, pectoral, purgative, tonic, diuretic, vermifuge, tenifuge, and anthelmintic. The fatty oil in the seed, along with aqueous and alcoholic extracts, paralyzes tapeworms and roundworms. When fully ripe or even when almost putrid, the fruit is used as a febrifuge. The fruit contains lycopine, found also in the skin of tomatoes, which is cardioprotective. Watermelon rind is also prescribed in cases of alcohol poisoning and diabetes. The root is purgative and in large doses is said to be emetic.

Watermelon is considered to be antemetic, anthelmintic, antiallergic, anticancer, antioxidant, antiprostatitic, antiseptic, aphrodisiac, cerebrotonic, chemopreventive, curare, demulcent, diuretic, febrifuge, hypocholesterolemic, hypotensive, laxative, litholytic, nephrotonic, purgative, snake repellant, and vermifuge.

Watermelon is used to treat bite, bronchosis, cancer, catarrh, cystitis, depression, dermatosis, diarrhea, dyspepsia, dysuria, fever, gas, gonorrhea, headache, hepatosis, high blood pressure, infection, inflammation, kidney stone, maculitis, malaria, nephrosis, pulmonosis, sinusitis, sore, sore throat, stomatosis, stone, strangury, typhus, urethrosis, vaginosis, sexually transmitted disease, roundworm, tapeworm, and various other worms.

SCIENTIFIC STUDIES: *Larvacidal Activity* According to a study conducted by Annamalai University in India, *Citrullus vulgaris* extract possesses larvicidal activity.[32]

Anti-Sickle Cell Activity According to a study conducted by Agricultural Research Service, watermelon rinds contain citrulline, an amino acid which plays an important role in the human body's urea cycle, removing nitrogen from the blood and converting it into urine. Citrulline helps to create arginine, an amino acid of which some people are deficient. Researchers are presently examining whether the cirtulline-arginine relationship can be exploited to create treatments for vascular tone problems associated with sickle-cell anemia. The discovery may lead to production of rind-based extract or dietary supplement products that address arginine or sickle cell–related deficiencies.[33]

Melons Notes

1. Abū Dāwūd S. *Ṣaḥīḥ Sunan Abū Dāwūd.* Riyyāḍ: Maktab al-Tarbiyyah, 1989; Tirmidhī M. *al-Jāmi' al-ṣaḥīḥ.* al-Qāhirah: Muṣṭafā al-Bābī al-Ḥalabī, [1937-].
2. Bāshā HS. *Qabasāt min al-Ṭibb al-nabawī wa-al-adillah al-'ilmiyyah al-ḥadīthah.* Jiddah: Maktabat al-Sawādī lil-Tawzī', 1991: 131.
3. Tirmidhī M. *al-Jāmi' al-ṣaḥīḥ.* al-Qāhirah: Muṣṭafā al-Bābī al-Ḥalabī, [1937-]; Bayhaqī A. *Sunan al-kubrā.* Bayrūt: Dār Ṣadīr, 1968; Abū Dāwūd S. *Sunan Abū Dāwūd.* Bayrūt: Dār Ibn Ḥazm, 1998; Ibn Qayyim al-Jawziyyah M. *al-Ṭibb al-nabawī.* Bayrūt: Dār al-Kitāb, 1985.
4. Chaghhaynī M. *Ṭibb al-nabī.* Trans. C Elgood. *Osiris* 1962; 14: 191.
5. Ibn Ṭulūn S. *al-Manhal al-rawī fī al-ṭibb al-nabawī.* Ed. 'Azīz Bayk. Riyyāḍ: Dār 'alam al-kutub, 1995. Quoting the *Kitāb al-Biṭṭīkh* of Nuqānī.
6. Daylamī S. *al-Firdaws.* Bayrūt: Dār al-Kutub al-'ilmīyyah, 1986.
7. Chaghhaynī M. *Ṭibb al-nabī.* Trans. C Elgood. *Osiris* 1962; 14: 191; Farooqi MIH. *Medicinal Plants in the Traditions of Prophet Muḥammad.* Lucknow: Sidrah Publishers, 1998: 128.
8. Chishti SHM. *The Book of Sufi Healing.* Rochester, Vermont: Inner Traditions, 1991: 60.
9. Chaghhaynī M. *Ṭibb al-nabī.* Trans. C Elgood. *Osiris* 1962; 14: 190; Chishti SHM. *The Book of Sufi Healing.* Rochester, Vermont: Inner Traditions, 1991: 60
10. Chaghhaynī M. *Ṭibb al-nabī.* Trans. C Elgood. *Osiris* 1962; 14: 189.
11. Chaghhaynī M. *Ṭibb al-nabī.* Trans. C Elgood. *Osiris* 1962; 14: 190.
12. Chaghhaynī M. *Ṭibb al-nabī.* Trans. C Elgood. *Osiris* 1962; 14: 189.
13. Chaghhaynī M. *Ṭibb al-nabī.* Trans. C Elgood. *Osiris* 1962; 14: 189.
14. Chaghhaynī M. *Ṭibb al-nabī.* Trans. C Elgood. *Osiris* 1962; 14: 189–90.
15. Chaghhaynī M. *Ṭibb al-nabī.* Trans. C Elgood. *Osiris* 1962; 14: 190.
16. Chaghhaynī M. *Ṭibb al-nabī.* Trans. C Elgood. *Osiris* 1962; 14: 191.
17. Chaghhaynī M. *Ṭibb al-nabī.* Trans. C Elgood. *Osiris* 1962; 14: 190.
18. 'Amilī H. *Wasā'il al-shī'ah.* Bayrūt: al-Mu'assasah, 1993.
19. Majlisī M. *Biḥār al-anwār.* Ṭihrān: Javad al-Alavi, 1956.
20. Iṣbahānī AN al-. *Mawsū'at al-ṭibb al-nabawī.* Ed. MKD al-Turkī. Bayrūt: Dār Ibn Ḥazm, 2006.
21. Sūyūṭī J. *As-Sūyūṭī's Medicine of the Prophet.* Ed. A Thomson. London: Ṭā-Hā Publishers, 1994: 41.
22. Johnstone P, trans. *Medicine of the Prophet.* Ibn Qayyim al-Jawziyyah. Cambridge: The Islamic Texts Society, 1998.
23. Ibn Ṭulūn S. *al-Manhal al-rawī fī al-ṭibb al-nabawī.* Ed. 'Azīz Bayk. Riyyāḍ: Dār 'ālam al-kutub, 1995.
24. Chaudhary SA. *Flora of the Kingdom of Saudi Arabia.* al-Riyyāḍ: Ministry of Agriculture and Water, 1999.
25. Biggs M, McVicar J, Flowerdew B. *Vegetables, Herbs, and Fruit: An Illustrated Encyclopedia.* Buffalo/Richmond Hill: Firefly Books, 2006: 480.

26. Toussaint-Samat M. *A History of Food.* New York: Wiley-Blackwell, 1994: 591.
27. Biggs M, McVicar J, Flowerdew B. *Vegetables, Herbs, and Fruit: An Illustrated Encyclopedia.* Buffalo/Richmond Hill: Firefly Books, 2006: 476.
28. Bianchini F, Corbettta F. *The Complete Book of Fruits and Vegetables.* New York: Crown, 1976: 140.
29. Toussaint-Samat M. *A History of Food.* New York: Wiley-Blackwell, 1994: 591.
30. Toussaint-Samat M. *A History of Food.* New York: Wiley-Blackwell, 1994: 591.
31. Ghazanfar SA. *Handbook of Arabian Medicinal Plants.* Boca Raton: CRC Press, 1994.
32. Prabakar, Jebanesan. Larvicidal efficacy of some Cucurbitacious plant leaf extracts against *Culex quinquefasciatus* (Say). *Bioresour* 2004; 95(1): 113–114.
33. Pons L. Exploring important medicinal uses for watermelon rinds. *Science Blog* Feb 21, 2003. http://www.scienceblog.com/community/older/archives/H/usda864.html; Rimando AM. Beyond pickles: medicine from watermelon rind? *Agricultural Research* Sept. 2003. http://http://findarticles.com/p/articles/mi_m3741/is_9_51 ai_108550683/

Millet / *Kasab*

Family: Poaceae

Botanical Name: *Pennisetum glaucum*

Common Names: *English* Pearl millet; *French* Millet perle; *Spanish* Mijo perla; *German* Perlhirse; *Urdu/Unānī* Bajra; *Modern Standard Arabic* Kasab

Safety Rating: Generally Safe Millet is generally considered safe for most people. However, since millet is a mild thyroid peroxidase inhibitor, its consumption should be limited by those who suffer from thyroid disease.

Prophetic Prescription: The Messenger of Allāh said, "Whoever has faith equal to a grain of millet will be taken out of the Fire."[1] Imām Ja'far al-Ṣādiq explained that "There are three which are not eaten but which fatten, and there are three which are eaten but do not fatten. The three which are eaten but do not fatten are the palm tree (*tala'*), pearl millet (*kasab*) [*Pennisetum glaucum*], and walnuts (*jawz*). The three which are not eaten but which fatten are lime (*nūrah*), the good one (*ṭayyib*), and flax seed (*labs al-kattān*)."[2]

Issues in Identification: It is the consensus that *kasab* is Arabic for pearl millet. During the time of the Prophet, millet was generally imported from southern Arabia.[3] Besides its use in bread, as well as boiled and steamed food, pearl millet is an important ingredient of couscous.

Properties and Uses: Millet is a tasty, mildly sweet, cereal with a nut-like flavor. Its seeds are demulcent and diuretic and are used in the treatment of kidney and urinary complaints while the inflorescence is astringent and hemostatic. Millet contains nearly 15 percent protein, high amounts of fiver, B-complex vitamins, including niacin, thiamin, riboflavin, the essential amino acid methionine, lecithin, and some vitamin E. It is also particularly high in iron, magnesium, phosphorus, and potassium.

Millet is also rich in phytochemicals, including phytic acid, which is believed to lower cholesterol, and phytate, which may reduce the risk of cancer. Due to its high magnesium content, millet may reduce the severity of asthma, the frequency of migraine headaches, as well as lowering blood pressure, reducing the risk of heart attack, and lowering cholesterol. The phosphorus in millet is essential to the development and repair of body tissue.

Millet, like other whole grains, can help substantially lower the risk of type 2 diabetes. The insoluble fiber in millet can also help prevent gallstones, protect against breast cancer, cardiovascular conditions, and childhood asthma. The consumption of cereals like millet may also have health-promoting activities equal to or even higher than that of vegetables and fruits. Since none of the millets are closely related to wheat, they may be consumed by people with celiac disease or other forms of wheat allergies or intolerance.

The immature plant, especially when wilted, is poisonous as it contains hydrogen cyanide and the alkaloid hordenine. These substances, however, are destroyed upon drying or when the plant is made into silage. Although hydrogen cyanide can stimulate the immune system, improve digestion, and perhaps treat cancer, in excess it can cause respiratory failure and even death.

Millet Notes

1. Muslim. *Jāmi' al-ṣaḥīḥ.* al-Riyyāḍ: Bayt al-Afkār, 1998.
2. Majlisī M. *Biḥār al-anwār.* Ṭihrān: Javad al-Alavi, 1956.
3. Tannahill R. *Food in History.* New York: Stein and Day, 1973: 174.

Miswak / *Miswāk*

Family: Salvadoraceae

Botanical Name: *Salvadora persica*

Common Names: *English* Toothbrush tree; *French* Arbre à brosse à dents; *Spanish* Salvadora pérsica, Mostaza arbel; *German* Zahnbürstenbaum, Salzbusch, Senfbaum, Arakbaum; *Urdu/Unānī* Darakht-e-Miswak, Pilu, Iraak, Jaal; *Modern Standard Arabic* shajarat al-miswāk

SAFETY RATING: GENERALLY SAFE The use of *Salvadora persica* to brush one's teeth is generally considered safe for most people. Extended use, however, can lead to discoloration of the teeth. Furthermore, the rough fibers of the miswak tend to scratch the tooth enamel, and cause the gums to bleed, thus allowing bacteria to enter. These undesirable effects can be eliminated by using a toothpaste made of *Salvadora persica* rather than using a branch from the plant.

PROPHETIC PRESCRIPTION: The Islamic religion places a great deal of stress on cleanliness. The importance of hygiene in the Muslim faith is summarized in a famous tradition in which the Prophet Muḥammad said, "Purification is half of faith."[1] Considering the Islamic dichotomy between physical and spiritual purity, it comes as no surprise that the Prophet Muḥammad would exhort his followers to observe proper oral hygiene as an act of devotion, "Use *miswāk* for it cleans the mouth and pleases the Lord."[2] He also said, "Using *miswāk* has tens of benefits."[3]

According to one tradition, Gabriel told the Prophet to use *miswāk* so often that the Prophet feared for his gums.[4] The Prophet regarded the use of *miswāk* prior to Friday prayer as important as bathing and applying perfume.[5] He also said, "Prayer with *miswāk* is seventy times better than prayer without it."[6] The Prophet Muḥammad even came close to making brushing and flossing a part of the obligatory religious ablutions: "If I did not think that it would be too burdensome to my *Ummah* [Nation]," stated Prophet Muḥammad, "I would have ordered them to brush their teeth with a *miswāk* before each prayer."[7]

Imām 'Alī ibn Abī Ṭālib stated that "Recitation of Qur'ān, *al-siwāk* [twig of *miswāk*], and storax are purifiers of phlegm."[8] Imām Ja'far al-Ṣādiq said, "Use *al-siwāk*. It is a purifier, and a good Sunnah."[9] The Imām also said, "There are twelve benefits in *al-siwāk*: it forms part of the Sunnah, it is a purifier of the mouth, it improves vision, it pleases the Merciful, it whitens the teeth, it removes holes, it strengthens the gums, it opens the appetite, it removes phlegm, it increases memory, it doubles blessings, and it pleases the angels."[10]

In a similar tradition, the Sixth Imām said, "There are ten benefits in *al-siwāk*: it is a purifier of the mouth, it pleases the Lord, it pleases the angels, it forms part of the Sunnah, it strengthens the gums, it improves vision, it removes phlegm, and it removes holes."[11] The Imām also said, "*Al-siwāk* and the recitation of the Qur'ān cut phlegm," and that "*Al-siwāk* takes away tears, and improves vision."[12] "Take *siwāk*," said the Imām, in another tradition, "for it removes heart murmurs."[13] He also said, "Use *al-siwāk* for it improves vision."[14] It was also reported by Muslim, the servant of Ja'far al-Ṣādiq, that "He stopped using *al-siwāk* two years before his death, and only because his teeth had become weak."[15] According to Imām 'Alī al-Riḍā, "*miswāk* ... freshens the breath, strengthens and thickens the gums, and fights calculus."[16]

The *miswāk* or toothbrush referred to in these prophetic traditions is often fashioned from the *Salvadora* genus made up of four or five species of salt-tolerant evergreen trees found in the more arid areas of Africa, the Middle East, India, and China. The *miswāk* is made from sections of the root. The bark is removed and the inner wood is frayed. It is then chewed and applied to the teeth and gums, serving simultaneously as both a toothbrush and floss.

Several species of *Salvadora* are used for making the *miswāk*, all sharing similar chemical properties, including *Salvadora persica*, which is commonly called Arak tree, toothbrush tree, salt bush, or mustard tree. According to Imām 'Alī al-Riḍā, "The best *miswāk* is made from *arak* branch."[17] According to the Prophet, "There are three types of *miswāk*. If *arak* is not available, then use *'anam* or *baṭm* (terebinth)."[18] He also said that the black fruit (*kabāth*) of *Salvadora* was the best.[19]

ISSUES IN IDENTIFICATION: The Arabic *arak* refers to *Salvadora persica* and not to aloeswood as Aḥmad Thomson, Elgood, and Akīlī claim.[20] Farooqi says that *arak* is *khamṭ*, *shajar al-miswāk*, and *khardal*. He is correct that *arak* is *shajar al-miswāk*. He is partially correct that it is also *khamṭ*. Quoting one of his sources, Bīrūnī says that *khamṭ* is a tree like the jujube with fruits which resemble mulberries. Another one of his sources says that *khamṭ* is the flower of *Salvadora persica*. As Said clarifies, *khamṭ* refers to anything bitter or sour, especially the fruit of the *arak* tree. Said identifies *arak* as both *kibāth* and *kabāth*, which is *Salvadora persica*. Besides *kibāth*, *kabāth*, Bīrūnī says that *arak* is also known as *mard*, and *siwāk*. The *barīrah* is the large-sized fruit, the *mard* is the green, fresh and tender, and the *kibāth* is the sweet, reddish, fully developed fruit.[21]

According to Mandaville, *Salvadora persica* is a rare plant in eastern Saudi Arabia, found only in coastal and inland sands. The plant is known as *rak* or *arak* in Saudi Arabic. Its twigs are known as *miswāk*, and its fruit as *barīr*.[22] The *mawāsik* used in Saudi Arabia is unquestionably *Salvadora persica*. As Ghazanfar mentions, *Salvadora persica* is found throughout Arabia, on coastal sands, and inland wadis.[23]

Properties and Uses: *Salvadora persica*, known as toothbrush tree, salt bush, and mustard tree, produces leaves which are astringent, stimulant, diuretic, expectorant, and which cleanse toxins. The leaves and root bark destroy parasites, while the wood promotes healing. The fruits improve appetite, and bowel function, and regulate the menstrual cycle. Both the fruit and seeds stimulate circulation.

Scientific Studies: *Multiple Activities Salvadora persica*, like other species of *Salvadora*, possesses numerous medicinal properties, several directly beneficial for oral hygiene. The leaves of *S. persica* are detoxicant. They are beneficial for cleansing toxins that exude from infections. The wood of *S. persica* promotes healing. Both its bark and roots are antimicrobial.[24] Abrasions and cuts resulting from brushing and flossing, as well as canker sores, cavities, abscesses, inflammation and infections, all benefit from the external use of its leaves. Research confirms that *S. persica* possesses significant anti-inflammatory activity.[25] An astringent herb, it precipitates proteins from the surface of cells, contracts tissues, forms a protective coating and reduces bleeding and discharges. It is also an expectorant, encouraging the expulsion of phlegm from the respiratory tract. *Salvadora persica* extract possesses significant protective action against ulcers.[26] Its roots and leaves are anti-parasitic. The regular use of *S. persica* may help prevent, reduce, and cure cases of intestinal parasitic infestation which are of particular concern in warmer climates.

Antimicrobial Activity Research has shown that *miswāk* extract is even more effective in removing plaque than chlorhexidine gluconate, which is one of the best-proven anti-plaque agents.[27] Studies indicate that *S. persica* extract is somewhat comparable to other oral disinfectants and anti-plaque agents like triclosan and chlorhexidine gluconate if used at a very high concentration.[28] *Salvadora persica* is indeed a "natural toothbrush."[29] In fact, the WHO recommended the use of *miswāk* in 1986 and in 2000 an international consensus report on oral hygiene concluded that further research was needed to document the effect of *miswāk*.

In a study conducted by the Shahid Beheshti University in Iran, the essential oil of *Dicyclophora persica* showed strong inhibition activity against *Bacillus subtilis*, *Staphylococcus aureus*, *Staphylococcus epidermidis*, *Enterococcus faecalis*, *Escherichia coli*, *Klebsiella pneumoniae*, and *Aspergillus niger*. It did not, however, inhibit *Pseudomonas aeruginosa*.[30] In a study conducted by the Jordan University of Science and Technology, the aqueous extracts of *miswāk* and derum enhanced the growth of fibroblasts and inhibited the growth of cariogenic bacteria, with the derum extract showing greater activity than *miswāk*.[31] In a controlled human trial of forty male subjects conducted by the College of Dentistry at New York University, use of a 50 percent *miswāk* extract solution significantly reduced the level of *Streptococcus mutans* in comparison to regular toothbrushing.[32] It may be concluded *miswāk* has an immediate antimicrobial effect.

Antifertility Activity In an animal study conducted by the Jordan University of Science and Technology, Irbid, Jordan, exposure of male mice to miswak extract resulted in a 72 percent reduction in pregnancies in untreated females impregnated by test males. The relative weights of the testes and preputial glands were significantly increased and that of the seminal vesicles was significantly decreased in test males. These results indicate that *miswāk* extract has adverse effects on the male and female reproductive system and fertility.[33]

Antiulcer Activity In an animal study conducted by the University of Messina in Italy, a decoction of *Salvadora persica* provided significant protective action against ethanol and stress-induced ulcers.[34] *Salvadora persica* appeared to normally reestablish the elements of gastric mucosa.

Miswak Notes

1. Qushayrī M. *Ṣaḥīḥ Muslim*. Bayrūt: Dār Ibn Ḥazm, 1995; Ibn Ḥanbal A. *Musnad al-Imām Aḥmad ibn Ḥanbal*. Bayrūt: Mu'assasat al-Risālah, 1993; Tirmidhī M. *al-Jāmi' al-kabīr*. Bayrūt: Dār al-Gharb, 1996.
2. This tradition and its variants are found in the following sources: Ibn Qayyim al-Jawziyyah M. *Natural Healing with the Medicine of the Prophet*. Ed. M al-Akīlī. Philadelphia: Pearl, 1994; Ibn Ḥanbal A. *Musnad al-Imām Aḥmad ibn Ḥanbal*. Bayrūt: Mu'assasat al-Risālah, 1993; Shāfi'ī M. *Musnad al-Imām al-Shāfi'ī*. Ed. M al-Sindī. Bayrūt: Dār al-Fikr, 1997–; Nasā'ī A. *Sunan al-Nasā'ī*. Cairo: Muṣṭafā al-Bābī al-Ḥalabī, 1964–65; Ibn Khuzaymah M. *Ṣaḥīḥ Ibn Khuzaymah*. Bayrūt: al-Maktab al-Islāmī, 1971–; Ḥākim al-Nīsābūrī M. *al-Mustadrak 'alā al-ṣaḥīḥayn*. N.p.: n.p., n.d.; Bayhaqī. *al-Sunan al-Kubrā*. Bayrūt: Dār al-Kutub al-'Ilmiyyah, 1994; Ibn Mājah M. *Sunan*. Trans. MT Anṣārī. Lahore: Kazi Publications, 1994; among others.
3. Iṣbahānī AN al-. *Mawsū'at al-ṭibb al-nabawī*. Ed. MKD al-Turkī. Bayrūt: Dār Ibn Ḥazm, 2006.
4. Ṭabarānī S. *al-Mu'jam al-awsaṭ*. 'Ammān: Dār al-Fikr, 1999.
5. Muslim. *Jāmi' al-ṣaḥīḥ*. al-Riyyāḍ: Bayt al-Afkār, 1998.
6. Ibn Mājah M. *Sunan*. Trans. MT Anṣārī. Lahore: Kazi Publications, 1994; Ibn Ḥanbal A. *Musnad al-Imām Aḥmad ibn Ḥanbal*. Bayrūt: al-Maktabah al-Islāmiyyah, 1969.
7. This tradition is found in Būkhārī, Muslim, Ibn Ḥibbān, Aḥmad, Ibn Khuzaymah, with variants cited in Bazar and Ṭabarānī. See: Ibn Ḥibbān M. *Ṣaḥīḥ Ibn Ḥibbān*. Bayrūt: Mu'assasat al-Risālah, 1984.
8. Nisābūrī A. *Islamic Medical Wisdom: The Ṭibb al-*

a'immah. Trans. B. Ispahany. Ed. AJ Newman. London: Muḥammadī Trust, 1991: 79.

9. Majlisī M. *Biḥār al-anwār*. Ṭihrān: Javad al-Alavi, 1956.

10. Majlisī M. *Biḥār al-anwār*. Ṭihrān: Javad al-Alavi, 1956.

11. Majlisī M. *Biḥār al-anwār*. Ṭihrān: Javad al-Alavi, 1956.

12. Majlisī M. *Biḥār al-anwār*. Ṭihrān: Javad al-Alavi, 1956.

13. Majlisī M. *Biḥār al-anwār*. Ṭihrān: Javad al-Alavi, 1956.

14. Majlisī M. *Biḥār al-anwār*. Ṭihrān: Javad al-Alavi, 1956.

15. Majlisī M. *Biḥār al-anwār*. Ṭihrān: Javad al-Alavi, 1956.

16. Riḍā, 'A al-. *Risālah fī al-Ṭibb al-nabawī*. Ed. MA Bār. Bayrūt: Dār al-Manāhil, 1991: 156.

17. Riḍā 'A al-. *Risālah fī al-ṭibb al-nabawī*. Ed. MA Bār. Bayrūt: Dār al-Manāhil, 1991: 156.

18. Farooqi MIH. *Medicinal Plants in the Traditions of Prophet Muḥammad*. Lucknow: Sidrah Publishers, 1998: 8.

19. Bukhārī M. *Ṣaḥīḥ al-Bukhārī*. al-Riyyāḍ: Bayt al-Afkār, 1998; Sūyūṭī J. *As-Sūyūṭī's Medicine of the Prophet*. Ed. A Thomson. London: Ṭā-Hā Publishers, 1994.

20. Elgood C. Trans. *Ṭibb al-nabī or Medicine of the Prophet*. Sūyūṭī J, M Chaghhaynī. *Osiris* 1962, 14; Ibn al-Qayyim al-Jawziyyah. *Natural Healing with the Medicine of the Prophet*. Pearl Publishing. Trans. M al-Akīlī. Philadelphia, 1993.

21. Bīrūnī, AR al-. *al-Bīrūnī's Book on Pharmacy and Materia Medica*. Ed. and trans. HM Said. Karachi: Hamdard National Foundation, 1973.

22. Mandaville JP. *Flora of Eastern Saudi Arabia*. London: Kegan Paul, 1990.

23. Ghazanfar SA. *Handbook of Arabian Medicinal Plants*. Boca Raton: CRC Press, 1994.

24. Almas K et al. The antimicrobial effects of bark and pulp extracts of miswak, *Salvadora Persica*. *Biomedical Letters* 1999; 60(235): 71–75; Almas K et al. In vitro antimicrobial effects of extracts of freshly cut and 1-month-old miswak (chewing stick). *Biomedical Letters* 1997; 56(223–24): 145–149; Al S et al. A study of the antimicrobial activity of the miswak ethanolic extract in Vitro. *Biomedical Letters* 1996; 53(212): 225–238.

25. Monforte MT et al. Antiulcer activity of *Salvadora Persica* on experimental ASA-induced ulcer in rats: ultrastructural modifications. *Pharmaceutical Biology* 2001; 39(4): 289–92; Zakaria MNM et al. Anti-inflammatory properties of *Salvadora Persica*. *46th Annual Congress of the Society for Medicinal Plant Research* (August 31- September 4 , 1998), Vienna; Abstract No. J54. .

26. Galati EM et al. Antiulcerogenic evaluation of the Persian tooth brush tree (*Salvadora persica*). *Pharmaceutical Biology* 1999; 37: 5; 325–328; Monforte MT et al. Antiulcer activity of *Salvadora persica* on experimental ASA-induced ulcer in rats: ultrastructural modifications. *Pharmaceutical Biology* 2001; 39: 4: 289–292; Islām, MW et al. Anti-gastric ulcer and cytoprotective effects of Arak Tree (*Salvadora persica*) in Rats. *46th Annual Congress of the Society for Medicinal Plant Research* (August 31-September 4 1998). Vienna; Abstract No. J55.

27. Almas K. The effect of *Salvadora persica* extract (miswak) and chlorhexidine gluconate on human dentin: A SEM Study. *J Contemp Dent Pract* 2002; 3(3): 27–35.

28. Almas K. The effect of *Salvadora persica* extract (miswak) and chlorhexidine gluconate on human dentin: a SEM study. *J Contemp Dent Pract.* 2002; 3(3): 27–35; Almas K, Skaug N, Ahmad, I. An in vitro antimicrobial comparison of miswak extract with commercially available non-alcohol mouthrinses. *Int J Dent Hyg.* 2005; 3(1): 18–24.

29. Hattab FN, Meswak. The natural toothbrush. *J Clinical Dentistry* 1997; 8: 5: 125–129.

30. Salehi, Sonboli, Mohammadi. Composition and antimicrobial activity of the essential oil of *Dicyclophora persica* Boiss. from Iran. *Z* 2006 May-Jun; 61(5–6): 315–318.

31. Darmani, Nusayr, Al-Hiyasat. Effects of extracts of miswak and derum on proliferation of Balb/C 3T3 fibroblasts and viability of cariogenic bacteria. *Int* 2006; 4(2): 62–6.

32. Almas, Al-Zeid. The immediate antimicrobial effect of a toothbrush and miswak on cariogenic bacteria: a clinical study. *J* 2004; 5(1): 105–14.

33. Darmani, Al-Hiyasat, Elbetieha, Alkofahi. The effect of an extract of *Salvadora persica* (Meswak, chewing stick) on fertility of male and female mice. *Phytomedicine.* 2003; 10(1): 63–65.

34. Sanogo, Monforte, Daquino, Rossitto, Maur, Galati. Antiulcer activity of *Salvadora persica* L.: structural modifications. *Phytomedicine.* 1999; 6(5): 363–366.

Mustard / *Khardal*

FAMILY: Brassicaceae

BOTANICAL NAME: *Brassica alba* (aka *Sinapis alba*)
COMMON NAMES: *English* White mustard, salad mustard, cultivated mustard; *French* Moutarde blanche; *Spanish* Mostaza blanca; *German* Echter Senf, Weißer Senf; *Urdu/Unānī* Safaid Rai, Aspandan; *Modern Standard Arabic* khardal abyaḍ, khardal

BOTANICAL NAME: *Brassica juncea*
COMMON NAMES: *English* Brown mustard, Indian mustard, Chinese mustard; *French* Moutarde brune; *Spanish* Mostaza de la india; *German* Indischer Senf; *Urdu* Rai, Khardal, Aahar, Jambo; *Unānī Medical Term* Rai, Lotni; *Modern Standard Arabic* khardal

BOTANICAL NAME: *Brassica nigra*
COMMON NAMES: *English* Black mustard; *French* Moutarde noire; *Spanish* Mostaza negra, Ajenabe; *German* Schwarzer Senf; *Urdu/Unānī* Rai, Benasari Rai, Khardal; *Modern Standard Arabic* khardal aswad

SAFETY RATING: GENERALLY SAFE Mustard is generally considered to be safe for most people when consumed as a condiment. Large doses, however, can irritate the intestinal lining while long-term use can lead to kidney and prostate damage. Externally, mustard should not be applied to the skin for too long or too often as it can cause blistering. All mustards contain substances that are extremely irritant to skin and mucous membranes.

As such, it should only be administered by a qualified practitioner. Undiluted mustard oil must never be allowed to touch the skin, mucous membranes or eyes. Internally or externally, large doses of mustard can cause severe inflammation and burns.

PROPHETIC PRESCRIPTION: Mustard is mentioned in the Qur'ān in the context of a parable (21:47, 31:16). The Messenger of Allāh said, "Whoever has faith the size of a mustard (*khardal*) seed will not go to Hell, and anyone who has pride as much as [a] mustard seed will not be allowed to enter Paradise."[1] He also said that Allāh would ask him to remove from Hell any person who has faith as small as a mustard seed.[2] The Prophet Muḥammad once asked, "What are the two basic cures?" He explained that "They are aloeswood and mustard seed (*khardal*)."[3] For pain in the ear, Imām Ja'far al-Ṣādiq prescribed the following:

> Take a handful of unhusked sesame (*simsim ghayr muqashshar*) and a handful of mustard (*khardal*). Grind each of them separately, then mix them together and extract the oil (*duhn*). Place the oil in a bottle and put an iron seal on it. Whenever you require, put two drops of it in the ear and bind it with a piece of cotton for three days. It will be cured, Allāh, the Exalted, willing.[4]

ISSUES IN IDENTIFICATION: Black, brown, and white mustard are believed to originate from the Middle East. According to Said, *khardal* is mustard. *Isfand* is *khardal abyaḍ* or white mustard seed. For Álvarez Morales and Girón Irueste, *khardal* refers to *Sinapis alba*.[5] Farooqi says that *khardal* refers to *Brassica nigra* or black mustard. Black mustard is known in Arabic as *khardal aswad* and *libsān*. In Bīrūnī, wild mustard (*Sinapis arvensis*) is called *al-harsha'*. Al-Rāzī mentions two types of mustard, the white (*Sinapis alba*) and the red (*al-ṣināb*, black mustard, *S. nigra*). As Said explains, Bīrūnī was also referred to a type of mustard which was yellowish-brown. American mustard is made with *Sinapis alba*. English mustard is made with a combination of *Sinapis alba* and *Brassica nigra*. French mustard is made with *Brassica nigra* or *Brassica juncea*.

According to Mandaville, *Brassica juncea* is found occasionally in eastern Arabia as a garden weed, in waste areas or on roadsides, and rarely in the desert or disturbed ground. *Sinapis arvensis* is also infrequent in eastern Arabia, where it is found as a weed of gardens or farms, and rarely in the desert around camp sites and roadsides.[6] According to Chaudhary, *Brassica juncea*, known as *khardal* in Saudi Arabic, exists in Arabia as a cultivated crop or an escapee. *Sinapis alba* or *Brassica alba* has only been collected once as a weed in Saudi Arabia.[7] Many herbalists treat black, brown, and white mustard (*Brassica nigra*, *Brassica juncea*, and *Sinapis alba*) synonymously.

According to Duke, the mustard mentioned in the Bible is believed to have belonged to the black variety. Black mustard as also the variety used medicinally by the Greeks and the Romans. Early herbalists preferred black mustard over the milder white-seeded species. The Native Americans also used black mustard medicinally. Based on historical medicinal use, it seems sound to conclude that the mustard referred to by the Prophet and the Imāms for medicinal purposes was the black-seeded variety.

PROPERTIES AND USES: *Brassica alba* or *Sinapis alba*, known commonly as white mustard, is a pungent, stimulant, warming herb that improves digestion and circulation, relieves pain, and is expectorant, diuretic, and antibiotic. White mustard acts directly on the gastric mucous membrane, stimulating secretion. It is also occasionally used as a laxative.

Brassica juncea, known as brown mustard, Indian mustard, and Chinese mustard, is a warming, stimulant herb, with antibiotic effects. It is considered digestive, laxative, decongestant, stimulant, rubefacient, vesicant, stimulant, and resolvent. In large quantities, it may act as an emetic.

Brassica nigra or black mustard is a pungent, warming herb that stimulates the circulatory and digestive systems, and irritates the skin and mucous membranes. *Brassica nigra*, which is also known as brown mustard, is stimulant, emetic, tonic, diuretic, laxative, rubefacient, irritant, epipastic, carminative, condiment, vesicant, dilates the vessels, causing redness, warmth, and irritates sensory nerves, giving burning pain. It is a potent emetic in large doses.

Black mustard is used to treat atonic dyspepsia with constipation, delirium tremens, atonic dropsy, hiccups, and narcotic poisoning. It is also used to treat fluid retention, intestinal gas, and to induce vomiting. Externally, it is used in poultices, mustard plasters, and baths for rheumatism, arthritis, muscular pain, chilblains, and respiratory tract infections. It is also used to treat gout, atrophy, neuralgia, colic, gastralgia, inflammation of throat or lungs, toothache, earache, headache, diarrhea, dysentery, amenorrhea, dysmenorrhea, and to stimulate the heart, vascular system, and respiratory system.

SCIENTIFIC STUDIES: *Antidiabetic Activity* In a review conducted by the All India Institute of Medical Sciences in India, *Brassica juncea* was one of 45 Ayurvedic plants found to possess anti-diabetic activity in experimental and clinical trials.[8]

Chemopreventive Activity According to an animal trial conducted at Jawaharlal Nehru University in India, the consumption of mustard seed oil was shown to reduce the incidence of tumors.[9] According to an animal study conducted by South Dakota State University, dietary mustard oil (which contains omega 3-polyunsaturated fatty acid) is more effective in preventing colon cancer in rats than dietary fish oil.[10] Another study, conducted by the University of Vienna, found that mustard juice is highly protective against induced DNA damage in human derived cells and that induction of detoxifying enzymes may account for its chemoprotective properties.[11]

Cholesterol-Lowering and Anticancer Activity In an animal study conducted by the University of Kerala in India, the consumption of mustard seeds was shown to reduce cholesterol levels and mean number of neoplasms in the colon intestine.[12]

Mustard Notes

1. Muslim. *Jāmi' al-ṣaḥīḥ.* al-Riyyāḍ: Bayt al-Afkār, 1998.
2. Muslim. *Jāmi' al-ṣaḥīḥ.* al-Riyyāḍ: Bayt al-Afkār, 1998.
3. Sūyūṭī J. *As-Sūyūṭī's Medicine of the Prophet.* Ed. A Thomson. London: Ṭā-Hā Publishers, 1994: 51.
4. Nisābūrī A. *Islamic Medical Wisdom: The Ṭibb al-a'immah.* Trans. B. Ispahany. Ed. AJ Newman. London: Muḥammadī Trust, 1991: 13.
5. Ibn Ḥabīb A. *Mujtaṣar fī al-ṭibb/Compendio de medicina.* Ed. C Álvarez de Morales and F Girón Irueste. Madrid: Consejo Superior de Investigaciones Científicas, 1992.
6. Mandaville JP. *Flora of Eastern Saudi Arabia.* London: Kegan Paul, 1990.
7. Chaudhary SA. *Flora of the Kingdom of Saudi Arabia.* al-Riyyāḍ: Ministry of Agriculture and Water, 1999.
8. Grover, Yadav, Vats. Medicinal plants of India with anti-diabetic potential. *J* 2002; 81(1): 81–100.
9. Hashim, Banerjee, Madhubala, Rao. Chemoprevention of DMBA-induced transplacental and translactational carcinogenesis in mice by oil from mustard seeds (*Brassica* spp.). *Cancer* 1998; 134(2): 217–226.
10. Dwivedi, Muller, Goetz-Parten, Kasperson, Mistry. Chemopreventive effects of dietary mustard oil on colon tumor development. *Cancer* 2003; 196(1): 29–34.
11. Uhl, Laky, Lhoste, Kassie, Kundi, Knasmüller S. Effects of mustard sprouts and allylisothiocyanate on benzo(a)-pyrene-induced DNA damage in human-derived cells: a model study with the single cell gel electrophoresis/Hep G2 assay. *Teratog* 2003; Suppl 1: 273–282.
12. Khan, Abraham, Leelamma. *Murraya koenigii* and *Brassica juncea:* alterations on lipid profile in 1–2 dimethyl hydrazine induced colon carcinogenesis. *Invest* 1996; 14(4): 365–369.

Myrobalan / *Halīlaj, Balīlaj, Amlaj*

FAMILY: Combretaceae
BOTANICAL NAME: *Terminalia chebula*

COMMON NAMES: *English* Black myrobalan, Chebulic myrobalan; *French* Myrobalan chébula, Chébule; *Spanish* Mirobálano; *German* Chebula-Myrobalane, Chebulische Myrobalane, Schwarze Myrobalane, Rispigermyrobalaneubaum; *Urdu/ Unānī* Halailah, Harr, Halailaj, Ahlilaj; *Modern Standard Arabic* shajar sha'īr hindī, ihlīlaj kābūlī

SAFETY RATING: GENERALLY SAFE *Terminalia chebula* is generally considered to be safe for most people when used for short periods of time, not extending beyond three months. The herb, however, should not be consumed by women who are pregnant or lactating.

PROPHETIC PRESCRIPTION: It is reported that the Messenger of Allāh said, "Myrobalan is from the trees of Paradise. It cures seventy diseases."[1] In some other traditions, the Prophet specifies the type of myrobalan, saying, "Eat black myrobalan. It is among the trees of Paradise, and it contains the cure for every disease"[2]; and "Use yellow myrobalan and drink it for it comes from the trees of Paradise. It is bitter in taste and cures every disease."[3]

Imām al-Ḥusayn said, "If people knew what was in yellow myrobalan (*al-halīlaj al-aṣfar*), they would buy it by its weight in gold." He said to one of his companions, "Take one grain of yellow myrobalan and seven grains of pepper. Grind and sieve them and use as kuḥl around the eyes."[4]

Imām Ja'far al-Ṣādiq related that "Mūsā [Moses], the son of 'Imrān, peace be upon them, complained to his Lord, the Most High, on account of moisture and humidity. Allāh ordered him to take black myrobalan (*al-halīlaj*), beleric myrobalan (*al-balīlaj*) and embelic myrobalan (*al-amlaj*), make them into a paste with honey, and then to take it." The Imām then said, "It is the medicine known among you as *al-ṭurayfil*."[5]

Imām Mūsā al-Kāẓim told a group of physicians, "Confine yourselves to the chief of these medicines: myrobalan (*al-ihlīlaj*), fennel (*al-rāziyānaj*), and sugar. [Take it] at the beginning of the summer for three months, three times a month, and at the beginning of the winter for three months, three days a month, three times. Let the place of the fennel be from near the gum mastic (*maṣṭakā*) and one will not fall ill except for the illness of death."[6] The Imāms used to prescribe beleric, black, embelic, and yellow myrobalan.

ISSUES IN IDENTIFICATION: According to Said, *halīlaj*, also known as *ihlīlis*, is myrobalan (chebulic myrobalan, *Terminalia chebula)* and *balīlaj* is beleric myrobalan, *Terminalia belerica.* The seeds can be white, black, red, or yellow. The Kābūlī variety are said to be superior. *Terminalia* originates in tropical Asia. One species, *Terminalia catappa*, is cultivated in Arabia.

PROPERTIES AND USES: Myrobalan is the dried fruit of *Terminalia chebula* (myrobalan, black chebulic). It is considered alterative, antidiarrheal, absorbent, astringent, aperient, carminative, stomachic, and cathartic. The fruit regulates colon function, improves digestion, is expectorant, controls bleeding and discharges, and destroys intestinal parasites. It also has a tonic, rejuvenative effect, especially on the digestive, respiratory, and nervous systems. Trees of the *Terminalia* genus are a source of secondary metabolites, cyclic triterpenes and their derivatives, flavanoids, tannins, and other aromatics, some of which have antifungal, antibacterial, anticancer, and hepaprotective indications. Internally, myrobalan is used for constipation, digestive and nervous disorders, diarrhea, dysentery, intestinal worms, hemorrhoids, rectal prolapse, abnormal uterine bleeding and inflammation, vaginal discharge, involuntary ejaculation, coughs, and asthma. It is not given to pregnant women or patients with severe exhaustion or dehydration.

SCIENTIFIC STUDIES: *Anti-inflammatory, Antioxidant, Antimicrobial, and Antiulcer Activity* High in tannin, myrobalan is used externally for ulcers, wounds, mouth inflammation, and gum disease. According to research, the ethanol extract of *Terminalia pallida* Brandis exhibits significant antiulcer activity by enhancing antioxidant potential of the gastric mucosa and reducing mucosal damage.[7] Research confirms the antifungal activity of *Terminalia* species.[8] Studies validate the healing properties of the plant, and corroborate the astringent effect of tannins by drawing tissues closer together.[9] Studies confirm that black myrobalan possesses significant antibacterial[10] and anti-inflammatory properties.[11] In fact, *Terminalia arjuna* and Triphal (mixture of *Emblica officinalis, T. chebula* and *T. belerica*) possess strong antimicrobial activity against multi-drug resistant *Salmonella*.[12]

Antidiabetic and Renoprotective Activity Studies clearly indicate significant antidiabetic and renoprotective effects with the chloroform extract of *Terminalia chebula*, lending support for its traditional usage.[13] In one study, extracts of *T. chebula* produced a significant antidiabetic activity on alloxan-induced diabetic rats.[14]

Anticancer Activity According to one study, *Terminalia chebula* extract shows potential as a therapeutic agent for cancer prevention as it blocks or suppresses the events associated with chemical carcinogenesis.[15] In a study of 18 healthy male smokers and an equal number of age-matched non-smokers, two weeks of *T. chebula* therapy lead to a significant regression of endothelial abnormality in chronic smokers.[16] *Terminalia chebula* has been found to have radioprotective properties in mice and human lymphocytes.[17] The antimutagenic activity of the aqueous extract of *T. chebula* results from its potent antioxidant properties which protect cellular organelles from radiation-induced damage.[18]

Antihyperglycemic Activity In an animal study conducted by Satsang Herbal Research and Analytical Laboratories in India, the oral administration of 95 percent ethanolic extract of *Terminalia belerica* was confirmed to possess blood glucose lowering effects.[19]

Myrobalan Notes

1. Ibn Ṭulūn S. *al-Manhal al-rawī fī al-ṭibb al-nabawī*. Ed. 'Azīz Bayk. Riyyāḍ: Dār 'ālam al-kutub, 1995.
2. Chaghhaynī M. *Ṭibb al-nabī*. Trans. C Elgood. *Osiris* 1962; 14: 191.
3. Ibn Ṭulūn S. *al-Manhal al-rawī fī al-ṭibb al-nabawī*. Ed. 'Azīz Bayk. Riyyāḍ: Dār 'ālam al-kutub, 1995.
4. Nisābūrī A. *Islamic Medical Wisdom: The Ṭibb al-a'immah*. Trans. B. Ispahany. Ed. AJ Newman. London: Muḥammadī Trust, 1991: 108.
5. Majlisī M. *Biḥār al-anwār*. Ṭihrān: Javad al-Alavi, 1956
6. Nisābūrī A. *Islamic Medical Wisdom: The Ṭibb al-a'immah*. Trans. B. Ispahany. Ed. AJ Newman. London: Muḥammadī Trust, 1991: 57.
7. Gupta M, Mazumder UK, Manikandan L, Bhattacharya S, Senthikumar GP, Suresh R. Antiulcer activity of ethanol extract of *Terminalia pallida* Brandis in Swiss albino rats. *J Ethnopharmacol* 2005; 97(2): 405–408.
8. Masoko P, Picard J, Eloff JN. Antifungal activities of six South African *Terminalia* species (Combretaceae). *J Ethnopharmacol* 2005; 99(2): 301–308.
9. Chaudari M, Mengi S. Evaluation of phytoconstituents of *Terminalia arjuna* for wound healing activity in rats. *Phytother Res.* 2006; 20(9): 799–805.
10. Malekzadeh F, Ehsanifar H, Shahamat M, Levin M, Colwell RR. Antibacterial activity of black myrobalan (*Terminalia chebula* Retz) against *Helicobacter pylori*. *Int J Antimicrob Agents* 2001; 18(1): 85–88.
11. Fan YM, Xu LZ, Gao J, Wang Y, Tang XH, Zhao XN, Zhang ZX. Phytochemical and anti-inflammatory studies on *Terminalia catappa*. *Fitoterapia* 2004; 75(3–4): 253–260.
12. Rani, Khullar. Antimicrobial evaluation of some medicinal plants for their anti-enteric potential against multi-drug resistant *Salmonella typhi*. *Phytother* 2004; 18(8): 670–673.
13. Rao NK, Nammi S. Antidiabetic and renoprotective effects of the chloroform extract of *Terminalia chebula* Retz. Seeds in streptozotocin-induced diabetic rats. *BMC Complement Altern Med* 2006; 6: 17; Tasduq SA, Singh K, Satti NK, Gupta DK, Suri KA, Johri RK. *Terminalia chebula* (fruit) prevents liver toxicity caused by sub-chronic administration of rifampicin, isoniazid, and pyrazinamide in combination. *Hum Exp Toxicol* 2006; 25(3): 1118.
14. Nagappa AN, Thakurdesai PA, Venkat Rao N, Singh J. Antidiabetic activity of *Terminalia catappa* Linn fruits. *J Ethnopharmacol* 2003; 88(1): 45–50.
15. Prasad L, Husain Khan T, Jahangir T, Sultana S.

Chemomodulatory effects of *Terminalia chebula* against nickel chloride induced oxidative stress and tumor promotion response in male Wistar rats. *J Trace Elem Med Biol* 2006; 20(4): 233–9; Sivalokanathan S, Ilayaraja M, Balasubramanian MP. Efficacy of *Terminalia arguna* (Roxb.) on N-nitrosodiethylamine induced hepatocellular carcinoma in rats. *Indian J Exp Biol.* 2005; 43(3): 264–267.
16. Bharani A, Ahirwar LK, Jain N. *Terminalia arjuna* reverses impaired endothelial function in chronic smokers. *Indian Heart J* 2004; 56(2): 123–128.
17. Gandhi NM, Nair CK. Radiation protection by *Terminalia chebula*: some mechanistic aspects. *Mol Cell Biochem* 2005; 277(1–2): 43–48.
18. Naik GH, Priyadarsini KI, Naik DB, Gangabhagirathi R, Mohan H. Studies on the aqueous extract of *Terminalia chebula* as a potent antioxidant and a probable radioprotective. *Phytomedicine* 2004; 11(6): 530–538.
19. Kar, Choudhary, Bandyopadhyay. Comparative evaluation of hypoglycaemic activity of some Indian medicinal plants in alloxan diabetic rats. *J* 2003; 84(1): 105–108.

Myrrh / *Murr*

Family: Burseraceae

Botanical Name: *Commiphora myrrha*

Common Names: *English* Myrrh; *French* Myrrhe; *Spanish* Mirra; *German* Myrre, Myrrhe; *Urdu* Mur, Mur Maki, Bol; *Unānī Medical Term* Murr; *Modern Standard Arabic* Murr, Murr baṭārikh

Safety Rating: Generally Safe Although it can cause diarrhea and irritate the kidneys, myrrh is generally considered to be safe for most people when used as directed. It should not, however, be used during pregnancy as it considered to have abortifacient effects. It can, however, be used when childbirth is imminent. Myrrh should not be used by women suffering from any kind of uterine bleeding. In large doses, myrrh acts as a purgative, causing vomiting, and may affect heart rate. Topical preparations containing myrrh are reported to cause contact dermatitis.[1] Interaction with antidiabetic therapy is possible as hypoglycemic properties have been documented.

Prophetic Prescription: The Messenger of Allāh stated, "Fumigate your houses with *al-shīḥ*, *murr*, and *sa'tar*."[2]

Issues in Identification: According to Bīrūnī, *murr* is "the gum-resin brought from Socotra."[3] According to Ghazanfar, *murr*, *mirr*, and *ṣubr* is *Commiphora myrrha*, which is found in sandy and rocky areas of southern Arabia, in both Saudi Arabia and Yemen. It is also found in Somalia, Ethiopia, and Kenya.[4] *Murr* is not *Commiphora africana*, which is known in Arabic as *adras*, nor is it *Commiphora habessinica*, which is known as *medigeh* and *'okor* in colloquial Arabic. As Duke confirms, the Arabic *murr* refers to *Commiphora myrrha*.

Properties and Uses: Myrrh, the oleo gum resin obtained from species of *Commiphora*, is well-known as a fragrance used in incense and perfumes. Myrrh is considered abortifacient, analgesic, anesthetic, anthelmintic, anticlastogeic, antiedemic, anti-inflammatory, antioxidant, antipyretic, atiradicular, antirheumatic, antiseptic, antispasmodic, antithrombotic, antitumor, antiulcer, and astringent. It is also viewed as bactericidal, carminative, collyrium, cytotoxic, decongestant, deobstruent, deodorant, dessicative, detersive, digestive, emmenagogue, and expectorant. It is equally considered a fasciolicide, fungicide, gastroprotective, haematogenic, hepatoprotective, hypocholesterolemic, hypoglycemic, hypotriclyceridemic, and immunostimulant. Finally, it is considered a lactagogue, laxative, larvicide, lipolytic, mitodepressant, mosquitocide, mucogenic, orexigenic, prostaglandigenic, resolvent, schistosomicide, stimulant, stomachic, thyrostimulant, tonic, and vulnerary.

Myrrh is used to treat abrasion, adnexitis, alopecia, amenorrhea, anemia, aphthae, arthrosis, arteriosclerosis, asthma, athlete's foot, bacteria, bedsores, bladder stone, boils, bronchosis, bruise, cancer, cancer of the abdomen and colon, candidiasis, canker sore, carbuncle, caries, catarrh, chilblain, chlorosis, circulosis, cold, congestion, consumption, cough, dandruff, decubitis, dermatosis, diabetes, diarrhea, dicrocoeliasis, dipheria, dropsy, dysentery, dyslactea, dysmenorrhea, dyspepsia, and dysuria. It is also used for earache, edema, enterosis, epilepsy, erysipelas, fascioliasis, fever, fracture, freckle, fungus, furunculosis, gangrene, gas, gastrosis, gingivosis, gleet, gonorrhea, HIV and AIDS, halitosis, hemorrhoids, hepatosis, hoarseness, hypothyroidism, impotence, indigestion and infection. It is equally used for infertility, inflammation, itch, laryngitis, leprosy, leucorrhea, menopause, menorrhagia, mononucleosis, mucososi, mycosis, odontosis, opththalmia, orchosis, osteoalgia, otosi, pain, parasites, pharyngosis, phthisis, pruritis, pulmonosis, rheumatism, rhinosis, salpingitis, schistosomiasis, sinusitis, snakebite, sore, sore throat, stich, stomatosis, and swelling. Finally, it is employed for thrombosis, tonsilosis, toothache, tuberculosis, tumor, ulcer, uterosis, uvulosis, sexually transmitted disease, water retention, weaning, worm, wounds, wrinkles, and yeast infections. Externally, it is used as a stimulant, disinfectant, and antiseptic to mucous membranes and ulcerated surfaces. It is used to treat abrasions, bed sores, gingivitis, hemorrhoids, sore throat, inflamed gums, ptyalism, mouth sores, wounds, cystitis, indolent ulcers, as well as chronic uterine and vaginal leucorrhea.

Scientific Studies: *Anti-inflammatory Activity* Studies have demonstrated the anti-inflammatory properties of myrrh.[5]

Anticancer Activity Sesquiterpenes, a constituent of the resin, have been shown to be potent inhibitors of certain cancers.[6] *Commiphora molmol* also inhibits the growth of Ehrlich carcinoma cells in mice. The cytotoxic activities appear to be as effective as cyclophosphamide in solid tumor-bearing mice. Results of one study reveal that the Na, K and Ca levels in cancer cells were reduced by treatment of *Commiphora molmol,* leading to inhibition of cellular proliferation and tumor growth.[7]

Antioxidative Activity In animal studies, aqueous suspension of *Commiphora molmol* has been found to protect against gastric mucosal damage caused by NSAIDs and ethanol. *Commiphora molmol* is thought to have free radical–scavenging, thyroid-stimulating and prostaglandin-inducing properties. In a controlled animal study conducted by Alexandria University Research Development in Egypt, myrrh was found to be a useful herbal remedy for controlling oxidative damages and genotoxicity induced by lead acetate intoxication.[8]

Antimicrobial Activity In a study conducted by Alexandria University in Egypt, it was confirmed that myrrh has considerable antimicrobial activity and is medicinally useful in a variety of diseases.[9]

Antihelminthic Activity In a human trial conducted by Mansoura University in Egypt, 204 patients with schistosomiasis, a widespread helminthic disease, were given myrrh at a dose of 10mg/kg of body weight/day for three days, inducing a 91.7 percent cure rate. Re-treatment of cases who did not respond with a dose of 10 mg/kg of body weight/day for six days gave a cure rate of 76.5 percent, increasing the overall cure rate to 98.09 percent. The drug was well tolerated, and side effects were mild and transient. Twenty cases provided biopsy specimens six months after treatment and none of them showed living ova.[10] Treatment of schistosomiasis is based on chemotherapy with praziquantel, which is the drug of choice. However, since resistance to praziquantel has been demonstrated, alternative drugs like myrrh must now be considered.

Myrrh Notes

1. Brinker F. *Herb Contraindications and Drug Interactions.* Sandy, OR: Eclectic Medical Publications, 2001; Lee TY, Lam TH. Allergic *Contact Dermatitis* 1993; 28: 89–90.

2. Ibn Ṭulūn S. *al-Manhal al-rawī fī al-ṭibb al-nabawī.* Ed. 'Azīz Bayk. Riyyāḍ: Dār 'ālam al-kutub, 1995.

3. Bīrūnī, AR al-. *al-Bīrūnī's Book on Pharmacy and Materia Medica.* Ed. and trans. HM Said. Karachi: Hamdard National Foundation, 1973: 304.

4. Ghazanfar SA. *Handbook of Arabian Medicinal Plants.* Boca Raton: CRC Press, 1994.

5. Tariq M, et al. Anti-inflammatory activity of *Commiphora molmol. Agents Actions* 1986; 17: 381–2; Qureshi S, et al. Evaluation of the genotoxic, cytotoxic, and antitumor properties of *Commiphora molmol* using normal and Ehrlich ascites carcinoma cell-bearing Swiss albino mice. *Cancer Chemother Pharmacol* 1993; 33: 130–8.

6. al Harbi MM, et al. Anticarcinogenic effect of *Commiphora molmol* on solid tumors induced by Ehrlich carcinoma cells in mice. *Chemotherapy* 1994; 40: 337–47; al Harbi MM, et al. Gastric antiulcer and cytoprotective effect of *Commiphora molmol* in rats. *J Ethnopharmacol* 1997; 55: 141–150.

7. Barnes J, et al. *Herbal Medicines.* London: Pharmaceutical Press, 2002.

8. El-Ashmawy, Ashry, El-Nahas, Salama. Protection by turmeric and myrrh against liver oxidative damage and genotoxicity induced by lead acetate in mice. *Basic* 2006; 98(1): 32–37.

9. El, Rashed, Salama, Saleh. Components, therapeutic value and uses of myrrh. *Pharmazie.* 2003; 58(3): 163–168.

10. Sheir, Nasr, Massoud, Salama, Badra, El-Shennawy, Hassan, Hammad. A safe, effective, herbal antischistosomal therapy derived from myrrh. *Am* 2001; 65(6): 700–704.

Myrtle/*Ās*

Family: Myrtaceae

Botanical Name: *Myrtus communis*

Common Names: *English* Myrtle; *French* Myrte; *Spanish* Mirto, Arrayán; *German* Echte Myrte, Braut-Myrte, Gewöhnliche Myrte; *Urdu/Unānī* Aas, Muwrad; *Modern Standard Arabic* ās (plant), hambalas (fruit)

Safety Rating: Generally Safe to Deadly While myrtle might be safe for most people in small quantities, it can cause nausea, vomiting, diarrhea, low blood pressure, and blood circulation disorders, as well as other problems. Due to the dangers posed by this plant, it should not be consumed by women who are pregnant or lactating. The oil of myrtle is dangerous for both adults and children. It can cause asthma-like attacks and lung failure leading to death. Myrtle should only be used as directed under expert supervision.

Prophetic Prescription: According to the Prophet Muḥammad, "If anyone offers you myrtle as a present, do not refuse it. It is from the Garden."[1] According to Ibn 'Abbās, myrtle was the first thing that was planted by Nūḥ (Noah) when he disembarked from the ark.[2] A man complained to Imām Mūsā al-Kāẓim that he suffered from excessive dirt (*wasakh kathīr*) making his garment filthy. The Imām said, "Grind myrtle and extract its water. Whisk it vigorously with the best wine vinegar available until it becomes foamy. Then wash your head and beard with it as vigorously as possible, after that, oil it with fresh sesame oil. It will remove it [the dirt], Allāh, the Exalted, willing."[3] Imām 'Alī al-Riḍā also recommended using the "comprehensive medicine" with a decoction of myrtle for an ailment of the belly.[4]

ISSUES IN IDENTIFICATION: *Myrtus communis* is found in the mountains of Spain, Italy, southern France, North Africa, and the Middle East. According to Dīnawarī, *ās* grows a lot in the sahel, the plains, and the mountains of Arabia.[5] Elgood, Turkī, Álvarez de Morales and Girón Irueste identify *ās* as myrtle.[6] According to Said, *al-ās* and *al-'amār* refer to *Myrtus communis*. Bīrūnī also speaks of *mūrid asfaram* which Said equally identifies as *Myrtus communis*. Bīrūnī also speaks of *māsifram*, and *mūrd isfaram*. *Isfaram* is a generic name for any odiferous plant in Arabic. According to Aṣma'ī, as is also known as *rand*, and it is known in Yemen as *al-hadas*.

As Ouassad notes, *Myrtus* is *al-āsiyyah*. According to Nehmé, *Myrtus* is *ās* and *rīḥān*, and *Myrtus communis* specifically is *ās shā'ī'*. Ghazanfar notes that *Myrtus communis* is known as *yās* in Oman and *hadās* in Yemen. *Myrtus communis* is found in Saudi Arabia and northern Oman. A southern European variety is also distributed and often cultivated in parts of Arabia. According to Ghazanfar, this foreign variety was probably introduced.[7]

PROPERTIES AND USES: *Myrtus communis*, commonly known as myrtle, is an aromatic, stimulant, astringent, styptic, antidiaphoretic, carminative, tonic herb that is antiseptic and an effective decongestant. Internally, it is used for urinary infections, vaginal discharge, bronchial congestion, sinusitis, diarrhea, dysentery, and dry coughs. It is also used to treat diabetes, and digestive disorders. Externally, it is used for acne, gum infection, bruises, wounds, hemorrhoids, and body odor. Myrtle oil is used externally to treat respiratory and bladder problems, as well as rheumatism. Myrtle oil is also used in soaps and skin-care products. Recent research has shown that myrtle contains a substance that has an antibiotic action.

SCIENTIFIC STUDIES: *Antibacterial, Antitumor, and Anti-inflammatory Activity* According to research, myrtle leaf lipid extracts exhibits antibacterial, antitumor, and anti-inflammatory activity.[8]

Antihypoglycemic and Antihypotriglyceridemic Activity According to an animal trial, myrtle exhibits hypoglycemic as well as mild hypotriglyceridemic activity in diabetic rabbits, supporting its use in Turkish folk medicine for the treatment of type 2 diabetes.[9] Other animal trials have also confirmed myrtle's anti-hyperglycemic activity.[10]

Antioxidative Activity Studies also suggest that myrtle extracts have a potent antioxidant activity.[11]

Myrtle Notes

1. Sūyūṭī J. *As-Sūyūṭī's Medicine of the Prophet*. Ed. A Thomson. London: Ṭā-Hā Publishers, 1994: 37.
2. Ibn Ṭulūn S. *al-Manhal al-rawī fī al-ṭibb al-nabawī*. Ed. 'Azīz Bayk. Riyyāḍ: Dār 'ālam al-kutub, 1995.
3. Nisābūrī A. *Islamic Medical Wisdom: The Ṭibb al-a'immah*. Trans. B. Ispahany. Ed. AJ Newman. London: Muḥammadī Trust, 1991: 102.
4. Nisābūrī A. *Islamic Medical Wisdom: The Ṭibb al-a'immah*. Trans. B. Ispahany. Ed. AJ Newman. London: Muḥammadī Trust, 1991: 115.
5. Dīnawarī AH. *Kitāb al-nabāt/The Book of Plants*. Ed. Bernhard Lewin. Uppsala/Wiesbaden: A.-B. Lundequistska Bokhandeln and Otto Harrassowitz, 1953: 10.
6. Elgood C. Trans. *Ṭibb al-nabī or Medicine of the Prophet*. Sūyūṭī J, M Chaghhaynī. *Osiris* 1962; 14; Iṣbahānī AN al-. *Mawsū'at al-ṭibb al-nabawī*. Ed. MKD al-Turkī. Bayrūt: Dār Ibn Ḥazm, 2006; Ibn Ḥabīb A. *Mujtaṣar fī al-ṭibb/Compendio de medicina*. Ed. C Álvarez de Morales and F Girón Irueste. Madrid: Consejo Superior de Investigaciones Científicas, 1992.
7. Ghazanfar SA. *Handbook of Arabian Medicinal Plants*. Boca Raton: CRC Press, 1994.
8. Wyatt RM, Hodges LD, Kalafatis N, Wright PF, Wynne PM, Macrides TA. Phytochemical analysis and biological screening of leaf and twig extracts from *Kunzea ericoides*. *Phytother-Res*. 2005; 19(11): 963–970; Al-Hindawi MK, et al. Anti-inflammatory activity of some Iraqi plants using intact rats. *J Ethnopharmacology* 1989; 26: 163–168.
9. Sepici-Dincel A, Acikgoz S, Cevik C, Sengelen M, Yesilada E. Effects of in vivo antioxidant enzyme activities of myrtle oil in normoglycaemic and alloxan diabetic rabbits. *J Ethnopharmacol*. 2007; 4; 110(3): 498–503.
10. Elfellah MS, et al. Anti-hyperglycemic effect of an extract of *Myrtus communis* in *Streptozotocin*-induced diabetes in mice. *J Ethnopharmacology* 1984; 11: 275–281.
11. Romani A, Coinu R, Carta S, Pinelli P, Galardi C, Vincieri FF. Franconi F. Evaluation of antioxidant effects of different extracts of *Myrtus communis* L. *Free Radic Res*. 2004; 38(1): 97–103; Rosa A, Deiana M, Casu V, Corona G, Appendino G, Bianchi F, Ballero M, Dessi MA. Antioxidative activity of oligomeric acylphloroglucinois from *Myrtus communis* L. *Free Radic Res*. 2003; 37(9): 1013–1019.

Narcissus/*Narjis*

FAMILY: Amaryllidaceae
BOTANICAL NAME: *Narcissus* spp.
COMMON NAMES: *English* Narcissus; *French* Narcisse; *Spanish* Narciso; *German* Narzisse, Osterglocke; *Urdu/Unānī* Narjis, Nargis; *Modern Standard Arabic* Narjis

Safety Rating: Dangerous to Deadly The poisonous nature of narcissus has been known since ancient times. Due to its narcotic effect, Socrates called it "the chaplet of the infernal gods." Homer asserted that it could cause torpor, insanity, and death. The very word narcissus derives from the Greek word *narke*, which means "stupor." Ibn al-Jawziyyah explained that eating the cooked flowers and stalks of narcissus or drinking its water stimulates vomiting.[1]

Farooqi is in error when he claims that "the bulbs have some toxicity and are a very mild poison."[2] All species of *Narcissus* contain lycorine, an alkaloid poison. Found mostly in the bulb, but also in the leaves, lycorine may be highly poisonous, if not lethal, when consumed in large doses. Nausea, acute abdominal pain, vomiting, diarrhea, trembling, and convulsions are symptoms of lycorine toxicity. Due to the dangers posed by this plant, its ingestion should be avoided. Contact with *Narcissus jonquilla* may cause severe skin irritation.

Prophetic Prescription: According to an uncorroborated tradition, the Messenger of Allāh is alleged to have said, "Smell a narcissus. For verily, in the heart of man there is the seed of insanity, leprosy, and vitiligo, which can only be prevented by smelling narcissus."[3] In a longer version, the Prophet says, "Smell a narcissus, even if only once a day or once a week or once a month or once a year or even once in a lifetime. For verily, in the heart of man there is the seed of insanity, leprosy, and leukoderma. And the scent of narcissus drives these away."[4] It is also related that the Prophet said, "Do not hesitate to smell narcissus, for it protects from the cold of winter, and so does black seed."[5]

Issues in Identification: It is the consensus that *narjis* is Arabic for *Narcissus*. Bīrūnī speaks of *narjis*, *abhar*, *sawsan*, and *qahd*, which Said identifies as *Narcissus tazetta* L. Aṣma'ī also says that *narjis* is a synonym for *abhar*. For Johnstone, *narjis* refers to *Narcissus poeticus*, and *Narcissus pseudonarcissus*.[6] For Álvarez de Morales and Girón Irueste, *narjis* is *Narcissus poeticus*.[7] Dīnawarī does not identify *sawsan* as *narjis*, but does state that it does not grow in Arabia, that it has many varieties, and the prettiest is white.[8] As Nehmé notes, *Narcissus* is *narjis*; *Narcisuss tazzetta* is *narjis ṭāsī*, and *narjis ṭāqī*, and *maḍ'af*.[9]

It is unlikely that the tradition refers to *Narcissus jonquilla*, known in English as narcissus, jonquil, and daffodil. It is found from Europe to the Mediterranean. It is equally unlikely that the tradition refers to *Narcissus poeticus* or poet's narcissus. Found from France to Greece, it was not readily available to the Arabs at the time of the Prophet. Furthermore, every part of the plant is poisonous, especially the bulbs, which are powerfully emetic and irritant. When present in any quantity in a close room, their mere smell is sufficient to produce headaches and vomiting in some persons. The bulb is powerfully emetic and irritant and is used as a homeopathic remedy.

Narcissus pseudonarcissus, known in English as wild daffodil, must also be discarded. Found in Western Europe and Britain. It is used as an emetic and to treat burns and other skin problems. All parts of the plant are poisonous. Although the toxins are found mainly in the bulb, even the flowers are mildly toxic. When applied to open wounds, an extract of the bulbs has produced staggering numbness of the whole nervous system, and paralysis of the heart. A small quantity of daffodil bulbs is sufficient to cause sudden death.

The flower referred to in the traditions above must be *Narcissus tazetta*, known as bunchflower daffodil, which ranges from Europe to East Asia.

Properties and Uses: Internally, *Narcissus tazetta* is a demulcent. The roots are emetic. It is also used to relieve headaches. Externally, it is employed as an antiphlogistic and analgesic poultice in the treatment of abscesses, boils, and other skin complaints, as well as mastitis. It is reputed to be effective against certain forms of cancer. This might be the result of benzaldehyde transforming into laetrile-like compounds or to lycorine turning into lycobetaine-like compounds in the body.

Scientific Studies: *Anticancer Activity* The anticancer activity of narcissus extracts have been known for many decades.[10] According to a study conducted by Xiangya Medical College in China, the extracts from *Narcissus tazetta* var. *chinensis* strongly decreased the survival rate of the following tumor cell lines: HL-60, K562, KT1/A3, and A3R.[11]

Antimalarial Activity According to a study conducted by Gazi University in Turkey, *Narcissus tazetta* alkaloids exhibit antimalarial activity.[12]

Anti-HIV Activity According to research conducted by the Katholieke Universiteit Leuven in Belgium, narcissus appears to contain a natural anti–HIV agent. The mannose-specific plant lectins from narcissus would primarily be targeted at the virus-cell fusion process.[13]

According to a study conducted by the Universitat de Barcelona, mannose-specific lectins isolated from bulbs of fifteen wild narcissus species growing in Spain almost all possess HIV-1 inhibitory activity in MT-4 cells, with some being comparable to dextran sulfate without significant cytotoxicity. On a molar basis almost all of the MSLs tested exhibited lower EC50 values than dextran sulfate while six MSLs had values lower than AZT. The most efficacious anti–HIV-1 activity was exhibited by the *Narcissus tortifolius* MSL, which was 10- (microg/mL) and 100- (molarity) fold more potent than dextran sulfate. Significantly, although this MSL was 15-fold less potent than AZT in terms of quantity, it was 68-fold more potent on a molar basis. The antiviral indices, a ratio of the concentrations that produce cytotoxicity and HIV-1 replication, were calculated and three of the MSLs, *Narcissus confusus*, *Narcissus leonensis* and *Narcissus tortifolius* reported 1.5-, 2- and 8.5-fold greater AI values than dextran sulfate or AZT. Comparison of MSL haemagglutination activities (HAA) to their anti–HIV-1 activities showed that there was no significant correlation. It was suggested that this may be due to dissociation between both activities as a consequence of multiple isolectin composition.[14]

Acetylcholinesterase Inhibitory Activity According to a study conducted by the Universitat de Barcelona, amaryllidaceous plants produce pharmacologically active alkaloids. The most interesting of them is galanthamine which shows potential in the treatment of Alzheimer's disease as a cholinesterase inhibitor. In this particular study, researchers tested 23 pure Amaryllidaceae alkaloids and 26 extracts from different species of the genus *Narcissus* for their acetylcholinesterase inhibitory activity. Only seven alkaloids, belonging to the galanthamine and lycorine skeleton types, exhibited such an effect, sanguinine being the most active, even more than galanthamine. All the extracts with the highest acetylcholinesterase inhibitory activity contained galanthamine except that of *Narcissus assoanus*, a lycorine type alkaloid-bearing species.[15]

Anti-Rabies Activity According to a study conducted by the Universita La Sapienza in Italy, rabies virus attachment to susceptible cells was prevented by *Narcissus pseudonarcissus* agglutinin.[16]

Antileukemic Activity According to an animal trial, a narcissus alkaloid, pretazettine hydrochloride, has been shown to be active against spontaneous AKR leukemia. The long-term treatment with pretazettine hydrochloride significantly prolonged the life span of the group.[17]

Anti-Alzheimer Activity According to a study conducted by the University of London in the UK, galanthamine isolated from several members of the Amaryllidaceae family (*Leucojum* spp., *Narcissus* spp., *Galanthus* spp.) has become an important therapeutic option used to slow down the process of neurological degeneration in Alzheimer's disease. This review traces aspects of the history of its development from little-known observational studies in the Caucasus Mountains (Southern Russia), to the use of this drug in Eastern European countries (esp. Bulgaria) in the treatment of poliomyelitis and ultimately to the recent introduction onto Western markets in the treatment of Alzheimer's disease.[18]

Galanthamine, an alkaloid present in the Amaryllidaceae, is currently undergoing clinical trials for the treatment of Alzheimer's. Common daffodils contain galanthamine and other alkaloids. Four commercial narcissus cultivars were evaluated as potential sources of galanthamine. Planting depths, planting densities, bulb size or flower bud removal did not affect galanthamine content.[19]

Narcissus Notes

1. Ibn Qayyim al-Jawziyyah M. *al-Ṭibb al-nabawī*. Bayrūt: Dār al-Kitāb, 1985.
2. Farooqi MIH. *Medicinal Plants in the Traditions of Prophet Muḥammad*. Lucknow: Sidrah Publishers, 1998: 97.
3. Sūyūṭī J. *As-Sūyūṭī's Medicine of the Prophet*. Ed. A Thomson. London: Ṭā-Hā Publishers, 1994: 106.
4. Chaghhaynī M. *Ṭibb al-nabī*. Trans. C Elgood. *Osiris* 1962; 14: 191.
5. Bār MA. *al-Imām al-Riḍā wa risālatuhu fī al-ṭibb al-nabawī*. Bayrūt: Dār al-manāhil, 1991: 172.
6. Johnstone P, trans. *Medicine of the Prophet*. Ibn Qayyim al-Jawziyyah. Cambridge: The Islamic Texts Society, 1998.
7. Ibn Ḥabīb A. *Mujtaṣar fī al-ṭibb/Compendio de medicina*. Ed. C Álvarez de Morales and F Girón Irueste. Madrid: Consejo Superior de Investigaciones Científicas, 1992.
8. Dīnawarī AH. *Kitāb al-nabāt: Le dictionaire botanique d'Abū Ḥanīfa al-Dīnawarī*. al-Qāhirah: Institut Français d'Archéologie Orientale du Caire, 1973.
9. Nehmé M. *Dictionnaire étymologique de la flore du Liban*. Bayrūt: Librairie du Liban, 2000.
10. Furusawa, Suzuki, Tani, Furusawa, Ishioka, Motobu. Anticancer activity of narcissus extracts in mice. *Proc* 1973; 143(1): 33–38.
11. Liu, Li, Ren, Hu. Apoptosis of HL-60 cells induced by extracts from *Narcissus tazetta* var. *chinensis*. *Cancer* 2006; 242(1): 133–140.
12. Sener, Orhan, Satayavivad. Antimalarial activity screening of some alkaloids and the plant extracts from Amaryllidaceae. *Phytother* 2003; 17(10): 1220–1223.
13. De. Current lead natural products for the chemotherapy of human immunodeficiency virus (HIV) infection. *Med* 2000; 20(5): 323–349.
14. Lopez, Armand-Ugon, Bastida, Viladomat, Este, Stewart, Codina. Anti-human immunodeficiency virus type 1 (HIV-1) activity of lectins from *Narcissus* species. *Planta* 2003; 69(2): 109–112.
15. Lopez, Bastida, Viladomat, Codina. Acetylcholinesterase inhibitory activity of some Amaryllidaceae alkaloids and *Narcissus* extracts. *Life* 2002; 71(21): 2521–2529.
16. Marchetti, Mastromarino, Rieti, Seganti, Orsi. Inhibition of herpes simplex, rabies and rubella viruses by lectins with different specificities. *Res* 1995; 146(3): 211–215.
17. Furusawa, Lockwood, Furusawa, Lum, Lee. Therapeutic activity of pretazettine, a narcissus alkaloid, on spon-

taneous AKR leukemia. *Chemotherapy.* 1979; 25(5): 308–315.
18. Heinrich, Lee. Galanthamine from snowdrop — the development of a modern drug against Alzheimer's disease from local Caucasian knowledge. *J* 2004; 92(2–3): 147–162.
19. Moraes-Cerdeira, Burandt, Bastos, Nanayakkara, Mikell, Thurn, McChesney. Evaluation of four Narcissus cultivars as potential sources for galanthamine production. *Planta* 1997; 63(5): 472–474.

Nuts (Almonds, Walnuts) / *Mukassarāt* (*Jawz, Lawz*)

FAMILY: Rosaceae

BOTANICAL NAME: *Prunus dulcis*

COMMON NAMES: *English* Almond tree; almond; *French* Amandier; amande; *Spanish* Almendro; almendra; *German* Echte Mandel; *Urdu/Unānī* Badam, Badam Shireen, Lauz; *Modern Standard Arabic* lawz

FAMILY: Juglandaceae

BOTANICAL NAME: *Juglans regia*

COMMON NAMES: *English* Walnut tree; walnut (nut); *French* Noyer; noix (nut); *Spanish* Nogal común; nuez (nut); *German* Echte Walnuss, Baumnuss, Walnussbaum; *Urdu/Unānī* Akhrot, Jawz, Gardgan; *Modern Standard Arabic* jawz, 'ayn al-jamal

SAFETY RATING: GENERALLY SAFE TO DEADLY In the absence of allergies, nuts are considered safe when consumed in moderation. Allergic reactions to nuts, however, tend to be severe, easily leading to death. Since 1 percent of Americans suffer from tree nut and peanut allergies, caution is always indicated. Even when allergies are absent, certain nuts should only be consumed in small quantities. Due to their high selenium content, consumption of Brazil nuts should be limited to one to two servings a maximum of twice per week. Since they are high in oxalate, they should not be overconsumed by individuals suffering from oxalate-containing kidney stones. Cashew nuts also contain oxalate and should be consumed in moderation by sensitive people. Due to their high moisture content, chestnuts are prone to the development of mold and bacteria. As such, they should always be kept covered and refrigerated. Cashews and pistachios contain oleoresins which can cause allergic reactions. Care should be taken when consuming bitter almonds as they contain highly poisonous amounts of prussic acid, the same toxic substance found in cyanide or hydrocyanic acid.

PROPHETIC PRESCRIPTION: The Messenger of Allāh is alleged to have said, "Cheese is a disease and walnuts (*jawzāt*) are a medicine. Taken together, they become a remedy."[1] The Imāms also prescribed almonds (*lawz*), blue almonds (*lawz azraq*) and pine nuts (*ṣanawbar*) for medicinal purposes.

According to Imām Ja'far al-Ṣādiq, "There is a remedy contained in both (fresh saltless) cheese and walnuts (*jawz*). However, when taken apart, they contain sickness."[2] The Imām also explained, "There are four things which improve vision. They are beneficial and contain no harm." He was asked what they were. He responded, "Thyme (*za'tar*) and salt when taken together, bishop's weed (*nānkhwāh*) and nuts (*jawz*) when taken together." He continued,

> Bishop's weed and nuts burn hemorrhoids, chase the wind, they improve the color, wrinkle the stomach, and warms the kidneys. Thyme and salt chase the wind from the heart (*fu'ād*), open that which is closed, burn phlegm, increase urine (*mā'*), increase flavor, softens the stomach, removes the bad wind (*riḥ al-khabīthah*), and give an erection.[3]

On another occasion, Imām Ja'far al-Ṣādiq explained that "There are three which are not eaten but which fatten, and there are three which are eaten but do not fatten. The three which are eaten but do not fatten are the palm tree (*tala'*), pearl millet (*kasab*) [*Pennisetum glaucum*], and walnuts (*jawz*). The three which are not eaten but which fatten are lime (*nūrah*), the good one (*ṭayyib*), and flax seed (*labs al-kattān*)."[4]

ISSUES IN IDENTIFICATION: There is no question that *jawz* is walnut and *lawz* is almond. According to Ghazanfar, walnut is pronounced as *joz* in Saudi Arabia, where it is also known as *naksh*. It exists in Arabia as a cultivated tree in the south west mountains.[5] The widespread use of nuts among the Arabs was the result of their contact with the Persians and Spaniards during the early period of Islamic expansion.[6]

PROPERTIES AND USES: *Juglans regia* or English walnut is a bitter, astringent herb that is expectorant and laxative, soothes irritated tissues, and dissolves kidney stones. It controls many disease-causing organisms, and has anticancer properties. Internally, walnut leaves are used for constipation, chronic coughs, asthma, and urinary stones. Walnut rind is used for diarrhea and anemia, and walnut oil is used for menstrual problems and dry skin conditions. Externally, walnut oil is used for eczema, herpes, eruptive skin complaints, eye inflammations, and hair loss. It is astringent, anthelmintic, cathartic, and tonic. A decoction of walnut tree leaves is used to treat leucorrhea, scrofula, rickets, and meningitis, while the rind or bark is used to check mammary secretions, ulcers, diarrhea, sore mouth, swollen tonsils, uterine hemorrhages, carbuncles, and scrofula.

Almonds are very high in minerals, including calcium, magnesium, potassium and iron, and are the only nut that is alkaline-forming in the body. They are also rich in protein and vitamins B2 and B3. Almonds are also thought to contain a compound that is anti-carcinogenic and for this purpose it is recommended that six almonds be consumed daily. Brazil nuts are 65 percent fat and 14 percent protein. They are rich in the sulfur containing amino acids and selenium. Selenium has an important function as an antioxidant and is involved in immunity. The kernels of cashews are nearly half fat and one-fifth protein. Pecans are rich in oils and vitamins B1 and B2.

Both sweet and bitter almonds come from trees of the same species, the first from *Prunus dulcis* var. *dulcis*, and the last from *Prunus dulcis* var. *amara*. Amygdalin, however, is only found in the bitter almond, which is more prized in medicine. *Prunus dulcis* or almond is a soothing, laxative herb that relaxes spasms. Almonds have sedative and antispasmodic effects making them useful in the treatment of nervous coughs, insomnia, and diseases of the respiratory organs. Internally, sweet almond oil acts as a demulcent while in larger doses it is a laxative. It is traditionally used to treat cough, intestinal irritation, and to mitigate the acrimony of the urine in calculus affections, cystitis, and gonorrhea. Externally, sweet almond oil is used for dry skin conditions and is used in the manufacture of emulsions for medicines, massage oils, skincare preparations, and cosmetics. Al-Kindī has *lawz*, most likely sweet almond, together with jasmine oil, costus, and sandalwood in a salve.[7] Bitter almond is slightly pain relieving and reduces irritation. Bitter almond oil is used in commercial food flavoring, especially in cakes, biscuits, candy, ice cream, maraschino cherries, and marzipan.

Nuts and seeds are concentrated sources of protein, fats, B vitamins, vitamin E, iron, magnesium and other minerals. Some of them contain omega 3 fatty acids and as such can help to improve the balance of cholesterol and the blood lipid profile and reduce the risk of heart disease.

Hazelnuts are very rich in oil calcium, magnesium, iron, potassium, phosphorus, folic acid and vitamin E. Hazelnuts act as a general tonic and strengthen the stomach. Macadamia nuts are very high in fat and can contribute to weight gain if consumed in excess. However in moderation they can help to improve the balance of cholesterol due to their abundance of monounsaturated fats. They are also very low in carbohydrates and as such are suitable for low carbohydrate diets.

Pistachio nuts are rich in oil. In Ayurvedic medicine, they are considered a tonic for the whole body. They purify the blood, lubricate the intestines and can be used for constipation. Walnuts are rich in oil, high in protein, iron and contain omega 3 fatty acids. The husks contain much vitamin C. They can reduce inflammation and pain, lubricate the lungs and intestines, and nourish the brain and adrenal glands.

Peanuts are officially a legume but share many characteristics with nuts. They are rich in B vitamins, vitamin E, iron, zinc, protein, and monounsaturated fats. These healthy fats found in peanuts can help to improve blood cholesterol balance. Peanuts can potentially exacerbate gall bladder conditions and may reduce the metabolic rate and as such peanuts are best avoided if weight loss is desired. Recent evidence suggests that peanuts contain a compound that may provide protection against stomach, colon and breast cancers.

Nuts Notes

1. Sūyūṭī J. *As-Sūyūṭī's Medicine of the Prophet*. Ed. A Thomson. London: Ṭā-Hā Publishers, 1994: 49; Chaghhaynī M. *Ṭibb al-nabī*. Trans. C Elgood. *Osiris* 1962; 14: 188. This tradition is considered *munkar* by Sunnī authorities.
2. Majlisī M. *Biḥār al-anwār*. Ṭihrān: Javad al-Alavi, 1956.
3. Majlisī M. *Biḥār al-anwār*. Ṭihrān: Javad al-Alavi, 1956.
4. Majlisī M. *Biḥār al-anwār*. Ṭihrān: Javad al-Alavi, 1956.
5. Ghazanfar SA. *Handbook of Arabian Medicinal Plants*. Boca Raton: CRC Press, 1994.
6. Tannahill R. *Food in History*. New York: Stein and Day, 1973: 175.
7. Levey M, al-Khaledy N, eds. *The Medical Formulary of al-Samarqandī*. Philadelphia: University of Pennsylvania Press, 1967: 192.

Olive/*Zayt, Zaytūn*

FAMILY: Oleaceae

BOTANICAL NAME: *Olea europaea*

COMMON NAMES: *English* Olive; *French* Olivier; *Spanish* Olivo; *German* Olive, Ölbaum, Olivenbaum; *Urdu/Unānī* Zaitoon; *Modern Standard Arabic* zaytūn

SAFETY RATING: GENERALLY SAFE Olives and olive oil are generally considered to be safe for most people.

Prophetic Prescription: While the Qur'ān draws our attention to the olive, the Prophet Muḥammad often focused on its practical medicinal applications, encouraging his followers to "[e]at olive oil, and anoint yourselves with it, for it comes from a blessed tree."[1] He said, "[t]here is olive oil for you, eat it, apply it, since it is effective for hemorrhoids."[2] He also stated, "[y]ou have the olive oil from this blessed tree, treat yourself with it, since it cures hemorrhoids [*basūr*]."[3] On another occasion, the Prophet said, "[e]at olive oil and apply it, since it is a cure for seventy diseases, one of which is leprosy."[4]

Zayd ibn Arqam narrated that the Prophet directed the companions to treat pleurisy with *kust baḥrī* and olive oil.[5] He also treated the illness with pseudo-saffron and olive oil.[6] The Messenger of Allāh also said, "A mourning woman can rub herself with lotus leaves and olive oil."[7]

In a detailed tradition, Imām 'Alī ibn Abī Ṭālib extols the values of olive oil in the following terms:

> You have olive oil: take it, moisten your bread with it, anoint yourselves with it, and enlighten yourselves with it. It is the oil of the best of men, the condiment of the elect, and your ointment and condiment. It comes from a tree blessed by Jerusalem since the time it appeared from the time it will disappear. Satan is powerless against this oil.[8]

When a man mentioned that olives cause wind, Imām Ja'far al-Ṣādiq corrected him, saying "No, they chase winds."[9] In another tradition, he said, "Olives increase water."[10]

Issues in Identification: It is the consensus that *zayt* is Arabic for olive. Since olives do not grow in Arabia, they need to be imported from the Mediterranean region. During the time of the Prophet, olives were generally imported by caravan from Palmyra.[11]

Properties and Uses: The olive has been cultivated since prehistoric times. While its culinary uses are well-known, its medicinal applications, which involve the leaves and the oil, are less familiar, particularly outside of the Islamic and Mediterranean world. The Muslim world, however, has always revered the olive as a source of food, oil, and medicine. The full appreciation of the olive was the direct result of both Qur'ānic and Prophetic guidance. The Holy Qur'ān, on the one hand, speaks of the olive on numerous occasions, presenting it as a sign of God, and inciting Muslims to ponder upon its properties (6:99, 6:141, 16:11, 23:20; 24:35, 80:29, 95:1). The Prophet Muḥammad, on the other hand, lauded the benefits of the blessed olive tree that provided food, oil, and various internal and external medicinal applications. The Qur'ānic and Prophetic guidance regarding the olive was followed by the companions of the Prophet, the followers of the companions, and the Imāms of the Muslims. Islamic scholars and scientists, inspired by the Qur'ān and the teachings of the Prophet, dedicated themselves to the study of the olive and its various medicinal applications. As a result, the olive became an integral part of Islamic/Unānī phytotherapy and was indicated as an effective treatment for numerous conditions from dry skin to leprosy and from hemorrhoids to pleurisy. Time, experience, and scientific studies have all confirmed the medical applications of the olive.

The olive is considered nutritive, emollient, demulcent, and laxative. Internally, olive oil is used to treat constipation, flatulence, and colic, as well as peptic and gastro-intestinal ulcers. It reduces gastric secretions, which is beneficial to patients suffering from hyperacidity and acid reflux. Middle Eastern, Japanese and North African doctors endorse the opinion that regular consumption of olive oil prevents incidences of gastrointestinal carcinoma.

Externally, olive oil is used to relieve pruritis, to soothe stings, burns, eczema, psoriasis, rheumatism, sciatica, alopecia, mouth and lip ulcers and dermatitis. In Cuba, research has shown the effectiveness of ozonized olive oil in treating herpes zoster, epidermofitosis, onychomycosis, chronic external otitis, ulcers, hemorrhoids, herpes simplex, genital herpes, vulvovaginitis, vaginitis, gingivostomatitis, keratitis, and other dermatological problems.[12] Applications of olive oil and henna leaves twice daily can help heal hemorrhoids while the concentrated aqueous extract of olive leaves and fruits is effective against dental cavities and leukoplakia in the mouth.[13]

Scientific Studies: *Cholesterol-Lowering Activity* In the United States, producers of olive oil may place the following health claim on product labels: "Scientific evidence suggests that eating about two tablespoons (23 grams) of olive oil daily may reduce the risk of coronary due to the monounsaturated in olive oil. To achieve this possible benefit, olive oil is to replace a similar amount of saturated and not increase the total number of calories you eat in a day." This decision was announced November 1, 2004 by the Food. Similar labels are permitted for omega-3 and walnuts, which also contain monounsaturated oil.[14]

Arterial Elasticifying Activity A health study in 2005 compared the effects of different sorts of olive oil on arterial elasticity. Probands were given a serving of 60 grams of white bread and 40 milliliters of olive oil each morning for two consecutive days. The study was conducted in two stages. During the first stage, the probands received polyphenol-rich oil ("extra virgin" oil contains the highest amount of polyphenol), during the second, they received oil with only one-fifth the phenolic content. The elasticity of the arterial walls of each proband was measured using a pressure sleeve and a Doppler laser. It was discovered that after the probands had consumed olive oil high in polyphenol antioxidants, they exhibited increased arterial elasticity, while after the consumption of olive oil containing less polyphenols, they exhibited no significant change in arterial elasticity. It is supposed that, in the long term, increased elasticity of arterial walls reduces vascular stress and consequentially the risk of two common causes of death —heart and stroke. This could, at least in part, explain the lower incidence of both ailments in regions where olive oil and olives are consumed on a daily basis. Animal tests have shown a hypotensive, antiarrythmic, and spasmolytic effect on the smooth muscle of the intestine.[15] Olive oil is a vasodilator, increases HDL, lowers the risk of cardiovascular disease, reduces blood pressure, and has potent antioxidative activity. As a cardiotonic, it is indicated in cases of sexual weakness due to a debilitated cardiovascular system and diabetes.

Respiratory Tract Enhancing Activity Olive oil is a good supportive treatment for diseases of the respiratory tract, including pleurisy and tuberculosis and helps reduce incidences of the common cold, coryzha and pneumonia.

Febrifugal Activity Both leaves and bark, for example, have valuable febrifugal qualities.[16] To this day, people in the Levant treat obstinate fevers with a tea made from olive leaves.

Antihelminthic Activity The anthelmintic oil procured from olive wood is particularly effective in eradicating ringworm and *Tinea versicolor*.

Anticancer Activity In a study conducted by the Universitat de Barcelona, olive fruit extracts were shown to inhibit proliferation and induce apoptosis in human colon cancer cells.[17]

Emollient Activity Olive oil is an excellent emollient. Grieve explains, "[d]elicate babies absorb its nourishing properties well through the skin."[18] This is consistent with Imām Muḥammad al-Bāqir's saying that "oil [applied] at night passes into the blood vessels and nourishes the skin."[19] As a lubricant it is valuable in skin, muscular, joint, kidney and chest complaints, abdominal chill, typhoid and scarlet fevers, plague and dropsy as well as sciatica and arthritis. The leaves of the olive tree are astringent, antiseptic and antimicrobial.[20] They are also smashed and applied externally to check excessive perspiration. Olive oil is also good vehicle for liniments. It is indicated for dry hair and dandruff and is often combined with industrial alcohol to make a good hair-tonic. It is also applied in eyes to relieve inflammation. The powder of the seeds mixed with butter is effective in brittle nails. Combined with honey, the water extracted from the leaves is used as eardrops.

Anti-Leprosy Activity In Aztec herbalism, a mixture of annatto/lipstick tree powder and olive oil is indicated for the treatment of leprosy. In ancient times, in Greece, Crete, and the Levant, olive oil was also used to treat the same dreaded disease. In one preliminary study completed in Cuba, 30 patients suffering from lepromatous leprosy were treated with ozonized olive oil. Four patients recovered, 15 improved satisfactorily, and 13 had to suspend the treatment.[21]

Olive Notes

1. This tradition is found with slight variants in Tirmidhī M. *al-Jāmi' al-kabīr*. Bayrūt: Dār al-Gharb, 1996; Ibn Mājah M. *Sunan*. Trans. MT Anṣārī. Lahore: Kazi Publications, 1994; Bayhaqī, A. *al-Sunan al-kubrā*. Bayrūt: Dār Ṣadīr, 1968.

2. Sūyūṭī J. *Jāmi' al-aḥādīth*. Bayrūt: Dār al-Fikr, 1994; Muttaqī A. *Kanz al-'ummāl*. 2nd ed. Ḥaydarabād: Dairat al-ma'ārif al-'Uthmāniyyah, 1945–75.

3. Sūyūṭī J. *Jāmi' al-aḥādīth*. Bayrūt: Dār al-Fikr, 1994; Ibn Qayyim al-Jawziyyah M. *al-Ṭibb al-nabawī*. Bayrūt: Dār al-Kitāb, 1985.

4. Sūyūṭī J. *Jāmi' al-aḥādīth*. Bayrūt: Dār al-Fikr, 1994; Muttaqī A. *Kanz al-'ummāl*. 2nd ed. Ḥaydarabād: al-Dikin Dairat al-ma'arif al-'Uthmaniyah, 1945–75; Iṣbahānī AN al-. *Mawsū'at al-ṭibb al-nabawī*. Ed. MKD al-Turkī. Bayrūt, Lubnān: Dār Ibn Ḥazm, 2006.

5. Tirmidhī M. *al-Jāmi' al-kabīr*. Bayrūt: Dār al-Gharb, 1996; Ibn Ḥanbal A. *Musnad al-Imām Aḥmad ibn Ḥanbal*. Bayrūt: Mu'assasat al-Risālah, 1993; Ibn Mājah M. *Sunan Ibn Mājah*. Bayrūt: Dār al-Jil, 1998.

6. Tirmidhī M. *al-Jāmi' al-ṣaḥīḥ*. al-Qāhirah: Muṣṭafā al-Bābī al-Ḥalabī, [1937-].

7. Ibn Anas M. *al-Muwaṭṭa'*. Bayrūt: Dār al-Gharb, 1999.

8. Ibn Ḥabīb A. *Mujtaṣar fī al-ṭibb/Compendio de medicina*. Ed. C Álvarez de Morales and F Girón Irueste. Madrid: Consejo Superior de Investigaciones Científicas, 1992: 75.

9. Majlisī M. *Biḥār al-anwār*. Ṭihrān: Javad al-Alavi, 1956.

10. Majlisī M. *Biḥār al-anwār*. Ṭihrān: Javad al-Alavi, 1956.

11. Tannahill R. *Food in History*. New York: Stein and Day, 1973: 126.

12. Biological oil and "active" oxygen: applications. http://www.pannomagico.it/eng/olioapp.htm

13. Khan MLA. Zaitoon (olive): cure for seventy diseases. http://www.crescentlife.com/dietnutrition/olives.htm

14. Olive oil makers win approval to make health claim on label. *New York Times*. Nov. 2, 2004. http://www.nytimes.com/2004/11/02/politics/02olive.html?ex=1187064000&en=4cf2c6 b8 bafcc869&ei=5070

15. Gehrmann B, Wolf-Gerald K, Tshirch CO, Brinkmann H. *Medicinal Herbs: A Compendium*. New York: Haworth Press, 2005: 144.

16. Hanbury D. On the febrifuge properties of the olive

(*Olea europaea* L.). *Pharmaceutical Journal of Provincial Transactions* 1854: 353–354.
17. Juan, Wenzel, Ruiz-Gutierrez, Daniel, Planas. Olive fruit extracts inhibit proliferation and induce apoptosis in HT-29 human colon cancer cells. *J* 2006; 136(10): 2553–2557
18. Grieve M. *A Modern Herbal.* Ed. C.F. Leyel. Middlesex, England: Penguin, 1980.
19. Nisābūrī A. *Islamic Medical Wisdom: The Ṭibb al-a'immah.* Trans. B. Ispahany. Ed. AJ Newman. London: Muḥammadī Trust, 1991: 118.
20. Juven B et al. Studies on the mechanism of the antimicrobial action of oleuropein. *J. Appl. Bact.* 1972; 35: 559–67; Fleming HP, Walter WM, Etchells JL. Isolation of a bacterial inhibitor from green olives. *Appl Microbiol* 18; 856–60; 1969; Fleming HP, Walter WM, Etchells JL. Antimicrobial properties of oleuropein and products of its hydrolysis. *Appl Microbiol* 26(5); 777–82: 1973.
21. Hernández N et al. Applications of the ozonized oil in the treatment of ulcer in patients suffering from leprosy. http://www.pannomagico.it/eng/olioapp.htm.

Onion / *Baṣal*

Family: Alliaceae

Botanical Name: *Allium cepa*

Common Names: *English* Onion; *French* Oignon; *Spanish* Cebolla; *German* Zwiebel; *Urdu/Unānī* Piyaz, Basl; *Modern Standard Arabic* baṣal

Safety Rating: Generally Safe Although onion is generally considered safe in food quantities, excessive consumption may produce stomach irritation. Theoretically, since onion has some antiplatelet activity, it may increase the risk of bleeding, and should not be consumed in large quantities prior to surgery. For the same reason, concurrent use of warfarin medications should also be avoided.

Prophetic Prescription: Garlic and onion, known as *fūm* and *baṣal*, are mentioned in the Qur'ān in the context of the Exodus (2:61). When garlic and onions were mentioned to the Prophet, he said, "The strongest is garlic." When asked whether it should be forbidden, he responded: "Eat it. And he who eats it should not come near this mosque until its odor goes away."[1] It is reported that the Messenger of Allāh forbade the consumption of fresh garlic and onions prior to interacting with people in the public sphere. As he explained, "He who eats them (garlic and onions) should not come near our mosque. If it is necessary to eat them, make them dead by cooking, that is, onions and garlic."[2]

When Imām Ja'far al-Ṣādiq was asked about eating garlic and onion, he responded that "It is all right to eat them uncooked."[3] The Imām spoke highly of the medicinal benefits of onion in several traditions, saying, "Eat onion for it contains three benefits: it improves the taste, it strengthens the gums, it increases semen (*al-mā'*), as well as intercourse"; and "Onion removes fatigue (*naṣab*), strengthens the nerves, increases the steps (*khaṭā*), increases semen (*al-mā'*), and removes fever."[4] He also stated that "Onion gives good taste, strengthens the back, and clarifies the skin."[5] When the Imām was approached by a client requesting a sexual stimulant, he told him to "Take a white onion (*baṣal*), but it into small pieces, and fry it in olive oil. Then take an egg and break it into a bowl. Put some salt on it, add it to the onion, then fry it and eat it."[6]

The Prophet also advised that "If you go into any town, eat of its vegetables and onions, for they drive away the sickness special to that town. They also remove weariness, strengthen the nerves, increase sexual powers, and remove fever."[7] According to one tradition, Allāh's Messenger said, "Whoever eats wild leek before retiring to bed will be free from flatulence."[8] In a tradition related by Mu'āwiyyah, the Prophet offered food with onions to some delegates, and said, "He who eats not of seasoning or of what diffuses the odor of the earth, such a man will suffer harm from its waters, and will suffer injury."[9] According to 'A'ishah, a wife of the Prophet, Muḥammad's last meal contained onions.[10]

Issues in Identification: It is the consensus that *baṣal* is the Arabic term for onion. As Ghazanfar explains, onion is cultivated throughout Arabia.[11] Although onions have been consumed since the Bronze Age, most of the varieties we are familiar today have been developed in the last century. Even the oldest heirloom varieties like the Flat of Italy, the Jaune Paille des Vertus, and the Australian Brown only trace back to one to two hundred years.

Properties and Uses: Onion has resolvent, suppurative, expectorant, detersive, aphrodisiac, deobstruent, antidotary, diuretic, stimulant, rubefacient, and antiseptic properties. It is used internally for loss of appetite, to treat cough, fever, dropsy, catarrh, chronic bronchitis, cardiovascular diseases, and as an arterioscleoris prophylactic. Combined with equal amounts of mustard oil, onion is applied externally to treat rheumatic pains and other inflammatory swellings. Onions possess properties similar to garlic, but in lesser degrees. According to Ibn Buṭlān, white, watery, and juicy onions are diuretic and facilitate coitus.[12] They are said to be a diuretic, and an aphrodisiac, which generate milk and sperm. The onions we are familiar with in the West are all modern varieties. Even the oldest heirlooms date from the late 1700s to mid 1900s. The garlic, onions, and leeks the Prophet was familiar with differed from the ones we find in the supermarket today. According to ancient authorities like Camerario, leeks (*Allium porrum*) used to have a clearly distinct bulb, which is no longer the case.[13]

SCIENTIFIC STUDIES: *Wound Healing Activity* According to a study conducted by the Chinese University of Hong Kong, onion extract was found effective in scar prevention in Chinese patients having laser removal of tattoos.[14]

Memory Enhancing Activity In a study conducted at Hokkaido Tokai University in Japan, behavioral experiments showed that onion extract had a highly ameliorative effect on memory impairment as a result of its antioxidant effect.[15]

Anthelmintic Activity One study found that *A. cepa* oil has an anthelmintic effect in rats infected with *Trichinella spiralis*, as well as increasing the production of antibodies generated during the life cycle of this parasite.[16]

Antispasmodic Activity One study found that certain saponins found in onion possess antispasmodic activity, explaining the traditional use of onion in the treatment of disturbances of the gastrointestinal tract.[17]

Antithrombotic Activity One particular variety of onion, the Toyohira, was found to possess antithrombotic effects.[18]

Antidiabetic Activity Studies have shown that onion and garlic juices exert antioxidant and antihyperglycemic effects in diabetic rats, showing potential to alleviate liver and renal damage caused by diabetes.[19] Garlic and onion have been experimentally documented to possess antidiabetic properties.[20] One study showed that only garlic, and not onion or fenugreek, is able to significantly lower blood glucose levels in diabetic rats.[21]

Antimutagenic and Anticarcinogenic Activity According to Justus-Liebig-University in Germany, diallyl disulfide, an oil-soluble constituent of garlic, has been reported to cause antimutagentic and anticarcinogenic effects in vitro and in vivo. The study also mentions that white, red, and, particularly, yellow onions have been shown to possess antimutagenic properties.[22] Dietary supplementation with raw brown onions has been shown to have moderate lipid-modulating and immunostimulatory properties.[23] According to one study the alkenyl thiosulfates found in onion and garlic have an antitumor effect.[24]

Aphrodisiacal Activity In a recent study, it was determined that FRS 1000, a beverage containing flavanoids extracted from onion peel, showed unexpected improvement of male sexual function. An in vitro enzyme assay clearly showed that FRS 1000 has a strong phosphodiesterase 5A (PDE 5A) inhibitory activity, which is considered to be important for treatment of erectile dysfunction. Detailed assays of each major ingredient indicated that the antioxidative flavonoid quercetin was responsible for the activity.[25]

Onion Notes

1. Abū Dāwūd S. *Ṣaḥīḥ Sunan Abū Dāwūd.* Riyyāḍ: Maktab al-Tarbiyyah, 1989.

2. Abū Dāwūd S. *Ṣaḥīḥ Sunan Abū Dāwūd.* Riyyāḍ: Maktab al-Tarbiyyah, 1989.

3. Majlisī M. *Biḥār al-anwār.* Ṭihrān: Javad al-Alavi, 1956.

4. 'Amilī H. *Wasā'il al-shī'ah.* Bayrūt: al-Mu'assasah, 1993.

5. Majlisī M. *Biḥār al-anwār.* Ṭihrān: Javad al-Alavi, 1956.

6. Nisābūrī A. *Islamic Medical Wisdom: The Ṭibb al-a'immah.* Trans. B. Ispahany. Ed. AJ Newman. London: Muḥammadī Trust, 1991: 172.

7. Chaghhaynī M. *Ṭibb al-nabī.* Trans. C Elgood. *Osiris* 1962; 14: 191.

8. Ibn Ṭulūn S. *al-Manhal al-rawī fī al-ṭibb al-nabawī.* Ed. 'Azīz Bayk. Riyyāḍ: Dār 'ālam al-kutub, 1995.

9. Ibn Qayyim al-Jawziyyah M. *al-Ṭibb al-nabawī.* Bayrūt: Dār al-Kitāb, 1985.

10. Abū Dāwūd S. *Ṣaḥīḥ Sunan Abū Dāwūd*, Riyyāḍ: Maktab al-Tarbiyyah, 1989.

11. Ghazanfar SA. *Handbook of Arabian Medicinal Plants.* Boca Raton: CRC Press, 1994.

12. Ibn Buṭlān, *The Medieval Health Handbook: Tacuinum sanitatis.* Ed. L Cogliati Arano. Trans. O Ratti and A Westbrook. New York: George Braziller, 1976: 134.

13. Bianchini F, Corbetta F. *The Complete Book of Fruits and Vegetables.* New York: Crown, 1976: 86.

14. Ho, Ying, Chan, Chan. Use of onion extract, heparin, allantoin gel in prevention of scarring in Chinese patients having laser removal of tattoos: a prospective randomized controlled trial. *Dermatol* 2006; 32(7): 891–896.

15. Nishimura, Higuchi, Tateshita, Tomobe, Okuma, Nomura. Antioxidative activity and ameliorative effects of memory impairment of sulfur-containing compounds in *Allium* species. *Biofactors.* 2006; 26(2): 135–146.

16. Abū. Effect of *Nigella sativa* and *Allium cepa* oils on *Trichinella spiralis* in experimentally infected rats. *J* 2005; 35(2): 511–523.

17. Corea, Fattorusso, Lanzotti, Capasso, Izzo. Antispasmodic saponins from bulbs of red onion, *Allium cepa* L. var. *Tropea. J Agric Food Chem.* 2005; 53(4): 935–940.

18. Yamada, Naemura, Sawashita, Noguchi, Yamamoto. An onion variety has natural antithrombotic effect as assessed by thrombosis/thrombolysis models in rodents. *Thromb* 2004; 114(3): 213–220.

19. El-Demerdash, Yousef, El-Naga. Biochemical study on the hypoglycemic effects of onion and garlic in alloxan-induced diabetic rats. *Food* 2005; 43(1): 57–63.

20. Srinivasan. Plant foods in the management of diabetes mellitus: spices as beneficial antidiabetic food adjuncts. *Int* 2005; 56(6): 399–414.

21. Jelodar, Maleki, Motadayen, Sirus. [Effect of fenugreek, onion and garlic on blood glucose and histopathology of pancreas of alloxan-induced diabetic rats.] *Indian* 2005; 59(2): 64–69.

22. Shon, Choi, Kahng, Nam, Sung. Antimutagenic, an-

tioxidant and free radical scavenging activity of ethyl acetate extracts from white, yellow and red onions. *Food* 2004; 42(4): 659–666.

23. Ostrowska, Gabler, Sterling, Tatham, Jones, Eagling, Jois, Dunshea. Consumption of brown onions (*Allium cepa* var. *cavalier* and var. *destiny*) moderately modulates blood lipids, haematological and haemostatic variables in healthy pigs. *Br* 2004; 91(2): 211–218.

24. Chang, Yamato, Yamasaki, Ko, Maede. Growth inhibitory effect of alkenyl thiosulfates derived from onion and garlic in human immortalized and tumor cell lines. *Cancer* 2005; 223(1): 47–55.

25. Lines, Ono. FRS 1000, an extract of red onion peel, strongly inhibits phosphodiesterase 5A (PDE 5A). *Phytomedicine.* 2006; 13(4): 236–39.

Orange/*Naranj, Turunj, Utruj*

Family: Rutaceae

Botanical Name: *Citrus aurantium*

Common Names: *English* Bitter orange, Seville orange; *French* Orange amère; *Spanish* Naranjo amargo; Naranja amarga (fruit); *German* Bitterorange, Apfelsine, Pomeranze, Sevilla-Orange, Saure Orange; *Urdu/Unānī* Naranj; *Modern Standard Arabic* naranj, kubād

Safety Rating: Generally Safe Oranges are generally considered to be safe for most people.

Prophetic Prescription: It is reported that the Messenger of Allāh said, "Eat oranges, for they tighten the strings of the heart, and increase the brain."[1] According to one tradition, a companion of Imām Ja'far al-Ṣādiq ate bitter orange (*utruj*) with honey, and it gave him indigestion. As a result, the Imām recommended that he eat dry bread. He did so, and it relieved his indigestion.[2] On another occasion, it was mentioned that it was good to eat bitter orange (*utruj*) on an empty stomach. The Imām stated, "If you take it before you eat, it is good. However, if you take it after you eat, it is the best, it is the best, it is the best."[3] On the same note, the Imām asked one of his companions, "When do your medical doctors recommend you to eat bitter orange (*utruj*)?" The companion responded, "Before eating." The Imām said "No. I order you to take it after you eat."[4] In a similar tradition, Imām Ja'far al-Ṣādiq asked his companions, "Tell me what do your medical doctors recommend for bitter orange (*utruj*)?" They responded, "They order us to eat it before meals." He said, "There is nothing worst than eating it before meals, and there is nothing better than taking it after meals. Use its jam. It perfumes the inside just like musk."[5]

Issues in Identification: According to Dīnawarī, *al-utruj* and *al-turunj* are synonymous, and are the same as *mutq*. He explains that during his time, oranges were widely cultivated in villages throughout Arabia. He describes oranges as having flowers like *rayḥān*, a thin peel, and a fruity taste.[6] He says that *turunj* is a colloquial synonym for *utruj*.

The word "orange" derives from the Sanskrit *nārangaḥ* or "orange tree." The Sanskrit word was borrowed into European languages through the Persian *nārang*, Armenian *nārinj*, Arabic *naranj* (Spanish *naranja* and Portuguese *laranja*), Late Latin *arangia*, Italian *arancia* or *arancio*, and Old French *orenge*, in chronological order. The Spanish *naranja* is derived from the Arabic *naranj* while the Spanish *toronja* is derived from the Arabic *turunj*. If the Spanish meaning is any indication, *naranj* referred to orange while *turunj* referred to grapefruit in the Arabic spoken in al-Andalus. However, based on the description of *naranj* provided by Ibn al-Bayṭar, Said has identified the fruit as *Citrus aurantium*. The terms *naranj*, *turunj*, and *utruj* may all refer to this specific citrus fruit. In Unānī *ṭibb*, however, the term *turunj* applies to *Citrus medica*.

Citrus appears to have originated in Asia and was transported westward to the ancient cultures of Mesopotamia (4000 B.C.). From there, they spread to Turkey, Egypt, Greece, and North Africa. The Romans were acquainted with lemons, as well as sour oranges and citron. As a result of the disintegration of the Roman Empire, however, many citrus groves were abandoned and simply vanished. It was only with the spread of Islām into Europe that citrus was re-introduced into Sicily, where it was recorded as growing in the year 1002, and the Iberian Peninsula.[7] According to some scholars, citron, sour orange, lemon, and pomelo were brought to North Africa and Spain by 1150 C.E.[8] For Biggs, McVicar, and Flowerdew, "[t]he lemon reached Egypt and Palestine in the tenth century, and was cultivated in Genoa by the mid-fifteenth century."[9] According to some scholars, the bitter orange was brought back to Italy by the Crusaders.[10] For others, the introduction dates from before the 9th century. Citrus fruit may very well have been brought into Andalusia in 711 C.E.

According to botanists, the oranges grown in Islamic Europe were not the sweet oranges we know today, but bitter oranges, known as sour oranges or Seville oranges, after the city of Seville, which was the center of Arabic culture in the Iberian Peninsula. According to Biggs, McVicar, and

Flowerdew, the sweet orange was first seen in India in 1330, and was first planted in Versailles in 1421. Another, planted in Lisbon in 1548, became the "mother" of most European sweet orange trees and was still living in 1823.

According to most botanists, it was only in the 1500s that Portuguese traders introduced sweet oranges from India or China to Europe and spread them throughout the world. Some of these scholars assert that it was Vasco de Gama (1460 or 1469–1524) himself who brought the first sweet orange tree root to Portugal.[11] Since sweet oranges came from China via India and Portugal, this may explain why they are known to North Africans as *lisin* or *latshīn* (Chinese) and *burtuqāl* (Portuguese) and many languages have different words for bitter and sweet orange, such as the Persian *narang* and *porteghal*.

Although the sour orange of Persian provenance may have predominated in the Mediterranean until the 1500s, the sweet orange also clearly existed, since Dīnawarī (828–896) spoke of two varieties of *utruj*, the sweet (*ḥalū*) and the sour (*ḥāmiḍ*).[12] Overlooked by botanists until the present, this information requires writers to rectify their theories regarding the history and spread of citrus. Sweet oranges may have first been seen by Europeans in 1330; however, they clearly existed in the seventh century as the words of Dīnawarī demonstrate.

PROPERTIES AND USES: *Citrus aurantium*, known as bitter or Seville orange, is a bitter, aromatic, expectorant herb that has diuretic effects, lowers blood pressure, improves digestion, reduces inflammation, and controls bacterial and fungal infections. It is used internally for flatulent indigestion and diarrhea, stubborn coughs, colic in babies, and shock. Externally, it is used in aromatherapy to treat tension, depression, and skin problems.

Citrus bergamia, known as bergamot orange, is a bitter, aromatic herb that relieves tension, relaxes spasms, and improves digestion. Its seeds produce neroli oil, which is stimulant and reputedly aphrodisiac, as well as bergamot oil which is more sedative and healing. Internally, orange blossom water is used for colic in babies. It is used externally in douches and baths for vaginal infections, and in aromatherapy for stress-related complaints and skin conditions.

Citrus reticulata, known as mandarin orange, tangerine, and clementine, is a bitter, spicy, warming herb that stimulates digestion, lungs, and spleen. It acts mainly upon the liver, gall bladder, and breasts. It is an energy stimulant, affecting the liver and kidneys. It also relieves pain. It is used internally for indigestion, flatulence, vomiting, wet coughs, liver and gall bladder disorders, bronchial congestion, mastitis, breast cancer, and pain in the liver, chest or breasts. It is also used to treat lumbago and orchitis.

SCIENTIFIC STUDIES: *Weight-Loss Promoting Activity* According to a review of research conducted by John Hopkins University, the use of *Citrus aurantium* as a diet is promising. However, larger and more rigorous clinical trials are necessary before adequate conclusions can be drawn regarding its safety and efficacy in promoting weight loss.[13] The Surgeon General of Canada, however, has issued a warning against the consumption of synephrine, the main active compound in bitter orange, as it is structurally related to ephedrine, which has been restricted in Canada because of adverse cardiovascular and cerebrovascular reactions.[14] This decree, however, seems premature and reactionary, considering the fact that *Citrus aurantium* has been used safely in Chinese medicine for thousands of years.

Anticancer Activity According to a study conducted by Mazandaran University of Medical Sciences in Iran, citrus extract from *Citrus aurantium* appears to protect bone marrow cells and reduce genotoxicity.[15] *Citrus aurantium* also contains monoterprenes, such as d-limonene, which help to prevent liver tumors. Animal trials have shown that d-limonene stops the spread of cancer of the liver to the colon, and slows the growth of cancerous tumors originating in the liver.[16]

Cardiovascular Toxic Activity In a case study of a single patient reported by Mercer University in Atlanta, the use of *Citrus aurantium*–containing supplements may present as a risk for cardiovascular toxicity; however, additional studies/case reports are needed to validate this conclusion.[17]

Radioprotective Activity In a controlled animal trial conducted by Mazandaran University of Medical Sciences in Iran, the citrus extract of *C. aurantium* was shown to possess radioprotective properties, reducing the clastogenic effect of radiation on mice bone marrow.[18] Another study conducted by Kinki University in Osaka, Japan, demonstrated the antimutagenic activity of bitter orange.[19]

Orange Notes

1. Chaghhaynī M. *Ṭibb al-nabī*. Trans. C Elgood. *Osiris* 1962, 14: 190.
2. 'Amilī H. *Wasā'il al-shī'ah*. Bayrūt: al-Mu'assasah, 1993.
3. 'Amilī H. *Wasā'il al-shī'ah*. Bayrūt: al-Mu'assasah, 1993.
4. 'Amilī H. *Wasā'il al-shī'ah*. Bayrūt: al-Mu'assasah, 1993.
5. Ṭabarsī H. *Mustadrak al-Wasā'il*. Bayrūt: Mu'assasat Āl al-Bayt, 1987–1988.
6. Dīnawarī AH. *Kitāb al-nabāt/The Book of Plants*. Ed. Bernhard Lewin. Bayrūt: Dār al-Qalam, 1974: 217–18.

7. Biggs M, McVicar J, Flowerdew B. *Vegetables, Herbs, and Fruit: An Illustrated Encyclopedia*. Buffalo/Richmond Hill: Firefly Books, 2006: 482.
8. Scora RW. On the history and origin of citrus. *Bulletin of the Torrey Botanical Club* 1975; 102(6): 370.
9. Biggs M, McVicar J, Flowerdew B. *Vegetables, Herbs, and Fruit: An Illustrated Encyclopedia*. Buffalo/Richmond Hill: Firefly Books, 2006: 482.
10. Bianchini F, Corbetta F. *The Complete Book of Fruits and Vegetables*. New York: Crown, 1976: 182.
11. Bianchini F, Corbetta F. *The Complete Book of Fruits and Vegetables*. New York: Crown, 1976: 182.
12. Dīnawarī AH. *Kitāb al-nabāt/The Books of Plants*. Ed. Bernhard Lewin. Uppsala/Wiesbaden: A.-B. Lundequistska Bokhandeln and Otto Harrassowitz, 1953: 46.
13. Haaz, Fontaine, Cutter, Limdi, Perumean-Chaney, Allison. *Citrus aurantium* and synephrine alkaloids in the treatment of overweight and obesity: an update. *Obes* 2006; 7(1): 79–88.
14. Bitter orange: synephrine warning. *Canadian Forces Personnel Newsletter* Jan. 26, 2005; 1: 5.
15. Hosseinimehr, Karami. Citrus extract modulates genotoxicity induced by cyclophosphamide in mice bone marrow cells. *J* 2005; 57(4): 505–509.
16. Balch PA. *Prescription for Herbal Healing*. New York: Avery, 2002: 33.
17. Nykamp, Fackih, Compton. Possible association of acute lateral-wall myocardial infarction and bitter orange supplement. *Ann* 2004; 38(5): 812–816.
18. Hosseinimehr, Tavakoli, Pourheidari, Sobhani, Shafiee. Radioprotective effects of citrus extract against gamma-irradiation in mouse bone marrow cells. *J* 2003; 44(3): 237–241.
19. Miyazawa, Okuno, Fukuyama, Nakamura, Kosaka. Antimutagenic activity of polymethoxyflavonoids from *Citrus aurantium*. *J* 1999; 47(12): 5239–5244.

Palm Tree / *Nakhl*

Family: Arecaceae

Botanical Name: *Phoenix dactylifera*

Common Names: *English* Date Palm; palm pith, heart of palm; *French* Palmier; chou palmiste; *Spanish* Palmera datilera; palmito (pith); *German* Palme, Dattelpalme; *Urdu/Unānī* Khajoor Ka Paid, Darakht-e Khurma; *Modern Standard Arabic* nakhl, jummār, qalb al-nakhlah

Safety Rating: Generally Safe Heart of palm is generally considered to be safe for most people.

Prophetic Prescription: The palm tree is mentioned many times in the Qur'ān (50:10, 26:148, 2:266, 6:99, 6:141, 13:4, 26:11, 26:67, 27:91, 28:32, 19:23, 19:25, 20:71, 23:19, 26:148, 26:34, 50:10, 54:20, 55:11, 55:68, 69:7, 80:29). According to 'Abd Allāh ibn 'Umār, while the Messenger of Allāh was sitting with a group of believers, someone offered him some palm-marrow (*jummār*), and he commented, "Among trees, there is one that resembles a Muslim. It is an evergreen that does not shed its leaves."[1] He is also reported to have said, "Eat marrow, for it causes an increase of the brain."[2]

Issues in Identification: It is the consensus that *nakhl* refers to the palm tree and that *jummār*, also known as *qalb al-nakhlah* and *qalb al-nakhallāh*, is the pith of the palm tree.

Properties and Uses: Heart of palm, also known as palm heart, palmito or swamp cabbage, is a vegetable harvested from the inner core and growing bud of several species of palm trees, including the coconut (*Cocos nucifera*), Palmito Juçara (*Euterpe edulis*), Açaí palm (*Euterpe oleracea*), sabal (*Sabal* spp.) and pejibaye (*Bactris gasipaes*) palms. When the vegetable is taken from the inner core of wild palm trees, the tree must be killed to be harvested. This problem does not arise with domesticated palm trees, from which only the growing bud is removed. Because heart of palm is labor-intensive to harvest, it is quite costly. Heart of palm contains 25 percent protein, 15 percent vitamin C, 1 percent calcium, and 4 grams of protein. It is also a good source of protein and contains virtually no fat.

Scientific Studies: *Vitamin A* Many studies suggest that palm fruit and its derivatives provide plenty of opportunities to alleviate endemic vitamin A deficiency.[3] As part of their marketing campaign, palm oil producers attempt to present their product as natural and healthy. Most fail to address the fact that palm tree plantations are responsible for destroying the forests of Malaysia and Indonesia and putting the orangutan in peril.[4]

Cholesterol-Lowering Activity According to a World Health Organization report released in 2003, there is convincing evidence that palmitic oil consumption contributes to an increased risk of developing cardiovascular diseases.[5] An epidemiological study of Chinese in Hong Kong and Singapore suggest that the higher rate of cardiovascular mortality in Singapore may be the result of a higher consumption of coconut and palm oil.[6] The vast body of evidence, however, suggests that palm oil does indeed reduce cholesterol levels.[7]

Cardioprotective Activity According to an animal study conducted by the All India Institute of Medical Sciences, dietary palm olein oil protects rat heart from oxidative stress associated with ischemic-reperfusion injury.[8] According to another study conducted by the same institute, dietary palm oil causes augmentation of myocardial antioxidant enzymes and protects against isoproterenol-induced myocardial necrosis and associated oxidative stress.[9]

Multiple Activity According to a report released by Ohio State University Medical Center, the tocotrienol forms of natural vitamin E possess powerful hypocholesterolemic, anticancer and neuroprotective properties that are often not exhibited by tocopherols. Oral tocotrienol protects against stroke-associated brain damage in vivo.[10]

Anticancer Activity A large body of evidence has shown that palm oil is antimutagenic and anticarcinogenic,[11] suppressing colon cancer,[12] prostate cancer,[13] skin cancer,[14] and breast cancer.[15]

Palm Tree Notes

1. Bukhārī M. *Ṣaḥīḥ al-Bukhārī.* al-Riyyāḍ: Bayt al-Afkār, 1998; Muslim. *Jāmi' al-ṣaḥīḥ.* al-Riyyāḍ: Bayt al-Afkār, 1998.

2. Chaghhaynī M. *Ṭibb al-nabī.* Trans. C Elgood. *Osiris* 1962; 14: 190.

3. Solomons, Orozco. Alleviation of vitamin A deficiency with palm fruit and its products. *Asia* 2003; 12(3): 373–384; Benade. A place for palm fruit oil to eliminate vitamin A deficiency. *Asia* 2003; 12(3): 369–372; Radhika, Bhaskaram, Balakrishna, Ramalakshmi. Red palm oil supplementation: a feasible diet-based approach to improve the vitamin A status of pregnant women and their infants. *Food* 2003; 24(2): 208–217; van Stuijvenberg ME, Dhansay MA, Lombard CJ, Faber M, Benadé AJ. The effect of a biscuit with red palm oil as a source of beta-carotene on the vitamin A status of primary school children: a comparison with beta-carotene from a synthetic source in a randomised controlled trial. *Eur* 2001; 55(8): 657–662; van Stuijvenberg ME, Faber M, Dhansay MA, Lombard CJ, Vorster N, Benadé AJ. Red palm oil as a source of beta-carotene in a school biscuit used to address vitamin A deficiency in primary school children. *Int* 2000; 51 Suppl: S43–50.

4. Murdoch G. Palm oil puts squeeze on endangered Orangutan. *ENN* May 28, 2007. http://www.enn.com/anim.html?id=1821; Palm oil plantations decimating orang-utans says report Friends of the Earth release. *Mongobay* Sept. 23, 2005. http://news.mongabay. com/2005/0923-foe.html

5. World Health Organization. *Diet, Technical Report Series* 916. Geneva. 2003. pages 82, 88 &c.

6. Zhang, Kesteloot. Differences in all-cause, cardiovascular and cancer mortality between Hong Kong and Singapore: role of nutrition. *Eur* 2001; 17(5): 469–477.

7. Koh, C.S. 2006. Comments on draft document: diet, nutrition, and the prevention of chronic diseases. http://www.who.int/dietphysicalactivity/media/en/gsfao_cmo_068.pdf; Hornstra G. Effects of dietary lipids on some aspects of the cardiovascular risk profile. *Lipids and Health*. Ed. G Ziant. Brussels: European Commission on Lipids and Cancer, 1990; van Jaarsveld PJ, Smuts CM, Benadé AS. Effect of palm olein oil in a moderate-fat diet on plasma lipoprotein profile and aortic atherosclerosis in non–human primates. *Asia* 2002; 11 Suppl 7: S424–32; van Jaarsveld PJ, Benadé AJ. Effect of palm olein oil in a moderate-fat diet on low-density lipoprotein composition in non–human primates. *Asia* 2002; 11 Suppl 7: S416–23; Qureshi AA, Qureshi N, Wright JJ, Shen Z, Kramer G, Gapor A, Chong YH, DeWitt G, Ong A, Peterson DM, et al. Lowering of serum cholesterol in hypercholesterolemic humans by tocotrienols (palmvitee). *Am* 1991; 53(4 Suppl): 1021S-1026S; Ng TK, Hassan K, Lim JB, Lye MS, Ishak R. Nonhypercholesterolemic effects of a palm-oil diet in Malaysian volunteers. *Am* 1991; 53(4 Suppl): 1015S-1020S; Elson, Qureshi. Prostaglandins. Coupling the cholesterol- and tumor-suppressive actions of palm oil to the impact of its minor constituents on 3-hydroxy-3-methylglutaryl coenzyme A reductase activity. *Prostaglandins Leukot Essent Fatty Acids.* 1995; 52(2–3): 205–207.

8. Narang, Sood, Thomas, Dinda, Maulik. Effect of dietary palm olein oil on oxidative stress associated with ischemic-reperfusion injury in isolated rat heart. *BMC* 2004; 4(1): 29.

9. Narang, Sood, Thomas, Dinda, Maulik. Dietary palm olein oil augments cardiac antioxidant enzymes and protects against isoproterenol-induced myocardial necrosis in rats. *J* 2005; 57(11): 1445–1451.

10. Sen, Khanna, Roy. Tocotrienols in health and disease: The other half of the natural vitamin E family. *Mol* March 2007.

11. Azuine Antimutagenic and anticarcinogenic effects of carotenoids and dietary palm oil. *Nutr Cancer.* 1992; 17(3): 287–295; *Goh, Hew, Norhanom, Yadav*. Inhibition of tumor promotion by various palm-oil tocotrienols. Inhibition of tumor promotion by various palm-oil tocotrienols. *Int J Cancer.* 1994; 15; 57(4): 529–531.

12. Boateng, Verghese, Chawan, Shackelford, Walker, Khatiwada, Williams. Red palm oil suppresses the formation of azoxymethane (AOM) induced aberrant crypt foci (ACF) in Fisher 344 male rats. *Food* 2006; 44(10): 1667–1673;

13. Srivastava, Gupta. Tocotrienol-rich fraction of palm oil induces cell cycle arrest and apoptosis selectively in human prostate cancer cells. *Biochem* 2006; 346(2): 447–453.

14. Azuine, Goswami, Kayal, Bhide. Palm oil alleviates 12-O-tetradecanoyl-phorbol-13-acetate-induced tumor promotion response in murine skin. *Cancer* 2003; 192(2): 151–160.

15. Nesaretnam, Ambra, Selvaduray, Radhakrishnan, Canali, Virgili. Tocotrienol-rich fraction from palm oil and gene expression in human breast cancer cells. *Ann* 2004; 1031: 143–157; Nesaretnam, Radhakrishnan, Selvaduray, Reimann, Pailoor, Razak, Mahmood, Dahliwal. Effect of palm oil carotene on breast cancer tumorigenicity in nude mice. *Lipids.* 2002; 37(6): 557–560; McIntyre, Briski, Gapor, Sylvester. Antiproliferative and apoptotic effects of tocopherols and tocotrienols on preneoplastic and neoplastic mouse mammary epithelial cells. *Proc* 2000; 224(4): 292–301; Nesaretnam, Dorasamy, Darbre.Tocotrienols inhibit growth of ZR-75-1 breast cancer cells. *Int* 2000; 51 Suppl: S95–103; Nesaretnam, Stephen, Dils, Darbre. Tocotrienols inhibit the growth of human breast cancer cells irrespective of estrogen receptor status. *Lipids.* 1998; 33(5): 461–469; Guthrie, Gapor, Chambers, Carroll. Inhibition of proliferation of estrogen receptor-negative MDA-MB-435 and -positive MCF-7 human breast cancer cells by palm oil tocotrienols and tamoxifen, alone and in combination. *J* 1997; 127(3): 544S-548S; Nesaretnam, Guthrie, Chambers, Carroll. Effect of tocotrienols on the growth of a human breast cancer cell line in culture. *Lipids.* 1995; 30(12): 1139–1143.

Pear / *Kūmīthrā*

FAMILY: Rosaceae
BOTANICAL NAME: *Pyrus* spp.
COMMON NAMES: *English* Pear tree, pear;

French Poire; *Spanish* Pera; *German* Echter Birnbaum; *Urdu/Unānī* Nashpati, Kamussara; *Modern Standard Arabic* ijjāṣ, kūmīthrā, injāṣ

Safety Rating: Generally Safe Pears are generally considered to be safe for most people.

Prophetic Prescription: Imām 'Alī ibn Abī Ṭālib said, "Eat pears (*al-kamathrā*), for they burnish the heart."[1] Imām Ja'far al-Ṣādiq said to a man who complained to him of a pain he felt in his heart, "Eat pears."[2] He also said: "The pear purifies the heart, and it calms internal pains."[3] On another occasion, a man complained to the Imām about heart pain and pressure. He advised him to "Eat pear."[4] "Pear burnishes the stomach, and strengthens it. It is the same as quince. It is more beneficial to take it on a full stomach than on an empty one. He who is affected by disease (*ṭakhā'*) should eat it [after a meal]."[5]

Issues in Identification: In both classical and colloquial Arabic there is confusion between plums, pears, and apricots. Bīrūnī speaks of *ijjāṣ, injāṣ, kumtharā*, and *'ayn al-baqar*, all of which are identified by Said as *Prunus domestica*, including plum, pear, and apricot, the later referring to the pear tree, *Pyrus communis* L. If the Hebrew word *agass* is of any indication, then the Arabic word *ijjāṣ* may have meant pear originally, only to have been generalized to include plums at some later point. Among the ancient Greek writers, Cato (234–149 B.C.E.) mentioned six varieties of pear while Virgil (70–19 B.C.E.) spoke of three. By the time of Pliny (23–79 C.E.), there were close to forty varieties of pears.[6]

Properties and Uses: The fruit of *Pyrus communis*, the pear, is used primarily as a nutrient. Pears are used internally as a diuretic and, as a sauce, are equally effective as prunes to treat constipation. In Chinese medicine, the pear is considered a *yin* or calming fruit. Externally, they are used as an analgesic.

Scientific Studies: *Iron Absorption Enhancing Activity* According to a human trial of 234 women, the consumption of pear juice moderately enhanced the absorption of iron from a rice meal.[7]

Pear Notes

1. Nisābūrī A. *Islamic Medical Wisdom: The Ṭibb al-a'immah.* Trans. B. Ispahany. Ed. AJ Newman. London: Muḥammadī Trust, 1991: 179.
2. Nisābūrī A. *Islamic Medical Wisdom: The Ṭibb al-a'immah.* Trans. B. Ispahany. Ed. AJ Newman. London: Muḥammadī Trust, 1991: 179.
3. Majlisī M. *Biḥār al-anwār.* Ṭihrān: Javad al-Alavi, 1956.
4. Majlisī M. *Biḥār al-anwār.* Ṭihrān: Javad al-Alavi, 1956.
5. 'Amilī H. *Wasā'il al-shī'ah.* Bayrūt: al-Mu'assasah, 1993.
6. Bianchini F, Corbetta F. *The Complete Book of Fruits and Vegetables.* New York: Crown, 1976: 130.
7. Ballot, Baynes, Bothwell, Gillooly, MacFarlane, MacPhail, Lyons, Derman, Bezwoda, Torrance, et al. The effects of fruit juices and fruits on the absorption of iron from a rice meal. *Br* 1987; 57(3): 331–343.

Plums/*Ijjāṣ*

Family: Rosaceae

Botanical Name: *Prunus domestica*

Common Names: *English* Plum tree, plum; *German* Hauspflaume, Zwetschgenbaum; *French* Prunier, Prunier de Damas; *Spanish* Ciruelo; Ciruela, Pruna (fruit); *Urdu/Unānī* Alu Bukhara, Ijjas; *Modern Standard Arabic* barqūq, ijjāṣ

Safety Rating: Generally Safe Plums are generally considered to be safe for most people.

Prophetic Prescription: Imām Ja'far al-Ṣādiq recommended his followers to eat plums as "[t]hey are beneficial for bitterness and relax the joints."[1] In a longer version, he advises against eating too much plum as they may cause wind in one's joints.[2] A man complained to Imām Ja'far al-Ṣādiq of gall (*al-marār*) which inflamed in him until he was almost bent over. The Imām said to him, "Make it subside with plums (*al-ijāṣ*)."[3] The Imām also said, "Plums on an empty stomach calm the bile but stir up the wind."[4] The Imāms from the Household of the Prophet also said to "Eat mellowed (*al-'atīq*) plums, for the benefit of mellowed plums remain and the harm is removed. Eat them peeled, for they are beneficial for every [kind of] gall and heat, and the blaze stirred up from it."[5]

Issues in Identification: In both classical and colloquial Arabic there is confusion between plums, pears, and apricots. The same occurs in European languages where the word for "plum" has a long history of ill-defined use. As Davidson explains, "In the Middle Ages it seems to have meant virtually any dried fruit."[6]

According to Muḥsin 'Aqīl, *ijjāṣ* is known as *barqūq* in Egypt, and as *ijjāṣ, injāṣ*, and *anjāṣ* in Syria. The *Encyclopedia of Fruits and Nuts* also asserts that *Prunus domestica* is known as *barqūq* in Arabic.[7] In the Maghrib, *ijjāṣ* refers to pear.[8] According to Batool Ispahany, the term *ijjāṣ* is Arabic for plum.

The Arabic *ijjāṣ* may have referred originally to pear, only to have been generalized to include plum or *barqūq* at some later point. For most Arabs, the most precise word for plum in Arabic is *barqūq* which derives from the Latin *praecox*, which means "precocious." Although it means plum at the present, it originally referred to apricot; hence, we have the Spanish *albaricoque* or apricot, which evolved from the Arabic *al-barqūq*. Apricot fruit is now known by Arabs as *mishmish*.

The plums that were prevalent during the time of the Prophet and the Imāms was the Damson plum or *Prunus domestica* ssp. *insititia*, a blue-skinned, rather acid variety with a tart flavor; it was ideal for making preserves and jams, and was often dried.

Properties and Uses: *Prunus domestica* or plums are considered nutritive, antibilious, refrigerant, demulcent, cooling, laxative, and digestive. They are typically eaten dried, soaked, and cooked, preserved in brandy or vinegar, and in sauces or stews, especially in Arab dishes, as well as in stuffing, desserts, and cakes. Internally, prunes are used for constipation, and are often added to laxative preparations. The laxative effect of prunes is the result of various compounds present in the fruits, such as dietary, sorbitol, and isatin. Prunes and prune juice are often used to help regulate the functioning of the digestive.

Scientific Studies: *Hypoglycemic Activity* In a two-month controlled animal trial conducted by the Indian Institute of Technology, *Prunus dulcis* seeds showed a definite hypoglycemic effect. The active factor appeared to be a non oil fraction which is only partly soluble in ethyl ether.[9]

Aphrodisiacal Activity According to a 3-month animal trial conducted by King Saud University in Saudi Arabia, *Prunus dulcis* showed no toxicity while the extract significantly increased sperm motility and sperm contents in epididymides without producing any spermatotoxic effect.[10]

Plums Notes

1. Nisābūrī A. *Islamic Medical Wisdom: The Ṭibb al-a'immah*. Trans. B. Ispahany. Ed. AJ Newman. London: Muḥammadī Trust, 1991: 181.
2. Ṭabarsī H. *Mustadrak al-Wasā'il*. Bayrūt: Mu'assasat Āl al-Bayt, 1987–1988.
3. Nisābūrī A. *Islamic Medical Wisdom: The Ṭibb al-a'immah*. Trans. B. Ispahany. Ed. AJ Newman. London: Muḥammadī Trust, 1991: 181.
4. Nisābūrī A. *Islamic Medical Wisdom: The Ṭibb al-a'immah*. Trans. B. Ispahany. Ed. AJ Newman. London: Muḥammadī Trust, 1991: 181; Ṭabarsī H. *Mustadrak al-Wasā'il*. Bayrūt: Mu'assasat Āl al-Bayt, 1987–1988.
5. Nisābūrī A. *Islamic Medical Wisdom: The Ṭibb al-a'immah*. Trans. B. Ispahany. Ed. AJ Newman. London: Muḥammadī Trust, 1991: 181.
6. Davidson A. *The Oxford Companion to Food*. Oxford: Oxford University Press, 1999.
7. Janick J. Paull RE. *The Encyclopedia of Fruits and Nuts*. Wallingford, UK: CABI, 2008: 695.
8. 'Aqīl M. *Ṭibb al-Imām al-Ṣādiq*. Bayrūt: Mu'assasat al-A'lamī, 199.
9. Teotia S, Singh M. Hypoglycemic effect of *Prunus amygdalus* seeds in albino rabbits. *Indian J Exp Biol*. 1997; 35(3): 295–6.
10. Qureshi, Shah, Tariq, Ageel. Studies on herbal aphrodisiacs used in Arab system of medicine. *Am* 1989; 17(1–2): 57–63.

Pomegranate / *Rummān*

Family: Punicaceae

Botanical Name: *Punica granatum*

Common Names: *English* Pomegranate, Carthagian apple; *French* Grenadier; Grenade (fruit); *Spanish* Granado; granada (fruit); *German* Echter Granatbaum, Granatapfelbaum; granatapfel; *Urdu/Unānī* Anar, Rumman; *Modern Standard Arabic* rummān

Safety Rating: Generally Safe to Dangerous Pomegranate fruit and juice are generally considered to be safe for most people. Some people, though, are allergic to pomegranate. This is particularly the case with people who suffer from plant allergies. Pomegranate juice seems safe for women who are pregnant or lactating. However, pomegranate extract should be avoided by such women. Pomegranate should not be consumed in medicinal doses by patients suffering from low blood pressure nor should it be consumed by women who are pregnant or breastfeeding. Pomegranate should not be consumed for two weeks prior to surgery. In large doses, pomegranate juice is emetic, nauseant, and vertigogenic. Stronger doses of over 80 g may cause chills, collapse, dizziness, hematemesis, visual disturbances, and death. Externally, when applied to the skin, pomegranate juice may cause itching, swelling, runny nose, and breathing difficulties. Pomegranate rind, however, is a potential carcinogenic substance. The bark of the root can be poisonous is taken in excess.

Prophetic Prescription: According to the Qur'ān, the pomegranate is one of the fruits of Paradise (6:99, 6:141, 55:68). As Almighty Allāh says, "Therein fruits, and palm trees, and pomegranates" (55:68). The Messenger of Allāh is reported to have said, "The palm tree and the pomegranate were created with what was left over from the dust of Adam."[1] According to the Prophet, "There is not a pomegranate (*rummān*) which is not cross-fertilized by a seed of a pomegranate from paradise."[2] He also said, "No pomegranate (*rummān*) grows ripe without being watered by a drop of the water of the Garden" and that "No pomegranate (*rummān*) seed enters into any one of you but that it enlivens the heart, and cleanses you from the Devil and from evil aspirations for forty days."[3] The Messenger of Allāh also said, "Pomegranate (*rummān*) and sumac (*summāq*) are effective in cases of bilious diseases"[4] and that "Pomegranate (*rummān*) and its rind strengthens digestion."[5] He is also reported to have said, "No one eats pomegranates without causing the Devil forty days of sickness" and "He who eats a pomegranate and finishes it, verily Allāh will enlighten his heart for forty days."[6] Imām 'Alī spoke highly of the benefits, both spiritual and medicinal, of the pomegranate:

> Eat pomegranate (*rummān*) with its pulp for it is good for the abdomen. Every grain of it which settles in the abdomen is life for the heart and illumination for the soul, and the temptations of Satan are quelled for forty mornings. The pomegranate (*rummān*) is among the fruits of Paradise. Allāh, the Mighty and Exalted, has said, "Therein are fruits, and palm trees, and pomegranates" [55:68].[7]

The Imām also stated that "Whoever eats pomegranates (*rummān*) has the light of Allāh in his heart."[8] He also said that the pomegranate was the best of fruit, satisfying hunger and helping digestion.

Imām Ja'far al-Ṣādiq said, "Feed your children pomegranates (*rummān*) for it speeds up their growth."[9] When sweet pomegranate was mentioned in his presence, he said, "The bitter one is the best for the belly."[10] The Imām recommended his followers to "Eat pomegranate with its pulp for it burnishes the stomach and it increases the intellect."[11] In a similar tradition, he said, "Eat bitter pomegranate with its flesh for it burnishes the stomach."[12] He also assured his followers that "[w]hoever eats pomegranate (*rummān*) before sleeping is secure until morning."[13] When one of his followers complained of indigestion due to overeating, the Imām said, "Take this sweet pomegranate (*rummān*) and eat it with its pulp, for it burnishes the stomach, cures indigestion, digests your food, and swims in your inside."[14]

According to Imām Ḥasan al-'Askarī, "Every pomegranate (*rummān*) is a sweet pomegranate, for it calms the blood and purifies it in the chest."[15] According to Imām Mūsā al-Kāẓim, a person who eats one pomegranate first thing on Friday morning, his heart will remain enlightened for forty days, if he eats two, it will remained enlightened for 80 days and so on.

Issues in Identification: It is the consensus that *rummān* is Arabic for pomegranate. According to Bīrūnī, *maẓẓ*, also known as *rummān al-barr*, is wild pomegranate. As Nehmé explains, *Punica* is *rummān*, and *Punica granatum* is *rummān shā'ī*.[16] As Ghazanfar explains, *Punica granatum* is indigenous to Asia. It is cultivated in southern Arabia and parts of the mountainous areas of northern Oman.[17] In all likelihood, the pomegranates consumed by the Prophet were of Egyptian provenance, probably from Hulwan.[18]

Properties and Uses: *Punica granatum* is considered a bittersweet astringent, refrigerant, styptic, stomachic, antidiarrheal, anthelmintic, antiviral, demulcent, and febrifugal herb. Internally, *P. granatum* is used for diarrhea, both common and chronic, amebic dysentery, intestinal worms, digestive disorders, kidney and gall bladders stones and fever. For tapeworm, a tea is made from the bark, taken at one hour intervals on an empty stomach. The rind is also astringent in diarrhea, leucorrhea, hemorrhage, cancer and ulcers of the uterus and rectum, as well as intermittent fever. In India, the rind is used to treat diarrhea and chronic dysentery, and is often combined with opium. The pomegranate's astringent properties make it effective in cases of diarrhea and dysentery. The leaves and flowers are styptic, and tonic. Large doses cause vomiting, purging, cramps, numbness in legs, giddiness, dim vision, and increased urine. The rind is also used for tanning, and dying. The fruit is used as cooling article of food.

Externally, *P. granatum* is used for anal itching, vaginal discharge, mouth sores, and throat infections. The roasted and powdered skin of the pomegranate fruit, combined with a little vegetable oil, is considered highly beneficial in the treatment of anal itching. Powder of the dry rind mixed with pepper and common salt is applied as a very good dentifrice. Its regular application strengthens the gums, stops bleeding, prevents pyorrhea, cleans the teeth and preserves them for a long time. Ibn Buṭlān stated that sour pomegranates are good for an inflamed liver.[19] *Jullinār* or pomegranate flower was used by al-Kindī in a poultice for the liver and the stomach, to relieve pain of the spleen and to strengthen it.[20]

Scientific Studies: *Antihelminthic Activity* The bark is highly effective as a vermifuge and may be used fresh or dried. *Punica granatum* is effective in destroying intestinal parasites because it contains unusual alkaloids, known as pelletierines, which paralyze tapeworms so that they are easily expelled in conjunction with a laxative. The root-bark is preferred to the stem-bark as it contains greater quantities of punicine, an alkaloid that is highly toxic to tapeworms. A decoction of the bark is used for expelling tapeworm.

Antimicrobial Activity According to one study, pomegranate possesses antimicrobial activity.[21]

Anti-Diarrheal Activity According to an in vitro study, pomegranate acts against some causes of diarrhea, including certain fungi, viruses, and intestinal worms.[22]

Cancer-Causing Activity Some studies suggest that pomegranate seeds and peels increase the risk of certain cancers because the dried peel contains high amounts of aflatoxin B-1, a known carcinogen.[23] Scientists have discovered that women in Northern Iran have the highest rate of esophageal cancer in the world, possibly due to their consumption of *majur* or *majoweh* during pregnancy.[24] The combination of pomegranate seeds, black pepper, dried raisins, and sometimes garlic, seems to be so harsh that it injures the esophagus, leading to cancer. Other factors may include eating foods at higher-than-normal temperatures, preserving food by sun-drying, and eating few fruits and vegetables.[25]

Pomegranate Notes

1. Chaghhaynī M. *Ṭibb al-nabī.* Trans. C Elgood. *Osiris* 1962; 14: 189.
2. Iṣbahānī AN al-. *Mawsū'at al-ṭibb al-nabawī.* Ed. MKD al-Turkī. Bayrūt: Dār Ibn Ḥazm, 2006.
3. Sūyūṭī J. *As-Sūyūṭī's Medicine of the Prophet.* Ed. A Thomson. London: Ṭā-Hā Publishers, 1994: 63; Chaghhaynī M. *Ṭibb al-nabī.* Trans. C Elgood. *Osiris* 1962; 14: 190; Chishti SHM. *The Book of Sufi Healing.* Rochester, Vermont: Inner Traditions International, 1991: 62.
4. Ibn Qayyim al-Jawziyyah M. *al-Ṭibb al-nabawī.* Bayrūt: Dār al-Kitāb, 1985.
5. Ibn Qayyim al-Jawziyyah M. *al-Ṭibb al-nabawī.* Bayrūt: Dār al-Kitāb, 1985.
6. Chaghhaynī M. *Ṭibb al-nabī.* Trans. C Elgood. *Osiris* 1962; 14: 190.
7. Nisābūrī A. *Islamic Medical Wisdom: The Ṭibb al-a'immah.* Trans. B. Ispahany. Ed. AJ Newman. London: Muḥammadī Trust, 1991: 178.
8. Sūyūṭī J. *As-Sūyūṭī's Medicine of the Prophet.* Ed. A. Thomson. London: Ṭā-Hā Publishers, 1994: 63.
9. Majlisī M. *Biḥār al-anwār.* Ṭihrān: Javad al-Alavi, 1956.
10. 'Amilī H. *Wasā'il al-shī'ah.* Bayrūt: al-Mu'assasah, 1993.
11. Majlisī M. *Biḥār al-anwār.* Ṭihrān: Javad al-Alavi, 1956; 'Amilī H. *Wasā'il al-shī'ah.* Bayrūt: al-Mu'assasah, 1993.
12. 'Amilī H. *Wasā'il al-shī'ah.* Bayrūt: al-Mu'assasah, 1993.
13. Nisābūrī A. *Islamic Medical Wisdom: The Ṭibb al-a'immah.* Trans. B. Ispahany. Ed. AJ Newman. London: Muḥammadī Trust, 1991: 178; 'Amilī H. *Wasā'il al-shī'ah.* Bayrūt: al-Mu'assasah, 1993.
14. Nisābūrī A. *Islamic Medical Wisdom: The Ṭibb al-a'immah.* Trans. B. Ispahany. Ed. AJ Newman. London: Muḥammadī Trust, 1991: 178; 'Amilī H. *Wasā'il al-shī'ah.* Bayrūt: l-Mu'assasah, 1993.
15. Nisābūrī A. *Islamic Medical Wisdom: The Ṭibb al-a'immah.* Trans. B. Ispahany. Ed. AJ Newman. London: Muḥammadī Trust, 1991: 69.
16. Nehmé M. *Dictionnaire étymologique de la flore du Liban.* Bayrūt: Librairie du Liban, 2000.
17. Ghazanfar SA. *Handbook of Arabian Medicinal Plants.* Boca Raton: CRC Press, 1994.
18. Tannahill R. *Food in History.* New York: Stein and Day, 1973: 126.
19. Ibn Buṭlān. *The Medieval Health Handbook: Tacuinum sanitatis.* Ed. L Cogliati Arano. Trans. O Ratti and A Westbrook. New York: George Braziller, 1976: 165.
20. Levey M, al-Khaledy N, eds. *The Medical Formulary of al-Samarqandī.* Philadelphia: University of Pennsylvania Press, 1967: 185, note 108.
21. Navarro V, et al. Anti-microbial evaluation of some plants used in Mexican traditional medicine for the treatment of infectious diseases. *Journal of Ethnopharmacology* 1996; 53: 143–147.
22. Segura JJ, et al. Growth inhibition of *Entamoeba histolytica* and *E. invadens* produced by pomegranate root. *Archivos de investigación médica* 1990; 21: 235–239.
23. Selim MI, et al. Aflatoxin B-1 in common Egyptian foods. *Journal of AOAC International* 1996; 79: 1124–1129.
24. Ghadirian P. Food habits of the people of the Caspian littoral of Iran in relation to esophageal cancer. *Nutrition and Cancer* 1987; 9: 147–157.
25. Fetrow CW, Avila JR. *The Complete Guide to Herbal Medicines.* Springhouse: Springhouse Corporation, 2000.

Pseudo-Saffron / *Waras*

FAMILY: Fabaceae

BOTANICAL NAME: *Flemingia grahamiana*

COMMON NAMES: *English* Bastard saffron; *French* No common name; *Spanish* Flemingia; *German* No common name; *Urdu/Unānī* Waras, Ikhwan-u Zafran, Kurkuma, Khus; *Modern Standard Arabic* waras

SAFETY RATING: UNKNOWN *Flemingia* is generally considered to be safe when used as a dye. Internally, the safety of the plant has not been established.

PROPHETIC PRESCRIPTION: The Messenger of Allāh said, "Do not press the throats of your children when you have costus (*qusṭ*) and pseudo-saffron (*waras*)."[1] According to Tirmidhī, "The Prophet, may Allāh bless him and grant him peace, used to recommend olive oil and pseudo-saffron (*waras*) as a remedy for pleurisy."[2] During the time of the Prophet, women would douche themselves with pseudo-saffron for forty days after giving birth.[3] They would also wash their faces with pseudo-saffron to remove spots from their faces. According to Ibn Ṭūlūn and Abū Nu'aym al-Iṣbahānī, when the head of Imām al-Ḥusayn was brought to Yazīd, it was covered in pseudo-saffron (*wasmah*).

ISSUES IN IDENTIFICATION: Elgood identifies *waras* as pseudo-saffron.[4] According to Said, *waras*, which is also known as *ghumr*, *bādirah*, *huss*, and *gindīr*, is produced from the roots of

Ceylon cornel tree (*Memeceylon tinctorium*), a tree indigenous to Yemen. Its roots are of two kinds: a deep red which is the most desired *al-bādirah*, and the inferior with white color combined with the red. Johnstone and Turkī equally identify *waras* as *Memecyclon tinctorium.*[5] According to Akīlī *waras* and *qinbīl* refers to mallotus obtained from the coating from the seed pods of the *Kamala* tree or *Mallotus philippinensis.*[6] Álvarez de Morales and Girón Irueste identity *waras* as curcuma, although this seems unlikely.[7]

Dīnawarī, however, says that *waras* is very yellow, that it stains clothing, that it is used as a dye, and that it is known as *mūris.*[8] He also explains that a cultivated plant, not a wild one, grows a lot in Yemen, and resembles *simsim.*[9] For Farooqi, *warus* is the name of a yellow dye obtained from the pods of *Flemingia grahamiana.* According to *King's American Dispensatory* from 1898, *waras, wurras,* and *warras,* though properly referring to saffron, has been applied to *kamala,* but more especially to a certain powder, the botanical source of which is not definitely known, though thought to come from *Flemingia grahamiana.*[10] However, in 1887, David Hooper had identified *waras* as *Flemingia grahamiana* on the basis of field work in southern India.[11]

PROPERTIES AND USES: The leaves and flowers of *Flemingia strobilifera* are used to treat tuberculosis. A decoction of flowers is used as a post-partum bath. It is used in Arabia to treat chills and coughs and is considered a vermifuge. Its roots are used in African medicine for male impotence and to lower fever. It is found in the Middle East, Yemen, Africa, and Asia.

SCIENTIFIC STUDIES: *Anthelmintic Activity* According to studies conducted by North Eastern Hill University in India, the crude root-peel extract of *Flemingia vestita* is highly effective against *Fasciolopsis buski*, the giant intestinal trematode.[12] In other studies study conducted by the same institution, the root-tuber peel of *F. vestita* was equally efficient in treating the cestode *Raillietina echinobothrida.*[13] In another study conducted by the same university, the root-tuber-peel extract of *F. vestita* was shown to be effective against a host of helminth parasites.[14]

Pseudo-Saffron Notes

1. Ḥākim al-Nīsābūrī M. *al-Mustadrak 'alā al-ṣaḥīḥayn.* N.p.: n.p., n.d.; Iṣbahānī AN al-. *Mawsū'at al-ṭibb al-nabawī.* Ed. MKD al-Turkī. Bayrūt: Dār Ibn Ḥazm, 2006.

2. Sūyūṭī J. *As-Sūyūṭī's Medicine of the Prophet.* Ed. A Thomson. London: Ṭā-Hā Publishers, 1994: 109.

3. Tirmidhī M. *al-Jāmi' al-ṣaḥīḥ.* al-Qāhirah: Muṣṭafā al-Bābī al-Ḥalabī, [1937-]; Bayhaqī A. *al-Sunan al-kubrā.* Bayrūt: Dār Ṣadīr, 1968; Ibn Mājah M. *Sunan.* Trans. MT Anṣārī. Lahore: Kazi Publications, 1994; Ibn Ḥanbal A. *Musnad al-Imām Aḥmad ibn Ḥanbal.* Bayrūt: al-Maktabah al-Islāmiyyah, 1969.

4. Elgood C. Trans. *Ṭibb al-nabī or Medicine of the Prophet.* Sūyūṭī J, M Chaghhaynī. *Osiris* 1962: 14.

5. Johnstone P, trans. *Medicine of the Prophet.* Ibn Qayyim al-Jawziyyah. Cambridge: The Islamic Texts Society, 1998.

6. Ibn al-Qayyim al-Jawziyyah. *Natural Healing with the Medicine of the Prophet.* Pearl Publishing. Trans. M al-Akīlī. Philadelphia, 1993.

7. Ibn Ḥabīb A. *Mujtaṣar fī al-ṭibb/Compendio de medicina.* Ed. C Álvarez de Morales and F Girón Irueste. Madrid: Consejo Superior de Investigaciones Científicas, 1992.

8. Dīnawarī AH. *Kitāb al-nabāt: Le dictionaire botanique d'Abū Ḥanīfa al-Dīnawarī.* al-Qāhirah: Institut Français d'Archéologie Orientale du Caire, 1973.

9. Dīnawarī AH. *Kitāb al-nabāt/The Book of Plants.* Ed. Bernhard Lewin. Bayrūt: Dār al-Qalam, 1974: 165.

10. Felter HW. Lloyd JU. *King's American Dispensatory.* 1898. http://www.henriettes herbal.com/eclectic/kings/mallotus-phil.html#rel-sp

11. Cooper D. Waras: its composition and relation to *Kamala. The Pharmaceutical Journal and Transactions* 1887: 213–215.

12. Kar, Tandon, Saha. Anthelmintic efficacy of genistein, the active principle of *Flemingia vestita* (*Fabaceae*): alterations in the free amino acid pool and ammonia levels in the fluke, *Fasciolopsis buski. Parasitol* 2004; 53(4): 287–291; Kar, Tandon, Saha. Anthelmintic efficacy of *Flemingia vestita*: genistein-induced effect on the activity of nitric oxide synthase and nitric oxide in the trematode parasite, *Fasciolopsis buski. Parasitol* 2002; 51(3): 249–257.

13. Das, Tandon, Saha. Anthelmintic efficacy of *Flemingia vestita* (*Fabaceae*): alterations in glucose metabolism of the cestode, *Raillietina echinobothrida. Parasitol* 2004; 53(4): 345–350; Das, Tandon, Saha. Anthelmintic efficacy of *Flemingia vestita* (*Fabaceae*): alteration in the activities of some glycolytic enzymes in the cestode, *Raillietina echinobothrida. Parasitol* 2004; 93(4): 253–261.

14. Tandon, Pal, Roy, Rao, Reddy. In vitro anthelmintic activity of root-tuber extract of *Flemingia vestita*, an indigenous plant in Shillong, India. *Parasitol* 1997; 83(5): 492–498.

Purslane/ *Baqalah al-Ḥamqā'*

FAMILY: Portulacaceae

BOTANICAL NAME: *Portulaca oleracea*

COMMON NAMES: *English* Purslane, Garden purslane, Common purslane; *French* Pourpier, Pourpier potager, Pourcellaine; *Spanish* Verdolaga; *German* Gartenportulak, Sommer-Portulak, Gewürz-Portulak, Gemüse-Portulak, Sommer-Postelein, Burzelkraut, Bürzelkraut, Bürzelkohl, Kreusel, Sauburtzel, Portulak; *Urdu/Unānī* Khurfa, Khulfa, Rajlah, Rijla; *Modern Standard Arabic* ḥurfah, rijlah

SAFETY RATING: GENERALLY SAFE Although

purslane is generally considered to be safe for most people even in high doses, individuals with a history of kidney stones should use it with caution as it can increase kidney filtration, urine production, and possibly cause a stone to move. Purslane injections have been found to induce powerful contractions of the uterus while oral use is said to weaken them. In any event, purslane should be avoided during pregnancy.

ISSUES IN IDENTIFICATION: *Portulaca oleracea* originates from India where it has been eaten for thousands of years. It is also found in the Middle East where it is a cultivated plant. As Chaudhary explains, *Portulaca oleracea* is known as *rijlah* and *baqlah* in Saudi Arabia. It is grown as a pot-herb and is a serious weed of cultivated areas.[1]

PROPHETIC PRESCRIPTION: It is related that the Prophet had an ulcer on his leg. He passed by some purslane, applied it to his leg, and exclaimed, "Praise be to Allāh for you, O purslane (*baqalah al-ḥamqā'*), wherever you may be!"[2] In another tradition, the Prophet said, "Purslane (*al-rijlah*) is a cure against ninety diseases, the first of which is headache."[3]

ISSUES IN IDENTIFICATION: According to Hans Wehr, *baqala* is an Arabic verb meaning "to sprout" in the context of a plant. The dictionary identifies *al-baqalah al-ḥamqā'* as purslane. Elgood and Turkī also identify it as purslane.[4] Nehmé explains that *Portulaca* is *farfaḥīn* and *rijlah*, and *Portulaca oleracea* is *farfaḥīn baqlī*, as well as *baqlah*.[5] As Álvarez de Morales and Girón Irueste explain, *baqlah* refers to *Portulaca oleracea* L.[6] According to Bīrūnī, the plant is also known as *farfakh* and Said says that it refers to *Portuluca obracea* L. Sūyūṭī says that it is also known as *rajlah*, *farfakh*, or *farfakhīn*.[7] Ibn Ṭūlūn says that it is known as *al-rijlah al-farfaj*.[8]

According to Ghazanfar, *Portulaca oleracea* is found in Arabian cities and as a weed of cultivated areas and farmlands.[9] According to Mandaville, *Portulaca oleracea* is common in eastern Arabia where it is a weed of gardens and walk edges. It is known as *barbīr*. The entire plant is edible, either raw or cooked. When sold as a salad vegetable, it is known by various names, including *baql*. According to Ghazanfar, *Portulaca oleracea* is known as *al-khaleqah* and *farfena*. It is also known as *ḥumḍeh* in Saudi, Omani, and Dhofari Arabic.[10]

PROPERTIES AND USES: *Portucula oloracea*, known commonly as purslane, is a sour, diuretic, cooling herb that lowers fever and clears toxins. It is considered demulcent, refrigerant, slightly astringent, sedative, emollient, alterative, and antibacterial. It is also regarded as a purgative, cardiotonic, muscle relaxant, and anti-inflammatory.

Internally, it is used for dysentery, acute enteritis, appendicitis, mastitis, hemorrhoids, urinary discharge, diarrhea, dysentery, piles, and postpartum bleeding. It is used for headaches, stomach, intestinal and liver ailments, cough, asthma, shortness of breath and arthritis. It is not given to pregnant women or to patients with digestive disorders. Externally, it is applied to boils, burns, psoriasis, snakebites, bee stings, and eczema.

SCIENTIFIC STUDIES: *Antioxidative Activity* Purslane has been recently identified as an excellent source of alpha-linolenic acid.[11] Alpha-linolenic is an omega-3 fatty acid, also found in fish oil. This crucial content in purslane plays an important role in human growth, development and preventing diseases. Since this fatty acid cannot be synthesized by humans it has to be ingested. Purslane leaves contain omega-3 fatty acids which regulate the body's metabolic activities. Purslane is known to have one of the highest known concentrations of omega-3 fatty acids in any plant. It is also an excellent source of vitamins A, C and E, and essential amino acids. Reports describe purslane as a "power food of the future" because of its high nutritive and antioxidant properties. Purslane is richer than spinach in many nutrients, containing ten times more alpha-linolenic acid and six times the vitamin E. According to the Center for Genetics, Nutrition and Health, in Washington, D.C., one hundred grams of fresh purslane leaves contains about 300–400 mg of 18:3w3; 12.2 mg of alpha-tocopherol; 26.6 mg of ascorbic acid; 1.9 mg of beta-carotene; and 14.8 mg of glutathione.[12]

Antidiabetic Activity According to a study conducted by the University of Victoria in Canada, *Portulaca oleracea* has sufficient scientific evidence in its favor to support its traditional use for urinary problems and high cholesterol.[13]

Broncho-Dilatory Activity According to a study conducted by Mashhad University of Medical Sciences in Iran, *P. oleracea* has a relatively potent but transient bronchodilatory effect on asthmatic airways.[14]

Analgesic and Anti-inflammatory Activity In a study conducted by Zayed Complex for Herbal Research and Traditional Medicine, in the United Arab Emirates, 10 percent ethanolic extract of the aerial parts of purslane showed significant anti-inflammatory and analgesic properties after intraperitoneal and topical but not oral administration when compared with the synthetic drug diclofenac sodium as the active control. Results indicate this cultivar species of *Portulaca* also possesses some of the claimed traditional uses of the wild species in the relief of pain and inflammation.[15]

Purslane Notes

1. Chaudhary SA. *Flora of the Kingdom of Saudi Arabia.* al-Riyyāḍ: Ministry of Agriculture and Water, 1999.
2. Sūyūṭī J. *As-Sūyūṭī's Medicine of the Prophet.* Ed. A Thomson. London: Ṭā-Hā Publishers, 1994: 42.
3. Ibn Ḥabīb A. *Mujtaṣar fī al-ṭibb/Compendio de medicina.* Ed. C Álvarez de Morales and F Girón Irueste. Madrid: Consejo Superior de Investigaciones Científicas, 1992: 78/46.
4. Elgood C. Trans. *Ṭibb al-nabī or Medicine of the Prophet.* Sūyūṭī J, M Chaghhaynī. *Osiris* 1962; 14; Iṣbahānī AN al-. *Mawsū'at al-ṭibb al-nabawī.* Ed. MKD al-Turkī. Bayrūt: Dār Ibn Ḥazm, 2006.
5. Nehmé M. *Dictionnaire étymologique de la flore du Liban.* Bayrūt: Librairie du Liban, 2000.
6. Ibn Ḥabīb A. *Mujtaṣar fī al-ṭibb/Compendio de medicina.* Ed. C Álvarez de Morales and F Girón Irueste. Madrid: Consejo Superior de Investigaciones Científicas, 1992.
7. Sūyūṭī J. *As-Sūyūṭī's Medicine of the Prophet.* Ed. A Thomson. London: Ṭā-Hā Publishers, 1994.
8. Ibn Ṭulūn S. *al-Manhal al-rawī fī al-ṭibb al-nabawī.* Ed. 'Azīz Bayk. Riyyāḍ: Dār 'ālam al-kutub, 1995.
9. Ghazanfar SA. *Handbook of Arabian Medicinal Plants.* Boca Raton: CRC Press, 1994.
10. Ghazanfar SA. *Handbook of Arabian Medicinal Plants.* Boca Raton: CRC Press, 1994.
11. Simopoulos, Tan, Manchester, Reiter. Purslane: a plant source of omega-3 fatty acids and melatonin. *J* 2005; 39(3): 331–332.
12. Simopoulos, Norman, Gillaspy, Duke. Common purslane: a source of omega-3 fatty acids and antioxidants. *J* 1992; 11(4): 374–382.
13. Lans. Ethnomedicines used in Trinidad and Tobago for urinary problems and diabetes mellitus. *J* 2006; 2: 45.
14. Malek, Boskabady, Borushaki, Tohidi. Bronchodilatory effect of *Portulaca oleracea* in airways of asthmatic patients. *J* 2004; 93(1): 57–62.
15. Chan, Islam, Kamil, Radhakrishnan, Zakaria, Habibullah, Attas. The analgesic and anti-inflammatory effects of *Portulaca oleracea* L. subsp. *sativa* (Haw.) Celak. *J* 2000; 73(3): 445–451.

Quince/*Safarjal*

Family: Rosaceae

Botanical Name: *Cydonia oblonga*

Common Names: *English* Quince; *French* Cognassier, Coignassier; *Spanish* Membrillero; Membrillo (fruit); *German* Echte Quitte, Birnquitte; *Urdu/Unānī* Bahi, Bihi; *Modern Standard Arabic* safarjal

Safety Rating: Generally Safe Quince is generally considered safe for most people when consumed as food. Little is known, however, about is safety in medicinal doses. Since the seeds contain cyanide, they are certainly not safe to consume. Quince should not be taken medicinally by women who are pregnant or lactating.

Prophetic Prescription: The Islamic religion is concerned with both the spiritual disease of the heart, and the physical disease of the heart. For the latter, the Prophet Muḥammad recommended the use of *Cydonia oblonga*, or quince, an anti-inflammatory and anti-spasmodic herb that acts mainly as a circulatory and digestive stimulant. The Messenger of Allāh stated, "Eat quince as it helps the heart. There has not been a single Prophet of Allāh who has not eaten it."[1] The Messenger of Allāh said of quince, "Take this, O Ṭalḥa, for it rests and relaxes the heart."[2] It is also related that he gave a quince to one of his companions, saying, "Here you are, Abū Dharr, for it strengthens the heart, refreshes the soul, and dispels heaviness of the chest."[3] He also said, "Feed quince to your women-folk when they are pregnant, for it makes the heart tender, and it makes the heart better."[4] Regarding the preferred manner of consuming the fruit for medicinal purposes, the Prophet said, "Eat quince on an empty stomach."[5]

According to the Messenger of Allāh, not only is quince beneficial for the heart, it gives a great deal of physical strength. "Eat quince," he advised, "for it softens the heart, and Allāh has not sent any prophet as His Messenger without giving him the quince of the Garden to eat, for that quince gives him the strength of at least forty men."[6] In another tradition, he described quince as "a tonic that musters the strength of the heart, lifts up one's spirit, satisfies one's desire for food, dissipates uptightness of the chest, and softens the heart."[7] When the Prophet was given a quince from Ṭā'if, he said, "Quince is an excellent food: it perfumes the mouth, eliminates *al-dujjā'* [darkness], which is the sadness which oppresses the heart."[8] The Prophet also believed that quince was beneficial for the eyesight. As he expressed, "To eat quince is to drive away dimness of vision."[9]

The "uptightness of the chest" in the prophetic tradition refers to conditions such as angina and is symptomatic of heart disease. The Prophet explained that the use of quince can "soften the heart" which is metaphorical for "healing the heart" but may also allude to the ability of quince to lower high cholesterol levels and possibly inhibit excessive platelet aggregation while helping promote fibrinolysis. Bown has noted that the fruit of *Chaenomeles*, or flowering quince, is an "anti-inflammatory and anti-spasmodic herb that acts mainly as a circulatory ... stimulant."[10] According to Ibn Buṭlān, quince cheers people up and stimulates them.[11] The anti-inflammatory effect of quince may assist in reducing the risk of myocardial infarctions. Its antispasmodic and stimulating effect on the circulatory system may help regulate and strengthen cardiac function.

The "softening of the heart" may refer to the ability of the mucilage of quince to soothe the sore breasts of women.

The Imāms from the Household of the Prophet also stressed the importance of quince in the treatment of cardiovascular conditions. Imām ʿAlī ibn Abī Ṭālib stated that "[e]ating quince increases a man's strength and removes his weakness."[12] Echoing the words of the Prophet, Imām Jaʿfar al-Ṣādiq explained that quince removes grief: "Quince removes sadness," he said, "like the hand which wipes sweat from the forehead."[13]

The Imām also recommended the use of quince saying that it "purifies the stomach and makes it fragrant."[14] He promoted the use of quince, saying, "Eat sweet quince with its seeds, for it fortifies what is weak, and makes fragrant and purifies the stomach."[15] He asserted that "Eating quince strengthens the heart, smartens the intellect (*qalb*), and emboldens the coward."[16] In a similar tradition, the Imām said: "In quince there is a quality not found in other fruits.... It emboldens the coward from the knowledge of the prophets, blessings be upon them all."[17] The Imām lauded the beautifying, strengthening, and sexually stimulating properties of quince, saying, "Quince helps the stomach, and strengthens the heart (*fu'ād*)" and "Quince beautifies the face, and strengthens the heart."[18] He also affirmed that "He who eats quince on an empty stomach improves the quality of his semen (*mā'*), and beautifies his face."[19]

Issues in Identification: It is the consensus that *safarjal* is Arabic for quince. During Dīnawarī's time, quince was grown abundantly in Arabia (*bilād al-ʿarab*).[20] The Andalusian Ibn Ḥabīb was familiar with many kinds of quince, some sweet, and some slightly acidic.[21] In all likelihood, the quince consumed by the Prophet and the Imāms was brought by caravan to Arabia from Isfahan in Persia.[22]

Properties and Uses: *Cydonia oblonga*, commonly known as quince, is nutritive, tonic, astringent, diuretic, vulnerary, antipyretic, expectorant, appetitive, thirst-quenching, galactalogue, antispasmodic, and cholagogue. Internally, it is used to treat coughs, rheumatism, gallbladder problems, flatulence, diarrhea, headache, and insomnia. It is also used to treat cancer, canker sores, dysentery, gonorrhea, aphthous affections, excoriations, gum problems, sore throat, and thrush. It is equally used to prevent dental cavities. Its juice is used to dissolve biliary calculi. A syrup from the fruit is used to treat patients with febrile diseases, and nausea. Quince is not used when the stomach or bowels are inflamed.

Scientific Studies: *Antioxidant, Antiulcerative Activity* In a study conducted by Shinshu University in Japan, the health benefits of Chinese quince (*Pseudocydonia sinensis*) and quince phenolics were evaluated for their antioxidant properties and anticulcerative activity in comparison with apple phenolics as a reference.[23] In the ethanol-induced gastric ulcer, preadministration of Chinese quince and quince phenolics suppressed the occurrence of gastric lesions in rats, whereas apple phenolics seemed to promote ulceration. The results showed that Chinese quince and quince phenolics might have health benefits by acting both in blood vessels and on the gastrointestinal tract.

Antidiarrheic Activity Research shows that preparations made from quince or its seed may provide minor relief from diarrhea and sore throat.[24]

Quince Notes

1. Ibn Mājah M. *Sunan*. Trans. MT Anṣārī. Lahore: Kazi Publications, 1994.
2. Ibn Mājah M. *Sunan*. Trans. MT Anṣārī. Lahore: Kazi Publications, 1994.
3. Nasā'ī A. *Sunan al- Nasā'ī*. al-Qāhirah: Muṣṭafā al-Bābī al-Ḥalabī, 1964–65.
4. Sūyūṭī J. *As-Sūyūṭī's Medicine of the Prophet*. Ed. A Thomson. London: Ṭā-Hā Publishers, 1994; Ibn Mājah, M. *Sunan*. Trans. MT Anṣārī. Lahore: Kazi Publications, 1994; Dhahabī S. *al-Ṭibb al-nabawī*. Bayrūt: Dār al-Nafā'is, 2004.
5. Sūyūṭī J. *As-Sūyūṭī's Medicine of the Prophet*. Ed. A Thomson. London: Ṭā-Hā Publishers, 1994.
6. Ibn Mājah, M. *Sunan*. Trans. MT Anṣārī. Lahore: Kazi Publications, 1994.
7. Nasā'ī A. *Sunan al-Nisā'ī*. Misr: Muṣṭafā al-Bābī al-Ḥalabī, 1964–65; Ibn Mājah M. *Sunan* Ibn Mājah. Bayrūt: Dār al-Jīl, 1998.
8. Ibn Ḥabīb A. *Mujtaṣar fī al-ṭibb/Compendio de medicina*. Ed. C Álvarez de Morales and F Girón Irueste. Madrid: Consejo Superior de Investigaciones Científicas, 1992: 81.
9. Chaghhaynī M. *Ṭibb al-nabī*. Trans. C Elgood. *Osiris* 1962; 14: 189.
10. Bown D. *Encyclopedia of Herbs and their Uses*. Westmount: RD Press, 1995: 258.
11. Ibn Buṭlān. *The Medieval Health Handbook: Tacuinum sanitatis*. Ed. L Cogliati Arano, Trans. O Ratti and Adele Westbrook. New York: George Braziller, 1976: 9.
12. Nisābūrī A. *Islamic Medical Wisdom: The Ṭibb al-a'immah*. Trans. B. Ispahany. Ed. AJ Newman. London: Muḥammadī Trust, 1991: 180.
13. Majlisī M. *Biḥār al-anwār*. Ṭihrān: Javad al-Alavi, 1956
14. Nisābūrī A. *Islamic Medical Wisdom: The Ṭibb al-a'immah*. Trans. B. Ispahany. Ed. AJ Newman. London: Muḥammadī Trust, 1991: 180.
15. Nisābūrī A. *Islamic Medical Wisdom: The Ṭibb al-a'immah*. Trans. B. Ispahany. Ed. AJ Newman. London: Muḥammadī Trust, 1991: 180; Ṭabarsī H. *Mustadrak al-Wasā'il*. Bayrūt: Mu'assasat Āl al-Bayt, 1987–1988.
16. Majlisī M. *Biḥār al-anwār*. Ṭihrān: Javad al-Alavi, 1956.
17. 'Amilī H. *Wasā'il al-shīʿah*. Bayrūt: al-Mu'assasah, 1993.
18. 'Amilī H. *Wasā'il al-shīʿah*. Bayrūt: al-Mu'assasah, 1993.
19. Ṭabarsī H. *Mustadrak al-Wasā'il*. Bayrūt: Mu'assasat Āl al-Bayt, 1987–1988.

20. Dīnawarī AH. *Kitāb al-nabāt/The Book of Plants*. Ed. Bernhard Lewin. Bayrūt: Dār al-Qalam, 1974: 218.
21. Ibn Ḥabīb A. *Mujtaṣar fī al-ṭibb/Compendio de medicina*. Ed. C Álvarez de Morales and F Girón Irueste. Madrid: Consejo Superior de Investigaciones Científicas, 1992: 93.
22. Tannahill R. *Food in History*. New York: Stein and Day, 1973: 126.
23. Hamauzu, Inno, Kume, Irie, Hiramatsu. Antioxidant and antiulcerative properties of phenolics from Chinese quince, quince, and apple fruits. *J* 2006; 8; 54(3): 765–772.
24. Fetrow CW, Avila JR. *The Complete Guide to Herbal Medicines*. Springhouse: Springhouse Corporation, 2000.

Radish / *Fujl*

FAMILY: Brassicaceae

BOTANICAL NAME: *Raphanus sativus*

COMMON NAMES: *English* radish; *French* Radis cultivé, Daïkon; *Spanish* Rábano; *German* Gartenrettich, Rettich, Radieschen; *Urdu/Unānī* Mooli, Turb; *Modern Standard Arabic* fujl

SAFETY RATING: GENERALLY SAFE Although radish is generally considered safe for most people, it can irritate the digestive track when consumed in large amounts. Radish should not be used in medicinal doses by people who have gallstones, nor should it be consumed by women who are pregnant or lactating.

PROPHETIC PRESCRIPTION: Imām Ja'far al-Ṣādiq said, "Eat radish (*fujl*) for it contains three benefits: the leaves chase the wind, its flesh increases urine, and its roots cut phlegm."[1] He also said, "Radish (*fujl*) roots cut phlegm, its flesh promotes digestion, and its leaves increase the flow of urine."[2] As for Imām Muḥammad al-Taqī, he recommended the "comprehensive medication" along with a decoction of radish (*al-fujl*) for people suffering from stones.[3]

ISSUES IN IDENTIFICATION: It is the consensus that *fujl* is Arabic for radish. As Nehmé notes, *Raphanus sativus* is known as *fujl zirā'ī* in Modern Standard Arabic.[4] According to Mandaville, *R. sativus* is occasionally found in eastern Arabia where it is known outside of cultivation as an escapee or weed around farms. It is known in the Saudi vernacular as *fujl* and *fujul*, though it is often pronounced as *fijal*. According to Ghazanfar, it is also known as *qusmī* in colloquial Arabic. Radish is commonly cultivated in Arabia and used as a salad vegetable.[5] It should be stressed, however, that "the small, round radishes that are now common in supermarkets are not of ancient origin."[6] The radishes described by the ancient Greeks were long-rooted, with fully developed seed pods (296).

PROPERTIES AND USES: *Raphanus sativus*, commonly known as radish, is a sweet, slightly pungent, tonic herb that is considered expectorant, antibacterial, antifungal, carminative, diuretic, resolvent, and astringent. Its seeds are used internally for indigestion, abdominal bloating, flatulence, acid reflux, diarrhea, and bronchitis.

SCIENTIFIC STUDIES: *Anticarcinogenic Activity* The anticarcinogenic properties of radish have been the subject of several studies. According to a study of 150 gallbladder cancer patients and 153 controls with gallstone disease, a low consumption of vegetables increased the odds of developing gallbladder cancer while a high consumption of green leafy vegetables, including radish leaves, decreased the odds.[7] In another study of 64 newly diagnosed cases of gallbladder cancer and 101 cases of gallstones, a significant reduction in carcinogenesis was seen with the consumption of radish.[8] The carcinopreventive property of radish seems to be due to the presence of isothiocyanates, which inhibit the development of tumors in many experimental models.[9] In an extensive examination of sixty-two Egyptian foods and medicinal preparations for antimutagenic and anticarcinogenic activity, radish was found to inhibit 29 percent of mutagenicity produced in direct antimutagenic assay and to inhibit 89 percent of mutagenicity induced in host-mediated assay.[10]

Antidiabetic Activity Japanese radish sprouts also show potential to alleviate hyperglycemia in cases where diabetes is present and to serve in the primary prevention of diabetes mellitus.[11]

Anti-Hyperlipidemia In one study, the juice of black radish (*Raphus sativus* L. var. *niger*) showed a beneficial effect in alimentary hyperlipidemia.[12]

Radish Notes

1. 'Amilī H. *Wasā'il al-shī'ah*. Bayrūt: al-Mu'assasah, 1993.
2. 'Amilī H. *Wasā'il al-shī'ah*. Bayrūt: al-Mu'assasah, 1993.
3. Nisābūrī A. *Islamic Medical Wisdom: The Ṭibb al-a'immah*. Trans. B. Ispahany. Ed. AJ Newman. London: Muḥammadī Trust, 1991: 115.
4. Nehmé M. *Dictionnaire étymologique de la flore du Liban*. Bayrūt: Librairie du Liban, 2000.
5. Ghazanfar SA. *Handbook of Arabian Medicinal Plants*. Boca Raton: CRC Press, 1994.
6. Weaver WW. *Heirloom Vegetable Gardening*. New York: Henry Holt, 1997: 296.
7. Rai A, Mohapatra SC, Shukla HS. Correlates between vegetable consumption and gallbladder cancer. *Eur J Cancer Prev.* 2006; 15(2): 134–137.
8. Pandey M, Shukla VK. Diet and gallbladder cancer: a case-control study. *Eur J Cancer Prev.* 2002; 11(4): 365–368.
9. Conaway CC, Yang YM, Chung FL. Isothiocyanates as cancer chemopreventive agents: their biological activities

and metabolism in rodents and humans. *Curr Drug Metab.* 2002; 3(3): 233–255.
10. Badria, FA. Is man helpless against cancer? An environmental approach: antimutagenic agents from Egyptian food and medicinal preparations. *Cancer Lett.* 1994; 84(1): 1–5.
11. Taniguchi H, Kobayashi-Hattori K, Tenmyo C, Kamei T, Uda Y, Sugita-Konishi Y, Oishi Y, Takita T. Effect of Japanese radish (*Raphanus sativus*) sprout (Kaiware-daikon) on carbohydrate and lipid metabolisms in normal and streptozotocin-induced diabetic rats. *Phytother Res.* 2006; 20 (4): 274–278.
12. Lugasi A, Blazovics A. Hagymasi K, Kocsis I, Kery A. Antioxidant effect of squeezed juice from black radish (*Raphanus sativus* L. var. *niger*) in alimentary hyperlipidaemia in rats. *Phytother Res.* 2005; 19(7): 587–591.

Raisin / *Zabīb*

FAMILY: Vitaceae

BOTANICAL NAME: *Vitis vinifera*

COMMON NAMES: *English* Grape vine (source); raisin (dried fruit); *French* Vigne, Vigne noble; raisin (dried fruit); *Spanish* Vid, Parra; pasa, pasita (dried fruit); *German* Weinrebe; Rosine (dried fruit); *Urdu/Unānī* Angoor, Anab; Kishmish, Maweez, Zabeeb (dried fruit); *Modern Standard Arabic* zabīb

SAFETY RATING: GENERALLY SAFE With the exception of allergic individuals, raisins are generally considered to be safe for most people. When consumed in large quantities, however, raisins can cause diarrhea. Other potential side effects of excessive use include stomach upset, indigestion, nausea, vomiting, cough, dry mouth, sore throat, infections, headache, and muscular problems. Raisins should not be consumed in medicinal amounts by women who are pregnant or lactating.

PROPHETIC PRESCRIPTION: The Messenger of Allāh asked Muslims to honor the raisin, saying, "Treat your aunts with honor: the palm tree and the raisin."[1] It is reported that he gave raisins to his companions, saying "Eat."[2] The Prophet is also reported to have said, "The condiment of bread is raisins."[3] The Messenger of Allāh advised that "Raisins (*zabīb*) and dates (*tamr*) should not be eaten together."[4]

The Messenger of Allāh recommended the consumption of raisins for a host of illnesses, saying, "Whoever eats twenty-one raisins at the beginning of the day, Allāh will repel from him every disease and illness."[5] The Prophet said, "Eat raisins (*zabīb*), but spit out the stones, for there is illness in the stones but healing in the flesh."[6] He said, "Eat raisins (*zabīb*). They brighten the face and are antiphlegmatic."[7] He also said, "Eat raisins for they extinguish bile, assuage phlegm, strengthen the nerves, drive away weariness, and beautify the heart."[8]

According to Imām 'Alī ibn Abī Ṭālib, "Whoever eats twenty-one raisins every day, will never find anything upsetting in his body."[9] Imām Ja'far al-Ṣādiq said, "Consuming twenty-one red raisins every day on an empty stomach prevents every illness but death."[10] He also explained that "Raisins strengthen the nerves, removes pride, and freshens the breath."[11] In a similar tradition, the Imām said the same while specifically referencing the raisins from Ṭā'if in the Arabian Peninsula.[12] The Imām also approved the use of raisins boiled in water with honey and cooked until two-thirds of it evaporates to treat a certain pain.[13]

ISSUES IN IDENTIFICATION: It is the consensus that *zabīb* is Arabic for raisins. Bīrūnī says that raisins are also known as *kishmish*. During the time of the Prophet and the Imāms, the cities of Jerusalem and Damascus were famous for their raisins.[14] As Ghazanfar explains, *Vitis vinifera* is currently cultivated in Arabia in the lower hills.[15]

PROPERTIES AND USES: Raisins are high in glucose and are thus an excellent food in cases of debility and convalescence. Studies conducted at the University of California have shown that daily consumption of raisins can greatly reduce the acidity of the urine. The free use of raisins is valuable in combating chronic acidosis which generally results from the excessive consumption of meat and cereals. Raisins are also highly beneficial in the treatment of constipation, anemia and febrile conditions. Raisins are also considered an aphrodisiac.

SCIENTIFIC STUDIES: *Antibacterial* Raisins have been found to contain several chemical compounds that may assist in fighting oral bacteria. In a laboratory, extracts from raisins were found to slow the growth of Streptococcus, the main bacteria behind tooth decay. Five chemicals in raisins — oleanolic, oleanolic, betulin, betulinic, and 5-(hydroxymethyl)-2-furfural — seem to be responsible for slowing the bacteria.[16] In addition, oleanic acid prevents *S. mutans* from sticking to tooth enamel.

Raisin Notes

1. Chaghhaynī M. *Ṭibb al-nabī.* Trans. C Elgood. *Osiris* 1962; 14: 189.
2. Sūyūṭī J. *As-Sūyūṭī's Medicine of the Prophet.* Ed. A Thomson. London: Ṭā-Hā Publishers, 1994: 65.
3. Chaghhaynī M. *Ṭibb al-nabī.* Trans. C Elgood. *Osiris* 1962; 14: 190.
4. Abū Dāwūd S. *Ṣaḥīḥ Sunan Abū Dāwūd.* Riyyāḍ: Maktab al-Tarbiyyah, 1989
5. Nisābūrī A. *Islamic Medical Wisdom: The Ṭibb al-*

a'immah. Trans. B. Ispahany. Ed. AJ Newman. London: Muḥammadī Trust, 1991: 181.
6. Sūyūṭī J. *As-Sūyūṭī's Medicine of the Prophet.* Ed. A Thomson. London: Ṭā-Hā Publishers, 1994.
7. Iṣbahānī AN al-. *Mawsū'at al-ṭibb al-nabawī.* Ed. MKD al-Turkī. Bayrūt: Dār Ibn Ḥazm, 2006.
8. Chaghhaynī M. *Ṭibb al-nabī.* Trans. C Elgood. *Osiris* 1962; 14: 190.
9. Iṣbahānī AN al-. *Mawsū'at al-ṭibb al-nabawī.* Ed. MKD al-Turkī. Bayrūt: Dār Ibn Ḥazm, 2006.
10. Majlisī M. *Biḥār al-anwār.* Ṭihrān: Javad al-Alavi, 1956.
11. Majlisī M. *Biḥār al-anwār.* Ṭihrān: Javad al-Alavi, 1956.
12. 'Amilī H. *Wasā'il al-shī'ah.* Bayrūt: al-Mu'assasah, 1993.
13. Nisābūrī A. *Islamic Medical Wisdom: The Ṭibb al-a'immah.* Trans. B. Ispahany. Ed. AJ Newman. London: Muḥammadī Trust, 1991: 72.
14. Tannahill R. *Food in History.* New York: Stein and Day, 1973: 174.
15. Ghazanfar SA. *Handbook of Arabian Medicinal Plants.* Boca Raton: CRC Press, 1994.
16. C. D. Wu, J. F. Rivero-Cruz, M. Zhu, B. Su, A. D. Kinghorn. Antimicrobial Phytochemicals in Thompson Seedless Raisins (*Vitis vinifera* L.) Inhibit Dental Plaque Bacteria. *American Society for Microbiology meeting.* June 5–9. Atlanta, 2005.

Rice/*Aruz*

Family: Poaceae

Botanical Name: *Oryza sativa*

Common Names: *English* Rice; *French* Riz; *Spanish* Arroz; *German* Reis; *Urdu/Unānī* Chawal, Chanwal, Birinj, Urz; *Modern Standard Arabic* aruz

Safety Rating: Generally Safe Rice is generally considered safe for most people in quantities normally consumed as food. Rice, however, should not be consumed in medicinal quantities by women who are pregnant or lactating.

Prophetic Prescription: According to the Messenger of Allāh, "The best of your food is meat, and rice."[1] There are also two apocryphal traditions which state that "Were it a man, it would be clement" and "Everything which the earth brings forth has both illness and healing, except rice; for it contains healing and no illness."[2]

According to Imām Ja'far al-Ṣādiq, rice is a wholesome and filling food. As he explained, "Nothing remains in one's inside from morning (*ghadwah*) until night except rice bread (*khubz al-aruz*)." The Imām also praise the medicinal values of rice, saying, "Rice is the best of medicine. It is cold, wholesome (*ṣaḥīḥ*), and free from sickness."[3] The Imām also stated that "Rice is the best of food. It enlarges the intestines. It removes hemorrhoids. We are very happy for the people of Iraq because they eat rice and unfertilized female dates (*bisr*) for they both enlarge the intestines and remove hemorrhoids."[4]

Imām Ja'far al-Ṣādiq recommended rice for stomach ailments of all kinds. He ordered his companions to "Feed rice bread (*khubz al-aruz*) to those of you who suffer from belly problems. Verily, there is nothing more beneficial for it burnishes the stomach and eradicates sickness."[5] Once, a man came to the Imām, complaining about pain in his belly. The Imām told him, "Take rice, wash it, dry it in the shade, ground it, and take a handful to eat every afternoon."[6] On another occasion, a man complained to the Imām that he had loose bowels. The Imām told him to "Take rice porridge (*sawīq al-aruz*) and to drink it."[7] On another occasion, the Imām, who was suffering from loose bowels, asked his servant to prepare rice for him.

A man came to Imām Ja'far al-Ṣādiq and said, "O son of the Messenger of Allāh, my daughter is wasting away and her body has become thin (*naḥīl*). Her illness has been protracted and she has a loose belly." The Imām replied, "What keeps you from eating this rice with the blessed fat? Allāh only made fat unlawful for the Banū Isra'īl [the Children of Israel] because of its great blessing in eating it, until Allāh removed what was in it. Perhaps you think it will be harmful because of the amount of treatment she has had?" The Imām described to him how to prepare the rice: cooking it and adding the fat from two kidneys. He said she should eat it when it was neither hot nor cold and she would be cured, Allāh, the Mighty and Sublime, willing. The man did as instructed and said, "By Allāh, there is no god but Him, she ate it only once and recovered."[8]

When the Imām was suffering from pain in the belly, he ordered his servant to boil some rice for him, and add sumac (*summāq*) on it.[9] When the Imām was suffering from loose bowels, he told his servant that "I was inspired in my illness to eat rice, and was commanded to eat it. So wash it and dry it, then roast it, crush it, and cook it, for I eat it with fat and Allāh will remove the pain from me."[10] According to several other traditions, the Imām used dried ground rice, whole cooked rice, or rice soup, to treat looseness of the bowels.[11]

When one of the Imām's companions complained to him of a loose belly, he ordered him to take rice porridge (*sawīq al-aruz*) and to drink it.[12] On one occasion, the Imāms said that "[Rice] porridge (*sawīq*) [*al-aruz*] creates flesh and strengthens the bone." He also added, "The feverish person should be given [rice] porridge (*sawīq*) that has been washed three times for it removes fever, dries the bitterness and phleghm, and strengthens the legs."[13] On another occasion, he said, "When taken on an empty stomach, dry [rice] meal (*sawīq*) [*al-aruz*] extinguishes the temperature, and calms the bitterness. However, if it is moistened and drunk, it will not do so."[14] Finally, he also recommended that Muslims have [rice] porridge and dates as an early morning meal prior to fasting, saying, "The best of your breakfast (*suḥūr*) [during Ramaḍān] is [rice] porridge (*sawīq*) and dates (*tamr*)."[15]

Issues in Identification: It is the consensus that *al-aruz* is Arabic for rice. According to Dīnawarī, rice was one of the plants that was grown in Arabia.[16] While it is possible to grow rice in oases with abundant water, as is done in the Yemen, the vast majority of rice consumed by the Arabs during the time of the Prophet was brought to Arabia by caravans from southern Iraq. After the rise of Islām the cultivation of rice spread north to Nisibin, the southern shores of the Caspian sea, and into the valley of the Volga. Rice was also eventually grown in the Jordan valley in Palestine.

Properties and Uses: *Oryza sativa*, commonly known as rice, is a nutritive, soothing, tonic herb that is diuretic, reduces lactation, improves digestion, and controls sweating. Boiled in water until perfectly soft, rice is useful in cases of debilitated stomach or bowels, as well as diarrhea. Internally, its seeds are used for urinary dysfunction. Both the seeds and germinated seeds are used to treat excessive lactation. The germinated seeds are also used for poor appetite, indigestion, and abdominal discomfort and bloating. The rhizomes are used especially in tuberculosis and chronic pneumonia. In Chinese medicine, grains are often cooked with herbs to make a medicinal gruel. According to Bakhru, rice is beneficial for high blood pressure, digestive disorders, diarrhea in children, and skin inflammation.

Scientific Studies: *Demulcent Activity* According to Maude Grieve, a decoction of rice, commonly called rice water, is recommended in the Pharmacopeia of India as an excellent demulcent, refrigerant drink in febrile and inflammatory diseases, and in dysuria, and similar affections. It may be acidulated with lime-juice and sweetened with sugar. This may also be used as an enema in affections of the bowel.

Antianaphylatic Activity According to an animal study conducted by Wonkwang University in South Korea, the methanol extract of *Oryza sativa* L. subsp. *hsien Ting* possesses strong antianaphylactic activity by inhibition of histamine release from mast cells in vivo and in vitro.[17]

Anticancer Activity According to a study conducted by Chung Shan Medical University in Taiwan, *Oryza sativa* L. *indica* contains compounds that exert an inhibitory effect of cell invasion on various cancer cells.[18] According to an animal study conducted by the University of Leicester, brown rice appears to interfere with the development of tumors. In the study in question, the consumption of rice bran reduced numbers of intestinal adenomas by 51 percent compared to mice on a control diet. In parallel, dietary rice bran decreased intestinal hemorrhage in these mice. The low-fiber rice bran (30 percent in the diet) did not affect intestinal carcinogenesis, suggesting that the fibrous constituents of the bran mediate chemopreventive efficacy. The results suggest that rice bran might be beneficially evaluated as a putative chemopreventive intervention in humans with intestinal polyps.[19] According to a controlled animal study conducted by Gifu University in Japan, *Aspergillus oryzae* (the fungus used in fermented rice) contains a potent anticarcinogenic compound which is promising for human urinary bladder cancer.[20] According to an animal study conducted by Tokyo Noko University, pre-germinated brown rice suppresses hypercholesterolemia.[21]

According to a study conducted by Gifu University in Japan, these observations indicate for the first time that FBRA inhibits NMBA-induced esophageal tumor development in rats possibly through inhibition of cell proliferation in the post-initiation phase, and suggest that FBRA is a promising dietary agent for prevention of human esophageal cancer.[22]

According to a study conducted by Gifu University in Japan, administration of 2.5 and 5 percent FBRA in the diet continuously during initiation and post-initiation period significantly inhibits colon tumor development in rats. These results seem to confirm that rice components, particularly rice germ, play a key role in preventing cancer. As a result, researchers suggest that it is a promising dietary supplement for prevention of human colon cancer.[23]

According to a prospective case-control study of dietary risks for stomach cancer conducted by the Regional Cancer Center in India, the consumption of rice was observed to pose a higher risk. The risk was also high for those who consumed spicy food, chili, and high-temperature food.[24]

According to an animal study conducted by the Technical Research Institute of Snow Brand Milk Products in Japan, a diet containing 2 or 4 percent of rice bran hemicellulose significantly lowered the incidence of colon tumors.[25]

According to a study conducted by Aichi-Gakuin University in Japan, the anthocyanidins found in grape rinds and red rice is effective in suppressing cancerous cell growth.[26]

Rice Notes

1. Sūyūṭī J. *As-Sūyūṭī's Medicine of the Prophet*. Ed. A Thomson. London: Ṭā-Hā Publishers, 1994 36, Ibn Qayyim al-Jawziyyah M. *al-Ṭibb al-nabawī*. Bayrūt: Dār al-Kitāb, 1985; Ibn Ṭulūn S. *al-Manhal al-rawī fī al-ṭibb al-nabawī*. Ed. 'Azīz Bayk. Riyyāḍ: Dār 'ālam al-kutub, 1995.

2. Ibn Qayyim al-Jawziyyah M. *al-Ṭibb al-nabawī*. Bayrūt: Dār al-Kitāb, 1985.

3. Ṭabarsī H. *Mustadrak al-Wasā'il*. Bayrūt: Mu'assasat Āl al-Bayt, 1987–1988.

4. Majlisī M. *Biḥār al-anwār*. Ṭihrān: Javad al-Alavi, 1956.

5. 'Amilī H. *Wasā'il al-shī'ah*. Bayrūt: al-Mu'assasah, 1993.

6. 'Amilī H. *Wasā'il al-shī'ah*. Bayrūt: al-Mu'assasah, 1993.

7. Ṭabarsī H. *Mustadrak al-Wasā'il*. Bayrūt: Mu'assasat Āl al-Bayt, 1987–1988.

8. Nisābūrī A. *Islamic Medical Wisdom: The Ṭibb al-a'immah*. Trans. B. Ispahany. Ed. AJ Newman. London: Muḥammadī Trust, 1991: 128; Ṭabarsī H. *Mustadrak al-Wasā'il*. Bayrūt: Mu'assasat Āl al-Bayt, 1987–1988.

9. 'Amilī H. *Wasā'il al-shī'ah*. Bayrūt: al-Mu'assasah, 1993.

10. Nisābūrī A. *Islamic Medical Wisdom: The Ṭibb al-A'imma*. Trans. B. Ispahany. Ed. AJ Newman. London: The Muḥammadī Trust, 1991: 128.

11. 'Amilī H. *Wasā'il al-shī'ah*. Bayrūt: al-Mu'assasah, 1993.

12. Ṭabarsī H. *Mustadrak al-Wasā'il*. Bayrūt: Mu'assasat Āl al-Bayt, 1987–1988.

13. Ṭabarsī H. *Mustadrak al-Wasā'il*. Bayrūt: Mu'assasat Āl al-Bayt, 1987–1988.

14. Ṭabarsī H. *Mustadrak al-Wasā'il*. Bayrūt: Mu'assasat Āl al-Bayt, 1987–1988.

15. Majlisī M. *Biḥār al-anwār*. Ṭihrān: Javad al-Alavi, 1956.

16. Dīnawarī AH. *Kitāb al-nabāt/The Book of Plants*. Ed. Bernhard Lewin. Uppsala/Wiesbaden: A.-B. Lundequistska Bokhandeln and Otto Harrassowitz, 1953: 70.

17. Kim, Kang, Lee, Shin. The evaluation of the antianaphylactic effect of Oryza sativa L. subsp. hsien Ting in rats. *Pharmacol* 1999; 40(1): 31–36.

18. Chen, Kuo, Chiang, Chiou, Hsieh, Chu. Black rice anthocyanins inhibit cancer cells invasion via repressions of MMPs and u-PA expression. *Chem* 2006; 163(3): 218–229.

19. Verschoyle, Greaves, Cai, Edwards, Steward, Gescher. Evaluation of the cancer chemopreventive efficacy of rice bran in genetic mouse models of breast, prostate and intestinal carcinogenesis. *Br* 2007; 96(2): 248–254.

20. Kuno, Hirose, Yamada, Hata, Qiang, Asano, Oyama, Zhi, Iwasaki, Kobayashi, Mori. Chemoprevention of mouse urinary bladder carcinogenesis by fermented brown rice and rice bran. *Oncol* 2006; 15(3): 533–538.

21. Miura, Ito, Mizukuchi, Kise, Aoto, Yagasaki. Hypocholesterolemic action of pre-germinated brown rice in hepatoma-bearing rats. *Life* 2006; 79(3): 259–264.

22. Kuno, Hirose, Hata, Kato, Qiang, Kitaori, Hara, Iwasaki, Yoshimura, Wada, Kobayashi, Mori. Preventive effect of fermented brown rice and rice bran on N-nitrosomethylbenzylamine-induced esophageal tumorigenesis in rats. *Int* 2004; 25(6): 1809–1815.

23. Katyama, Yoshimi, Yamada, Sakata, Kuno, Yoshida, Qiao, Vihn, Iwasaki, Kobayashi, Mori. Preventive effect of fermented brown rice and rice bran against colon carcinogenesis in male F344 rats. *Oncol* 2002; 9(4): 817–822.

24. Mathew, Gangadharan, Varghese, Nair. Diet and stomach cancer: a case-control study in South India. *Eur* 2000; 9(2): 89–97.

25. Aoe, Oda, Tojima, Tanaka, Tatsumi, Mizutani. Effects of rice bran hemicellulose on 1,2-dimethylhydrazine-induced intestinal carcinogenesis in Fischer 344 rats. *Nutr* 1993; 20(1): 41–49.

26. Koide, Kamei, Hashimoto, Kojima, Hasegawa. Antitumor effect of hydrolyzed anthocyanin from grape rinds and red rice. *Cancer* 1996; 11(4): 273–277.

Rose / *Ward*

FAMILY: Rosaceae

BOTANICAL NAME: *Rosa* spp.

COMMON NAMES: *English* Rose; *French* Rose; *Spanish* Rosa; *German* Rose; *Urdu/Unānī* Gulab, Gul-e Surkh, Ward; *Modern Standard Arabic* ward

SAFETY RATING: GENERALLY SAFE Although they can cause side effects such as nausea, vomiting, diarrhea, heartburn, stomach cramps, fatigue, headache, inability to sleep, and other side effects in sensitive individuals, rose hips are generally considered to be safe for most adults. In some people, inhaling rose hip dust can cause an allergic reaction. Rose hips should not be consumed by women who are pregnant or lactating. They should not be consumed by persons with diabetes, sickle-cell disease, glucose-6-phosphate dehydrogenase deficiency, or iron-related disorders such as hemochromatosis, thalassemia, or some types of anemia.

PROPHETIC PRESCRIPTION: It is reported that the Messenger of Allāh said, "He who desires to smell my own perfume, let him smell the red rose."[1]

ISSUES IN IDENTIFICATION: It is the consensus that the Arabic *ward* means rose. It is believed that roses originated in northern Persia. From there, the flower spread across Mesopotamia to Palestine and across Asia Minor to Greece, being brought to Italy by Greek colonists, and then spreading to the rest of southern Europe. Álvarez de Morales and Girón Irueste identify *ward* as *Rosa gallica* which, in the context of al-Andalus makes perfect sense. During the time of the Prophet, the type of rose cultivated by the Romans was *Rosa gallica*. If we limit ourselves to roses that are native to Palestine, the two most likely candidates for the Prophet's ward would be *Rosa can-*

ina and *Rosa phoenicia*. During the early centuries of Islām, there were rose gardens in many areas which provided the rose water that Arabs loved to use in their cookery.[2]

Properties and Uses: *Rosa canina*, known as dog rose, is an acidic, astringent, and tonic herb which is rich in vitamins. It is used internally to treat colds, influenza, minor infectious diseases, scurvy, diarrhea, and gastritis.

Rosa rugosa or Japanese rose is an aromatic, tonic herb, which stimulates the liver, improves circulation, and acts as an antidote in antimony poisoning. It is used internally to treat poor appetite and digestion, as well as menstrual complaints. It is combined with *Leonurus cardiaca* or *L. sibiricus* for excessive menstruation. The fruits are an excellent source of vitamin C.

Rosa gallica, known as the red rose, is an aromatic, tonic, mildly astringent herb that controls bacterial infections, promotes healing, and improves morale. Internally, the petals are used to treat colds, bronchial infections, gastritis, diarrhea, depression, and lethargy. In the United States, they used to be used to treat passive hemorrhages, excessive mucous, and bowel complaints. Rose petals are used to treat inflammations, circulatory congestion, sore throat, mouth sores, and menstrual problems. For the treatment of menstrual irregularity, rose petals are combined with *Asparagus racemosus*, as a tonic, and with *Hibiscus rosa-sinensis* or *Carthamus tinctorius*. Externally, rose hips are used as a poultice to treat ophthalmic diseases. They are also used in aromatherapy to counter depression, anxiety, and negative feelings. Rose hips are particularly high in vitamin C. They also contain carotenoid pigments, plant sterols, tocotrienols, and a very high level of anthocyanins, catechins, and other polyphenolics, which help protect against cancer and cardiovascular diseases.

Rosa damascena is considered cooling, mildly laxative, aphrodisiac, antipyretic, and cardiotonic. Fresh rose petals are used as a tonic, to treat bad breath, to improve the appetite, and relieve headaches and toothaches. They are also used to treat stomatitis, inflammation, as well as kidney, liver, and intestinal problems. Dried rose petals are used to give fragrance in perspiration.

Scientific Studies: *Anti-inflammatory Activity* According to an in vivo study conducted by Gazi University in Turkey, the ethanolic extract of *Rosa canina* L. fruits and the fractions prepared from the fruits was shown to possess significant inhibitory activity against inflammatory models and on a pain model based on the inhibition of p-benzoquinone-induced writhing in mice.[3]

According to a double-blind, placebo-controlled, randomized, crossover study of 112 patients with osteoarthritis conducted by the Institute for Clinical Research in Denmark, treatment of 5 g daily of Hyben Vital produced significantly more improvement for pain and stiffness than placebo. After the first three months of active treatment, 66 percent of patients showed improvement as opposed to 36 percent with those on placebo, indicating that Hyben Vital, a standardized powder of a subspecies of *Rosa canina* fruits, reduces the symptoms of osteoarthritis.[4]

According to an animal trial conducted by Yonsei University in South Korea, *Rosa* x *hybrida* extract clearly exhibited inhibitory effects against acute and subacute inflammation by oral administration. *Rosa* x *hybrida* extract also showed an analgesic effect. As the researchers conclude, these results support the use of *Rosa* x *hybrida* in relieving inflammatory pain and provides insight into the development of new agents for treating inflammatory diseases.[5]

According to an animal study conducted by Hanyang University in Korea, the administration of rosmarinic acid to mice with induced arthritis dramatically reduced the arthritic index and number of affected paws, suppressing synovitis, showing benefit for treatment of rheumatoid arthritis in clinical settings.[6]

According to a study conducted by the Danish Institute of Agricultural Sciences, the dried and milled fruits of *Rosa canina* contain a galactolipid with inhibitory effects on chemotaxis of human peripheral blood neutrophils in vitro. As researchers explain, the presence of galactolipid 1 in rose hips may explain the clinically observed anti-inflammatory properties of rose hip herbal remedies.[7]

According to a study conducted by Sangji University in Korea, the roots of *Rosa rugosa* contain anti-inflammatory triterpenoids which are responsible for the anti-inflammatory and antinociceptive action of *Rosa rugosa* roots.[8]

Cardioprotective Activity According to an animal study conducted by Yonsei University in Korea, *Rosa* x *hybrida* flower significantly increased antioxidant enzyme activity and HDL-cholesterol, as well as decreasing malondialdehyde, which may reduce the risk of inflammatory and heart disease.[9]

Anti-HIV Activity In a study conducted by Nankai University in China, 18 medicinal herbs traditionally used in China were screened for their ability to inhibit HIV in vitro. Of all the herbs studies, the ethanol precipitate of the aqueous extract of *Rosa rugosa* showed the strongest inhibition.[10]

According to a study conducted by MRC Collaborative Centre in the United Kingdom, water and methanol extracts of *Rosa damascena* exhibited moderate anti–HIV activity. One compound was shown to reduce the maturation of infectious progeny virus, while three other compounds appear to inhibit HIV infection.[11]

Antioxidative Activity In a study of Turkish medicinal plants conducted by Ataturk University in Turkey, the aqueous extract of *Rosa pimpinellifolia* was shown to have one of the highest peroxidation inhibition activity.[12]

According to a study conducted by Toyama Medical and Pharmaceutical University in Japan, compounds from *Rosa rugosa* were shown to possess marked and dose-dependent inhibitory effects on lipid peroxidation.[13]

According to a 5-week randomized, placebo-controlled, single-blind trial of 36 young, healthy, and non-smoking individuals conducted by North-West University in South Africa, *Rosa roxburghii* supplementation significantly increased plasma antioxidant capacity. These findings support the beneficial properties linked to *Rosa roxburghii* as a dietary supplement that can enhance antioxidant status.[14]

Antiulcer Activity In an in-vivo study conducted by Gazi University in Turkey, five herbal medicines used as Turkey as gastroprotective drugs were assessed for antiulcer activity. Among other ingredients, the crude drugs contained the fresh fruit of *Rosa canina*. Prepared according to traditional indications in experimental conditions, all extracts exhibited statistically significant gastroprotective effect, with *Rosa canina* showing 100 percent effectiveness. In fact, at the concentration under study, both crude drugs were more effective than the reference compound misoprostol.[15]

Antibacterial Activity According to a study conducted by The Robert Gordon University in the United Kingdom, *Rosa canina* is active against one bacterial species.[16]

Antiviral Activity In a study conducted by the University of British Columbia, one hundred methanolic plant extracts were screened for antiviral activity against seven viruses. The extract of *Rosa nutkana* was found to be very active against an enteric coronavirus.[17]

Rose Notes

1. Chaghhaynī M. *Ṭibb al-nabī*. Trans. C Elgood. *Osiris* 1962; 14: 191.

2. Tannahill R. *Food in History*. New York: Stein and Day, 1973: 174.

3. Deliorman. In vivo anti-inflammatory and antinociceptive activity of the crude extract and fractions from *Rosa canina* L. fruits. *J Ethnopharmacol.* 2007; 112(2): 394–400.

4. Rein, Kharazmi, Winther. A herbal remedy, Hyben Vital (standard powder of a subspecies of *Rosa canina* fruits), reduces pain and improves general wellbeing in patients with osteoarthritis — a double-blind, placebo-controlled, randomised trial. *Phytomedicine.* 2004; 11(5): 383–391.

5. Choi, Hwang. Investigations of anti-inflammatory and antinociceptive activities of *Piper cubeba, Physalis angulata* and *Rosa hybrida. J* 2003; 89(1): 171–175.

6. Youn, Lee, Won, Huh, Yun, Cho, Paik. Beneficial effects of rosmarinic acid on suppression of collagen induced arthritis. *J* 2003; 30(6): 1203–1207.

7. Larsen, Kharazmi, Christensen, Christensen. An anti-inflammatory galactolipid from rose hip (*Rosa canina*) that inhibits chemotaxis of human peripheral blood neutrophils in vitro. *J* 2003; 66(7): 994–995.

8. Jung, Nam, Choi, Lee, Park. 19 Alpha-hydroxyursane-type triterpenoids: antinociceptive anti-inflammatory principles of the roots of *Rosa rugosa. Biol* 2005; 28(1): 101–104.

9. Choi, Hwang. Effect of some medicinal plants on plasma antioxidant system and lipid levels in rats. *Phytother* 2005; 19(5): 382–386.

10. Fu. Compounds from rose (*Rosa rugosa*) flowers with human immunodeficiency virus type 1 reverse transcriptase inhibitory activity. *J Pharm Pharmacol.* 2006; 58(9): 1275–1280.

11. Mahmood, Piacente, Pizza, Burke, Khan, Hay. The anti–HIV activity and mechanisms of action of pure compounds isolated from *Rosa damascena. Biochem* 1996; 229(1): 73–79.

12. Mavi, Terzi, Ozgen, Yildirim, Coskun M. Antioxidant properties of some medicinal plants: *Prangos ferulacea* (*Apiaceae*), *Sedum sempervivoides* (*Crassulaceae*), *Malva neglecta* (*Malvaceae*), *Cruciata taurica* (*Rubiaceae*), *Rosa pimpinellifolia* (*Rosaceae*), *Galium verum* subsp. *verum* (*Rubiaceae*), *Urtica dioica* (*Urticaceae*). *Biol* 2004; 27(5): 702–705.

13. Cho, Yokozawa, Rhyu, Kim, Shibahara, Park. The inhibitory effects of 12 medicinal plants and their component compounds on lipid peroxidation. *Am* 2003; 31(6): 907–917.

14. Janse, Erasmus, Loots, Oosthuizen, Jerling, Kruger, Louw, Brits, van. *Rosa roxburghii* supplementation in a controlled feeding study increases plasma antioxidant capacity and glutathione redox state. *Eur* 2005; 44(7): 452–457.

15. Gürbüz I, Ustün O, Yesilada, Sezik, Kutsal. Anti-ulcerogenic activity of some plants used as folk remedy in Turkey. *J* 2003; 88(1): 93–97.

16. Kumarasamy, Cox, Jaspars, Nahar, Sarker. Screening seeds of Scottish plants for antibacterial activity. *J* 2002; 83(1–2): 73–77.

17. McCutcheon, Roberts, Gibbons, Ellis, Babiuk, Hancock, Towers. Antiviral screening of British Columbian medicinal plants. *J* 1995; 49(2): 101–110.

Rue / *Sadhāb*

FAMILY: Rutaceae

BOTANICAL NAME: *Ruta chalepensis*

COMMON NAMES: *English* Aleppo rue, Eastern rue, Egyptian rue, Fringed rue; *French* Rue d'Alep,

Rue ailée fétide; *Spanish* Ruda; *German* Raute; *Urdu/Unānī* Sudab; *Modern Standard Arabic* sadhāb

Botanical Name: *Ruta graveolens*

Common Names: *English* Common rue, Herb of grace; *French* Rue des jardins, Rue officinale, Rue fétide; *Spanish* Ruda; *German* Gartenraute, Raute; *Urdu/Unānī* Sudab; *Modern Standard Arabic* fayjān, sadhāb

Safety Rating: Dangerous to Deadly Excessive intake of rue, particularly in its fresh form, affects the central nervous system and may prove fatal. In animal experiments, rue causes strong uterine stimulation, and the extract acts as an abortive agent in large doses.[1] Rue is toxic to both embryo and fetus. Due to its spasmolytic and abortifacient properties, the herb is never administered to women who are pregnant or lactating. The abortifacient quality of rue is caused by its toxicity. Using rue to terminate unplanned pregnancies is a perilous practice which can cause death, not only to the baby, but to the mother herself. Rue should not be used internally by small children, the elderly, nor by patients suffering from cardiac or kidney ailments. Rue should not be used while taking medications to lower blood pressure as it may increase their effects. When applied externally to the skin or handled in the garden, rue can cause serious photodermatatis as well as contact dermatitis in sensitive people.

Symptoms of rue poisoning include retching, vomiting, violent pain in the stomach, headache, cerebral oppression and fullness, heat flushes, uncertain locomotion, somnolence, prostration, feeble pulse, at first rapid, then slow, coldness and twitching of the extremities, and frequent desire to pass urine, which is strongly impregnated with the peculiar odor of rue. German health authorities have concluded that neither rue nor any of its preparations should be utilized in medicine as it has an unfavorable risk-benefit ratio.[2] Rue should only be taken medicinally under expert supervision.

Prophetic Prescription: Imām Muḥammad al-Ṭaqī used to prescribe the "comprehensive medication" with rue water for people suffering from stones.[3] It is also reported that a few drops of rue, cooked with olive oil, helps subside throbbing ear pain.[4]

Issues in Identification: According to Hans Wehr, *sadhāb* is Arabic for rue. For Álvarez Morales and Girón Irueste, the term refers to *Ruta graveolens*.[5] Bīrūnī says that *kuft fayjān* is rue while Said identifies it as *Nasturtium indicum* (Indian cress). Dīnawarī also says that *sadhāb* is known as *fayjān*.[6] As Nehmé explains, ruta is *sadhāb* and *fayjān*; *Ruta chalepensis*, known as Aleppo rue or fringed rue, is known as *sadhāb ḥalab* or *khuft*.[7]

Ruta chalepensis is the type of rue commonly known in Arab countries as *sadhāb*, and which occurs as a ruderal in southwestern Saudi Arabia. According to Ghazanfar, the distribution of *R. chalepensis* ranges from the Mediterranean region to Pakistan, Somalia, and Ethiopia. It is found throughout Arabia, in gravelly and rocky places. In Omani, Saudi Arabian, and Yemeni Arabic, the plant is known as *saḍab*, *sadhāb*, *shadhab*, and *shathāb*.[8] Although both *R. chalepensis* and *R. graveolens* could grow in parts of Arabia, the latter is more temperate and would thrive better in the Mediterranean zone.

Properties and Uses: *Ruta graveolens* is a bitter, pungent, warming herb that stimulates the uterus, relaxes spasms, improves digestion, increases perspiration, and strengthens capillaries. Rue is considered irritant, detersive, expectorant, calorific, resolvent, antiseptic, antispasmodic, narcotic, hypnotic, anodyne, emetic, emmenagogue, ebolic, deobstruent, carminative, desiccative, astringent, antispasmodic, stimulant, alterative, aphrodisiac, lactagogue, anthelmintic, and, in large quantities, abortifacient and toxic.

Internally, it is used in small doses for menstrual problems, colic, epilepsy, rheumatism, nervous headaches, heart palpitations, high blood pressure, to help harden bones and teeth, and to expel intestinal parasites. Rue is also used to treat mental illnesses, hysteria, epilepsy, hemorrhoids, intermittent fevers, colic, retention of urine, hiccup, rheumatism, calculi or ureter, gallstones, jaundice, dysmenorrheal, neuralgia, lumbago, and as an ointment for baldness. It is also used to treat arthritis, joint disorders, lack of menstruation, menstrual pain, muscle disorders, nervousness, spasms, sports injuries, sprains and strains, and to promote lactation in breast-feeding women. The powdered seeds are an excellent vermifuge, particularly efficient in expelling tapeworms. Externally, rue is used in the treatment of strained eyes.

Scientific Studies: *Anti-inflammatory, Vasorelaxant, Antihypertensive, Bone-Hardening, Cardioregulating, and Antispasmodic Activity* Studies have confirmed that rue is anti-inflammatory[9] and a vasorelaxant.[10] The most important component in rue is a crystalline body called rutin. According to the United States Department of Agriculture, rutin is very effective in treating high blood pressure, and it also helps to harden the bones and teeth. It also is useful for heart palpitations. Its oil and alkaloids are antispasmodic which explains its use in the treatment of nervous digestion and colic.

Antitumor Activity In a study conducted by the Danish University of Pharmaceutical sciences, in Copenhagen, Denmark, extract of *Ruta graveolens* exhibited moderate inhibition of acetylcholinesterase enzyme.[11] In a study conducted by the Amala Cancer Research Centre in India, an extract of *R. graveolens* was found to be cytotoxic to Dalton's lymphoma ascites, Ehrlich ascites carcinoma and L929 cells in culture, as well as increasing the lifespan of tumor-bearing animals. The extract further decreased solid tumors from developing. A homeopathic preparation of *R. graveolens* was equally effective. Neither was effective, however, for reducing already developed tumors. The *R. graveolens* extract was found to scavenge hydroxyl radicals and inhibit lipid peroxidation at low concentrations. At higher concentrations, however, the extract acted as a prooxidant as inhibition of lipid peroxidation and scavenging of hydroxyl radicals was minimal. These data indicates that the prooxidant activity of *R. graveolens* may be responsible for the cytocidal action of the extract, and its ability to produce tumor reduction.[12]

Antimicrobial Activity A study conducted by the Bulgaria Academy of Sciences confirmed that the methanol, petroleum ether, ethyl acetate and water-methanol extracts of *Ruta graveolens* possess antimicrobial and cytotoxic activities.[13]

Antifertility Activity In an animal study conducted by the Universidad Nacional Mayor de San Marcos in Peru, the oral administration of *Ruta graveolens* extract was shown to interfere with preimplantation development and embryo transport.[14] According to an animal study, the chloroform extracts of the root, stem and leaf of *R. graveolens* shows significant anti-fertility activity in rats when administered intragastrically on days 1–10 post-coitum.[15] In another animal study, *R. graveolens* was shown to inhibit pregnancy in 50–60 percent of rats.[16]

Antinociceptive Activity According to a study conducted by Jordan University of Science and Technology, *Ruta graveolens* possesses antinociceptive effects. This data affirms the traditional use of the plants for painful and inflammatory conditions.[17]

Rue Notes

1. Compton MS. *Herbal gold.* St. Paul: Llewellyn, 2000: 270.

2. Tyler VE, Foster S. *Tyler's Honest Herbal.* 4th ed. New York: Haworth Press, 1999: 326.

3. Nisābūrī A. *Islamic Medical Wisdom: The Ṭibb al-a'immah.* Trans. B. Ispahany. Ed. AJ Newman. London: Muḥammadī Trust, 1991: 115.

4. Nisābūrī A. *Islamic Medical Wisdom: The Ṭibb al-a'immah.* Trans. B. Ispahany. Ed. AJ Newman. London: Muḥammadī Trust, 1991: 89.

5. Ibn Ḥabīb A. *Mujtaṣar fī al-ṭibb/Compendio de medicina.* Ed. C Álvarez de Morales and F Girón Irueste. Madrid: Consejo Superior de Investigaciones Científicas, 1992.

6. Dīnawarī AH. *Kitāb al-nabāt: Le dictionaire botanique d'Abū Ḥanīfa al-Dīnawarī.* al-Qāhirah: Institut Français d'Archéologie Orientale du Caire, 1973.

7. Nehmé M. *Dictionnaire étymologique de la flore du Liban.* Bayrūt: Librairie du Liban, 2000.

8. Ghazanfar SA. *Handbook of Arabian Medicinal Plants.* Boca Raton: CRC Press, 1994.

9. Raghav, Gupta, Agrawal, Goswami, Das. Anti-inflammatory effect of *Ruta graveolens* L. in murine macrophage cells. *J* 2006; 104(1–2): 234–9.

10. Shi, Chen, Wang, Liao, Chen. Vasorelaxant effect of harman. *Eur* 2000; 390(3): 319–325.

11. Adsersen, Gauguin, Gudiksen, Jager. Screening of plants used in Danish folk medicine to treat memory dysfunction for acetylcholinesterase inhibitory activity. *J* 2006; 104(3): 418–422.

12. Preethi, Kuttan, Kuttan. Anti-tumor activity of *Ruta graveolens* extract. *Asian* 2006; 7(3): 439–443.

13. Ivanova, Mikhova, Najdenski, Tsvetkova, Kostova. Antimicrobial and cytotoxic activity of *Ruta graveolens. Fitoterapia.* 2005 Jun; 76(3–4): 344–347.

14. Gutierrez-Pajares, Zuniga, Pino. *Ruta graveolens* aqueous extract retards mouse preimplantation embryo development. *Reprod* 2003; 17(6): 667–672.

15. Kong, Lau, Wat, Ng, But, Cheng, Waterman. Antifertility principle of *Ruta graveolens. Planta* 1989; 55(2): 176–178.

16. Prakash, Saxena, Shukla, Tewari, Mathur, Gupta, Sharma, Mathur. Anti-implantation activity of some indigenous plants in rats. *Acta* 1985; 16(6): 441–448.

17. Atta, Alkofahi. Anti-nociceptive and anti-inflammatory effects of some Jordanian medicinal plant extracts. *Ethnopharmacol.* 1998; 60(2): 117–124.

Saffron / *Za'farān*

FAMILY: Iridaceae

BOTANICAL NAME: *Crocus sativus*

COMMON NAMES: *English* saffron, crocus; *French* Safran, Safran cultivé; *Spanish* Azafrán; *German* Echter safran; *Urdu/Unānī* Zafran, Kurkum, Kesar; *Modern Standard Arabic* za'farān

SAFETY RATING: GENERALLY SAFE TO DANGEROUS *Crocus sativus* is generally considered to be safe for most adults when used as a spice and in medicinal doses. Besides potential allergic reactions, side effects may include anxiety, drowsiness, change in appetite, and headache. In large doses, *Crocus sativus* is poisonous, causing yellowing of the skin, eyes, and mucous membranes, vomiting, dizziness, bloody diarrhea, bleeding from the nose, lips, and eyelids, as well as numbness and other serious side effects. The herb should not be ingested by people suffering from bipolar disease. Since the plant is abortifacient and poisonous, it should not be consumed in any quantity by women who are pregnant or lactating

Saffron is prone to adulteration with safflower, coreopsis, marigold, turmeric rhizomes, corn stigma, paprika, and other powders used as diluting fillers. Different saffron grades are also mixed and mislabeled. Since saffron is worth its weight in gold, if it is inexpensive, it is fake. The highest grade saffron is from Kashmir. The Iranian variety is cheaper. The so-called saffron from Mexico is actually marigold or safflower.

PROPHETIC PRESCRIPTION: According to Imām 'Alī al-Naqī, "The best thing for quartan fever is to eat sweet flummery and a lot of saffron on the day the fever occurs, and not to eat anything else on that day."[1]

ISSUES IN IDENTIFICATION: Bīrūnī gives many names for the plant, including *za'furān, za'farān, jādī, jisād, jayhumān, rādin, rayhaqān, ra'bal, 'abīr*, and *ramhuqān*, all of which are identified by Said as *Crocus sativus*. Saffron was cultivated in Darband and Isfahan in the 10th century. According to Chinese sources, the plant was spread there by the Muslims. The saffron employed by the Imāms was likely of Persian provenance.

PROPERTIES AND USES: *Crocus sativus*, commonly known as saffron, is a pungent, bittersweet herb that improves digestion, increases perspiration, stimulates circulation and menstruation, and reduces high blood pressure. It is stomachic, emmenagogue, diaphoretic, sedative, aphrodisiac, slightly anodyne, antispasmodic, resolvent, detersive, and carminative. It is used for coughs, whooping cough, asthma, flatulent colic, insomnia, measles, depression, and conjunctivitis. It is also said to benefit amenorrhoea, dysmenorrhea, chlorosis, hysteria, and suppression of the lochial discharge. It is also used for depression and menstrual disorders. Externally, it is used in compounds for rheumatism and neuralgic pains, as well as for dry skin.

SCIENTIFIC STUDIES: *Neuroprotective Activity* In an animal trial conducted by Fukuoka University in Japan, *Crocus sativus* was confirmed to possess neuroprotective properties.[2]

Antidepressant Activity In a double-randomized 8-week human trial on forty depressed outpatients conducted by the University of Tehran in Iran, saffron was shown to be equally effective as fluoxetine in the treatment of mild to moderate depression.[3]

In a 6-week double-blind, placebo-controlled and randomized human trial of forty patients with major depression conducted by Arak University of Medical Sciences, and the Psychiatric Research Center of Roozbeh Hospital in Iran, petals of *Crocus sativus* produced a significantly better outcome on Hamilton Depression Rating Scale than placebo, indicating the efficacy of *Crocus sativus* petals in the treatment of mild to moderate depression.[4] (It should be noted that the petals of *C. sativus* are not usually used for culinary or medicinal purposes; rather, the stigmas of the flower are used.)

Tehran University of Medical Sciences conducted a 6-week pilot, double-blind, single-center, randomized human trial of thirty adult outpatients meeting the DSM IV for major depression, and scoring at least 18 on the Hamilton Rating Scale for Depression. They found that 30 mg/day of saffron was found to be similar to 100 mg/day of imipramine in the treatment of mild to moderate depression.[5]

Antioxidative Activity In a study conducted by the University of Patras in Greece, *Crocus sativus* stigmas were shown to possess good antioxidant properties, higher than those of tomatoes and carrots, which inhibited Abeta fibriollogenesis in a concentration and time-dependent manner.[6]

Respiratory Tract Relaxing Activity In a controlled animal trial conducted by the Mashhad University of Medical Sciences in Iran, the potent relaxant effects of aqueous-ethanolic extracts of *Crocus sativus* were confirmed.[7]

Memory-Enhancing Activity In a study conducted by the University of Thessaly in Greece, the effects of extracts of *Crocus sativus* on memory were investigated in the rat by using the object recognition and the step-through passive avoidance task. In the first study, post-training administration of saffron extract successfully counteracted extinction of recognition memory in the normal rat, suggesting that saffron extract modulates storage and/or retrieval of information. In a subsequent study, pre-training treatment with *C. sativus* extract significantly antagonized the scopolamine-induced performance deficits in the step-through passive avoidance test. These results support and extend prior findings about the implication of *C. sativus* extract in learning and memory mechanisms.[8]

According to the University of Tokyo, recent behavioral and electrophysiological studies demonstrate that saffron extract affect learning and memory in experiments with animals. Studies have shown that saffron extract improves ethanol-induced impairments of learning behaviors in mice, and prevents ethanol-induced inhibition of hippocampal long-term potentiation, a form of activity-dependent synaptic plasticity that may underlie learning and memory. This effect of saffron extract is attributed to crocin (crocetin digentiobiose ester), but not crocetin. The study concludes that saffron extract or its active constituents, crocetin and crocin, could be useful as a treatment for neurodegenerative disorders accompanying memory impairment.[9]

Cholesterol-Lowering Activity In a 10-day animal study conducted by the China Pharmaceutical University, the hypolipidemic mechanism of crocin, an active ingredient in *Crocus sativus*, significantly reduced serum triglyceride, total cholesterol, low density lipoprotein (LDL) cholesterol and very low density lipoprotein (VLDL) cholesterol levels in the daily dose range of 25 to 100 mg/kg. Results of the modified fat-loading method indicated that crocin inhibited the absorption of fat and cholesterol and this inhibition is closely related to the hydrolysis of fat. Although crocin did not directly block the absorption of cholesterol, it could selectively inhibit the activity of pancreatic lipase as a competitive inhibitor. These findings suggest that crocin yielded its hypolipidemic effect by inhibiting pancreatic lipase, leading to the malabsorption of fat and cholesterol.[10]

Anticonvulsant Activity In a study conducted by Mashhad University of Medical Sciences in Iran, the effects of safranal, an active constituent of *Crocus sativus* L. stigmas, were studied on seizures induced by pentylenetetrazol. Protection against generalized tonic-clonic seizures was 30 percent, 100 percent and 100 percent and mortality protection was 40 percent, 100 percent and 100 percent. These results indicate that safranal could exert anticonvulsant activity.[11]

Antigenotoxic, Antioxidant, and Chemopreventive Activity In a study conducted by the University of Madras in India, the chemoprotective potential of saffron was tested against the genotoxicity of three well-known antitumor drugs: cisplatin, cyclophosphamide, and mitomycin-C. Three doses of saffron (20, 40 and 80 mg/kg b.w.) were orally administered to mice for five consecutive days prior to the administration of antitumor drugs under investigation. Pre-treatment with saffron significantly inhibited antitumor drugs induced cellular DNA damage as revealed by decreased comet tail length, tail moment and percent DNA in the tail. These findings, together with previous results, suggest a potential role for saffron as an antigenotoxic, antioxidant and chemopreventive agent and could be used as an adjuvant in chemotherapeutic applications.[12]

Antioxidative Activity In a study conducted by Aristotle University of Thessaloniki in Greece, saffron showed a high radical scavenging activity, supporting its use in functional foods, drinks with antioxidative activity, in pharmaceutical and cosmetic preparations for their antioxidative activity, and probably for their antiaging activity.[13]

In a study conducted by Fukuoka University in Japan, a pharmacologically active component of *Crocus sativus* was shown to have greater antioxidant effects than alpha-tocopherol at the same concentration. These results, together with previous data, suggest that crocin is a unique and potent antioxidant that combats oxidative stress in neurons.[14]

Anticancer Activity According to the Chittaranjan National Cancer Institute in India, pharmacological studies have demonstrated that *Crocus sativus* L. possesses many health-promoting properties including radical scavenging, antimutagenic and immuno-modulating effects. In an animal study, an aqueous infusion of saffron was shown to prevent chemically induced skin carcinogenesis.[15]

In a study conducted by the Amala Cancer Research Centre in India, the topical application of *Nigella sativa* and *Crocus sativus* extracts inhibited two-stage initiation/promotion of skin carcinogenesis in mice. Intraperitoneal administration of *Nigella sativa* and oral administration of *Crocus sativus* for 30 restricted tumor incidence to 33.3 percent and 10 percent, respectively.[16]

In a study conducted by the Amala Cancer Research Centre, in Kerala, India, the oral administration of saffron to tumor-bearing mice increased their life spans by 111 percent, 83.5 percent, and 112.5 percent respectively. These results indicate the potential use of saffron as an anticancer agent.[17]

In a review produced by the National Institute of Pediatrics in Mexico reports that a growing body of research has demonstrated that saffron extract itself and its main constituents, the carotenoids, possess chemopreventive properties against cancer.[18] According to an in-vitro study, crocin, safranal, and picrocrocin from saffron inhibits the growth of human cancer cells.[19]

Antihypertensive Activity In an animal trial conducted by Mashhad University of Medical Sciences in Iran, aqueous and ethanol extracts of *Crocus sativus* petals were shown to reduce blood pressure in a dose-dependent manner.[20]

Antinociceptive and Anti-inflammatory Activity In an animal trial conducted by Mashhad University of Medical Sciences in Iran, the aqueous and ethanolic extracts of saffron stigma and petal showed an antinociceptive effect, as well as acute and/or chronic anti-inflammatory activity.[21]

Vasodilatory Activity In a study conducted by

Texas A&M University College of Medicine, crocin analogs isolated from *Crocus sativus* L. were found to significantly increase the blood flow in the retina and choroid and to facilitate retinal function recovery. Increased blood flow due to vasodilation presumably improves oxygenation and nutrient supply of retinal structures. These results indicated that crocin analogs could be used to treat ischemic retinopathy and/or age-related macular degeneration.[22]

Anti-Premature Ejaculation Activity In Germany, a patent has been granted for a combination of saffron, quinine, and opium, for the treatment of premature ejaculation.[23]

Saffron Notes

1. Nisābūrī A. *Islamic Medical Wisdom: The Ṭibb al-a'immah*. Trans. B. Ispahany. Ed. AJ Newman. London: Muḥammadī Trust, 1991: 59.
2. Ochiai, Shimeno, Mishima, Iwasaki, Fujiwara, Tanaka, Shoyama, Toda, Eyanagi, Soeda. Protective effects of carotenoids from saffron on neuronal injury in vitro and in vivo. *Biochim* 2007; 1770(4): 578–584.
3. Akhondzadeh, Moshiri, Noorbala, Jamshidi, Abbasi, Akhondzadeh. Comparison of petal of *Crocus sativus* L. and fluoxetine in the treatment of depressed outpatients: A pilot double-blind randomized trial. *Prog* 2007; 30; 31(2): 439–442.
4. Moshiri, Basti, Noorbala, Jamshidi, Hesameddin, Akhondzadeh. *Crocus sativus* L. (petal) in the treatment of mild-to-moderate depression: a double-blind, randomized and placebo-controlled trial. *Phytomedicine.* 2006; 13(9–10): 607–611.
5. Akhondzadeh, Fallah-Pour, Afkham, Jamshidi, Khalighi-Cigaroudi. Comparison of *Crocus sativus* L. and imipramine in the treatment of mild to moderate depression: a pilot double-blind randomized trial. *BMC* 2004; 4: 12.
6. Papandreou, Kanakis, Polissiou, Efthimiopoulos, Cordopatis, Margarity, Lamari. Inhibitory activity on amyloid-beta aggregation and antioxidant properties of *Crocus sativus* stigmas extract and its crocin constituents. *J* 2006; 15; 54(23): 8762–8768.
7. Boskabady, Aslani. Relaxant effect of *Crocus sativus* (saffron) on guinea-pig tracheal chains and its possible mechanisms. *J* 2006; 58(10): 1385–1390.
8. Pitsikas, Sakellaridis. *Crocus sativus* L. extracts antagonize memory impairments in different behavioral tasks in the rat. *Behav* 2006; 173(1): 112–115.
9. Abe, Saito. Effects of saffron extract and its constituent crocin on learning behavior and long-term potentiation. *Phytother* 2000; 14(3): 149–152.
10. Sheng, Qian, Zheng, Xi. Mechanism of hypolipidemic effect of crocin in rats: crocin inhibits pancreatic lipase. *Eur* 2006; 543(1–3): 116–1122.
11. Hosseinzadeh, Sadeghnia. Protective effect of safranal on pentylenetetrazol-induced seizures in the rat: Involvement of GABAergic and opioids systems. *Phytomedicine.* 2007; 14(4): 256–262.
12. Premkumar, Thirunavukkarasu, Abraham, Santhiya, Ramesh. Protective effect of saffron (*Crocus sativus* L.) aqueous extract against genetic damage induced by anti-tumor agents in mice. *Hum* 2006; 25(2): 79–84.
13. Assimopoulou, Sinakos, Papageorgiou. Radical scavenging activity of *Crocus sativus* L. extract and its bioactive constituents. *Phytother* 2005; 19(11): 997–1000.
14. Ochiai, Ohno, Soeda, Tanaka, Shoyama, Shimeno. Crocin prevents the death of rat pheochromyctoma (PC-12) cells by its antioxidant effects stronger than those of alpha-tocopherol. *Neurosci* 2004; 362(1): 61–64.
15. Das, Chakrabarty, Das. Saffron can prevent chemically induced skin carcinogenesis in Swiss albino mice. *Asian* 2004; 5(1): 70–76.
16. Salomi, Nair, Panikkar. Inhibitory effects of *Nigella sativa* and saffron (*Crocus sativus*) on chemical carcinogenesis in mice. *Nutr* 1991; 16(1): 67–72.
17. Nair, Pannikar, Panikkar. Antitumor activity of saffron (*Crocus sativus*). *Cancer* 1991; 57(2): 109–114.
18. Abdullaev. Cancer chemopreventive and tumoricidal properties of saffron (*Crocus sativus* L.). *Exp* 2002; 227(1): 20–25.
19. Escribano J, et al. Crocin, safranal, and picrocrocin from saffron (*Crocus sativus* L.) inhibits the growth of human cancer cells in-vitro. *Cancer Letters* 1996; 100: 23–30.
20. Fatehi, Rashidabady, Fatehi-Hassanabad. Effects of *Crocus sativus* petals' extract on rat blood pressure and on responses induced by electrical field stimulation in the rat isolated vas deferens and guinea-pig ileum. *J* 2003; 84(2–3): 199–203.
21. Hosseinzadeh, Younesi. Antinociceptive and anti-inflammatory effects of *Crocus sativus* L. stigma and petal extracts in mice. *BMC* 2002; 2: 7.
22. Xuan, Zhou, Li, Min, Chiou. Effects of crocin analogs on ocular blood flow and retinal function. *J* 1999; 15(2): 143–152.
23. Fetrow CW, Avila JR. *The Complete Guide to Herbal Medicines*. Springhouse: Springhouse Corporation, 2000.

Senna/*Sanā*

FAMILY: Fabaceae

BOTANICAL NAME: *Cassia angustifolia*

COMMON NAMES: *English* Indian senna, Tinnevelly senna plant, Alexandrian senna; *French* Casse trompeuse, Casse à feuilles étroites; *Spanish* Sen; *German* Senneskassie; *Urdu/Unānī* Sana, Sanna-e Makki; *Modern Standard Arabic* sanā, sanā ḥindī, sanā makkī, sanā ḥijāzī

SAFETY RATING: GENERALLY SAFE When used as directed for short periods, senna is generally considered safe for most adults and children over the age of two. Some of the side effects of senna include stomach discomfort, cramps, and diarrhea. Senna should not be used for more than two weeks as it may cause abnormal bowel function and may lead to dependency on laxatives. Furthermore, long-term use can cause low electrolytes which can cause heart problems, muscle weakness, liver damage, and other adverse effects. Senna should not be used by pregnant women unless advised to do so by their physician. People with stomach or bowel disorders, low electrolytes, and hemorrhoids should also avoid using the herb, as should people who are dehydrated or suffering from diarrhea or loose stools.

Prophetic Prescription: The Prophet Muḥammad said, "Senna (*sanā*) and dill (*sannūt*) are for you, for there is a cure in these two for every disease except death."[1] He said, "If there was anything that could cure death, that cure would be senna."[2] He said, "If there is any remedy against death, then it is senna, the gladdening one, the gentle one."[3] He said, "There are three things which are a cure for every disease except death"[4] (senna, dill, and a third cure not identified in the tradition). As for the meaning of *sannūt*, scholars are divided on the issue, some suggesting that it means honey, a mixture of Meccan fat, a seed similar to cumin or dates.[5] They were evidently unaware of the Prophet's saying that: *Al-thuffā' al-ḥurf wa al-sannūt shbit* or "*Thuffā'* is garden-cress and *sannūt* is dill."[6]

The Messenger of Allāh once inquired from Asmā' bint Amīs what she used to keep her in good health. She replied, "I drink warm milk." The Prophet said, "But this is very hot for the body." She replied, "I also use senna herbs." On hearing this, the Prophet said, "If there was any cure in that, it would have been the senna (*sanā*)." The Prophet asked 'Ā'ishah "What do you use for a purgative?" She replied, "I use Euphorbia." The Prophet responded that "It is too hot and strong. I myself use senna seed (*sanā*)."[7] According to Ibn Ḥabīb, the Prophet used to cook senna in olive oil before administering it. He also relates that Ḥārith ibn Kaladah, the famous herbalist who lived during the time of the Prophet, used to cook senna with olive oil and use it to treat phlegm and back pain.[8] According to Imām Ja'far al-Ṣādiq,

> If people knew what was in senna, they would pay double its weight in gold. It is a protection against *Tinaea versicolor* (*al-bahaq*), *psoriasis* (*baraṣ*), leprosy (*al-judhām*), madness, semi-paralysis (*fālij*), and facial paralysis (*luqwah*).[9] It is taken with seedless dried red raisins. Add Kabūlī embelic myrobalan to it, along with the same portion of the yellow and the black one. The quantity of three dirhams is taken on an empty stomach, and similarly when you go to sleep. It is the best of medicine.[10]

Issues in Identification: Bīrūnī and Dīnawarī speak of *sanā makkī* which Said identifies as the leaves of senna, including at least two possible varieties (*Cassia angustifolia*, *Cassia acutifolia*, and *Cassia oborata*).[11] Ibn al-Jawziyyah claims that *sanna* means honey, a variety of cumin called *kammūn karmanī*, the essence of fat which accumulates as fine dark lines on top of ghee, a fruit similar to a date or even a variety of fennel called *rāzyanj* or *shomār*.[12]

According to Ghazanfar, *Cassia senna* (also known as *Cassia alexandrina*, *Senna alexandrina*, *Cassia angustifolia*) is called *sanā*, *sannā makkī*, *senā*, and *sennā makkī* in Arabic. Barr, however, holds that *sanā* and *sanā makkī* refer to *Cassia cacutifolia* while *sanā al-hindī* refers to *Cassia angustifolia*.[13] The plant is native to Arabia, Somalia, Sind, and the Punjab. It is found in the Western and southern regions of Saudi Arabia.[14]

Properties and Uses: Senna is a sweet, cooling, laxative herb with antibacterial effects. A cathartic and cholagogue, it acts on nearly the entire intestinal tract, especially the colon, increasing peristalsis and intestinal secretions, producing copious stools in four to six hours, with griping and flatulence. The griping and flatulent qualities of senna are often lessened by addition of carminatives like ginger, coriander, peppermint, tamarind, fennel, or Epsom salt. While large doses cause vomiting, it never results in poisoning. Senna should never be administered to children under 12, women who are pregnant or lactating, people suffering from inflammatory intestinal illness (Crohn's disease, ulcerative colitis, appendicitis, abdominal pains of unknown cause).[15] Senna is also considered a blood purifier, anthelmintic, and detersive. Wild senna (*Cassia marilandica*), which is found in North America, is milder than its cousin from the Old World. Senna is used also used to treat fever, tumors, and to promote menstruation. Externally, senna is used for skin afflictions such as burns, psoriasis, and boils.

Scientific Studies: *Peristaltic Stimulating Activity* Senna contains a number of chemical substances that stimulate peristaltic movements in the lower bowel, thus acting as a laxative. While it is good for constipation, it must be used with great care in its natural form as it is a cathartic drug and its dosage is difficult to adjust. Since it can be damaging in cases of spastic constipation or colitis, causing severe nausea and pain, the use of standardized over the counter products is recommended. Because of the presence of anthraquinones, senna species are used as the primary ingredient in certain commercial stimulant laxatives. It is also the primary ingredient found in most "dieter's tea." Even with standardized preparations, habitual dosing should be avoided as excessive colonic irritation can occur. The German Ministry of Health warns that chronic abuse may result in electrolyte disturbances due to potassium loss may interfere with or potentiate the activity of cardiac glycosides.[16]

Senna Notes

1. Sūyūṭī J. *As-Sūyūṭī's Medicine of the Prophet.* Ed. A Thomson. London: Ṭā-Hā Publishers, 1994: 70; Ibn Mājah M. *Sunan.* Trans. MT Anṣārī. Lahore: Kazi Publications, 1994.
2. Ibn Ḥabīb A. *Mujtaṣar fī al-ṭibb/Compendio de medicina.* Ed. C Álvarez de Morales and F Girón Irueste. Madrid: Consejo Superior de Investigaciones Científicas, 1992: 67/34.
3. Sūyūṭī J. *As-Sūyūṭī's Medicine of the Prophet.* Ed. A Thomson. London: Ṭā-Hā Publishers, 1994: 71.
4. Sūyūṭī J. *As-Sūyūṭī's Medicine of the Prophet.* Ed. A Thomson. London: Ṭā-Hā Publishers, 1994: 71.
5. Sūyūṭī J. *As-Sūyūṭī's Medicine of the Prophet.* Ed. A Thomson. London: Ṭā-Hā Publishers, 1994: 71.
6. Ibn Ḥabīb A. *Mujtaṣar fī al-ṭibb/Compendio de medicina.* Ed. C Álvarez de Morales and F Girón Irueste. Madrid: Consejo Superior de Investigaciones Científicas, 1992: 78/46.
7. Sūyūṭī J. *As-Sūyūṭī's Medicine of the Prophet.* Ed. A Thomson. London: Ṭā-Hā Publishers, 1994: 70. There are various versions of this tradition featuring either Asmā', Ā'ishah or Umm Salamah.
8. Ibn Ḥabīb A. *Mujtaṣar fī al-ṭibb/Compendio de medicina.* Ed. C Álvarez de Morales and F Girón Irueste. Madrid: Consejo Superior de Investigaciones Científicas, 1992: 67/35.
9. As Aḥmad al-Sharīf has shown, ancient Arabic medical terms were confused in pre–Islamic times, and this confusion has continued to the present. I agree with Sharīf that *judhām* refers to leprosy, that black *bahaq* refers to *Tinaea versicolor*, that black *baras* refers to psoriasis, that white *baraṣ* refers predominantly to vitiligo, and occasionally to leprosy, and that both white *bahaq* and *wadah* refer to vitiligo. See: Sharīf A. *Judhām, baraṣ, wadah, bahaq,* and *quwaba'*: a study of terms and concepts in *al-Qanūn fī al-ṭibb* of Ibn Sīnā. *JISHIM* 2006; 5: 30–39. Like many Arabs who are fond of used shortened forms, the Imāms did not specify the type *baraṣ* or *bahaq*, as the particular case is usually evident based on context. In this case, *baraṣ* could refer to psoriasis or vitiligo.
10. Majlisī M. *Biḥār al-anwār.* Ṭihrān: Javad al-Alavi, 1956.
11. Dīnawarī AH. *Kitāb al-nabāt: Le dictionaire botanique d'Abū Ḥanīfa al-Dīnawarī.* al-Qāhirah: Institut Français d'Archéologie Orientale du Caire, 1973.
12. Ibn Qayyim al-Jawziyyah M. *al-Ṭibb al-nabawī.* Bayrūt: Dār al-Kitāb, 1985.
13. Ibn Ḥabīb A. *al-Ṭibb al-nabawī.* Ed. MA Barr. Bayrūt: Dār al-Qalam, 1993.
14. Ghazanfar SA. *Handbook of Arabian Medicinal Plants.* Boca Raton: CRC Press, 1994.
15. Gehrmann, B, Wolf-Gerald K, Tshirch CO, Brinkmann H. *Medicinal Herbs: A Compendium.* New York: Haworth Press, 2005: 178.
16. German Ministry of Health. *Senna: Commission E. Monographs for Phytomedicines.* Bonn: German Ministry of Health, 1984.

Sesame / *Simsim*

FAMILY: Pedaliaceae

BOTANICAL NAME: *Sesamum indicum*

COMMON NAMES: *English* Sesame, benne, gingili; *French* sésame; *Spanish* sésamo; *German* Sesam; *Urdu/Unānī* Til, Kunjad, Simsim; *Modern Standard Arabic* simsim

SAFETY RATING: GENERALLY SAFE Sesame seeds are generally considered to be safe for most people. They do, however, produce an allergic reaction in a small percentage of the population. They are associated with nut allergy in children, and may be the main allergen in some cases.

PROPHETIC PRESCRIPTION: It is reported that the Messenger of Allāh gave some sesame seeds (*simsim*) and some dates (*tamr*) to one of his companions. He consumed some of them and made a supplication.[1] According to Ibn Ṭūlūn, Imām Muḥammad al-Bāqir and Imām Ja'far al-Ṣādiq said that the Prophet used to apply sesame seed oil.[2] According to Ibn Ḥabīb, the Prophet used to apply sesame (*simsim*) (oil) inside his nose.[3] The Imāms often used sesame seed oil in their medicine.

ISSUES IN IDENTIFICATION: It is the consensus that the Arabic *sismim* means sesame.

PROPERTIES AND USES: Sesame is a sweet, warming, soothing herb that fortifies the bones and teeth, moisturizes dry tissues, relaxes spasms, is mildly laxative, and has a tonic effect on the liver and kidneys. Sesame seeds are astringent, diuretic, emollient, galactogogue, lenitive, and nutritive. Sesame seeds are used internally to treat premature hair loss and graying, convalescence, chronic dry constipation, tooth decay, osteoporosis, stiff joints, dry cough, and symptoms such as tinnitus, poor vision, dizziness, headache, infantile cholera, diarrhea, dysentery, bladder troubles and excess mucus. The leaves are used to treat cystitis. The oil is used as a laxative, to promote menstruation, and to treat constipation in the elderly. The root is used in a decoction to treat asthma and coughs, and the seeds have a marked ability to increase maternal milk production. Externally, sesame seed oil is used to treat hemorrhoids. Mixed with lime water, the oil is used to treat burns, boils, and ulcers.

SCIENTIFIC STUDIES: *Antitumor Activity* According to an animal study conducted by Jinan University in China, the alcohol extract from *Sesamum indicum* flower showed an obvious antitumor effect.[4]

Hypoglycemic Activity According to an animal study conducted by Shizuoka University in Japan, the hot-water extract from defatted *Sesamum indicum* seeds reduced plasma glucose concentration caused perhaps by delayed glucose absorption.[5]

Sesame Notes

1. Iṣbahānī AN al-. *Mawsū'at al-ṭibb al-nabawī.* Ed. MKD al-Turkī. Bayrūt: Dār Ibn Ḥazm, 2006.

2. Ibn Ṭulūn S. *al-Manhal al-rawī fī al-ṭibb al-nabawī.* Ed. ʿAzīz Bayk. Riyyāḍ: Dār ʿālam al-kutub, 1995.
3. Ibn Ḥabīb A. *Mujtaṣar fī al-ṭibb/Compendio de medicina.* Ed. C Álvarez de Morales and F Girón Irueste. Madrid: Consejo Superior de Investigaciones Científicas, 1992: 56/23.
4. Xu, Yang, Yang, Qi, Liu, Yang. Antitumor effect of alcohol extract from *Sesamum indicum* flower on S180 and H22 experimental tumor. *Zhong* 2003; 26(4): 272–273.
5. Takeuchi, Mooi, Inagaki, He. Hypoglycemic effect of a hot-water extract from defatted sesame (*Sesamum indicum* L.) seed on the blood glucose level in genetically diabetic KK-Ay mice. *Biosci* 2001; 65(10): 2318–2321.

Sneezewort / *Kundus*

Family: Compositae/Asteraceae

Botanical Name: *Achillea fragrantissima*

Common Names: *English* Lavender cotton; *French* Garda-robe, aurone gemelle, santoline; *Spanish* Guardaroba, santolina; *German* Cypressengarbe; *Urdu/Unānī*; *Modern Standard Arabic* qayṣūm

Botanical Name: *Achillea millefolium*

Common Names: *English* Yarrow; *French* Achilée, herbe à la copure; *Spanish* Cientoenrama, flor de pluma, maquilea, milenrama, mil hojas, hierba de las heridas, hierba del carpintero, hierba de aquiles; *German* Garbe, schafgarbe; *Urdu/Unānī* Biranjaasif, Gomadar; *Modern Standard Arabic* Huzambil

Botanical Name: *Achillea ptarmica*

Common Names: *English* Sneezewort; *French* Achillée sternutatoire; *Spanish* Botón de plata; *German* Sumpfschafgarbe, Bertram-Schafgarbe, Deutscher Weißer Dorant, Sumpf-Garbe; *Urdu/Unānī* Qaisoom; *Modern Standard Arabic* kundus

Safety Rating: Generally Safe to Dangerous *Achillea millefolium* is generally considered safe when used in moderation as a carminative and diaphoretic. Although *Achillea millefolium* is not generally considered toxic, it is an emmenagogue and an abortive. As such, its volatile oil must not be used during pregnancy. The most commonly reported side effect of *Achillea millefolium* is contact dermatitis. It can also cause headache and vertigo in large doses. Although symptoms are generally slow to develop, *Achillea ptarmica* is poisonous to cattle, sheep, and horses. Symptoms include fever, rapid pulse, breathing difficulties, weight loss, drooling, spasms, loss of muscular control, and convulsions.

Prophetic Prescription: A man complained to Imām Jaʿfar al-Ṣādiq of the common cold. The Imām said, "It is one of the workings of Allāh and one of the armies of Allāh. Allāh has sent it to an illness in your body to remove it. When it has been removed, you must take one *daniq* [⅙ of a *dirham*] weight of fennel flower, and half a *daniq* weight of sneezewort (*kundus*). Grind it and inhale it all. It will get rid of the cold. If it is possible that you not treat it with something else then do that, for it [the cold] has many benefits."[1]

Issues in Identification: *Achillea ptarmica* or sneezewort, which is known as *kundus* in Arabic, should not be confused with *Achillea millefolium* or yarrow, which is known as *huzambil* in Arabic, or with *Achillea fragrantissima*, which is known as *qayṣūm*. However, since the three flowers belong to the same family, we have commented upon all of them in the sections below. In India, *nakk chhikni* or *Centipeda orbicularis* is also known as sneezewort, and should not be confused with *Achillea ptarmica.*

According to Mandaville, *Achillea fragrantissima* is the most powerfully fragrant plant in eastern Arabia. Although not widespread, it is found in silt-floored basins, usually in rocky country. The sedentary Arabs use it to treat renal calculi, high blood sugar, diabetes, and for urinary tract infections. The Bedouin use the leaves to treat diabetes, chest, stomach, and kidney problems, muscular rheumatism, cough, snake and scorpion bites. They also use *Achillea conferta*, called *qūysī mah*, and *Achillea santolina* for practically the same purposes, although they are considered weaker than *Achillea fragrantissima.*

Achillea millefolium is considered astringent, anesthetic, carminative, diaphoretic, hemostatic, and tonic.

Properties and Uses: Traditionally used as a tonic, diaphoretic, and errhine, *Achillea ptarmica* or sneezewort is valuable for chills, fevers, and other febrile diseases. The whole plant possesses errhine properties, but the flowers, particularly the florets of the disk, are the most active, and may be used, in powder, as a snuff, in headache, incipient coryza, catarrh, deafness, and other affections where errhines are desired. *A. ptarmica* is anti-inflammatory, and is used in the treatment of sore throat, diarrhea, flatulence, dysentery, gastrointestinal inflammation, blurred vision, bruises, the common cold, influenza, and stomach cramps. *A. ptarmica* is also diuretic and is used to treat chronic urinary diseases.

Achillea millefolium, the most common type of *Achillea* used in Unānī and Ayurvedic medicine, is described as stimulant, tonic, carminative, emmenagogue, antispasmodic, and anti-inflammatory. It is used internally to treat amenorrhea, menorrhagia, and leucorrhoea. It is also given to treat dyspepsia, flatulence, diarrhea, hemorrhoids, and parasitic infestation. An infusion of the whole plant is used as a disinfectant gargle. For Native Americans, yarrow is abortive, analgesic, emmenagogue, febrifuge, laxative, stimulant, and tonic. They use the plant to treat coughs, colds, throat irritations, toothaches, bowel and urinary complaints, headache, indigestion, and respiratory diseases. Externally, Native Americans use yarrow to treat bruises, burns, sprains, and wounds, as well as to stop bleeding. Since the active ingredients in *Achillea millefolium* are choline and achilleine, which are regarded as lipotropic and suforific, the herb is used to treat infectious hepatitis.

SCIENTIFIC STUDIES: *Hypoglycemic Activity* According to an animal study conducted by the University of Tehran, *Achillea santolina* has a high hypoglycemic activity which may be attributed to its antioxidative potential.[2]

Antiparasitic Activity According to a study conducted by the Instituto Oswaldo Cruz in Brazil, the essential oil of *Achillea millefolium* inhibits parasite growth.[3]

Anti-inflammatory Activity According to an animal study conducted by Al-Isra University in Jordan, *Achillea* extract reduced edema by 48.1 percent while diclosal Emulgel produced a 47 percent reduction of edema.[4]

Spasmolytic Activity In an animal study conducted by the University of Vienna, the concentration of the flavonoids is high enough in *Achillea millefolium* tea to exert a spasmolytic effect in the gut. The spasmolytic effect of yarrow tea is mainly caused by blockade of the calcium inward current, but additionally by mediator-antagonistic effects.[5]

*Anti–*H. Pylori *Activity* As part of an ongoing screening program conducted by the University of Illinois at Chicago, methanol extract of *Achillea millefolium* had a minimum inhibitory concentration of 50 microg/mL against 15 *Helicobacter pylori* strains.[6]

Antitumor Activity According to research, *Achillea millefolium* contains antitumor compounds.[7]

Anti-inflammatory Activity Research has confirmed the anti-inflammatory activity of *Achillea millefolium.*[8]

Antispermatogenic Activity Research has confirmed the antispermatogenic activity of *Achillea millefolium* in mice.[9]

Sneezewort Notes

1. Nisābūrī A. *Islamic Medical Wisdom: The Ṭibb al-a'immah*. Trans. B. Ispahany. Ed. AJ Newman. London: Muḥammadī Trust, 1991: 77.

2. Yazdanparast, Ardestani, Jamshidi. Experimental diabetes treated with *Achillea santolina*: Effect on pancreatic oxidative parameters. *J* 2007; 112(1): 13–18.

3. Santoro, Cardoso, Guimaraes, Mendonca, Soares. Trypanosoma cruzi: Activity of essential oils from *Achillea millefolium* L., *Syzygium aromaticum* L. and *Ocimum basilicum* L. on epimastigotes and trypomastigotes. *Exp* 2007; 116(3): 283–290.

4. Maswadeh, Semreen, Naddaf. Anti-inflammatory activity of *Achillea* and *Ruscus* topical gel on carrageenan-induced paw edema in rats. *Acta* 2006; 63(4): 277–280.

5. Lemmens-Gruber, Marchart, Rawnduzi, Engel, Benedek, Kopp. Investigation of the spasmolytic activity of the flavonoid fraction of *Achillea millefolium* s.l. on isolated guinea-pig ilea. *Arzneimittelforschung.* 2006; 56(8): 582–588.

6. Mahady, Pendland, Stoia, Hamill, Fabricant, Dietz, Chadwick. In vitro susceptibility of *Helicobacter pylori* to botanical extracts used traditionally for the treatment of gastrointestinal disorders. *Phytother* 2005; 19(11): 988–991.

7. Tozyo T, et al. Novel antitumor sesquiterpenoids in *Achillea millefolium. Chemical and Pharmaceutical Bulletin (Tokyo)* 1994; 42: 1096–1100.

8. Goldberg AS, Mueller EC, Eigen E. Isolation of the anti-inflammatory principles from *Achillea Millefolium Compositae. Journal of Pharmacological Science* 1969; 58: 938–941.

9. Montanari T, De Carvalho JE, Dolder H. Antispermatogenic effect of *Achillea millefolium* L. in mice. Contraception 1998; 58(5): 309–313.

Spurge / *Shubrum*

FAMILY: Euphorbiaceae

BOTANICAL NAME: *Euphorbia* spp.

COMMON NAMES: *English* Spurge; *French* Euphorbe; *Spanish* Euforbio; *Spanish* hierba de golondrina, golondrina; *German* Wolfsmilch; *Urdu/Unānī* Farfiyun, Farbiyun; *Modern Standard Arabic* farbayūn

SAFETY RATING: DANGEROUS TO DEADLY All types of *Euphorbia* are dangerous, and some are capable of causing cancer. The type most commonly used by herbalists is *Euphorbia hirta* or asthma weed, known in Unānī medicine as *Dudhi Kalan* and *Sheer Ghiyah*, which should only be administered in extreme cases under expert supervision. Even in such cases, it is best to avoid *Euphorbia* altogether as plenty of safe alternatives exist.

PROPHETIC PRESCRIPTION: The Prophet asked 'Ā'ishah "What do you use as a purgative?" She replied, "Euphorbia (*shubrum*)." The Prophet responded that it was *ḥārrun jārrun* which means that it is a very hot and a powerful laxative.[1] In another tradition, he is reported to have said, "You have senna and euphorbium (*shubrum*), which is a hot and powerful laxative, that is, it flushes out disease."[2]

Issues in Identification: According to Ibn Sīnā, *shubrum* is the latex of *Euphorbia pithyusa*. Akīlī identifies it simply as *Euphorbia*, while Thomson suggests that it is *Euphorbia resinifera*.[3] There are many types of *Euphorbia* native to Arabia. Generally known as *farbayūn* in Modern Standard Arabic, none of the numerous species of *Euphorbia* are known as *shubrum*. Bīrūnī mentions *shubrum*, which Said takes to be a species of *Tithymalus*, also spelled as *shibran* and *shilram*. The only plant known as *shubrum* is *Alhagi maurorum*, the Sinai manna or Hebrew manna plant, which is also known as *'āqul, shawk al-jimāl*, among many other Arabic dialectical names. This is certainly not the plant the Prophet warned against. *Alhagi maurorum* is a legume, not a spurge, and it is not a violent purgative. Rather, its roots are used in traditional medicine to make an infusion used for kidney or liver ailments.

Properties and Uses: *Euphorbia* is a violent purgative containing terpenic. Most spurges contain carcinogenic, highly irritant diterpene esters and are powerful purgatives. The Chinese species *Euphorbia kansui* is used as a purgative, as it is *Euphorbia pekinensis*, which also has diuretic and antibacterial effects. The North African *Euphorbia resinifera* is another drastic purgative, which is now considered far too dangerous for medicinal use. *Euphorbia lathyrus* is also far too toxic to consume as it contains a violent purgative oil similar to croton oil.

The spurge most regularly employed by herbalists is *Euphorbia hirta*, which is ester-free. The plant is anodyne, anti-asthmatic, anticatarrhal, anti-pruritic, antispasmodic, anthelmintic, carminative, a bronchodilator, demulcent, depurative, depressant, diuretic, febrifugal, galactogogue, purgative, sedative, and vermifuge. It is used to treat acute and chronic dysentery, colic, worms, cough, coryza, bronchial catarrhal affections, asthma, and emphysema. It is also used to treat warts, athlete's foot, syphilis, and skin conditions. It should only be used under expert supervision as large doses cause gastro-intestinal irritation, nausea, and vomiting.

Although animal studies on *Euphorbia hirta* suggest that it has some ability to treat certain infections and reduce pain, fever, inflammation, nervousness, and anxiety, no research has been conducted on human beings. One study, however, showed that *Euphorbia hirta* is neither safe nor effective in treating asthma. Although spurges were used by the ancient Arabs as a purgative, the Prophet warned against this dangerous use, recommending the use of henna instead. The general symptoms of ingestion are abdominal pains, blistering/irritation of the mouth/throat and vomiting. The Prophet was right to err on the side of caution as the sap of *Euphorbia hirta* is carcinogenic in nature.

Scientific Studies: *Analgesic, Antipyretic, and Anti-inflammatory Activity* According to one study, *Euphorbia hirta* possesses analgesic, antipyretic, and anti-inflammatory properties.[4]

Antimicrobial Activity According to a study conducted by Shri Vishnu College of Pharmacy in India, the ethanolic extract of the aerial parts of *Euphorbia hirta* exhibits a broad spectrum of anti-microbial activity, particularly against *Escherichia coli* (enteropathogen), *Proteus vulgaris, Pseudomonas aeruginosa* and *Staphylococcus aureus*.[5]

Antidiarrheic Activity According to a study conducted by G.B. Pant University of Agriculture and Technology in India, the aqueous leaf extract of *Euphorbia hirta* decreased the gastrointestinal motility in rats and decreased the effect of castor oil-induced diarrhea in mice.[6] In another study, conducted by the Universidad de Granada in Spain, a lyophilized decoction of *Euphorbia hirta* whole plant demonstrated anti-diarrheic activity in experimental models of diarrhea induced by castor oil, arachidonic acid, and prostaglandin E2, delaying the small intestinal transit. Researchers isolated a flavonoid, known as quercitrin, with anti-diarrheic activity from this crude drug.[7]

*Anti–*Helicobacter pylori *Activity* According to a study conducted by National Chung-Hsing University in Taiwan, ninety-fiver percent ethanol extract of *Euphorbia hirta* showed moderate anti–*H. pylori* activity.[8]

Antiplasmodial Activity In an in-vitro study conducted by the University of Kinshasa in the Democratic Republic of the Congo, extracts from the whole *Euphorbia hirta* plant exhibited antiplasmodial activity, showing its potential for use in the treatment of malaria.[9]

Antimalarial Activity According to an in-vitro study conducted by the University of Kinshasa in the Democratic Republic of the Congo, the extract of *Euphorbia hirta* whole plant produced more than 60 percent inhibition of *P. falciparum* growth at a test concentration of 6 microg/ml. Extracts from *Euphorbia hirta* also showed a significant chemosuppression of parasitemia in mice infested with *P. berghei* with oral doses of 100–400 mg/kg per day.[10]

Anti-amebic and Spasmolytic Activity According to an in-vitro study conducted by the University of Kinshasa in the Democratic Republic of Congo, the anti-amebic and spasmolytic activity of *Eurphorbia hirta* are concentrated in the polyphenolic fraction, and not in the saponin or alkaloid containing fractions.[11]

Diuretic Activity According to an animal study conducted by Ahmadu Bello University in Nigeria, the water and ethanol extracts of *Euphorbia hirta* plant produced time-dependent increase in urine output with significant electrolyte excretion. The study suggests that the active component(s) in the water extract of *E. hirta* leaf had similar diuretic spectrum to that of acetazolamide, validating the use of *E. hirta* as a diuretic agent.[12]

Spurge Notes

1. Sūyūṭī J. *As-Sūyūṭī's Medicine of the Prophet.* Ed. A Thomson. London: Ṭā-Hā Publishers, 1994: 70.
2. Ibn Ḥabīb A. *Mujtaṣar fī al-ṭibb/Compendio de medicina.* Ed. C Álvarez de Morales and F Girón Irueste. Madrid: Consejo Superior de Investigaciones Científicas, 1992: 67.
3. Ibn al-Qayyim al-Jawziyyah. *Natural Healing with the Medicine of the Prophet.* Pearl Publishing. Trans. M al-Akīlī. Philadelphia, 1993.
4. Lanhers MC, et al. Analgesic, anti-pyretic, and anti-inflammatory properties of *Euphorbia hirta. Planta Medica* 1991; 57: 225–231.
5. Sudhakar, Rao, Rao, Raju, Venkateswarlu. Antimicrobial activity of *Caesalpinia pulcherrima, Euphorbia hirta* and *Asystasia gangeticum. Fitoterapia.* 2006; 77(5): 378–380.
6. Hore, Ahuja, Mehta, Kumar, Pandey, Ahmad AH. Effect of aqueous *Euphorbia hirta* leaf extract on gastrointestinal motility. *Fitoterapia.* 2006; 77(1): 35–38.
7. Galvez, Zarzuelo, Crespo, Lorente, Ocete, Jiménez J. Anti-diarrheic activity of *Euphorbia hirta* extract and isolation of an active flavonoid constituent. *Planta* 1993; 59(4): 333–336.
8. Wang, Huang. Screening of anti-*Helicobacter pylori* herbs deriving from Taiwanese folk medicinal plants. *FEMS* 2005; 43(2): 295–300.
9. Tona, Cimanga, Mesia, Musuamba, De, Apers, Hernans, Van, Pieters, Totté J, Vlietinck. In vitro antiplasmodial activity of extracts and fractions from seven medicinal plants used in the Democratic Republic of Congo. *J* 2004; 93(1): 27–32.
10. Tona, Ngimbi, Tsakala, Mesia, Cimanga, Apers, De, Pieters, Totté J, Vlietinck. Antimalarial activity of 20 crude extracts from nine African medicinal plants used in Kinshasa, Congo. *J* 1999; 68(1–3): 193–203.
11. Tona, Kambu, Ngimbi, Mesia, Penge, Lusakibanza, Cimanga, De, Apers, Totte, Pieters, Vlietinck. Anti-amebic and spasmolytic activities of extracts from some antidiarrheal traditional preparations used in Kinshasa, Congo. *Phytomedicine.* 2000; 7(1): 31–38.
12. Johnson, Abdurahman, Tiam, Abdu-Aguye, Hussaini. *Euphorbia hirta* leaf extracts increase urine output and electrolytes in rats. *J* 1999; 65(1): 63–69.

Sumac / *Summāq*

FAMILY: Anacardiaceae

BOTANICAL NAME: *Rhus* spp.

COMMON NAMES: *English* Sumac, tanner's sumac; *French* Sumac, Sumac des corroyeurs, Vinaigrier; *Spanish* Sumaque, Zumaque; *German* Gerbersumach, Essigbaum; *Urdu/Unānī* Sumaaq; *Modern Standard Arabic* summāq, summāq al-dibāghah

SAFETY RATING: GENERALLY SAFE TO DEADLY While *Rhus coriaria* and *Rhus glabra* are considered safe for most people, some species, such as *Rhus radicans* (poison ivy), *Rhus diversiloba* (poison oak), and *Rhus vermix* (poison sumac), contain the allergen urushiol and can cause severe skin and mucous membrane irritation. Of the latter three, poison sumac is the most virulent. Some botanists consider it the most toxic plant species in the United States. Inhalation of the smoke of poison sumac can cause delirium, inflammation of the kidneys and digestive track, as well as a rash on the lining of the lungs, resulting in extreme pain, and possibly fatal respiratory difficulty. Since poison sumac can be fatal in even small doses, mistaking poison sumac for sumac can result in death. This mistake can be made easily since the poisonous and non-poisonous sumac species have similar leaves. The key to distinguishing between both varieties is based on its fruits. The non-poisonous species have red fruits that form distinctive, erect, cone-shaped terminal heads, while the poisonous variety produces hanging, whitish green fruits.

PROPHETIC PRESCRIPTION: The Messenger of Allāh also said, "Pomegranate (*rummān*) and sumac (*summāq*) are effective in cases of bilious diseases."[1] A woman wrote to Imām 'Alī al-Riḍā complaining of the continuous flow of menstrual blood. He wrote to her, "Take one handful of coriander (*kuzbarah*) and one of sumac (*summāq*) and soak it for one night in the open air. Then put it on the fire and sieve it. Drink a saucer of it and the blood will case, Allāh, the Exalted, willing."[2]

ISSUES IN IDENTIFICATION: There is no question that the *summāq* mentioned by the Prophet is *Rhus.* It is not entirely clear, however, whether he was referring to *Rhus coriara* or another *Rhus* species. Farooqi, Álvarez Morales and Girón Irueste hold that it is *Rhus coriaria,* which is found in Syria, Iran, and the Mediterranean.[3] As Nehmé explains, the first is known in Arabic as *summāq,* while the second bears the name of *summāq al-dabbāghīn.*[4]

PROPERTIES AND USES: *Rhus coriari* is an astringent, antiseptic, repercussive, antibilious, styptic, mucilaginous herb with tonic effects. The bark is regarded as alterative; the fruits are cooling and diuretic. The root bark from *Rhus coriari* or smooth sumac is used internally for diarrhea, nausea, vomiting, dysentery, and to alleviate thirst. The fruits are used to stimulate the appetite, to relieve bilious diarrhea, scurvy, ophthalmia, dysentery, nausea, vomiting, haemoptysis, haematemis, dieresis, leucorrhoea, feverish illnesses, and urinary complaints. The root bark is also used externally for skin irritations, sores, ulcers, vaginal discharge, and hemorrhoids. Various sumacs are high in tannins and are valued for their astringent properties.

In Unānī medicine, the most common type of *Rhus* employed is *Rhus aromatica* or dwarf sumac, which is indigenous to North America. *Rhus aromatica* is astringent, diuretic, emmenagogue, febrifuge, refrigerant, and tonic. It is used internally for sore throat, diarrhea, lekorrhea, urinary problems, inflammation of the bladder, and gonorrhea. Externally, its leaves are applied as poultice to relieve symptoms of poison ivy.

SCIENTIFIC STUDIES: *Antimicrobial Activity* Numerous scientific studies have confirmed the antimicrobial, antibiotic, and antifungal properties of *Rhus glabra*.[5]

Anti-Hyperglycemic Activity According to a study conducted by the University of Calabria in Italy, the ethyl acetate extract of sumac poses potential in the treatment and prevention of hyperglycemia, diabetes and obesity.[6]

Antioxidative Activity In a study of *Rhus coriaria* conducted by the University of Cumhuriyet in Turkey, the methanolic extract (water-soluble part) was prepared and investigated using free radical-generating systems in vitro. The methanolic extracts of *R. coriaria* L. fruits have considerable antioxidative activity against free radicals and lipid peroxidation in vitro, a fact that may encourage in vivo studies.[7]

Sumac Notes

1. Ibn Qayyim al-Jawziyyah M. *al-Ṭibb al-nabawī*. Bayrūt: Dār al-Kitāb, 1985.
2. Nisābūrī A. *Islamic Medical Wisdom: The Ṭibb al-a'immah*. Trans. B. Ispahany. Ed. AJ Newman. London: Muḥammadī Trust, 1991: 130.
3. Farooqi; Ibn Ḥabīb A. *Mujtaṣar fī al-ṭibb/Compendio de medicina*. Ed. C Álvarez de Morales and F Girón Irueste. Madrid: Consejo Superior de Investigaciones Científicas, 1992.
4. Nehmé M. *Dictionnaire étymologique de la flore du Liban*. Bayrūt: Librairie du Liban, 2000.
5. Saxena, McCutcheon, Farmer, Towers, Hancock. Antimicrobial constituents of *Rhus glabra*. *J* 1994; 42(2): 95–99; *McCutcheon, Ellis, Hancock, Towers*. Antibiotic screening of medicinal plants of the British Columbian native peoples. *J* 1992 Oct; 37(3): 213–223; *McCutcheon, Ellis, Hancock, Towers*. Antifungal screening of medicinal plants of British Columbian native peoples. *J* 1994; 44(3): 157–169.
6. Giancarlo, Rosa, Nadjafi, Francesco. Hypoglycaemic activity of two spices extracts: *Rhus coriaria* L. and *Bunium persicum* Boiss. *Nat* 2006; 20(9): 882–886.
7. Candan, Sokmen. Effects of *Rhus coriaria* L. (Anacardiaceae) on lipid peroxidation and free radical scavenging activity. *Phytother* 2004; 18(1): 84–86.

Sweet Flag/*Dharīrah*

FAMILY: Acoraceae

BOTANICAL NAME: *Acorus calamus*

COMMON NAMES: *English* Sweet flag, calamus, myrtle flag; *French* Roseau aromatique; *Spanish* Ácoro, Cálamo aromático; *German* Kalmus, Deutscher Zitwer, Deutscher Ingwer, Echter Kalmus, Magenwurz; *Urdu/Unānī* Waj Turki, Bach, Agar Turki, Ood-al waj; *Modern Standard Arabic* Dharīrah, 'irq aykar, al-wajj

SAFETY RATING: **DANGEROUS** With the exception of possible skin rash, the external use of *Acorus calamus* appears to be generally safe for most people. Its internal use, however, can be potentially dangerous. Besides its potential to cause stomach upset and constipation from calcium channel blockers, the ingestion of *Acorus calamus* can affect heart rhythm and interfere with heart medications and other herbs such as digoxin and foxglove. *Acorus calamus* may also interact with immunostimulating agents, hyponotics, antispasmodics, antifungals, antibiotics, amphetamines, cholesterol-lowering agents, anti-inflammatories, anticholinergics or antioxidants. Although the effects of *Acorus calamus* on cancer are controversial, it should be used cautiously in cancer patients and in patients using antineoplastic agents, as animal studies showed it to cause heart and liver damage, as well as cancer. According to the FDA, the oil of calamus of the Jammu variety is a carcinogen. *Acorus calamus* should not be consumed by women who are pregnant or lactating. Since sweet flag has hallucinogenic potential and can cause euphoria, it has the potential for abuse. Excessive consumption of the herb causes vomiting. Sweet flag, particularly in the form of oil of calamus, is subject to legal restrictions in some countries. Since safer herbs exist, the use of sweet flag for medicinal purposes should be discouraged.

PROPHETIC PRESCRIPTION: One of the Prophet's wives had a boil on her finger. The Prophet asked her, "Do you have *dharīrah*?" She responded affirmatively. He then told her to "Apply *dharīrah* to the boil and pray to Allāh."[1] According to both Bukhārī and Muslim, 'Ā'ishah perfumed the Messenger of Allāh with *dharīrah* with her own hand at the Farewell Pilgrimage, before and during the state of *iḥrām*. It is also reported that the Prophet used to apply *dharīrah* to his beard.[2]

ISSUES IN IDENTIFICATION: Bīrūnī refers to this plant as *qālamūs* and *aqirun*, which Said identifies as *Acorus calamus*. Bīrūnī also mentions *qaṣab*

al-dharīrah which, according to Said, refers to any odiferous reed, but in Egypt today, it may be the *wajj*, which is the rhizome of *Acorus calamus*.

PROPERTIES AND USES: *Acorus calamus*, known as sweet flag, calamus, and myrtle flag, is an aromatic, bitter, stimulant herb that is and apperitive, increases the secretion of gastric juices, relaxes spasms and relieves indigestion. The root and rhizome are carminative, slightly tonic, expectorant, antispasmodic, emetic, nauseant, and nervine sedative.

Internally, it is used for digestive complaints, flatulent colic, atonic dyspepsia, pain, bronchitis, sinusitis, and to help control diabetes. Externally, it is used for skin eruptions, indolent ulcers, blisters, rheumatic pains, and neuralgia. It is an important herb in Ayurvedic medicine, regarded as a restorative for the brain and nervous system, particularly after a stroke. It is also given for bleeding disorders. It is used in Chinese medicine for vomiting, diarrhea, abdominal pain, and dysentery. It is combined with *Elettaria cardamomum* to help with the digestion of dairy products. It is also used as a snuff for nasal congestion, polyps, shock, or coma.

SCIENTIFIC STUDIES: *Genotoxic Activity* Sweet flag has been banned as a food additive and supplement in the United States because it can cause genetic mutations.[3]

Renoprotective Activity According to an animal study conducted by Hamdard University in India, *Acorus calamus* appears to possess a protective effect on nickel chloride nephrotoxicity.[4]

Spasmolytic Activity According to a study conducted by the Aga Khan University Medical College in Pakistan, *Acorus calamus* possesses a spasmolytic effect, strongly supporting its traditional use in gastrointestinal disorders such as colic pain and diarrhea.[5]

Hypolipidemic Activity In a study conducted by SNDT Women's University in India, the ethanolic extract of *Acorus calamus* and its saponins demonstrate significant hypolipidemic activity. The aqueous extract, however, showed hypolipidemic activity only at a dose of 200 mg/kg.[6]

Sweet Flag Notes

1. Ibn al-Sunnī; Ḥākim al-Nīsābūrī M. *al-Mustadrak 'alā al-ṣaḥīḥayn*. N.p.: n.p., n.d.

2. Bukhārī M. *Ṣaḥīḥ al-Bukhārī*. al-Riyyāḍ: Bayt al-Afkār, 1998; Muslim. *Jāmi' al-ṣaḥīḥ*. al-Riyyāḍ: Bayt al-Afkār, 1998.

3. Hasheninejad G, Caldwell J. Genotoxicity of the alkylbenzenes alpha- and beta-asarone, myristin and elmicin as determined by the UDS assay in cultured rat hepatocytes. *Food and Chemical Toxicology* 1994; 32: 223–231.

4. Prasad, Khan, Jahangir, Sultana. *Acorus calamus* extracts and nickel chloride: prevention of oxidative damage and hyperproliferation response in rat kidney. *Biol* 2006; 113(1): 77–92.

5. Gilani, Shah, Ahmad M, Shaheen. Antispasmodic effect of *Acorus calamus* Linn. is mediated through calcium channel blockade. *Phytother* 2006; 20(12): 1080–1084.

6. Parab, Mengi. Hypolipidemic activity of *Acorus calamus* L. in rats. *Fitoterapia*. 2002; 73(6): 451–455.

Tamarisk / *Ṭarfā', Ghaz, Athal*

FAMILY: Tamaricaceae

BOTANICAL NAME: *Tamarix gallica*

COMMON NAMES: *English* Tamarisk, French tamarisk; *French* Tamaris; *Spanish* Tamarisco; *German* Tamariske; *Urdu/Unānī* Maayeen Kalan; *Modern Standard Arabic* Shajarat al-'adhabah, ṭarfā'

BOTANICAL NAME: *Tamarix mannifera*

COMMON NAMES: *English* Manna tree; *French* Tamaris à manne; *Spanish* Tamarisco, Taray; *German* Tamariskenmanna, Manna-Tamariske; *Urdu/Unānī* Mayeen Kalaan, Bari Mayeen; *Modern Standard Arabic* ṭarfā' al-mann, Ḥaṭab aḥmar

BOTANICAL NAME: *Tamarix orientalis*

COMMON NAMES: *English* Tamarisk, Tamarisk salt tree; *French* Tamaris; *Spanish* Tamarisco; *German* Tamariske; *Urdu/Unānī* Mayeen Khurd, Choti Mayeen; *Modern Standard Arabic* 'ablah, athal

SAFETY RATING: GENERALLY SAFE Tamarisk is generally considered safe for most people when used as directed. It should not, however, be taken by women who are pregnant or lactating.

PROPHETIC PRESCRIPTION: It is related by companions of the Prophet that while at war, they had nothing to eat except the leaves of tamarisk (*ṭarfā'*) and acacia (*samrah*).[1] The tamarisk or *athal* is mentioned in the Qur'ān (34:16).

ISSUES IN IDENTIFICATION: According to some translators and commentators, the manna mentioned in the Qur'ān (5:57, 5:160, and 5:80–81) in the context of the exodus refers to a type of tamarisk, probably *Tamarix mannifera*. According to Chaudhary, there are seven species of tamarisk in Saudi Arabia. Tamarisk is widely distributed in Egypt, Jordan, Saudi Arabia, Yemen, and surrounding countries. *Tamarix aphylla* is widely distributed and cultivated as a tall shade tree, and in coastal areas to prevent soil erosion. However, it is native to Egypt and southwest Asia.[2]

According to Chaudhary, *athal* refers to tree

forms of *Tamarix* while *ṭarfah* refers to shrubby forms.[3] According to Nehmé, *ṭarfā'* and *athal* are *Tamarix*, while *ṭarfā' al-nīl* is *Tamarix nilotica*. Said says that *athal* also refers to *Tamarix dioica*. Elgood identified *athal* as *Tamarix articulata*.[4] Bīrūnī also speaks of *arṭā*. Said identifies *ṭarfā'* as *Tamarix aphylla* Kars, *Tamarix dioica*, and *Tamarix jallica*. According to Yusuf 'Ali, the famous translator of the Qur'ān, *mann* is the sweet gum obtained from the tamarisk trees from the Sinai Peninsula. Farooqi, Álvarez de Morales, and Girón Irueste identify the plant as *Tamarix mannifera*. According to Bīrūnī, *mann* is also known as *taranjubin*, which Said identifies as the tamarisk tree.

According to Ghazanfar, *Tamarix aphylla* is found from the Mediterranean region to southern Africa.[5] As Mandaville explains, *Tamarix aphylla* is common in eastern Arabia, where it is cultivated in saline or non-saline sills where water table is within reach of its roots. It is sometimes seen at sites of ruins or remote wells but never, apparently, self-propagating in the eastern part of the country. It is known in Saudi Arabic as *athal*.

Tamarix aucheriana is known as *ṭarfā'*. It is found on saline ground at roadsides and *sabkhah* (saline flat) edges. It seems to be less frequent than the other tamarisk species in eastern Arabia. *Tamarix macrocarpa* is also known as *ṭarfā'* and occurs frequently in saline ground near wells or margins of *sabkhahs*. *Tamarix mannifera* is known as *ṭarfā'*. It occurs on saline grounds at roadsides or *sabkhah* edges. Its frequency is not well-known, but it is apparently less common than *Tamarix arabica*. *Ṭarfā'* is also *Tamarix pycnocarpa* and *Tamarix ramosissima*. Although it is certain that the Prophet was referring to a species of tamarisk, it is difficult to determine the particular type with exactitude.

PROPERTIES AND USES: According to Ghazanfar, the leaves of *Tamarix aphylla* are used in childbirth, and for treating sores and wounds.[6] *Tamarix articulata* is abrasive, astringent, and tonic. It is used to check secretions. It is also used as tooth powder to polish teeth, and to treat bad breath.

SCIENTIFIC STUDIES: *Antibacterial Activity* According to a study conducted by the School of Horticulture and Animal Production in Tunisia, the volatile oils of *Tamarix boveana* exhibit an interesting antibacterial activity.[7]

Anticancer Activity According to a study conducted by Hamdard University in India, *Tamarix gallica* is a potent chemopreventive agent.[8]

Tamarisk Notes

1. Muslim. *Jāmi' al-ṣaḥīḥ*. al-Riyyāḍ: Bayt al-Afkār, 1998.
2. Chaudhary SA. *Flora of the Kingdom of Saudi Arabia*. al-Riyyāḍ: Ministry of Agriculture and Water, 1999.
3. Chaudhary SA. *Flora of the Kingdom of Saudi Arabia*. al-Riyyāḍ: Ministry of Agriculture and Water, 1999.
4. Elgood C. Trans. *Ṭibb al-nabī or Medicine of the Prophet*. Sūyūṭī J, M Chaghhaynī. Osiris 1962: 14.
5. Ghazanfar SA. *Handbook of Arabian Medicinal Plants*. Boca Raton: CRC Press, 1994.
6. Ghazanfar SA. *Handbook of Arabian Medicinal Plants*. Boca Raton: CRC Press, 1994.
7. Saïdana D, Mahjoub, Boussaada, Chriaa, Chéraif I, Daami, Mighri, Helal. Chemical composition and antimicrobial activity of volatile compounds of *Tamarix boveana* (*Tamaricaceae*). *Microbiol* 2007 Jan 12.
8. Sehrawat *Tamarix gallica* ameliorates thioacetamide-induced hepatic oxidative stress and hyperproliferative response in Wistar rats. *J Enzyme Inhib Med Chem*. 2006 Apr; 21(2): 215–23.

Terebinth / *Baṭm, Buṭm*

FAMILY: Anacardiaceae

BOTANICAL NAME: *Pistacia terebinthus*

COMMON NAMES: *English* Turpentine tree, Terebinth tree; *French* Térébinthe, Pistachier térébinthe; *Spanish* Terebinto, Cornicabra; *German* Terpentinpistazie, Terpentinbaum; *Urdu/Unānī* Mastagi, Mastagi Rumi, Ilak-ul Butm; *Modern Standard Arabic* buṭm sāfis, buṭm, fustuq

BOTANICAL NAME: *Pistacia vera*

COMMON NAMES: *English* Pistachio; *French* Pistachier, Pistachier cultivé; *Spanish* Alhócigo, pistacho; *German* Echte pistazie; *Urdu/Unānī* Pista Ka Darakht (tree); Pista, Fustuq (nut); *Modern Standard Arabic* buṭm, fustuq baladī, fustuq karmidī

SAFETY RATING: GENERALLY SAFE TO DEADLY *Pistacia vera* is generally considered safe. *Pistacia terebinthus* is also considered to be safe for most people when used as directed for short periods of time. It should be avoided by individuals who are allergic to members of the Anacardiaceae family, including pistachio, Chinese pistache, and *Schinus terebinthifolius* (Brazilian pepper). When used with ACE inhibitors, terebinth may have addictive effects. Since *Pistacia lentiscus* may lower blood pressure, it should not be taken with any herbs, supplements, or medications that alter blood pressure. As it may potentially cause fetal injury or death, terebinth should not be consumed by women who are pregnant or lactating.

PROPHETIC PRESCRIPTION: The Messenger of Allāh said, "If you do not have *miswāk*, use *'anam* or *baṭm*."[1]

ISSUES IN IDENTIFICATION: It is the consensus

that *buṭm* or *buṭum* is Arabic for terebinth. According to Dīnawarī, *baṭm* is the tree of *ḥabb al-khadrā* or "seed of a green plant" and has a pleasant scent. He says that it contains *'alak* or chewing gum, and that it does not grow in Arabia.[2] On the basis of this description, the Prophet may have been referring to *Pistacia terebinthus*, which grows in Iran, northern Arabia, and the Mediterranean. He may also have been referring to *Pistacia lentiscus*. Known in English as mastic tree and lentisk, its Arabic names include *mastīk*, *ḍarw*, and *sarīs*. It is also possible that the Prophet was referring to *Pistacia palaestina* (Palestine pistachio), known in Arabic as *fustuq filasṭīnī* and *buṭm*, or even *Pistacia vera*, which provides the pistachio nut. This latter is the most likely as it continues to be known as *boṭnim* and *buṭm* in various Arabic dialects.

PROPERTIES AND USES: *Pistacia terebinthus*, known as terebinth tree and Cyprus turpentine, is a bitter, aromatic, anti-inflammatory, and antiseptic herb that is expectorant, relaxes spasms, controls bleeding, promotes healing, and is effective against various parasitic organisms. Internally, it is used for streptococcal, urinary, and renal infections. It is also used for chronic bronchial and streptococcal infections, hemorrhage, gallstones, tapeworm, and rheumatism. Externally, it is used for arthritis, gout, sciatica, scabies, and lice. It has also been used in the treatment of cancer.

SCIENTIFIC STUDIES: *Anti-inflammatory Activity* According to a study by the Universitat de Valencia, an extract from the galls of *Pistacia terebinthus* proved to be effective against chronic and acute inflammation.[3]

Terebinth Notes

1. Iṣbahānī AN al-. *Mawsū'at al-ṭibb al-nabawī*. Ed. MKD al-Turkī. Bayrūt: Dār Ibn Ḥazm, 2006.
2. Dīnawarī AH. *Kitāb al-nabāt/The Book of Plants*. Ed. Bernhard Lewin. Bayrūt: Dār al-Qalam, 1974: 216; Dīnawarī AH. *Kitāb al-nabāt/The Book of Plants*. Ed. Bernhard Lewin. Uppsala/Wiesbaden: A.-B. Lundequistska Bokhandeln and Otto Harrassowitz, 1953: 74.
3. Giner-Larza, Manez, Giner, Recio, Prieto, Cerda-Nicolas, Rios. Anti-inflammatory triterpenes from *Pistacia terebinthus* galls. *Planta* 2002; 68(4): 311–315.

Thyme/*Sa'tar*

FAMILY: Lamiaceae

BOTANICAL NAME: *Thymus serpyllum*

COMMON NAMES: *English* Mother of thyme, Wild thyme, Creeping thyme; *French* Serpolet, Thym sauvage, Thym serpolet; *Spanish* Serpol; *German* Feldquendel, Wilder Thymian, Betony, Quendel, Sand-Thymian, Thyme, Feldkümmel; *Urdu/Unānī* Haasha, Saatar-ul Hamer, Sanobar-ul Himaar, Jaroob Gandah; *Modern Standard Arabic* sa'tar

BOTANICAL NAME: *Thymus vulgaris*

COMMON NAMES: *English* Common thyme, Garden thyme, Pot-herb thyme; *French* Thym, Thym commun, Serphyllum, Frigoule; *Spanish* Tomillo sanjuanero; *German* Thymianquendel, Thymian, Gartenquendel, Gartenthymian; *Urdu/Unānī* Hasha, Saatar-ul Hamer, Pudina Kohi; *Modern Standard Arabic* al-'abs, sa'tar rasmī

SAFETY RATING: GENERALLY SAFE Thyme is generally considered to be safe for most people when consumed in food, and as medicine for short periods of time. In some cases, it can cause digestive system upset. Although it can cause irritation in some people, thyme oil seems to be safe when applied to the skin. Thyme should not be consumed by individuals who are allergic to oregano. Thyme should not be consumed in medicinal quantities by women who are pregnant or lactating, nor should it be consumed two weeks prior to surgery as it may increase the risk of bleeding.

PROPHETIC PRESCRIPTION: The Messenger of Allāh said, "Fumigate your homes with thyme (*sa'tar*) and olibanum."[1] He also said, "Fumigate your homes with myrrh (*murr*), *shīḥ*, and thyme (*sa'tar*)."[2] According to Imām Ja'far al-Ṣādiq, "Thyme and salt chase the wind from the heart (*fu'ād*), open that which is closed, burn phlegm, increase urine (*mā'*), increase flavor, softens the stomach, removes the bad wind (*rīḥ al-khabīthah*), and give an erection."[3]

ISSUES IN IDENTIFICATION: It is difficult to discern the type of thyme that was referred to in ancient herbals since there are over one hundred species found in Europe, western Asia, North Africa, and the Canary Islands. It may have been common thyme, known variously as creeping thyme, mountain thyme, wild thyme or mother-of-thyme. According to Hans Wehr, *ṣa'tar* is wild thyme or *Thymus serpyllum*. Bīrūnī writes of *sa'tar*, *za'tar* and *thayyil*, which Said identifies as *Thymus vulgaris* L. Said says that *sa'tar* may also refer to oregano since Bīrūnī said that it was *arighanun* in Latin. Kamal identifies *Thymus vulgaris* as *hāshā* and *za'tar al-ḥamīr*. According to Hans Wehr, *sa'tar* is wild thyme or *Thymus serpyllum*. Turkī also holds that *sa'tar* and *za'tar* is *Thymus serpyllum*.[4] However, according to Bīrūnī, wild thyme is *nimmām* or *nammām*. According to Nehmé, thyme is known as *sa'tar*, *ṣa'tar*, and *za'tar*. Ouassad said that *Thymus vulgaris* is *ṣa'tar al-shā'i'*.

It should be stressed that the Arabs do not make a clear distinction between aromatic herbs of the mint family. As Gernot Katzer explains, words like *za'tar*, for example, which is often used in conjunction with qualifying or descriptive adjectives, can be applied to a variety of native herbs, including, but not restricted to, oregano, marjoram, thyme, and savory.[5] According to Kowalchik and Hylton, *za'tar* refers to *Thymbra spicata*, a type of savory which is native to Turkey and Palestine. The herb has a long history of use in the region. The herb was mentioned by Dioscorides, and remains of it were found in the tomb of Tutankhamun.

Properties and Uses: While there are many types of thyme, the main medicinal ones are *Thymus vulgaris* and *Thymus serpyllum*. *Thymus vulgaris*, known as common thyme, is an aromatic, warming, astringent herb that is expectorant, improves digestion, relaxes spasms, and controls coughing. It is also tonic, carminative, emmenagogue, antispasmodic, strongly antiseptic, and antifungal. Common thyme is used internally for dry coughs, lack of appetite, colic, flatulence, whooping cough, bronchitis, excess bronchial mucus, asthma, laryngitis, indigestion, gastritis, and diarrhea and enuresis in children. It is also used to treat headache, hysteria, intestinal gas, painful menstruation, worm infections, and to induce sweating. Externally, common thyme is used to treat tonsillitis, gum disease, fungal infections, rheumatism, athlete's foot, arthritis, wounds, as well as fungal and yeast infections.

Thymol, the highly antiseptic volatile oil from thyme, is an important ingredient in many toothpastes, mouthwashes, and topic antirheumatic preparations. Common thyme is often combined with *Lobelia inflata* and *Ephedra* species for asthma, and with *Marrubium vulgare*, *Prunus serotina*, and *Drimia maritima* (commonly described as *Urginea maritima*), for whooping cough. Its oil is used in aromatherapy for aches and pains, exhaustion, depression, upper respiratory tract infections, and skin and scalp complaints. Common thyme is never administered internally to pregnant women. Thyme oil may cause irritation to skin and mucous membranes, as well as allergic reactions.

Scientific Studies: *Antifungal Activity* In a study conducted by the University of Zagreb thyme essential oil demonstrated a wide range spectrum of fungicidal activity. The vaporous phase of the oil exhibited long-lasting suppressive activity on molds from damp dwellings. In low concentration, essential oil of thyme and thymol could be used for disinfection of moldy walls in the dwellings.[6]

Antiherpetic Activity In a study conducted by the University of Heidelberg in Germany, *Thymus vulgaris* extract was shown to possess high antiviral activity against HSV-1, HSV-2 and an acyclovir resistant strain. Both types of herpes virus including the acyclovir resistant strain were considerably neutralized after treatment with the extract prior to infection. At maximum noncytotoxic concentrations of the extracts, plaque formation was significantly reduced by > 90 percent for HSV-1 and HSV-2 and > 85 percent for the acyclovir resistant strain. In time-response studies over a period of two hours, a clearly time-dependent activity was demonstrated. These results indicate that the extracts affect HSV before adsorption but have no effect on the intracellular virus replication. Therefore, the extract exerts its antiviral effect on free HSV and offers a chance to use it for topical therapeutic application against recurrent herpes infections.[7]

Anticold Activity In a human trial of 62 patients with the common cold, bronchitis or respiratory tract diseases with formation of mucus, the daily intake of 10 ml of ivy and thyme syrup for 12 days, the 13 doctors and 62 patients assessed the efficacy of the treatment as good or very good in 86 percent and 90 percent of the cases, respectively. The tolerability was assessed as good or very good by 97 percent of the doctors and patients. In light of its traditional use in cough syrup, its reduction in the symptom score, and the tolerability of the syrup, the scientists concluded that ivy and thyme syrup appeared to alleviate cough in consequence of the common cold, and bronchitis or respiratory tract diseases with mucus formation.[8]

Antitumor Activity A study conducted by the Beijing University of Traditional Chinese Medicine, found that ethyl acetate is the major antitumor fraction in ethanol extracts from *Thymus quinquecostatus* Celak.[9]

Sedative Activity In an animal study conducted by Hanbul Cosmetics in Korea, it was demonstrated that the inhalation by mice of essential oils such as thyme, ginger, and peppermint, resulted in 5 percent to 22 percent of immobility, confirming their sedative effects in aromatherapy.[10]

Antibacterial Activity In a study of 11 essential oils from commercial origin conducted by the Instituto Nacional de Antropología e Historia in Mexico, the essential oil of *Thymus vulgaris* exhibited the highest and broadest antibacterial activity against prevalent pathogenic bacteria strains which were resistant to selected antibiotics.[11]

Antimicrobial Activity Research has confirmed the anti-microbial activity of thyme.[12]

Thyme Notes

1. Ibn Qayyim al-Jawziyyah M. *al-Ṭibb al-nabawī*. Bayrūt: Dār al-Kitāb, 1985.
2. Bayhaqī A. *al-Sunan al-kubrā*. Bayrūt: Dār Ṣadīr, 1968.
3. Majlisī M. *Biḥār al-anwār*. Ṭihrān: Javad al-Alavi, 1956.
4. Iṣbahānī AN al-. *Mawsū'at al-ṭibb al-nabawī*. Ed. MKD al-Turkī. Bayrūt: Dār Ibn Ḥazm, 2006.
5. Katzer G. Marjoram (*Majorana hortensis* Moench.) http://www.uni-graz.at/~katzer/engl/Maio_hor.html
6. Segvic, Kosalec, Mastelic, Pieckova, Pepeljnak. Antifungal activity of thyme (*Thymus vulgaris* L.) essential oil and thymol against moulds from damp dwellings. *Lett* 2007; 44(1): 36–42.
7. Nolkemper, Reichling, Stintzing, Carle, Schnitzler. Antiviral effect of aqueous extracts from species of the *Lamiaceae* family against herpes simplex virus type 1 and type 2 in vitro. *Planta* 2006; 72(15): 1378–1382.
8. Buechi, Vogelin, von, Ramos, Melzer. Open trial to assess aspects of safety and efficacy of a combined herbal cough syrup with ivy and thyme. *Forsch* 2005; 12(6): 328–332.
9. Sun, Zhang, Cheng, Ma, Guo, Zhang. Anti-tumor effect of ethanol extracts from *Thymus quinquecostatus* Celak on human leukemia cell line. *Zhong* 2005; 3(5): 382–385.
10. Lim, Seo, Lee, Pyo, Lee. Stimulative and sedative effects of essential oils upon inhalation in mice. *Arch* 2005; 28(7): 770–774.
11. Hersch-Martinez, Leanos-Miranda, Solorzano-Santos. Antibacterial effects of commercial essential oils over locally prevalent pathogenic strains in Mexico. *Fitoterapia*. 2005; 76(5): 453–457.
12. Hammer KA, Carson CF, Riley TV. Antimicrobial activity of essential oils and other plant extracts. *Journal of Applied Microbiology* 1991; 86(6): 985–990.

Truffles / *Kamā'*

FAMILY: Terfeziaceae

BOTANICAL NAME: *Tirmania* spp.; *Terfezia* spp.

COMMON NAMES: *English* Truffle; *French* Truffle; *Spanish* Trufa; *German* Trüffel; *Urdu/Unānī* Khumbhi, Kumaat; *Modern Standard Arabic* kamā'

SAFETY RATING: GENERALLY SAFE Truffles are generally considered to be safe for most people.

PROPHETIC PRESCRIPTION: The Prophet said, "Truffles are from manna and manna is from Paradise."[1] He said, "Truffles are the manna of manna, and their water contains a cure for the eyes."[2] He said, "Truffles are a manna which Allāh sent to the children of Israel. Their water is a cure for the eyes."[3] One of the Prophet's companions commented that truffles were the pox of the earth. The Messenger of Allāh responded that "No, they are a type of manna. Their water is a useful remedy for the eyes."[4] He also said, "The Fire laughed, and out came truffles, and the Earth laughed, and out came capers."[5]

ISSUES IN IDENTIFICATION: Bīrūnī speaks of *kamā'*, *bīamī*, *shaḥmat al-arḍ*, *bayḍat al-arḍ*, *bayḍat al-balad*, and *nibāt al-ra'd*, which Said identifies broadly as mushroom. The white one is *faqa'* and *'asqal*. According to Hans Wehr and Turkī, *kamā'* means both truffle and mushroom.[6] Muḥammad 'Alī Barr also translates *kamā'* as both truffles and mushrooms.[7]

While the term may have acquired a more general meaning over time, *kamā'* referred exclusively to truffles in classical Arabic. In his chapter on truffles, Abū Ḥanīfa al-Dīnawarī, the foremost authority on classical Arabic botanical nomenclature, explains that *kamā'* grows under the earth.[8] Farooqi cites traditions in which the term *kamā'* is translated at times as truffle, and at other times as mushroom. It is clear from both linguistic context and phytogeography that the Prophet was referring to truffles, and not mushrooms, which are known as *fuṭr*. Álvarez de Morales and Girón Irueste are correct in identifying *kamā'* as truffles. For them, the species is *Tuber album* Sow.[9] As Stobart explains,

> The terfezias are fungi related to the truffles and to be distinguished from them only by botanists. They grow to some extent in southern Europe, but are very plentiful in North Africa and the Middle East, where travelers are likely to come across them. They are abundant in the Syrian desert, in places like Palmyra, and also in the Libyan desert. Although usually pale in color, dark varieties are also found, and these are considered superior. They are somewhat tasteless when compared to true truffles, but still excellent when cooked in local ways or eaten raw as salad.[10]

As Chaudhary explains, *kamā'* refers to desert truffles, which are also known as *fugī'*.[11] Desert truffles are known in Morocco as *terfās*. In Egypt, the Bedouin of the Western Desert call them *terfās*. In Kuwait, they are known as *fagga*. In Saudi Arabia, they are known as *faq'*, and in Syria they are known by their classical Arabic name *kamā'*. The Iraqis call them *kamā'* (or *kima* or *chima* depending on local dialects) while the Omanis call them *faqah* or *zubaydī*.

PROPERTIES AND USES: Desert truffles occur in wild areas of Arabia and North Africa. Rich in carbohydrates, protein, potassium, and phosphate, they are a good source of fiber and essential amino acids. Desert truffles also contain an appreciable amount of ascorbic acid and fair amount of iron. An important edible resource in arid regions, desert truffles often serve as a meat substitute. In fact, some varieties contain 20 to 27 percent protein, 85 percent of which is digestible by humans. Since *Terfezia africana* flour is so filled with nutrients, some scholars have suggested that it be added to wheat flour at a rate of 5 to 10 percent in order to enrich it. Arab Bedouins have traditionally employed truffles to treat eye diseases and to activate the synthesis of sex hormones in the body.

SCIENTIFIC STUDIES: *Antimicrobial Activity* Research has confirmed that the aqueous extract of the truffle *Terfezia claveryi* contains a potent antimicrobial agent that is protein in nature, and may be used in the treatment of eye infections caused by *Pseudomonas aeruginosa.*[12]

Antibacterial Activity In an in-vitro study conducted by Jordan University of Science and Technology, a 5 percent aqueous extract of *Terfezia claveryi* inhibited the growth of *Staphylococcus aureus* by 66.4 percent.[13] According to a study published in Kuwait, truffle extract is effective against trachoma, a bacterial infection of the eye.[14] Several other studies have demonstrated the broad antibiotic activity of truffle extracts.[15]

Truffles Notes

1. Nisābūrī A. *Islamic Medical Wisdom: The Ṭibb al-a'immah.* Trans. B. Ispahany. Ed. AJ Newman. London: Muḥammadī Trust, 1991: 103.

2. Bukhārī M. *Ṣaḥīḥ al-Bukhārī.* al-Riyyāḍ: Bayt al-Afkār, 1998; Nasā'ī, A. *Sunan al-Nisā'ī.* al-Qāhirah: Muṣṭafā al-Bābī al-Ḥalabī, 1964–65.

3. Muslim. *Jāmi' al-ṣaḥīḥ.* al-Riyyāḍ: Bayt al-Afkār, 1998; Ibn Mājah M. Sunan. Trans. MT Anṣārī. Lahore: Kazi Publications, 1994; Iṣbahānī AN al-. *Mawsū'at al-ṭibb al-nabawī.* Ed. MKD al-Turkī. Bayrūt: Dār Ibn Ḥazm, 2006.

4. Farooqi MIH. *Medicinal Plants in the Traditions of Prophet Muḥammad.* Lucknow: Sidrah Publishers, 1998: 137; Farooqi MIH. *Plants of the Qur'ān.* Lucknow: Sidrah, 2000: 29; Tirmidhī M. *al-Jāmi' al-ṣaḥīḥ.* al-Qāhirah: Muṣṭafā al-Bābī al-Ḥalabī, [1937-]; Bayhaqī A. *Sunan al-kubrā.* Bayrūt: Dār Ṣadīr, 1968.

5. Sūyūṭī J. *As-Sūyūṭī's Medicine of the Prophet.* Ed. A Thomson. London: Ṭā-Hā Publishers, 1994: 88; Ibn Qayyim al-Jawziyyah M. *al-Ṭibb al-nabawī.* Bayrūt: Dār al-Kitāb, 1985.

6. Iṣbahānī AN al-. *Mawsū'at al-ṭibb al-nabawī.* Ed. MKD al-Turkī. Bayrūt: Dār Ibn Ḥazm, 2006.

7. Ibn Ḥabīb A. *al-Ṭibb al-nabawī.* Ed. MA Barr. Dimashq: Dār al-Qalam, 1993.

8. Dīnawarī AH. *Kitāb al-nabāt/The Book of Plants.* Ed. Bernhard Lewin. Bayrūt: Dār al-Qalam, 1974.

9. Ibn Ḥabīb A. *Mujtaṣar fī al-ṭibb/Compendio de medicina.* Ed. C Álvarez de Morales and F Girón Irueste. Madrid: Consejo Superior de Investigaciones Científicas, 1992.

10. Stobart T. *Herbs, Spices, and Flavoring.* Woodstock, NY: Overlook Press, 1982: 271.

11. Chaudhary SA. *Flora of the Kingdom of Saudi Arabia.* al-Riyyāḍ: Ministry of Agriculture and Water, 1999.

12. Janakat SM, Al-Fakhiri SM, Sallal AK. Evaluation of antibacterial activity of aqueous and methanolic extracts of the truffle *Terfezia claveryi* against *Pseudomonas aeruginosa.* Saudi Med J 2005; 26(6): 952–955.

13. Janakat Al-Fakhiri Sallal. A promising peptide antibiotic from *Terfezia claveryi* aqueous extract against *Staphylococcus aureus* in vitro. *Phytother* 2004; 18(10): 810–813

14. Al-Marzooky MA. Proceedings of the International Conference on Islamic Medicine. 1981; 353–57.

15. Janakat S, Al-Fakhiri S, Sallal AK. *Phototherapy Research.* 2004; 18: 810–13; Janakat S, Al-Fakhiri S, Sallal AK. *Saudi Medical Journal* 2005; 26: 952–55.

Turnip / *Saljam*

FAMILY: Brassicaceae

BOTANICAL NAME: *Brassica rapa* var. *rapa*

COMMON NAMES: *English* Rape, Turnip; *French* Rave, Grosse rave; *Spanish* Nabo; *German* Wasserrübe, Weiße Rübe, Rübsamen, Rübsen; *Urdu/ Unānī* Shaljam, Shalgham, Lift; *Modern Standard Arabic* lift

BOTANICAL NAME: *Brassica napobrassica*

COMMON NAMES: *English* Field cabbage, Swede turnip; *French* Chou champêtre; *Spanish* Repollo chino; *German* Feldkohl, Raps, Rübenkohl; *Urdu/ Unānī* Lahee; *Modern Standard Arabic* lift, shaljam

SAFETY RATING: GENERALLY SAFE Turnips are generally considered to be safe for most people.

PROPHETIC PRESCRIPTION: According to Imām Ja'far al-Ṣādiq, "Whoever has a root of leprosy (*judhām*), then he should eat turnip (*shaljam*) when it is in season for it will take it away from you."[1] The Imām also said, "Eat turnip (*shaljam*), and continue to eat it regularly. Hide it from anyone but its owner, for we all have the root of leprosy (*judhām*). Dissolve it by eating it."[2] According to Imām Mūsā al-Kāẓim, "Eat turnips (*al-lift*), which is *al-shaljam*, for there is not one who has a strain of leprosy (*'irq min al-judhām*) but that the eating of turnips (*al-shaljam*) dissolves it." When asked whether they should be consumed raw or cooked, he replied, "Both."[3]

ISSUES IN IDENTIFICATION: Bīrūnī speaks of both *lift* and *shaljam*, which Said identifies as *Brassica campestris* L., or wild turnip. According to Nehmé, *Brassica rapa* is known as *lift* and *suljum* in Modern Standard Arabic.

PROPERTIES AND USES: *Brassica campestris*, or wild turnip, is high in vitamin C and is used as an antiscorbutic. Internally, it is used in the treatment of bile stones, coughs, colds, bronchitis, and whooping cough. Externally, it is used for the treatment of itchy skin. Erucic acid, which is found in the seed oil of some varieties, is toxic. Modern cultivars, however, have been selected to be virtually free of erucic acid. Turnip seed oil is used as a lubricant, luminant, and in soap making.

SCIENTIFIC STUDIES: *Anticancer Activity* In a population-based case-control study among Chinese women in Shanghai researchers found that breast cancer declined with an increased intake of dark yellow-orange vegetables, including Chinese white turnips.[4]

Aphrodisiacal Activity According to a three-month animal trial conducted by King Saud University in Saudi Arabia, *Brassica rapa* extract significantly increased both sperm motility and sperm contents without producing a spermatoxic effect.[5]

Turnip Notes

1. Majlisī M. *Biḥār al-anwār*. Ṭihrān: Javad al-Alavi, 1956.
2. 'Āmilī H. *Wasā'il al-shī'ah*. Bayrūt: al-Mu'assasah, 1993.
3. Nisābūrī A. *Islamic Medical Wisdom: The Ṭibb al-a'immah*. Trans. B. Ispahany. Ed. AJ Newman. London: Muḥammadī Trust, 1991: 136.
4. Malin AS, Qi D, Shu XO, Gao YT, Friedman JM, Jin F, Zheng W. Intake of fruits, vegetables, and selected micronutrients in relation to the risk of breast cancer. *Int J Cancer* 2003; 105(3): 413–418.
5. Qureshi, Shah, Tariq, Ageel. Studies on herbal aphrodisiacs used in Arab system of medicine. *Am* 1989; 17(1–2): 57–63.

Violet / *Banafsaj*

FAMILY: Violaceae

BOTANICAL NAME: *Viola odorata*

COMMON NAMES: *English* Violet, sweet violet; *French* Violette, Violette odorante; *Spanish* Violeta; *German* März-Veilchen, Veilchen, Duft-Veilchen, Echtes Veilchen, Wohlreichendes Veilchen, Veil; *Urdu/Unānī* Banafshah, Banafsaj, Banafshu, Farfir; *Modern Standard Arabic* banafsaj

SAFETY RATING: GENERALLY SAFE Violet is generally considered to be safe for most people when used as directed. It should not, however, be consumed by women who are pregnant or lactating.

PROPHETIC PRESCRIPTION: The Prophet Muḥammad recommended the use of violet oil in the following terms, "Use the oil of violets, for the excellence of violet over all the oils is as the excellence of the *Ahl al-Bayt* over people."[1] He is also quoted as saying "You have violet oil which is better than other oils like my excellence is superior to your lowly condition."[2] The Prophet is also reported to have said, "Anoint yourselves with violets, for they are cold in summer and hot in winter."[3] The Messenger of Allāh is also reported to have said, "The excellence of the violet is like the excellence of Islām over other religions."[4] According to many scholars, however, this is actually a popular saying, which has been erroneously attributed to the Prophet.

According to Imām Ja'far al-Ṣādiq, "The oil of violets is the chief oil."[5] He said, "There is nothing dearer to us than the violet from your region."[6] He said, "The most excellent oil is violet," recommending his followers to "anoint yourselves with it, for its excellence over the rest of the oils is like our excellence over men."[7] He also stated that "The excellence of violet oil over other oils is like the excellence of Islām over other religions."[8] He said, "Oil of violets among the oils is as the believer among men." Then he said, "It is hot in the winter and cold in the summer. The rest of the oils do not have this merit."[9] He also stated that "The violet is hot in the winter and cold in the summer, gentle for our Shī'ah, and dry for our enemies. If people knew what is in the violet, every ounce would be sold for a dinar."[10] The Imām also said, "There are four things which improve habits: Sūrānī pomegranate (*rummān sūrānī*), boiled unfertilized female dates (*bisr*), violet, and endive (*hindibā'*)."[11] He also explained that "The best of oil is violet oil. It removes sickness from the head."[12]

ISSUES IN IDENTIFICATION: Bīrūnī speaks of *banafsaj* and Said identifies it as blue violet or *Viola odorata*. Álvarez de Morales, Girón Irueste, and Barr also identify *banafasaj* as *Viola odorata* L.[13] As Nehmé explains, *Viola* is *banafsaj*, and *Viola odorata* is *banafsaj 'aṭir*.[14] As Mandaville explains, *Viola tricolor* is rare in eastern Arabia, existing only as an introduction. The nearest native violet population in Arabia is the drought-tolerant *Viola cinerea*, found in the rocky foothills and mountains of Oman. According to Chaudhary, *Viola cinerea* is the only wild variety found in Saudi Arabia, growing in the southern heights.[15]

PROPERTIES AND USES: *Viola odorata* is a bittersweet, mucilaginous cooling herb that cleanses toxins and has expectorant, antiseptic, and anticancer effects. It is considered pectoral, antipyretic, diaphoretic, diuretic, astringent, aperient, demulcent, alterative, cathartic, laxative, and suforific. In large doses, its rhizomes are emetic and purgative. The flowers, leaves and roots are rich in vitamins A and C.

Viola odorata is used internally for bronchitis, excess respiratory mucus, coughs, whooping cough and asthma. It possesses emollient and soothing expectorant properties which are similar to, but lesser than, ipecacuanha. It is used to treat fever, constipation, cough, inflammation, nervousness, as well as cancer of the breasts, lungs, and digestive tracts. Violet has a reputation for treating tumors, both benign and cancerous. It is reputed to be slightly sedative. The flowers are useful in cases of anxiety and insomnia. The flowers and seeds also act as laxatives.

Viola odorata is used externally for mouth and throat infections. In aromatherapy, it is used for bronchial complaints, exhaustion, or skin problems. It is applied to scrofula, syphilis, and nephritis. According to Ibn Buṭlān's aromatherapy, the scent of violets calm frenzies; when consumed, they purify.[16] Ibn Sīnā applied violet oil to the head to treat convulsion.[17] As for Samarqandī, he used a combination of violet and pomegranate juice for the treatment of eye inflammations.[18]

SCIENTIFIC STUDIES: *Antipyretic Activity* According to animal studies, sweet violet leaf extracts may reduce fever as effectively as aspirin.[19]

Antiplasmodial Activity In a study conducted by the University of Mississippi, a species of the *Viola* genus from South Korea, *Viola verecunda*, was found to contain epi-oleanic acid which displays high antiplasmodial activity.[20]

Antibacterial Activity According to a study conducted by the University of Medical Sciences in Poland, the infusion, decoction, and ethanol extract of *Viola tricolor* were found to be most effective against tested microorganisms.[21] In another study, conducted by the Chinese Academy of Medical Sciences in Beijing, the petroleum ether and ethyl acetate extracts of *Viola yedoensis* showed activity against *Bacillus subtilis* and *Pseudomonas syringae*.[22]

Anti-HIV Activity Most promising of all is a study conducted by the Chinese University of Hong Kong, in which twenty-seven medicinal herbs reputed in ancient Chinese folklore to have anti-infective properties were extracted were tested for inhibitory activity against the human immunodeficiency virus.[23] Of the twenty-seven herbal extracts, eleven were found to be active. One of these extracts, *Viola yedoensis*, was studied in greater depth. It was found that its extract completely shut off the growth of HIV at a subtoxic concentration in virtually every experiment. On the basis of this study, the group of scientists concluded that *Viola yedoensis*, and other Chinese medicinal herbs, appear to be a rich source of potentially useful materials for the treatment of human immunodeficiency virus infection.

Violet Notes

1. Nisābūrī A. *Islamic Medical Wisdom: The Ṭibb al-a'immah*. Trans. B. Ispahany. Ed. AJ Newman. London: Muḥammadī Trust, 1991: 118.
2. Ibn Ḥabīb A. *Mujtaṣar fī al-ṭibb/Compendio de medicina*. Ed. C Álvarez de Morales and F Girón Irueste. Madrid: Consejo Superior de Investigaciones Científicas, 1992: 69.
3. Chaghhaynī M. *Ṭibb al-nabī*. Trans. C Elgood. *Osiris* 1962; 14: 188.
4. Chaghhaynī M. *Ṭibb al-nabī*. Trans. C Elgood. *Osiris* 1962; 14: 191; Iṣbahānī AN al- *Mawsū'at al-ṭibb al-nabawī*. Ed. MKD al-Turkī. Bayrūt: Dār Ibn Ḥazm, 2006: 760.
5. Nisābūrī A. *Islamic Medical Wisdom: The Ṭibb al-a'immah*. Trans. B. Ispahany. Ed. AJ Newman. London: Muḥammadī Trust, 1991: 118.
6. Majlisī M. *Biḥār al-anwār*. Ṭihrān: Javad al-Alavi, 1956.
7. Nisābūrī A. *Islamic Medical Wisdom: The Ṭibb al-a'immah*. Trans. B. Ispahany. Ed. AJ Newman. London: Muḥammadī Trust, 1991: 118.
8. Majlisī M. *Biḥār al-anwār*. Ṭihrān: Javad al-Alavi, 1956.
9. Nisābūrī A. *Islamic Medical Wisdom: The Ṭibb al-a'immah*. Trans. B. Ispahany. Ed. AJ Newman. London: Muḥammadī Trust, 1991: 118.
10. Nisābūrī A. *Islamic Medical Wisdom: The Ṭibb al-a'immah*. Trans. B. Ispahany. Ed. AJ Newman. London: Muḥammadī Trust, 1991: 118; Majlisī M. *Biḥār al-anwār*. Ṭihrān: Javad al-Alavi, 1956.
11. Majlisī M. *Biḥār al-anwār*. Ṭihrān: Javad al-Alavi, 1956.
12. Majlisī M. *Biḥār al-anwār*. Ṭihrān: Javad al-Alavi, 1956.
13. Ibn Ḥabīb A. *Mujtaṣar fī al-ṭibb/Compendio de medicina*. Ed. C Álvarez de Morales and F Girón Irueste. Madrid: Consejo Superior de Investigaciones Científicas, 1992; Ibn Ḥabīb A. *al-Ṭibb al-nabawī*. Ed. MA Barr. Dimashq: Dār al-Qalam, 1993.
14. Nehmé M. *Dictionnaire étymologique de la flore du Liban*. Bayrūt: Librairie du Liban, 2000.
15. Chaudhary SA. *Flora of the Kingdom of Saudi Arabia*. al-Riyyāḍ: Ministry of Agriculture and Water, 1999.
16. Ibn Buṭlān. *The Medieval Health Handbook: Tacuinum sanitatis*. Ed. Luisa Cogliati Arano, Trans. Oscar Ratti and Adele Westbrook. New York: George Braziller, 1976: 241.
17. Ibn Sīnā H. *The Canon of Medicine*. Ed. O. Cameron Gruner. London: Luzaz, 1930: 373.
18. Samarqandī N. *The Medical Formulary of al-Samarqandī*. Philadelphia: University of Pennsylvania Press, 1967: 139.
19. Khattak SG, et al. Antipyretic studies on some indigenous Pakistani medicinal plants. *Journal of Ethnopharmacology* 1985; 14: 45–51.
20. Moon HI, Jung JC, Lee J. Antiplasmodial activity of triterpenoid isolated from whole plants of *Viola* genus from South Korea. *Parasitol* 2007; 100(3): 641–644.
21. Witkowska-Banaszczak, Bylka, Matlawska, Goslinska, Muszynski. Antimicrobial activity of *Viola tricolor* herb. *Fitoterapia* 2005; 76(5): 458–461.
22. Xie, Kokubun, Houghton, Simmonds. Antibacterial activity of the Chinese traditional medicine, Zi Hua Di Ding. *Phytother* 2004; 18(6): 497–500.
23. Chang, Yeung. Inhibition of growth of human immunodeficiency virus in vitro by crude extracts of Chinese medicinal herbs. *Antiviral* 1988; 9(3): 163–175.

Walnuts *see* Nuts

Watercress / *Jirjīr*

FAMILY: Brassicaceae
BOTANICAL NAME: *Nasturtium officinale*

Common Names: *English* Watercress; *French* Cresson officinal; *Spanish* Berro, Mastuerzo de agua; *German* Brunnenkresse; *Urdu/Unānī* Jirjir, Qurrah-al Ain; *Modern Standard Arabic* jirjīr, qurrah makhzaniyyah, qurrat al-'ayn, ḥurf, ḥurf al-mā', rashād, ḥab al-rashād

Safety Rating: Generally Safe to Dangerous Watercress is generally considered to be safe for most people so long as it is produced in fresh, clean water. Consumption of uncooked water plants like watercress, which provide shelter for liver flukes, particularly when animal waste is present in the water, should be avoided in order to prevent *fascioliasis*. A parasitic infection caused by *Fasciola hepatica* or *Fasciola gigantica*, fascioliasis can cause damage and enlargement of the liver during the acute phase, and can later cause severe pain in the upper right abdomen, yellowing of the skin, and skin inflammation.

Prophetic Prescription: According to the Prophet Muḥammad, "Watercress (*jirjīr*) is an herb from Ethiopia, and I have seen it growing in the fire of Hell."[1] He also said, "Watercress (*jirjīr*) is a painful plant. It seems to have been created from Fire."[2] He also said, "Do not consume watercress (*jirjīr*) since this plant spreads the source of elephantiasis."[3] Imām 'Alī al-Riḍā used to say "Lemon balm (*al-bādharūj*) for us and watercress (*al-jirjīr*) for the Banū Umayyah."[4]

Issues in Identification: The identification of *jirjīr* has been a source of a great deal of confusion for both classical and contemporary commentators and translators since the term is used to describe *Eruca sativa* (rocket), *Lepidium sativum* (garden cress), as well as *Nasturtium officinale* (water cress). This might explain why Elgood simply translates it as "cress" without being more specific.[5]

According to Ibn Ṭūlūn, doctors used to call the plant *baqalah 'Ā'ishah*.[6] Farooqi suggests that it may be *Eruca sativa*, known in English as rocket, as its seed contains very bitter oil. Álvarez Morales and Girón Irueste also identify *jirjīr* as *Eruca sativa*.[7] And, although the *National Formulary of Unānī Medicine* equates *jirjīr* with *Nasturtium*, C.P. Khare insists that it is *Eruca sativa*. For Nehmé, *jarjīr* refers to *Eruca sativa* in Modern Standard Arabic. According to Mandaville, *jarjīr* is also the colloquial Saudi Arabian peasant name for *Eruca sativa*. Although shared by many, the view that *jirjīr* represents *Eruca sativa* is unconvincing as it is only known in Eastern Arabia as a weed in farm fields, and occasionally along roads. *Nasturtium officinale*, however, is found in the southwestern heights of Saudi Arabia where it is also known as *qurat al-'ayn* and *ḥurf*.[8]

According to Bīrūnī, *jarjīr* is known as *arzūmūn* in Latin, and Said has identified it as *Lepidium sativum*. According to one of Bīrūnī's sources, however, there were two varieties of *jarjīr*, one of which was fragrant, and the other of which was sharp and pungent. Bīrūnī also speaks of *jarjīr al-mā'*, which he also calls *karafs al-mā'* and *qurrat al-'ayn*. His authorities state that it is a fragrant aquatic herb, with foliage like celery, having a sticky liquid which adheres to the hands. Said identifies it as *Nasturtium indicum*.

When the Prophet Muḥammad described *jirjīr*, he said that it was so hot that it seemed to have been made in hell. This is a perfect description of watercress as its generic Latin name, *Nasturtium*, is derived from the words *nasus tortus* (a convulsed nose) on account of its pungency. As the *Larūs* dictionary describes, *jarjīr* "burns the mouth and the tongue." Although the Prophet Muḥammad simply said *jirjīr*, which means cress, and did not specify *al-mā'*, which means water, he was unequivocally describing *jirjīr al-mā'* (watercress) and not *jirjīr* (gardencress). According to Nehmé, *jarjīr al-mā'* refers to *Nasturtium officinale* in Modern Standard Arabic. The usage of *jirjīr* for watercress instead of *jirjīr al-mā'* has been preserved in both Egyptian and Syrian colloquial Arabic, as attested by Hans Wehr. Turkī also agrees that the *jirjīr* of the Prophet refers to watercress or rocket.[9]

Properties and Uses: *Nasturtium officinale* is a source of phytochemicals and antioxidants. Rich in vitamins and minerals, watercress contains vitamin A, vitamin C, iron, iodine, folic acid, and calcium. Due to its high vitamin C content, watercress has been used as an antiscorbutic for centuries. Watercress is considered mildly stimulant, diuretic, expectorant, appetitive, diuretic, emmenagogue, galactagogue, anthelmintic, ecbolic and abortifacient, aphrodisiac, vesicant, resolvent, aperient, alterative, tonic, carminative, and digestive.

It is used internally for edema, excess mucus, bronchitis, wet coughs, acne, eczema, rheumatism, and anemia, as well as debility associated with chronic disease, scurvy, and gall bladder complaints. According to Ibn Buṭlān, watercress augments the production of sperm and is thus good for coitus.[10] The seeds are used to treat hiccup, dysentery, diarrhea, flatulence, leucorrhea, and skin problems.

Scientific Studies: *Anticancer Activity* Many studies have shown that watercress contains anticancer compounds.[11] According to the University of Minnesota Cancer Center, a large amount of data demonstrate that isothiocyanates, which are released in substantial quantities upon consumption of normal amounts of cruciferous vegetables, act as cancer chemopreventive agents.[12] Some of these naturally occurring isothiocyanates are effective inhibitors of cancer in rodents and have quite specific effects, including the prevention of lung tumorigenesis. Similar effects have been observed in smokers who consumed watercress. On the basis of these observations and knowledge of the carcinogenic constituents of cigarette smoke, scientists believe that a strategy for chemoprevention of lung cancer can be developed. In another study, crude watercress extract proved to be significantly protective against the three stages of the carcinogenesis process: initiation, proliferation, and metastasis.[13]

Watercress Notes

1. Sūyūṭī J. *As-Sūyūṭī's Medicine of the Prophet.* Ed. A Thomson. London: Ṭā-Hā Publishers, 1994: 48.
2. Dhahabī S. *al-Ṭibb al-nabawī.* Bayrūt: Dār al-Nafā'is, 2004.
3. Ibn Ḥabīb A. *Mujtaṣar fī al-ṭibb/Compendio de medicina.* Ed. C Álvarez de Morales and F Girón Irueste. Madrid: Consejo Superior de Investigaciones Científicas, 1992: 66/25.
4. It is translated as "mountain balm" by Ispahany. See: Nisābūrī A. *Islamic Medical Wisdom: The Ṭibb al-a'immah.* Trans. B. Ispahany. Ed. AJ Newman. London: Muḥammadī Trust, 1991: 185.
5. Elgood C. Trans. *Ṭibb al-nabī or Medicine of the Prophet.* Sūyūṭī J, M Chaghhaynī. *Osiris* 1962; 14.
6. Ibn Ṭulūn S. *al-Manhal al-rawī fī al-ṭibb al-nabawī.* Ed. 'Azīz Bayk. Riyyāḍ: Dār 'ālam al-kutub, 1995.
7. Ibn Ḥabīb A. *Mujtaṣar fī al-ṭibb/Compendio de medicina.* Ed. C Álvarez de Morales and F Girón Irueste. Madrid: Consejo Superior de Investigaciones Científicas, 1992.
8. Chaudhary SA. *Flora of the Kingdom of Saudi Arabia.* al-Riyyāḍ: Ministry of Agriculture and Water, 1999.
9. Iṣbahānī AN al-. *Mawsū'at al-ṭibb al-nabawī.* Ed. MKD al-Turkī. Bayrūt: Dār Ibn Ḥazm, 2006.
10. Ibn Buṭlān. *The Medieval Health Handbook: Tacuinum sanitatis.* Ed. LC Arano, Trans. OR Ratti and A Westbrook. New York: George Braziller, 1976: 150.
11. Chung FL, et al. Chemopreventative potential of Thiol Conjugates of Isothio-cyanates for lung cancer and a urinary biomarker of dietary isothiocyanates. *J Cellular Biochemistry Supplement.* 1997; 27: 76–85; Hecht SS. Effects of watercress consumption on metabolism of a tobacco-specific lung carcinogen in smokers. *Cancer Epidemiology, Biomarkers, and Prevention* 1995; 4: 877–884.
12. Hecht. Chemoprevention of cancer by isothiocyanates, modifiers of carcinogen metabolism. *J* 1999; 129(3): 768S-774S.
13. Boyd, McCann, Hashim, Bennett, Gill, Rowland IR. Assessment of the anti-genotoxic, anti-proliferative, and anti-metastatic potential of crude watercress extract in human colon cancer cells. *Nutr* 2006; 55(2): 232–241.

Wheat / *Ḥinṭah*

Family: Poaceae
Botanical Name: *Triticum* spp.
Common Names: *English* Wheat; *French* Blé, froment; *Spanish* Trigo; *German* Weizen; *Urdu/Unānī* Gehun, Gandum; *Modern Standard Arabic* ḥinṭah

Safety Rating: Generally Safe Wheat is generally considered to be safe for most people.

Prophetic Prescription: The Messenger of Allāh once said, "I would love to have bread made from brown wheat."[1] After reaching Medina, the Prophet Muḥammad is said to have never consumed wheat bread for three consecutive days.[2] According to Farooqi, this was because "Wheat was costlier and barley was cheaper."[3] However, there may be a medical reason for this dietary choice. As several studies have shown, there appears to be a link between wheat intake and diabetes. Reducing his intake of wheat may have been a preventative measure taken by the Prophet. When a companion mentioned to him that he had applied nutgrass (*al-su'd*) to his sore teeth, Imām 'Alī al-Riḍā advised him to "Take wheat (*al-ḥinṭah*), husk it, and extract the oil. It the tooth is decayed and rotten, put two drops of the oil in it. Put some oil on a piece of cotton and place it in the ear near the tooth for three nights. It will stop [the decay], Allāh, the Exalted, willing."[4]

Issues in Identification: It is the consensus that *ḥinṭah* and *burr* are Arabic for wheat. It is known in Saudi Arabic as both *ḥinṭah* and *qamḥ*. During biblical times, the wheat that was grown in the Holy Land was *Triticum durum* or durum wheat as well as *Triticum dicoccum* or emmer. As Duke explains, *Triticum aestivum* (common wheat), and *Triticum spleta* (spelt) do not even grown in Palestine. It is quite possible then that the wheat of the Prophet was durum or awned wheat. If it was *Triticum aestivum*, known as common wheat or bread wheat, it was certainly imported from wheat-growing regions such as Egypt, the bread basket of Imperial Rome, and was a whole wheat, as opposed to a white wheat.[5]

Properties and Uses: Wheat is antibilious, antihydrotic, antipyretic, antivinous, sedative, and stomachic. The young stems are used to treat intoxication and the ash is used to remove skin blemishes, while the fruit is antipyretic and sedative. The light grain is antihydrotic and is used to treat night sweats and spontaneous sweating. The seed is said to contain sex hormones and is used in China to promote female fertility. The seed sprouts, which are antibilious and antivinous, are used to treat malaise, sore throat, throat, thirst, abdominal coldness and spasmic pain, constipation and cough. The plant also possesses anticancer properties.

Scientific Studies: *Diabetes-Inducing Activity* According to a study conducted by Virginia

Polytechnic Institute and State University, wheat gluten may be one of the elusive environmental triggers in type 1 diabetes.[6] According to a U.S. Environmental Protection Agency report, the underlying cause of mortality from myocardial infarction and type 2 diabetes increased, and the underlying cause of mortality from coronary atherosclerosis decreased, in countries where a large proportion of the land area is dedicated to spring and durum wheat farming.[7] Several other human trials have suggested a link between insoluble dietary fiber and diabetes.[8]

Wheat Notes

1. Ibn Qayyim al-Jawziyyah M. *al-Ṭibb al-nabawī*. Bayrūt: Dār al-Kitāb, 1985; Abū Dāwūd S. *Ṣaḥīḥ Sunan Abū Dāwūd*, Riyyāḍ: Maktab al-Tarbiyyah, 1989.
2. Bukhārī M. *Ṣaḥīḥ al-Bukhārī*. al-Riyyāḍ: Bayt al-Afkār, 1998.
3. Farooqi MIH. *Medicinal Plants in the Traditions of Prophet Muḥammad*. Lucknow: Sidrah Publishers, 1998: 149.
4. Nisābūrī A. *Islamic Medical Wisdom: The Ṭibb al-a'immah*. Trans. B. Ispahany. Ed. AJ Newman. London: Muḥammadī Trust, 1991: 16.
5. Tannahill R. *Food in History*. New York: Stein and Day, 1973: 174.
6. Barbeau, Bassaganya-Riera, Hontecillas. Putting the pieces of the puzzle together: a series of hypotheses on the etiology and pathogenesis of type 1 diabetes *Med* 2007; 68(3): 607–619.
7. Schreinemachers. Mortality from ischemic heart disease and diabetes mellitus (type 2) in four U.S. wheat-producing states: a hypothesis-generating study. *Environ* 2006; 114(2): 186–193.
8. Weickert, Mohlig, Koebnick, Holst, Namsolleck, Ristow, Osterhoff, Rochlitz, Rudovich, Spranger, Pfeiffer. Impact of cereal fiber on glucose-regulating factors. *Diabetologia*. 2005; 48(11): 2343–2353; Ezenwaka, Kalloo. Carbohydrate-induced hypertriglyceridaemia among West Indian diabetic and non-diabetic subjects after ingestion of three local carbohydrate foods. *Indian* 2005; 121(1): 23–31; Montonen, Knekt, Jarvinen, Aromaa, Reunanen. Whole-grain and fiber intake and the incidence of type 2 diabetes. *Am J Clin Nutr*. 2003; 77(3): 622–629.

Wormwood / *Shīḥ*

FAMILY: Asteraceae

BOTANICAL NAME: *Artemisia arborescens*
COMMON NAMES: *English* Shrubby wormwood, tree wormwood; *French* Armoise arborescente; *Spanish* No common name; *German* Halbstrauchiger Wermut, Strauch-Wermut; *Modern Standard Arabic* Shīḥ mushajjir, Shaybah, Dhaqn al-shaykh, Rayḥān abyaḍ

BOTANICAL NAME: *Artemisia absinthium*
COMMON NAMES: *English* Wormwood, Absinthe, artemisia; *French* Absinthe, Grande absinthe, Absinthe amère, Herbe aux vers; *Spanish* Ajenjo, Ajorizo, Artemisia amarga, Hierba santa; *German* Wermut, Absinth; *Urdu/Unānī* Afsanteen; *Modern Standard Arabic* Afsantīn, Dasīsah, Shīḥ rūmī, Kushūth rūmī, Shwaylā, Shaybah

BOTANICAL NAME: *Artemisia herba-alba*
COMMON NAMES: *English* herba-alba, white wormwood; *French* Armoise herbe-blance; *Spanish* Ajenjo moruno; *German* Weißer Wermut, Pyrenäen-Wermut; *Modern Standard Arabic* Shīḥ, Ghurayrah

BOTANICAL NAME: *Artemisia judaica*
COMMON NAMES: *English* Judean wormwood; *French* Absinthe de Judée, Semen-contra, Armoise de Judée; *Spanish* Artemisia judaica, Chihai; *German* Wermut aus Judaea; *Modern Standard Arabic* shīḥ, shīḥān, ḥashīshah khurasāniyyah

BOTANICAL NAME: *Artemisia monosperma*
COMMON NAMES: *English* One-seeded wormwood, sand wormwood; *French* Armoise à une graine; *Spanish* Artemisia monosperma; *German* Einsamiger Wermut; *Modern Standard Arabic* Shīḥ Uḥādī al-bizrah, 'Adhir

BOTANICAL NAME: *Artemisia santonicum*
COMMON NAMES: *English* Holy wormwood, Semen-contra; *French* Armoise santonique, Semen-contra; *Spanish* Artemisia Santónico, Ajenjo Marino; *German* Wurmsamen, Heiliger Beifuß, Salz-Wermut, Salz-Beifuß, Salzsteppenbeifuß; *Modern Standard Arabic* Shīḥ khurasānī, qayṣūm al-ānshī

BOTANICAL NAME: *Artemisia scoparia*
COMMON NAMES: *English* Broom wormwood; *French* Armoise à balais; *Spanish* Artemisia scoparia; *German* Besen-Beifuß; *Urdu/Unānī* Baranjasif, Balanjasif, Bua-e Madaran; *Modern Standard Arabic* Shīḥ miknāsī, Silmās

BOTANICAL NAME: *Artemisia vulgaris*
COMMON NAMES: *English* Mugwort, common wormwood; *French* Armoise, Herbe à cents gouts; *Spanish* Altamisa, Hierba de San Juan; *German* Echter Beifuß, Gewöhnlicher Beifuß, Mugwurz, Beinweich, Besenkraut, Donnerkraut, Gänsekraut, Gürtlerkaurt, Jungfernkraut, Sonnenwdel, Sonnwendgürtel, Throwurz, Wilder Wermut; *Modern Standard Arabic* Barnajāsaf, Shūwilā', Ḥabqu al-rā'ī

SAFETY RATING: GENERALLY SAFE TO DEADLY
The occasional consumption of wormwood in small quantities is generally considered to be safe for most adults. Even small quantities, however, can cause nervous disorders, insomnia, and convulsions in some cases. In sensitive people, the mere smell of the plant can cause headaches and

nervousness. Large and long-term consumption of wormwood, however, can be potentially perilous as it contains a volatile oil which is an active narcotic poison. Habitual or large doses of wormwood is toxic to the nervous system, causing convulsions, insomnia, nausea, nightmares, restlessness, tremors, and vertigo. As such, it should not be used by patients who suffer from nervous disorders or who are taking medicine for seizures. Since wormwood is a uterine stimulant, it must be avoided during pregnancy and lactation. Due to its dangers, wormwood should not be consumed by small children, particularly those under the age of six. It should not be ingested by those who suffer from cirrhosis, hepatitis, gall bladder obstruction or kidney disease. Due to its potentially irritating action, it should be avoided by people with stomach or intestinal ulcers. Treatment with wormwood tea should not surpass more than a few days.

The essential oil of wormwood is toxic and must never be used internally. Absinthe or Green Fairy, an alcoholic beverage made from wormwood, is addictive and highly toxic to the nervous system. As a result, it is banned in many countries. Since the term wormwood applies to many species, positive identification should not be attempted by non-experts due to the dangers posed by erroneous identification. For the sake of safety, wormwood should only be used in medicinal doses under expert supervision. Symptoms of wormwood overdose include restlessness, vomiting, vertigo, tremors, and convulsions.

Prophetic Prescription: The Messenger of Allāh said, "Fumigate your homes with *Olibanum* and wormwood (*shīḥ*)."[1] He also said, "Fumigate your homes with wormwood (*shīḥ*), myrrh (*murr*), and thyme (*ṣaʿtar*)."[2]

Issues in Identification: In Modern Standard Arabic, *Artemisia* is known as *shīḥ* and *ḥabaq al-rāʿī*. According to Bīrūnī, the plant was known in classical Arabic as *Arṭamasiyā*, *Arṭamāsā*, *Afsantīn*, *ifsintīn*, *rayḥān abyaḍ*, *shawaṣarā*, *qayṣūm*, *marwah*, *misk al-jān*, and *khutruq*, which Said identifies as *Artemisia absinthium*. Bīrūnī says that the plant is also known as *shaybah*, *ifsintīn*, *rayḥān abyaḍ*, *shawaṣarā*, *qayṣūm*, *marwah*, *misk al-jān*, and *khutruq*, which Said identifies as *Artemisia absinthium* L. According to Hans Wehr, *shībah* is *Artemisia arborescens* L., while *shīḥ* is an Oriental variety of *Artemisia*. Said identifies *shīḥ* as Armenian wormwood or *Artemisia abrotanum* L. Farooqi believes that it refers to *Artemisia maritima*. For Turkī, *shīḥ* refers to *Artemisia herba-alba*, known by the common name of herbaceous absinthe. Álvarez Morales and Girón Irueste simply identify *shīḥ* as *Artemisia*.[3] Thomson translated *shīḥ* as thyme.[4]

According to Mandaville, *Artemisia sieberi* is often referred to as *Artemisia herba-alba*. However, this taxon is now considered by authorities to be restricted to the western Mediterranean. Next to *Achillea fragrantissima*, it is the strongest aromatic plant of the northern plains and Summan. According to Ghazanfar, *Artemisia sieberi* is found in Saudi Arabia, and northern Oman, in rocky, gravelly, and silty wadi beds. It is also found in Northern Africa, and Southwest Asia.[5] According to Mandaville, it is occasional to locally frequent in eastern Arabia, particularly on silt floors of wadis and basins, usually in rocky country. It is known colloquially as *shīḥ*. It is used by Bedouin as a medicinal, often by inhaling the smoke.

As Mandaville explains, *Artemisia judaica* is a northwestern Arabian species of *Artemisia*, which is known in the colloquial as *buʿaythirān*. *Artemisia monosperma* is locally common in deep sands in the northern and central Dahna and the red sand bodies of central Arabia. It is known in the colloquial as *ʿadhir*. *Artemisia scoparia* is infrequent in eastern Arabia, found in silt-floored basins of the northern plains and Summan, sometimes at roadsides on disturbed ground. It is known in the vernacular as *ʿuwaydhirān*, a diminutive of *ʿadhir*.

As we read in Duke, biblical wormwood was most likely *Artemisia herba-alba*, although *Artemisia judaica* is similarly used. Egyptian bedouins sell both species in Cairo markets. Duke also relates that the Lebanese use *A. arborescens*, *A. herba-alba*, *A. judaica*, and *A. maritima* interchangeably. In all likelihood, the Prophet was using the term *shīḥ* as a generic common name without pointing to a specific species.

Properties and Uses: There are several hundred types of *Artemisia*, many of which are used medicinally. Known as wormwood and, in the U.S., as sage brush, they are among the most bitter of herbs. If we limit ourselves to the most prevalent species of wormwood found in Arabia, the *shīḥ* referred to by the Prophet may include *Artemisia abyssinica*, a perennial, sand-stabilizing species common in the great inland deserts, or *Artemisia maritima*, known as sea wormwood. *Artemisia maritima* is an anthelmintic, antiseptic, antispasmodic, carminative, cholagogue, emmenagogue, febrifuge, stimulant, stomachic, tonic, and vermifuge. Although not often used in herbal medicine, its medicinal properties are similar to *A. absinthium*, the type of wormwood most commonly used in Unānī medicine, though milder in action. *Artemisia absinthium* is considered resolvent, deobstruent, diuretic, tonic, antiperiodic, vermicidal, febrifuge, stomachic, diaphoretic, antiseptic, anti-inflammatory, and slightly narcotic.

Artemisia maritima is used primarily as a tonic for the digestive system, treating intermittent fevers, and as a vermifuge. The leaves and flowering shoots are anthelmintic, antiseptic, antispasmodic, carminative, cholagogue, emmenagogue, febrifuge, stimulant, stomachic, tonic, and vermifuge, while the unexpanded floral heads contain the vermicide santonin. *Artemisia maritima* is more powerful than chloroquine.

SCIENTIFIC STUDIES: *Potential Health Hazards* In an animal study conducted King Saud University in Saudi Arabia, *Artemisia abyssinica* leaves, a traditional medicine for the treatment of various disorders, were fed to male Wistar rats at 2 percent and 10 percent of the standard diet for 6 weeks. At 2 percent the *A. abyssinica* leaf diet was not toxic to rats. Depression in growth, hepatopathy and nephropathy were observed in rats fed a diet containing 10 percent of *A. abyssinica* leaves. These findings were accompanied by leukopenia, anemia and alterations of serum aspartate aminotransferase, alanine aminotransferase and gamma glutamyl transferase activities with changes in concentrations of total protein, albumin, cholesterol and urea.[6]

Insecticidal Activity According to one study, *Artemisia absinthium* contains insecticidal agents.[7]

Antifertility Activity In an animal study conducted by King Saud University in Saudi Arabia, significant sperm damage was observed in *A. abyssinica*-treated mice while *A. inculta* failed to produce any significant spermatotoxic effect.[8]

A study conducted by the University of the Philippines suggest that aqueous and chloroform extracts from leaves of *A. vulgaris* have antihypertensive actions but have no significant effects on cardiovascular hemodynamics under basal conditions.[9]

Antimalarial Activity Although the tea from *Artemisia annua* is used to treat malaria, modern artemesinin preparations have been shown to be more effective. The antimalarial drug Coartem produced by Novartis stems from this plant. Knowledge of the antimalarial properties of *A. annua* was found in a Chinese medical book written on silk and unearthed from a tomb of the West Han Dynasty, which started around 200 B.C. The drug was developed by Chinese military scientists in the 1970s to treat soldiers suffering from malaria in Vietnam. Novartis struck a deal with the Chinese in the early 1990s to buy the rights to Coartem. Artemisinin drugs are extensively used in Southeast Asia, and increasingly in Africa.[10] There also exists a charity called Anamed which trains people in the Tropics to cultivate *Artemisia annua* and to employ their harvest in the form of a tea to treat malaria and other diseases.

In an open, randomized, controlled pilot trial conducted by the German Institute for Medical Mission, traditional tea preparations of *A. annua* resulted in a quick resolution of parasitaemia and of clinical symptoms. After seven days of medication, cure rates were on average 74 percent for the *Artemisia* preparations compared with 91 percent for quinine. The *Artemisia* groups, however, had high recrudescence rates. As a result, researchers could not recommend the use of *A. annua* as an alternative to modern antimalarials. Due to its rapid resolution of parasitaemia and clinical symptoms, the scientists concluded that *A. annua* deserved further investigation.[11]

In a study conducted by Virtual Campus Rhineland-Palatinate in Germany, Artesunate, a semi-synthetic derivative of artemisinin, the active principle of the Chinese herb *A. annua*, revealed remarkable activity against multidrug-resistant *Plasmodium falciparum* and *P. vivax* malaria.[12]

In a study conducted by Hopital Nebobongo in the Congo, five malaria patients who were treated with *Artemisia annua* tea showed a rapid disappearance of parasitaemia within 2 to 4 days. An additional trial with 48 malaria patients showed a disappearance of parasitaemia in 44 patients (92 percent) within 4 days. Both trials showed a marked improvement of symptoms. In our opinion, these results justify further examinations of the antimalarial effect of *Artemisia annua* preparations.[13]

Hepaprotective and Antioxidative Activity In an animal study conducted by Bahauddin Zakariya University in Pakistan, the hepatoprotective activity of the aqueous-methanolic extract of *Artemisia maritima* was demonstrated against acetaminophen and carbon tetrachloride-induced hepatic damage.[14] A study conducted by the Chemistry Department, Faculty of Science, Beni-Suef, Egypt, also suggested that *Artemisia maritima* acts as both a hepaprotective and antioxidant agent.[15]

Anticancer Activity Artemisinin induces apoptosis in human cancer cells. *Artemisia annua* has also been shown to possess anticancer properties. It is said that it has the ability to be selectively toxic to breast cancer cells and some forms of prostate cancer. There have also been some exciting preclinical trials against leukemia, and other cancer cells.[16] Studies have shown that Artemisinin is most active against leukemia and colon cancer cell lines. Its toxicity was also shown to be in line with those of established antitumor drugs.

Due to its promising results and low toxicity, Artemisinin may be a promising novel candidate for cancer chemotherapy.[17]

Wormwood Notes

1. Bayhaqī A. *al-Sunan al-kubrā*. Bayrūt: Dār Ṣadīr, 1968.

2. Bayhaqī A. *al-Sunan al-kubrā*. Bayrūt: Dār Ṣadīr, 1968.

3. Ibn Ḥabīb A. *Mujtaṣar fī al-ṭibb/Compendio de medicina*. Ed. C Álvarez de Morales and F Girón Irueste. Madrid: Consejo Superior de Investigaciones Científicas, 1992.

4. Iṣbahānī AN al-. *Mawsū'at al-ṭibb al-nabawī*. Ed. MKD al-Turkī. Bayrūt: Dār Ibn Ḥazm, 2006.

5. Ghazanfar SA. *Handbook of Arabian Medicinal Plants*. Boca Raton: CRC Press, 1994.

6. Adam, Al-Qarawi, Elhag. Effects of various levels of dietary *Artemisia abyssinica* leaves on rats. *Lab* 2000; 34(3): 307–312.

7. Sherif A, et al. Drugs, insecticides and other agents from *Artemisia*. *Medical Hypotheses* 1997; 23: 187–193.

8. Qureshi, Ageel, al-Yahya, Tariq, Mossa, Shah. Preliminary toxicity studies on ethanol extracts of the aerial parts of *Artemisia abyssinica* and *A. inculta* in mice. *J* 1990; 28(2): 157–162.

9. Tigno, de, Flora. Phytochemical analysis and hemodynamic actions of *Artemisia vulgaris* L. *Clin* 2000; 23(2–4): 167–175.

10. Van, Eggelte, van. Artemisinin drugs in the treatment of malaria: from medicinal herb to registered medication. *Trends* 1999; 20(5): 199–205.

11. Mueller, Runyambo, Wagner, Borrmann, Dietz, Heide. Randomized controlled trial of a traditional preparation of *Artemisia annua* L. (annual wormwood) in the treatment of malaria. *Trans* 2004; 98(5): 318–321.

12. Efferth, Dunstan, Sauerbrey, Miyachi, Chitambar. The anti-malarial artesunate is also active against cancer. *Int* 2001; 18(4): 767–773.

13. Mueller, Karhagomba, Hirt, Wemakor. The potential of *Artemisia annua* L. as a locally produced remedy for malaria in the tropics: agricultural, chemical and clinical aspects. *J Ethnopharmacol.* 2000; 73(3): 487–493.

14. Janbaz, Gilani. Evaluation of the protective potential of *Artemisia maritima* extract on acetaminophen- and CCl4-induced liver damage. *J* 1995; 23; 47(1): 43–47.

15. Ahmed, Khater. Evaluation of the protective potential of *Ambrosia maritima* extract on acetaminophen-induced liver damage. *J* 2001; 75(2–3): 169–174.

16. Mueller MS, Runyambo, Wagner I, et al. Randomized controlled trial of a traditional preparation of *Artemisia annua* L. (annual wormwood) in the treatment of malaria. Trans R Soc *Trop Med Hyg*. 2004; 98: 318–321; Räth K, Taxis K, Walz GH, et al. Pharmacokinetic study of artemisinin after oral intake of a traditional preparation of *Artemisia annua* L. (annual wormwood). *Am J Trop Med Hyg* 2004; 70: 128–132.

17. Efferth, Dunstan, Sauerbrey, Miyachi, Chitambar. The anti-malarial artesunate is also active against cancer. *Int* 2001; 18(4): 767–773.

Glossary of Technical Terms

While this glossary may adequately define some of the technical terms employed in the encyclopedia, it is intended merely to supplement a good medical or scientific dictionary.

Adaptogen: Increase the body's resistance to physical, biological, emotional and environmental stressors.
Adjuvant: Agents which modify the effect of other agents while having few if any direct effects when given by themselves.
Abortifacient: Causes abortion.
Abrasive: Causing abrasion.
Allergen: Produces an allergic reaction.
Alkalizing: Neutralizes acids.
Alopecia: Baldness; an absence of normal body hair.
Alterative: Improves vitality by improving breakdown and excretion of waste products; a medicinal substance that gradually restores health.
Amenorrhea: The absence or suppression of menstruation.
Amoeba: A single-celled protozoan that is widely found in fresh and salt water. Some types of amoebas cause diseases such as amoebic dysentery.
Analgesic: Relieves pain.
Anaphylaxis: A rapidly progressing, life-threatening allergic reaction.
Angiogenesis: A physiological process involving the growth of new blood vessels from pre-existing vessels.
Anodyne: Relieves pain.
Anaphrodisiac: Represses sexual desire.
Anesthetic: Causes local or general loss of sensation.
Anodyne: A pain-relieving medicine, milder than analgesic.
Anthelmintic: An agent which is destructive to parasitic intestinal worms; vermifuge.
Anthemorrhagic: Prevents, reduces or halts hemorrhage.
Antiallergenic: Helps prevent or combat allergies.
Antianaphylaxis: Allergic reaction. In severe cases, this can include potentially deadly anaphylactic shock.
Antiangiogenic: Of or relating to a naturally occurring substance, drug, or other compound that can destroy or interfere with the fine network of blood vessels needed by tumors to grow and metastasize.
Antiarrhythmic: An agent alleviating cardiac arrhythmias
Antiarthritic: Prevents or relieves arthritis.
Antibacterial: Destroys or hinders the growth of bacteria.
Antibilious: An herb that combats biliousness, a group of symptoms consisting of nausea, abdominal discomfort, headache, constipation, and gas.
Antibiotic: Destroys or inhibits growth of microorganisms.
Anticandidial: Prevents or relieves Candida or vaginal yeast infection.
Anticarcinogenic: A source of the prevention, or delay of the development of cancer.
Anticolic: Prevents or relieves colic or abdominal pain.
Antidiarrheal: Prevents or relieves diarrhea.
Antifertility: Contraceptive: capable of preventing conception or impregnation.
Antigenotoxic: Protects against carcinogens, specifically those capable of causing genetic mutation and or contributing to the development of tumors.
Antihemorrhagic: Prevents or combats hemorrhage or bleeding.
Antihepatotoxic: A substance with protects the liver from toxins, or clears toxins from the liver; a liver detoxifier
Antihydrotic: A substance that reduces or suppresses perspiration.
Antihypertensive: Reducing or controlling high blood pressure.
Anti-infective: Combats infection.
Anti-inflammatory: Reduces inflammation.
Antimicrobial: A substance that kills or inhibits

the growth of microbes such as bacteria (antibacterial activity), fungi (antifungal activity), viruses (antiviral activity), or parasites (antiparasitic activity).
Antimutagenic: Inhibits mutation.
Antioxidant: Prevents or slows the deterioration of cells by oxidization.
Antiparasitic: Prevents or destroys parasites.
Antiproliferative: Counteracting a process of proliferation.
Antipruritic: Prevents or relieves itching.
Antipyretic: An agent effective against fever.
Antirheumatic: Prevents or treats rheumatism.
Antiscorbutic: Combats scurvy or vitamin C deficiency.
Antiseptic: Prevents or controls infection; prevents the growth of germs.
Antispasmodic: Prevents or reduces spasms or tension, especially involuntary muscle spasms.
Antithrombotic: Prevents blood clots from forming in blood vessels, particularly inside the brain.
Antitumor: Prevents or combats tumors or cancers.
Antiurolithiatic: Prevent the formation of stones in the kidney, bladder, and urethra.
Antiviral: An effective agent inhibiting a virus.
Anxiolytic: A drug prescribed for the treatment of symptoms of anxiety.
Aperitive: Stimulates the appetite for food.
Aphrodisiac: Promotes sexual excitement.
Aphthous: A small sensitive painful ulcer crater in the lining of the mouth.
Apoptosis: Process of suicide by a cell in a multicellular organism.
Aperient: A mild laxative; causes a gentle bowel movement.
Aromatic: Agents which emit a fragrant smell and produce a pungent taste. Used chiefly to make other medicines more palatable.
Astringent: Precipitates proteins from the surfaces of cells, causing contraction of tissues; forms a protective coating, and reduces bleeding and discharges.
Atherogenesis: The process of forming atheromas, plaques in the inner lining (the intima) of arteries.
Atherosclerosis: Hardening of the arteries.
Atrophy: Wasting away of any part, organ, tissue or cell.
Bacillus: Any rod-shaped bacterium.
Bactericidal: A substance that kills bacteria and, preferably, nothing else. Bactericides are either disinfectants, antiseptics or antibiotics.
Bitter: Stimulates the flow of saliva and the secretion of digestive juice, improving appetite and aiding the process of digestion.
Bronchial: Relating to the air passages in the lungs.
Bronchocele: An indolent swelling of the thyroid gland; goitre; tracheocele.
Bronchodilator: Dilates the lungs.
Bursitis: Inflammation of a bursa, often associated with pain and swelling. Most frequently occurs near shoulder, elbow or hip joints.
Calculi: Stones or solid lumps such as gallstones.
Calmative: An agent with mild sedative or calming effects.
Carcinogenic: Causes cancer.
Cardioactive: Affecting the heart.
Cardio-inhibitory: Depress cardiac function by decreasing heart rate (chronotropy) and myocardial contractility (inotropy), which decreases cardiac output and arterial pressure.
Cardiotonic: Substance that strengthens or regulates heart metabolism without overt stimulation or depression. It may increase coronary blood supply, normalize coronary enervation, relax peripheral arteries (thereby decreasing back-pressure on the valves), or decrease adrenergic stimulation.
Carminative: Relieves flatulence, colic, and digestive discomfort; a drug that removes flatus from the gastrointestinal tract.
Catharsis: A purging of the bowels.
Cathartic: Pertaining to catharsis.
Cattarrh: Inflammation of the mucous membranes with a discharge of mucus secretions; particularly from the upper respiratory tract. This has special reference to the air passages of the head and throat. For example: hayfever, rhinitis, influenza, bronchitis, pharyngitis, and asthma.
Cephalic: Referring to diseases affecting the head and upper part of the body.
Chelation: To remove a heavy metal, such as lead or mercury, from the bloodstream by means of a chelate, such as EDTA.
Chemopreventive: Inhibits, delays, or reverses carcinogenesis.
Chilblain: Inflammation, swelling, and itching of the ears, fingers, and toes produced by frostbite.
Cholagogue: An agent that increases bile flow to the intestines.
Cholesterol: A fatlike material, present in the blood and in most tissues, which is an important constituent of cell membranes, steroid hormones, and bile salts.
Cholinergic: Related to the neurotransmitter acetylcholine.
Chondroprotective: Compounds that stimulate chondrocyte synthesis of collagen and proteoglycans, as well as synoviocyte production of hyaluronan, inhibit cartilage degradation and prevent fibrin formation in the subchondral and synovial vasculature.

Circulatory stimulant: Dilates the blood vessels and increases blood flow.

Cirrhosis: Inflammation or an organ characterized by degenerative changes, particularly the liver.

Conjunctivitis: Inflammation of the conjunctiva or mucous membranes lining the eyelids and covering the anterior surface of the eyeball.

Cooling: A remedy, often based on bitter or relaxant herbs, that reduces internal "heat" or physiological hyperactivity.

Cordial: A stimulating medicine or drink.

Coryza: Nasal catarrh resulting from inflammation of the mucous membranes; common head cold.

Cystitis: Inflammation of the bladder due to infection, usually by *E. coli* bacteria transferred from the bowel; it is particularly common in the early stages of pregnancy, and attacks tend to recur. In men, cystitis is usually secondary to prostate problems, bladder tumors, bladder stones, or congenial abnormality of the bladder or urethra.

Cytopathogenicity: Of, relating to, or producing pathological changes in cells.

Cytoprotective: Cytoprotective agents (or "cell" protective agents) are medications used in the treatment of peptic ulcer disease (PUD) because they help protect the lining of the stomach and the upper small intestine (duodenum) to allow ulcer healing to occur.

Delirium tremens: An acute, psychotic state usually occurring during reduction or cessation of alcohol intake after a prolonged or copious intake of alcohol; characterized by symptoms such as tremors, hallucinations, or seizures. Requires immediate treatment; may be life threatening.

***Demodex folliculorum*:** A mite that infests hair follicles, contributing to a skin condition called rosacea.

Demulcent: Soothes and softens damaged, irritated, or inflamed tissues (especially of the digestive tract); a substance that soothes or softens the skin.

Depressant: Reduces nervous or functional activity.

Depurative: Promotes the elimination of waste products from the body; purifying or cleansing of the blood, detoxifying.

Dermatitis: Inflammation of the skin.

Dermatophyte: A parasitic fungus that infects the skin.

Detoxicant: Removes poisons (especially waste products) from the body.

Diaphoretic: Induces profuse perspiration, thus eliminating toxins and lowering fever.

Digestive: Stimulates digestion.

Diuretic: Increases volume of urine.

Diuresis: Abnormal secretion of urine.

Dropsy: *see* Edema

Dysentery: A group of intestinal disorders characterized by inflammation and irritation of the colon, with diarrhea, abdominal pain, and the passage of mucous or blood.

Dyslipidemia: An abnormal concentration of lipids or lipoproteins in the blood.

Dysmenorrhea: Painful menstruation.

Dyspepsia: Indigestion.

Dysuria: Any difficulty in urination, sometimes accompanied by pain.

Edema: Swelling from excessive accumulation of serous fluid in tissue.

Emetic: Causes vomiting.

Emmenagogue: A medicine that stimulates menstrual functioning.

Emollient: An agent that softens or smoothens the skin.

Enuresis: Involuntary urination.

Epidermophytosis: A disease (as athlete's foot) of the skin or nails caused by a dermatophyte.

Epididymides: A long, narrow, convoluted tube in the spermatic duct system that lies on the posterior aspect of each testicle and connects with the vas deferens.

Epigastric: Pertaining to the upper middle part of the abdomen, including the area over and in front of the stomach.

Epstein-Barr virus: A virus causing diseases ranging from mononucleosis to several kinds of cancer.

Errhine: Bringing on sneezing, increasing flow of mucus in nasal passages.

Estrogenic: Similar in effects to the hormone estrogen, which plays an important role in the development and functioning of female sexual organs.

Euphoric: Causing an increased sense of well-being.

Excitant: Causes stimulation.

Excoriation: An erosion or destruction of the skin by mechanical means, which appears in the form of a scratch or abrasion of the skin.

Expectorant: Encourages the expulsion of phlegm from the respiratory tract; an agent which liquefies sputum or phlegm.

Febrifuge: An agent that relieves or lowers fever.

Febrile: Related to fever.

Fibrinolysis: The process where a fibrin clot, the product of coagulation, is broken down. Its main enzyme, plasmin, cuts the fibrin mesh at various places, leading to the production of circulating fragments that are cleared by other proteinases or by the kidney and liver.

Flatulence: Excessive gas in the stomach and the alimentary canal.

Fungal: Caused by a fungus.
Fungicide: A substance that destroys fungi.
Furuncle: Boil; a painful nodule in the skin caused by inflammatory sequestration of staphylococci and core formation.
Galactofuge: Suppresses milk flow.
Galactogogue: Increases milk flow.
Genotoxic: Any substance that leads to chromosomal damage.
Germicidal: Destroys germs.
Gingivostomatitis: Gingivostomatitis is a viral infection of the mouth and gums that causes swelling and sores. It is common, particularly in children.
Grave's disease: Toxic goiter characterized by diffuse hyperplasia of the thyroid gland, a form of hyperthyroidism; exophthalmos is a common, but not invariable, concomitant.
Helminth: A worm classified as a parasite.
Hemoptysis: Coughing up blood from the lungs.
Hemostatic: An agent that checks bleeding.
Hepaprotective: Protects the liver.
Hepatic: An herb that promotes the well-being of the liver and increases the secretion of bile.
Hepatocarcinoma: Adult primary liver cancer.
Histological: Referring to histology, microscopical presentation of biological tissues.
Homocystinuri: An inherited disorder of the metabolism of the amino acid methionine, often involving cystathionine beta synthase. It is an inherited autosomal recessive trait, which means a child needs to inherit the defective gene from both parents to be affected. Also known as cystathionine beta synthase deficiency.
Hydragogue: Producing a watery discharge from the bowels; a drug which acts as a cathartic causing a watery evacuation of the bowels.
Hypercholesterolemia: Chronic high levels of cholesterol in the bloodstream.
Hyperglycemic: A condition characterized by elevated blood glucose levels.
Hyperinsulinemia: An endocrine disorder characterized by a failure of our blood sugar control system (BSCS) to work properly.
Hypertension: High blood pressure.
Hypertensive: Causing or marking a rise in blood pressure.
Hyperthyroidism: Overactive thyroid gland.
Hypertonia: Increased tightness of muscle tone.
Hypertrophy: The increase of the size of an organ or in a select area of the tissue.
Hypnotic: An agent that can induce hypnosis or sleep.
Hypoglycemic: A condition characterized by lower than normal blood glucose levels.
Hypolipidemic: Lowers cholesterol.
Hypotensive: Causing or marking a lowering of blood pressure.
Hypoglycemia: A deficiency of blood sugar marked by fatigue, restlessness, malaise, irritability, muscular weakness, mental confusion, sweating, and weakness.
Immune system: The body's defense mechanisms against infectious organisms and other foreign materials, such as allergens.
Immunomodulator: A drug used for its effect on the immune system.
Immunostimulant: Stimulating various functions or activities of the immune system.
Insecticidal: Destroys insects.
Intraperitoneal: Within the peritoneal cavity, the area that contains the abdominal organs.
Keratitis: Inflammation of the cornea.
Lactation: Secretion of milk by the mammary glands, which usually begins at the end of pregnancy.
Lacto-dyspepsia: Abdominal discomfort caused by milk. Particularly common in babies.
Lactogogue: Stimulates the production of milk.
Larvicidal: Destroys larvae.
Laxative: Encourages bowel movements.
Lenitive: Assuasive, emollient; remedy that eases pain and discomfort; alleviative; moderating pain or sorrow.
Leucorrhea: Discharge of white mucous material from the vagina; often an indication of infection.
Leukoplakia: A condition that involves the formation of white leathery spots on the mucous membranes of the tongue and inside of the mouth.
Ligand: An ion, a molecule, or a molecular group that binds to another chemical entity to form a larger complex.
Lipids: Fatlike substances, such as cholesterol, which are important structural materials in the body, and present in most tissues (especially the blood).
Lochial: Relating to lochia or post-partum vaginal discharge, containing blood, mucus, and placental tissue or menstrual blood.
Lumbago: A non-medical term signifying pain in the lumbar region. Archaic term meaning back pain.
Lymphedema: Chronic swelling of an arm or leg due to a blockage of the lymph vessels.
Lymphocyte: Any of the nearly colorless cells found in the blood, lymph, and lymphoid tissues, constituting approximately 25 percent of white blood cells.
Macular degeneration: A medical condition predominantly found in elderly adults in which the

center of the inner lining of the eye, known as the macula area of the retina, suffers thinning, atrophy, and in some cases bleeding.

Menstruation: The "period" in the menstrual cycle, occurring at approximately monthly intervals, in which the lining of the womb breaks down and is discharged as blood and debris.

Micturition: Urination.

Mucilaginous: An agent characterized by a gummy or gelatinous consistency.

Muscarinic receptor: Membrane-bound acetylcholine receptors that are more sensitive to muscarine than to nicotine.

Myelocytic leukemia: A malignant neoplasm of blood-forming tissues; marked by proliferation of myelocytes and their presence in the blood.

Myocardial infarction: Heart attack.

Narcotic: An addicting substance that reduces pain and produces sleep.

Nasopharyngeal carcinoma: A poorly differentiated carcinoma that may appear at any site in the upper respiratory tract, but most commonly, in the lateral wall of the nasopharynx around the ostium of the Eustachian tube — the fossa of Rosenmulle.

Nematocidal: Destroys nematodes (unsegmented worms some of which are disease-causing parasites, such as hookworm).

Neoplasm: A tumor, benign or malignant; an abnormal growth of tissue.

Nephritis: Inflammation of the kidneys.

Nerve tonic: A remedy that supports the proper functioning of the nervous system. Also called nervine.

Nervine: An agent that affects, strengthens, or calms the nerves.

Neuralgia: A sharp, shooting pain along a nerve pathway.

Nutritive: An herb which provides nutrition.

Odontalgic: Used for the treatment of toothache.

Oleolite: A medicine with an oily base.

Onychomycosis: The invasion of the nail plate by a dermatophyte, yeast or nondermatophyte mold.

Ophthalmic: Heals disorders and diseases of the eye.

Orexigenic: Stimulates appetite.

Osteoarthritis: Degenerative arthritis; a joint disease caused by the breakdown and loss of the cartilage of one or more joints.

Otitis: Inflammation of the middle ear.

Oxytocic: A medicinal drug used to hasten parturition or stimulate uterine contractions.

Papilloma: A benign epithelial tumor.

Pathogen: A microorganism that causes disease; a biological agent that causes disease or illness to its host.

Pectoral: Pertaining to the chest or breast; an expectorant which relieves respiratory tract disorders.

Periodontosis: A degenerative disturbance of the periodontium, characterized by degeneration of connective-tissue elements of the periodontal ligament and by bone resorption.

Peristalsis: Waves of involuntary muscle contraction in the digestive tract that push the contents along.

Peritumoral: Around the tumor.

Phagocytes: Cells that ingest (and destroy) foreign matter, e.g., microorganisms or debris, via phagocytosis, i.e., a process by which these cells ingest and kill offending cells by cellular digestion. They are extremely useful as an initial immune system response to tissue damage.

Phagocytic: Pertaining to or produced by phagocytes.

Phlegm: Thick mucus, secreted by the walls of the respiratory tract.

Photodermatitis: A condition in which the skin becomes sensitized to a certain substance that, when exposed to sunlight, causes dermatitis.

Phytotherapy: Treatment of diseases using plants.

Piscicide: A substance which is poisonous to fish.

Plasmolysis: The shrinking and separation of the cytoplasm from the cell wall due to exosmosis of water from the protoplast.

Platelet aggregation: The clumping together of platelets in the blood.

Pleurisy: An inflammation of the pleura, the lining of the pleural cavity surrounding the lungs, which can cause painful respiration and other symptoms; also known as **pleuritis**.

Postprandial glycemia: A rise in blood sugar after consuming a meal.

Poultice: A moist, usually warm or hot mass of plant material applied to the skin, or with cloth between the skin and plant material, to effect a medicinal action.

Productive coughing: Resulting in expulsion of phlegm.

Prokinetic: Agents used to treat heartburn caused by gastroesophageal reflux disease.

Prophylactic: Agent which wards off disease.

Prostration: Exhaustion.

Ptyalism: Excessive flow of saliva.

Puerperal: After childbirth.

Pungent: Having an acrid smell or strong, bitter flavor.

Purgative: A substance that evacuates the bowels; a cathartic; an agent that causes cleansing or watery evacuation of the bowels, usually with griping (painful cramps).

Pyorrhea: The advanced stage of periodontal disease in which the ligaments and bones that support the teeth become inflamed and infected. It is usually a result of gingivitis, a periodontal disease that infects the gum through plaque leading to the formation of a pocket between the teeth that trap the plaque.

Refrigerant: Relieves fever and thirst; a cooling remedy; lowers body temperature.

Rejuvenative: Restores vitality.

Relaxant: Relaxes tense, overactive tissues.

Resolvent: An agent that causes dispersion of inflammation.

Restorative: Revives health or strength; causing a return to health or to consciousness; a remedy or substance that is effective in the regaining of health or strength.

Rhinitis: Inflammation of the nasal mucous membranes.

Rhizomes: Stem, usually underground, often horizontal, typically non-green and root-like in appearance but bearing scale leaves and/or foliage leaves.

Rubefacient: Causes reddening of the skin, thus increasing blood flow and cleansing the tissues of toxins.

Schistosomiasis: A parasitic disease caused by several species of flatworm; also known as bilharzia.

Sciatica: Irritation of the sciatic nerve resulting in pain or tingling running down the inside of the leg.

Scrofula: Tuberculosis involving the lymph nodes of the neck, usually occurs in early life. Now very rarely seen.

Sedative: Reduces anxiety and tension; a tranquilizer; an agent allaying irritation or excitement; quieting; calms the nerves, allays excitement, induces relaxation, and is conducive to sleep.

***Shigella dysenteriae*:** A highly communicable, strictly human pathogen spread by the fecal-oral route.

Sialogogue: An agent that stimulates secretion of saliva.

Somnolence: Drowsiness; a state of near-sleep, a strong desire for sleep, or sleeping for unusually long periods.

Soporific: Induces drowsiness or sleep.

Spasmogenic: Causing spasms.

Spasmolytic: Checking spasms or cramps.

Spermicidal: Destroys spermatozoa.

Sternutatory: Tending to cause sneezing.

Stimulant: Increases physiological activity.

Stomachic: A medicine which aids functional activity of the stomach.

Styptic: Contracting the tissues or blood vessels; astringent; tending to check bleeding by contracting the tissues or blood vessels; hemostatic.

Sudorific: Herbs that cause heavy perspiration.

Synergistic: Two or more compounds acting together in such a way that the total effect is greater than if each compound acted alone.

Synovitis: Inflammation of a synovial membrane, which line those joints which possess cavities (synovial joints).

Tenesmus: A physiological condition by which one has trouble urinating or especially defecating. It is marked by painful spasms of the anal sphincter, occurring with an urgent desire to defecate and an inability to do so.

Tenifuge: An agent that causes the expulsion of tapeworms.

Thrombotic: Forming a clot of coagulated blood in blood vessel or in the heart that remains at the site of formation, impeding blood flow.

Thrush: An infection of the mouth caused by the candida fungus, also known as yeast. Candida infection is not limited to the mouth; it can occur in other parts of the body as well, causing diaper rash in infants or vaginal yeast infections in women. Although it occurs most commonly in babies and toddlers, older adults, and people with weak immune systems, thrush can affect anyone.

Thyroid: Relating to the thyroid gland, near the base of the neck, which controls metabolism and growth.

Tinnitus aurium: Ringing in the ear.

Tonic: Improves physiological functions and sense of well-being; an ambiguous term referring to a substance thought to have an overall positive medicinal effect of an unspecified nature.

Topical: Applied to the body surface.

Torpor: Listlessness; inactivity resulting from lethargy and lack of vigor or energy.

Toxic: Harmful or poisonous.

Toxicity: The degree of strength of a toxic substance.

Tuberculostatic: Arresting the tubercle bacillus (the germ responsible for causing tuberculosis).

Tumorigenesis: A collection of complex genetic diseases characterized by multiple defects in the homeostatic mechanisms that regulate cell growth, proliferation and differentiation.

Ureter: Thin walled tube that drains urine from the kidney to the bladder.

Urethritis: Inflammation of the urethra caused by infection.

Uterine: Pertaining to the uterus.

Uterotonic: Having a positive effect on an unspecified nature of the uterus.

Vaginosis: Very common vaginal infection characterized by symptoms such as increased vaginal discharge or itching, burning, or redness in the genital area.

Vasoconstrictor: An agent that causes blood vessels to constrict, or narrow the caliber.
Vasodilator: An agent that causes blood vessels to relax and dilate.
Vermifuge: Destroys of expels intestinal worms.
Viral: Caused by a virus.
Virus: A disease-causing organism, capable of replication only within the cells of an animal or plant.
Vulnerary: An agent or herb used for healing wounds, fresh cuts, etc., usually used as a poultice.
Vulvovaginitis: An inflammation of the vagina and vulva, most often caused by a bacterial, fungal, or parasitic infection.
Warming: A remedy, often based on spicy, pungent herbs, that dispels internal "coldness" or hypoactivity, and increases vitality, mainly by stimulating digestion and circulation.

Bibliography

Abū Dāwūd, S. *Sunan Abū Dāwūd.* Bayrūt: Dār Ibn Ḥazm, 1998.

_____. *Sunan Abū Dāwūd.* Riyyāḍ: Maktab al-Tarbiyyah, 1989.

Ahmad, F, Nizami Q, Aslam M. *Classification of Unānī Drugs with English and Scientific Names.* Delhi: Maktaba Eshaatul Qur'ān, 2005.

Albānī, M al-. *Ṣaḥīḥ al-Jāmi'.* Dimashq: al-Maktab al-Islāmī, 1970.

'Alī, Abdullāh Yūsuf, trans. *The Holy Qur'ān.* Brentwood: Amana Corp., 1983.

'Amilī, *Wasā'il al-shī'ah.* Bayrūt: al-Mu'assasah, 1993.

Amin, M. *Wisdom of the Prophet Muḥammad.* Lahore: Lion Press, 1945.

'Aqīl, M. *Ṭibb al-Nabī.* Bayrūt: Dār al-Maḥajjah al-Bayḍā,' 2000.

_____. *Ṭibb al-Imām al-Ṣādiq.* Bayrūt: Mu'assasat al-A'lamī, 1998.

_____. *Ṭibb al-Imām 'Alī.* Bayrūt: Dār al-Maḥajjah al-Bayḍā,' 1996.

Aristotle. *Historia animalium: The Works of Aristotle.* Trans. D'A W. Thompson. Ed. J.A. Smith and W.D. Ross. Oxford: Oxford University Press, 1910.

al-Aṣma'ī, A.M. *Kitāb al-nabāt.* Cairo: Maktabat al-mutanabbī, 1972.

Assouad, M.W. *Dictionnaire des termes botaniques.* Librairie du Liban: Bayrūt, 2002.

Azraqī, I. *Tashil al-manafi' fī al-ṭibb wa al-ḥikmah.* al-Qāhirah: Muḥammad 'Alī Ṣabiḥ, 1963.

Bakhru, H.K. *Foods that Heal: The Natural Way to Good Health.* Delhi: Orient Paperbacks, 1997.

Balch, P.A. *Prescription for Herbal Healing.* New York: Avery, 2002.

Ba'lī M. *Saḥīḥ al-ṭibb al-nabawī.* Bayrūt: Dār Ibn Ḥazm, 2004.

Bār, M.A. *al-Sanā wa al-sanawāt.* Jiddah: Maktabat al-Sharq al-Islāmī, 1992

_____. *Hal hunāk ṭibb nabawī.* Jiddah: al-Dār al-Sa'ūdiyyah, 1409 [1988].

_____. *Al-Imām al-Riḍā wa risālatuhu fī al-ṭibb al-nabawī.* Bayrūt: Dār al-manāhil, 1991.

Barnes, J., et al. *Herbal Medicines.* London: Pharmaceutical Press, 2002

Bāshā, H. *Qabasāt min al-ṭibb al-nabawī.* Jiddah: Maktabat al-Sawādī, 1991.

Bayhaqī, A. *Shu'ab al-imān.* al-Riyyāḍ; al-Qāhirah: Maktabat al-Rushd, Nāshirūn, 2003.

_____. *al-Sunan al-Kubrā.* Bayrūt: Dār al-Kutub al-'Ilmiyyah, 1994.

Bellamy, D., and A. Pfister. *World Medicine: Plants, Patients and People.* Oxford: Blackwell, 1992.

Benenson, V. *Extract of Aloe: Supplement to Clinical Data.* Moscow: Medexport: Moscow Stomatologic Inst.

Bianchini, F., and F. Corbetta. *The Complete Book of Fruits and Vegetables.* New York: Crown, 1976.

Bible. *Good News.* New York: American Bible Society, 1976.

Biggs, M., J. McVicar and B. Flowerdew. *Vegetables, Herbs, and Fruit: An Illustrated Encyclopedia.* Buffalo/Richmond Hill: Firefly Books, 2006.

Bīrūnī, A.R. al-. *al-Bīrūnī's Book on Pharmacy and Materia Medica.* Ed. and trans. HM Said. Karachi: Hamdard National Foundation, 1973.

Blumenthal, M. *The ABC Clinical Guide to Herbs.* Austin: American Botanical Council, 2003.

Bown, D. *Encyclopedia of Herbs and Their Uses.* Montreal: RD Press, 1995.

Bratman, M.D., and D. Kroll. *The Natural Pharmacist: Natural Health Bible.* New York: Prima, 1999.

Brinker, F. *Herb Contraindications and Drug Interactions.* Sandy, OR: Eclectic Medical Publications, 2001.

Browne, E.G. *Arabian Medicine.* Cambridge: Cambridge University Press, 1962.

Bruneton, J. *Pharmacognosy: Phytochemistry of Medicinal Plants.* Paris: Tec & Doc, 1999.

Budge, E.A. *The Divine Origin of the Craft of the Herbalist.* London: Society of Herbalists, 1928.

Bukhārī, M. *Saḥīḥ al-Bukhārī.* Al-Riyyāḍ: Bayt al-Afkār, 1998.

Burgel, J.C. *Secular and Religious Features of Medieval Arabic Medicine. Asian Medical Systems: A Comparative Study.* Ed. C. Leslie. Berkeley and Los Angeles: University of California Press, 1972.

Buxó, R. *Arqueología de las plantas.* Barcelona: Crítica, 1997.

Campbell, D. *Arabian Medicine and its Influence on the Middle Ages*. Vol. 1. Kegan Paul. London: Trench, Trübner, 2001.

Castleman, M. *The New Healing Herbs: The Classic Guide to Nature's Best Medicines*. Emmaus, PA: Rodale Press, 2001.

Chaghhaynī, M. *Ṭibb al-nabī or Medicine of the Prophet*. Trans. C Elgood. *Osiris* 1962; 14.

Chan, H., and P. But, eds. *Pharmacology and Applications of Chinese Materia Medica*. Singapore: World Scientific, 1986.

Chaudhary, S.A. *Flora of the Kingdom of Saudi Arabia*. al-Riyyāḍ: Ministry of Agriculture and Water, 1999

Chevallier, A. *The Encyclopedia of Medicinal Plants*. New York: DK, 1996.

Chishti, S.H.M. *The Book of Sufi Healing*. Rochester, Vermont: Inner Traditions International, 1991.

_____. *The Traditional Healer's Handbook: A Classic Guide to the Medicine of Avicenna*. Rochester, Vermont: Healing Arts Press, 1991.

Compton, M.S. *Herbal Gold*. St. Paul: Llewellyn, 2000.

Conrad, L.I. *The Western Medical Tradition*. Cambridge: Cambridge University Press, 2006.

Coyle, L.P. *The World Encyclopedia of Food*. New York: Facts on File, 1982.

Cowan, J.M., ed. *Arabic-English Dictionary: The Hans Wehr Dictionary of Modern Written Arabic*. New York: Spoken Language Service, 1976.

Crelli, J.K., and J. Philpott. *Herbal Medicine: Past and Present*. Vol. 2. Durham and London: Duke University Press, 1990.

Davidson, A. *The Oxford Companion to Food*. Oxford: Oxford University Press, 1999.

Daylamī, S. *al-Firdaws*. Bayrūt: Dār al-Kutub al-'ilmīyah, 1986.

Dhahabī, S. *al-Ṭibb al-nabawī*. Bayrūt: Dār al-Nafā'is, 2004.

Dīnawarī, A.H. *Kitāb al-nabāt/The Book of Plants*. Ed. Bernhard Lewin. Bayrūt: Dār al-Qalam, 1974.

_____. *Kitāb al-nabāt: Le dictionaire botanique d'Abū Ḥanīfah al-Dīnawarī*. al-Qāhirah: Institut Français d'Archéologie Orientale du Caire, 1973.

_____. *Kitāb al-nabāt/The Book of Plants*. Ed. Bernhard Lewin. Uppsala/Wiesbaden: A.-B. Lundequistska Bokhandeln and Otto Harrassowitz, 1953.

Duke, J.A. *Duke's Handbook of Medicinal Plants of the Bible*. Boca Raton: CRC Press, 2008.

_____. *The Green Pharmacy: The Ultimate Compendium of Natural Remedies from the World's Foremost Authority on Healing Herbs*. New York: Macmillan, 1998.

_____. *Handbook of Medicinal Plants of the Bible*. Boca Raton: CRC Press, 2007.

Ebadi, M.S. *Pharmacodynamic Basis of Herbal Medicine*. Boca Raton: CRC Press, 2006.

Eldin, S. Dunford A. *Herbal Medicine in Primary Care*. Amsterdam: Elsevier Health Sciences, 1999.

Elgood, C., Trans. *Ṭibb al-nabī or Medicine of the Prophet*. Sūyūṭī J, M Chaghhaynī. *Osiris* 1962; 14.

Farooqi, M.I.H. *Medicinal Plants in the Traditions of Prophet Muḥammad*. Lucknow: Sidrah Publishers, 1998.

_____. *Plants of the Qur'ān*. Lucknow: Sidrah Publishers, 2000.

Felter, H.W., and J.U. Lloyd. *King's American Dispensatory*. 1898. http://www.henriettesherbal.com/eclectic/kings/index.html.

Fern, K. *Plants for a Future: Edible, Medicinal, and Useful Plants for a Healthier World*. Clanfield: Permanent Publications, 1997. http://www.pfaf.org/

Fetrow, C.W., and J.R. Avila. *The Complete Guide to Herbal Medicines*. Springhouse, PA: Springhouse Corporation, 2000.

Fortin, F. *The Visual Food Encyclopedia*. New York: Macmillan, 1996.

Gehrmann, B., K. Wolf-Gerald, C.O. Tshirch, and H. Brinkmann. *Medicinal Herbs: A Compendium*. New York: Haworth Press, 2005.

Germany. Ministry of Health. *Senna: Commission E. Monographs for Phytomedicines*. Bonn: German Ministry of Health, 1984.

Ghazanfar, S.A. *Handbook of Arabian Medicinal Plants*. Boca Raton: CRC Press, 1994.

Goldberg, B. *Alternative Medicine: The Definitive Guide*. Fife, Washington: Future Medicine, 1995.

Grieve, M. *A Modern Herbal: The Medicinal, Culinary, Cosmetic and Economic Properties, Cultivation and Folklore of Herbs, Grasses, Fungi, Shrubs, and Trees, with all their Modern Scientific Uses*. 1931. New York: Dover Publications, 1982. http://www.botanical.com/botanical/mgmh/mgmh.html.

_____. *A Modern Herbal*. Ed. C.F. Leyel. Middlesex, England: Penguin, 1980.

Gunther, R.T. *The Greek Herbal of Dioscorides*. Trans. J Goodyear. New York: Hafner, 1959.

Ḥākim al-Nīsābūrī, M. *al-Mustadrak 'alā al-ṣaḥīḥayn*. N.p.: n.p., n.d.

Hamarneh, S., and M.A. Anees. *Health Sciences in Early Islām*. San Antonio: Noor Health Foundation and Zahra Publications, 1983.

Ḥamīdullāh, M. Introduction. *Kitāb al-nabāt: Le dictionnaire botanique d'Abū Ḥanīfah al-Dīnawarī*. Cairo: Institute Français d'Archéologie Orientale du Caire, 1973.

Heinrich, M., J. Barnes, S. Gibbos, and E.M. Williamson. *Fundamentals of Pharmacognosy and Phytotherapy*. London: Churchill Livingstone, 2004.
Herbal Medicine Handbook. Springhouse, PA: Springhouse, 2001.
Holmes, C. *Summary Report for the European Union: 2000–2005*. York: Agricultural and Rural Strategy Group, 2005.
Ibn ʻAbd al-Barr Y. *Jāmiʻ bayān al-ʻilm*. al-Dammām: Dār Ibn al-Jawzī, 1994.
Ibn al-ʻArabī. *Mujarrabāt ibn ʻArabī fī al-ṭibb al-rūḥānī*. Ed. M. ʻAqīl. Bayrūt: Dār al-Maḥajjah, 2006.
Ibn Anas, M. *al-Muwaṭṭa'*. Bayrūt: Dār al-Gharb, 1999.
Ibn Buṭlān, *The Medieval Health Handbook: Tacuinum sanitatis*. Ed. L Cogliati Arano. Trans. O. Ratti and A. Westbrook. New York: George Braziller, 1976.
Ibn Ḥabīb A. *Mujtaṣar fī al-ṭibb/Compendio de medicina*. Ed. C. Álvarez de Morales and F Girón Irueste. Madrid: Consejo Superior de Investigaciones Científicas, 1992.
_____. *al-Ṭibb al-nabawī*. Ed. MA Barr. Dimashq: Dār al-Qalam, 1993.
Ibn Ḥanbal, A. *Musnad al-Imām Aḥmad ibn Ḥanbal*. Bayrūt: Mu'assasat al-Risālah, 1993.
_____. *Musnad al-Imām Aḥmad ibn Ḥanbal*. Bayrūt: al-Maktabah al-Islāmiyyah, 1969.
Ibn Ḥibbān, M. *Ṣaḥīḥ Ibn Ḥibbān*. Bayrūt: Mu'assasat al-Risālah, 1984.
Ibn Khaldūn. *The Muqaddimah: An Introduction to History*. Vol. 3. Trans. F Rosenthal. Princeton: Princeton University Press, 1967: 150.
Ibn Khuzaymah, M. *Ṣaḥīḥ Ibn Khuzaymah*. Bayrūt: al-Maktab al-Islāmī, 1971.
Ibn Mājah, M. *Sunan*. Trans. MT Anṣārī. Lahore: Kazi Publications, 1994.
_____. *Sunan Ibn Mājah*. Bayrūt: Dār al-Jīl, 1998.
Ibn Mufliḥ al-Maqdisī, M. *Khamsūn faṣlan fī al-tadāwī wa-al-ʻilāj*. al-Riyyaḍ: Dār ʻĀlam al-Kutub, 2000.
Ibn al-Qayyim al-Jawziyyah. *Medicine of the Prophet*. Trans. P. Johnstone. Cambridge: The Islamic Texts Society, 1998.
_____. *Natural Healing with the Medicine of the Prophet*. Trans. M. al-Akīlī. Philadelphia: Pearl Publishing, 1993.
_____. *al-Ṭibb al-nabawī*. Bayrūt: Dār al-Kitāb, 1985.
Ibn Sīnā. *The Canon of Medicine*. Ed. O. Cameron Gruner. London: Luzaz, 1930.
Ibn al-Sunnī. *Ṭibb al-nabī*. Ed. Omer Recep. Marburg/Lahn: Philipps-Universität, 1969.
Ibn Ṭulūn, S. *al-Manhal al-rawī fī al-ṭibb al-nabawī*. Ed. ʻAzīz Bayk. Riyyaḍ: Dār ʻālam al-kutub, 1995.
India. Ministry of Environment and Forests. *State of the Environment Report*. New Delhi: Ministry of Environment and Forests, Government of India, 2001.
_____. National Institute of Industrial Research. *The Handbook on Unānī Medicines with Formulae, Processes, Uses and Analysis*. Delhi: Asia Pacific Business Press, 2004.
Iṣbahānī A.N. al-. *Mawsūʻat al-ṭibb al-nabawī*. Ed. M.K.D. al-Turkī. Bayrūt: Dār Ibn Ḥazm, 2006.
Janick, J., and R.E. Paull. *The Encyclopedia of Fruits and Nuts*. Wallingford, UK: CABI, 2008.
Johnstone, P., trans. *Medicine of the Prophet*. Ibn Qayyim al-Jawziyyah. Cambridge: The Islamic Texts Society, 1998.
Juniper, B.E., and D.J. Mabberley. *The Story of the Apple*. Portland: Timber Press, 2006.
Kamal, Ḥ. *Encyclopedia of Islamic Medicine*. Cairo: General Egyptian Book Organization, 1975: 87.
Khaṭīb al-Baghdādī, A. *al-Riḥlah fī ṭalab al-ḥadīth*. [S.l.: s.n.], 1975.
Kayne, S.B. *Complementary Therapies for Pharmacists*. London: Pharmaceutical Press, 2002.
Keville, K. *Herbs: An Illustrated Encyclopedia*. New York: Friedman/Fairfax, 1994.
Khare, C.P. *Indian Medicinal Plants*. New York: Springer, 2007.
Khumaynī, R. *Forty Ḥadīth: An Exposition of Ethical and Mystical Traditions*. Trans. M. Qarā'ī. Islamic Propagation Organization, 1989.
_____, M. Mutahharī, and M.H. Ṭabāṭabā'ī. *Luz interior*. Trans. A.D. Manzolillo. Buenos Aires: Editorial Jorge Luis Vallejo, 1997.
Kīlanī, N. Fī. *Riḥāb al-ṭibb al-nabawī*. Bayrūt: Mu'assasat al-Risālah, 1980.
Komarov, V.L., et al. *Flora SSSR* 1934–1964. N.p.: N.p., n.d.
Kowalchik, C., and W. Hylton. *Rodale's Illustrated Encyclopedia of Herbs*. Emmaus, PA: Rodale Press, 1987.
Kulaynī, M. *al-Kāfī*. Ṭihrān: Maktabat al-Ṣadūq, 1961.
Labarta, A. *Libro de dichos maravillosos: misceláneo morisco de magia y adivinación*. Madrid: Consejo Superior de Investigaciones Científicas/Instituto de Cooperación con el Mundo Árabe, 1993.
Lambert Ortiz, E. *The Encyclopedia of Herbs, Spices, and Flavourings: A Cook's Compendium*. New York: DK, 1992.
Lawless, J., and J. Allan. *Aloe Vera: Natural Wonder Cure*. Thorsons: London, 2000.
Leung, A., et al. *Encyclopedia of Common and Natural Ingredients used in Food, Drugs, and Cosmetics*. New York: John Wiley and Sons, 1996.
Levey, M., and N. al-Khaledy, eds. *The Medical*

Formulary of al-Samarqandī. Philadelphia: University of Pennsylvania Press, 1967.

Lowbury, E.J.L., and G.A.J. Ayliffe. *Drug Resistance in Antimicrobial Therapy*. Springfield: Thomas, 1974.

Lucas, R.M. *Miracle Medicine Herbs*. West Nyack: Parker, 1991.

Majlisī, M.B. *Usages et bons comportements en Islām*. Trans. A.A. al-Bostani. Paris: Séminaire Islamique, 1990.

_____. *Biḥār al-anwār*. Ṭihrān: Javad al-Alavi, 1956.

Majno, G. *The Healing Hand: Man and Wound in the Ancient World*. Cambridge: Harvard University Press, 1975.

Mandaville, J.P. *Flora of Eastern Saudi Arabia*. London: Kegan Paul, 1990.

Meulenbeld, G.J., and D. Wujastyk. *Studies on Indian Medical History*. New Delhi: Motilal Banarsidass, 2001.

Miki, W. *Index of the Arab Herbalist's Materials*. Tokyo: Institute for the Study of Languages and Cultures of Asia and Africa, 1976.

Ministry of Health and Family Welfare. *The Ayurvedic Pharmacopoeia of India*. New Delhi: Ministry of Health & Family Welfare, 1978–2000.

_____. *National Formulary of Unānī Medicine*. Delhi: Ministry of Health and Family Welfare, 1983.

Moerman, D. *Native American Ethnobotany*. Portland: Timber Press, 1998. *Native American Ethnobotany: A Database of Foods, Drugs, Dyes, and Fibers of Native American Peoples, Derived from Plants*. http://herb.umd.umich.edu/.

_____. *Native American Medicinal Plants: An Ethnobotanical Dictionary*. Portland: Timber Press, 1998.

Murata, S. *The Tao of Islam*. Albany: SUNY Press, 1992.

Murray, M.T., and L. Pizzorno. *The Encyclopedia of Healing Foods*. New York: Simon & Schuster, 2005.

Mūsawī Lārī, M. *Problèmes moraux et psychologiques*. Trans. Nahid Chahbazī. Qum: Mūsawī Lārī, 1987.

Muslim. *Jāmi' al-ṣaḥīḥ*. al-Riyyāḍ: Bayt al-Afkār, 1998.

Muttaqī. *Kanz al-'ummāl*. Bridgeview, IL: Bayt al-Afkar al-Dawliyyah, 1999.

Narāqī, M.M. *L'Éthique musulmane*. Trans. A.A. al-Bostani. Paris: Séminaire Islamique, 1991.

_____. *Jāmi' al-sa'ādāt*. Najaf: Jāmi'at al-Najaf al-Dīniyyah, 1963.

Nasā'ī, A. *Sunan al-Nasā'ī*. al-Qāhirah: Muṣṭafā al-Bābī al-Ḥalabī, 1964–65.

Nasā'ī, M. *al-Ṭibb al-nabawī wa-al-'ilm al-ḥadīth*. Dimashq: al-Sharikah al-Muttaḥidah, 1984.

Nehmé, M. *Dictionnaire étymologique de la flore du Liban*. Bayrūt: Librairie du Liban, 2000.

Nīsābūrī. *Islamic Medical Wisdom: The Ṭibb al-a'immah*. Trans. B. Ispahany. Ed. A.J. Newman. London: Muḥammadī Trust, 1991.

_____. *Ṭibb al-a'immah*. Bayrūt: Dār al-Maḥajjah al-Bayḍā', 1994.

PDR for Herbal Medicines. Montvale, NJ: Medical Economics Company, 2000.

Perho, I. *The Prophet's Medicine: A Creation of the Muslim Traditionalist Scholars*. Helsinki: Kokemäki, 1995.

Plants for a Future: Edible, Medicinal, and Useful Plants for a Healthier World. http://www.pfaf.org/index.php.

Prioreschi, P. *A History of Medicine: Byzantine and Islamic Medicine*. Omaha: Horatius Press, 2001.

Rāzī, M. *La Médecine spirituelle/Ṭibb al-rūḥānī*. Trans. R. Brague. Paris: Flammarion, 2003.

_____. *The Spiritual Physick of Rhazes*. Trans. A. Arberry. N.p.: n.p., n.d.

Reeve, E.C.R., and I. Black. *Encyclopedia of Genetics*. New York: Taylor & Francis, 2001.

Riḍā, 'A. *Il trattato aureo sulla medicina attribuito all'Imām 'Alī al-Riḍā*. Trans. F. Speziale. Palermo: Officina di Studi Medievali, 2009.

Riḍā, 'A al-. *al-Risālah al-dhahabiyyah*. Qum: Maṭba'at al-Khayyām, 1982.

_____. *Risālah fī al-ṭibb al-nabawī*. Ed. M.A. Bār. Bayrūt: Dār al-Manāhil, 1991.

Riddle, J.M. *Eve's Herbs: A History of Contraception and Abortion in the West*. Cambridge: Harvard University Press, 1997.

Said, H.M. *Hamdard Pharmacopoeia of Eastern Medicine*. Karachi: Times Press, 1969. *Hamdard Pharmacopoeia of Eastern Medicine*. Delhi: Sri Satguru Publications, 1997.

_____. *al-Ṭibb al-Islāmī: A Brief Survey of the Development of Ṭibb (Medicine) during the Days of the Holy Prophet Moḥammad and in the Islamic Age, and Presented on the Occasion of the World of Islām Festival, London, April-June 1976*. Karachi: Hamdard National Foundation, 1976.

Samarqandī, N. *The Medical Formulary of al-Samarqandī*. Trans. M. Levey and M. Khaledy. Philadelphia: University of Pennsylvania Press, 1967.

Sarton, G., ed. *Introduction to the History of Science*. Baltimore: Williams & Wilkins, 1953.

Satyavati, G.V., A.K. Gupta, and N. Tandon. *Medicinal Plants of India*. New Dehli: Indian Council of Medical Research, 1987.

Schleicher, P., and M. Saleh. *Black Cumin: The Magical Egyptian Herb for Allergies, Asthma, and Immune Disorders*. Rochester, Vermont: Healing Arts Press, 2000.

Schulz V., et al. *Rational Phytotherapy.* New York: Springer-Verlag, 1998.
Selin, H., and H. Shapiro. *Medicine Across Cultures: History and Practice of Medicine in Non-Western Cultures.* New York: Springer, 2003.
Sengers, G. *Women and Demons: Cult Healing in Islamic Egypt.* Leiden: Brill, 2003.
Shāfi'ī, M. *Musnad al-Imām al-Shāfi'ī.* Ed. M al-Sindī. Bayrūt: Dār al-Fikr, 1997.
Shatzmiller, M. *Labour in the Medieval Islamic World.* Leiden: Brill, 1984.
Siddiqui, A.W. *The Qur'ān and Science.* http://www.thequranandscience.com/display.php?book/39/4
Sinclair Rohde, E. *The Old English Herbals.* New York: Dover, 1971.
Skidmore-Roth, L. *Mosby's Handbook of Herbs and Natural Supplements.* St. Louis: Mosby, 2001.
Skrabanek, P., and J. McCormick. *Sofismas y desatinos en medicina.* Barcelona: Doyma, 1992.
Speziale, F. *Le médecin du cœur: soufisme, religion et médecine en Islām indien.* Paris: Karthala, 2009.
_____. *Il trattato aureo sulla medicina attribuito all'Imām 'Alī al-Riḍā.* Palermo: Officina di Studi Medievali, 2009.
Stobart, T. *Herbs, Spices, and Flavoring.* Woodstock, NY: Overlook Press, 1982.
Sūyūṭī, J. *As-Sūyūṭī's Medicine of the Prophet.* Ed. A. Thomson. London: Ṭā-Hā Publishers, 1994.
Sūyūṭī, J. *Jāmi' al-aḥādīth.* Bayrūt: Dar al-Fikr, 1994.
_____. *al-Raḥmah fī al-ṭibb wa al-ḥikmah.* al-Qāhirah: al-Maktabah al-Muḥammadiyyah, 1960.
_____, and M. Chaghhaynī. *Ṭibb al-nabī or Medicine of the Prophet.* Trans. C. Elgood. *Osiris* 1962; 14: 33–192.
Swerdlow, J.L. *Nature's Medicine: Plants that Heal.* Washington: National Geographic, 2000.
Symons, M. *A History of Cooks and Cooking.* Chicago: University of Chicago Press, 2000.
Ṭabarānī, S. *al-Mu'jam al-awsaṭ.* 'Ammān: Dār al-Fikr, 1999.
Ṭabarsī, H. *Mustadrak al-Wasā'il.* Bayrūt: Mu'assasat Āl al-Bayt, 1987–1988.
Tannahill, R. *Food in History.* New York: Stein and Day, 1973.
Tiamat, U.M. *Herbal Abortion: The Fruit of the Tree of Knowledge.* Peoria, IL: Safe-femme!, 1994.
Tirmidhī, M. *al-Jāmi' al-ṣaḥīḥ.* al-Qāhirah: Muṣṭafā al-Bābī al-Ḥalabī, [1937-].
Thomson, R. *The Grosset Encyclopedia of Natural Medicine.* New York: Grosset & Dunlap, 1980.
Toby, H. *The Rise of Early Modern Science: Islām, China, and the West.* Cambridge: Cambridge University Press, 2003.
Toussaint-Samat, M. *A History of Food.* New York: Wiley-Blackwell, 1994.
Tyler, V.E., and S. Foster. *Tyler's Honest Herbal.* 4th ed. New York: Haworth Press, 1999.
Ullmann, M. *Islamic Medicine.* Edinburgh: Edinburgh University Press, 1978.
United States. Dept. of the Army. *U.S. Army Survival Manual.* Washington: Dept. of the Army, 1957.
Usmanghani, K. *Indusyunic Medicine.* Karachi: University of Karachi, 1997.
Van Alphen, J., and A. Aris. *Oriental Medicine: An Illustrated Guide to the Asian Arts of Healing.* London: Serindia Publications, 1995.
Vázquez de Benito, M.C., and C.A. Morales, trans. *El libro de las generalidades de la medicina.* Madrid: Trotta, 2003.
Vehling, J.D. *Apicuis: Cookery and Dining in Imperial Rome.* New York: Dover Publications, 1977.
Watson, A. *Agricultural Innovation in the Early Islamic World.* New York: Cambridge University Press, 1983.
Weaver, W.W. *Heirloom Vegetable Gardening.* New York: Henry Holt, 1997.
Weed, S. *Wise Woman Herbal for the Child Bearing Year.* Woodstock, NY: Ash Tree Publishing, 1985.
White, L.B., and S. Foster. *The Herbal Drugstore.* Emmaus, PA: Rodale, 2000.
Winston, D. *Cherokee Herbal Medicine.* Medicines from the Earth Conference 2001; 01ME07. http://www.botanicalmedicine.org/Tapes/01me/01me07.htm
Wu Zheng-yi, P.H. Raven, et al., eds. *Flora of China.* N.p.: 1994.
Wujastyk, D. *Oriental Medicine: An Illustrated Guide to the Asian Arts of Healing.* J. Van Alphen, and A. Aris, eds. London: Serindia Publications, 1995.
Yaḥyā, Adam ibn. *Kitāb al-Kharāj.* al-Qāhirah: Dār al-Shurūq, 1987.
Zahedi, E. *Botanical Dictionary: Scientific Names of Plants in English, French, German, Arabic, and Persian Languages.* Tehran: University of Tehran Press, 1959.

Index